MYTHOLOGY AND THE ROMANTIC TRADITION
IN ENGLISH POETRY

MYTHOLOGY AND THE ROMANTIC TRADITION IN ENGLISH POETRY

DOUGLAS BUSH

HARVARD UNIVERSITY PRESS

CAMBRIDGE , MASSACHUSETTS

Reissued, with a new preface, 1969

Publication of this book has been aided by a grant from
the Hyder Edward Rollins Fund

Distributed in Great Britain by Oxford University Press, London

Library of Congress Catalog Card Number 72–85071

SBN 674-59825-3

Printed in the United States of America

FOR

H. C. B. AND S. E. B.

PREFACE TO THE 1969 PRINTING

This book was first published by the Harvard University Press in 1937. Both it and its predecessor, *Mythology and the Renaissance Tradition in English Poetry*, were reissued in 1957 by the Pageant Book Company and in 1963 by W. W. Norton & Company (for this last issue the Renaissance volume was revised). After two such recent revivals it is very gratifying to me that the Harvard University Press should have spontaneously (and optimistically) undertaken to give a further lease of life to the book it originally brought out.

Thinking of that first publication calls up memories of composition. A good deal of the reading, especially of swarms of small poets, was done at the British Museum, a good deal of the writing in a Hampstead house owned by Mrs. T. F. Tout, widow of the eminent Manchester historian, and on a huge table which had belonged to Mrs. Gaskell the novelist (whose characters were signally given to dying). I recall these minute personal data because a glance through my book and through American, English, French, and German reviews seems to warrant the agreeable feeling that, in spite of the table's mortuary associations and the depressing effect of much dead verse (mainly confined to the Appendix), I kept up a fair degree of liveliness; in these days I, like most other people, would find that hard to compass, since, not without reason, melancholy is now the only wear. I cannot exclaim, like the fading Swift at the sight of his early *Tale of a Tub*, "Good God! what a genius I had when I wrote that book!" but perhaps I can murmur "How bright I was in that far-off time!" At one point, by the way, brightness overreached itself. The opening bit of the section on Wordsworth (p. 56) was prompted by exasperation over much literary chatter about the discovery of Wordsworth's French daughter and its redeeming of the poet's stuffy image; but irony missed fire (as it so often does), and two distinguished American critics took my remarks as a revelation of the low state of morality at Harvard.

In 1937 "myth-and-symbol" criticism was still far from reaching its peak, although the anthropological and psychological conception of myth had already manifested itself in literature. The influence of Frazer's *The Golden Bough* (1890 and later editions) had been conspicuous in *The Waste Land* (1922), and in his famous review of *Ulysses* (the prose epic of the same year) Eliot had celebrated Joyce's creation of a new mythic method for imaginative dealing with the complex materials of the modern world. Growing criticism of these writers and of Yeats and Pound and others made more and more specific applications of such ideas. An early, full-scale, literary exploration of "myth" was Maud Bodkin's Jungian *Archetypal Patterns in Poetry: Psychological Studies of Imagination* (1934). The most comprehensive and canonical analysis and synthesis came in 1957, in Northrop Frye's *Anatomy of Criticism*. These years had meanwhile brought forth general and particular studies of the origins of myth in ritual and story, the nature of tragedy, and such universal themes as "the hero," "the quest," "the eternal return"; and these inquiries continue to multiply. In the modern spectrum Greek and Roman myths are only one band of color, though a central one, and they have been enriched in becoming part of a larger whole.

But the broad modern view of myth is only the latest phase in a process which, focused mainly on classical myths, has been going on throughout the history of Western culture and was well established in Greece before Plato. The main road followed for roughly twenty centuries was that of allegory. The impulse to disinfect or to rationalize the immoral divinities of Homer and Greek myth led to various kinds of interpretation: the gods and goddesses were deified mortals or the elements and forces of nature or — often obliquely — they exemplified moral lessons. In the early Christian era troublesome things in the Bible were reinterpreted with partly similar motives. Then the well-tried method of allegorical reading attested its efficacy in making pagan literature and myth safe for Christian readers and writers, and not only the almost blameless Virgil but the dubious Ovid acquired new moral and religious authority. The accommodation to Christian use of the great pagan heritage was furthered also by the principle of typology: just as persons and ideas of the Old Testament were seen to be prefigurations of the New, so the figures of pagan myth (notably Orpheus and Hercules, who had descended to hell) were partial anticipations of Christ. Unsophisticated pioneers in comparative religion could not miss the parallels between pagan and Judeo-Christian story — the wars of the Titans and the gods and the revolt of Satan, the great flood that drowned the wicked inhabitants of the earth and left only a righteous remnant, and so on. Such parallels suggested that pagan myth, however garbled, was a reflection or refraction of the true history of God's ways with man. These various approaches did not at all preclude imaginative and aesthetic enjoyment; they only added strong religious and moral sanctions, or, at times, protective coloring.

In the sixteenth and the earlier seventeenth century both poets and the very popular handbooks of allegorized mythology — ably described in Jean Seznec's *Survival of the Pagan Gods* (1953) — carried on ancient and medieval traditions, with more classical learning and with emphasis on moral interpretation, though religious typology was by no means dead. But in the latter half of the seventeenth century, in England as elsewhere, some lines of conflict became

clear. For one thing, the Reformation and the Counter-
Reformation had strengthened anti-pagan sentiments which
had always, but ineffectually, existed. This was not merely
a fundamentalist groundswell; poets from Tasso to Cowley
and Milton felt the need of Christian epic themes. Even
secular writers, reacting against both Renaissance classicism and the legacy of medieval romance, affirmed that
poetry should concern itself with the realistic delineation
of men and manners (and the Augustan age was the great
age of English satire). That doctrine was in harmony with
a far more dynamic phenomenon, the rapid growth of
science and the scientific temper, which apparently had a
chilling effect on the mythic imagination of poets. In
prose, moreover, one impulse of the critical spirit, especially
among emerging Deists, was toward rationalistic inquiry
into the origins and universal elements of myth and religion
— a movement most fully set forth in F. E. Manuel's *The
Eighteenth Century Confronts the Gods* (1959). Such causes
contributed to what is an evident fact, that, in England,
in the whole period from about 1650 (the epic Milton was a
partial anachronism) up to Coleridge and Wordsworth,
there were only two or three poets who had a real spark of
mythic or mythological imagination. The early part of the
period yielded a crop of travesties, and eighteenth-century
poets still made references to myth, but these were usually
anemic and less attractive than the personifying of abstractions. It depends on our point of view whether, as friends
or foes of mythology, we see a long period of sterility or the
Enlightenment. But, among the many Christian or anti-
Christian writers on mythology, two who were in different
ways friends of poets were the enthusiast Thomas Blackwell
(*Letters Concerning Mythology*, 1748) and John Lempriere,
the scholarly compiler of the long-lived *Classical Dictionary*
(1st ed., 1788), which we associate chiefly with the young
Keats.

The revival of Greek myth in Europe generally was an integral part of the Romantic reaction against a rationalistic and mechanistic view of the world and man. Of that nothing needs to be said here, since so much of my book is an attempt to describe it. But we may note a few interesting particulars. The full allegorical commentary that George Sandys in 1632 added to his translation of Ovid's *Metamorphoses* was, after generations of neglect, read and utilized by Keats; the fact is a reminder that the old allegorical tradition led quite naturally into modern symbolism. Another suggestive fact is that William Godwin, the most hard-headed doctrinaire rationalist of his age, produced (under the pseudonym "Edward Baldwin") a handbook of mythology, *The Pantheon* (1806), in which Greek myth was taken seriously as a religion; this book also was used by Keats. But the most central facts are that Coleridge nostalgically deplored the extinction of myth by "the faith of reason," that Wordsworth, whatever his Christian consciousness of pagan error, could revivify Greek myths in a spirit akin to his own religion of nature, and that the younger Keats and Shelley could make them vehicles for their most personal and exalted visions of nature and man and poetry.

Poets of the Renaissance from Spenser to Milton had — in their own distinctive ways — drawn upon a public treasury of mythological symbols, but a larger infusion of personal interpretation was to be a main characteristic of mythological poetry of the nineteenth and twentieth centuries. However, the promise of continued vitality of any kind did not at first seem assured. Apart from those who — like the authoritative editor, Francis Jeffrey — found mythological themes wanting in human interest, such diverse writers as Hazlitt, Keats, Peacock, and the young Macaulay and Tennyson were more or less oppressively conscious that the progress of science and civilization was bound to clip the wings of poetry and myth. The threat only grew

stronger with the growth of Utilitarianism and industrialism. Matthew Arnold's first volume, published two years
before the Great Exhibition of 1851, drew criticism even
from his friends about his use of classical myth, and his first
critical essay (1853) was a reply to the multiplying voices
that called upon poets to leave "the exhausted past" and
embrace the modern world.

In the course of the next two generations Nietzsche declared that modern man, stripped of unifying myths and
starving for want of roots, was groping frantically for a
usable past; the young Yeats lamented grey Truth's sup-
pression of Arcadian dreams; and the explosive D. H.
Lawrence cried that we must get back Apollo and the other
divinities, the symbols of the unified world our souls live
in, and resist the sterile, disintegrating abstractions of reason and science. During the last two generations most of
the leading British and American poets (not to mention
Rilke and others) have renewed the mythic or mythological
tradition with fresh power. Thus, in spite of the accumulated pressures and threats of our time, the vitality and the
necessity of myth remain. It will doubtless survive those
contemporary rebels who would annul the whole past and
whose visionary utopia appears to be a cultural void.

The past thirty years have brought forth innumerable
scholarly and critical books, articles, and essays on all
phases of the mythological tradition from antiquity to the
present. These writings obviously fall into two categories:
general studies of poetry and of individual poets, and
studies of the classical tradition, classical mythology, and
individual myths. Two notable examples of the last kind
— which take in far more than our present concern, the
nineteenth and twentieth centuries — are W. B. Stanford's
*The Ulysses Theme: A Study in the Adaptability of a Tradi-
tional Hero* (1954; 2nd ed., 1963) and Raymond Trousson's
Le Thème de Prométhée dans la littérature européenne (2 vols.,

1964). The latest work — also notable — is Patricia Merivale's *Pan the Goat-God: His Myth in Modern Times* (1969),
which begins in antiquity but deals mainly with Pan's great
revival in the poetry of the nineteenth century and in
modern fiction (especially, as we might expect, that of
D. H. Lawrence).

To return to my own book, I wish that I could revise the
multitudinous footnotes and the bibliographies so as to
take account of the whole library I have briefly referred to;
but I am too deeply mired in other large jobs for any such
enterprise. I may remark that bibliographical deficiencies
are considerably made up in a recent and much shorter
book of mine, *Pagan Myth and Christian Tradition in
English Poetry* (published by the American Philosophical
Society, 1968), a rapid survey in three lectures that run
from the Renaissance to the present; or perhaps I should
say that the discourses flow through a bibliographical forest
set out for readers of scholarly zeal. The third lecture in
that book, by the way, may offset some faults of proportion
in my earlier and fuller account of the twentieth century.
However, to come back again to the book in hand, I doubt,
even if time allowed, whether I should be inclined to make
many changes (I have altered a very few phrases in the text
and a few details in the notes); on the whole, my inner light
being still very limited, I agree with what I said in 1937,
although now I might put a number of things with more
sober and becoming flatness. I do regret, for instance, that
I still cannot see Shelley plain, or as devout Shelleyans see
him, but that blind spot is past praying for; and various
readers may have various other regrets. At any rate, as I
said at the beginning, I am grateful to the Harvard University Press for a very pleasant surprise.

D.B.

Cambridge, Massachusetts
February 3, 1969

PREFACE TO THE FIRST PRINTING

THIS book is intended to be complete in itself, though it is a sequel to my *Mythology and the Renaissance Tradition in English Poetry* (University of Minnesota Press and Humphrey Milford, 1932). That volume stopped at 1680; this one struggles up to 1935. The multitude of poets, especially minor poets, in the modern period made the problem of selection and proportion more difficult, and, if any reader thinks some writers are unjustly slighted or ignored, it may be said that that cause of complaint would not have been warranted by the original manuscript, which, in consideration of the cost of printing and the brief span of human life, has been greatly abridged. After spending so much of my own brief span on the history of mythological poetry I could almost rise to a Gibbonian leave-taking, but I have no summer-house and no garden, and possibly a more appropriate citation would be the Duke of Gloucester's celebrated remark: "Another damned thick, square book! Always scribble, scribble, scribble! Eh! Mr. Gibbon?" However, before my notes are collected for a funeral pyre, I may return to mythology once more, since everyone, sooner or later, collapses in the bosom of Shakespeare.

For a list of abbreviations used in footnotes, see the first page of the bibliography. The place of publication of all books cited is London, unless some other reference is given.

For help of various kinds I am indebted to the officers and attendants of the University of Minnesota Library and the Harvard College Library, and especially to those of the British Museum who so patiently shoveled tons of verse across my table; to the Guggenheim Memorial Foundation and the University of Minnesota, which provided a year's absence from students, a lucid interval but for which the world would have had to wait some time longer for this book; to my friends Professors A. S. P. Woodhouse and E. K. Brown, for allowing me to incorporate articles on Wordsworth and Tennyson published in the *University of Toronto Quarterly*; to my friends of the University of Minnesota, Professors J. W. Beach, C. A. Moore, and E. E. Stoll, who read several chapters in only too amiable a mood; and to Professors James B. Munn and Hyder Rollins of Harvard University, who might be called the godfathers of this book, though their generous beneficence has far outrun that degree of responsibility. As for the godmother, she declines to stand at the font.

DOUGLAS BUSH

CAMBRIDGE, MASSACHUSETTS

CONTENTS

Introduction

IF THE benevolent reader will ascribe the statement to economy rather than complacency, I will say that the best introduction I can give to the present volume is the conclusion of the former one; and I will not overtax his benevolence by repeating that summary of the fundamental elements of the Renaissance tradition in mythological verse. (One may wish it were possible to emulate Thomas Rymer's compendious survey of English poetry: "Chaucer refin'd our English. Which in perfection by Waller.") Poets of the Renaissance were characterized, on the classical side, by their instinctive mingling of the antique, the medieval, and the Italianate, and, further, by their steadily growing consciousness of disharmony between Christian and pagan ideals. The Renaissance tradition is therefore complex enough, yet the main line of development, represented by Chaucer, Spenser, and Milton, is clear and logical. Nor was it less logical that exhaustion and reaction should, in Milton's own time, have resulted in a flood of travesties and burlesques of classical themes.

While the great bulk of Renaissance poems were more purely (or impurely) Ovidian than philosophic, the *Cantos of Mutabilitie* and *Comus* show what a weight of metaphysical and ethical seriousness, along with a wealth of sensuousness, the mythological poem could bear. When after many almost fruitless generations the mythological poem was reborn in the early nineteenth century, it was no less sensuous and was much more predominantly serious. The relation of the artist to society, and the problems involved in that, became all-important in the era of the French and the industrial revolutions, and they never weighed more heavily upon poets than they do at present. The questions Keats asked are being asked by the young poets of to-day,

> Chin-deep in Eternal Flux,
> Angling for reassurance.[1]

What is the place of poets in modern civilization? Have they a right to exist, and, if they have, what is their function? Are poets the unacknowledged legislators of the world, the guardians and the makers of civilization, or are they merely tolerated practitioners of an outmoded luxury trade, piping little songs for one another? The great ancients, from Pindar to Aristophanes, and Dante and Spenser and Milton, were not troubled by such paralyzing questions; they were citizens, teachers, artists, all at once and as a matter of course. (If Chaucer and Shakespeare were not of that company, they had at least a sound bourgeois sanity and an insatiable curiosity about and satisfaction in the perpetual drama of life.) Spenser and Milton, who may stand for the Renaissance attitude, were conscious leaders and teachers; in their art and in their message they were relatively secure in the strength of a tradition, a literary, ethical, and religious culture, which was aristocratic but was also, in a real sense, universally valid. The eighteenth century achieved its own uniformity and culture, rich and solid within its limits, but it did so at a high price. When the comparative stability of that era broke down, the romantic poets, while seeking to enlarge the contracted range of poetry, to regain the lost leadership, brought to the task no Miltonic mastery of knowl-

---

[1] C. Day Lewis, *Transitional Poem* (1929). See, for example, Mr. Lewis' *A Hope for Poetry* (Oxford, 1934); Stephen Spender, "The Problems of Poet and Public," *Spectator*, CXLIII (1929), 152; "The Artistic Future of Poetry," *New Republic*, LXXVIII (1934), 268–70; *The Destructive Element* (1935); Ronald Bottrall, *Arion Anadyomenos* (*The Loosening And other Poems*, Cambridge University Press, 1931).

edge, they had behind them no such substantial European tradition, no such universal authority. In an indifferent or hostile world they were groping for private and personal revelations, for the effect of both the romantic and the industrial movements was to make the artist, if not an antisocial figure, at any rate an isolated one. And, because the world was not only indifferent or hostile to poetry but sick and troubled, the poets felt, some of them, an inner as well as an outer conflict. Who were they to be cultivating poesy in solitude when the sufferings of mankind demanded sympathy and action? Besides, if the artist had a social function to perform, could he, in the interest of his own art, afford to live to himself, not sharing the common lot? Hence such various answers, to consider them only from one point of view, as *The Prelude* and *The Excursion*, *Endymion* and *The Fall of Hyperion*, *Alastor* and *The Triumph of Life*, *The Palace of Art* and *Sordello*, *The Scholar Gipsy* and *The Earthly Paradise* — or, to sum up these and other problems under one comprehensive name, the second part of *Faust*. The poets who possessed a mythological instinct were likely to hold the Apollonian creed, but the modern world seemed to require the Faustian; which was the truer faith, and could they be united? Such large questions are not very specifically mythological, to be sure, yet they cannot be avoided in a discussion of mythological poetry in the nineteenth century, whether in a poet who is tormented by them, like Keats, or in one who tries to escape from them, like William Morris.

When mythological poetry carries the weight of such preoccupations, forthright story-telling, at least for the philosophically minded writers who matter most, ceases to be a main object. For better or worse, Ovid lost his ancient sway. In deriving their mythological impulse and method from the Elizabethans, Keats and Shelley did not catch the gift for narration that Milton and even Spenser possessed, for these earlier poets, though they had philosophies to expound, were still in the authentic tradition of epic and romance. But in most other respects the nineteenth-century poets continued the Renaissance manner. The Elizabethans followed two fashions in mythological poems, the merely sensuous, represented by Marlowe and Shakespeare, and the sensuously symbolic or allegorical, represented by Spenser, Drayton, Chapman, and the Milton of *Comus*. It was of course the latter method which appealed to Keats and Shelley and many of their successors. Picture-making was as lavish as ever, and what Spenser and his fellows owed to tapestries the moderns owed to painting and sculpture. Landscapes continued to be mainly English, though the mythological figures placed in them acquired a more classical costume. Renaissance poets took a large license in reworking ancient material, but they were more or less controlled by a learned and international tradition; modern writers have been inclined to handle myth either with the same freedom of decorative and symbolic invention or, at times, with a much stricter classical purism.

The romantic poets, and indeed most English poets of the nineteenth century, were not European in the sense that Spenser and Milton were; they were not consciously writing in an international tradition. But the Hellenic revival, which directly or indirectly touched them all, was international; it was part of that tidal wave of primitivistic and idealistic sentiment which moved over Europe. In general the Latin culture which had been dominant since Roman times, and which was associated with neoclassic formalism, gave way, in the latter half of the eighteenth century, to a worship of all things Greek, or supposed to be Greek. The English temperament, in literature as in politics, seldom leads to fighting on the barricades, and the rebirth of classic myth which accompanied the Elizabethan

and Hellenic revival was a slow, quiet, almost imperceptible process. Until we reach Wordsworth we can hardly
point to any man, book, or date as a really significant
turning-point, and even the fourth book of *The Excursion*
was not exactly a ringing battle-cry. But in Germany the
revolt against French neoclassicism, and the idealizing of
Greek art, life, and myth, were most intense and self-
conscious. There, in a few decades, we pass from death to
life, from the mythology of Versailles to the mythology of
Homer, somewhat Teutonized and Titanized, to be sure.
The phases of revolution which carry us from Gottsched to
Goethe are clearly marked, and it was a revolution in
which almost every man of letters bore arms. The importance of that epoch-making change of heart extended
of course far beyond the confines of mythology. Even
though in Germany itself anti-pagan reaction and the
troubles of 1848 almost extinguished Hellenism, the gods
of Greece had returned to European poetry.

As for Hellenism in another sense of the word, the approximation to standards of Greek poetic art, our glance
at the romantic revival of the Elizabethans is sufficient
reminder that there is no essential relation between a love
of Greek myth and a love of order and measure, of clarity
and precision. For those qualities (which, we may remember, are not omnipresent in the Greek poets themselves),
we must turn back to the Restoration and the early eighteenth century. That there had been no such relation in the
poetry of the English Renaissance my former volume en-
deavored at some length to illustrate, and it would be difficult to frame a definition of Hellenism which would
include, to name a few poets who knew Greek, Byron,
Shelley, the Brownings, Swinburne and Morris. Obviously the modern poetic genius has not lost its English
capacity for resisting the discipline of Greek thought and
expression. Of late years the reaction against Victorian

luxuriance and Victorian sentiment has been more "metaphysical" than classical, but some classical virtues have been regained in the process.

The Hellenic revival brings us to two other questions, the last that can be raised here, which we find being asked and answered from the early nineteenth century up to our own time. Christian poets of the Renaissance had been troubled by their own instinctive response to pagan allurements, and, while Spenser could reach a flexible compromise, Milton was more openly aware of a gulf. In nineteenth-century England, Anglican and Nonconformist pietism, soon reinforced by the Oxford Movement, led to a consciousness of conflicting claims between Christian and antique subjects and between Christian and antique (usually Dionysian) ways of life. The antithesis was sometimes keenly felt, sometimes it was only literary; at any rate the numerous Christian champions were mostly inferior as poets to the few pagans. Often that conflict was bound up with another, between the claims of the antique and of modern realism. This second problem was not a problem for Renaissance poets, but the ugliness of the modern industrial world has forced upon modern writers a vivid sense of the contrast between the actual present and the ideal past. Most of the important poets consciously or unconsciously, philosophically or sentimentally, solved the problem for themselves by investing ancient myths with modern significance, yet that solution has never satisfied the realist. And here we come to a difficult question, that is, how far the poetry of our modern world can or should be confined within classical modes and categories.

MYTHOLOGY AND THE ROMANTIC
TRADITION IN ENGLISH POETRY

CHAPTER I

The Eighteenth Century

IT HAS long been the misfortune of eighteenth-century poets, both good and bad, to be treated not simply as eighteenth-century poets but as either stragglers or forerunners, as neoclassic Pharisees or romantic John the Baptists.[1] Yet such a subject as the mythological tradition compels us to take something like that attitude, for this chapter is largely a description of the hiatus between the end of the Renaissance and the beginning of romanticism, and the poets of the eighteenth century (for us the period 1680–1800) inevitably appear as weak links in the chain of evolution, or as steps to the romantic temple — even though nowadays the foundations of that temple may seem to have been partly of sand. Of late years the very real virtues of eighteenth-century poetry have been abundantly recognized, especially by those who had just discovered its existence, and it is no longer necessary to be apologetic about clear-eyed, intelligent, urbane artists who were free from aberrations and hysterias and mistiness. To read normal eighteenth-century verse and prose is to have a cleansing and refreshing bath — not a Carlylean

---

[1] A generous critic complained mildly about the use in my earlier book of such barren and obsolete terms as "classical," "neoclassic," and "romantic." While sharing such dislike for words often employed both loosely and dogmatically, I do not know what substitutes we have as established terms for brief reference. "Classical" and "romantic," however their content may alter from age to age, do in essence indicate permanent attitudes of mind. And although, in England at any rate, the "neoclassic" critic who applied Procrustean rules is as much a figment of the imagination as the later "economic man," still the word does suggest the outline of a fairly definite esthetic code.

"Baphometic Fire-baptism" — in cool and masculine rationality, to be persuaded that man is a civilized and cosmopolitan being in an orderly, uniform, and rather comfortable world, and the writers who have such qualities and induce such moods deserve better praise than Arnold's damaging "our excellent and indispensable eighteenth century." I have not forgotten that the age of Locke and Hume and Gibbon was also the age of Bunyan and Berkeley and Wesley, but I am speaking here of the dominant conservative tendencies.

At the same time the recent reaction in favor of an abused period has sometimes ignored the fact that in poetry the virtues of craftsmanship, sanity, and good taste are in themselves secondary virtues, that they become fundamental ones only when united with the supreme creative gifts. It may be granted that these writers, from Dryden and Pope down, have more emotion than they have commonly been allowed, that they wrote some poems which are great by any standard, but it remains true, to reaffirm another platitude, that most of the delightful writing put forth in that age is not great poetry; or, if it is, some other name must be found for the writings of the ancients, and Dante, and others of that class. There is not much eighteenth-century verse which, in poetic emotion, imagination, and beauty, equals, say, Gibbon's prose account of his conceiving the subject of his history as he "sat musing amidst the ruins of the Capitol, while the barefooted friars were singing vespers in the Temple of Jupiter." The great themes of life and the universe are seldom touched, the great questions seldom asked, in the neoclassic age; they are mostly taken as settled. For the poets of the Renaissance tradition, man was an actor in a drama whose stage was earth and heaven. In the eighteenth century that stage has immeasurably contracted. Even Calvinism, with its terrible and poetic conception of human life, for the most part dwindled into placid or gloomy pietism. Milton had exalted reason with religious fervor because it was divine; the Augustans endorsed it because it was reasonable. It was no accident that the narrowing, or deflecting, of the poetic imagination synchronized with the decline of the spiritual force which the Renaissance had inherited from the Middle Ages; or, to put it in another way, with the rise of a scientific and mechanical view of the world. The Augustan poets as a rule are at ease in Zion. Sitting in the middle of his clock-like universe man may address the Creator Spirit, he does not cry in agony of soul to the Clock-maker: "Batter my heart, three person'd God...." No heroic poet offers Miltonic prayers to the Holy Spirit for divine aid; if Blackmore did, he was not answered.

It is quite natural and inevitable, then, and only superficially paradoxical, that the neoclassic age, instead of yielding a harvest of mythological poems, is almost completely barren, at least of good ones. The fundamental reason, as usual, is that the right kind of genius did not happen to be born; some other reasons will be touched upon a little later. But certain poets do demand attention, and, besides, I must try to give a brief account of eighteenth-century taste in classical matters, of some great pieces of translation, of the place occupied by mythology in the eighteenth-century mind, and of the changing conceptions of poetry and the antique which made possible, in the romantic poets, a rebirth of the mythological imagination. Thus the chapter is both an autopsy and an accouchement, if the terms are not too pretentious for a slight sketch, from a particular point of view, of a long and varied period; I can only pray that the officiating Dr. Slop may not evoke the curse of Ernulphus from eighteenth-century specialists.

I. Classical Taste in the Earlier Eighteenth Century

It would be easy to drop into large generalizations about eighteenth-century estimates of the classical authors and the general status and significance of classical culture. One could find support for the idea that Virgil's essential qualities were missed, that the *Aeneid* had become only a pallidly decorous and graceful model for an epic poem; but one might be checked by the recollection that no English critic has shown more sympathetic insight into the mind and art of Virgil than Dryden. Homer, especially in the earlier neoclassic period, was often censured, in comparison with Virgil, for "incorrectness" ("the porter-like language of Homer's heroes" is the phrase of the conservative Chesterfield [2]), yet what critic, old or new, has written more worthily of Homeric fire than Pope? (And whatever Dryden and Pope owed to French criticism, they felt what they said.) There is abundant evidence for the critical formalism, partly right and partly misguided, which had come down from the Renaissance as a conscious effort to civilize and Europeanize English poetry. On the other hand almost every English critic protested against "the rules," and it was the Augustan age which, following Boileau, welcomed the one ancient critic (apart from Plato) who exalted creative power and emotional intensity, "Longinus."

Or, taking one's cue from Gibbon and Gray, one might describe the Oxford and Cambridge of the period as temples of Morpheus and Bacchus, but in what age have exceptional men not damned their universities? And institutions in which Gibbon and Gray, and Thomas Warton

---

[2] *Letters of Philip Dormer Stanhope, 4th Earl of Chesterfield*, ed. Bonamy Dobrée (1932), no. 1734 (1750), IV, 1610. Addison, commenting on Homer's lapses into the "low," remembers "but one Laugh in the whole *Aeneid*" (*Spectator*, 279).

and many others, could pursue their studies unmolested may, to the harassed modern teacher, seem ideal temples of learning. The House of Commons, too, however infested by Welbore Ellises, was after all the best club in Europe, an assembly which enjoyed debates flavored by quotations from Horace and Virgil and Lucretius. Chesterfield's definition of education, despite its ironical barb, indicates the general state of affairs: "Classical knowledge, that is, Greek and Latin, is absolutely necessary for everybody; because everybody has agreed to think and to call it so. And the word *illiterate*, in its common acceptation, means a man who is ignorant of those two languages." [3] In the academic, literary, clerical, and political world of eighteenth-century London (and Edinburgh), a world that might be called cozy if one forgot the strong intellectual breeze blowing through it, familiarity with the classics was the great bond of cultural uniformity and social solidarity; it gave the entrée to all the best houses, including the established church. A gentleman was a man who read Horace and rode to hounds, though the Squire Westerns of the age, not always "lash'd into Latin by the tingling rod," may have emphasized one of these avocations. For of course when one thinks of the classics in the eighteenth century one thinks of Horace first of all, not the Horace who can at moments emulate Pindar, but the well-bred, dignified, cultivated man of the world, who enjoys the good things of life and love with urbane discrimination, who can express feeling but frowns on "enthusiasm," who likes to moralize on the decencies and has a real respect for religion but whose cheerfully mundane temper is not soured by a sense of sin — it was this Horace whom the Augustans

[3] *Letters*, no. 1564 (1748), III, 1155. For some doubts concerning the complete adequacy of classical education, see Spence's *Polymetis*, Dialogue XVII (ed. 1755, pp. 287–91); and the remarks of James Beattie quoted by Joseph E. Brown, *Critical Opinions of Samuel Johnson* (Princeton University Press, 1926), p. lii.

cherished, and no ancient author would have felt so much at home in London or a not too remote country house.

Chesterfield has been cited already, and one could hardly find a better index to standards of classical taste in the great world than the *Letters*. When one compares the ideals of culture and the gentleman set forth by Castiglione and by Chesterfield, one is aware of an immense loss in solidity and breadth and sincere disinterestedness. (Of course Chesterfield was writing *ad hominem*, or rather *ad puerum*, and it was besides an *experimentum in corpore vili*.) Such different things as fitness for public service and a sense of beauty have become less important than drawing-room manners, and one need not contrast Castiglione's Neo-Platonic rhapsody on love with Chesterfield's more realistic observations. Yet there is quite enough to remind us that Chesterfield is writing in the same tradition. His ideal is the cultivated amateur and man of the world, not the professional pedant, but he knows the worth as well as the decorative value of the classics. Since God has apparently not made young Philip a poet (and, as we shall see, without higher aid his father's precepts would not have taken him far), "for God's sake, make yourself an orator, which you may do"; and the best books in the world for that purpose are Quintilian and the *De Oratore*.[4] Since Philip does not want to be a diplomat abroad, he might take a Greek professorship at home; "It is a very pretty sinecure, and requires very little knowledge (much less than, I hope, you have already) of that language"[5] — an interesting comment on the state of Greek in the age before Porson and Parr. A couple of years later Chesterfield urges daily study of Greek, not the Greek poets of whom every smatterer knows a little, but "Plato, Aristoteles, Demosthenes, and Thucydides, whom none but adepts know. It

---

4 *Letters*, no. 1672 (1749), IV, 1445–46.
5 *Ibid.*, no. 1518 (1748), III, 1084.

is Greek that must distinguish you in the learned world, Latin alone will not." [6] God, however, has not made Philip a scholar, not even scholar enough for a professorship, and in the following year the desperate or sagacious parent "had much rather that you were passionately in love with some determined coquette of condition (who would lead you a dance, fashion, supple, and polish you), than that you knew all Plato and Aristotle by heart." (Ten years earlier he had soberly remarked that Virgil in his fourth book calls Aeneas *dux* rather than *pius* "because making love becomes a general much better than a man of singular piety." [7] Young Philip did not become either.) As the young man grows up there is less insistence on books and more on "the great usage of the world"; let him study the *beau monde* with great application, but read Homer and Horace only when he has nothing else to do. [8]

Though endowed by Thomson with "all Apollo's animating fire," Chesterfield is obviously a man of prose and not of poetry. Achilles "was both a brute and a scoundrel, and, consequently, an improper character for the hero of an epic poem; for he had so little regard for his country, that he would not act in defence of it because he had quarrelled with Agamemnon about a whore." [9] Ariosto and Tasso should be read, but Dante is "not worth the pains necessary to understand him"; one remembers Horace Walpole's remark that Dante was a Methodist parson in Bedlam. [10] For Chesterfield, as for Walpole, heroic poetry is a bit *de longue haleine*. "In this disposition of mind, judge whether I can read all Homer through *tout de suite*. I admire his beauties; but, to tell you the truth, when he

[6] *Ibid.*, no. 1734 (1750), IV, 1610.
[7] *Ibid.*, no. 1785 (1751), IV, 1765; no. 690 (1741), II, 441.
[8] *Ibid.*, no. 1773 (1751), IV, 1729.
[9] *Ibid.*, no. 1621 (1749), IV, 1305–06.
[10] *Ibid.*, no. 1690 (1750), IV, 1504; *Letters of Horace Walpole*, ed. Mrs. Paget Toynbee (Clarendon Press, 1903–05), XII, 274.

slumbers I sleep. Virgil, I confess, is all sense, and therefore I like him better than his model; but he is often languid, especially in his five or six last books, during which I
am obliged to take a good deal of snuff." [11] After all, the
treatment of love in the *Aeneid* is no better than it is in the
Henriade.[12] Chesterfield, like Walpole, has the virtue of
honesty.

These epistolary scraps do not, to be sure, provide
a cross-section of eighteenth-century opinion, for which
there is no space, but, in and between the lines, they suggest a good deal of the temper of the age, a temper more
Ciceronian and Horatian than Platonic,[13] an instinctive
and all-embracing rationalism which is admirably adapted
for most phases of civilized life, and reveals its limitations
only when confronted with the highest imaginative, philosophic, and religious poetry. At times classical culture appears as a kind of substitute for the medieval law of nature, a justification of things as they are. The conception
of an orderly and uniform physical world is reflected in a
Deism sometimes placid, sometimes "enthusiastic," and
eighteenth-century Deism is reflected in eighteenth-cen-

---

[11] *Letters of Chesterfield*, no. 1858 (1752), V, 1952. Walpole, on the contrary,
finds in the *Aeneid* "such a dearth of invention . . . so little good sense, so little
variety, and so little power over the passions," that for him there remains
nothing but Virgilian harmony and grace (*Letters*, XIII, 280–81). For Walpole's
definition of epic poetry, see XII, 273.

[12] *Letters of Chesterfield*, no. 1858 (1752), V, 1953. Walpole thinks that the
Henriade "leaves Virgil, and even Lucan, whom he [Voltaire] more resembles,
by far his superiors" (*Letters*, XIII, 283).

[13] Gray, says Norton Nicholls, studied Plato "perhaps more than any other
person," and "lost all patience when he talked of the neglect of his favourite
author at the University," yet "what he admired in Plato was not his mystic
doctrines, which he did not pretend to understand, nor his sophistry, but his excellent sense, sublime morality, elegant style, and the perfect dramatic propriety
of his dialogues" (*Letters of Thomas Gray*, ed. D. C. Tovey, II [1904], 284). In
1789 Walpole railed at "this half-witted Taylor" who preferred absurd metaphysics to Bacon and Locke, though these "were as clear as Plato was unintelligible — because he did not understand himself" (*Letters*, XIV, 238).

tury classicism.[14] The peace of the Augustans was in fact less peaceful than it seems in the pages of Addison, or Pomfret, but, with all the preaching of reason and restraint, one would welcome more evidence of irrational and rebellious impulses to restrain. Here I may quote some brief and suggestive sentences from M. André Gide which might serve as a motto not only for this chapter but for almost every chapter on poets of the nineteenth century:

Il importe de considérer que la lutte entre classicisme et romantisme existe aussi bien à l'intérieur de chaque esprit. Et c'est de cette lutte même que doit naître l'œuvre; l'œuvre d'art classique raconte le triomphe de l'ordre et de la mesure sur le romantisme intérieur. L'œuvre est d'autant plus belle que la chose soumise était d'abord plus révoltée. Si la matière est soumise par avance, l'œuvre est froide et sans intérêt.[15]

In *Samson Agonistes* the victory is not won in advance; in poets of the eighteenth and even the nineteenth century it often is.

There is so much in eighteenth-century classicism that is not merely cool and attractive, but solid and fruitful, that one hesitates to say that on the whole, compared with the classicism of the Renaissance, it is somewhat attenuated and pallid. We think of the religious fervor with which many men of the Renaissance devoured classical wisdom, and we ask if the classics in the eighteenth century were a guide to life or only a hall-mark of gentility. The obvious answer is that they could be both. Chesterfield can say, with sober sincerity, that Horace teaches the art of life as well as of poetry: "To avoid extremes, to observe propriety, to consult one's own strength, and to be consistent

[14] See Arthur O. Lovejoy, "The Parallel of Deism and Classicism," *M.P.*, XXIX (1932), 281 ff.

[15] "Réponse à une enquête de la Renaissance sur le classicisme, 8 Janvier 1921" (*Morceaux Choisis*, Paris, 1922, p. 453). The passage is quoted in Mr. Herbert Read's *Reason and Romanticism* (1926), p. 93.

from beginning to end, are precepts as useful for the man as for the poet."[16] Properly understood, that is not an ignoble ideal, but if it seems a little lacking in warmth, take these words from a letter of Chatham's to his nephew:

I hope you taste and love those authors [Homer and Virgil] particularly. You cannot read them too much: they are not only the two greatest poets, but they contain the finest lessons for your age to imbibe: lessons of honour, courage, disinterestedness, love of truth, command of temper, gentleness of behaviour, humanity, and in one word, virtue in its true signification.[17]

Those are the lessons which, with or without allegorical coloring, the Renaissance humanist also found in Homer and Virgil. And, finally, there is the famous story, itself a poem, about the last hours of Lord Granville — how he refused to prolong his life by postponing business, and, repeating Sarpedon's speech on glory and death, "he dwelled with particular emphasis on the third line, which recalled to his mind the distinguishing part, he had taken in public affairs."[18] The incident shows, as Arnold said, "the English aristocracy at its very height of culture, lofty spirit, and greatness, towards the middle of the 18th century." And one may cite this anecdote, instead of, say, the death of Addison, because, as a dramatization of the words of Chatham, it shows also the Renaissance ideal of the statesman nourished and fortified by the example of classical magnanimity.

II. DRYDEN'S *Virgil* AND POPE'S *Homer*

While the study of translations does not properly come within the scope of this book, the fact that so much energy

---

[16] *Letters*, no. 914 (1746), III, 732.

[17] *Correspondence of William Pitt, Earl of Chatham* (1838), I, 62–63.

[18] Robert Wood, *Essay on the Original Genius and Writings of Homer* (1775), p. vii; see *Iliad*, xii. 324, and Arnold, *On Translating Homer*, etc. (New Universal Library, pp. 18–19).

in the Augustan age went into renderings of the classics and so little into mythological poems may warrant what is not entirely a digression. To judge from comparison of Dryden's *Miscellany* and Dodsley's, the literary public's appetite for translations had fallen off greatly by the middle of the century,[19] but all the eminent hands of the earlier generation contributed their quota. These few pages are given to Dryden and Pope, and mainly to Dryden, because he was the chief creator of Augustan poetic style, and because his *Virgil*, unlike Pope's *Homer*, has commonly received less than its due. As a general caution, we may remember that changes in taste seldom allow long life to translations, especially verse translations of poetry; translator slays translator, and then himself is slain. We must neglect Dryden's powerful rendering of Lucretius, and the versions from Ovid and the satirists in which his instinct for antithesis and epigram had full play. Further, we must take for granted his theories of translation and his criticism of Virgil, though a phrase or two will remind us of his sensitive insight. "Virgil has a thousand secret beauties," and he has "the gift of expressing much in little, and sometimes in silence"; quoting one untranslatable phrase, "amongst a thousand others," Dryden exclaims, born lover of great writing that he is, "For my part, I am lost in the admiration of it: I contemn the world when I think on it, and myself when I translate it."[20]

Echoing Denham, Dryden sought "to make Virgil speak such English as he would himself have spoken, if he had been born in England, and in this present age." There was, then, no artificial drag on the translator's native energy and

---

[19] Raymond D. Havens, "Changing Taste in the Eighteenth Century: A Study of Dryden's and Dodsley's Miscellanies," *P.M.L.A.*, XLIV (1929), 501 ff., especially pp. 502, 532. See Gay's advice in his *On a Miscellany of Poems: To Bernard Lintott*.

[20] *Essays of John Dryden*, ed. W. P. Ker (Clarendon Press, 1900), II, 183, 13, 233; see *Aen*. viii. 364.

rapidity. He himself thought that if he anywhere copied the majestic style of his original, it was in the first *Georgic*, which he considered more sublime than any other part of Virgil.[21] We might take first a few lines from Thomson's Virgilian paraphrase in *Winter*, on the signs of a coming storm:

> Seen through the turbid, fluctuating air,
> The stars obtuse emit a shivering ray;
> Or frequent seem to shoot athwart the gloom,
> And long behind them trail the whitening blaze.

This is Dryden:

> And oft, before tempestuous winds arise,
> The seeming stars fall headlong from the skies,
> And, shooting through the darkness, gild the night
> With sweeping glories, and long trails of light. . . .

One need not make obvious comments.

The learned Dr. Trapp said that when you most admired Dryden you saw the least of Virgil, but Dr. Trapp was a rival translator. As a rule Dryden seems to be most adequate when Virgil is on his middle level, in narrative of action, and in many passages of elevated rhetoric. He is less happy in most of the essentially and intimately Virgilian lines, those expressions of wistful sadness, pity, tenderness, wavering faith and hope, which have meant so much to Newman, Tennyson, and other modern readers. If nowadays we tend a little to sentimentalize Virgil, Dryden's robust nature did not incline him to shed tears, idle tears. He cherished truth, according to his lights, but his pulse was not too obviously stirred when he rendered the famous lines in the second *Georgic*:

> Happy the man, who, studying nature's laws,
> Through known effects can trace the secret cause —
> His mind possessing in a quiet state,
> Fearless of Fortune, and resigned to Fate![22]

---

[21] *Works of John Dryden*, ed. Scott and Saintsbury (Edinburgh, 1882–93), XIV, 21. In quoting Dryden's text I have used the volume in the World's Classics series.

[22] *Georg*. ii. 490 ff.; Dryden, p. 397. The Scott-Saintsbury edition (XIV, 66, l. 699) erroneously prints "sacred" for "secret."

And this is what becomes of *sunt lacrimae rerum et mentem mortalia tangunt*:

> E'en the mute walls relate the warrior's fame,
> And Trojan griefs the Tyrians' pity claim.

Everyone knows Wordsworth's "Yet tears to human suffering are due," and his rendering of

> largior hic campos aether et lumine vestit
> purpureo . . . ,[23]

but no other-worldly yearnings trouble Dryden. He is as matter-of-fact as a commercial artist advertising desirable building lots:

> The verdant fields with those of heaven may vie,
> With ether vested, and a purple sky.[24]

Often it is not Dryden's words that disappoint us, for he wields strong, easy, unaffected, classic English, but the structure and movement of his verse. In the translation of the beautiful simile evoked by the death of Pallas we may miss Dryden's genuine feeling when the melancholy undulations of the hexameters are cut into brisk antithetical couplets with emphatic rhymes.[25] When Virgil retires, as it were, into the chapel of his soul for meditation or the rites of piety, the master of the long majestic march sweeps on with drums and trumpets doubtfully muted. Then, too, though Dryden fully realized the difficulty, or rather the impossibility, of translating Virgil, he forgot his own precepts in making him "copious." The especially

[23] In a letter to Scott, Wordsworth remarked that whenever Virgil can be fairly said to have his eye upon his object, Dryden always spoils the passage; see *Early Letters of William and Dorothy Wordsworth (1787–1805)*, ed. E. de Selincourt (Clarendon Press, 1935), p. 541; *Letters of the Wordsworth Family*, ed. W. Knight (Boston and London, 1907), I, 209, II, 119 ff., 123 ff., 494–95. In his own Virgilian translation, done about 1816, Wordsworth was at least as pseudo-Miltonic as Dryden, and frequently had his eye upon Dryden. To mention only the chief example, compare Dryden's "Nor pass unpraised . . . entwine" (p. 26), and ll. 77–78 in Wordsworth (*Poems*, ed. T. Hutchinson, Oxford University Press, 1926, p. 624).

[24] P. 160; *Aen.* vi. 640.   [25] P. 290; *Aen.* xi, 68 ff.

Virgilian qualities of condensation, suggestion, and intricate delicacy are dissolved in a broad, clear, uniform, smoothly flowing stream of heroic verse.   However, we can overlook such a gratuitous addition to a night-piece as "And Peace, with downy wings, was brooding on the ground," when we come to such splendidly Virgilian lines as these:

> Obscure they went through dreary shades, that led
> Along the waste dominions of the dead.[26]

There is no room to consider Dryden's debts to his predecessors.   All of them, except the baldly literal Sandys, would encourage his freedom of handling, and some furnished striking and un-Virgilian antitheses.   Denham's "Darkness our Guide, Despair our Leader was," is improved into "Night was our friend; our leader was despair"; Godolphin's "The earth is faithless, faithless are the skies," becomes "Faithless is earth, and faithless are the skies!" [27]   Nor can we look back to Sir Richard Fanshawe's rendering of the fourth book (*ca.* 1640), except for one brief comparison.   This is Dido's appeal to her sister, in Dryden:

> But do not you my last request deny;
> With yon perfidious man your interest try;
> And bring me news, if I must live or die.

That does not sound like a desperate woman.   This is Fanshawe:

> Yet try for me this once; for only thee
> That perjur'd soul adores, to thee will show
> His secret thoughts: thou when his seasons be,
> And where the man's accessible dost know.[28]

---

[26] Dryden, pp. 101, 147; *Aen.* iv. 522 ff., vi. 268.

[27] *Aen.* ii. 360, iv. 373; Dryden, pp. 41, 95; Denham, l. 348; Godolphin, l. 384.   For general and particular discussion of Dryden's work and borrowings, see Mark Van Doren, *The Poetry of John Dryden* (New York, 1920), and Charles Macpherson, *Über die Vergil-Übersetzung des John Dryden* (Berlin, 1910).

[28] *Aen.* iv. 420 ff.; Dryden, p. 97; Fanshawe, *The Fourth Book of Virgil's Aeneid on the Loves of Dido and Aeneas*, ed. A. L. Irvine (Oxford, 1924), p. 53. See my other volume, pp. 233–36.

After reading Dryden's criticism one cannot possibly doubt the depth of his feeling for Virgil, and he was certainly a greater poet than Fanshawe; one can only conclude, in spite of Fanshawe's conceits, that the poetic medium of his age had virtues which that of Dryden's age had lost. But then Dryden was not translating a single book, he had to gird himself for a long journey; one feels sure that Tennyson could have done parts of Virgil with entire fidelity and felicity, and one feels hardly less sure that a complete Virgil from his hand would have been a failure. Dryden's *Virgil*, with all the inadequacies that have been observed, is in its general texture a splendid achievement. I may say that my own experience was parallel to that lately reported by Mr. Stuart Bates, who began his study of Virgilian translations "with a prejudice against Dryden," and ended "with the conviction that his merits as a translator of Virgil surpass those of all his fellow translators put together." [29] (One must, however, make an exception of Gavin Douglas.)

Dryden hoped to finish the *Iliad*, but he did not get beyond the first book and part of the sixth. He found Homer more congenial than Virgil, and Homer's rapid, objective story-telling and forthright style gave scope for Dryden's special virtues. He is more diffuse than Pope, though Pope often echoes and follows Dryden, sometimes when Dryden is not exactly following Homer — to borrow Pope's phrase about Dryden's dependence on Chapman. [30] One line in

[29] *Modern Translation* (Oxford University Press, 1936), p. 29.

[30] *The Iliad of Homer. Translated by Alexander Pope*, ed. Gilbert Wakefield (1796), I, lxi. Both Dryden and Pope echo Ogilby's translation of Homer, and Dryden's translation is even colored by Ogilby's notes.

To mention a pleasant example of something more than diffuseness, in the last speech of Zeus to the inquisitive Hera, in the first book of the *Iliad*, the harassed deity begins with the expressive but restrained "*daimonie.*" In Dryden the word is amplified by a Restoration husband:

"My Household Curse, my lawful Plague, the Spy
Of Jove's Designs, his other squinting Eye. . . ."

Dryden, by the way, in Hector's speech to Andromache — "And Universal Ruine cover all" — was remembered in the last line of *The Dunciad*.

Pope is of course a superlative artist, and his *Homer* is alive, but Bentley's dictum and Arnold's critique stand firm. In prolonged reading his style and movement become intolerable, much more so than Dryden's in his *Virgil*. We may take an illustration of Pope at his best. In his rendering of the parting of Hector and Andromache, says Mr. Mackail, "there are about two hundred continuous lines without a single inadequate phrase, a single flat or jarring note, even after two hundred years." Well, here are some of the opening lines:

> Pensive she stood on Ilion's towery height,
> Beheld the war, and sicken'd at the sight;
> There her sad eyes in vain her lord explore,
> Or weep the wounds her bleeding country bore.
>   But he who found not whom his soul desired,
> Whose virtue charm'd him as her beauty fired. . . .

Dryden translated thus:

> From whence with heavy Heart she might survey
> The bloody business of the Dreadful day.
> Her mournful Eyes she cast around the Plain,
> And sought the Lord of her Desires in vain.
>   But he, who thought his peopled Palace bare,
> When she, his only Comfort, was not there. . . .[31]

In which version is the diction more simple and natural, the thought more unsophisticated, the movement more free and flowing? Or one might use the two couplets Tennyson cited, to show "how much more real poetic force

---

[31] J. W. Maçkail, *Studies of English Poets* (1926), pp. 70 ff.; Pope's *Iliad* (World's Classics ed.), p. 125; *Poems of John Dryden*, ed. John Sargeaunt (Oxford University Press, 1913), p. 419.

there is in Dryden," and there is no need to say which belongs to which:

> He said, observant of the blue-eyed maid;
> Then in the sheath return'd the shining blade.

> He said; with surly Faith believ'd her Word,
> And, in the Sheath, reluctant, plung'd the Sword.[32]

The lack of salience in Pope's couplet might be illustrated in his lines describing the departure of the priest
Chryses:

> Disconsolate, not daring to complain,
> Silent he wander'd by the sounding main.

Tickell (whose Homeric skiff, as Gay observed, "set forth
for Greece, but founder'd in the way") rightly preferred
his own version, which renders the pictorial and onomato-
poeic quality of Homer that Pope largely misses:

> Silent he pass'd amid the deaf'ning Roar
> Of tumbling Billows on the lonely Shore.[33]

However, one may now say things about Pope that one
might not have said when *The Dunciad* was in process of
incubation, and I am not trying in a few paragraphs to
topple an illustrious classic from his throne. But in the
field of translation, while Dryden may have more faults,
his best things are quite beyond Pope's reach. At any rate
the cordial welcome extended to Mr. Pope on his return
from Greece was prolonged through many generations. As
for the influence of his *Homer* on the style and diction of
eighteenth-century verse, no discussion is needed here. All
his artificialities — and he was perhaps as much of a col-

---

[32] *Alfred Lord Tennyson: A Memoir By His Son* (1897), II, 287; Pope, p. 9
(*Il.* i. 219–20); Dryden, p. 412, ll. 328–29.

[33] R. Eustace Tickell, *Thomas Tickell and the Eighteenth Century Poets* (1931),
pp. 211–12; Pope's *Iliad*, ed. Wakefield, I, 18.

lector as a creator — were heightened and multiplied by scores of poetasters who had nothing of his art and fire.[34]

III. The Status of Mythology

In 1549 Du Bellay had described the art of mythological periphrasis — "the thundering father" for "Jupiter," and so on — with the fresh enthusiasm of an early Renaissance classicist eager to elevate the style of French poetry.[35] In 1739 Lord Chesterfield explained to his unpoetic son, now engaged with his longs and shorts, that "poetry is a more noble and sublime way of expressing one's thoughts" than prose:

For example, in prose, you would say very properly, "it is twelve of the clock at noon," to mark the middle of the day; but this would be too plain and flat in poetry; and you would rather say, "the Chariot of the Sun had already finished half its course." In prose you would say, "the beginning of the morning or the break of day"; but that would not do in verse; and you must rather say, "Aurora spread her rosy mantle." Aurora, you know, is the goddess of the morning. This is what is called poetical diction.[36]

These Longinian precepts for the attaining of sublimity were delivered, not by an owlish country schoolmaster, but

[34] I might smuggle in a not unilluminating note about eighteenth-century versions of the tale of Hero and Leander, summarized from a catalogue in *M.L.N.*, XLIII (1928), 101–04. A list of a dozen versions in which the chief poetical names are those of Eusden and Theobald is not inviting. Eusden's poem, which appeared in Dryden's *Miscellany*, was more plagiarized than any other. The most significant fact is the negative one that Marlowe's poem has dropped completely out of sight. That translator-of-all-work, Francis Fawkes, said in his preface of 1760 that the first English translation of Musaeus was Stapylton's. All these pieces are in the glossiest poetic diction. Hero is "the angry Fair"; the tragic story will soothe "a modern Belle of Taste" and "charm a Prude." And one writer who is full of things like "the tear Neptunian" naturally considers that Homer had much "false wit."

[35] See *La défense et illustration de la langue française*, ed. L. Séché (Paris, 1905), pp. 152–53; Boileau, *L'art poétique*, iii. 165 ff.; and my other volume, p. 93.

[36] *Letters*, no. 641 (1739), II, 362.

by the leader of fashion, who was, incidentally, one of the great masters of English prose. We hardly need further evidence of what had happened to poetry and mythology toward the end of the two centuries since Du Bellay.

The mythology of Milton shows an evolution from the sensuous sweetness and richness of the Elizabethans to something like Alexandrianism, and as Milton's influence rolled like a tidal wave up the shores of the eighteenth century it deposited everywhere the bleached seaweed of mythology and poetic diction from which the Miltonic life had departed. In Thomson's *Summer* we are told that, in an Arcadian South America, the natives have "their powerful herbs, and Ceres void of pain"; it is rather sad after "which cost Ceres all that pain. . . ." But nothing could be more congenial to an age which preferred the general and abstract to the particular and concrete, and which usually abhorred the realistic and "low." In 1738 Henry Pemberton praised Glover because in his *Leonidas* he had not named such vulgar things as hay and straw but had used periphrasis: "This is a refinement, which seems to have arisen by time. In Homer we often find the commonest things expressed by their plain names." [37] Some years later Joseph Warton remarked that "among the other fortunate circumstances that attended Homer, it was not one of the least, that he wrote before *general* and *abstract* terms were invented." [38] In keeping with this inflated Miltonese was the vogue of personified abstractions, which became notable about 1742 and which, as a cure for mythological measles, was worse than the disease; Inoculation, heavenly maid, did descend, and infected everyone.[39]

[37] *Observations on Poetry*, pp. 86–87; Raymond D. Havens, *The Influence of Milton on English Poetry* (Harvard University Press, 1922), pp. 141–42.
[38] *An Essay on the Genius and Writings of Pope* (ed. 1806), II, 160–61. Cf. *ibid.*, I, 318–19.
[39] See George Dyer, *Poetics* (1812), I, 148–49; Havens, *Influence of Milton*, p. 441.

Since this chapter is largely a series of reminders, I trust that the reader does not crave a body of evidence to prove, first, that many writers continued to employ frigid mythological allusions, and, secondly, that many critics continued to object to the practice. Some samples of bad verse may be encountered in the next section, but here we may listen to the critics. The serious or humorous protests of Addison,[40] the repeated trumpetings of Dr. Johnson,[41] and numerous other expressions of hostility, were mostly based on a few fundamental principles. One was that puerile and effete mythological fictions could not be reconciled with standards of universal truth, reason, and reality. No reader of Augustan verse, especially pastorals, will question the rightness of the verdict. At the same time, though the fairy way of writing was allowed (as the spoiled child of poetry), the prevailing notion of truth was too much limited to the immediate and actual, and the universal and typical were often confused with the obvious. The rationalism which could be so sane and civilized, and which illuminated so clearly the well-oiled machine of the universe, left few dark corners for the spirit of wonder and mystery, for the mythologizing of the forces of nature and the ideals of man. Before the cool stare of good sense, nymphs melted away like Lamia under the eye of the sage, or were reduced, like Armstrong's naiads, to a "gelid reign." Yet somehow mythology stubbornly refused to die. Even toward the end of the century, about the time when James Boyer was administering his — shall we say "fundamental"? — lessons of truth and simplicity to the

---

[40] *Spectator*, 523.
[41] Johnsonian dicta on mythology are conveniently assembled by Joseph E. Brown, *The Critical Opinions of Samuel Johnson* (1926), pp. 154–60; see also Sir Walter Raleigh, *Six Essays on Johnson* (Clarendon Press, 1910), pp. 149–50. Johnson would have endorsed at least one remark of Maurice Morgann's, that about "the decayed remnants and fripperies of antient mythology"; see *Shakespeare Criticism*, ed. D. Nichol Smith (World's Classics), p. 196.

young Coleridge and Leigh Hunt, Dr. Moore, the worthy author of *Zeluco*, advised Burns to acquire learning, among other things heathen mythology, "on account of its charming fancifulness." [42]

Of course the same rationalism, the same unblinking intelligence, made satire and burlesque the dominant strain in Augustan literature. Classical travesty was especially popular from about the middle of the seventeenth century to the middle of the eighteenth. Apart from travesties proper, which are only too numerous, the majority of mythological poems of the period move on various levels of facetiousness, from that of Prior down to that of scurrilous pot-poets. Much of the salt has lost its savor, but we shall pause, later on, for a momentary taste. Obviously the widespread spirit of satire and burlesque, a matter of the head rather than the heart, acted as a corrosive agent upon the mythological imagination. In the paper of Addison's already mentioned, one exception is made to the general condemnation of mythology; in mock-heroic poems it "is not only excusable but graceful, because it is the Design of such Compositions to divert, by adapting the fabulous Machines of the Antients to low Subjects, and at the same time by ridiculing such kinds of Machinery in modern Writers."

Another corrosive agent, which likewise had begun to work during the Renaissance, was very different but not less powerful. In the later sixteenth century many puritans, Catholic and Protestant, continental and English, had objected to fables about pagan and immoral deities. In England, especially from the middle of the seventeenth century through the first three quarters of the eighteenth, pagan tastes were frowned upon by both the Nonconformist conscience and the more easy-going Anglican con-

[42] Catherine Carswell, *Life of Robert Burns* (1930), p. 247.

science.[43] Thus we have many religious complaints, shrill or sober, against the use of pagan fable or the mixing of it with Christian truth, from such various persons as Blackmore, Addison, Isaac Watts, Joseph Spence, Dr. Johnson of course, and Cowper.[44]

The conflict between poetic myth and religion had begun in ancient Greece, and Renaissance poets and critics commonly followed the ancient and medieval method of saving poetry by resorting to a more or less allegorical interpretation. One has only to think of Spenser and Chapman, and the Milton of *Comus*, to remember how vital and integral a part of their poetic thought and feeling the ethical application of myth could be. And, further, one has only to think of *Paradise Lost* and *Paradise Regained* to remember how difficult, in the latter half of the seventeenth century, the situation of a Renaissance humanist and puritan had become, to remember how uneasy a compromise Milton achieved between his artistic and his religious instincts.[45] During Milton's lifetime the allegorical conception of myth had been dwindling from an accepted and inspiring orthodoxy into an insignificant gloss on the poetic creed. Without citing the opinions of Dryden, Pope, Addison, Garth, and many others,[46] one may say that of the Augustan

---

[43] A brief sketch of anti-pagan sentiment in the seventeenth century is given in my earlier volume, pp. 244–47. For a full account of hostility to pagan epic machinery, and the problem of the Christian epic, see A. F. B. Clark, *Boileau and the French Classical Critics in England* (Paris, 1925), especially pp. 308 ff.

[44] For Blackmore, see Chalmers, *English Poets*, X, 332; for Addison, *Spectator*, 297; Watts' preface to *Horae Lyricae* (1706); Spence's *Polymetis* (ed. 1755), p. 302; Cowper's *Conversation*, ll. 815 ff. (*Poetical Works*, ed. H. S. Milford, 1913, p. 107), and *The Task*, ii. 534 ff., vi. 231 ff. For Dr. Johnson, see note 41 above.

[45] See Basil Willey, *The Seventeenth Century Background* (1934), ch. X, "The Heroic Poem in a Scientific Age," ch. XII, "On Wordsworth and the Locke Tradition," and also pp. 290 ff. See the chapter on Milton in my other volume.

[46] For some of Dryden's remarks on the didactic purpose of Homer and Virgil, see *Essays*, ed. W. P. Ker, II, 127, 154, 167, 171–72; and, for remarks on gods and spirits and Ovid's "instructive mythologies," *ibid.*, I, 152–53, II, 194. For Pope, see Wakefield's edition of Pope's *Iliad* (1796), I, xiv–xv (for Parnell's opinions,

writers some ignored allegory entirely, some gave it a half-hearted, conventional endorsement, and only a few still appealed to it seriously. Even the conception of the poet as the teacher of mankind, which had been held with such high and responsible idealism by Renaissance poets, including Milton, in the eighteenth century shrank for the most part into the notion of prosaic moralizing.

Thus in the Augustan age mythological allegory and symbolism were largely in a state of suspended animation; the return of the divine spark to the almost lifeless body will be described in pages to come.[47] Of the numerous prose works of moralized or descriptive mythology which carried on, however thinly, the tradition of the Renaissance mythographers, I might mention two; these are of special interest because, at a more propitious time, they furnished at least dry tinder for the youthful imaginations of Keats and Leigh Hunt. One was Andrew Tooke's popular *Pantheon*, which the ironical Swift described as "that nasty Pantheon" and as undesirable food for the female mind.[48] The other and much more elaborate work was

---

pp. clxii, clxxxiii); A. F. B. Clark, *Boileau*, p. 247; Austin Warren, *Alexander Pope as Critic and Humanist* (Princeton University Press, 1929), pp. 81, 100–01. See *The Spectator*, 183, 315, 369, and, for Addison's gibes at Alexander Ross, *Miscellaneous Works of Joseph Addison*, ed. A. C. Guthkelch (1914), I, 135. In his preface to the chief Augustan version of the *Metamorphoses*, Garth endorsed with apparent sincerity the allegorical interpretations of George Sandys, but he himself was not endorsed by Dr. Johnson (*Lives of the English Poets*, ed. G. Birkbeck Hill, Clarendon Press, 1905, II, 61–62). Cf. Warton, *Pope* (ed. 1806), II, 25.

Lord Chesterfield extracts edifying allegories from a number of myths. See the *Letters*, nos. 619–21, II, 327–30; no. 651, II, 376; no. 658, II, 387.

[47] In the preface to his lifeless *Judgment of Paris* (1765), James Beattie anticipates the charge that it will be thought absurd to introduce pagan theology into a serious modern poem, but he assures the reader that the names Juno, Pallas, and Venus do not represent the Homeric goddesses; they are "the Patronesses of *Ambition*, of *Wisdom*, and of *Effeminate Pleasure*."

[48] See Swift's *Poems*, ed. William E. Browning (1910), II, 97. The *Pantheon*, translated from the *Pantheum Mythicum* of Father Pomey, first appeared in 1698.

Spence's *Polymetis* (1747).⁴⁹ While it can hardly be said that such writers as Tooke and Spence nourished eighteenth-century poets as Natalis Comes nourished Chapman and Spenser, yet Spence's descriptions, however prosy, of statues, paintings, and medals may remind us that shortly before *Polymetis* appeared the *Odes* of one fine plastic artist, William Collins. And Collins might be taken as the first and most signal illustration in the whole period of a truth enunciated in 1812 by George Dyer (who was never quite in the van of the literary movement), namely, that ancient myth cannot be natural and beautiful "with us moderns, till men either paganize their divinity, or spiritualize their philosophy." ⁵⁰

IV. Mythology in Verse

In my former volume some pages were given to classical travesties of the Restoration, and any reader of the travesties or of that chapter will share my unwillingness to return to the subject here.⁵¹ The later writers of travesty or burlesque continued to exploit the established formulas, degrading romantic or heroic poems and themes to the level of bourgeois farce, and relying less on wit and satire than on comic anachronisms and boisterous animal spirits. But while the classical travesty proper may be neglected without loss — though there are agreeable exceptions such as

⁴⁹ It tells us something about the classical taste of the age, not to mention the condition of scholarship, that in a work dealing with Greek myths Spence concerned himself almost entirely with Latin literature, a procedure which was criticized by such an exceptional scholar as Gray. See *Correspondence of Gray, Walpole, West and Ashton*, ed. Paget Toynbee (Clarendon Press, 1915), II, 71, 76; *Letters of Thomas Gray*, ed. D. C. Tovey, I (1900), 165–67; *Correspondence of Thomas Gray*, ed. P. Toynbee and L. Whibley (Clarendon Press, 1935), I, 268–70.

⁵⁰ *Poetics* (1812), I, 148–49.

⁵¹ For full accounts of burlesque in the late seventeenth and early eighteenth centuries, see, in the bibliography to this chapter, the books by Messrs. Albert H. West, Richmond P. Bond, Friedrich Brie, and George Kitchin.

William King's *Orpheus and Eurydice* (1704) and *The Art of Love* (1709) — we cannot overlook the great abundance of mock-heroic, satirical, or merely playful mythology scattered through the verse of Prior, Gay, Swift, Pope, Parnell, and many others. One quatrain of Lady Winchilsea's *Answer to Pope's Impromptu* is enough to suggest the tone of a mass of poems and allusions in writers too familiar with the classics to ignore mythology, and too sophisticated to take it to their hearts as well as their heads. Thus she sings, with other notes than to the Orphean lyre:

> You of one Orpheus sure have read,
> Who would like you have writ
> Had he in London town been bred,
> And polish'd too his wit.

So many men bred in London town have polished their wit on the same grindstone (the lighter ancients and the French) that, so far as our subject is concerned, they might almost be taken as Augustan Poets, Incorporated, but two or three representatives must be briefly noticed.

Like most men of his time Prior could use classical reference in the most frigid and hyperbolical style, but in the *vers de société* by which he lives the most exalted classical themes are reduced to the polished and facetious trifling of the well-bred scholar and man of the world:

> Prometheus forming Mr Day
> Carv'd something like a man in clay.

In *Daphne and Apollo* the god retains his divinity and his dignity so far as he can when pleading with an emancipated nymph, and the conditions which she lays down for marriage with an immortal are closer to the marriage articles of Millamant than to the romantic renunciation of Stephen Phillips' Marpessa. The Elizabethans had delighted to weave Anacreontic themes into luxuriantly decorative tapestries which were mixtures of French and Italianate pastoral conventions and fresh English pastoral realism. When Prior reports the vagaries of Venus and Cupid and Cloe, he turns the Anacreontic formula into elegant and playful compliment (if "elegant" be stretched far enough to include such things as *The Dove*). The Elizabethans had domesticated Venus and Cupid in the English countryside; Prior has established them in town, and they stray no farther than St. James's Park.

It is an obvious fact that nearly all the poets who handle myth both seriously and humorously are vastly better in the lighter vein. When they accept their limitations and are content to flutter within them, they are at least entertaining; when they try to soar, as in Pindaric odes, their wings melt. Such lines as these are incomparable:

> Or, as Ixion fix'd, the wretch shall feel
> The giddy motion of the whirling Mill,
> In fumes of burning Chocolate shall glow,
> And tremble at the sea that froths below!

But we may wish to invoke a worse sentence upon the author when, in the *Ode on St. Cecilia's Day*, he can write in more sublime vein of Ixion and his fellows in the midst of

> Dreadful gleams,
> Dismal screams,
> Fires that glow,
> Shrieks of woe.

Pope celebrates Orpheus' victory over death and hell in strains which, as Warton observed, have "the air of a drinking song at a county election." [52] Second to *The Rape of the Lock* in influence on the heroi-comical poem was *The Fan* (1714), but Gay's smooth playfulness and lack of satirical edge result in very mild amusement. And while Pope's theme, tone, and details are all of a piece, Gay appears to have had less interest in the situation of his hero

---

[52] *Pope* (ed. 1806), I, 54. In *The Rambler* for July 30, 1751, Johnson suggested, giving parallels (along with remarks on the dangers of parallel-hunting), that Pope's account of Orpheus was indebted to Boethius (bk. iii, met. 12).

and heroine than in the pictures to be painted on the fan,
a series of "saints of Cupid," from Ariadne and Dido to
Leda and Venus, whose fortunes in love, pathetic or happy,
yield useful lessons for the young and fair. Gay's serious
efforts at luxuriant mythological description, if not often
in King Cambyses' vein, are commonplace Augustan
Ovidianism. Altogether, as Dr. Johnson said of *The Fan*,
"the attention naturally retires from a new tale of Venus,
Diana, and Minerva."

In general, to attempt a vain summary of a mass of
material, the comic application of myth in the Augustan
age ranges from, say, the use of Pandora's box in Parnell's
Hesiod: or, the Rise of Woman, a somewhat arch and elegant satire on "the fair," to the less fanciful piece of furniture in a poem neither arch nor elegant, *The Lady's
Dressing-Room*. It is pleasanter to recall the most humane
and benevolent of all Swift's poems, *Baucis and Philemon*,
in which Ovidian myth is made not only English but ec-
clesiastical. The gods are "hermits, saints by trade," the
cottage becomes a church, and the kindly old pair, before
their arboreal metamorphosis, enjoy themselves as a dignified parson and his wife. Swift was fond of myth,
whether in a personal poem like *Cadenus and Vanessa* or
in such a satire on Marlborough as *The Fable of Midas*. He
could burlesque the mythological fripperies of conventional gallantry in *A Love Song in the Modern Taste*, but,
in addressing Stella, he could use them himself with a kind
of mock-heroic sincerity and real warmth of feeling.
Swift's facetious and satirical mythology often reminds
one of Byron's, and these lines from *Apollo Outwitted*, with
a change of meter, might occur in *Don Juan*:

> Ovid had warn'd her to beware
>   Of strolling gods, whose usual trade is,
> Under pretence of taking air,
>   To pick up sublunary ladies.

In turning to the serious use of mythology one is confronted by that towering monument, *The Epigoniad* (1757), but one may be forgiven for not surveying the work of "the Scottish Homer," who was rather less close to the ancient poet than pounds Scots were to pounds sterling.[53] In many shorter if not lighter poems myths provided a nominal framework for moral essays. The unwary reader might be deceived by such a title as *Chiron to Achilles* (1732), but only the first two lines are concerned with the characters; from there on we have a sermon. The ancient fable of Hercules, Pleasure, and Virtue was treated at least four times in thirty years, notably by Shenstone and Robert Lowth.[54] The theme had been brought into prominence by Shaftesbury's esthetic treatise, and the two poems seem to be slightly indebted to it.[55] These moral discourses, among which may be mentioned Beattie's *Judgment of Paris* (1765), are the work of authors who think justly but think faintly, and they invite unhappy comparisons with such Elizabethan poems as Daniel's *Ulysses and the Siren.* Some of these poets or poems remind us that one of the newer vehicles for Augustan moralizing was imitation of Spenser. A more complex example of both the Spenserian manner and more or less Spenserian mythological allegory was Gloster Ridley's *Psyche* (1747). What set out to be a casual imitation of Spenser's stanza and style turned, says the author, into "a kind of Heathen

---

[53] Wilkie's preface, which deals at length with the place of myth in poetry, survives as a document in the history of primitivistic theories of epic origins. See Chalmers, *English Poets*, XVI, 123 ff.; Georg Finsler, *Homer in der Neuzeit* (Leipzig and Berlin, 1912), pp. 337 ff.

[54] See the Appendix, 1741, 1747, 1752, and 1769. Lowth's *Choice of Hercules* was the only English poem Spence chose to include in *Polymetis* (1747); it appeared also in Dodsley's *Collection* (1748), III, 1–12.

[55] "Notion of the Historical Draught of Hercules," in Shaftesbury's *Second Characters*, ed. B. Rand (Cambridge University Press, 1914), pp. 30 ff. In Shenstone, Virtue is armed with an "imperial sword," as she is in Shaftesbury (pp. 42, 45), though not in Xenophon (*Memorabilia*, ii. 1. 21). A few identical phrases in Lowth and Shaftesbury may or may not be accidental. The fable was alluded to in *The Spectator*, 183.

Paradise Lost"; the long sequel *Melampus* (1781) accordingly had to be "the Heathen *Paradise Regained."* [56] But
the mythological allegory is a Christian sermon, and on the
literary side the work is a mixture of standard ingredients,
Spenserian, Miltonic, and Augustan.

Of non-didactic mythological poems there were enough
throughout the period to preserve the genre in a twilight
life-in-death. Dryden's popular *Fables,* through its Ovidian and still more through its Italian stories, ministered to
a taste for the exotic and erotic, the romantic and the sensational; the generally hard tone and style proclaimed a
robust extrovert. But again, as the century advances, we
find the influence of Spenser operating, and in a less thin
and superficial way than in either the didactic or the facetious Spenserians. In contrast to the "gelid reign" of
Armstrong's naiads, Joseph Warton's fair nymphs bathe
"their sun-brown limbs." William Thompson's *Hymn to
May* is a sometimes charming revival of the soft Elizabethan pastoral note, and his more Miltonic *Coresus and
Callirhoe* (1757) is one of the few tolerable "Hellenics" of
the age.[57] William Whitehead wrote a somewhat similar
pair of poems, a *Hymn to the Nymph of Bristol Spring* and
Atys and Adrastus; the former, partly inspired by Akenside's *Hymn to the Naiads,* was an English parallel to the
Homeric *Hymns* and the hymns of Callimachus, while the
latter was avowedly modeled on Dryden's *Fables.*[58]

[56] *Melampus* (1781), introduction, p. ii. This volume includes *Psyche,* which
first appeared in Dodsley's *Museum* (1746–47), III, 80–97, and was reprinted in
Dodsley's *Collection.* The fullest discussion of Ridley is that of Adolf Hoffmann
(see my bibliography, "General").

[57] Chalmers, *English Poets,* XV, 22 ff., 32 ff. *Coresus and Callirhoe* was
based, the author says, on a passage translated from Pausanias (ed. Frazer, VII.
xxi. 1–5, I, 359) in Sir George Wheler's *Journey into Greece* (ed. 1682, p. 292).

[58] Chalmers, XVII, 201 ff., 210 ff. For the story of Atys and Adrastus, see
Herodotus, i. 34–35. Adrastus, by the way, may be said to illustrate the eighteenth-century strain in Wordsworth's Protesilaus; he is

"studious to controul
With Reason's Calm the Tumult of the Soul."

Narrative poems naturally turn one's mind to the treasury of Renaissance poets, the *Metamorphoses*, and one symptom of altered taste, to be inferred from silence as well as from express statements, is the loss of prestige that Ovid underwent, a loss which he has never quite recovered. For seventeen hundred years Ovid had held a high place in the tradition of European poetry, during long periods he had outshone the greater ancients; in England he had had the devotion of Chaucer and Gower, of Shakespeare, Spenser, and their fellows, and of Milton. The response of the early Augustans was less ardent, but it was exceedingly voluminous; every gentleman of letters translated parts of the *Metamorphoses* or the *Heroides* or the *Ars Amatoria*.[59] But the appeal of Ovid quickly declined. As a boy Pope liked Sandys' *Metamorphoses* extremely, and his affection for Ovid lasted longer than it should have, so that Spence felt apologetic about his hero's old-fashioned attitude, and "what seemed to Spence 'mistaken taste' was to Warton, or by Warton's time, 'bad taste.'" [60]

Of the incidental mythology in most serious eighteenth-century verse a sufficient description might be found in these lines of Pope's:

> Flow, Welsted, flow! like thine inspirer, Beer,
> Tho' stale, not ripe; tho' thin, yet never clear;
> So sweetly mawkish, and so smoothly dull;
> Heady, not strong; o'erflowing, tho' not full.

[59] As evidence of scholarly conscientiousness I may say that I once read in all the translations of Ovid made during the period 1550–1800 which are in the British Museum, and even wrote extensive comparative notes on them. My regret for these youthful wild oats is greater than I can express, and the only proof I can give of increased discretion is the resolve to keep my knowledge to myself.

A translation of the *Metamorphoses* much less known than that edited by Garth appeared about the same time. The most important contributors were Pope and Gay, though the bulk of the work was by G. Sewell and Theobald; both Pope and Gay contributed also to Garth's version. See *T.L.S.*, May 21, 1931, p. 408, June 4, p. 447; George Sherburn, *Early Career of Alexander Pope* (Clarendon Press, 1934), p. 183.

[60] Austin Warren, *Alexander Pope*, p. 193. See Joseph Spence, *Anecdotes*, ed. S. W. Singer (1820), pp. 274, 276; J. Warton, *Pope*, II, 25.

Mythology was then, as it often has been since, a mighty leveler; it had the advantage Sir Robert Walpole is said to have
discerned in bawdy conversation, that all could join in on
equal terms. It appeared in verse of every kind, from Dryden's songs to what might be called a sequel to most of those
songs, *Callipaedia: or, The Art of Getting Beautiful Children*
(a translation by Rowe and others); from Dyer's *The Fleece*,
in which the transportation of wool is thus made poetical —

> And spiry towns, where ready Diligence
> The grateful burden to receive, awaits,
> Like strong Briareus, with his hundred hands —

to Darwin's *Botanic Garden*, where "the Proteus-lover,"
to wit, *Conferva polymorpha*, "woos his playful bride":

> To win the fair he tries a thousand forms,
> Basks on the sands, or gambols in the storms.[61]

But we must turn to some poets who at their best did
more than reflect contemporary tastes and tendencies.
Gray did not do more than that in his "rosy-bosom'd
Hours," for the difference between the Miltonic original
and the echo is the difference between convention informed
by poetic feeling and convention as a substitute for poetic
feeling. As for "redning Phoebus," Wordsworth and
Coleridge said enough. But here is an example of Gray's
mythology at its best:

> Thee the voice, the dance, obey,
> Temper'd to thy warbled lay.
> O'er Idalia's velvet-green
> The rosy-crowned Loves are seen
> On Cytherea's day
> With antic Sports, and blue-eyed Pleasures,
> Frisking light in frolic measures.

---

[61] Part II (ed. 1794), p. 178. In the Apology to Part I (p. vii) Darwin says:
"Many of the important operations of Nature were shadowed or allegorized in
the heathen mythology, as the first Cupid springing from the Egg of Night, the
Marriage of Cupid and Psyche, the Rape of Proserpine, the Congress of Jupiter
and Juno, Death and Resuscitation of Adonis, &c. many of which are ingeniously
explained in the works of Bacon. . . ." Darwin's theory was better than his
practice, and nymphs were not forgotten in *The Loves of the Triangles*.

This is a pleasantly bookish Arcady, and Gray follows, with a slight stiffness of joints, the dancing movement of the earlier Milton, but what he lacks is apparent when we remember Collins:

> They would have thought who heard the Strain,
> They saw in Tempe's Vale her native Maids,
> Amidst the festal sounding Shades,
> To some unwearied Minstrel dancing.

For Gray is reminiscent, descriptive, external, while the quality of Collins' rapturous and romantic vision is best indicated by the evident fact that it stayed in Keats's memory. Sometimes Collins is mainly descriptive too; his nymph "Chearfulness," otherwise Diana, is presented with a wealth of sensuous detail. Indeed *The Passions* as a whole is a series of pictures constantly suggesting the work of allegorical painters as well as the traditional doctrine *ut pictura poesis*.[62] At the time of Collins' *Odes* that doctrine was being reaffirmed by Spence and many others. "Scarce any thing," Spence remarks, "can be good in a poetical description; which would appear absurd, if represented in a statue, or picture." [63]

Though Collins wrote no poem around a classical myth, some of his incidental mythology, as well as his use of

[62] Here and later I am indebted to the learned and critical study of my friend Mr. A. S. P. Woodhouse, "Collins and the Creative Imagination," *Studies in English by Members of University College* (University of Toronto Press, 1931), pp. 59–130. See especially pp. 95 ff.

[63] *Polymetis*, p. 311. For Pope's emphasis on picturesque qualities in Homer, see Austin Warren, *Alexander Pope*, pp. 108 ff. In his *Essay on the Genius and Writings of Pope*, Joseph Warton draws frequent parallels between poetry and painting, and insists on the importance in poetry of picturesque detail. Among general studies of the subject are William G. Howard, "*Ut Pictura Poesis*," *P.M.L.A.*, XXIV (1909), 40–123; Elizabeth W. Manwaring, *Italian Landscape in Eighteenth Century England* (Oxford University Press, 1925); Christopher Hussey, *The Picturesque* (1927); Cicely Davies, "Ut Pictura Poesis," *M.L.R.*, XXX (1935), 159–69; Herbert Read, "Parallels in English Painting and Poetry" (*In Defence of Shelley*, 1936, pp. 225–48). See also C. V. Deane, in my bibliography.

native folklore, testifies to his true mythological instinct. His desire to liberate the imagination and the emotions from bondage to the actual implies an understanding of the elements of mystery in the universe and in man, and without that understanding mythology could not be reborn. Collins is least happy in his rather melodramatic references to Greek tragedy, but his sense of an historical or imaginary classic past is very real, whether his mood be rich and glowing or cool and tranquil. That vivid apprehension of an antique world, along with his faculty of wonder, made his use of myth inevitably and spontaneously symbolic. Not that such symbolism is confined within classical limits; it is only one aspect or expression of a fundamentally mythological conception of nature and experience. Lines like these are nearer to Shelley than to Gray:

> Thou, to whom the World unknown
> With all its shadowy Shapes is shown;
> Who see'st appall'd th' unreal Scene,
> While Fancy lifts the veil between. . . .[64]

Nowhere, of course, are nature and myth so quietly and perfectly blended as in the *Ode to Evening*. The myth-making faculty is rare in any age — in the nineteenth century it virtually died with Keats and Shelley — and such passages as those cited are different in imaginative quality, in the mode of apprehension (as well as felicity of phrase), from many a superficially similar rhapsody in enthusiasts of Collins' time. That quality Collins himself explained best in his *Ode on the Poetical Character*. He takes Spenser's girdle of Florimell as a symbol of the poetic, that is, the creative imagination, which makes its own world, and goes on to celebrate Milton as the great exemplar. What gives Collins' view of poetry its emotional and half-mystical elevation is his conception of God as the supreme poet —

[64] *Ode to Fear.* See also the *Ode to Liberty*, ll. 101 ff.

not the supreme clock-maker. The creation of the world was "itself a flight of the Divine Imagination": [65]

> The Band, as Fairy Legends say,
> Was wove on that creating Day,
> When He, who call'd with Thought to Birth
> Yon tented Sky, this laughing Earth,
> And drest with Springs, and Forests tall,
> And pour'd the Main engirting all. . . .
>
> And Thou, Thou rich-hair'd Youth of Morn,
> And all thy subject Life was born!

It is not far from such lines to Shelley's *Hymn of Apollo* or "Tiger, tiger, burning bright."

In some essential respects Akenside is parallel with Collins. In an age of predominantly Latin culture both drew their classical inspiration mainly from Greek poetry and Greek ideals of freedom. (Gray of course knew Greek literature thoroughly, but its influence was more apparent in his Pindaric style than in his imagination.) Both Akenside and Collins achieved at times the Attic simplicity that many men praised; witness some of the former's Landorian inscriptions. Both repudiated their immediate predecessors and turned back to find the true poetic imagination in Milton and Spenser. Akenside's defect, and it is not merely a defect in style, is that he usually lacks the indefinable magic which is omnipresent in Keats and sometimes takes possession of Collins. [66]

Akenside's *Hymn to the Naiads* (written in 1746 and published in Dodsley's *Collection* in 1758) is probably the most notable mythological poem of the century, a fact which is partly a testimony to the author and partly a re-

---

[65] Woodhouse, p. 62. On the reference to Apollo in the *Ode*, see *ibid.*, pp. 63, 66.

[66] For instance, with Collins' lines on Tempe from *The Passions*, which were quoted above, compare Akenside's on the same theme, in *The Pleasures of Imagination* (i. 299 ff., *Works*, ed. Dyce, 1884). Akenside's Miltonic picture is nearer Gray than Collins.

flection on the age. It has some faults characteristic of Akenside and of his time. Even with the aid of the prose argument one does not readily follow the rather prolix development of the various themes, and the nymphs minister to health, commerce, and maritime power in addition to their more primitive functions. There are occasional reminders of the flat topographical and moralizing poems which everybody could and did write. The author's classical learning is not always vitalized, but may remain undigested and pebbly, an effect to which the pseudo-Miltonic language contributes. These are liabilities, and one may define as either a liability or an asset the impression Akenside often gives, that his feelings and intuitions are richer than in his verse they appear to be. He has been labeled a frozen Keats and also a small Landor, and these not incompatible references suggest the nature of his qualities of perception and expression. If, to leave Keats and Landor out of account, we compare the *Hymn* with Leigh Hunt's *The Nymphs*, we see that, though Akenside does not communicate Hunt's eager exuberance of immediate sensuous impressions, on the other hand his intelligence is at work.[67] Further, along with his tendency toward inflated and coagulated diction, Akenside attains at moments, sometimes in whole passages, a rare purity, economy, and even nobility of style.

But if Akenside now and then suggests the *Hellenics*, he is in general not content with Landorian objectivity in the treatment of myth. His model in the *Hymn* is Callimachus, "whose hymns are the most remarkable example of that mythological passion, which is assumed in the preceding poem, and have always afforded particular pleasure to the author of it, by reason of the mysterious solemnity

---

[67] Hunt, by the way, said he had as cold a recollection of Akenside's *Hymn* as of a morning in November, or one of old Panope's washing days ("The Nymphs of Antiquity and of the Poets," *A Day by the Fire*, Boston, 1870, p. 179).

with which they affect the mind." [68]   Since the modern
reader would be little interested in the mere genealogy or
adventures of the gods, Akenside has sought "to employ
these ancient divinities as it is probable they were first
employed; to wit, in personifying natural causes, and in
representing the mutual agreement or opposition of the
corporeal and moral powers of the world; which hath been
accounted the very highest office of poetry." Apart from
a degree of dryness in the language, the man who held such
a view of myth was an obvious forerunner of Wordsworth,
Keats, and Shelley.   Akenside's conception of external
nature as a revelation of the divine was not of course peculiar to him — it was the accepted doctrine of Deism on
its more "enthusiastic" and "poetic" side — and, like
Collins, he thought of God as the first poet.[69]   But, so far
as I am aware, he is the only poet except Collins who, in a
serious and significant way, carries that religion of nature
into mythological symbolism.   He follows Shaftesbury not
only in identifying beauty with truth, but, to mention an
incidental yet illuminating item, in his conception of
Prometheus as the creative artist.[70]

In comparison with romantic poetry Akenside's mythology may be cool and pallid, yet it is commonly touched
with something symbolic, or at least mysterious.   There is
such power of suggestion in the simple and perfect opening
of his fifteenth ode, *To the Evening Star*:

> To-night retired, the queen of heaven
> With young Endymion stays. . . .

---

[68] Akenside's notes, pp. 266–67.

[69] It is needless to refer to Mr. C. A. Moore's standard essay, "The Return
to Nature in English Poetry of the Eighteenth Century," *S.P.*, XIV (1917),
243 ff.; especially, for Akenside, pp. 273 ff. See also Margaret Sherwood, *Undercurrents of Influence in English Romantic Poetry* (Harvard University Press,
1934), p. 79.

[70] *The Pleasures of Imagination*, ii. 1 ff. And cf. iii. 410 ff.

It appears, intermittently, in the *Hymn to the Naiads*, in the opening apostrophe, in the finely Pindaric picture of Apollo and the Muses, and elsewhere, but there is room for only one quotation. In pleading for fit audience, though few, Milton had besought Urania to drive far off the barbarous dissonance of Bacchus and his revelers. With the Miltonic motive and the Miltonic symbolism, Akenside uses the same Bacchic theme,[71] and he addresses the Naiads, who dwell "far from that unhallowed rout," as the source and symbol of true poetic inspiration:

> The immortal Muse
> To your calm habitations, to the cave
> Corycian, or the Delphic mount, will guide
> His footsteps; and with your unsullied streams
> His lips will bathe: whether the eternal lore
> Of Themis, or the majesty of Jove,
> To mortals he reveal; or teach his lyre
> The unenvied guerdon of the patriot's toils,
> In those unfading islands of the blessed,
> Where sacred bards abide.

It is perhaps sufficient praise of such lines to say that they recall Tennyson's nostalgic visions of a classical Elysium.

If this were a book on the eighteenth century and not a chapter, one could yield to the temptation to quote other poets and poems. William Broome's fine expression of the Renaissance feeling for mutability, *The Rose-bud* (1727), has no such flash of magic as Nashe's "Brightness falls from the air," but it calls up the names of Helen and Cleopatra with moving sobriety.[72] Or there is Thomas Russell's great sonnet on Philoctetes, *Suppos'd to be Written at Lemnos*, which Landor declared would authorize the poet

---

[71] Ll. 285 ff. In a note on l. 83 (p. 265) Akenside says that Milton was "the only modern poet (unless perhaps it be necessary to except Spenser) who, in these mysterious traditions of the poetic story [a myth of Bacchus], had a heart to feel, and words to express, the simple and solitary genius of antiquity."

[72] *Oxford Book of Eighteenth Century Verse*, pp. 187–88; Chalmers, *English Poets*, XII, 22.

"to join the shades of Sophocles and Euripides." [73] Or, finally, one might quote some lines from a greater poet than Broome or Russell which combine a Miltonic echo with modern overtones:

> Whether on Ida's shady brow,
> Or in the chambers of the East,
> The chambers of the sun, that now
> From antient melody have ceas'd. . . . [74]

Devotees of Blake worship him as he is, but others may wish that he had not felt obliged to invent a private mythology.

V. Mythology and the Romantic Revival

Before embarking on the broad stream of ideas which led to the revival of mythology, we may notice some tangible evidence of English interest in classical antiquities. As the narrative manner of Keats's *Lamia* was partly modeled on Dryden's *Fables*, so the classical background of the poem was, as we shall see, derived from a learned work of the same age, John Potter's *Archaeologia Graeca*

---

[73] *Poems of Cuthbert Shaw and Thomas Russell*, ed. Eric Partridge (1925), p. 128; *Oxford Book of Eighteenth Century Verse*, p. 609. The primary inspiration, of course, is from Sophocles, but Russell may well have got hints from Fénelon's immensely popular *Aventures de Télémaque* (ed. Paris, 1784, bk. xv, II, 89–91); see also Gilbert West's translation of Pindar's first Pythian ode (Chalmers, *English Poets*, XIII, 162). With Russell's last lines compare *Paradise Lost*, ii. 660–61 (and see Havens, *Influence of Milton*, p. 507).

For Landor's tribute, see the preface to *Simonidea* (1806), p. vii. Landor may have remembered the sonnet in a passage of his own on Philoctetes; see his *Poems*, ed. Wheeler (1933), I, 109.

In an inferior and less "romantic" sonnet Wordsworth used the story of Philoctetes as a text for moralizing (*Poems*, ed. T. Hutchinson, 1926, p. 273). The sonnet is of uncertain date; it was published in 1827. In a letter to Landor of 1822 Wordsworth spoke of "the fine conclusion" of Russell's sonnet (*Letters of the Wordsworth Family*, ed. W. Knight, 1907, II, 180).

[74] Blake's *To the Muses* (*Oxford Book of Eighteenth Century Verse*, p. 617). Cf. the lines in *Comus* (98 ff.) about the sun pacing toward the other goal "Of his chamber in the east," and *Psalms*, xix. 5 (and my other volume, p. 95, note 15).

(1697–98). From the middle of the eighteenth century there was a great advance in the study of every branch of classical and oriental archaeology and topography, which is marked by the writings of Robert Wood, "Athenian" Stuart, Chandler, Revett and others; thanks to Byron, the most familiar books of this kind are those of Sir William Gell, such as *The Topography of Troy* (1804) and *The Geography and Antiquities of Ithaca* (1807). And the mention of Byron and Keats brings us to the story of the Elgin Marbles, which evoked such different and such characteristic reactions in the two poets, and which enabled Haydon almost to forget himself in passionate devotion to a great cause; but I shall not try to summarize Haydon's explosive account of his defence of the true antique and his combat with that esthetic Apollyon, Richard Payne Knight.

Childe Harold was of course both a symptom and a cause of increasing interest in the scenes and monuments of Italy, Greece, and the Orient. But the poetic exploitation of such themes had begun early in the eighteenth century; indeed it had never entirely ceased since the beginning of the Renaissance, when Giovanni Villani, contemplating the baths and amphitheaters of Rome, thought of the buried grandeur of the ancient state. In English verse of the eighteenth century there were such landmarks as Addison's *Letter from Italy*, large sections of Thomson's *Liberty*, Dyer's *Ruins of Rome* (which is better than its best-known line, "Neptunian Albion's high testaceous food"), and the digression on Greece in the third canto of Falconer's *Shipwreck*. In spirit and style parts of Thomson and Dyer are not very far from Byron. Further, when the Greek war of independence came, external stimulus only added revolutionary and personal ardor to a familiar theme, for ideals of Hellenic freedom had been celebrated, in more academic style, by Thomson, Glover, and Collins.

From these few concrete items we may turn to the more complex subject of the romantic movement in general and the mythological revival in particular. In earlier sections of this chapter some aspects of orthodox classical taste have been outlined. Here I shall try to recall, with equal brevity, some of the opposed tendencies which were gathering momentum throughout the eighteenth century, and which finally resulted in the romantic conception and treatment of classic myths. If one could imagine two histories of eighteenth-century literature in England, one tracing the decline of neoclassicism and the other the rise of romanticism, they would be very different, but they would be concerned almost entirely with the same men. It was, for instance, the author of that typical piece of Augustan moralizing, *The Choice of Hercules*, whose discourses on the sacred poetry of the Hebrews contributed to Herder's immensely fruitful conception of myth, poetry, and religious symbolism; [75] it was the author of *Night Thoughts* who helped to kindle the romantic rebels in Germany with his attack on literary imitation and his glorification of original genius; it was the conservative Gray who most notably signalized the arrival of northern mythology in English poetry. If it will not do to say that such writers were facing both backward and forward, one can say of them what is true of most writers of any age, that some looked further back than others; in this case they looked beyond Pope to a larger and richer tradition which had in some respects become impoverished. They were seldom conscious or single-hearted rebels, even when they demanded more freedom for the emotions and the creative imagination, or praised "Gothic" art, or cele-

[75] See Fritz Strich, *Die Mythologie in der deutschen Literatur von Klopstock bis Wagner* (Halle, 1910), I, 115 ff., and *passim*. One need not, at this date, emphasize the value of this comprehensive work for the mythological side of German Hellenism.

brated the divine beauty of the physical universe and the divine beauty of man's soul. After all, they were only carrying on impulses which were visible, some clearly, some obscurely, during the time when neoclassicism was at whatever height of authority it attained. The appeal of Gothic art lay not only in its supposed individuality and wildness but in its being more in conformity with nature and truth than classical art. Most of the Wordsworthian gospel of nature was implicit, though in a much less subtle form, in the verse of the Augustan Deists. Nor was the meaning of "nature" as typical human experience entirely altered between Pope and Wordsworth, for Wordsworth's peasants were representatives of universal humanity, even if not to advantage dressed. Collectively and in the long run, the romantic movement in England was a matter of emphasis and proportion, of the reinterpretation of familiar catchwords. Some affirmations, faint or ardent, here, some repudiations, faint or ardent, there, and in a few decades the whole spiritual landscape was altered beyond recognition. For there were not only different degrees, but very different kinds, of romanticism.[76]

The romantic movement involved, to attempt a compendious summary, a change from a mechanical conception of the world to an enthusiastic religion of nature, from rational virtue to emotional sensibility, from Hobbesian egoism to humanitarian benevolence, from realism to optimism, from acceptance of things as they are to faith in progress, from contentment with urban civilization to sentimental primitivism, from traditional doctrines of literary imitation to conceptions of the naïve and original,

[76] On some of the questions touched in this paragraph, see the article by C. A. Moore cited above (note 69); R. D. Havens, "Thomas Warton and the Eighteenth Century Dilemma," *S.P.*, XXV (1928), 36–50; Arthur O. Lovejoy, "The First Gothic Revival and the Return to Nature," *M.L.N.*, XLVII (1932), 419–46; "On the Discrimination of Romanticisms," *P.M.L.A.*, XXXIX (1924), 229–53.

from poetic preoccupation with the normal, the true, and the actual to dreams of the strange, the beautiful, and the ideal. . . . The catalogue might be lengthened, but this will serve. It is clear that most of the potent ideas which are called romantic were more or less essential to a rebirth of the mythological imagination, and we have seen some of them at work in Collins and Akenside. It is clear also that some of the primary ideas, such as an optimistic faith in progress and the goodness of man, had begun during the Renaissance.

However, we must take in sail and come to what especially concerns us, the growth of interest in folklore, ballads, and "primitive" epics. The evolution of opinion can be most obviously illustrated from the history of Shakespearean criticism: the great but irregular genius of the stricter formalists became the great and irregular genius, at first a supreme "original," a child of nature whose warblings wild were better than cold correctness, and then a great artist who makes his own laws, whose works are growths of nature, to be sure, but organic growths. In regard to popular ballads, Addison's attitude was much the same as Sir Philip Sidney's (even if his pulse beat less heroically), but later in the eighteenth century, when everyone was eager to discover primitive bards, the rude simplicity of ballad poetry had become a virtue; classical analogues and smoothing editorial work were no longer necessary. The criticism of Homer went through a similar cycle. While Homeric fire and invention had never been questioned, Homeric judgment and decorum had been, and here too the defects of irregularity and "naïveté" became the glory of an inspired child of nature. In carrying a step further the conventional neoclassic contrast between Homer and Virgil, Thomas Blackwell partly anticipated Schiller's distinction between naïve and sentimental po-

etry.[77] And he did more than that. With a new enthusiasm, and with a method historical at least in intention, he
developed the notion, which had been touched by earlier
scholars, of Homer as a strolling bard. All circumstances
combined to produce Homer in the right geographical and
spiritual climate at exactly the right time. He came between periods of barbarism and sophistication. The people
he knew were simple and spontaneous in feeling and expression — like Cumberland dalesmen, one might add.
The Greek language happily still retained "a sufficient
Quantity of its Original, amazing, metaphoric Tincture."
As an extemporizing bard, Homer was at once stimulated
and guided by the responsive audience before him, and
when, to the sound of his lyre, he told of Saturn and the
golden age and the gods, his listeners "conceived a high
Reverence for their Teacher, and were struck with an Awe
and Dread of the Deities which he sung." [78] For the "Alle-
gorical Religion" of the Greeks was universally believed;
"It had attained its Vigour, and had not lost the Grace of
Novelty and Youth." Knowledge in Homer's time

was wholly fabulous and allegorical. "The Powers of Nature,
and Human Passions were the Subject; and they described their
various Effects with some Analogy and Resemblance to Human
Actions. They began with the Rise of Things, their Vicissitudes
and Transformations, defined their Nature and Influence; and,
in their metaphorical Stile, gave to each a Person, a Speech, and
Method of Operation, conformable to their fancied Qualities."
This they called a History of the Birth of the Gods; of the
Heaven, to wit, the Earth, Air, and Sea; of the Sun, Moon, and

---

[77] *An Enquiry into the Life and Writings of Homer* (ed. 1736), pp. 336 ff. The
book appeared in 1735. See Finsler, *Homer in der Neuzeit*, p. 334; and the writings of Miss Lois Whitney cited in my bibliography. An account of Homeric
criticism in Germany is given by Marshall Montgomery, *Friedrich Hölderlin
and the German Neo-Hellenic Movement* (Oxford University Press, 1923),
pp. 106–99.
[78] *Enquiry*, pp. 34, 47, 55–56, 120, 156, 336 ff.

Divisions of the Stars; of the Rivers, Woods, Rocks, Fountains, and the other constituent Parts of the Universe. . . .[79]

In his *Letters Concerning Mythology* (1748) Blackwell writes in a similar strain. In its grandest form mythology

> was a various enchanted Robe of triple Texture, with Heaven and Earth, Air and Sea, and all they contain, represented in every possible Attitude, varying as it changed Lights, and according to the different Positions in which you held it to your Eye. The History of the Creation, or Rise of the Universe, what we call natural Philosophy, and the Ancients called Theogony, was the Ground-work of the Garment. The Powers that govern the World, for which We have no separate Name, framed the Figures and planned the Design; while the Passions of Men, the Harmony of the human Breast (moral Philosophy) gave the Gloss and Colouring, and as they languish or glow, it is tarnished and fades or blooms with Life, and by a secret Magic seems at times to take fire, and mount into a Blaze.[80]

Since our interest is in mythology, we cannot follow the subsequent course of Homeric criticism through Wood and others down to Wolf. But the notion of the bardic Homer was bound up with the whole new conception of folk-poetry and myth, of which we have had a misty glimpse in Blackwell's rhapsodies on the wisdom, grandeur, and mystery of Greek interpretations and personifications of the elements of nature. The new Homeric and mythological ideas were carried further in Germany by the dithyrambic Herder and the scholarly Heyne.[81] Herder was stirred by

[79] *Ibid.*, pp. 51, 102.

[80] *Letters Concerning Mythology*, p. 79. As one would expect, Blackwell praises Akenside's *Pleasures of Imagination* (p. 68).

[81] For the background of mythological scholarship, see Otto Gruppe, *Geschichte der klassischen Mythologie und Religionsgeschichte während des Mittelalters im Abendland und während der Neuzeit* (Leipzig, 1921); on Herder, pp. 96 ff., on Heyne, pp. 107 ff. (and Finsler, pp. 458 ff.). Gruppe's very learned work neglects Blackwell and Wood. I may refer again to Fritz Strich (see note 75 above).

Wood and Blackwell, and, with his much larger philosophic vision, he was a sort of wild west wind that scattered seeds far and wide. On the subject of mythological allegory and symbolism Blackwell had cited not only ancient mythographers but such names as Cartari, Bacon, and Bochart, and Herder likewise appealed to the mythological ideas and traditions of antiquity and the Renaissance.[82] But Herder widened and deepened the conception of the improvising bard by linking it with his general theory of *Volkslieder*. Not only were saga, *märchen*, and myth all products of the folk-mind confronted with nature, but poetry, myth, and religion were, if not quite identical, at any rate closely related.[83]

In the neoclassic age in England, as we have seen, mythology had been atrophied through being cut off from religion and "truth." The Augustan Deists had found in nature a revelation of God, but they had in general failed to re-create the mythological imagination, though some direct or indirect disciples of Shaftesbury, such as Akenside, Collins, and Blackwell, did have a "primitive" vision of a mythological world. Now, in Germany, mythology of all kinds gained a new depth and inwardness when it was seen as not only a primitive but a permanently fruitful phase in the religious evolution of humanity. The process was in part a return to ancient, medieval, and Renaissance conceptions of myth, but the passionate modern reinterpretation had behind it all the momentum of the "storm and stress." The gods of Greece, no longer a set of rococo toys, were enthroned as Titanic symbols of power and beauty and harmony.

[82] *Herders Sämmtliche Werke*, ed. B. Suphan, III (Berlin, 1878), 226 ff.; Finsler, p. 433.

[83] *Werke*, IX, 525, 534; Finsler, p. 434. Such ideas had been anticipated by Vico, who, reacting against the whole rationalistic movement, considered myth as the primitive and poetic conception of the divine, and emphasized the place of imagination in the religious consciousness. See Gruppe, p. 87.

The first and chief contributor to the new idealism has not yet been mentioned. If Lessing destroyed pseudo-classicism by turning from France to Greece, and Herder and his fellows rediscovered the living gods, Winckelmann rediscovered their marble counterparts. "In his famous phrase, 'edle Einfalt und stille Grösse,' he revealed, as in a flash, what the whole Renaissance movement had failed to grasp, that Greek beauty is a serene thing, that its greatness lies in its simplicity." [84] However slight Winckelmann's knowledge of genuine Greek art, his faculty of divination was great, and however much his ideas lent themselves to sentimentalizing, his gospel was sorely needed. It was a gospel which, on the whole, dominated the late eighteenth and the nineteenth century — in spite of Nietzsche — until ousted by modern anthropology; nowadays we have accurate knowledge, without the passionate vision which made Hellenism a new religion. Finally, if we want a poetic manifesto from Greece-intoxicated Germany, we have it in that hymn of liberation and idealism, Schiller's *Die Götter Griechenlands* (1788).[85] And from there it is only a step to Coleridge and Wordsworth — whether or not that poem actually influenced them — and another step to Keats and Shelley.

But the golden age of German Hellenism proved to be brief. In Miss E. M. Butler's vivid book, *The Tyranny of Greece over Germany*,[86] the whole subject may be said to turn on two main conflicts, first, between the conscious Apollonian ideal of classical serenity and the unconscious creative instinct (of this the great representative is

[84] John G. Robertson, *The Gods of Greece in German Poetry* (Clarendon Press, 1924), p. 7; *Essays and Addresses on Literature* (1935), p. 122.

[85] *Schillers Sämtliche Werke* (Säkular-Ausgabe, Stuttgart and Berlin), *Gedichte*, I, 156 ff.

A few of the multitudinous books on German Hellenism are cited in my bibliography, "General."

[86] Cambridge University Press, 1935.

Goethe), and, secondly, the conflict between Dionysian paganism and Christianity, which is exemplified in Heine. At any rate in a few decades the conscience of German romanticism asserted itself, and the Greek gods faded — as they had so often in Europe since the wailing cry "Pan is dead!" — before the pale Galilean on the Cross.[87] In England, where Anglicanism has usually not been "enthusiastic," and where the Hellenic movement was proceeding quite placidly, never reaching German raptures, pangs, and antagonisms — unless over false quantities — we find a similar though less intense pietistic tendency. It lasted, as we have seen, throughout the eighteenth century, and, as we shall see, it lasted throughout the nineteenth; it appeared even in those poets who, before Keats and Shelley, had written most sincerely and beautifully of myth, Coleridge and Wordsworth.

Thus about 1800 a set of widely various but related impulses, from advancing Greek scholarship to a new primitivistic conception of the imagination, of myth, of nature, and of religion, these made not only possible but inevitable a revival of poetry inspired by a rich mythological symbolism. Although it was the Germans who brought back the gods from exile, actual contacts between German literature and English poets, apart from Coleridge, were few and slight. For us Wordsworth is far more important than Schiller or Goethe, Haydon than Winckelmann, and, it

[87] See, for example, Heine's *Reisebilder* (*Italien*: "Die Stadt Lucca," vi), in his *Gesammelte Werke*, ed. G. Karpeles (Berlin, 1887), III, 353–54; Robertson, *The Gods of Greece*, pp. 23–25 (*Essays and Addresses*, pp. 136–38); E. M. Butler, pp. 225–34 (on Hölderlin), pp. 243–300 (on Heine), etc.

Since France has had to be neglected in this sketch, I might quote Chateaubriand: "Or cette cause était la mythologie, qui, peuplant l'univers d'élégants fantômes, ôtait à la création sa gravité, sa grandeur et sa solitude. Il a fallu que le christianisme vînt chasser ce peuple de faunes, de satyres et de nymphes, pour rendre aux grottes leur silence, et aux bois leur rêverie . . . le vrai Dieu, en rentrant dans ses œuvres, a donné son immensité à la nature" (*La génie du christianisme*, Paris, 1865, p. 238).

may be added, Swinburne than Nietzsche. We may remember too that German Hellenism owed a great deal to
Shaftesbury, Blackwell, and Wood, to Young and Lowth
and Percy and Macpherson — not to mention Shakespeare
— and the English romantics inherited the English tradition. The next chapter must deal chiefly with the father of
English mythological poetry of the nineteenth century, the
author of *We Are Seven*.

CHAPTER II

Coleridge: Wordsworth: Byron

I. Coleridge

BEFORE we come to Wordsworth, who has been described as Coleridge's greatest work, and, like all his other works, left unfinished, a few pages must be given to Coleridge's writings. Mythology is perhaps not to be counted among the first score or two of his major interests, but some of his allusions to the subject in both prose and verse are very suggestive and important. He touched everything, and seldom touched anything that he did not either illuminate or befog. For an example of the latter result, it is enough to refer to the extraordinary essay "On the Prometheus of Aeschylus" (1825).[1] Much briefer and somewhat more lucid are his remarks on Asiatic and Greek mythologies. Whatever his immediate sources of information, ancient and modern, Coleridge might be summarizing Blackwell (not to mention the Germans) when he describes Greek mythology as being "in itself fundamentally allegorical, and typical of the powers and functions of nature, but subsequently mixed up with a deification of great men and hero-worship."[2] It is in

[1] *Miscellanies, Aesthetic and Literary*, ed. T. Ashe (1885), pp. 55 ff. Along with Coleridge's own rueful account of the lecture (*Letters*, ed. E. H. Coleridge, 1895, II, 740) one should mention Hazlitt's eloquent report of the poet's eloquent talk on the *Prometheus* and Greek tragedy in general (*The Spirit of the Age*). See also *Unpublished Letters of Samuel Taylor Coleridge*, ed. Earl L. Griggs (1932), II, 281–82, 336.

[2] *Miscellanies*, p. 150; *Coleridge's Miscellaneous Criticism*, ed. Thomas M. Raysor (Harvard University Press, 1936), p. 191. Cf. Blackwell, *Letters Concerning Mythology* (1748), pp. 171, 207 ff., and above, ch. I, part v. Coleridge

harmony with such ideas that Coleridge takes Bacchus not merely as the jolly god of wine but as "the symbol of that power which acts without our consciousness from the vital energies of nature, as Apollo was the symbol of our intellectual consciousness." [3] Here also he is in agreement with Schlegel and Heyne — and Nietzsche — though it is doubtful "whether Heyne taught Coleridge anything that he did not know before he went to Germany." [4]

Coleridge's scattered and of course repeated observations on the finite, anthropomorphic, and statuesque quality of the Greek gods and Greek art are more familiar and perhaps more significant. In his lecture on Dante he compares these Greek "finites," in which the form was the end, with their opposites, Christian symbols of moral truth and infinity:

Hence resulted two great effects; a combination of poetry with doctrine, and, by turning the mind inward on its own essence instead of letting it act only on its outward circumstances and communities, a combination of poetry with sentiment. And it is

---

goes on to discuss ancient mysteries, the Cabiri, and other twilight topics which attracted Blackwell also (*Letters*, pp. 277 ff.), but he seems here to be following the mazy track of Friedrich Schelling, *Ueber die Gottheiten von Samothrace* (Stuttgart and Tübingen, 1815).

[3] *Coleridge's Shakespearean Criticism*, ed. Thomas M. Raysor (Harvard University Press, 1930), II, 263; cf. *ibid.*, I, 184–85, II, 7. See also *Lectures and Notes on Shakspere and Other English Poets*, ed. T. Ashe (1908), pp. 234, 462; *Lectures and Notes on Shakespeare and Other Dramatists* (World's Classics ed.), p. 60. The phrase "vinum mundi" as applied to Bacchus occurs in the older texts of Coleridge, though not in Mr. Raysor's. While criticizing other Hellenic notions of Coleridge's, Mr. Gilbert Murray endorses his idea of the god as the wine of the world; see "What English Poetry May Still Learn from Greek," *Essays and Studies by Members of the English Association*, III (1912), 10.

[4] A. C. Dunstan, "The German Influence on Coleridge," *M.L.R.*, XVIII (1923), 196. Both Coleridge and Schlegel heard the lectures of Heyne. For Schlegel's conception of Bacchus as a symbol of higher aspirations, see Anna A. Helmholtz (Mrs. A. A. von Helmholtz Phelan), *The Indebtedness of Samuel Taylor Coleridge to August Wilhelm von Schlegel, Bulletin of the University of Wisconsin, Philology and Literature Series*, III (1907), 365 (and also p. 299); and Dunstan, pp. 194–95. Dunstan also quotes Heyne.

this inwardness or subjectivity, which principally and most fundamentally distinguishes all the classic from all the modern poetry.[5]

It may be said in the first place that this whole passage seems to be mainly a reproduction of Schiller and Schlegel, though the general distinction between the finiteness of the Greek mind and the insatiable longing for the infinite characteristic of Christianity was a commonplace of German romanticism;[6] we shall encounter the idea throughout the nineteenth century. Secondly, if we take Coleridge's definition of the two attitudes of mind without questioning its entire validity, it may be said that it is the union of those attitudes which distinguishes the mythological poetry of Keats and Shelley; for they (along with Elizabethan opulence of expression) combine, in different ways and degrees, this outwardness and inwardness, they make the beautiful forms of Greek myth symbols of infinity and progress.

Coleridge's comment on Gray's unfortunate "Phoebus" has a much wider bearing than its immediate topic:

That it is part of an exploded mythology, is an objection more deeply grounded. Yet when the torch of ancient learning was rekindled, so cheering were its beams, that our eldest poets, cut off by Christianity from all *accredited* machinery, and deprived of all *acknowledged* guardians and symbols of the great objects of nature, were naturally induced to adopt, as a *poetic* language, those fabulous personages, those forms of the supernatural in nature,

---

[5] *Miscellanies*, pp. 140–41; *Coleridge's Miscellaneous Criticism*, ed. Raysor, p. 148. Cf. *Lectures and Notes*, ed. Ashe, pp. 233 ff.; *Coleridge's Shakespearean Criticism*, ed. Raysor, I, 176, 222, II, 262–63; *Unpublished Letters*, ed. Griggs, II, 336.

[6] A. C. Dunstan (*M.L.R.*, XVII [1922], 274–75) quotes Schiller's *Über naive und sentimentalische Dichtung*; see *Schillers Sämtliche Werke* (Säkular-Ausgabe), XII, 184 (and 179 ff., 247 ff.). For Coleridge and Schlegel, see Mrs. von Helmholtz Phelan, pp. 310 ff., 326, 337, 365 ff. According to Dunstan (*M.L.R.*, XVIII, 193), both Schlegel and Coleridge drew their comparisons of classical and Gothic architecture and drama from Goethe's *Deutsche Baukunst*. See also Arthur O. Lovejoy, *P.M.L.A.*, XXXIX (1924), 243–46, and *M.L.N.*, XXXV (1920), 139.

which had given them such dear delight in the poems of their great masters. Nay, even at this day what scholar of genial taste will not so far sympathize with them, as to read with pleasure in Petrarch, Chaucer, or Spenser, what he would perhaps condemn as puerile in a modern poet? [7]

In a footnote Coleridge mentions the desiccating agent that we have noticed already, "the mechanical system of philosophy" which had made the world in relation to God like a building in relation to its mason, and had left "the idea of omnipresence a mere abstract notion in the state-room of our reason." In a similar, though more poetic and nostalgic, mood he had written the beautiful passage in *The Piccolomini* (1799–1800):

> The intelligible forms of ancient poets,
> The fair humanities of old religion,
> The Power, the Beauty, and the Majesty,
> That had their haunts in dale, or piny mountain,
> Or forest by slow stream, or pebbly spring,
> Or chasms and wat'ry depths; all these have vanished.
> They live no longer in the faith of reason!
> But still the heart doth need a language, still
> Doth the old instinct bring back the old names. . . .[8]

---

[7] *Biographia Literaria*, ch. XVIII (ed. Shawcross, Clarendon Press, 1907, II, 58). Cf. Dryden, *Essays*, ed. Ker, II, 30–33; and Wordsworth's note on his *Ode to Lycoris*, quoted below.

We may recall the conclusion of Coleridge's *The Garden of Boccaccio* (1828), and the characterization, both charming and true, of Renaissance mythologizing — Boccaccio with his manuscript of Homer, and "Ovid's Holy Book of Love's sweet smart," and the all-enjoying, all-blending fancy which mingles "fauns, nymphs, and wingéd saints."

[8] *Wallenstein*, Part II (*The Piccolomini*), II. iv. 123 ff. In the fourth line of the extract, "their" was "her" in the 1829 text; see *Complete Poetical Works*, ed. E. H. Coleridge (Clarendon Press, 1912), II, 649. For the German text, as we have it now, see Schiller's *Werke*, V, 132, *Die Piccolomini*, III. iv, ll. 1632 ff. In considering Coleridge's very free adaptation we may remember that "the manuscript used by Coleridge was carefully prepared by Schiller and differed in some respects from the text that has since become the standard" (John L. Haney, *The German Influence on Coleridge*, Philadelphia, 1902, p. 21). And then, as Mr. Haney remarked in a letter to me, Coleridge "had too lively a poetic imagination to stick very closely to any original that he translated."

One may wonder if the rendering of these lines was colored by recollections of

These lines are written, in a sense, from the outside, they are an expression of wistful regret, a comment, not a re-creation; yet Coleridge has so rich an understanding of beauty, both sensuous and philosophic, that in his religious imagination the figures of mythology can become symbols of divine omnipresence in nature and in the heart of man.

One reason for the nature and the uniqueness of that mood is that Coleridge was not "primitive" or "pagan" enough in temperament to have an instinctively mytho-logical intuition of the natural world such as, in varying degrees, Wordsworth, Keats, and Shelley had. A more positive reason we have met already, in the contrast be-tween Greek finiteness and Christian ideas of infinity. It would be pleasanter to end this sketch with a memory of the fair humanities of old religion, yet one would give an inadequate picture of Coleridge, and an inadequate intro-duction to much later verse and prose of the century, if one failed to emphasize the dominance of his Christian over his Hellenic impulses, of his philosophic desire for unity over what he conceived to be the Greek contentment with mul-tiplicity. In such moods he could be astringently and un-poetically hostile to Greek religion and myth.[9]

Schiller's *Die Götter Griechenlands*, a poem that he must surely have known. He translated Schiller's *Dithyrambe* (*Gedichte*, I, 7) as *The Visit of the Gods*. See Haney, p. 14; and F. W. Stokoe, *German Influence in the English Romantic Period* (Cambridge University Press, 1926), p. 122, note 4.

[9] In a letter to Sotheby, September 10, 1802, Coleridge writes: "It must occur to every reader that the Greeks in their religious poems address always the Numina Loci, the Genii, the Dryads, the Naiads, etc., etc. All natural objects were *dead*, mere hollow statues, but there was a Godkin or Goddessling *included* in each. In the Hebrew poetry you find nothing of this poor stuff, as poor in genuine imagination as it is mean in intellect. At best, it is but fancy, or the aggregating faculty of the mind, not imagination or the *modifying* and coadunat-ing faculty. This the Hebrew poets appear to me to have possessed beyond all others, and next to them the English. In the Hebrew poets each thing has a life of its own, and yet they are all our life" (*Letters*, ed. E. H. Coleridge, I, 405–06). See the severe condemnation of mythology in comparison with Christianity in a letter of December 17, 1796 (*ibid.*, I, 199–200).

II. WORDSWORTH

The Victorians, beset by science and skepticism, and groping for an undogmatic faith, reverenced the poet who gave them a natural religion. We, who have got far beyond such naïve gropings, and recoil from a plaster embodiment of virtue and nobility, have acquired a new respect for the poet who gave to society a natural daughter. Wordsworth has become, so to speak, one of ourselves; "Daddy Wordsworth" is, for a distinguished modern critic, "a reformed rake." Although the poet has been so happily revived and rehabilitated, the limitations of our subject forbid chatter about Annette and compel attention to what he wrote, and only a small portion of that. Nowadays we recognize Wordsworth, no matter how great his debt to Coleridge, as the most richly germinal of all the romantic poets, as the fountain-head from which flowed the main stream of nineteenth-century poetry. It is an obvious but less familiar fact that the poet of nature and the humble man was also the fountain-head of nineteenth-century poetry on mythological themes. In *Laodamia* he re-established the classical genre, and in the extended passages on the origins of myth in *The Excursion* he brought back to life what had been dead. When we think of the body of poetry which we call Wordsworth, we may be inclined to regard the offspring of his mythological Muse as another natural child, but his ideas of Greek myth were really rooted in his deepest intuitions.

Wordsworth was not a mere ruminating cow; he was from youth up, at least until weak eyes hampered him, an ardent reader of English and foreign literature; in his increasing preference for books of his own writing he was only more candid than most poets. Even as a child of the mountains, he says in the eleventh book of *The Prelude*, and before he had read the classics, he had "learnt to

dream of Sicily," and he goes on to salute Theocritus.
The boy who loved the *Arabian Nights* was the boy who
reveled in their Roman counterpart, Ovid's *Metamor-*
phoses, who was later thankful that his early passion for
romance had not been snuffed out by Rousseauistic edu-
cators, and who, later still, protested against Niebuhr's
scientific destruction of the heroic legends of Rome.[10] His
note on the *Ode to Lycoris* (1817) is too important not to be
quoted at length:

But surely one who has written so much in verse as I have done
may be allowed to retrace his steps in the regions of fancy which
delighted him in his boyhood, when he first became acquainted
with the Greek and Roman poets. Before I read Virgil I was so
strongly attached to Ovid, whose *Metamorphoses* I read at school,
that I was quite in a passion whenever I found him, in books of
criticism, placed below Virgil. As to Homer, I was never weary
of travelling over the scenes through which he led me. Classical
literature affected me by its own beauty. But the truths of
Scripture having been entrusted to the dead languages, and these
fountains having recently been laid open at the Reformation, an
importance and a sanctity were at that period attached to classical literature that extended, as is obvious in Milton's *Lycidas* for
example, both to its spirit and form in a degree that can never be
revived. No doubt the hacknied and lifeless use into which mythology fell towards the close of the 17th century, and which
continued through the eighteenth, disgusted the general reader
with all allusion to it in modern verse; and though, in deference
to this disgust, and also in a measure participating in it, I ab-
stained in my earlier writings from all introduction of pagan
fable, surely, even in its humble form, it may ally itself with real
sentiment, as I can truly affirm it did in the present case.[11]

[10] *Memorials of a Tour in Italy* (1837), sonnets iv–vi (*Poems of Wordsworth*,
ed. T. Hutchinson, Oxford University Press, 1926, p. 359). Unless some other
reference is given, Wordsworth is regularly quoted from this edition.
[11] *Poetical Works*, ed. W. Knight (1896), VI, 145–46. See the reference to
Basil Willey above (ch. I, note 45).

It was quite natural that the younger Wordsworth should prefer to sit on old gray stones rather than on "parlor" furniture of faded plush (though the *Evening Walk* and *Descriptive Sketches* exhibit every other vice of eighteenth-century style). But, like most artists who have rebelled against effete conventions of the immediate past, Wordsworth was in touch with an older and richer tradition. His chosen masters, Chaucer, Shakespeare, Spenser, and Milton, had all delighted in Ovid and classic story, and, apart from other reasons, it was inevitable that under their influence, especially that of Milton, Wordsworth's initial antipathy to myth should diminish. The poetry of his great decade certainly contains very little mythology in comparison with his later and generally inferior work, but what there is is important; and his increasing use of myth is partly but not wholly explained by age and failing inspiration, since he wrote more good stuff after 1807 than he is always given credit for.

The finest and most familiar of Wordsworth's mythological allusions is the impassioned outburst in *The world is too much with us*:

> Great God! I'd rather be
> A Pagan suckled in a creed outworn;
> So might I, standing on this pleasant lea,
> Have glimpses that would make me less forlorn;
> Have sight of Proteus rising from the sea;
> Or hear old Triton blow his wreathèd horn.

We have here a Miltonic complexity of literary reminiscence. Although Wordsworth was a reader of Plato, the Platonism of the *Intimations of Immortality* is rather that of Proclus and Coleridge. The sonnet was apparently written in 1802, at the same time as most of the *Ode*, and this sentence from Proclus, translated in Thomas Taylor's *Plato*, has connections with both the *Ode* and the sonnet:

It is requisite therefore that the soul which is about to be led properly from hence to that ever vigilant nature, should amputate those second and third powers which are suspended from its essence, in the same manner as weeds, stones, and shells, from the marine Glaucus; should restrain its externally proceeding impulses and recollect true beings and a divine essence, from which it descended, and to which it is fit that the whole of our life should hasten.[12]

Wordsworth's "Pagan" is of course a general symbol, but he undoubtedly is thinking of Proclus, one of the last opponents of Christianity; and Glaucus, who belongs originally to Plato's *Republic*, has become Proteus, a sea-god made more familiar by *Paradise Lost*, *The Faerie Queene*, and *Colin Clout*; this last poem furnishes also Triton's wreathed horn and, less happily, the pleasant lea.[13] But these borrowings are fused into a completely original whole, and the classical allusions, though beautifully decorative, are essential to the rendering of the idea. In this sonnet we may find the keynote of a mass of mythological poetry of the nineteenth and twentieth centuries; the old antagonism between Pan and Christ has become a contrast between the ugly materialism of our commercial and industrial civilization and the natural religion, the ideal beauty and harmony, of Hellenic life. Unlike many later poets, however, Wordsworth does not fall into sentimentalism.

In a similar though a more calm and philosophic mood Wordsworth wrote the passages on the origin and signifi-

---

[12] Frederick E. Pierce, "Wordsworth and Thomas Taylor," *P.Q.*, VII (1928), 62. For the Latin text see John D. Rea, "Coleridge's Intimations of Immortality from Proclus," *M.P.*, XXVI (1928–29), 208–09. See also Herbert Hartman, "The 'Intimations' of Wordsworth's *Ode*," *R.E.S.*, VI (1930), 1–20.

[13] Rea, p. 211; *Republic*, bk. x, 611; *Paradise Lost*, iii. 604; *Faerie Queene*, III. viii, IV. xii; *Colin Clout*, ll. 245, 248 ff., 283. For Triton see also *Comus*, l. 873. Miss Abbie F. Potts has pointed out many reminiscences of Spenser and Milton in the *Ode*; see *S.P.*, XXIX (1932), 607 ff.

cance of myth in the fourth book of *The Excursion.*[14] Reacting, like Coleridge, against eighteenth-century rationalism, and, like Coleridge, putting his faith in imagination
(as they understood that faculty), Wordsworth could not
despise ancient mythological religions as idle supersti-
tions; they were testimonies, however imperfect, of the
divine presence and of man's endeavor to apprehend it.
Here, then, for the first time in many generations a great
English poet set forth a really glowing conception of pagan
myths as vital symbols of the religious imagination and
established mythology as the language of poetic idealism.
The passages are too long for quotation, but the substance,
bereft of its beauty, is this. The Solitary, the disciple of
Voltaire, overcome by disillusionment and despair of truth,
has cut himself off from man and nature, has taken refuge
in cynical apathy. But, declares the Wanderer, even humble children of the ancient east possessed a natural piety,
a religious imagination. The rustic Greek, however ignorant and superstitious, lived close to the spirit of nature,
in intimate communion with the deities of sun and moon
and wood and stream. Through such forms of the divine
were nourished the admiration, hope, and love by which we
live, and perhaps too that faith in "Life continuous, Being
unimpaired," which strengthens and sustains the frail
creatures of a day.[15] When the mind admits the law of

[14] Ll. 717 ff., 847 ff. Later (vi. 538 ff.) Wordsworth mentions the stories of
Prometheus, Tantalus, and the line of Thebes, as fictions in form, but in their
substance tremendous truths.

[15] The image reminds us of the last sonnet of the Duddon series, where
Wordsworth splendidly echoes Milton and Moschus (*Poems*, pp. 384, 915).

For the lines in *The Excursion* on the casting of a lock of hair into the river,
Wordsworth would have found suggestions in various books that he possessed,
such as Taylor's translation of Pausanias (I. xxxvii. 3) and Pope's *Iliad*, xxiii.
175, note; see *Works*, ed. Knight, V, 396–97. For a parallel idea in Wordsworth's
Essay upon Epitaphs, see *Poems*, p. 928, col. 2; or *Prose Works*, ed. Knight
(1896), II, 128. He might also have got hints, especially for "Life continuous,
Being unimpaired" (l. 755), from Potter's *Archaeologia Graeca* (ed. Edinburgh,
1818), II, 278. His library in 1859 contained Potter's first volume (*Transactions
of the Wordsworth Society*, VI, 206, item 61); presumably he had owned the

duty, man gains dominion over experience, ascends in dignity of being and in spiritual power. As the moon rises behind a grove and turns all the dark foliage to silver,

> Like power abides
> In man's celestial spirit; virtue thus
> Sets forth and magnifies herself; thus feeds
> A calm, a beautiful, and silent fire.

The ethical import of this passage, of the whole poem in fact, was fully absorbed by Keats, and re-expressed particularly in *Hyperion*. It is more obvious that his senses and imagination would be delighted by Wordsworth's account of the way in which the myth-making faculty of the Greeks peopled heaven and earth with radiant or shaggy deities, from Apollo and Diana, naiads and oreads, to satyrs and Pan himself, "The simple shepherd's awe-inspiring God!" [16] It is doubtless an insoluble problem how much Wordsworth's general conception may have owed to Coleridge and, directly or through Coleridge, to such German Hellenists as Schiller. [17] At any rate he was not writ-

---

second, and possibly he had lent it to Coleridge. Potter says that both the watery deities and the sun were thought to deserve gratitude "for the first gift, as well as continuance of life."

[16] See also the perfect lines on Pan in *The Prelude*, viii. 180 ff. Except for one word they are the same in the version of 1805–06 as in the later one.

[17] Some scholars have found echoes of Schiller's *Gods of Greece* in these mythological passages of *The Excursion*, but the resemblances seem too slight and general to prove anything. Wordsworth of course knew, and admired, Coleridge's lines on the fair humanities of old religion (see *The Correspondence of Henry Crabb Robinson with the Wordsworth Circle*, ed. Edith J. Morley, Clarendon Press, 1927, I, 402), and they may well have been in his mind, but he is less close to Coleridge in *The Excursion* than in the fifth section of the *Ode* of 1816 (*Poems*, p. 325: "And ye, Pierian Sisters. . . ."). For various opinions on these points see, for example, Theodor Zeiger, *Studien zur vergleichenden Litteraturgeschichte*, I (1901), 287–89; Thomas Rea, *Schiller's Dramas and Poems in England* (1906), pp. 74–75; Max J. Herzberg, "William Wordsworth and German Literature," *P.M.L.A.*, XL (1925), 339–42; F. W. Stokoe, *German Influence in the English Romantic Period* (1926), p. 116; A. C. Bradley, "English Poetry and German Philosophy in the Age of Wordsworth," *A Miscellany* (1929), pp. 126–27; Frederic Ewen, *The Prestige of Schiller in England 1788–1859* (Columbia University Press, 1932), p. 80, note 154.

ing under any neo-pagan impulse. Though classic myth may seem remote from the Wordsworth we usually think of, it is not at all remote if we remember the animism which was for him, as it could not be for Coleridge, almost a religious faith.[18] For one who held such conceptions of nature and of imaginative intuition, myths inevitably embodied authentic tidings of invisible things.[19]

Laodamia (1814) was the chief poetic fruit of Wordsworth's renewed reading, with his son, of some ancient authors. Ovid supplied a few details, though his epistle of course could not treat the return of Protesilaus, and Ovid's heroine, while not without pathos, comes dangerously close to comedy when she urges her husband to remember that his prowess should be displayed not in war but in love. Catullus, one of the Roman poets with whom Wordsworth's acquaintance was "intimate," emphasizes the passion of Laodamia. But the essential classical source was the sixth book of the *Aeneid*.[20] While Tennyson is

[18] "It is interesting to notice that when Wordsworth began to write *The Prelude* he still delighted to conceive of Nature not merely as the expression of one divine spirit, but as in its several parts animated by individual spirits who had, like human beings, an independent life and power of action. This was obviously his firm belief in the primitive paganism of his boyhood . . . and long after he had given up definite belief in it, he cherished it as more than mere poetic fancy" (E. de Selincourt, *The Prelude*, Clarendon Press, 1926, p. 506). Cf. Melvin M. Rader, *Presiding Ideas in Wordsworth's Poetry* (*University of Washington Publications in Language and Literature*, VIII, 1931), especially pp. 175 ff., 186 ff.

[19] For one expression of Wordsworth's belief in the religious character of all true poetry, see his letter in reply to Landor's strictures on *Laodamia* (*Works*, ed. Knight, 1896, VI, 9; *Letters of the Wordsworth Family*, ed. Knight, 1907, II, 214–15).

[20] An obvious initial suggestion for the poem was the appearance of Laodamia among the shades of unhappy lovers. Some other items derived from the sixth book are the opening sacrifices to the infernal gods, the attitude of the suppliant Laodamia (modeled on that of the priestess), her vain attempt to embrace the ghost of her husband, and of course the passage quoted in the text. Wordsworth's translation of part of the *Aeneid* was noticed above, ch. I, note 23.

See Catullus, lxviii; and *Letters of the Wordsworth Family*, II, 179. In Hyginus (*Fab.* ciii–iv) Laodamia wins the favor from the gods; in Lucian

commonly accepted as the most Virgilian of nineteenth-century English poets, it is a less familiar fact that his nearest rival is the supposedly unbookish Wordsworth. The few lines in *Laodamia* are enough to convince one that no poet has absorbed with finer understanding, or rendered with more wistful beauty, the spirit of Virgil's picture of Elysium:

> In his deportment, shape, and mien, appeared
> Elysian beauty, melancholy grace,
> Brought from a pensive though a happy place.
>
> He spake of love, such love as Spirits feel
> In worlds whose course is equable and pure;
> No fears to beat away — no strife to heal —
> The past unsighed for, and the future sure;
> Spake of heroic arts in graver mood
> Revived, with finer harmony pursued;
>
> Of all that is most beauteous — imaged there
> In happier beauty; more pellucid streams,
> An ampler ether, a diviner air,
> And fields invested with purpureal gleams;
> Climes which the sun, who sheds the brightest day
> Earth knows, is all unworthy to survey.[21]

(*Dialogues of the Dead*, xxiii) it is the ardent Protesilaus. In Propertius (I. xix) Protesilaus is the passionate one of the pair. See also Servius, on *Aen.* vi. 447. For details about Ovid, Euripides, and Virgil, see *Works*, ed. Knight, VI, 11 ff.

[21] Cf. *Aen.* vi. 637 ff.:

> "His demum exactis, perfecto munere divae,
> devenere locos laetos et amoena virecta
> fortunatorum nemorum sedesque beatas.
> largior hic campos aether et lumine vestit
> purpureo, solemque suum, sua sidera norunt.
> pars in gramineis exercent membra palaestris,
> contendunt ludo et fulva luctantur harena;
> pars pedibus plaudunt choreas et carmina dicunt."

One might add two passages which show the difference between a dead convention and a convention brought to life. In *Descriptive Sketches* (1793 version, *Poems*, p. 613), Wordsworth echoes a hundred eighteenth-century versifiers:

"An ampler ether, a diviner air" is Virgil rendered with literal felicity, but touched also with the Platonic radiance which illumines this and other parts of the poem; and the second and third lines of the quotation, though not directly Virgilian, are the distilled essence of Virgil's melancholy grace of style, his high, grave pity, tenderness, and hope.

Wordsworth's treatment of his heroine is not altogether Virgilian. Laodamia, like Dido, is passionate, and, so far as conventions go, with more justification (though her vulgar outspokenness offended the modesty of that British matron, Sara Coleridge).[22] But Dido captured Virgil's sympathy to such a degree that for most modern readers she throws the poem out of focus — and perhaps did so for the author. Wordsworth, though at first lenient, grew more severe, as later versions of the ending show, in meting out punishment to Laodamia. And while Protesilaus has a sense of duty and discipline that is worthy of Aeneas, his moral seriousness, with its emphasis on chastity, is perhaps more puritan than Roman. His discourse on self-control and on the higher objects of love is partly Platonic, but it is Platonism that has, one may think, filtered through Milton.[23] The name of Milton suggests a central question in regard to *Laodamia*. Milton treated the conflict between

---

> "For come Diseases on, and Penury's rage,
> Labour, and Pain, and Grief, and joyless Age,
> And Conscience dogging close his bleeding way. . . ."

This is from *Yew-Trees* (1803; *Poems*, p. 185):

> ". . . ghostly Shapes
> May meet at noontide; Fear and trembling Hope,
> Silence and Foresight; Death the Skeleton
> And Time the Shadow. . . ."

Cf. *Aen*. vi. 273 ff.

[22] *Memoir and Letters* (1873), I, 396 ff.

[23] Compare *Laodamia*, ll. 73 ff., 145 ff., and *Paradise Lost*, viii. 586 ff. For the alterations in the conclusion see Wordsworth's *Poems*, p. 901.

human reason and mainly sensual temptation in his four
long poems. In *Comus* and *Paradise Regained* there is no
struggle and no sin, while in *Paradise Lost* and still more in
Samson Agonistes it is only after defeat that erring human beings win the victory which is a vindication of
man's divine gifts and possibilities. Hence the one pair
of poems (though their power has until lately been under-
estimated) do stir us less profoundly than the others.
With which group does *Laodamia* belong? Did Wordsworth conceive of his heroine as a woman or as an object
lesson, a sort of female Byron who dared to take "Life's
rule from passion craved for passion's sake"? [24] There is
an obvious gulf between the poet's appeal to rational self-
control and his early reliance for moral wisdom upon
emotional intuitions of nature, between the condemnation
of Laodamia's ardor and the ecstasies of *Vaudracour and
Julia*, though the change is not in itself evidence of decline.
Does Wordsworth's faith in reason and discipline mean
that the romanticist has become classical (whatever that
means!), or is this "classicism" a reversion to the mingled
timidity and moralizing of the eighteenth-century classicist, a mark of the poet's own advancing years? Has he
achieved a Sophoclean grasp of law and imaginative reason, or has he only put off the old man to put on the old
woman? [25]

Such questions are perhaps unanswerable, but an in-

[24] *Evening Voluntaries*, iv (1834), *Poems*, p. 455.
[25] I may recall the phrase quoted from William Whitehead in ch. I, note 58.
See Dean Inge's remarks, quoted by Miss Edith C. Batho, *The Later Wordsworth* (Cambridge University Press, 1933), p. 307; and Aubrey de Vere, *Essays
Chiefly on Poetry* (1887), I, 186–88.

Mr. Herbert Read (*Wordsworth*, 1930, pp. 214 ff.) and Mr. Hugh Fausset
(*The Lost Leader*, 1933, p. 443) are very severe upon *Laodamia*; they both see
behind the hero and heroine the figures of Wordsworth and Annette. It may be
so, but one has grown weary of Annette as the one key to the poetry of Wordsworth, and the tone of critics who lecture him is not entirely unlike that of the
Protesilaus they detest.

creasing distrust of spontaneous emotion and impulse, an increasing desire for rational self-discipline, are clearly revealed in many poems of the great decade, in *Ruth* (1799), in *Resolution and Independence* (1802), in the noble series of patriotic sonnets, where Wordsworth appeals to heroic minds and careers and to "pure religion breathing household laws," in the 1805–06 version of *The Prelude*.[26] Then there is the notable group of poems of 1804–06, the *Ode to Duty*, *Elegiac Stanzas Suggested by a Picture of Peele Castle*, and the *Character of the Happy Warrior*. The last two were written, like the conclusion of *The Prelude*, under the shadow of his brother's death, a loss which had thrown Wordsworth back upon his ultimate resources; to meet such a test the healing power of nature was not enough. In the reality of grief he submitted to a new control, the law of reason. The same lesson of high and composed endurance, with more religious coloring, is learned by the heroine of *The White Doe of Rylstone* (1807–08).[27] Some relevant sentiments in *The Excursion* have already been touched upon, and that poem is so largely concerned with "reason's steadfast rule" over passions that "hold a fluctuating seat," with submission to the law of conscience, with the search for the central peace that subsists at the heart of endless agitation, that it would be idle to cite passages.[28] Thus the doctrine which receives such stately expression in *Laodamia* does not represent a unique or isolated mood. Wordsworth did not, during some years at least, merely

[26] See, for example, book xiii, ll. 160 ff., 261 ff., pp. 482 and 488 in *The Prelude*, ed. De Selincourt (1926).

While in his early prime Wordsworth often disparaged books and reason, such sentiments were sometimes dramatic or playful, and sometimes they were the natural reaction of a man who had turned for salvation to Godwinism, the intellectual system *par excellence*, and had found it both inadequate and dangerous. Moreover, at the time of *Laodamia* or later he could on occasion cherish his early faith in impulses from the vernal wood.

[27] Canto vii, ll. 1621–28 (*Poems*, p. 414).

[28] See, for example, iv. 1270 ff., v. 1011 ff., and below, ch. III, notes 63–64.

grow old and timid. Under the shock of grief especially, he fought a real battle to arrive at "the top of sovereignty" — to quote, for variety, the words of Keats — the power

> to bear all naked truths,
> And to envisage circumstance, all calm.

The trouble is that in a number of Wordsworth's later poems, including *Laodamia,* that genuine struggle seems to have receded into the past, and a "classical" faith in reason, order, moderation, becomes at times indistinguishable from copy-book morality and conventional pietism. At any rate, whatever motives really prompted the final ending of *Laodamia,* it has been, since Arnold, too readily accepted as inferior to the first one; some readers may prefer not to have a marmoreal poem suddenly lapse into softness.[29]

Dion (1816) ought to be more satisfying than *Laodamia,* for the hero is an indubitable sinner. In *The Prelude,* Dion had been linked with Beaupuy.[30] Now he has, though with good intentions, "overleaped the eternal bars" of wisdom and moderation, and has "stained the robes of civil power with blood." But if we are to be moved by the workings of eternal justice we must be made to realize the behavior of the offender who is punished; and Dion is little more than a name, the lesson of his fate is not "carried alive into the heart by passion." Thus if the two poems are to be called partial failures, the cause is not so much lack of passion, for Wordsworth's half-mystical elevation of moral wisdom surely deserves that name, but the fact

[29] For Arnold's complaint about Wordsworth's tinkering see his *Letters,* ed. G. W. E. Russell (1895), II, 182–83.

[30] *The Prelude,* ix. 408 ff. See De Selincourt's edition, pp. 570, 589. For Wordsworth's use of Plutarch in the poem, see *Works,* ed. Knight, VI, 125 ff. The most detailed criticism of *Dion,* and the highest eulogy, that I have seen is that of Mr. Sturge Moore ("The Best Poetry," *Transactions of the Royal Society of Literature,* Second Series, XXXI [1912], 36 ff.).

that the passion lacks an "objective correlative," that the *raison d'être* is inadequately conceived.

Laodamia and *Dion* are often spoken of, and were in their own day, as *tours de force*, and certainly they appear un-Wordsworthian in style if one comes to them directly from the Lucy poems or *Michael*. But if we had time to trace Wordsworth's stylistic evolution through the splendors of *Intimations of Immortality* and the frequent sublimities of *The Excursion*, we should find a fairly steady increase in the amount of classicized diction. Sometimes there is a truly Miltonic afflatus, sometimes only pseudo-Miltonic inflation. The Miltonic Wordsworth can now and then gain effects impossible for the Wordsworth of homespun, and we could ill spare the ornate dignity of the best parts of these poems, and such scattered beauties as "An incommunicable sleep" and "the unimaginable touch of Time."[31] Not that Wordsworth lost his command of pregnant simplicity:

> How fast has brother followed brother,
> From sunshine to the sunless land!

The last phrase carries an aura of classical suggestion like that of Housman's "strengthless dead."

We cannot linger over the mythological allusions in Wordsworth's later verse. The imagination which had called up Proteus and Triton from the sea dwindled for the most part into uninspired bookishness, serious or playful; the poet who had been content with a simple Highland girl and a solitary reaper began to think of rustic maidens in terms of dryads.[32] But that the aging Wordsworth was

---

[31] This last phrase may be a reminiscence of the "unimaginable touches" of Milton's remarks on music in his *Of Education* (*Prose Works*, Bohn ed., III, 476). On the next page Milton says that in the spring "it were an injury and sullenness against nature, not to go out and see her riches"; with this compare *Excursion*, iv. 1190–91; *Intimations of Immortality*, l. 42.

[32] See, for example, the Miltonic conclusion of *The Brownie's Cell* (1814); *The Excursion*, vi. 826 ff.; *The Three Cottage Girls* (1821); the opening of the third part of *The Russian Fugitive* (1830).

capable of genuine mythological and sensuous ardor we have Hazlitt's testimony, in his account of the poet's glowing talk about Bacchus and Titian's painting; and we have such a surprising and pretty piece of paganism as the Bacchic procession in *On the Power of Sound* (1828).[33] It was not, however, pagan enough for Landor, who declared in his Landorian way that "after eight most noble Pindaric verses on Pan and the Fawns and Satyrs, he lays hold on a coffin and a convict, and ends in a flirtation with a steeple. We must never say all we think, and least so in poetry."[34] In general, Wordsworth's nymphs, unlike Swinburne's, are clothed to the neck in British woolens, and they haunt, not an antique brake, nor the Mount Ida of the nude goddesses, but "The chaster coverts of a British hill."[35]

The consciousness of an antithesis between Christianity and paganism seems to have grown upon Wordsworth; in a more pallid way, for the question was not central in him, he went through a sort of Miltonic cycle. Even in *The Excursion*, the poem in which he had given new life to myth by treating it as a manifestation of natural religion, he could, like Milton, reveal in the same passage his love of myth and his fear of it.[36] And in his preface of 1815 he

---

[33] See Hazlitt's *The Spirit of the Age*. Mr. De Selincourt has suggested that Hazlitt's account is colored by recollections of Keats's Bacchic lines (*Poems of John Keats*, 1926, p. 572).

[34] John Forster, *Walter Savage Landor* (1869), II, 323.

[35] *The Triad* (1828); see *Poems*, p. 220. One of the triad, Sara Coleridge, thought the poem "artificial and unreal" (*Memoir and Letters*, 1873, II, 352), but Wordsworth liked it (*Letters of the Wordsworth Family*, II, 351).

[36] Book vii, ll. 728 ff. The lines are uttered by the Pastor.

Doubtless too much should not be made of the anecdote told by Haydon and by Hazlitt, especially since both were masters of vivid corroborative detail. At Christie's, apparently in 1824, Wordsworth looked for some time, says Haydon, at "the group of Cupid and Psyche kissing," and then "he turned round to me with an expression I shall never forget, and said, 'The Dev-ils!'" (See *Autobiography and Memoirs of Benjamin Robert Haydon*, ed. Aldous Huxley, 1926, I, xviii, 351; *Works of William Hazlitt*, ed. P. P. Howe, VIII [1931], 343.) Miss Batho (*The Later Wordsworth*, p. 84) insists that "there are at least two impossible interpretations, that he hated art and hated or was afraid of passionate love."

expresses sentiments partly similar to those we have met in Coleridge. He names, as "the grand store-houses of enthusiastic and meditative Imagination," the prophetic and lyrical parts of the Bible, and Milton, and he cannot forbear to add Spenser:

I select these writers in preference to those of ancient Greece and Rome, because the anthropomorphitism of the Pagan religion subjected the minds of the greatest poets in those countries too much to the bondage of definite form; from which the Hebrews were preserved by their abhorrence of idolatry. This abhorrence was almost as strong in our great epic Poet, both from circumstances of his life, and from the constitution of his mind. However imbued the surface might be with classical literature, he was a Hebrew in soul; and all things tended in him towards the sublime. [37]

If, in regard to classic myth, the visionary gleam had fled in Wordsworth's old age, if he was in that as in other affairs a lost leader, at least he had been a leader. Whatever he may have owed to Coleridge or Germany, it was he who re-created mythological poetry for the nineteenth century. He passed on to the younger generation, especially to Keats, its most influential representative, a noble and poetic conception of mythology as a treasury of symbols rich enough to embody not only the finest sensuous experience but the highest aspirations of man. And it was Wordsworth who created a style, or rather styles, fit for the treatment of such subjects. Of course Keats and Shelley absorbed Shakespeare, Spenser, Milton, and others of the Renaissance tradition, but in the matter of mythology the earlier masters were not enough. After the eighteenth century the vitality of serious poetic myth needed to be demonstrated by a great poet who belonged to their own age, who wrote under similar conditions, and who wrestled with similar problems in philosophy and poetry.

[37] *Poems*, p., 957.

III. Byron

Byron's classical mythology was mainly so remote from the idealistic symbolism of his contemporaries that a discussion of him at this point amounts to a digression. But his use of myth has some lively aspects, and, besides, such a book as this could not pass by "Euphorion," the poet whose name and whose death are bound up with the revival of Hellenism and the cause of Greek freedom. Only one whole poem, *Prometheus*, comes within our range — since we cannot take account of the drama *Sardanapalus* — and though mythological allusions are abundant, a glance at this peripheral aspect of Byron's work must be in the nature of a squint, for it excludes a view of wholes and misses the earth-shaking power and spacious sweep which animate pages or cantos but are rarely concentrated in single unforgettable images and phrases. We are all agreed that Byron was a volcano; it is not agreed whether he is an extinct one. However, his mythology mostly belongs to that part of him which still lives, the eighteenth-century part.

Although Byron's early education left him with a "sickening memory" of "the daily drug," "the drilled dull lesson," [38] his writing owed a great deal to his knowledge of ancient literature and history. One genuine passion was early kindled and never extinguished, a passion for the *Prometheus Bound*. The Donna Inez who "dreaded the Mythology" resembled Lady Byron more than Mrs. Byron, and the "filthy loves of gods and goddesses" which embarrassed Juan's tutors were not all that the young Byron absorbed:

> The infant rapture still survived the boy,
> And Loch-na-gar with Ida looked o'er Troy,

---

[38] *Works of Lord Byron. Poetry*, ed. E. H. Coleridge (1903–04), I, 405, 424 (*Hints from Horace*, ll. 225–26, 513–14); II, 386–88 (*Childe Harold's Pilgrimage*, IV. lxxv ff.).

Mixed Celtic memories with the Phrygian mount,
And Highland linns with Castalie's clear fount.[39]

Whatever the sufferings involved in the process, Byron
learned about as much of the classics "as most school-boys
after a discipline of thirteen years," [40] as much at least as
sat gracefully on a peer. In literary matters the great
rebel was always a thorough conservative and well-bred
man of the world. To vary a phrase of Georg Brandes'
about Voltaire, the man who had little respect for anything
in heaven or earth respected the dramatic unities. Byron
never forgot his rank, and social prejudice apparently
counted as much as critical taste in aligning him with
Moore, Campbell, Rogers — "the last Argonaut of classic
English poetry" [41] — and the gentlemanly Popeian tradition; the Lake poets, clothed in homespun and moonshine,
were not familiar denizens of St. James's Street and Pall
Mall, and they undervalued Pope.

The romantics generally, even Keats, started out in the
eighteenth-century manner, but all except Byron soon cast
it off. While his non-satirical poems were seldom free from
the glossy and rhetorical, he was, as a hard-headed man of
this world commenting on society with realistic vigor, a
truer and more masculine heir of Dryden and Pope.[42] From
almost the beginning to the end of his career Byron employed myth both seriously and facetiously. Most allusions of the former kind are conventional tags, though a
few reach the level of memorable rhetoric or even poetry.
The flippant and satirical ones are nearly all good, very
often among the best of their kind; and when Byron uses

[39] The Island, ii. 290–93 (Works, V, 609–10); Don Juan, I. xli (Works, VI, 26).

[40] Works. Letters and Journals, ed. R. E. Prothero (1902–04), I, 172.

[41] Ibid., V, 270, note; V, 274.

[42] The early paraphrase, in Hours of Idleness (1807), of the Virgilian episode of Nisus and Euryalus often reads like an awkwardly heightened imitation of Dryden's rendering, which in fact it sometimes echoes. An odd conjunction of stars, by the way, was responsible for Byron's imitation of Ossian, The Death of Calmar and Orla (Works, I, 177–83), which is based on the Virgilian story.

the same reference in both ways, the witty one is almost invariably superior. The second canto of *The Bride of Abydos* opens with a serious, romantic recollection of the tale of Hero and Leander which might have been written by any poetaster; the humorous poem on his emulation of Leander (of which feat he was genuinely and inordinately proud) is at least worthy of Prior.[43] In the first canto of *Childe Harold*, Byron writes of Phoebus and "his amorous clutch" — a mauling, perhaps, of "Phoebus' amorous pinches" — but the deity is more than a verbal counter in the famous apostrophe: "Oh, Amos Cottle! — Phoebus! what a name...." [44]

We shall not try to follow Childe Harold as, with the brand of Cain on his brow and the taste of Dead Sea fruit in his mouth, he moved slowly about Europe, sighing or spouting before the appropriate landmarks. (It is true, as Mr. Grierson has said, "that Byron made his readers feel that he was large enough to stand thus face to face with these sublime topics — the Alps, Venice, Rome, the Sea — and comment in passionate tones, and in a single breath, on them and on himself.")[45] There were good reasons for his fame. He was a peer, a rake, and a romantic misanthrope; his impressionistic guide-book in verse had more animation than the placid pages of Eustace, Clarke, and Gell; and in taste and style he was, unlike Shelley and Keats, in happy accord with the mass of readers. We can praise an image (borrowed from Sabellicus) as worthy of Venice —

> She looks a sea Cybele, fresh from Ocean,
> Rising with her tiara of proud towers — [46]

---

[43] *Works*, III, 13. Cf. *Don Juan*, II. cv. In *Don Juan*, II. cciv, Byron seems to echo the passage in the *Hero and Leander* of Musaeus which describes the uncanonical union of the lovers.

[44] *Childe Harold*, I. lviii; *English Bards, and Scotch Reviewers*, l. 399; *Antony and Cleopatra*, I. v. 28.

[45] "Lord Byron: Arnold & Swinburne," *The Background of English Literature* (1925), p. 89.

[46] *Childe Harold*, IV. ii (*Works*, II, 328).

yet here, as often, we feel how completely Byron's style was lacking in distinction, magic, finality of phrase and rhythm.

His rhetorical energy appears in the faded purple patches on works of art. Byron's esthetic opinions were largely a compound of untutored instinct and personal or popular prejudice. Following in the wake of Payne Knight, he had gibed at Lord Elgin's "Phidian freaks," and in *The Curse of Minerva* prejudice was mingled with genuine devotion to Greece, of which Byron had a tendency to regard himself as proprietor.[47] But a literary member of the House of Lords had to combine correct taste with the good sense of the cosmopolite, he had to walk the zigzag path between "artiness" and Philistinism. Accordingly Childe Harold was bound to pause at intervals and declaim before the well-known statues, and he did so in the style of an admirer of Canova. In the dubiously Lucretian picture of Venus, whose "lava kisses" pour on Mars "as from an urn," we feel that we are reading "made" poetry, and we prefer the easy spontaneity, half idyllic, half mocking, of the lines on Haidée and Juan:

> And thus they form a group that's quite antique,
> Half naked, loving, natural, and Greek.[48]

In a stanza on "the Lord of the unerring bow" the Pythian of the age is seeing and feeling, yet we are still uncomfortably aware of being addressed by an unusually eloquent guide-lecturer.[49]

Now and then Byron's passion for freedom burns into a memorable phrase, as in the apostrophe to Rome, "The

[47] See, for instance, his defence of Pope's translation of the moonlight scene in Homer, and his strictures on Wordsworth's geography in the passage on Greece in *The Excursion* (*Letters*, III, 239 ff.). And see the remarks of Apollo-Byron in Disraeli's skit *Ixion in Heaven* (ed. 1927, p. 15).

[48] *Childe Harold*, IV. li; *Don Juan*, II. cxciv.

[49] *Childe Harold*, IV. clxi. Cf. Thomson, *Liberty*, iv. 163 ff.

Niobe of nations! . . . Childless and crownless, in her voiceless woe." Not many poets could equal his nonchalance in striking a different note; the Church, "Like Niobe, weeps o'er her offspring — Tithes." [50] So too we may pass from the romantic grandeur and solitude of Childe Harold's ocean, where "the dark Euxine rolled Upon the blue Symplegades," to "The new Symplegades — the crushing Stocks," or to the passage in *Don Juan* where the Symplegades are still blue but where "Euxine" rhymes with "pukes in." [51] If we had time to run through *The Island* (1823), Byron's chief contribution to romantic primitivism, we should observe how jejune and colorless the serious mythological allusions are when put beside satirical parallels in *Don Juan*. [52] Indeed it would add a welcome sparkle to these pages to quote dozens of bits from that great epic, such as the original euhemeristic interpretation of Pasiphae, or the linking of Castlereagh with Ixion in the savage stanzas of the Dedication, [53] but we have had more than enough evidence of the superiority of Byron's facetious over his serious mythology. The large element of earth and prose in Byron did not prevent his using myth with fluent triteness, but it contributed to his robust common sense, his firm grasp of realities. His cynicism was not unmixed with Calvinism. If we turn from *Epipsychidion* to *Don Juan*, we may at times recoil in disgust; but there are moods, not necessarily baser ones, in which we prefer Byron's anti-Platonic mockery. And however enraptured we may be by Shelley's visions of

[50] *Childe Harold*, IV. lxxix; *The Age of Bronze*, ll. 642–43.

[51] *Childe Harold*, IV. clxxv–clxxvi; *The Age of Bronze*, ll. 658–59; *Don Juan*, V. v. In this as in other respects Byron may have owed something to Frere, though he went far beyond him. See *The Monks and the Giants*, ed. R. D. Waller (Manchester University Press, 1926), II. li, III. ix and xi, IV. xiv–xv, xxxiii ff.

[52] For example, compare the allusions to the *Argo* in *The Island*, i. 229–30 (*Works*, V, 597), and *Don Juan*, II. lxvi, XIV. lxxvi; or the allusions to Aphrodite and Venus in *The Island*, ii. 132–33, and *Don Juan*, I. lv.

[53] *Don Juan*, II. clv; Dedication, xiii.

a golden age, we may find wisdom in such a stanza as
this:

> Oh, Mirth and Innocence! Oh, Milk and Water!
>   Ye happy mixtures of more happy days!
> In these sad centuries of sin and slaughter,
>   Abominable Man no more allays
> His thirst with such pure beverage. No matter,
>   I love you both, and both shall have my praise:
> Oh, for old Saturn's reign of sugar-candy! —
> Meantime I drink to your return in brandy.[54]

Byron's last expedition to Greece was inspired partly by
the desire of a man who was only half a poet to express in
action an impulse worthier of his better self than his recent
life had been. Like his own Sardanapalus, he "springs up
a Hercules at once." It was with more than an aristocratic disdain for Grub Street that Byron insisted that he
did not rank poetry and poets high in the scale of intellect.
He praised the few authors, from Aeschylus down, who had
been brave and active citizens, and preferred the capacity
for doing to all the speculations of mere dreamers and observers.[55] The desire to let inward lava erupt in action was
of course coupled with Byron's zeal for freedom and his old
love of Greece, "the only place," as he wrote to Trelawny,
that he "was ever contented in." Trelawny records too
that "he often said, if he had ever written a line worth pre-
serving, it was Greece that inspired it." [56] Yet even in
these last days Byron still possessed the two pairs of lenses
through which, according to his mood, he surveyed the
world. "If things are farcical, they will do for *Don Juan*; if
heroical, you shall have another canto of *Childe Harold*."[57]

---

[54] *Beppo*, lxxx (*Works*, IV, 185).

[55] *Letters*, II, 345, III, 405.

[56] *Trelawny's Recollections of the Last Days of Shelley and Byron*, ed. Dowden
(Oxford University Press, 1923), pp. 107, 22.

[57] *Ibid.*, p. 142.

One example must serve. When, at Ithaca, Trelawny wanted Byron to visit the scenes supposedly connected with Odysseus, he became the exasperated man of the world who detested "antiquarian twaddle." Yet it was during this very time that he wrote, at Cephalonia, the fragment *Aristomenes* which laments the death of Pan and other ancient deities.[58] Even if the lines seem little more than a halting imitation of Coleridge's regrets for the fair humanities of old religion, their testimony to a genuine vein of sentiment is borne out by many other things in Byron. Finally, there is no better illustration of the poet's two sides than *The Isles of Greece*. Here passion kindles rhetoric into poetry, yet Byron is so afraid of being caught shedding manly tears that he puts the poem into a flippant frame.[59]

If one who knew a good deal of Byron were told that he had written only one poem on a mythological character, a character into whom he could project himself, the answer would be an easy guess. As Mr. Garrod says, "Of this new Prometheus, all the world was the Caucasus, and all the men and women in it vultures; and the part of first vulture was taken by a preposterous mother." [60] *Prometheus* was written in Switzerland in 1816, during the days of Byron's companionship with Shelley, and the modern significance of the myth must have been a topic of conversation. While there was doubtless mutual influence, Shelley had so far used Prometheus only as an example of the ills that came with the cooking and eating of flesh, and Byron in 1814 had recorded his view of "him, the unforgiven," who "in his fall preserved his pride." [61] Moreover, Byron said that

---

[58] *Trelawny's Recollections*, pp. 136–37 (and cf. *Letters*, VI, 242); *Works*, IV, 566. The autograph manuscript of the fragment is dated September 10, 1823.
[59] *Don Juan*, III. lxxxvi, lxxxvii.
[60] *The Profession of Poetry* (Clarendon Press, 1929), p. 52.
[61] *Ode to Napoleon Buonaparte*, xvi (*Works*, III, 312).

Aeschylus' drama, of which he "was passionately fond as a boy," was always so much in his head that he could easily conceive its influence over all or anything that he had written; his works contain some seventeen allusions to Prometheus, of varying length and seriousness.[62]

The *Prometheus Bound* had been too vast and explosive for neoclassic taste — Dacier, for instance, comments on its monstrosities [63] — but as in the course of the eighteenth century the formal and the rococo gave way to the wild and strong and rebellious, Prometheus (like Milton's Satan) came to be a symbol of heroic individualism, of revolt against divine or human tyranny. The development of the theme followed two main lines, which were sometimes separate, sometimes united. One starts (if a scholar may safely use the word "start" about any idea) from Shaftesbury's description of the true poet or artist who imitates the Creator, who "is indeed a second *Maker*; a just Prometheus under Jove." [64] This partly esthetic conception, growing with the doctrine of original genius, may be said to culminate in the brief drama of Goethe (1773). Here Prometheus is more or less Goethe himself, a type of the free spirit of the artist who, emancipated from fear of the dull and idle gods, rejoices in the fullness of life as it is and in the exercise of his creative powers.[65]

[62] See notes on *Prometheus* (*Works*, IV, 48); *Letters*, IV, 174 (1817). Nearly all the allusions are collected by Mr. Chew, *M.L.N.*, XXXIII (1918), 306–09. One might refer to the Promethean ejaculation uttered by Byron when ill after a swim (*Trelawny's Recollections*, p. 101).

[63] *La poëtique d'Aristote traduite en françois* (Paris, 1692), p. 205.

[64] "Soliloquy or Advice to an Author," *Characteristics*, ed. J. M. Robertson (1900), I, 136; and see II, 15–16. For some studies of the Prometheus theme in modern literature, see the writings of John Bailey, Arturo Graf, Karl Heinemann, and Oskar Walzel, in my bibliography, "General."

[65] *Goethes Sämtliche Werke*, Jubiläums-Ausgabe (Stuttgart and Berlin, 1902–07), XV, 11 ff. As Strich observes, "dieses Gedicht bringt ein neues Element in die mythologische Dichtkunst: den Mythos als Erlebnis des Dichters" (*Die Mythologie in der deutschen Literatur*, I, 235).

The other main line of evolution, less esthetic than rebellious or humanitarian or both, is represented by Byron's
poem and Shelley's drama, and also by Goethe's great
monologue, "Bedecke deinen Himmel, Zeus." [66] Byron's
poem is of only fifty-nine lines, but he seldom maintains
through even that space such unfaltering dignity of
thought and expression. His Prometheus is a Titan, and
the poem, for all its brevity, has a massive effect. Byron's
hero is not Goethe's intellectual and creative spirit, nor is
he Shelley's humanitarian idealist and lover of Asia. He
embodies part of the conception that we have in Shelley, of
the god who endures punishment for befriending man, but
he is the Prometheus of Shelley's opening lines; he would
have uttered the curse against Jupiter, he would never
have retracted it. Byron's Prometheus is of course as
much of a self-portrait as the works of Goethe and Shelley,
and, though calm and restrained in manner, he anticipates
the heaven-storming rebellion of *Manfred, Cain,* and
Heaven and Earth. The poem "is a defiant and unshake-
able arraignment of the conception of Providence taught
him by Orthodox Evangelicalism," and Prometheus "becomes the symbol of humanity, humanity more sinned
against than sinning." [67] But though Byron denies the
Calvinistic God and the Calvinistic conviction of sin and
personal responsibility, he cannot find relief in a Shelleyan
gospel of love, for the sense of inward discord and the reality of evil is in his bones. A stanza on life and evil in
Childe Harold is echoed in *Prometheus Unbound,* and the

---

[66] *Werke,* II, 59. It is uncertain whether this monologue was intended for
incorporation in the play or not (J. G. Robertson, *Life and Work of Goethe,* 1932,
pp. 44–45). As Robertson remarks elsewhere, this magnificent *Prometheus* was
Goethe's "real reply to Wieland, a reply before which Wieland's whole would-be
Greek world shrivelled up" (*The Gods of Greece,* p. 10; *Essays and Addresses,*
p. 125).

[67] H. J. C. Grierson, "Byron and English Society," *The Background of English
Literature,* pp. 184–86.

iron lines at the end of Byron's *Prometheus* are echoed in Shelley's last stanza, but Byron cannot escape from his realistic dualism to rejoice in the triumphant and harmonious soul of man.[68]

[68] *Childe Harold*, IV. cxxvi; *Prometheus Unbound*, II. iv. 100 ff.

CHAPTER III

Keats

KEATS is probably the only romantic poet, apart from Blake, whose present rank is conspicuously higher than it was in the nineteenth century, and the rank given him by critics and poets of that period was not low. What is there in Keats that has enabled him to emerge from modern scrutiny a larger figure than ever before? In the first place, he carries relatively little excess baggage in the way of mediocre writing or "dated" ideas from which, in various ways and degrees, Wordsworth, Coleridge, Byron and Shelley must be cut loose. Keats speaks to us directly, almost as one of ourselves; we do not need to approach him through elaborate reconstructions of dead philosophies or dead poetical fashions. The romantic elements in him remained, so to speak, central, sane, normal — in everything but their intensity — and did not run into transcendental or pseudo-romantic or propagandist excesses. It is one of Keats's essential links with some poetic leaders of our own age that he, alone among the romantic poets, consciously strove to escape from self-expression into Shakespearean impersonality.

Moreover, there is nowadays a much more general understanding of the solid strength of Keats's mind and character, of his philosophic attitude toward life and art, of his astonishing self-knowledge and capacity for growth, of his unceasing struggle to achieve poetic integrity. In all these respects, and especially in the last, he is linked with the serious poets of the present. Certain fundamental questions are always tormenting him; he can neither put them aside nor finally answer them. Has the artist a right to exist at all in the midst of chaos and wrong and suffering? If his existence is justified, can he allow his imagination to be self-centered, in the large sense "lyrical," or should it be dramatic and rooted in the heart of man and human life? Is truth, the truth which is the soul of poetry, to be won by sensuous intuition or by study and conscious thought? From first to last Keats's important poems are related to, or grow directly out of, these inner conflicts, conflicts which are all the more acute because his poetic ambitions are so often at odds with his poetic gifts. This central problem has been expounded many times of late years, but, in a chapter which necessarily reviews a large part of Keats's work, one can hardly take hold of any other thread.

I

The *Ode to Apollo* (1815) may be taken as an illustration of one of his youthful eighteenth-century phases. It is not at all an ode in the richly meditative and introspective manner, but an objective declamatory sketch of the progress of poesy like many earlier imitations of the odes of Gray, Collins, and others on poetry, music, and kindred themes. In most of the poem Keats is only practising a worn-out convention, echoing the phrases of Dryden and Thomson, Gray and Beattie, but in the best lines, the first two, there is a gleam of mythological fancy:

> In thy western halls of gold
> When thou sittest in thy state. . . .[1]

These lines have caught richer echoes, from Jonson's *Queen and huntress* and Collins' *To Evening*:

[1] *Poems of John Keats*, ed. Ernest de Selincourt (fifth ed., 1926), p. 348. For some other echoes see *P.M.L.A.*, L (1935), 790–91.

O Nymph reserv'd, while now the bright-hair'd Sun
Sits in yon western Tent. . . .[2]

Keats's first line is a faint anticipation of "the realms of gold" and "western islands." The young bard's fealty to Apollo is as yet only a verbal inheritance; the deeper meaning it acquired during the next four years was to be set forth in *Hyperion*.

The *Epistle to George Felton Mathew* (November, 1815) is one of Keats's early poems of escape. His physical orbit is restricted to the Borough, and his increasingly irksome medical studies prevent his mind from flying away to nature and poetry:

> But 'tis impossible; far different cares
> Beckon me sternly from soft "Lydian airs,"
> And hold my faculties so long in thrall,
> That I am oft in doubt whether at all
> I shall again see Phoebus in the morning:
> Or flush'd Aurora in the roseate dawning!
> Or a white Naiad in a rippling stream;
> Or a rapt seraph in a moonlight beam.[3]

This is apparently Keats's first series of mythological allusions, and their quality is prophetic, however dimly, of his more mature manner. They are not merely eighteenth-century tinsel, they are symbols of the sensuous joys of nature and poetry. Nature and poetry, poetry and myth, are one.[4] Further, the poem contains the first embryonic statement of Keats's conflicting poetic impulses, though as yet they are scarcely in conflict. The more immediate

[2] Collins' ode seems to be remembered again in Keats's last stanza.

[3] The last line seems to combine the "rapt seraph" of Pope's *Essay on Man* (i. 278) with a more imaginative recollection of the seraph band who stood in the moonlight on the ship of the Ancient Mariner.

[4] The poem ends with an unhappy experiment in myth-making. Mathew may have rubbed his eyes on learning that he was "once a flowret blooming wild" which underwent some Ovidian metamorphoses at the hands of Diana and Apollo.

pleasures are those of the eye and the realm of sense, but he goes on to speak of humanity, of the harsh treatment accorded poets, whose genius has helped to cure the stings of the pitiless world; and, as a good disciple of Clarke and "Libertas," he celebrates great champions of national freedom. The epistles addressed to George Keats and Clarke (August and September, 1816) show a similar mixture of themes and motives, from maidens with breasts of cream to the inevitable Alfred and William Tell. Sensuous delights and humanitarian aspirations follow one another in wayward alternation — the scarlet coats of poppies even suggest the pestiferous soldiery — and, though the two poetic worlds are not set in opposition, there is no doubt which is the more instinctive and congenial.

I Stood Tip-toe (1816) is the work of a young man who is literally in a transport of sensuous intoxication. At first sight the poem may appear only "a posey of luxuries," sometimes described, however, with a new, sure delicacy and even largeness of expression, but the essential thing is Keats's first full affirmation of the identity of nature, myth, and poetry; hence the significance of the allusions to Psyche, Pan, Narcissus, and particularly Endymion and Cynthia, for the poem was, we remember, a first attempt on the theme of *Endymion*. Keats writes of Narcissus, for instance, almost as if he had himself invented the myth while gazing into a Hampstead pond, and when one thinks of his progressive adaptation of myth to humanitarian symbolism one may say, by way of definition, not disparagement, that he is as yet a self-centered Narcissus. These allusions are mostly in Keats's early vein of sugary softness, though the passage on Cynthia contains some pure, clear beauty, but they are not merely ornamental. His boyish passion for myth had been confirmed, as instinct ripened into understanding, by the potent authority of Wordsworth, whose inspiring discourse on mythology in

The Excursion was a fundamental chapter in Keats's poetic bible. Yet the identifying of nature and myth had
been, so to speak, incidental in Wordsworth. He was glad
to find in the origins of myth a traditional and religious
sanction for his own natural religion, but the element of
pure myth was far less important to him than to Keats; he
had deliberately excluded it from most of the poetry by
which he lives. Wordsworth did not, until his inner vision
faded, see a dryad behind every oak tree; he had little of
Keats's half-sophisticated, half-primitive delight in the
sheer beauty of mythological tales. And, so preoccupied
was Wordsworth in philosophizing what he saw, one may
doubt if he was able to surrender himself so completely and
ecstatically to the beauty of nature for its own sake, if he
could become, as Keats could, a stalk of waving grain.

For a better parallel, in some respects, one must go back
to Spenser, because, even if he did not view nature with
modern romantic eyes, Spenser more than any other English poet had equated poetry and myth, had used myth for
both decoration and symbol. Keats is commonly linked
with the Elizabethans by virtue of his sensuous richness,
but there are less obvious and not less important links than
that. For one thing, in Keats as in a number of Elizabethans, it is almost impossible to draw a line between
sensuous and spiritual experience. For another, Keats was
the only one among the romantic poets who could quite
naturally accept and carry on the allegorical interpretation
of myth as he found it in Spenser, Chapman, Sandys, and
others; of course he does not, with medieval and Elizabethan "naïveté," understand mythology in literal religious, ethical, and scientific applications, but he is, by
instinct and influence, in the same tradition. Like Spenser,
too, he loves beauty in its concrete and human forms, and
sees in myth a treasury of the "material sublime." Though
Cynthia, in *I Stood Tip-toe*, brings him "Shapes from

the invisible world," Keats is happier among visible things.[5]

In *Sleep and Poetry*, written in the autumn and winter of 1816, his contradictory impulses and ambitions reveal the beginnings of genuine conflict. The exposition of the three stages of poetic development, taken over from *Tintern Abbey* (and later paralleled, with deeper understanding, in the letter on the mansion of life), leads from the glad animal movements of the carefree schoolboy through the adolescent passion for the finer joys of nature and sense. Keats's symbols for this passion, however, are not the cataract, the rock, the mountain and the wood, but the realm of Flora and old Pan, and kisses won from white-shouldered nymphs. It is in this world, amid this store of luxuries, that he is now delightedly dwelling. The third stage, partly retrospective for Wordsworth, is for Keats an anticipation of the future, and he almost has to goad himself on. He "must pass" these joys for a nobler kind of poetry, that which deals with the agonies, the strife of human hearts. The poem has all the varieties of style that we expect in Keats's earlier work, from the Titianesque Bacchus

---

[5] There are some items of interest in these lines:

> "Stepping like Homer at the trumpet's call,
> Or young Apollo on the pedestal:
> And lovely women were as fair and warm,
> As Venus looking sideways in alarm."

The first line has puzzled commentators, and the best explanation is that Keats had in mind an anecdote of the youthful Homer told by Chapman in the preface to his *Iliad* (Temple Classics ed., I, xxviii); see Margaret P. Boddy, *T.L.S.*, February 2, 1933, p. 76, and J. M. Murry, *ibid.*, February 9, p. 92.

In the second line Keats is thinking of a statue of Apollo which suggests motion, and may be recalling Spence's account of the Apollo Belvedere: "The god, in the bloom of youth . . . holding his bow; and seeming not only going to move on, but to move on rapidly" (*Polymetis*, ed. 1755, p. 87, and see plate XI).

While the young Keats was fond of sidelong glances, his reference to Venus may also be a recollection of Spence (p. 68 and plate V); cf. Thomson, *Liberty*, iv. 177. Mr. Maurice R. Ridley suggests a number of parallels with Spence in *Endymion* (*Keats' Craftsmanship*, Clarendon Press, 1933, p. 299).

and the pretty descriptions of Hunt's pictures to the sculptural massiveness of "might half slumb'ring on its own right arm." In *Venus and Adonis* Shakespeare's Ovidian and Italianate mythology is only tapestry in comparison with the dew-bedabbled hare, the lark, and the snail, and in *Sleep and Poetry* the picture of Diana bathing is far inferior to that of the sea, which Keats had lately beheld with his own eyes, and the weeds that "Feel all about their undulating home." [6] Our old friends Alfred and Kosciusko appear, for a moment, sandwiched between Sappho and Petrarch and Laura, for in Keats's heart liberty is a noble but somewhat remote and chilly ideal compared with love. His desire to interpret sterner themes is wholly sincere, yet, for a poet untried by life, it is less strong than ardent youthful instinct for "the most heart-easing things."

No English poet has drawn more authentic inspiration from sculpture, painting, and literature, all of which are a part of "life," than Keats, and the sonnet *On an engraved gem of Leander* (March, 1816 or 1817) was an early proof of his gift for indirect description of a work of art, description which is the concentrated imaginative re-creation of both physical fact and human feeling. [7] As for the sonnet on Chapman's *Homer*, or rather, on the discovery of a new imaginative world and the discovery by a poetic aspirant of

[6] Cf. Tennyson (*Merlin and Vivien*, l. 230): "The blind wave feeling round his long sea-hall"; and *Iliad*, xiv. 16.

In ll. 230–35 Keats is (Leigh Hunt said) attacking the "morbidity" of the Lake poets. The themes of that kind of verse are ugly clubs, the poets are Polyphemes disturbing the grand sea. As Miss Boddy has suggested to me, the allusion may be colored by a memory of Sandys, who comments at length on "Polypheme" as a type of barbarous strength (*Ovids Metamorphosis*, 1640, pp. 251, 263). Chapman used the name "Cyclop" in his translation of the *Odyssey*, though "Polypheme" appears in the argument to Book ix.

[7] On the question of the date see Claude L. Finney, *The Evolution of Keats's Poetry* (Harvard University Press, 1936), I, 192. Mr. Finney's elaborate study appeared too late to allow me to do more than pay my respects in occasional footnotes; parts of his work of course had been printed in various journals.

his own genius, that can only be mentioned here, even though it started from ancient myth, the Homeric account of the wreck of Odysseus.[8]

II

The masculine and classic style of the sonnet on Chapman was not recaptured until Keats wrote *Hyperion*, and that poem's monumental grandeur is of a different kind. It was hardly to be expected that he should rid himself all at once of some congenital faults of taste and certain baneful literary influences, both Elizabethan and contemporary. The manner of *Endymion* is largely that of *I Stood Tip-toe* and *Sleep and Poetry*, luscious, half feminine, and often beautiful. There is a distinct growth in craftsmanship, but perhaps even more remarkable is the increased depth and breadth of his philosophic apprehension of myth. While his fresh, youthful, and personal mythological vision of nature is everywhere present, that now is only a background or a starting-point for a pattern of thought. *Endymion* is one of the longest poems on a classic myth in English, and its theme and its details have received endless and generally illuminating comment. The treatment of such a poem in a section of a chapter is a problem, and perhaps it may save time in the end to give a simple summary of what Keats says. One cannot hope to shed fresh light, but one can try, so far as the plan of this book demands or allows, to place the poem in relation to Keats's mind and work.

---

[8] Among the more recent general or particular discussions of the sonnet, see, in the bibliography, J. W. Beach, H. L. Creek, B. I. Evans, J. M. Murry, J. H. Wagenblass. Keats has many echoes of Coleridge, and, as I remarked in an obscure sentence (*P.Q.*, VIII [1929], 313), he probably took "pure serene" from the *Hymn before Sun-rise, in the Vale of Chamouni* (l. 72). See Mr. Lowes's independent discussion of the matter, *T.L.S.*, October 12, 1933, p. 691.

The description of the rites of Pan [9] establishes the scene and the atmosphere, and the conclusion of the *Hymn*, with its mystical conception of Pan, adumbrates the theme; the hero's "solitary thinkings" will lead him to "universal knowledge." When the stage is cleared, Endymion, who has been strangely melancholy, unfolds the cause to his sister; he has had a vision of a lovely goddess. Peona is sympathetic, but she cannot understand how a young man of his character, a leader of men, a doer, should have been led by a dream to sully high and noble life with thoughts so sick. Endymion's reply includes the passage which Keats's letter to his publisher marks as all-important. Endymion has always longed for the world's praises, but even ambition may be dwarfed by a higher hope. Happiness lies in that which becks our ready minds to fellowship divine, a fellowship with essence. When we behold the clear religion of heaven, when we feel the beauty of nature and human legend, then we have a consciousness of universal unity. But the path to the chief intensity lies through richer entanglements, enthrallments far more self-destroying; the crown of these is love and friendship, and of the two love is supreme. The first sensuous effects of love bring pain with them, but in the end we become a part of love, and life's self receives its proper nourishment. So rich is this food that even men who ruled the world have been content to lose the world for love. If earthly love is good, and has such power, what a trifle are the claims of ambition compared with an immortal love! And the dream, Endymion believes, was a reality.

In the badly written but deeply felt apostrophe to love which opens the second book, Keats proclaims his faith in

---

[9] In *Lamia*, Keats certainly made use of Potter's *Archaeologia Graeca, or The Antiquities of Greece*, a book that he owned, and it apparently contributed some details to this passage in *Endymion*. See my "Notes on Keats's Reading," *P.M.L.A.*, L (1935), 785–806.

a sovereign power which is eternally important, as mere historical events are not.[10] Then Endymion sets off in search of his dream-goddess and wanders through an underworld of endless passages; the general idea of an underworld might have come from many sources, such as the *Aeneid* or the cave of Mammon in *The Faerie Queene*, or *Gebir* or *Alastor*. Overcome by thoughts of self and solitude, and cut off from the beauties of nature in which he had delighted, Endymion prays to Diana,[11] chief representative of the clear religion of earth and heaven. (We may remember that Endymion does not know that his dream-goddess is Diana.) In answer to his prayer flowers spring up around him, but now he cannot linger to enjoy them, nor does music soothe the restless lover consumed by a flame of elemental passion. Endymion comes to a bower where Adonis sleeps. Adonis had shunned the joy of Venus' love — folly that the ardent Endymion is ready to condemn [12] — but now, awakened by Venus from his half-year's sleep, the once reluctant youth is a willing lover and shares in warm embracements.[13] On fire himself, Endymion is encouraged in his quest by Venus, and he soon has the joy of actually embracing his "known Unknown." With fruition love's madness leaves him, and all other depths seem shallow; other values, former hopes and

[10] The reference to Themistocles and the owl (ll. 22–23) probably comes from Potter's *Archaeologia Graeca* (ed. Edinburgh, 1818, I, 379–80). On pp. 378, 380, Potter mentions Alexander (Keats, ll. 24–25), but the terms of Keats's allusion to Alexander and the Indus suggest a misty recollection of his favorite Robertson (*History of America*, Dublin, 1777, I, 15–16).

[11] Colvin (*John Keats*, 1917, p. 233) observes that the prayer echoes the description of Diana in the mythological passage in the fourth book of *The Excursion*.

[12] Compare the canceled lines of *Fancy* (*Poems*, p. 480), written in December, 1818, after Keats had fallen in love, and see Mr. Murry's comments (*Keats and Shakespeare*, Oxford University Press, 1925, pp. 106–07).

[13] While Keats knew various Elizabethan treatments of Adonis, his picture of the youth asleep on a rich bed, with myrtles around, and a company of attendant Cupids, seems to be indebted to Bion. See Chalmers, *English Poets*, XX, 385, ll. 98 ff.

ambitions, are good only so far as they minister to love. Then Endymion hears the voice of Alpheus pleading passionately with Arethusa, who is eager to grant his wish but fears Diana. Endymion, who has witnessed the blissful reunion of Venus and Adonis, who has himself found relief from unsatisfied desire, prays to the goddess of his pilgrimage to make these lovers happy.

Near the opening of the third book Endymion, who is now wandering under the sea, apostrophizes the moon, and we learn what had been his state of mind before the poem begins. Since his childhood the moon had moved his heart with strange potency, she had blended with all the ardors of the growing boy. She was the beauty of nature, of philosophy, of poetry, she was the voice of friends, she was glory and great deeds, she was the charm of women. From all things beautiful his spirit had struck a wild and harmonized tune. But there came a nearer bliss, his strange love — that is, the goddess whom he has been seeking — and the moon faded, though not entirely. Now he feels the moon's power fresh upon him, but he entreats her to keep back her influence and not blind his sovereign vision.

Endymion then comes upon old Glaucus, and is saluted as a destined deliverer. Glaucus' sorrow wins sympathy from Endymion, who listens to a story partly similar to his own. At first a contented lover of nature, Glaucus had craved a larger life; then he had fallen in love with Scylla, but Scylla refused him. In seeking aid from Circe he had been seduced by a beautiful stranger, and had become a vassal of an arbitrary queen of sense. When he learned that this was Circe, and she knew that he knew, she put a curse of senile feebleness upon him.[14] After he had felt a

---

[14] Mr. De Selincourt has shown Keats's debt to the allegorical verses and commentary in Sandys' *Ovid*. The same allegorical tradition about Circe, and perhaps the same commentary, had been incorporated in *Comus*; see my other volume, p. 267.

keen desire to help some shipwrecked people, a means of salvation had been offered. If he would explore the essential meaning of all things, and especially if he would preserve the bodies of lovers lost at sea, a young man would appear who would assist him to complete the task. In performing the appointed rites and reviving the dead lovers, Endymion and Glaucus now taste a pure wine of happiness.[15] During a celebration at Neptune's palace Venus again encourages Endymion with hopes of regaining his love. Hymns are sung to Neptune, Venus, and Cupid, the god of warm pulses and disheveled hair and panting bosoms bare.[16] Stricken with passion for his goddess, Endymion swoons, but hears a voice assuring him that he has won immortal bliss for both herself and him.

At the beginning of the fourth book Endymion feels a new access of joy and pain when he sees, pities, and loves a forlorn Indian maiden. He condemns himself for having "a triple soul," and he knows that this human maid has stolen the wings wherewith he was to top the heavens. After she sings her roundelay, Endymion grows more and more ardent, and ominous words echo through the woods. While the two are carried on an airy voyage they sleep, and Endymion dreams that he is in heaven among the gods. For the first time he sees that the goddess he has loved is

[15] The nature of the humanitarian service might have been suggested by Jonson's *Masque of Lethe* (*Masques and Entertainments*, ed. Henry Morley, 1890, pp. 209 ff.), where we have the revival of a troop of ghosts who are the gentle forms of sea-tossed lovers.

[16] The episode at Neptune's palace is indebted, as De Selincourt showed, to Spenser and Sandys. At least one phrase, "the palace of his pride" (Keats, l. 833), probably comes from a passage in *Thalaba* which I think lies behind stanzas xiv–xv of *Isabella*; see Southey's *Poems* (Oxford University Press, 1909), i. 22, l. 238, i. 28, l. 363. Keats may also have derived hints from Jonson's *Neptune's Triumph*; for details concerning both Southey and Jonson, see *P.M.L.A.*, L, 795–96, 799. In the hymn to Neptune (ll. 943 ff.) Keats links some obvious reminiscences of Virgil's picture of Neptune calming the storm with a recollection of Milton's *At a Vacation Exercise*, ll. 34 ff. Cf. *Hyperion*, ii. 234 ff.

Diana. Torn between her and the Indian maid, he at last
cleaves to his mortal love, and the goddess of his dream
melts away. He cries out in misery. His soul does not
seem his own, he has no self-passion or identity. As the
pair continue their journey through the sky the moon
appears, and the body of the Indian maiden fades from
Endymion's grasp. In the "Cave of Quietude" the
tortured lover feels the desperate contentment of utter
apathy.

Rejoining his companion on the ground, he bitterly reproaches himself for having clung to nothing, loved nothing
but a great dream:

> There never liv'd a mortal man, who bent
> His appetite beyond his natural sphere,
> But starv'd and died. My sweetest Indian, here,
> Here will I kneel, for thou redeemed hast
> My life from too thin breathing: gone and past
> Are cloudy phantasms.[17]

Endymion bids farewell to his dream. He loves her still,
but she is not for earth; it is the Indian girl who will give
human kisses. Echoing Polyphemus' invitation to Galatea
to live with him and be his love,[18] Endymion pictures a life
of love and peace in the natural realm of Pan. But the
Indian is forbidden to love. The two return, silent and sad,
to the scenes of Endymion's earlier life. Peona meets them,
full of hopes for the future. But now Endymion would
have his Indian maid as a friend only. Deceptions that
pass for pleasures are, he knows, pleasures real as real may
be, but there are higher ones he may not see if he impiously
takes an earthly realm. So he will be a hermit, and the
Indian maid will serve Diana. Endymion upbraids him-

[17] Compare the *Epistle to Reynolds* (March, 1818), ll. 78 ff., and *The Excursion*, iv. 123 ff.

[18] Endymion may be echoing Caliban also. See *The Tempest*, II. ii. 173 ff., 180 ff., and Caroline F. E. Spurgeon, *Keats's Shakespeare* (Oxford University Press, 1928), pp. 12, 58–59.

self for having been a butterfly, a lord of flowers; yet it is an unjust fate for one who has been wedded to things of light from infancy. When the three meet again, Endymion resigns his will to that of heaven. Before his eyes the Indian maiden is transformed into Diana and his love. She had held back hitherto because of foolish fear, and fate, and because it was needful that Endymion should be spiritualized.

The poem has several though related meanings, and Keats's apparent intentions do not always seem to be in accord with the poetic result. The design of the whole is an organic unit, but the control of particular parts is uncertain, partly because Keats was a young and undisciplined artist, and partly because *Endymion* was a confessional poem growing out of immediate turmoil of spirit. Up to the last moment the hero is subject to conflicting desires and impulses, as his creator was to the end of his short life. And in addition to difficulties in the conscious exposition of inner conflict, there are unconscious implications, so that at times what is said in the lines seems to be partly contradicted by what can be read between them. *Endymion* was Keats's most serious early attempt to answer fundamental questions about the relation of the artist to his art and to the world. Shelley had asked similar questions in *Alastor*, and, without losing sight of other factors, one may perhaps understand *Endymion* best by taking it in part as a reply to Shelley, a reply which includes imitation and adaptation as well.[19] Shelley's hero is a romantic idealist who finds no satisfaction in the unlovely world of humanity, and, frustrated in his quest, dies in solitude; but it is better, says Shelley, so to pursue the vision and perish than to live, a finished and finite clod, untroubled by a spark. No search for ideal love and beauty

[19] See Leonard Brown, "The Genesis, Growth, and Meaning of *Endymion*," *S.P.*, XXX (1933), 618 ff.

could be unattractive to Keats, and there is something of Shelley's hero in Endymion. Yet that hero, for all his powers of locomotion, inhabited, as Keats would see, an ivory tower. It is a fundamental source of Keats's strength, and of his hold upon us, that he, despite his love of poetic luxuries and devotion to art, shared and understood the common experience of mankind as Shelley, with all his humanitarian zeal, never did. Although, then, Endymion does not learn his lesson until the very end, his whole previous pilgrimage has been leading him away from purely visionary idealism to the knowledge that the actual world of human life must be accepted, not denied, and that only through participation in that life can the ideal be realized. That thoroughly Wordsworthian doctrine is, to be sure, the moral Shelley expounded in the preface to *Alastor* (which ends with some lines from *The Excursion*), but Shelley seems to have largely forgotten it in the poem, which is in effect a glorification of the unique and isolated visionary.

Before the appearance of his dream-goddess Endymion had been a contented devotee of Diana, who is the source and symbol of all particular manifestations of beauty, natural and artistic, sensuous and intellectual. But she is also the incentive to great deeds, since all our passions, as well as love, are, in their sublime, creative of essential beauty. Endymion's abandonment of active life and public service, and Peona's censure of such conduct, along with her brother's plea for the contemplative ascent to reality, reflect Keats's uncertain view of the predicament of the artist. Can writing poetry be included among the ways of doing good to the world? And, in poetry, what are the just claims of the senses and of humanity at large? When *Endymion* was passing through the press, Keats wrote to Taylor: "I have been hovering for some time between an exquisite sense of the luxurious and a love for

Philosophy — were I calculated for the former I should be glad — but as I am not I shall turn all my soul to the latter." [20] In this particular utterance there is no doubt which is Keats's primary instinct (however mistaken he is, for once, in his judgment of himself), but, as countless other utterances show, his sterner ambitions were fundamental and lasting. We may remember that by "philosophy" Keats means not so much philosophical and literary learning, though that is included, but "a comprehension (and a comprehension of a peculiar kind) of the mystery of human life." [21] He wanted to be Shakespearean, and the thought of all he could never be did not comfort him, it left him perpetually dissatisfied with what his special gifts enabled him to do best.

The dream-goddess seems, in Keats's intention, to represent the supreme aspect of ideal beauty which is ideal love; what he mainly describes is in fact the sensuous earthly passion which, at least in its earlier stages, brings torment with it. A major part of his plan is to show love progressing from selfish passion to spiritual altruism, but his instincts partly defeat his purposes; love does not, even in the case of the Indian maiden, rise so far as it should above the warm embracements of Endymion and his goddess and Venus and Adonis. When the goddess is an abstraction in the background, she is a chaste ideal Diana; when with her worshiper, she is more like Venus. As in *Alastor* the imagination of a young man and a poet cannot help presenting the ideal as a breathing, desirable woman rather than a principle of beauty. A deliberately colorless outline of the poem should have made clear, so far as an outline can, the consistently earthly and sensuous character of Endymion's passion. The staid Bailey deplored the "indelicacy," and wished that Keats had not been inclined toward "that

[20] *Letters*, ed. Maurice B. Forman (Oxford University Press, 1935), p. 135.
[21] Murry, *Keats and Shakespeare*, p. 60.

abominable principle of Shelley! — that sensual love is the principle of things." [22] Though Miss Lowell's refusal to see symbolism in the poem was mere temperamental wrongheadedness, she did discern Keats's preoccupation with normal, youthful, amorous emotion. The dream-goddess is a symbol of the ideal, which Keats sincerely worshiped, but she is nine parts flesh and blood and one part Platonic. For Endymion, as for Philip Sidney, "Desire still cries, 'Give me some food,'" and he cannot, with high resignation, turn to a religious and philosophic second-best: "Leave me, O love which reachest but to dust."

To arrive at ideal friendship and finally love demands more than a sense of oneness with all nature and human story; sympathy for human suffering must be felt and actively displayed. Here, as critics have agreed, lies the significance of the episodes of Alpheus and Arethusa and Glaucus and the reviving of dead lovers. Glaucus' personal story is also a warning to Endymion, whose fancied disloyalty to his goddess is foreshadowed in Glaucus' desertion of Scylla for a sensual love. Moreover, although desirous of helping the distressed, Glaucus, like the hero of *Alastor*, had been reduced to impotence through a misguided passion which alienated him from mankind. If the dream-goddess had been kept wholly on the level of ideal love, the appearance of the Indian maiden would have been more logical; the goddess herself, however, comes so close to being a human love, except in her prolonged absences from her votary, that Keats might be said to have almost proved his case before the Indian maiden is introduced. But the episode makes the fourth book much clearer than the second and third. As Mr. Leonard Brown points out, the Arab maiden of *Alastor* was quite neglected by the hero, who had no thought for a mere human girl

[22] Amy Lowell, *John Keats* (Boston and New York, 1925), I, 398. See Murry, "The Meaning of 'Endymion,'" *Studies in Keats* (Oxford University Press, 1930).

who loved him; but in Keats's parable the value of a human love must be made of central significance. While Shelley's self-centered poet found solitude and death, Endymion, in achieving selflessness, finds love and service and more abundant life.[23] Ideal love or beauty is a transcendent divinity not to be immediately apprehended by man, or by man isolated from his fellows; mortals can win that heaven only through intermediaries, through experience of human love and sympathy with sorrow. (The altruistic motive ought to govern this incident, but, in spite of the maiden's situation and her song, it is her beauty rather than her distress that seems to excite Endymion.) The idealist thinks that the abstract and the concrete, the spirit and the flesh, are remote from and opposed to each other, that in loving the Indian maiden he has forfeited his highest hopes. But, after much painful vacillation, he learns that apparent defeat was real victory, that earthly love and beauty are identical with the divine; he learns, in short, "the holiness of the Heart's affections and the truth of Imagination." This, a primary article in Keats's creed, we may if we like label as only another statement of the romantic doctrine of the beautiful soul, but Keats was too normal and sane to hold such a faith in any extravagant or half-spurious way; he wrote no *Epipsychidion*.

Thus, while Keats's hopes and confessions and beliefs are sometimes blurred and obscure, sometimes waywardly decorative, one can hardly fail to see the outlines of a large and really impressive symbolic plan. Nor, on the other hand, can one slight the earthly and sensuous emotions in

---

[23] There is another aspect of this annihilation of self. When Endymion exclaims that he has no self-passion, no identity, he is expressing the bewilderment of a soul drawn in opposite directions. But, since his quest symbolizes a poet's life, is he not here and elsewhere touching on that favorite idea of Keats's, the negative capability, the chameleon nature, of the artist, who has no real identity, no rigid self, but may be at one moment a sparrow picking about the gravel, at another Achilles shouting in the trenches?

order to keep a young poet on the plane of abstract or even humanitarian philosophizing. The Platonism of the poem, so far as it goes, is entirely sincere and fundamental, but, whatever he had absorbed from Spenser and others, there is little more in *Endymion* than an instinctive personal devotion to the ideal which is in some degree, like amorous passion, the birthright of any youthful poetic nature. Keats would not be what he is if he were not kindled by an authentic beam from the white radiance of the One, but his habitation is the dome of many-colored glass. He has grown immensely since *Sleep and Poetry*, where he had looked forth from the realm of Flora and old Pan to contemplate the agonies of human hearts, yet his humanitarian and Platonic faith, however sincere an affirmation, is still beyond his experience, and, in general, the more spiritual parts of the poem are less real than the sensuous. The harmony of the solution comes home to us less than the author's troubled and ever-present consciousness of discord.

While it is clear that Keats made some use of Drayton's *The Man in the Moone*, the question of a much greater debt to *Endimion and Phoebe* remains a puzzle. The central device of Drayton's earlier poem is Phoebe's appearing to her votary in the form of a mortal and winning his love away from her divine self; he then learns the Platonic lesson that his human love was a step toward the ideal, that the two are one. Keats's plot has the further complication of a double disguise. What stands in the way of an entirely convincing case is the fact that *Endimion and Phoebe* was almost unknown and inaccessible; there are at present only three copies extant.[24] Without attempting to brush

[24] Could Dilke's neighbor, Park, the editor of *Heliconia*, have known of the copy in Westminster Abbey? For the parallels between Drayton and Keats, see Finney, *P.M.L.A.*, XXXIX (1924), 805–13, and *The Evolution of Keats's Poetry*, I, 252–55; Amy Lowell's chapter; and De Selincourt, pp. 567–68. The minor parallels seem to be negligible commonplaces; the blue mantle, for instance, is in Chapman and Adlington (see note 30 below).

aside what may in time be completely proved, one may think that *Endimion and Phoebe* was at any rate not necessary. If Drayton had a direct source for his own plot, none has so far turned up, and can we assume that Drayton could invent what Keats could not? Then, if a lover of the myth of Endymion and Diana and its traditional allegory sets out to show through that tale the ultimate identity of the real and the ideal, is not some such device almost inevitable? [25] And I think Colvin dismissed too quickly the possible suggestions, explicit or implicit, in Lyly's *Endimion*, which plays with the current Platonic notions of earthly and heavenly beauty; while the relations of Tellus and Cynthia to Endymion are not the same as in Keats's poem, such a reader as Keats might well see in Lyly's scheme some hints for his own.[26] Another contributory source might have been Mrs. Tighe's *Psyche*, for which Keats had an early admiration. When the story has left Apuleius entirely, a strange knight appears as the protector of Psyche, and he rescues her from time to time in the course of her allegorical adventures. After the final rescue Psyche prays for reunion with her heavenly spouse, and the knight reveals himself as none other than Cupid; the divine and the human are identified. Finally, if Keats was in

[25] In a letter written November 22, 1817, when he was finishing *Endymion*, Keats said: "The Imagination may be compared to Adam's dream — he awoke and found it truth. . . . Adam's dream will do here and seems to be a conviction that Imagination and its empyreal reflection is the same as human Life and its Spiritual repetition" (*Letters*, p. 68). See *Paradise Lost*, viii. 460–90.

[26] I may quote Mr. Percy W. Long's exposition of Lyly, made without reference to Keats: "Endimion thus becomes a devotee of that Heavenly Beauty, best typified by Cynthia, to the contemplation of which the lover by degrees is raised. By a series of steps he passes from the love of Earthly Beauty to the adoration of Heavenly Beauty. This ultimate infidelity of the lover to his primal passion for Earthly Beauty affords Lyly his opportunity for a plot. . . . Corsites is enamored of Tellus, is a devotee of Earthly Beauty, and therefore represents in contrast to Endimion, Earthly or Sensual Love" ("The Purport of Lyly's *Endimion*," *P.M.L.A.*, XXIV [1909], 164 ff.). Corsites and Tellus, by the way, are somewhat similar to Keats's Glaucus and Circe.

some sense replying to *Alastor*, his Platonic and humanitarian purpose would suggest the combining into one of Shelley's two separate characters, the ideal woman of the vision and the Arab maiden.[27] Thus, whether or not Keats knew Drayton's poem, and whether or not he had in mind these other variations on the Platonic motive, their mere existence would seem to show that his fable was not beyond his own capacity.

The last topic that can be touched is the incidental mythology, and two set pieces may be mentioned first, the *Hymn to Pan* and the *Ode to Sorrow*. The former was the most sustained good writing, and by far the richest mythological re-creation, that Keats had yet achieved. Some forced rhymes and other defects in detail are almost lost in the power of the whole. In the list of Pan's attributes Keats seems to be pouring out items gathered from a wide variety of reading — William Browne, Chapman, Spenser, John Fletcher, Sandys, Ben Jonson, Marston, and others — but there is mature art in the grouping and in the orchestration that mounts with such a grand crescendo to the last reverberating sounds. Wordsworth's grim, prim phrase, "A very pretty piece of Paganism," was not even true, for, as Colvin observed, the main "mystical" inspiration of the hymn came from Wordsworth himself. Keats's conception of Pan, however un-Greek, is in accordance with the allegorical tradition, but he so greatly enriches "the All" of the mythographers that his "Pan is, in fact, the symbol of romantic imagination, concrete in a thousand objective shapes, the very life itself of 'sensations

[27] As regards the vision, Mrs. Tighe might be cited also. Cupid wounds Psyche with his dart and she pines away with secret grief; she is haunted by a vision of a beautiful young man, and it proves to have been not altogether a dream, for she had awakened in time to catch a glimpse of the god. Though Mrs. Tighe says in her preface that she has not used La Fontaine, there is a parallel incident in his version; see *Œuvres*, ed. Marty-Laveaux, III (Paris, 1859), 37; Mrs. Tighe, *Psyche*, i. 30–32.

rather than thoughts.'"[28] More deserving of Wordsworth's judgment is the somewhat irrelevant picture of the
Bacchic procession in the fourth book, for that hardly does
get beyond exotic and multitudinous color and ornament.
But even if this is less satisfying than Keats's profounder
treatments of myth, simply as a bravura piece it lives
in the memory far more vividly than anything of Swinburne's.[29]

Most of the incidental mythology is of course in Keats's
early vein of Elizabethan luxuriance. Endymion's dream-
goddess, when first described, seems to have more than the
usual complement of lips and eyes, but the lines just following are better:

> Ah! see her hovering feet,
> More bluely vein'd, more soft, more whitely sweet
> Than those of sea-born Venus, when she rose
> From out her cradle shell. The wind out-blows
> Her scarf into a fluttering pavillion;
> 'Tis blue, and over-spangled with a million
> Of little eyes, as though thou wert to shed,
> Over the darkest, lushest blue-bell bed,
> Handfuls of daisies.[30]

Keats's eye is in a sense on the object, and in his fresh enjoyment of physical beauty he forgets his symbolic theme;

[28] H. W. Garrod, *Keats* (Clarendon Press, 1926), p. 81.

[29] Titian of course accounts for something in Keats's matter and manner.
Mr. De Selincourt quotes part of Sandys' translation of Ovid's tale of Bacchus,
but does not mention the suggestive passage of eighty-eight lines about the god
translated from Seneca's *Oedipus* and included in Sandys' commentary, which
itself contains a number of hints. See Sandys' *Ovid*, ed. 1640, pp. 61–62, and
52–53, 65, 73–75. On the sources of the whole poem see Finney, *Evolution*, I,
272–91, and, for a few possible details, *P.M.L.A.*, L, 797.

[30] Book i, ll. 624 ff. For various details compare Spenser, *F.Q.*, I. iv. 31 (a
passage marked by Keats; see Lowell, I, 100, II, 558); C. Spurgeon, *Keats's
Shakespeare*, pp. 10, 56–57; Chapman, *Hero and Leander*, iv. 26 ff.; J. H. Reynolds, *Devon* (1817), ll. 57–58, 65; Coleridge, *Christabel*, i. 63. With the picture as
a whole compare the description of Venus in *The Golden Ass*, x. 31 (trans. Adlington, ed. T. Seccombe, 1913, p. 251).

his goddess is soft white flesh. A parallel passage, in the chief work of Shelley's maturity, is at first a Botticellian picture of crystal purity and simplicity — though when he comes to love his canvas flares into a Turner sunrise — and Shelley's Asia or Venus is a symbol only.[31] A similar contrast, though the theme is not mythological, appears in the two poets' descriptions of wrecks and ruins of time, where Shelley certainly remembered Keats.[32] Shelley's relics symbolize the powers of destruction which the millennium has made obsolete. Keats's list, partly Shakespearean, partly Virgilian,[33] seems to be inspired mainly by the brevity and littleness of man's life and works; if he is thinking of symbols of human art his choice of items is rather confused. But of course Keats is not always concerned with the fact and Shelley with the thesis; the myth of Arethusa serves Keats for humanitarian symbolism and for Shelley means pure lyric ecstasy.

Much might be said about Keats's mixed sources, for he is as little of a purist in such matters as Chaucer or Spenser. And even if a myth remains "pure," he can distil the essence of romantic magic — "Aeaea's isle was wondering at the moon." To the unblinking objectivity of Ovid he adds warm human feeling, as in "Dryope's lone lulling of her child," or a depth of pictorial and emotional suggestion, as in the picture of Cybele or "blind Orion hungry for the morn." This last phrase, by the way, is one of those changes which make Keats's revisions an education in taste. But there are other poems to speak of and one must come to an end.

[31] *Prometheus Unbound*, II. v. 20 ff. For Shelley's possible recollection of Erasmus Darwin see Carl Grabo, *A Newton Among Poets* (University of North Carolina Press, 1930), pp. 46, 62–63, and J. W. Beach, *The Concept of Nature in Nineteenth-Century English Poetry* (New York, 1936), pp. 233–35.

[32] *Endymion*, iii. 123 ff.; *Prometheus Unbound*, IV. 287 ff.; *Letters of Shelley*, ed. Ingpen (1914), II, 829; Colvin, *John Keats*, pp. 239–40.

[33] See *Richard III*, I. iv. 24 ff.; *Aeneid*, vii. 183 ff.

III

The sensuous, imaginative and fanciful *Endymion* expressed the first virgin passion of a soul communing with the glorious universe. During 1818 Keats began really to learn that "Sorrow is Wisdom." The removal of George and his wife, reviewers' mauling of *Endymion*, physical ailments aggravated by the Scottish tour, the stings of sexual passion (not yet concentrated on Fanny Brawne), and, finally, the fatal decline of Tom, all these things compelled Keats to seek a "feverous relief" in "abstract images," "those abstractions which are my only life." "Poor Tom — that woman — and Poetry were ringing changes in my senses." In such circumstances the long-planned *Hyperion* got under way. That poem must be held over until we reach the revised version. Meanwhile we may very briefly take stock of Keats's position in regard to "sensation" and "thought," and then consider the great group of odes.

If Shakespeare was always the deity in Keats's poetic heaven, Wordsworth and Milton were saints under the throne. Shakespeare was the very opposite of the egotistical sublime, the great exemplar of negative capability, of undogmatic, unobtrusive, impersonal art, but Wordsworth and Milton were more approachable and more imitable. Keats's vacillating allegiance to these two poets is one of the clearest testimonies to the conflict in himself, the conflict he discerned in Milton, between the ardors and the pleasures of song. The letters record so many changes of attitude, so many fluctuating moods, sometimes ripples on the surface, sometimes not, that it is difficult to generalize,[34] but, with reservations, it may be said that when

[34] For instance, on January 23, 1818 (*Letters*, p. 86), Keats copies the poem on Milton he had written two days before; in it he longs to "grow high-rife With Old Philosophy." A month later (p. 104), in the lines on the thrush sent to

Wordsworth is in the ascendant Keats's mind and poetic ambition are turned to the human heart, the mysteries of pain and existence, the improvement of the world; and the ascendancy of Milton, though he sometimes appears as a humanitarian and champion of liberty, means that Keats is enjoying great art and fine phrases with the passion of a lover. But this is all a matter of emphasis and shading, not a clear-cut division. Keats was always striving for unity; in *Endymion* he had attempted to unite the ideal and the real, and in the two *Hyperions* he was to do so again. Where the odes stand in relation to that problem we may try to see.

The fragmentary *Ode to Maia* (May, 1818), and *To Autumn* (September, 1819), the first and the last of the great odes, stand apart in mood as well as in chronology from the group written in the spring of 1819. These two, in their pure, untroubled sensuousness, their objective directness and simplicity of feeling and expression, their lack of "spirituality," form, as it were, a serene frame for a troubled picture. *To Autumn* lies outside our range, though the delicate personifications of the second stanza exhibit Keats's myth-making instinct at its ripest and surest. The initial literary impulse for the *Ode to Maia* may have come from Barnabe Barnes's ode "Lovely Maya," but Keats is not here writing like an Elizabethan or like his earlier self; for a more lush and uneven handling of a similar theme one might compare the dedication of the 1817 volume. Instead of the exuberant catalogue of nature and myth and the Wordsworthian symbolism of the *Hymn to Pan*, the *Ode to Maia* is content with the quiet primrose and the simple worship of a day; we may remember what Severn liked to remember, Keats's talk about

---

Reynolds, he says: "O fret not after knowledge . . ."; he has none, and can sing as well without it. Two days later (p. 107) he is reading Voltaire and Gibbon, although he "wrote to Reynolds the other day to prove reading of no use."

Greek polytheism as a "religion of joy." The poem is as Greek in its sober simplicity of expression as it is un-Greek in its pure romantic nostalgia. And it takes its place among Keats's affirmations on the side of the senses.[35]

The *Ode to Psyche* is the least coherent and most uneven of the later group. The author of *Endymion* reveals himself in such phrases as "fainting with surprise" and "tender eye-dawn of aurorean love," and in the too lavish decoration. But it is only in comparison with himself that Keats suffers, and there is no lack of the magic with which he unites myth, nature, and literature. Psyche has not, like Maia, been rich in the simple worship and happy pieties of ancient times. Latest born of the faded hierarchy, she has had no priest or choir, no music or incense; only the poet can celebrate her now. The poem does not embody the traditional allegory of Cupid and Psyche. Keats's branched thoughts are far removed from the spirit of Milton's mystical allusion at the end of *Comus*; he is contemplating, not the Bride of the Lamb, but soft delight and warm love. And "Yes, I will be thy priest" is equally far from "Make me thy lyre, even as the forest is." The west wind of liberty is characteristic of the whole of Shelley; Keats's symbols are characteristic of that half of his mind which found its finest expression in these odes.[36]

[35] See the discussion in the letter of May 3 which contains the poem (*Letters*, pp. 140–41).

Students have sometimes wondered what connection there was between Maia and Baiae. In Lempriere (1804 ed.) there is a note on "Maiama, festivals in honor of Maia, celebrated on the first of May among the Romans," and it is said that "the principal inhabitants frequented Ostia to spend their time in greater festivity." Keats might have confused Ostia with Baiae, or might have substituted the latter name for the sake of meter and rhyme (however bad the rhyme). This note is not in the 1806 edition of Lempriere, the one now at the Keats House, but, as Mr. Forman remarks (*Letters*, p. 513), Keats apparently had two copies in his time.

[36] I may mention a few possible literary reminiscences in addition to those recorded by Mr. De Selincourt. Among Mr. Earle V. Weller's more plausible parallels with Mrs. Tighe's *Psyche* are "untrodden," "virgin choir," "dear re-

At first sight Keats's theme in the *Ode to a Nightingale* and the *Ode on a Grecian Urn* — the two cannot be separated — is the belief that whereas the momentary experience of beauty is fleeting, the ideal embodiment of that moment in art, in song, or in marble, is an imperishable source of joy. If that were all, these odes should be hymns of triumph, and they are not. It is the very acme of melancholy that the joy he celebrates is joy in beauty that must die. Even when Keats proclaims that the song of the bird is immortal, that the sculptured lover feels an enduring love that is beyond the pains of human passion, his deepest emotions are fixed on the obverse side of his theme. He tries to believe, and with part of his mind he does believe and rejoice, in the immortality of ideal beauty, but he is too intense a lover of the here and now, of the human and tangible, to be satisfied by his own affirmations. It is the actual moment that is precious, that brings ecstasy with it, and the moment will not stay. The truth that Keats embraces is not that of his large humanitarian aspirations, nor the smaller measure of truth granted to the philosophic intellect, it is the truth, that is, the reality, apprehended through the senses. The author of these odes hears the still, sad music of humanity, but he tries to escape from it. The bird's song, poetry, carries him away from the lazar-house of life and above the level of the dull, perplexing brain; the urn is a symbol of untroubled beauty in the midst of human woe and it teases him out of thought. Was

---

membrance" (*Keats and Mary Tighe*, New York, 1928, pp. 9, 27). The last phrase, however, has been related to the opening of *Lycidas*, along with "sweet enforcement"; cf. Horace's *lene tormentum* (*Odes*, III. xxi. 13). With "Yes, I will be thy priest . . . ," compare Spenser, *Amoretti*, xxii. Some small resemblances between the first stanza and Adlington's translation of Apuleius may be only coincidence. The historical note with which Keats introduces the poem (*Letters*, p. 340) suggests Lempriere, who says (ed. 1806): "The word signifies *the soul*, and this personification of Psyche first mentioned by Apuleius, is posterior to the Augustan age, though still it is connected with ancient mythology." This last item is noticed by Mr. Finney, II, 614.

it the ecstasies and torments of love that intensified and decided the conflict, or was it that in poetry the senses had for the time won the victory and released him from the half-paralyzing claims of "higher" poetry? At any rate, as in *Endymion*, Keats is not wholly happy with the ideal, his instinct seeks the particular object and experience. And his instincts are more honest than Shelley's, for he is always aware of the cleavage in himself. He may grasp at the ideal as an authentic and inspiring sanction for his love of the actual, but he does not deceive himself, or us, when he endeavors, with more than Shelley's occasional misgivings, to bridge the gap between them. He cannot so easily rhapsodize about Intellectual Beauty when he is thinking of holding the hands of Harriet or Mary or Emilia or Jane. Neither beauty nor truth is for Keats a real abstraction, a Platonic Idea; beauty is something beautiful, the "material sublime." When he tries to generalize from a melancholy ecstasy, he remains at odds with himself. The urn is a joy for ever, but the marble figures are cold.

Probably no one but William Michael Rossetti has found in the *Nightingale* "a surfeit of mythological allusions." [37] They are all so harmonious that one may forget they are there. Keats's taste in the matter of allusions is generally that of the Elizabethans and Jacobeans from whom he drew so much of his mythology. Quite Elizabethan, too, is his mingling of classical and native lore; Diana, the queen-moon, is "Cluster'd around by all her starry Fays." [38] Many readers of the *Grecian Urn* have wondered, no doubt,

[37] *Life of John Keats* (1887), p. 200.

[38] We are not accustomed to think of Keats as a reader of Horace, but he owned a copy and cited him a number of times. In noting some possible Horatian parallels with the *Nightingale*, Mr. Blunden has suggested that it may have been a volume of Horace that Keats had with him when he sat under the tree in the garden (*London Mercury*, XX [1929], 289 ff.). One such parallel is between Keats's last lines and *Odes*, III. iv. 5–8, but, since the poem contains clear Wordsworthian echoes, one may observe Wordsworth's "By waking sense or by the dreaming soul" (*Excursion*, ii. 833).

if Keats had ever heard Sidney's shepherd's boy "piping, as though he should never be old," but he must have known William Browne's echo of Sidney.[39] And, without forgetting the Elgin Marbles, several urns, and Claude's painting, one may add a bit from Sandys' *Ovid* to the citations given by Mr. De Selincourt; Cadmus followed a heifer which

> made a stand; to heaven her fore-head cast,
> With loftie horns most exquisitely faire;
> Then, with repeated lowings fill'd the ayre.[40]

But of course no array of parallels is of much account. When Keats mixes three sounds in his thought they become, not a fourth sound, but a star. The lines on the little town were quoted, or rather misquoted, by Arnold and praised for being Greek, "as Greek as a thing from Homer or Theocritus . . . composed with the eye on the object, a radiancy and light clearness being added." [41] But, as in the *Ode to Maia*, the concrete details are suffused with a rich nostalgia. The hard edges of classical Greek writing are softened by the enveloping emotion and suggestion. In his classical moments Keats is a sculptor whose marble becomes flesh.

IV

Keats was so right in his self-criticism that one hesitates to question any of his judgments, yet few modern readers

---

[39] Sidney's *Arcadia*, ed. A. Feuillerat (Cambridge University Press, 1912), p. 13; *Britannia's Pastorals*, Book ii, Song 2, ll. 33-36. The lines are quoted in *P.M.L.A.*, L, 803.

[40] Ed. 1640, p. 47. All the items of the similar sacrifice in the *Epistle to Reynolds* (ll. 20 ff.) are mentioned or suggested in Potter's *Archaeologia Graeca* (I, 251-73, especially 267-68). See Colvin, pp. 264, 416-17; De Selincourt, p. 586.

[41] *On the Study of Celtic Literature and On Translating Homer* (New York, 1883), p. 125.

seem to like *Lamia* as well as he did. It contains a great deal of sumptuous and admirable writing (along with some strange lapses), it shows a mastery of the couplet [42] and of coherent story-telling, and yet it is in essential ways the least satisfying of the longer poems. On the purely literary side *Lamia* is too much of a brilliant piece of tapestry. But the fundamental defect is that the poem has no emotional and philosophic unity. Clearly the story is not told merely for the story's sake, though the amount of ornament and the over-elaboration of the initial episode of Hermes might suggest that it is.[43] Whether or not it was his original intention, Keats gave the poem a meaning, so that it takes its place among the many poems which embody the inward struggle between the claims of self and the senses and the claims of the world and "philosophy." But here Keats does not seem to know which side he is on, and a plausible case can be, and has been, made out for *Lamia* as a condemnation of philosophy, as a condemnation of the senses, and as a condemnation of a divorce between the two. Each of these interpretations can be supported by chapter and verse from Keats's other poems and from his letters, yet each leaves difficulties in *Lamia* itself.

On the one hand Lamia is a sinister serpent woman; the house to which she takes her lover is a "purple-lined palace of sweet sin"; she is afraid when he hears the heroic sound of trumpets from the outside world, for she knows "that but a moment's thought is passion's passing bell." Such a conception is in general accord with the spirit of Burton's tale and his discussion of the destructive power of love; it

[42] The usual emphasis on the metrical influence of Dryden has been qualified by Mr. Ridley (pp. 241 ff.) and Mr. Charles A. Langworthy (see bibliography).

[43] This episode has been explained by Mr. Edward T. Norris as an integral part of the symbolism: "As Hermes represents the industrious poet in contrast to Lycius, the poet of sensation, so the nymph represents Keats's true ideal of poetry in contrast to Lamia, the poetry of sensation" (*ELH*, II [1935], 322–26). This seems to me quite unconvincing.

is also in accord with two poems which probably had some influence on *Lamia*, namely, *Christabel* and *Rhododaphne*.[44] On the other hand Keats obviously sympathizes with the sensuous or sensual passion, the "unperplex'd delight," of the young lovers; Apollonius the sage is the ghost of folly haunting the sweet dreams of his former disciple; and at the end, when Apollonius is about to cast a blight upon Lamia, the author lets himself go in an attack on "cold philosophy." [45] Thus Lamia is at the same time a beautiful woman who loves and should be loved, and an evil embodiment of the wasting power of love, a *belle dame sans merci*.

Such central contradictions cannot be reconciled. Spenser, with the easy flexibility of a Renaissance poet, could first exploit the sensuous and then condemn it; that compromise was impossible for Keats, a modern poet driven to seek for unity in himself and the world, yet we wonder, as we do in reading of the destruction of the bower of bliss, if Keats's stern conclusion expresses as much of himself as had gone into the tale of amorous enchantment. There is the essential difference, however, that Spenser was dealing largely with the world of imagination, as Keats was in *Endymion*. There Keats had arrived at a solution, a harmonizing of his instincts and his aspirations, yet the former element is so much the stronger, at that stage in the author's growth, that we doubt if the solution is final. The dilemma that faced Endymion, compared with that of Lycius, was esthetic and theoretical. The trouble in

[44] In the sixth and seventh cantos of Peacock's poem we have the description of a rich palace erected by magic and a banquet room sumptuously arrayed, and the enchantress who has seduced the hero is destroyed by Uranian Love.

[45] It has been plausibly suggested (De Selincourt, p. 573) that in the line "Philosophy will clip an Angel's wings" Keats remembered Hazlitt's remark in the first of his *Lectures on the English Poets*, that "the progress of knowledge and refinement has a tendency to circumscribe the limits of the imagination, and to clip the wings of poetry." The proverbial phrase occurs twice in Burton, a few pages before the story of Lamia (Bohn's Popular Library ed., III, 45–46), and in Dryden's *Theodore and Honoria* (l. 54) "Love had clipp'd his Wings."

Lamia is that, despite the exotic story and trappings, the poem is a too immediate transcript of actual experience; despite the technical skill, it is, spiritually, the raw material of a poem. The conflict has been interpreted wholly in terms of poetry, of the senses and the intellect, and the attack on cold philosophy certainly belongs to poetic theory; it embodies not only one of Keats's own moods but something of the general romantic protest against a purely scientific view of the world. Yet the fire that Keats was aware of in *Lamia* was not merely born of opposed literary desires, however intense, it came from the divided soul of a lover. The struggle between passion and the craving to escape from passion is felt too keenly and rendered too literally — the literalness is that of Keats, not of D. H. Lawrence — to result in a unified, integrated poem. "The truth about the Lamia," as Mr. Murry says, "is that Keats himself did not know whether she was a thing of beauty or a thing of bale. He only knew that if he were to be deprived of her, he would die, which he did, in the poem and in fact." [46] We may be moved, if we are not put off by the glittering surface, but we are moved in much the same way as we are in reading the letters to Fanny Brawne, which are after all the best commentary on the poem.[47]

Of the frequent beauty of the writing there is no room or need to speak. The magnificent allusion to Hermes as "the star of Lethe" drew a magnificent eulogy from Lamb.

[46] *Keats and Shakespeare*, p. 159. Mr. Murry's discussion of the autobiographical element in *Lamia* is illuminating but goes too far, much farther than, for example, Lucien Wolff (*John Keats*, Paris [1911], pp. 539 ff.). It is odd that a critic who sees the essential inwardness of the poem so sympathetically should so externalize Keats's inward struggle as to see Charles Brown behind Apollonius. Apart from the lack of evidence (see John H. Roberts, *P.M.L.A.*, L, 550–61), to take Apollonius as representing anything but one side of Keats is to empty the poem of its significance.

[47] See especially the letters of July 25 and August 16, 1819, which are among those written while Keats was at work on the revised *Hyperion*, *Lamia* apparently having been laid aside half-finished.

William Morris must have envied the mingled simplicity
and richness of the lines,

> Men, women, rich and poor, in the cool hours,
> Shuffled their sandals o'er the pavement white.

Keats could never, with the alcoholic fluency of Porson,
have hiccuped Greek like a Helot, but how near could
Porson have come to this?

> Soft went the music the soft air along,
> While fluent Greek a vowel'd undersong
> Kept up among the guests. . . .[48]

But random comment must give place to my ewe-lamb of
research. *Lamia* is the only classical story Keats reworked
which required definite information about ancient manners
and furniture, and he naturally turned to the standard
book on the subject, a book he owned himself, John Potter's *Archaeologia Graeca*. Virtually all of the material
background and customs described in *Lamia* appear to be
drawn, sometimes with verbal echoes, from Potter, and we
may observe Keats's selective memory and imagination
transforming the learned but pedestrian pages of his authority into the romantic glamor and opulence of the poem.
There is space for only one example of the process.

> Of wealthy lustre was the banquet-room,
> Fill'd with pervading brilliance and perfume:
> Before each lucid pannel fuming stood
> A censer fed with myrrh and spiced wood,
> Each by a sacred tripod held aloft,
> Whose slender feet wide-swerv'd upon the soft
> Wool-woofed carpets. . . .
> Twelve sphered tables, by silk seats insphered,
> High as the level of a man's breast rear'd
> On libbard's paws, upheld the heavy gold
> Of cups and goblets. . . .
> Thus loaded with a feast the tables stood,
> Each shrining in the midst the image of a God.

---

[48] "Undersong" might have come from the homely Wordsworthian "kettle
whispering its faint undersong" (*Personal Talk*, i); cf. Spenser, *Prothalamion*,
l. 110.

The relevant items from Potter may be lumped together:

And the room wherein the entertainment was made, was sometimes perfumed by burning myrrh or frankincense, or with other odours.

The form [of tables] was round, if we may believe Myrleanus in Athenaeus, who reports, that the ancient Greeks made their tables, and several other things, spherical. . . .

. . . the beds covered with cloth or tapestry, according to the quality of the master of the house.

They [the tables] were also adorned with plates of silver, or other metals, and supported by one or more feet, curiously wrought. . . . The most common support of these tables was an ivory foot, cast in the form of a lion, a leopard, or some other animal.

. . . their cups were made of silver, gold, and other costly materials.

It was customary to place the statues of the gods upon the table.[49]

But Potter was a doubtful source of inspiration, for Keats is at his best when he does not follow sources so closely. The sensuous beauties of *Lamia* are too often indoor and

---

[49] Ed. Edinburgh (1818), II, 383, 376, 373, 377, 390, 376. The chief passages in *Lamia* which seem to be related to Potter are i. 317 ff., ii. 106 ff., 191 ff., 208, 215 ff., 241 ff. For details see *P.M.L.A.*, L, 785 ff.; a number of the items are quoted in Finney, II, 674–77.

Southey's *Thalaba* has already been cited, and it includes these suggestive lines (vi. 25):

"And still the aloes and the sandal-wood
From golden censers, o'er the banquet room
Diffuse their dying sweets."

Some details of Keats's feast suggest Virgil (*Aen.* i. 701 ff., 723 ff.). Keats's overdone pictures of the snake (i. 47 ff., 146 ff.) also recall Virgil's more subdued descriptions. With Keats's first account compare *Aen.* v. 84 ff. (and *Paradise Lost*, ix. 494 ff.); with the second, *Aen.* ii. 206 ff. Routh (*M.L.N.*, XXV, 34) cited the water-snakes in *The Ancient Mariner*.

The episode of Hermes seems to be elaborated from the story of Mercury, Herse, and Aglauros, at the end of the second book of the *Metamorphoses*, and the picture of Lamia as she withers away under the eye of the sage perhaps owes something to the punishment of Aglauros in the same Ovidian tale. The passages from Sandys (ed. 1640, pp. 31, 32) are quoted in *P.M.L.A.*, L, 789.

artificial, too material and mundane, for a poet who has
taught us how high and deep the senses can reach.

V

Hyperion was begun in the autumn of 1818 and finished
by April, 1819. In August and September, and, according
to Charles Brown, in November and December, 1819,
Keats was engaged in remodeling the fragment in the form
of a vision, *The Fall of Hyperion*. The subject had been
conceived at least as early as September, 1817, and a number of references in the later books of *Endymion*, not to
mention the preface, show that the new project was considerably occupying Keats's thoughts.[50] What had been
called in September "a new Romance" is differently described in another letter to Haydon of January 23, 1818:

In Endymion I think you may have many bits of the deep and
sentimental cast — the nature of *Hyperion* will lead me to treat
it in a more naked and grecian Manner — and the march of
passion and endeavour will be undeviating — and one great contrast between them will be — that the Hero of the written tale
being mortal is led on, like Buonaparte, by circumstance;
whereas the Apollo in Hyperion being a fore-seeing God will
shape his actions like one.[51]

The first half of the fragment at least reveals few lapses
from the naked and Grecian manner. To say, as critics
often do, that *Hyperion* is not Keats, that it is a splendid
tour de force, seems rather idle; we do not find fault with
Paradise Lost because it is not in the style of *Comus*. Of
course Keats had, in Milton, a single dominating literary
model, as Milton had not, and one may therefore, if one
likes, regard *Hyperion* as derivative and artificial. But
Hyperion and its complement are, in important respects,

---

[50] De Selincourt, pp. 451, 484.
[51] *Letters*, pp. 82–83, and p. 51.

entirely original — *Paradise Lost* was likewise, though it absorbed a thousand tributaries — and they are the culmination of Keats's poetic progress, the last and greatest statement of his conflicting instincts and ambitions. In finally abandoning the *Fall*, which not only retained most of the old Miltonisms but added new ones, Keats was moved less by a distaste for the Miltonic manner than by deeper reasons. I shall not attempt to speak here of Milton's influence, for I have nothing to add to the many discussions of style and diction, story and structure. But one may mention a subtle lesson that Keats learned from Milton, and put greatly into practice, the "stationing" of figures which his notes on Milton show that he had studied.[52]

Along with Milton other influences contributed to the strength and massiveness which are such an astonishing change from the lush and fanciful luxuriance of *Endymion*. Landor, the master of the definite line, may have been one of those influences; we remember that Shelley had a passion for *Gebir*, though his own writing was hardly Landorian. When, for instance, the undefeated Titan moves "With stride colossal, on from hall to hall," we feel certain that Keats had Shakespeare in mind, but he may also have known Landor's "The parting Sun's gigantic strides." [53]

---

[52] "But in no instance is this sort of perseverance more exemplified, than in what may be called his *stationing or statuary*. He is not content with simple description, he must station, — thus here we not only see how the Birds '*with clang despised the ground*,' but we see them '*under a cloud in prospect*.' So we see Adam '*Fair indeed, and tall — under a plantane*' — and so we see Satan '*disfigured — on the Assyrian Mount*'" (*Works*, ed. Forman, 1889, III, 28–29).

[53] *Hyperion*, i. 195; *Julius Caesar*, I. ii. 134–36; *Gebir*, iii. 18 (Landor's *Poems*, ed. Wheeler, 1933). The "faded eyes" of *Hyperion*, i. 90, may combine the "faded cheek" of *Paradise Lost*, i. 602, with the "faded eyes" of *Gebir*, v. 57. Keats's "O lank-eared Phantoms of black-weeded pools!" (i. 230) might embody a recollection of the sights seen by Gebir in the underworld, particularly a giant "flound'ring mid the marshes, yellow-flower'd," "His bosom tossing with black weeds besmear'd" (*Gebir*, iii. 201 ff.). Keats's lines about the shell (ii. 270–71), though slight, suggest Landor's famous passage or Wordsworth's adap-

The results of Keats's familiarity with the Elgin Marbles
are none the less important for not being precisely demonstrable. *Hyperion* contains a number of Egyptian allusions, and the vast bulk of the Titans, which suggests beings more primeval than Phidian, may owe something to
Keats's interest in Egyptian statuary.[54] *Hyperion's* palace, too, is more Egyptian, or at least oriental, than Greek;
in some respects it resembles a glorified mosque.[55] Finally,
not the least important influence that helped to create a
setting worthy of the Titans, "a Stonehenge of reverber-
ance," was the huge, rugged masses of northern scenery.
The change from the soft richness and sweetness of *Endymion* to the bare grandeur of *Hyperion* is partly the result
of a change from the Isle of Wight and Oxford and Box
Hill to the lake country and Scotland. In a letter from the
north of June 27, 1818, Keats said: "I cannot think with
Hazlitt that these scenes make man appear little. I never
forgot my stature so completely — I live in the eye; and
my imagination, surpassed, is at rest." These last phrases
perfectly describe the purely esthetic experience of reading
Hyperion.

Though *Hyperion* is completely his own, Keats, like
Virgil and Milton, was often most original when refining
the ore, or engraving the gold, of other poets. While
Shakespearean influence ranges from the conception of
Saturn to versification, the chief group of Shakespearean
details is the list of evil omens, for which Keats would go
as naturally to Shakespeare as Shakespeare went to Plu-

tation of it. If there be any connection between "My life is but the life of winds
and tides" (*Hyperion*, i. 341) and "We are what suns and winds and waters make
us," Landor would be the debtor, since *Regeneration* was written later.

54 Helen Darbishire, "Keats and Egypt," *R.E.S.*, III (1927), 1 ff.

55 In addition to *Paradise Lost*, i. 710 ff., and the description of the halls of
Eblis in *Vathek*, Keats may have taken hints from an unexpected picture in *The
Excursion* of a fabric of diamond and gold, with alabaster domes, blazing ter-
races, and serene pavilions bright (ii. 830 ff.). Cf. *Hyperion*, i. 176 ff., 220, 238.

tarch and others.[56] Landor, Southey, and Sandys may all have contributed to that Miltonic turn:

> How beautiful, if sorrow had not made
> Sorrow more beautiful than Beauty's self.[57]

But I need not venture upon comments which Mr. Lowes will shortly render obsolete, and for the same good reason I shall not summarize what has so far been discovered about the special sources of Keats's classical material.[58] The probable or possible sources are as heterogeneous as ever — Chapman's *Homer*, Sandys' *Ovid*, Hyginus, Hesiod, Ronsard, Davies' *Celtic Researches*, the *Arabian Nights*, *Vathek*, and other books. Like medieval and Elizabethan poets, Keats altered mythology freely, and he welcomed post-classical accretions that old stories had gathered in passing through many hands.[59] To mention one more topic which must be passed by, Keats was never a finer artist than when improving on himself; *Hyperion* is full of inspired revisions.

By Milton's time, indeed by Virgil's, the conventional mold of the heroic epic had become inadequate for the increasingly abstract themes of modern and philosophic poets. Whatever Keats originally had in mind, his final

[56] Finney, *Evolution*, II, 520 ff.; *P.Q.*, III (1924), 139 ff. The chief items are summarized in De Selincourt, pp. 580–81.

[57] De Selincourt (p. 496) quotes *Gebir*, i. 68–71 (Wheeler ed.). See Southey, *Thalaba*, xi. 31, ll. 383–84; and Sandys, ed. 1640, p. 129 (and *P.M.L.A.*, L, 800).

[58] See Finney, II, 494 ff.

[59] In *The Indicator* of December 8, 1819, Hunt wrote thus of a friend whom he later identified as Keats: "Talking the other day with a friend about Dante, he observed, that whenever so great a poet told us any thing in addition or continuation of an ancient story, he had a right to be regarded as classical authority. For instance, said he, when he tells us of that characteristic death of Ulysses in one of the books of his Inferno, we ought to receive the information as authentic, and be glad that we have more news of Ulysses than we looked for." "More News of Ulysses," *The Indicator* (1820), I, 65; W. E. Peck, "Keats on Poet-Historians," *Books, New York Herald-Tribune*, October 16, 1927. Incidentally, in regard to the date of *The Fall of Hyperion*, it is perhaps of some interest to find Keats citing Dante in November or December, 1819.

plan avoided epic battles by starting after the defeat of the Titans and referring to war only in allusive retrospect, a method in harmony with his poetic temper and with his symbolic conception of the subject; how he would have ended the poem we can only guess.[60] Yet his method, however wise and necessary, involved difficulties. The first two books are a series of magnificent sculptural friezes, but the figures can hardly be set moving. They seem to be too much a stage setting for Apollo, who first appears in the third book and whose significance does not become entirely clear until we turn to the *Fall*. The chief reason for the abandonment of *Hyperion* may well have been, as Mr. Abercrombie in particular has said, that Keats perceived his poem to be mainly façade, that his elaboration of a semi-Miltonic pattern, though grand in itself, was smothering his idea under decoration. He must have known as well as we do that for stately elevation and beauty the first two books had no superior or equal since Milton, but, to a man of Keats's poetic conscience, it would have meant more that he was not getting his theme expressed. When the poem takes a fresh start in the fragmentary third book, he seems determined to come to grips with his central story, to set forth his "message"; by that time, however, if the poem was to comprise four books, the architecture was so much out of proportion that Keats did not see his way to a satisfactory ending or recasting. Milton and Wordsworth had been the two poles of Keats's poetical orbit, and, to change metaphors, the wedding of Miltonic technique to Wordsworthian inwardness was almost bound to be an unequal union.

If *Endymion* was in the philosophic sense Keats's *Prel-*

---

[60] Mr. De Selincourt (p. 488) suggests that Apollo, after being confirmed in his supremacy by Jove, "would have gone forth to meet Hyperion who, struck by the power of supreme beauty, would have found resistance impossible." For Woodhouse's account of the original plan, which involved war and the dethronement of a number of Titans, see De Selincourt, p. 486.

ude, Hyperion was his *Excursion.* Apollo, like Endymion, is John Keats. But the author of *Hyperion* has emerged from the chamber of maiden-thought. The untried idealism of *Endymion* has not weakened; it has, under the stress of realities, become stronger, sterner, less self-centered. The facts of death and love have been proved on the author's pulses. "Sensations" without knowledge have ripened and deepened into sensations with knowledge. Although the mere "poetical" beauty of the fragment is completely satisfying even now, when so much merely beautiful poetry has faded, description is not simply description; it carries a weight of magnanimity and compassion which the author of *Endymion* could not yet have felt or expressed. And Keats has not, like the elder Wordsworth, cut himself off from some of his youthful and essential roots; even though Keats did not solve his problem, the two *Hyperions* represent the consummation of his growth.

As a poem of evolution *Hyperion* has both social and personal aspects. We no longer think of Keats as the one great poet of his time who turned away from a troubled present to find esthetic refuge in a romantic Middle Age or romantic Greece. Letters and poems alike bear ample witness to his critical interest in public affairs and the state of society and to his vigorous liberal opinions. The author of *Hyperion*, like Wordsworth and Shelley, was a child of revolutionary optimism, but while Wordsworth literally and poetically lived through the vicissitudes of the French Revolution, and Shelley was often a shrill doctrinaire on the platform, Keats was always an artist and viewed his world, so to speak, with the eyes of posterity. In *Hyperion* Keats's treatment of myth is more like Spenser's than Shelley's. Spenser had made the war of the gods and Titans the vehicle for his deepest thoughts and feelings about the riddle of the one and the many, the possibility of permanence in the midst of flux. From a world of medieval fixities, if I may repeat myself, he contemplated the melancholy spectacle of endless change, and he arrived at a compromise half Christian, half scientific, the doctrine that all things work out their own perfection under divine control, until the process of change shall give way to the changelessness of eternity. Keats was no "Godwin perfectibility Man," and in *Hyperion* his faith in progress was put in a way peculiarly his own. The Jupiter whom Shelley overthrows is a wholly evil embodiment of superstition, tyranny, and custom, whose reign must give way to the rule of universal love. Keats's Titans, though beneficent rulers of the world, must yield to a race of gods superior in beauty and magnanimity. However familiar the speech of Oceanus, it must be partly quoted:

And first, as thou wast not the first of powers,
So art thou not the last; it cannot be:
Thou art not the beginning nor the end. . . .

Then thou first-born, and we the giant-race,
Found ourselves ruling new and beauteous realms.
Now comes the pain of truth, to whom 'tis pain;
O folly! for to bear all naked truths,
And to envisage circumstance, all calm,
That is the top of sovereignty. Mark well!
As Heaven and Earth are fairer, fairer far
Than Chaos and blank Darkness, though once chiefs;
And as we show beyond that Heaven and Earth
In form and shape compact and beautiful,
In will, in action free, companionship,
And thousand other signs of purer life;
So on our heels a fresh perfection treads,
A power more strong in beauty, born of us
And fated to excel us, as we pass
In glory that old Darkness: nor are we
Thereby more conquer'd, than by us the rule
Of shapeless Chaos. . . .
            . . . for 'tis the eternal law
That first in beauty should be first in might.

The passage hardly needs corroboration, but one may quote two more personal bits of prose. In the important letter of May 3, 1818, Keats had compared Milton and Wordsworth in regard to their zeal for humanity and their knowledge of the human heart, and he had put Wordsworth first, not because of individual superiority but because of a general advance among mankind. "What is then to be inferr'd? O many things — It proves there is really a grand march of intellect —, It proves that a mighty providence subdues the mightiest Minds to the service of the time being, whether it be in human Knowledge or Religion." [61] On September 18, 1819, Keats wrote: "All civil[iz]ed countries become gradually more enlighten'd and there should be a continual change for the better." One might add some brief queries from *The Excursion* which epitomize a good deal of Wordsworth:

> Is Man
> A child of hope? Do generations press
> On generations, without progress made? [62]

If Keats's notion of the enlightened progress of the race is partly Wordsworthian, still more so is the ideal of individual progress summed up in the speech of Oceanus, the power to bear all naked truths and face circumstance with calm. All through *The Excursion* Wordsworth is pleading for self-discipline achieved through reason and the law of duty, and for the "pagan" Keats Wordsworth's stoicism would be detachable from his Christian faith. The soul, says Wordsworth, craves a life of peace, "Stability without regret or fear," the central peace subsisting at the heart of endless agitation.[63] Possessions, opinions, passions change, but duty remains, "by the storms of circumstance unshaken." Reason is "A crown, an attribute of sovereign

[61] *Letters*, pp. 144–45. For the second epistolary item see *ibid.*, p. 406.
[62] *Excursion*, v. 465–67. Cf. vii. 999 ff.
[63] *Ibid.*, iii. 385–86, iv. 1146–47.

power," and a life of discipline may enable Age, "in awful sovereignty," to sit on a superior height, disencumbered from the press of near obstructions.[64] One may dismiss all this as Polonian moralizing and say that Keats had no such stuff in mind when he named *The Excursion* as one of the three things in the age to rejoice at.[65] But one can hardly read *Hyperion* or the letters and not believe that the attaining of such stability of soul was a reality to him. Again I must limit myself to two inadequate scraps. "The best of Men have but a portion of good in them — a kind of spiritual yeast in their frames which creates the ferment of existence — by which a Man is propell'd to act and strive and buffet with Circumstance." [66] "Circumstances are like Clouds continually gathering and bursting — While we are laughing the seed of some trouble is put into the wide arable land of events — while we are laughing it sprouts [it] grows and suddenly bears a poison fruit which we must pluck." [67]

The words of Oceanus are no incidental exhortation, they cast back to the speech of Coelus in the first book, and they are essential to Keats's whole conception of the Titans and the significance of their defeat. He does not think of them as primitive deities of brute force and tyranny. Saturn laments that he is

> buried from all godlike exercise
> Of influence benign on planets pale,
> Of admonitions to the winds and seas,
> Of peaceful sway above man's harvesting,
> And all those acts which Deity supreme
> Doth ease its heart of love in.

Even Enceladus gives similar testimony.[68] The myth of a steady decline from the golden age is not for Keats. The

---

[64] *Ibid.*, iv. 69–73, v. 503, ix. 55, 70. Cf. iv. 1070 ff., 1266 ff.

[65] *Letters*, p. 79 (January 10, 1818).

[66] *Ibid.*, p. 84 (January 23, 1818).

[67] *Ibid.*, pp. 315–16 (March 19, 1819). See also p. 345.

[68] *Hyperion*, ii. 335 ff.

Titans are superior to their predecessors; they are one link, not the first, in the upward succession. Indeed the principal Titans are so completely majestic and sublime that Keats would have been sorely tried in creating gods who could win our sympathy away from them. But his intention is clear. The Titans, however benign and beneficent, had in a crisis behaved not like deities but like frail mortals; they had lost, and deserved to lose, the sovereignty of the world because they had lost the sovereignty over themselves.

> Divine ye were created, and divine
> In sad demeanour, solemn, undisturb'd,
> Unruffled, like high Gods, ye liv'd and ruled:
> Now I behold in you fear, hope, and wrath;
> Actions of rage and passion; even as
> I see them, on the mortal world beneath,
> In men who die. — This is the grief, O Son!
> Sad sign of ruin, sudden dismay, and fall! [69]

Coelus, who belongs to the old order and does not understand the situation, exhorts Hyperion, the one unconquered Titan, to use force. Later we see Saturn himself,

> the supreme God
> At war with all the frailty of grief,
> Of rage, of fear, anxiety, revenge,
> Remorse, spleen, hope, but most of all despair.

Thus, even though the Titans were

> symbols divine,
> Manifestations of that beauteous life
> Diffus'd unseen throughout eternal space,

---

[69] *Ibid.*, i. 329 ff. Cf. Sandys (ed. 1640, p. 15): "The Giants were the sonnes of the Earth (for so they called of old the ignorant, and earthly minded: as those the sonnes of heaven, who were admired for their vertues) said to be of a huge proportion; in that commonly such are prone to intemperance, wrath, and injustice; seldome yeelding unto reason, but are carried with the swinge of their lusts and affections." Like many poets before him, Keats confuses Giants and Titans (De Selincourt, pp. 486, 505–06).

they failed to justify the continuance of their reign. Hence the larger vision and wisdom of Oceanus, who alone among them has "wandered to eternal truth," and who now is able to envisage circumstance, all calm. He alone, except weak Clymene, whose glimpse of truth is only sensuous and emotional, can see the glow of superior beauty in the eyes of his successor and acknowledge the rightness of defeat.

When Apollo passes from aching ignorance to knowledge, the god, the true poet, is born.

> Knowledge enormous makes a God of me.
> Names, deeds, gray legends, dire events, rebellions,
> Majesties, sovran voices, agonies,
> Creations and destroyings, all at once
> Pour into the wide hollows of my brain,
> And deify me, as if some blithe wine
> Or bright elixir peerless I had drunk,
> And so become immortal.

The most important passage in the first book of *Endymion* — the answer to the question "Wherein lies happiness?" — contained a similar list of symbols of human history, but there the emphasis was on the clear religion of heaven, the "oneness" enjoyed by the soul that felt a bond with nature and legend, and that oneness was the first stage of experience leading to friendship and love. The lines in *Hyperion* have less of nature and of self, and more of the rise and fall of nations, the whole chaotic story of man's troubled past. Keats is not here concerned with the source of happiness, or with love, but with the knowledge that is sorrow, the sorrow that is wisdom. And the bright elixir that Apollo has drunk is no opiate that carries him Lethewards, away from the fever and fret of the world of man, for Keats has attained, potentially, his poetic manhood. "Was there a Poet born?" he had asked in *I Stood Tip-toe*, as he thought, with a charming mythological fancy, of the marriage night of Diana and Endymion. The poetic birth of Apollo takes place on the farther side of the vale of soul-making.

In addition to the reasons already indicated for the abandonment of *Hyperion*, Keats may have had one of his revulsions against a too high and hard conception of poetry. At any rate he wrote *The Eve of St. Agnes* and the odes; late in the summer he wrote *Lamia*, and set about the recasting of *Hyperion*. *The Fall of Hyperion* was his last effort to integrate his faculties and impulses, and to set forth his conception of the poet and the poet's function in the world. In *Hyperion* the meaning of Apollo's spiritual birth-pangs had been left somewhat obscure; the objective manner of presentation was not natural to one who had always written directly out of his own feelings, and perhaps he did not quite know what to do with the god when he had got him. The narrative in the *Fall* seems to carry out the general intention of *Hyperion*, but, by the late summer of 1819, Keats's failing health, the prolonged fever of his love for Fanny Brawne, pecuniary troubles, perhaps most of all the conviction that the topmost heights of poetry were not to be won by a divided soul, such causes as these had deepened and embittered his despair over himself, his past and his future.[70] In the symbolism of the garden, the temple, and the shrine, we have perhaps another variation on the three Wordsworthian stages of development, from sensuous pleasure to humanitarian concern for the world.[71] But the sketch of poetic evolution is not now, as in *Sleep and*

---

[70] On November 19 we have a gloomy letter to George, who needs money; Mr. Abbey wants John "to turn Bookseller"; he has tried to write lately but cannot get on while George is in such low water. Looking back over his *annus mirabilis*, he can say: "Nothing could have in all its circumstances fallen out worse for me than the last year has done, or could be more damping to my poetical talent — I comfort myself in the idea that you are a consolation to each other" (*Letters*, pp. 442–43).

[71] Mr. De Selincourt's interpretation is questioned by Mr. Ridley (p. 268). Mr. Lowes has shown that the structural background and texture of the *Fall* are derived from Dante's *Purgatorio* (*T.L.S.*, January 11, 1936, p. 35).

Poetry, partly wishful prophecy. Keats is here looking back on what seem to him to be the facts of his brief career, and he condemns himself, with harsh sincerity, for having dwelt in an ivory tower, for having given to men the illusive balm of dreams, whereas true poets, by intense effort, seize upon the reality which is not illusive. To them, as to active benefactors of humanity, the miseries of the world are misery, and will not let them rest.[72]

One need not be a sentimentalist to feel the profound personal tragedy not only in the self-laceration of this last effort to feel the giant agony of the world, but also in Keats's turning aside from the *Fall* to enjoy a last serene "sensation" in *To Autumn*. We do not endorse his condemnation of a large part of his work, but we can understand his attitude, can even see that the whole course of his development made it inevitable. As he said himself, the genius of poetry must work out its own salvation in a man, and we cannot guess, if he had had health and some measure of contentment, what would have been his ultimate solution and achievement. His house was, most of the time, divided against itself, but his consciousness of the fissure, his unceasing endeavor to solve the problem of sense and knowledge, art and humanity, are in themselves

---

[72] These lines seem to embody a recollection of the preface to *Alastor*, as Bradley suggested (*Oxford Lectures on Poetry*, 1920, pp. 242–43). In connection with active benefactors of humanity, and poets, one may quote from a letter written at this time: "I am convinced more and more day by day that fine writing is next to fine doing, the top thing in the world, the Paradise Lost becomes a greater wonder" (*Letters*, p. 374; August 24, 1819).

The reference to "gray cathedrals" (*Fall*, i. 67) may well be to Winchester Cathedral, since Keats was living in Winchester during part of August and September, and frequently mentioned the cathedral in letters. While allusions to Byron occur at various times in the letters, we may notice, in connection with the anti-Byronic lines in the *Fall* (i. 207–09), the hostile remarks in letters of September (pp. 405, 413). Some of the opening lines of the *Fall* may echo *The Excursion*; cf. ll. 2–7, and *Excursion*, iv. 1277 ff.; ll. 11 ff., and *Excursion*, i. 77 ff. Keats's outburst against dreamers recalls such passages as *Excursion*, i. 635–36, iii. 333 ff.

an index of his stature. No other English poet of the century had his poetic endowment, and no other strove so intensely to harmonize what may, without undue stretching of the terms, be called the Apollonian and the Faustian ideals of poetry. However high one's estimate of what he wrote, one may really think — to use an often meaningless cliché — that Keats was greater than his poems.

CHAPTER IV

Shelley

THOUGH the name of Shelley is the very symbol of a spontaneous singer, he was not, like Keats, a born poet, he may be said to have become one almost by accident. As late as January, 1819, at the beginning of his *annus mirabilis*, he could write thus to Peacock:

My first act of "Prometheus" is complete, and I think you would like it. I consider poetry very subordinate to moral and political science, and if I were well, certainly I would aspire to the latter; for I can conceive a great work, embodying the discoveries of all ages, and harmonising the contending creeds by which mankind have been ruled. Far from me is such an attempt, and I shall be content, by exercising my fancy, to amuse myself, and perhaps some others, and cast what weight I can into the scale of that balance, which the Giant of Arthegall holds.[1]

In his earlier years Shelley made zealous if ineffectual efforts as a practical reformer, but it was with the realization of his loneliness as a lover of man, and woman, and of his failure to move an inert world, that he discovered his true vocation, to teach in song what he had learned in suffering. If he could not in his own person, by speeches and proclamations (delivered or bottled), achieve freedom for mankind, he could win partial solace in endless descriptions of Utopia and himself, and perhaps bring the millennium somewhat nearer by expressing his faith in radiant verse.

[1] *Letters of Percy Bysshe Shelley*, ed. Roger Ingpen (1914), II, 660.

For almost all his major poems are propaganda or apologia or both.

Shelley differed from many young radicals of our day in having the courage of his convictions. To feel or to think, at least in his earlier years, was to act, and the action might be noble, or grotesque, or, at times, inhuman. If he never possessed, as Mr. Brailsford finely says, that sanity which consists in becoming accustomed to the monstrous, it is also true that, through most of his life and in the face of many self-deceptions, he seems hardly ever to have had any doubt concerning the absolute rightness of all his acts and opinions. With much more than the usual undergraduate enthusiasm for dead causes, and with much less than the usual undergraduate knowledge of life, he embraced one faded literary fashion or humanitarian creed after another, from the fiction of "Monk" Lewis and Rosa Matilda to the fiction of Godwinian perfectibility. What is more important is that he cherished and fought for ideals which, after a hundred years, are still only ideals. If he had been born in 1892, gone to Eton in 1904, and to Oxford in 1910, he would probably have passed through a Wilde-Beardsley phase, would have gone on to harangue from Fabian platforms, would have transferred his discipleship to Edward Carpenter, and in 1914 would have been arrested as a conscientious objector.

One might not expect such a young man to become the author of some enchanting mythological lyrics and the most beautiful of lyrical dramas on a mythological theme. Left to himself, Shelley might have continued to nourish his soul too long or too exclusively on the rather moldy husks of anti-Christian and perfectibilarian philosophy. (He would doubtless at all times have described himself as a modern poet does in *Who's Who*: "*Educ*.: Eton . . . Oxford; mainly self-educated.") Now that compulsory Latin and Greek have ceased to be, we may feel the gratitude that Shelley did not feel for "the grand, old, fortifying, classical curriculum." Whatever the defects of Eton and Oxford, they gave him the key to two literatures — even if the key needed to be oiled by Peacock — and Greek especially did more than anything else to turn a mixture of magnanimous crusader and eccentric crank into a poet. Shelley's real discovery of classical literature came some years after he had left Oxford, but even in his school and college days the apathy with which he absorbed the prescribed books was sometimes stirred into eager enthusiasm by authors like Lucretius who appealed to his growing hatred for the tyranny of custom in religion, morality, and social institutions.[2] To the militant young radical Antigone appeared as a sort of Mary Wollstonecraft. "But is the Antigone immoral?" he writes to Hogg in 1811. "Did she wrong, when she acted in direct, in noble violation of the laws of a prejudiced society?" Ten years later, when ideal passions have come and gone, and Shelley has retired more and more into the world of dreams, Antigone is not a figure in a problem play but a vision of the unattainable: "Some of us have, in a prior existence, been in love with an Antigone, and that makes us find no full content in any mortal tie."[3]

For a time, in 1812, when Shelley was more Godwinian than Godwin, he could discern little good in ancient civilization or in a modern system of education based on it. He might not have echoed Blake's ejaculation — "The Clas-

---

[2] Medwin tells of Shelley's early dislike of the dead languages, and of the ease with which he acquired them; see his *Life of Percy Bysshe Shelley*, ed. H. B. Forman (Oxford University Press, 1913), p. 20. It is needless to refer to modern biographers' accounts of his classical reading. See Adolf Droop, *Die Belesenheit Percy Bysshe Shelley's* (Weimar, 1906). There was doubtless some perverse boyish egotism in Shelley's declaration to Godwin that he probably gained more knowledge of Latin from poring over Albertus Magnus than from all the discipline of Eton — and some Cicero might have been better for him. See *Letters*, I, 314.

[3] *Letters*, I, 76, II, 921.

sics! it is the Classics, & not Goths nor Monks, that Desolate Europe with Wars" [4] — but he saw in the vindicators of ancient learning, apart from Godwin, a set of literary despots, and, worse still, a body of children of the established fact, narrow, unreasoning bigots and reactionaries. (Some idealists of our own time have found an insidious connection between the classical discipline and British imperialism, an argument which quite fails to explain American imperialism.) However, this passing phase is of interest mainly in showing that the young Shelley's somewhat gritty rationalism needed richer nourishment. Before the end of the year he was ordering classical texts by the dozen from his bookseller; it is of interest to observe the relative proportions of pure literature and the literature of ideas and doctrine.[5] Vastly more important than this brief anti-classical measles was Shelley's ardent conception of Greece and Rome as the nurseries of freedom. Even his first doubts concerning the genuineness of Christian revelation, he wrote to Godwin, had been excited by contemplation of ancient virtues and genius.[6] It was Shelley's passion for liberty which first kindled his Hellenic fervor, and which remained, in spite of increasing literary and artistic appreciation, the most powerful motive in his reading.

I

As Shelley's early interests and literary models would lead one to expect, the conventional use of classical themes and allusions did not at first attract him; indeed, apart from his mythological poems, classical reference never was a normal strain in his writing as it was in that of Keats. In *Queen Mab* (1813) mythology appears in the course of

---

[4] *Prophetic Writings of William Blake*, ed. D. J. Sloss and J. P. R. Wallis (Clarendon Press, 1926), I, 640.

[5] See, for example, the letter of December 24, 1812 (*Letters*, I, 371–72).

[6] *Ibid.*, I, 320.

a denunciation of religion. The childhood of the human race was the era of a false but beautiful polytheism, the personification of the forces of nature. With less than Wordsworthian sympathy a poet who was to become one of the few modern myth-makers writes thus of the myth-making imagination:

> Thou [religion] taintest all thou look'st upon! — the stars,
> Which on thy cradle beamed so brightly sweet,
> Were gods to the distempered playfulness
> Of thy untutored infancy: the trees,
> The grass, the clouds, the mountains, and the sea,
> All living things that walk, swim, creep, or fly,
> Were gods: the sun had homage, and the moon
> Her worshipper.[7]

The notes to *Queen Mab* contain an item as remarkable as anything in Fulgentius or Boccaccio. No one could predict *Prometheus Unbound* from Shelley's interpretation, borrowed from Newton's *Defence of Vegetable Regimen*, of the myth of Prometheus as an allegory of the evils that cooking animal food brought upon mankind.[8]

In later works Shelley moralizes or reinterprets classic myths as Spenser and others had done before him.[9] But

---

[7] *Queen Mab*, vi. 72 ff. Shelley's poems are quoted from the one-volume edition of Thomas Hutchinson (Oxford University Press, 1927), which is cited as *Works*.

[8] *Works*, p. 817 (note on *Queen Mab*, viii. 211–12). Shelley's admired Erasmus Darwin discerned in Prometheus "an allegory for the effects of drinking spirituous liquors" and the resulting diseases; see *The Botanic Garden* (ed. 1794), Part II, p. 120. See also Peacock's Mr. Escot in *Headlong Hall*, ch. II; and Hoxie N. Fairchild, *The Noble Savage* (Columbia University Press, 1928), pp. 348 ff.

Whether or not Shelley at this time knew Bacon's *De Sapientia Veterum*, the more general part of his remarks is not unlike Bacon's account of Pandora (*Works*, ed. Spedding *et al.*, Boston, 1860, XIII, 153). Bacon is here following Natalis Comes, *Mythologiae*, IV. vi (ed. Padua, 1616, p. 169); C. W. Lemmi, *The Classic Deities in Bacon* (Johns Hopkins University Press, 1933), p. 130.

[9] In his edition of Mary Shelley's classical dramas (Oxford University Press, 1922, pp. xxiv ff.), M. Koszul quotes a fragmentary "draft of an Essay, which occurs, in Mrs. Shelley's handwriting, as an insertion in her Journal for the Italian period." Its thesis is that heathen mythology rests on as good proofs as

whereas the poets of the Renaissance commonly borrowed from, or wrote in the spirit of, the orthodox allegorical handbooks, Shelley treats the myths with more subjective coloring and freedom of intuition. Orpheus is a Shelleyan poet whose tempestuous grief finds utterance in song.[10] The music of Amphion is a symbol not merely of magic melody but of truth and freedom.[11] The "Cimmerian Anarchs" who oppose the liberty of Naples shall be Actaeons, "devoured by their own hounds." [12] Shelley is closer to the Renaissance interpretation of Actaeon, though the added subtlety is modern, when in *Adonais* he describes himself as one who (unlike his own Peter Bell) had gazed on Nature's naked loveliness, "Actaeon-like," and fled astray, pursued by the raging hounds of his own thoughts.[13] In the same poem the line "Wisdom the mirrored shield, or scorn the spear" recalls the story of Perseus and Medusa in Shelley's admired Lucan, or no less admired Bacon, where Pallas gives the hero a mirror in which he may look at the Gorgon without harm.[14] And the name of Medusa suggests the very different mood of the poem on the paint-

---

Christianity, that they do not contradict one another, and that therefore a person who believes in one must believe in the other. M. Koszul thinks the intention more conciliatory than destructive. It is uncertain whether Mrs. Shelley was setting down a theory of equal "inspiration" original with herself, or suggested by her husband, or developed in conversation.

[10] *Orpheus* (*Works*, p. 621, especially ll. 81–83). This poem has been regarded as an attempt at imitating the improvisations of Sgricci, and some scholars have taken it to be mainly the work of Mary Shelley.

[11] *Revolt of Islam*, Dedication, st. x; *Hellas*, ll. 1002 ff.

[12] *Ode to Naples*, ll. 77 ff. Shelley's use of "Cimmerian" recalls the traditional locating of that people not far from Naples; he may have remembered the discussion in Eustace's *A Classical Tour Through Italy* (1815), II, 401–02.

[13] *Adonais*, st. xxxi; *Peter Bell the Third*, IV. xi. See Mr. Walter E. Peck's *Shelley: His Life and Work* (Boston, 1927), II, 4, 182; *Epipsychidion*, ll. 272–74. For a common Renaissance moralizing of Actaeon, which is most familiar through *Twelfth Night* (I. i. 19), see my other volume, p. 71, note 11.

[14] *Adonais*, st. xxvii; Lucan, *Pharsalia*, ix. 669–70; Bacon, *De Sapientia Veterum*, c. vii. For Shelley's knowledge of Bacon's work, see Peck, II, 348, and note 34 below.

ing attributed to Leonardo; the fascination felt by Shelley in the mingling of beauty and pain, "the tempestuous loveliness of terror," carries us forward through many sadistic imaginings to Swinburne and to Pater's reverie over Monna Lisa.[15]

Shelley's handling of mythological allusion, and also his gift for the spontaneous creation of myths, are most richly illustrated in *Prometheus Unbound* and *The Witch of Atlas*, but two or three decorative bits from other poems may be noticed here. If some allusions cited in the last paragraph had a shrill or strident note, there is nothing of that quality in the lines on the departed glories of Venice in the *Euganean Hills* (1818); Amphitrite and Apollo are serene symbols of an ideal past. Apart from a few cold naiads, Shelley's mythology is usually fresh and radiant and sometimes inspired. The decorative impulse may be the only one, or it may, with an addition rather than a loss of beauty, subserve a larger purpose. One might compare two of Shelley's many references to the Bacchic Maenads. Here is one of the glowing stanzas of *The Sensitive Plant*:

> And the wand-like lily, which lifted up,
> As a Maenad, its moonlight-coloured cup,
> Till the fiery star, which is its eye,
> Gazed through clear dew on the tender sky.

This is beautiful picture-making, but the quiet miniature falls far short of the cosmic personification, the demonic rush and power, of the simile in the *Ode to the West Wind*.

II

We turn from scattered allusions to the group of mythological lyrics written in 1820.[16] To comment on *Arethusa*

[15] *Works*, p. 577; Mario Praz, *The Romantic Agony* (English translation, Oxford University Press, 1933), pp. 25–26.

[16] *Arethusa* and the perfect little *Song of Proserpine* were written for Mrs. Shelley's drama *Proserpine*, the *Hymn of Pan* and the *Hymn of Apollo* for her

is like trying to describe a waterfall. Shelley evidently had Ovid in mind, but he took over little more than the outline of the myth (and altered that), and some proper names which, mere geographical labels in Ovid, become melodious incantations in the lyric.[17] The Latin version has all its author's realistic detail, and, though Ovid is a poet, it seems strangely prosy after one has been caught up in a shimmering network of colored light. Ovid's Arethusa has robust rustic charms, Shelley's is a divinity or a stream, we hardly know which. Here as in *The Cloud* (where science becomes ethereal), the poet's delight in playing with the elements of nature allows no intrusive thought of the unregenerate world or of himself. Keats's episode of Arethusa, which Shelley may have remembered, is more in Ovid's manner, and is used also as a link in humanitarian symbolism; Shelley surrenders completely to the myth, he becomes the stream itself.[18] Of course not even Shelley can place himself in the myth-making age of the human mind, and *Arethusa* and *The Cloud* are not really primitive; but no other poet has approached Shelley's magical deceptions.

Midas. See M. Koszul's elaborate edition of these dramas; the notes in Mr. Newman I. White's *The Best of Shelley* (New York, 1932), pp. 494–97; and my few remarks on the dramas at the beginning of the next chapter.

[17] The associations of Enna were of course familiar to Shelley, and in Ovid the myth of Arethusa forms part of the episode of Ceres; for some of Shelley's proper names, see *Metam.* v. 385, 499, 608, 640. Shelley's felicitous "Acroceraunian" may be remembered from a commonplace line of Byron's (*Childe Harold*, IV. lxxiv). The picture of Alpheus with his trident opening a chasm in the rocks was doubtless transferred from the Ovidian Pluto (*Metam.* v. 420 ff.) or the Virgilian Aeolus (*Aen.* i. 81 ff.). For other details, compare Shelley, ll. 4–5, and Ovid, ll. 612–13; Shelley, ll. 37–39, and Ovid, ll. 617–20; Shelley, ll. 52–54, and Ovid, ll. 605–06; Shelley, l. 81, and Ovid, l. 591. Ll. 47–48 were evidently suggested by Virgil, *Ecl.* x. 4–5; cf. Shelley's translation of part of that eclogue. Shelley's "as soft as sleep" (l. 15), if not original, may go back to Virgil, *Ecl.* vii. 45 (*somno mollior herba*); cf. Theocritus, v. 51, xv. 125. For the possible influence of Hunt's *The Nymphs*, a poem Shelley liked, see my next chapter, note 16.

[18] If only as an example of the difference in poetic instinct and method in description, compare *Arethusa*, ll. 64–72, and *Endymion*, ii. 988 ff.

The *Hymn of Apollo*, in its cool purity of imagination, its large, serene stateliness, recalls the poem ascribed to Ralegh, *Praised be Diana's fair and harmless light*. The god whose footsteps pave the clouds with fire retains his mythological attributes, which inspire a series of beautiful pictures, but they are touched with mystical suggestion. Ovid's Apollo, *Mundi oculus*, is transcendentalized, and embodies a thoroughly Shelleyan conception of the light of imagination:

> I am the eye with which the Universe
> Beholds itself and knows itself divine.[19]

The *Hymn of Pan* also starts from Ovidian motives and far transcends them, even in the material details of the scenic background. Browning liked to think of Pan as the shaggy goat-god, benevolent or amorous; Keats in his *Hymn* reveled in details, half real, half fanciful, of primitive pastoral life, and toward the end mounted from the concrete to the mystical; the sweet pipings of Shelley's Pan are a purely lyrical rapture, the goat-god is as disembodied as Ariel. And in his third stanza Shelley leaves the Ovidian world altogether in giving a more than allegorical turn to the myth of Pan and Syrinx. Its first four lines are perhaps an echo of the songs of Silenus and Iopas in Virgil.[20] Then, with a marked change of rhythm, we hear the voice of Shelley himself, who so eagerly pursued so many Antigones, to find that they were brown demons or noble animals or clouds instead of Junos. But the sadness is not

---

[19] *Metam.* iv. 226–28. Miss Winstanley does not notice Ovid, but compares the tenth book of Plato's *Laws* ("Platonism in Shelley," *Essays and Studies by Members of the English Association*, IV [1913], 86). Cf. *Paradise Lost*, v. 171: "Thou Sun, of this great world both eye and soul."

Shelley apparently took some hints from the Homeric *Hymn to the Delian Apollo* (e.g., ll. 22 ff., 140 ff.), and from the *Metamorphoses, passim*. See also his translation of the *Symposium* (*Prose Works*, ed. Shepherd, 1912, II, 82–83).

[20] *Ecl.* vi. 31 ff., *Aen.* i. 742 ff. Shelley alludes to the former passage in *Prometheus Unbound*, II. ii. 90 ff.

merely of disappointment in love, it is the fundamental disillusion of the idealist.[21]

III

Before we come to *The Witch of Atlas*, a word may be said of Shelley's translations from the Greek. We have enthusiastic testimony from such witnesses as Medwin and Thornton Hunt to the ease and charm of his oral renderings, and the published versions — which he did to while away hours of idleness — might have made a reputation for a smaller poet. The only fault in the *Cyclops* of Euripides, except for occasional errors due in part at least to a defective text, is a too consistent refinement of style for a satyric play. The renderings of the Homeric *Hymns* are often better than the originals. Apart from some omissions and more expansions, most of the *Hymn to Mercury*, in spite of the *ottava rima*, is remarkably faithful.[22] Shelley forgets the troubles of the inner and outer world and gives himself up whole-heartedly to enjoyment of the impudent knavery of the childish thief. With perfect flexibility of mood and style, he can pass from the Byronic

> He sung how Jove and May of the bright sandal
> Dallied in love not quite legitimate,

to such Shelleyan lines as these:

> His left hand held the lyre, and in his right
> The plectrum struck the chords — unconquerable
> Up from beneath his hand in circling flight
> The gathering music rose — and sweet as Love
> The penetrating notes did live and move
>
> Within the heart of great Apollo. . . .[23]

[21] E. M. W. Tillyard, *Poetry: Direct and Oblique* (1934), pp. 158–59.
[22] See *Letters*, II, 802.
[23] Shelley, ll. 72–73, 558 ff.; Homeric *Hymn*, ll. 57–58, 418 ff. For a detailed

Like Spenser's *Muiopotmos*, *The Witch of Atlas* (1820) has been treated as a gossamer cobweb of pure fancy and also as an elaborate and serious allegory. But, with such instinctively mythological and decorative artists as Spenser and Shelley, a poem can be both at once. While the manner of *The Witch of Atlas* is that of the most ethereal extravaganza, it is clear that Shelley has a meaning, or a number of meanings. What they are is another question. For not here only, but in such an obviously serious work as *Prometheus Unbound*, Shelley anticipates poets of our own time in "playing by himself in public," to borrow Mr. Max Eastman's phrase. He will, unlike our contemporaries, make his principal conception fairly clear, and then he feels at liberty to adorn or obscure it with a multitude of details which, we often feel sure, have significance for him but remain hazy to us. It is always safe to assume that a beautiful woman in Shelley has some relation to the earthly or heavenly Venus, the spirit of love and beauty in nature and the mind of man, and the witch embodies all these and other attributes.[24] She is Asia (and Prometheus) on a

---

comparison of Shelley's translation with the Greek, see Florian Asanger, *Percy Bysshe Shelley's Sprach-Studien* (Bonn, 1911), pp. 89 ff.

In January, 1818 (*Letters*, II, 584), Shelley asked Ollier to send him Chapman's *Hymns*. He could not have got much real help from Chapman, whose versions are stiff and strained in diction and syntax, though of course Chapman could not write anything without forging some fine phrases. The evidence for Shelley's use of Chapman is slight. The line, "Where the immortal oxen of the Gods," appears in Shelley, with "God" instead of "Gods"; Chapman's "and in the end Never deceive thee" is in Shelley, "And even at the end will ne'er deceive thee." See Chapman's *Poems and Minor Translations* (1875), pp. 290, 298; Shelley, ll. 90, 618; and below, note 50. Sometimes a word or turn of phrase suggests Chapman. These items seem to have been overlooked in Theodor Vetter's comparison of Chapman and Shelley (see my bibliography).

[24] Among special studies of the poem see A. M. D. Hughes, "Shelley's 'Witch of Atlas,'" *M.L.R.*, VII (1912), 508–16; E. E. Kellett, "The Witch of Atlas," *Suggestions* (Cambridge University Press, 1923); and Mr. Carl Grabo's elaborate monograph, *The Meaning of The Witch of Atlas* (University of North Carolina Press, 1935). Mr. Grabo has many valuable interpretations of Neo-Platonic and scientific matters, but he ignores the literary background, even the Homeric hymns.

holiday. But many things in the poem, and the allusion in *Mont Blanc* to "the still cave of the witch Poesy," suggest that the witch also represents, more specifically, the creative imagination of the poet, and here the *Defence of Poetry* becomes the best commentary. Like medieval allegorizers of myth, Shelley moves on more than one plane, and metaphysical Neo-Platonic symbols are mingled with the forces of the physical world — though he is perhaps less preoccupied with electricity than Mr. Grabo would have him. In any case Shelley is content for the most part to let his reforming zeal slumber, and the witch's soul is undisturbed by the workings of "Custom's lawless law." This mood of untroubled serenity, even irresponsible gayety, which is so genuine and yet so rare in him, was partly the result of his excursion to the top of Monte San Pellegrino; his response to the buoyant stimulus of Italian scenery was unfailing. On the literary side that spirit was carried over, along with the *ottava rima*, from his recent translation of the Homeric *Hymn to Hermes*. Indeed *The Witch of Atlas* is itself a sort of Homeric hymn, of Shelleyan spirituality, subtlety, and color, and it owes a number of hints to the Homeric hymns to Hermes and Aphrodite.

The nature of the sources and symbolism can only be touched upon here. Along with Shelley's favorite and more or less Neo-Platonic symbols, the ideal woman, the cave, the veil, the boat, the stream, literary borrowings are given a metaphysical significance in relation to the many-faceted theme of beauty, love, and imagination. The witch lives on Atlas' mountain, like the sorceress consulted by Dido who had power over love and the elements, and like the Minerva of Thomas Taylor's Neo-Platonic commentary.[25] The sun, the creative principle (and the god of poetry), was

---

[25] *Aen.* iv. 480 ff. Among those attracted by the witch are "the rude kings of pastoral Garamant" (xi. 2); cf. *Aen.* iv. 198, and a poet Shelley preferred to Virgil, Lucah, *Phars.* ix. 369, 460. For Minerva, see Grabo, pp. 24, 137–38.

her father, as he was the father of the twin Spenserian in-
carnations of virginity and love, Belphoebe and Amoret.[26]
Wild beasts grow tame and follow her, as they follow
Aphrodite and Una.[27] In Spenser the wood-gods reverence
Una, perhaps because true faith finds a welcome among the
humble; Silenus and the rest attend the witch perhaps — I
use the word "perhaps" once for all — because "the wild-
est and most vulgar fancies, when touched with true Imagination, are transformed into unaccustomed beauty." [28]
Una, who has her Platonic aspect, is veiled because her
untried knight is not yet fit to look upon the dazzling face
of Truth; the witch weaves her veil, "a shadow for the
splendour of her love," because her beauty makes the
actual world seem dim and shadowy, and those who see
her can love nothing else.[29] In the Homeric *Hymn*, Maia,
the mother of Hermes, like the witch dwelt alone in a dim
cave, and there Zeus visited her.[30] Shelley's cave seems to
be the world of the soul, a realm midway between the pure
intellect and the body, and the material properties become
partly immaterial. The witch has lamps and chalices corresponding to Maia's tripods and cauldrons, but instead of
Maia's nectar and ambrosia, gold, silver, and shining
raiment, the witch's cave is filled with visions of love,
thought-stirring odors, life-giving liquors. There are
strange scrolls, "the works of some Saturnian Archimage,"

[26] *Faerie Queene*, III. vi. 2–9. Cf. also *Witch*, ii–iii, and Ovid, *Metam*. iv.
247 ff.
[27] *Witch*, vi–vii; *Hymn to Aphrodite*, ll. 69–74; *Faerie Queene*, I. iii. 5–6 (and
I. vi. 26). Droop (*Belesenheit*, p. 78) cites Southey's *Curse of Kehama*, xiii. 10–12.
[28] Kellett, p. 122. Cf. *Witch*, viii–xi and xxii, and *Faerie Queene*, I. vi. 7 ff.,
14 ff., and *Witch*, viii, and Virgil, *Ecl*. x. 24–27 (see Shelley's translation of part
of this eclogue, *Works*, pp. 715–16).
[29] *Witch*, xii–xiii; *Faerie Queene*, I. iii. 4, vi. 4, xii. 21–23 (and *Amoretti*, xxxv).
Shelley's phrase, "the fleeting image of a shade," is too Shelleyan to need a
source, but one may mention Lucan's *Stat magni nominis umbra* (*Phars*. i. 135);
cf. *Hellas*, l. 568.
[30] *Witch*, i–iii; *Hymn to Hermes*, ll. 4 ff.

which tell how men may win back a golden age of innocence and control the elements, and they reveal also "the
inmost lore of Love." [31]

In the Homeric *Hymn to Aphrodite* the goddess' love for
Anchises is embittered by the knowledge that he is mortal,
and the witch, who represents eternal principles, grieves
because the earthly creatures who love her must decay.[32]
Tempering fire and snow with liquid love, the witch makes
a beautiful hermaphrodite. Spenser's snowy Florimell
represented false beauty, spurious chastity; the meaning
of Shelley's sexless creature, in spite of all the explanations,
remains dubious.[33] Is it simply that the witch, in her immortal loneliness, must create for herself a companion of
ideal perfection? But of many details the earnest critic
(who "wants to know, you know") can only say, in Shelleyan language, "Each to itself must be the oracle." The
mainly playful and satirical conclusion of the poem is lucid
enough.

The Witch of Atlas may be called Shelley's most Elizabethan poem, though the adjective has only to be used to
demand qualification. In Drayton's Platonic *Endimion
and Phoebe* the story is told in a richly Ovidian style, with
an abundance of pastoral and mythological "realism," and
the didactic and Platonic layers could be removed without
disturbing the narrative. Spenser, a much more instinctive and philosophic Platonic idealist than Drayton, often
writes poetry with his right hand and allegory with his
left, though sometimes the two are perfectly fused. Shel-

---

[31] *Witch*, xiv–xx; *Hymn to Hermes*, ll. 60–61, 246–51; Hughes, p. 512; Grabo,
pp. 44 ff. See *Faerie Queene*, II. ix. 50–51, 53, 57. Cf. also *Witch*, xl. 4, and *F.Q.*,
II. ix. 51.

[32] *Witch*, xxiii–xxiv; *Hymn to Aphrodite*, ll. 239 ff.

[33] *Witch*, xxxv ff.; *Faerie Queene*, III. viii. 5 ff. (and I. i. 45). Cf. the canceled
fragments of *Epipsychidion* (*Works*, pp. 421–22, ll. 57–61). See Edward Carpenter and George Barnefield, *The Psychology of the Poet Shelley* (1925), pp. 18 ff.
Ovid's Hermaphroditus, by the way, was a scion of Atlas (*Metam*. iv. 368).

ley's poem is almost all of a piece; transcendental symbolism is the very warp and woof of a tapestry of incomparable lightness and grace. It is in keeping with the spirit
of the whole that the mythological allusions are rarely of
Elizabethan concreteness. Of the two dozen mythological
characters alluded to only a few are given anything like a
local habitation, the rest are airy nothings, bright phantoms; universal Pan is an invisible spirit who dwells with
the *anima mundi*. Spenser, or Keats, would linger over
physical background or attributes, or endow divinities
with human feeling; Shelley touches a name, awakens an
association, and skims on his winged way. The witch is
related to the One of Shelley's Platonic heaven, but here,
as often in more serious poems, he is most poetically satisfying when he is flitting, a radiant butterfly, among the
Many.

IV

We have observed Shelley's early interest in the myth
of Prometheus, in unpromising relation to a vegetable
regimen. For a conception more fruitful than Mr. Newton's, and one very much in the air in the romantic period,
Shelley may, as we have seen, have owed something to in-
tercourse with Byron in 1816.[34] At any rate *Prometheus*

---

[34] See the last section of ch. II. Medwin (*Life*, ed. Forman, p. 161) makes
Byron the debtor to Shelley, and he may have been in part, but Medwin is a
dubious witness. The external history of Shelley's acquaintance with the
Aeschylean drama is briefly this. In December, 1812, he ordered a copy of
Aeschylus from his bookseller (*Letters*, I, 372), and he read *Prometheus Bound*
in 1816 (Dowden, *Life of Shelley*, 1886, II, 75, 185). On March 26, 1818 (*Letters*,
II, 590–91), he wrote of an Alpine scene "like that described in the Prometheus
of Aeschylus." Apart from these items and the note to *Queen Mab*, Shelley does
not seem to have referred to the myth or the drama until October, 1818, when he
wrote to Peacock that he had just finished the first act of *Prometheus Unbound*,
and asked "what there is in Cicero about a drama supposed to have been written
by Aeschylus under this title" (*Letters*, II, 630). Shelley was thinking here of the

Unbound is Shelley's finest work; it was, along with *Adonais*, his own favorite. Critics have worked out fairly complete and conflicting expositions of the allegory, but I have
neither the space nor the courage for an effort which does
not find much warrant in the comments of either Shelley
or his wife. The symbolic significance of the principal
figures is made sufficiently clear by the text and by Mrs.
Shelley's notes. Prometheus retains something of his
mythological character as the champion of mankind, but he
is mainly the ideal type of mankind itself, the highest and
noblest result of human evolution. Asia, mentioned by
Herodotus as the wife of Prometheus,[35] is, according to
Mrs. Shelley, "the same as Venus and Nature." She is,
then, one of Shelley's names for the spirit of love or beauty
"which penetrates and clasps and fills the world"; as such,
and as the creative spirit in nature, she is the ideal, the
complement, and the ally of evolving man.[36] Jupiter is
partly the anthropomorphic God of theology whom Shelley
abhorred; but in a larger way, since the hateful Jehovah
himself is man's creation, Jupiter represents petrified custom, superstition, tyrannic power, all the evil that man has
brought upon man. In a word, Shelley is again treating
his one great theme, the eternal conflict between the spirit
of good and the spirit of evil. To go much beyond these
generalities is to be involved in endless puzzles, and no
mind as subtle and penetrating as Shelley's own has
yet appeared to elucidate them satisfactorily.[37] However

---

passage in the *Tusculan Disputations* (II. x) which is regularly quoted among the
fragments of Aeschylus.

For Shelley's knowledge of Bacon's interpretation of Prometheus (*De Sapi-
entia Veterum*, xxvi), see note 14 above; R. Ackermann's edition of *Prometheus
Unbound* (Heidelberg, 1908), p. 129, note on *P.U.*, III. iii. 148; D. L. Clark,
P.M.L.A., XLVIII (1933), 545.

[35] Herodotus, iv. 45. Cf. Aeschylus, *Prometheus Bound*, ll. 555–60.
[36] Cf. *Queen Mab*, vi. 39 ff.
[37] Among recent critics Mr. Carl Grabo has made perhaps the most heroic,
because the most detailed, attempts to explain much that the usual Shelleyan is

familiar the drama is, I fear that even my brief discussion must begin with an outline of the more lucid and tangible parts of the fable.

Aeschylus' drama opens with the grimly realistic business of nailing Prometheus to the rocks, and the hero maintains a silence almost unendurable for even the modern reader. Shelley starts with Prometheus' grand denunciation of Jupiter, whose long reign has filled men "With fear and self-contempt and barren hope"; the words are recalled, with a difference, in the last lines of the poem. There is the difficulty that Shelley cannot forgo an occasion for cursing tyranny and yet has to dramatize his hero's change of heart. So Prometheus defies and denounces Jupiter; declares that he no longer feels hate or any evil wish; craves to hear again the curse he had once launched against the tyrant; and, after hearing it repeated, repents and wishes "no living thing to suffer pain." [38] His unregenerate mother, Earth, who has not learned the law of love, laments his weakness. When Mercury urges him to submit and reveal the secret which he alone knows of the danger threatening Jupiter's sovereignty, Prometheus refuses to seal mankind's captivity by yielding; he will await "the retributive hour." The tortures to which he is subjected are chiefly mental, pictures of the evil which has come out of good — Christ "wailing for the faith he kindled," and the bloody excesses of the French Revolution. The earth is a hell of superstition, wrong, and suffering. When the Furies have gone, vanquished by Prometheus'

content to pass by; see *A Newton Among Poets* and *Prometheus Unbound: An Interpretation* (University of North Carolina Press, 1930 and 1935). Mr. Grabo is a devout and learned expositor, but the more one might accept of his scientific and Neo-Platonic parallels, the more one would be driven to wonder how Shelley could have expected even five or six readers to follow him.

[38] "A robe of envenomed agony" (l. 289) is an obvious allusion to Nessus' shirt, and probably an echo of *Paradise Lost*, ii. 543. The two lines following may recall the vengeance taken by Euripides' Medea on the new bride of Jason (*Medea*, ll. 1186–87).

endurance and infinite pity, Earth summons a chorus of spirits who try to cheer the martyr with songs of love, self-sacrifice, wisdom, and the poetic imagination; they assure him that he shall conquer. He, feeling "most vain all hope but love," yearns for Asia, and Panthea reminds him that Asia, in exile "in that far Indian vale," waits and watches over him.

Nearly all that can be called drama is found in Shelley's first act, where most of his borrowings from Aeschylus occur. With the second act, and the recital of various dreams, difficulties begin. Shelley's main theme, the regenerating power of love, is of course not Aeschylean at all. The sympathy of nature is suggested in Aeschylus, in the hero's great appeal to the elements, and through the chorus, but for Shelley the division between man and nature is much less distinct than for Aeschylus, and Prometheus as a character is gradually submerged in the background. Shelley is not content with a nameless chorus of Oceanides, he gives Prometheus a wife and two sisters-in-law, a typical Shelleyan household. The significance of Panthea and Ione is too speculative for discussion here; in some vague way they represent aspects of love.[39] At any rate whenever the seraglio of feminine abstractions appear, they dissolve what elements of hardness belong to the fable and to Prometheus himself.

In the third scene Asia and Panthea have reached the realm of Demogorgon. This dread power is a fusion of several related conceptions. He stands for the mysterious reality, the eternal order, behind and above the temporal world, and he is something like Greek fate, with a strong coloring of Shelleyan "necessity."[40] The cryptic dialogue

[39] See the article by M. Koszul cited in the bibliography, and Grabo, *Prometheus Unbound*, pp. 52 ff.

[40] See J. F. C. Gutteling, *Neophilologus*, IX (1924), 283–85. Some other discussions of Demogorgon, by A. R. Benham, E. Ebeling, H. G. Lotspeich, M. M. Rader, are mentioned in my bibliography. Denis Saurat labels Demogorgon

between Asia and Demogorgon on the nature of God leads
to Asia's account of two of the three ages of man as Shelley
liked to think of them. First there was the Saturnian
golden age, when man's happiness, though real, was im-
mature and incomplete; [41] he was only like the flowers and
leaves. Then Prometheus made Jupiter ruler of the world
and human suffering and strife began. But Prometheus
gave to man hope and love and knowledge and power —
the Aeschylean catalogue of benefits is in part reproduced,
with spiritual and scientific embellishments — and now the
giver hangs on Caucasus, while man, who looks on his glorious creation like a god, is pursued by "Evil, the immedi-
cable plague." The answer is that "man, having enslaved
the elements, remains himself a slave." [42] Jupiter still
reigns, yet he is the servant of evil, and he cannot hold out
against the servant of love.

The destined Hour arrives and carries Asia and Panthea
upward. Asia is transfigured; the full radiance of Aphrodite Urania is unveiled, and sounds in the air proclaim that
the whole world feels the power of love. Then we come to
the two lyrics, "Life of Life" and "My soul is an enchanted boat." At this point all good Shelleyans face the
east, and regard an attempt to discern the meaning as both

"the Minister of the Absolute" (*Literature and Occult Tradition*, New York,
1930, pp. 15-16). Miss Maud Bodkin calls him "the Unconscious" (*Archetypal
Patterns in Poetry*, Oxford University Press, 1934, p. 255). Demogorgon is not
a figure in classical mythology, but Shelley would have met him in Spenser and
Milton. For the mythological side of the conception, he had enough material in
Peacock's note on *Rhododaphne*; Peacock mentions Milton, Natalis Comes, and
Boccaccio. I might add a sentence from an authority on deities, Samuel Boyse:
"Lactantius informs us, that the Father of all Nature was call'd *Demigorgon*, or
God of the Earth, (by which the Heathens meant no doubt the *Anima Mundi*)
and assigns him Eternity for his Companion" (*A New Pantheon*, 1753, p. 2).

[41] Shelley's notion of the ages was apparently indebted to Plato's *Statesman*,
270 ff.; see L. Winstanley, "Platonism in Shelley," pp. 98-100. For a more historical view see Shelley's "Essay on Christianity" (*Shelley's Literary and Philosophical Criticism*, ed. J. Shawcross, Oxford University Press, 1909, p. 114).

[42] *A Defence of Poetry* (Shawcross, pp. 151-52). For the echo of Byron in the
lines on evil (II. iv. 100 ff.), see the last paragraph of ch. II above.

prosaic and profane; those who desire more in poetry than rapturous reverie, who ask that feeling shall have direction as well as intensity, must not enter the temple with their thick-soled shoes. The journey of Asia and Panthea has been a journey backward through the world of matter and sense to ultimate reality, and the idea is recapitulated in the last stanza of the second lyric. Transcendentalizing a bit of Plato's *Statesman*,[43] Shelley reverses the "Platonic" process of Wordsworth's *Ode*; the soul, borne on the wings of music and love, passes backward and forward beyond mortal bars, "Through Death and Birth, to a diviner day," to the world of pre-existence.

The third act discloses Jupiter on his throne, with his consort Thetis, rejoicing, like Ozymandias, in his omnipotence.[44] The dramatic display of *hybris* is followed by Jupiter's quite undramatic tribute, which Shelley cannot resist putting in, to the invincible soul of man. Then, by way of dramatic irony, Jupiter reveals his expectation that, after the overthrow of Demogorgon, an Hour will bring Demogorgon's ever-living limbs to heaven to be united with the spirit of the son of himself and Thetis; the new being thus created will extinguish the last spark of man's rebellion.[45] But Demogorgon himself arrives, for a

[43] *Statesman*, 270 *d, e*; E. M. W. Tillyard, *T.L.S.*, September 29, 1932, p. 691. And see *ibid.*, p. 762. Cf. *Queen Mab*, ix. 149 ff.

[44] Among various Shelleyan parallels to the moral of *Ozymandias* cf. *Queen Mab*, ix. 23 ff. The Egyptian monarch, unlike Jupiter, is "vanquished by Time, not man" (M. A. Bald, "Shelley's Mental Progress," *Essays and Studies by Members of the English Association*, XIII [1928], 114). But "Necessity" has a part in the overthrow of Jupiter, though that power was more and more being transformed in Shelley's mind into Love.

[45] Shelley may have been influenced by the Christian doctrine of incarnation (see J. F. C. Gutteling, note 40 above), but ancient mythology included the "popular fancy that some day a new order of things would come into being, with the return of Kronos or the advent of some divine child," so that Shelley's Demogorgon was "imaginatively right" (J. A. K. Thomson, "The Religious Background of the *Prometheus Vinctus*," *Harvard Studies in Classical Philology*, XXXI [1920], 6).

different purpose, and, after a momentary resistance, Jupiter sinks into the abyss. (With another undramatic impulse, Shelley has the abject tyrant beg that Prometheus, the "gentle, and just, and dreadless," be made his judge.) This easy toppling over of Jupiter has often been called grotesque, and it is that if one takes the incident as in itself representing Shelley's solution of the problem of evil. However unsatisfying his real solution may be, he had here much the same difficulty that Milton encountered in rendering abstract ideas through a concrete fable. Jupiter of course does not fall because Demogorgon pushes him off his throne; that act is only the culmination and the symbol of the process whereby the spirit of love has prevailed in Prometheus and in the world and has made impossible the continued reign of evil. "Yet slow and gradual dawned the morn of love." [46] The awkwardness results from the exigencies of dramatic foreshortening.

After an idyllic scene, parallel to that of the fauns in the second act, Hercules unbinds Prometheus and restores him to Asia. Ideal man is reunited with the creative spirit of life and love and nature; in full and harmonious possession of all his powers, he can in time become master of the universe. And now begins Shelley's picture of the third age of man, the golden age of the dim future or of dreams. What, we ask, will the all-wise Prometheus have to say on this occasion of the rebirth of mankind? It is that he knows of a pretty cave where he and Asia will twine flowers and

> will sit and talk of time and change,
> As the world ebbs and flows, ourselves unchanged.

Even William Michael Rossetti, perceiving the horrors of such an eternity, reluctantly admitted that Prometheus

[46] *Queen Mab*, ix. 38. On the possible influence of Southey's *Curse of Kehama* (xxiii–xxiv), see Droop, *Belesenheit*, pp. 75–76. Peck (*Shelley*, II, 138) cites *Thalaba*, xii. 259–77.

here comes perilously close to "an idealized Leigh Hunt."[47] Although the products of man's mind include "Painting, Sculpture, and rapt Poesy," the whole passage is a sentimental reverie; Shelley's cave is a world away from Plato's. So enthusiastic a Shelleyan as Mrs. Olwen Campbell remarks that the drama might well have ended with the second scene of the third act. "It is when Shelley rushes on into descriptions of earthly paradises and rejoicing eternity that we are compelled to know that the real hero of the whole play was that invariable hero of Shelley's, the Millennium . . . and in the third and fourth scenes of Act III we see him [Prometheus] slowly asphyxiated before our eyes in the vapours of a universal carouse." [48]

The rest of the third act describes the regenerated world of nature and man. All things have put their evil nature off; even kingfishers have become vegetarians.[49] Thrones are kingless, the temples of religious superstition are moldering; liberty, equality, and fraternity prevail under the dominion of love. Women are free from old inhibitions. Man is

> Exempt from awe, worship, degree, the king
> Over himself.

Human nature being what it is in this new world, it is not clear what subjects the king has to rule over. And if Shelley remembered the phrase "Exempt from awe" from Chapman's *Hymn to Apollo*, he may not have cared to remember that Chapman used it of runaway horses.[50]

In the last act, an after-thought, Shelley gives free rein to his happy imagination and rejoices in the spectacle of beneficent man and the beneficent universe he inhabits and

[47] "Shelley's Prometheus Unbound," Part II, *Shelley Society's Papers*, I, 160.
[48] *Shelley and the Unromantics* (1924), p. 220.
[49] The phrase is Rossetti's (Part I, p. 56).
[50] See above, note 23, and Chapman's *Poems and Minor Translations* (1875), p. 282, col. 2.

controls. With the victory of love in the soul of Prometheus the energies of the physical world are directed to the good of man, whose Baconian sovereignty lieth hid in knowledge as well as love. Shelley's blending of the metaphysical and the physical has a concrete and recurring illustration in his linking of love with electricity in a thought-created world. Berkeley and Newton are met together, Plotinus and Edison have kissed each other. But this song of the morning stars is commonly read "for the poetry," and one may suspect that it is more often praised than read through; it reminds us that *Prometheus Unbound* as a whole is not a drama but a sustained emotional lyric. And if we turn back from the choruses of spirits and songs of the earth and moon to the cataclysm of nature which engulfs the Prometheus of Aeschylus, we may feel the difference — even after digesting Mr. Grabo's expositions of Shelley's scientific knowledge — between the idyllic and the cosmic imagination.

Shelley justly claimed the license that the Greek dramatists enjoyed of adapting mythological material to their own purpose. But the contrast between his purpose and that of Aeschylus is illuminating. He apparently knew no more of the lost parts of the Aeschylean trilogy than that they recorded the submission of Prometheus to Zeus, and he "was averse from a catastrophe so feeble as that of reconciling the Champion with the Oppressor of mankind. The moral interest of the fable, which is so powerfully sustained by the sufferings and endurance of Prometheus, would be annihilated if we could conceive of him as unsaying his high language and quailing before his successful and perfidious adversary." The only imaginary being at all resembling Prometheus is Satan, "the Hero of *Paradise Lost*," but Satan's bad qualities lessen our sympathy for him, whereas Prometheus "is, as it were, the type of the highest perfection of moral and intellectual nature, impelled by the purest and the truest motives to the best and noblest ends." Thus while such a notion of Satan was common in the romantic age, Shelley has no thought of Milton's or Aeschylus' total philosophic design but only of individual character isolated from the plot,[51] and, with his usual Manicheism, he sees the antagonists in terms of black and white. He recoils or withdraws so far from the evil world that he must have a perfect hero. The notion of a perfect hero was no more congenial to the Greek dramatists than to Aristotle, and it was not in such terms that Aeschylus conceived of Prometheus and Zeus. His Prometheus is a benefactor of the human race who has acted with noble motives and is suffering unjustly cruel punishment; but, since Greek tragedy is concerned less with motives than with acts and consequences, Prometheus has taken too much on himself, has overstepped the sacred limits set by law as embodied in Zeus. Aeschylus' drama is built on an idea more Greek than modern, the inviolable sanctity of law and order. Yet Zeus, though he is Law incarnate, has done wrong. In presenting him as a ruthless tyrant, Aeschylus reiterates that Zeus is a new ruler governing with the despotic harshness born of insecurity. Thus Prometheus and Zeus are both right and both wrong; the one is not an unreal saint nor the other an unreal monster. And the Aeschylean reconciliation involves no feeble catastrophe, no quailing of a noble nature before a successful and perfidious adversary. For, in the end, Zeus releases Kronos and the Titans whom he had imprisoned, and Prometheus is unbound. With time, for Aeschylus conceives of an evolving God, Zeus has become just and merciful; and Prometheus, on the other hand, has learned by suffer-

[51] Tillyard, *Poetry: Direct and Oblique*, p. 228. In *A Defence of Poetry* (Shawcross, pp. 129–30), Shelley conceals the imperfections of Homer's heroes under sentimental drapery; the tone of his remarks is quite different from that of even the idealistic and semi-allegorical critics of the Renaissance. See A. C. Bradley, *Oxford Lectures on Poetry* (1920), p. 166.

ing the virtues of wisdom, moderation, and obedience to a law higher than himself.[52]

Thus Aeschylus' drama is rooted always in human nature and human values, it combines imaginative splendor with lucid concreteness and a firmly unified pattern, and it remains invincibly modern. Shelley's much more complex work, despite some passages of moving realism, is too far from humanity, too wayward and obscure and uneven, to make an effect as a whole, except as a youthful song of love and hope. Shelley said that his poems did not attempt "a reasoned system on the theory of human life," that he intended to set forth such a system in prose, and that the poems aimed simply at familiarizing readers "with beautiful idealisms of moral excellence." Such words are a virtual repudiation of the office of the poetic legislators of the world, for a poet who offers a serious interpretation of life cannot afford to be content with beautiful idealisms. In his best prose Shelley writes like a rational man of this world who has had marvelous glimpses of another; in most of his poetry he gives himself up to the intoxications of wish-fulfilment. His emotional idealism, whatever metaphysics and science may be mixed with it, is far removed from the "imaginative reason" of Aeschylus.[53]

Comparison of *Prometheus Unbound* and *Queen Mab* shows an immeasurable enrichment of poetic inspiration and craftsmanship and some important philosophic changes, but, in the stock of millennial ideas, hardly any change at all. The dry soil of Godwinism, to be sure, has

[52] For some modern discussions by classical scholars of the mythological and religious ideas of Aeschylus' drama, see, in the bibliography, "General," J. T. Sheppard, H. W. Smyth, George Thomson, J. A. K. Thomson, and O. J. Todd. I may add a discussion by a devotee of Shelley much better informed than most devotees are, Mr. William R. Rutland, *Swinburne* (Oxford, 1931), pp. 70 ff.

[53] For an illustration outside of Aeschylus, one might compare Shelley's picture of the harmonious soul of emancipated man with the mingled idealism and humanistic reality of the chorus in *Antigone* on the achievements and the limitations of man (*P.U.*, IV. 382 ff.; *Antigone*, ll. 332 ff.).

been irrigated by Rousseauistic and Neo-Platonic streams, there is a fuller recognition of human responsibility for evil, and "necessity" is allied with love, but Shelley is still what Keats (whose faith in the holiness of the heart's affections was ballasted with Shakespearean wisdom) would call "a Godwin-methodist." He still believes that man can purify and discipline his soul by bestowing a kiss on the universe. One cannot avoid quoting the familiar words of Mrs. Shelley, which are sometimes set aside by modern critics more intimately and intelligently acquainted with Shelley's mind than she was:

The prominent feature of Shelley's theory of the destiny of the human species was that evil is not inherent in the system of the creation, but an accident that might be expelled. . . . Shelley believed that mankind had only to will that there should be no evil, and there would be none. . . . That man could be so perfectionized as to be able to expel evil from his own nature, and from the greater part of the creation, was the cardinal point of his system.[54]

The main conflict between Prometheus and Jupiter is that between good and evil in the mind of man, but, in a manner more in accord with the myth, Shelley sees also an external conflict between, as it were, God and Satan — with their rôles reversed — and he shifts from one conception to the other in a somewhat disconcerting way. It is especially disconcerting when the conquest of evil by the individual and by the race is bound up with the conquest of nature and ideas of progress.[55]

[54] Cf. *Julian and Maddalo*, ll. 170 ff. A similar account of Shelley's doctrine was given by Horace Smith, whose intelligence is as unquestionable as his admiration for his friend (Arthur H. Beavan, *James and Horace Smith*, 1899, p. 173).

[55] Shelley might reply: "It imports little to inquire whether thought be distinct from the objects of thought. The use of the words *external* and *internal*, as applied to the establishment of this distinction, has been the symbol and the source of much dispute. This is merely an affair of words. . . ." ("Speculations on Metaphysics," Shawcross, p. 69.)

A romantic has been succinctly defined as a person who does not believe in the fall of man. That sentimental optimism, of which Shelley is the chief exponent in English poetry, had begun with the sometimes exuberant faith of Renaissance humanists in man's essential goodness. In such humanists, however, as the early Erasmus and the late Milton, who were rooted in both classical and Christian traditions, that faith had been kept within bounds by a realistic consciousness of the portion of evil and unreason in man's nature. In addition to a heightening of the classical view of human dignity, the late Renaissance saw the beginnings of a theory of progress quite different from the religious and static conception of the world which commonly prevailed in the Middle Ages. The golden age of man's happiness, an idyllic inheritance from classical and biblical myth, was, with the mundane hopefulness engendered by the rise of science, transferred from a mythological past to a mythological future. In the eighteenth century the advancing tide of sentimental optimism and monism gradually washed away, in emancipated minds, the dualism established by traditional religion and morality.[56] But if man is naturally good, and yet evil persists, it is clear that he has been corrupted by the restraints of civilized society; as Paine expressed it, "Government, like dress, is the badge of lost innocence." If then the irksome man-made institutions and conventions of politics, religion, and sexual morality are cast off, human nature will be free to flourish in its native goodness and beauty. This brief and crude summary of primitivist and perfectibilarian doctrine may serve to remind us not only of how much the

[56] The romantic movement included anti-naturalistic as well as naturalistic tendencies, but our concern is with the latter. See Arthur O. Lovejoy, "On the Discrimination of Romanticisms," *P.M.L.A.*, XXXIX (1924), 229 ff., especially 247 ff.; and Ronald S. Crane, *P.Q.*, XI (1932), 204–06.

mature Shelley abandoned, but of how much he never outgrew.

It may be said that Shelley's flaming gospel of love and human brotherhood atones, if any atonement be needed, for much Utopian day-dreaming. We are always being told that *Prometheus Unbound* in particular gives magnificent expression to the faith of Plato and of Christ. Shelley does frequently give magnificent expression to a partly Platonic sense of an immaterial reality behind the world of flux, but he has little or nothing of Plato's austere ethical temper, and in place of the discipline of Platonic dialectic he has only undisciplined emotion. For a long time critics have perpetuated the bad habit of describing as a Platonist anyone who is rapt out of this world by the *Symposium* and the *Phaedrus*; there are a good many other works. Much of the "Platonism" in Shelley is only poetic hypnotism; why call it Plato? [57]

[57] Miss Winstanley (see note 19 above) makes Shelley a complete Platonist by ignoring a number of fundamental distinctions. For more critical estimates see S. F. Gingerich, *Essays in the Romantic Poets* (New York, 1929), pp. 205 ff., and J. W. Beach, *The Concept of Nature in Nineteenth-Century English Poetry* (New York, 1936), pp. 242–75. See also Mr. Grabo's *Prometheus Unbound*, *passim*.

The predominant inspiration of Plato is reasserted in Mr. Herbert Read's recent essay, *In Defence of Shelley* (1936). Like many ideas in the essay, this is an unsupported statement, although the critic complains of Mr. Eliot's anti-Shelleyan utterances as mere suggestions, not demonstrations. One begins the essay with the hopes warranted by the author's name, and one finishes the eighty-four pages wondering what has been accomplished by a not too well-informed rehash of commonplace generalities. Not that it is all commonplace; Mr. Read, with the aid of the scriptural revelations of psychology, devotes some thirty-five pages to proving that Shelley was an unconsciously homosexual narcissist. What with that and Harriet and such things, he has little space for the poetry he set out to vindicate, and can meet the Victorian hostility of Arnold and Mr. Eliot with little more than a repetition of Victorian eulogy. One of the worst things about Shelley is the effect he has on his admirers; nearly all of them are reduced to a common denominator, of which the outward evidence is perhaps a wild glitter in the eye. Those of us who are conscious of imperfect sympathy cannot hurt Shelley, but those who were born to understand him . . . !

As for the faith of Christ, one must quote the *locus classicus*:

> To suffer woes which Hope thinks infinite;
> To forgive wrongs darker than death or night;
>   To defy Power, which seems omnipotent;
> To love, and bear; to hope till Hope creates
> From its own wreck the thing it contemplates;
>   Neither to change, nor falter, nor repent;
> This, like thy glory, Titan, is to be
> Good, great and joyous, beautiful and free;
> This is alone Life, Joy, Empire, and Victory.

A greater poet than Shelley had labored for twenty years to create a new England inspired by a new ideal of liberty; he had failed, but he put into verse his vision of regenerated man, whose inner victory does not open the way to an earthly paradise but raises him above the need of one:

> Henceforth I learn that to obey is best,
> And love with fear the only God, to walk
> As in his presence, ever to observe
> His providence, and on him sole depend,
> Merciful over all his works, with good
> Still overcoming evil, and by small
> Accomplishing great things, by things deem'd weak
> Subverting worldly strong, and worldly wise
> By simply meek; that suffering for truth's sake
> Is fortitude to highest victory,
> And to the faithful, death the gate of life;
> Taught this by his example whom I now
> Acknowledge my Redeemer ever blest.
>   . . . Only add
> Deeds to thy knowledge answerable; add faith,
> Add virtue, patience, temperance; add love,
> By name to come called charity, the soul
> Of all the rest: then wilt thou not be loth
> To leave this Paradise, but shalt possess
> A Paradise within thee, happier far.

Of these two all-important summaries, which in some respects are at one, Shelley's is more typical than Milton's, since the latter lacks the emphasis on human reason which is everywhere in Milton's major poems; moreover, Milton is not the most Christian poet one could quote. But there is no question which passage is closer to the faith of Christ. (Shelley, by the way, echoes the resolve of Milton's Satan never to "repent, or change."[58]) Granted that Shelley, like Abou Ben Adhem, loved his neighbor, one looks in vain in a poet exempt from awe for any recognition of Christ's first and great commandment. The God of Christianity, a primitive projection of man's mind, Prometheus destroys when he learns the lesson of love, and the new God of evolving humanity is humanity itself; this is not quite equivalent to "The kingdom of God is within you." Shelley does certainly glorify a Spirit of Good, but there is a difference between being the father and being the child of one's deity. Besides the love of man, a frequent substitute in Shelley for the love of God is the love of woman, which involves among other things a reversion to polytheism. Altogether, as Aubrey de Vere remarked, we find in *Prometheus Unbound* "ideas at once exactly parallel with Christian, and exactly their opposite." [59] We may doubt if Christ would have understood the love which "makes the reptile equal to the God," or would have rejoiced that man's "nature is its own divine control." But to the Shelleyan devotee the fact that Shelley had no personal sense of sin is only the crowning likeness between him and Christ.

Shelley's love of man, however sincere, is sicklied over with sentimentality. His heroes and martyrs are all alike, all physically weak and spiritually lonely, pale youths who perish, or are ready to perish, unupbraiding. They are all variations on the portrait of himself as an effeminate romantic idealist which he so often put into verse, a portrait which is partly true but misses that Shelley who always

58 *Paradise Lost*, i. 96.
59 Wilfrid Ward, *Aubrey de Vere: A Memoir* (1904), p. 335.

went on until he was stopped and who never was stopped. The genuine admiration which he came to feel for Christ must be somewhat discounted, for he saw in Christ only a Judaean Shelley. The Prometheus of Aeschylus, along with his godlike greatness of soul, has a healthy human truculence, even humor, and we may be sure that the learning of his lesson did not make him soft. But it is painful, doubly painful when we remember that Christ is in the background, to think of the Aeschylean god in terms of "pale feet," "pale wound-worn limbs," "soft and flowing limbs And passion-parted lips"; [60] of a god who feels "faint, like one mingled in entwining love," and who appears in Panthea's eyes arrayed "in the soft light of his own smiles." The great Prometheus dwindles into another Laon or Lionel — or should one say another Asia? Tertullian's God, *verus Prometheus*, is rather different. [61]

I must pass by a number of elements in Shelley, partly of ancient origin, such as his recurring symbols, the eagle and the snake [62] and the rest, and those images which reverse the normal process and compare the concrete with the abstract. Shelley's unique genius for myth-making has already been touched on. It is not of course a mere poetic trick, it arises out of his belief in the life of matter, which leads to the constant blending of the natural and mental

[60] Although Shelley is fond of parted lips, he is evidently recalling here Correggio's Christ, whose lips are "parted, but scarcely parted, with the breath of intense but regulated passion" (*Letters*, II, 637). "Soft limbs" belong more appropriately to Sophia Stacey (*Works*, p. 576).

[61] *Apologeticus*, xviii. 3.

[62] This symbol has been derived from Ovid, *Metam.* iv. 449–52 (Peck, *Shelley*, I, 430; Michele Renzulli, *La Poesia di Shelley*, Rome, 1932, p. 91); the passage meant is presumably *Metam.* iv. 714–17. A more probable source is the more elaborate description in Homer (*Il.* xii. 200–07) or Virgil (*Aen.* xi. 751 ff.); see A. H. Gilbert, *M.L.N.*, XXXVI, 505–06, and C. W. Lemmi, *ibid.*, L, 165–68. One might quote Richard Payne Knight, *An Inquiry into the Symbolical Language of Ancient Art and Mythology* (1818), p. 82: "The eagle is sometimes represented fighting with a serpent, and sometimes destroying a hare. . . . In these compositions the eagle must have represented the destroying attribute."

worlds. Hence his original myths in *Prometheus* and elsewhere are not conceits or Ovidian imitations, such as the
Elizabethans delighted in, but, whether mixed with science
or not, they combine primitive freshness with sophisticated
subtlety. Of the details of Shelley's classical mythology
there is no room to speak adequately, even if one could. It
is completely of the open air, and the rich display in *Prometheus* of cool, iridescent, and magical images of light and
color in earth and sky and water is best suggested in Shelley's own words: "The bright blue sky of Rome, and the
effect of the vigorous awakening spring in that divinest
climate, and the new life with which it drenches the spirits
even to intoxication." No one but Shelley could write

> See where the child of Heaven, with winged feet,
> Runs down the slanted sunlight of the dawn.

He may be recalling Virgil's picture of Iris, but the speed
and lightness are pure Shelley.[63] Or, for a less merely
decorative bit, a description in mythological terms of the
serene joy and peace which follow the overthrow of Jupiter,
there is the stately speech of Ocean, who hears "the un-
pastured sea hungering for calm," and beholds the nereids
under the green sea,

> Their wavering limbs borne on the wind-like stream,
> Their white arms lifted o'er their streaming hair.[64]

Shelley's un-bookish mythology is colored not merely by
Italian and Swiss scenery but by vivid recollections of
plastic art and architecture. One need only mention the
well-known example of the figures of Victory on the arch
of Titus which were described in a letter to Peacock and,
in verse, became notable even in Shelley as images of daz-

[63] *Aen.* iv. 700–02.
[64] III. ii. 39 ff.

zling speed.[65] Shelley's appreciation of ancient art was in the Winckelmann tradition; it was also, in some fundamental ways, Wordsworthian. After visiting Pompeii, he wrote to Peacock:

I now understand why the Greeks were such great poets; and, above all, I can account, it seems to me, for the harmony, the unity, the perfection, the uniform excellence, of all their works of art. They lived in a perpetual commerce with external nature, and nourished themselves upon the spirit of its forms.[66]

This last sentence is in the spirit of the mythological discourse in the fourth book of the *Excursion*, and Shelley's phrasing seems to echo other passages in a poem he knew well.[67]

Needless to say, Shelley's ardent delight in Greek literature and art, and the general inspiration he derived therefrom, had little direct formative influence — apart from Plato — on his own thought and style. As we have seen, in *Prometheus Unbound* he repudiates the religious and philosophic solution of Aeschylus. On the side of poetic art Shelley is generally as remote as possible from Aeschylus or anything Greek. After the first act the structure becomes, if not nebulous, at any rate more musical than dramatic. Instead of concrete, realistic characterization we have a host of phantoms, all of whom, even the bad ones, speak like Shelley. Instead of restrained and distinct images Shelley expands Aeschylean suggestions of nature's sympathy into a Turneresque panorama of atmospheric

---

[65] *Letters*, II, 680, 684 (March 23, 1819); *P.U.*, II. iv. 135 ff. See Peck, II, 118–19; I. O'Sullivan-Köhling, *Shelley und die bildende Kunst* (Halle, 1928), p. 157.

[66] *Letters*, II, 666.

[67] *Excursion*, i. 267 ff., iv. 1207 ff. One may recall too the paragraph in the *Defence of Poetry*: "Poetry turns all things to loveliness . . . it strips the veil of familiarity from the world, and lays bare the naked and sleeping beauty, which is the spirit of its forms."

pageantry. However grateful we are for what the sun-treader alone can give, the very richness of his shimmering web makes it a dubious medium for serious ideas, which appear "like stars half quenched in mists of silver dew." For example, in Aeschylus the hero says that he made it impossible for men to foresee their fate: "I caused blind hopes to dwell in them." In contrast with this grim and impressive brevity, Shelley muffles and softens the idea with decoration:

> Prometheus saw, and waked the legioned hopes
> Which sleep within folded Elysian flowers,
> Nepenthe, Moly, Amaranth, fadeless blooms,
> That they might hide with thin and rainbow wings
> The shape of Death. . . .[68]

Modern poets, said Arnold in 1852, in censuring Keats and Shelley for reviving Elizabethan profusion of ornament, need to use greater plainness of speech than the older writers, since modern poetry, which like the ancient must include religion, must interpret the whole of life, cannot afford to spend itself in embellishment; it ought to be "very plain direct and severe." [69] Most modern poets and critics would endorse this view, which need not be prejudiced by comparisons between *Prometheus Unbound* and *Merope*.

V

Shelley's normal sympathy for the under dog was stirred to the utmost when the under dog was Greece struggling for freedom. The preface to *Hellas* (1821) expressed his boundless admiration for the ancient Greeks; if the modern descendants of those glorious and almost superhuman beings have somewhat degenerated, it is because of slavery,

---

[68] Aeschylus, ll. 250 ff.; Shelley, II. iv. 59 ff.

[69] *Letters of Matthew Arnold to Arthur Hugh Clough*, ed. Howard F. Lowry (Oxford University Press, 1932), p. 124.

and when it disappears the Greeks' vices will disappear too.[70] Byron's attitude was more realistic. For the general plan of the drama Shelley was of course chiefly indebted to Aeschylus. The scene of *Hellas*, like that of the *Persae*, is laid in the country of the enemy. While Aeschylus has a chorus of aged Persians, Shelley's chorus is made up of Greek captive women, since he needs a mouthpiece for his songs of freedom. The summoning of the ghost of Mahomet the Second and his prophecy are conceived in imitation of the similar incident in Aeschylus, and perhaps owe something also to Lucan.[71] Many details are borrowed from the *Persae* and some from the *Agamemnon* as well. Shelley's treatment of the war is bewildering to the reader who expects a modicum of truth. The various messengers' accounts of battles, peppered with proper names, recall Dr. Johnson's verdict on Arthur Murphy's *Zenobia* — "too much *Tig* and *Tirry* in it." A more serious matter is the mingling of newspaper reports, Aeschylus' description of the battle of Salamis, and pure fancy.[72] Greek valor and success are magnified or invented, and Greek cowardice, fraud, and barbarity are glossed over, with the selective instinct and transforming power of impassioned idealism.

In spite of the contemporaneous theme and much realistic detail, the Greeks and Turks are only a starting point for another Shelleyan vision of the war between right and wrong. The cause of right is upheld by "Necessity," which appears as oriental fatalism, but also, on the lips of

[70] We may remember Trelawny's pointing out to Shelley the squalid crew of a Greek ship at Leghorn and asking if this realized his idea of Hellenism: "No!" said Shelley, "but it does of Hell" (*Trelawny's Recollections*, ed. Dowden, 1923, pp. 54–55).

[71] *Phars.* vi. 776 ff. These invokings of the dead may have contributed to the phantasm of Jupiter in *Prometheus Unbound*.

[72] See Newman I. White, "The Historical and Personal Background of Shelley's Hellas," *South Atlantic Quarterly*, XX (1921), 52–60; Richard Ackermann, *Quellen, Vorbilder, Stoffe zu Shelley's Poetischen Werken*, *Münchener Beiträge*, II (1890), 44 ff.

a dying Greek, as "the Omnipotence of God." Its human manifestation is "the Spirit that lifts the slave before his lord." *Hellas* is hastier and shallower than *Prometheus Unbound*, and has more of mere rebellion against tyranny and less of the regenerating power of love, but there is the figure of Christ, the "Promethean conqueror," and love is somehow associated with peace and freedom in America. The contrast between good and evil, white and black, is not so complete as it is in Shelley's other long poems. Mahmud is not merely an unthinking barbarous despot, he has thoughts that wander through eternity; he can echo Bacon, and, more than once, *Macbeth*. Under the influence of Ahasuerus, he passes from fatalistic despair to something like acquiescence in the rightness of his own defeat. Ahasuerus himself, that Wandering Jew who exercised such a fascination over Shelley, is not the ranting radical of *Queen Mab*, the defier of the "omnipotent Fiend" of heaven, but a mystic who re-utters Prospero's speech in the spirit of Berkeley. And Shelley does not now picture a world of freedom and love as something which, however remote and dim, can be thought of as within reach of man's will. He has retreated still further from actualities into a solitude of pure idealism where alone he can remold the sorry scheme of things nearer to the heart's desire.

Through the choruses of *Hellas* hope and disillusion ebb and flow. In the opening lyrics freedom is celebrated with the old fervor. In "Worlds on worlds" the flux of the external universe is contrasted with the immortality of the thinking beings who inhabit it, especially such a spirit as Christ, the great exemplar of love. "The cross leads generations on." As in Milton's *Nativity*, the classical divinities "Fled from the folding-star of Bethlehem." (Lest we might suspect him of being a Christian, Shelley explains in a note that he is here representing popular notions of

Christianity.) The third group of lyrics returns to the theme of liberty; Greece and her foundations are based on "thought and its eternity." [73] Revolution means bloodshed, but love may be paid for hate and tears for blood. Cries of victory from the Turks lead up to the last group of choral lyrics, which lament the extinction of Greek independence. Westward the course of freedom takes its way, following "Love's folding-star," but the America in which the fragments of Greece are rebuilt is rather what Shelley had called it earlier in the play, Atlantis. And the last chorus, with its echoes of Virgil's fourth eclogue, Byron's *Isles of Greece*, and perhaps Wordsworth, has no relation to anything attainable on earth. [74] The mythological allusions make the vision less impalpable than it usually is — for Virgil's linking of Saturn and Astraea, by the way, Shelley substitutes "Saturn and Love" — but a brighter Hellas rears its mountains only in the poet's world of dreams, and before the chorus ends the radiant mirage has faded:

> Oh, cease! must hate and death return?
> Cease! must men kill and die? [75]

---

[73] With ll. 696 ff., compare *Manfred*, III. iv. 36–41; with ll. 221 ff., compare *Childe Harold*, II. iii. "Let the tyrants rule the desert they have made" (l. 1008) may come directly from the famous phrase of Tacitus (*Agricola*, xxx), or from Byron's "He makes a solitude, and calls it — peace" (*The Bride of Abydos*, ii. 913).

[74] See *Excursion*, iii. 756–58; for other echoes, A. S. Cook, *M.L.N.*, XX (1905), 161–62. Mr. T. S. Eliot (*Selected Essays*, 1932, p. 292) contrasts Shelley's first stanza with Dryden's "All, all of a piece throughout" (*Poems*, ed. J. Sargeaunt, 1913, p. 203), much to the advantage of the latter. While one may often prefer Dryden's majestic common sense to Shelley's visions, it seems hardly profitable to compare lines so different in scope and intention. See William Empson, *Seven Types of Ambiguity* (1930), p. 201. For the snake one may quote Virgil, *Ecl.* iv. 24; Ovid, *Ars Amat.* iii. 77; and R. Payne Knight (see note 62 above): ". . . the principle of life . . . was represented by the serpent; which having the property of casting its skin, and apparently renewing its youth, was naturally adapted for that purpose" (*Inquiry*, p. 16).

[75] In commenting on Mr. Yeats's *Two Songs from a Play* (*The Tower*), in which the poet echoes this chorus, Mr. Tillyard remarks on the tremendous effect of his fierce irony "set against the background of Shelley's most serene and pas-

VI

Classical mythology is not of much account in *Adonais* (1821), but the last great example of the English pastoral elegy cannot be passed over without a word. Most of what is bad in *Adonais*, and there is a good deal, results from imitation of Bion and the elegy on Bion. The pastoral convention had become increasingly difficult to use — Arnold virtually abandoned it — and some readers have been offended by *Lycidas*. But Milton's fabric is so closely and consistently woven, he works so greatly within the convention, that *Lycidas* remains a unified work, with that remoteness and isolation which distinguish the greatest art. Shelley's handling of the convention rather heightens than diminishes its artificiality; besides, he is very diffuse and full of conceits, and he gives way to his youthful instinct for the macabre and the melodramatic. While *Lycidas* is firm and substantial, Shelley's personified abstractions pass before us "Like pageantry of mist on an autumnal stream." [76] And when he shatters the thin woof of his pastoral tapestry to assail reviewers, we feel a greater shock of incongruity than we do in *Lycidas*, for anticlerical invective had become a part of the Renaissance convention and Milton makes it seem an integral part of his poem.

Some of Shelley's characteristic weaknesses, quite apart from the pastoral business, are illustrated in the forty-fifth stanza, which celebrates three flesh-and-blood poets who had died young. These inheritors of unfulfilled renown

---

sionate idealism" (*Poetry: Direct and Oblique*, p. 196). One may surely question "most serene."

It seems unnecessary to discuss the third work of Shelley's which is related, distantly, to Greek drama. It might be said that the water-drinking author of *Swellfoot the Tyrant* had gone to a gin-shop for a leg of pork.

[76] See George Rylands, "English Poets and the Abstract Word," *Essays and Studies by Members of the English Association*, XVI (1931), especially pp. 68 ff.

rise from their thrones "Far in the Unapparent." After
sentimentalized pictures of Chatterton and Sidney we
come to "Lucan, by his death approved," and this phrase
of Roman ring, an echo of Lucan himself, stands out like
a bar of iron from the soft context. But the next line
sinks back into the not very intense inane of the eighteenth
century: "Oblivion as they rose shrank like a thing re-
proved." [77] This stanza illustrates not only the uneven
style, the admixture of frigid rhetoric and padding, but the
vesture of sentimentality in which almost all the poets
Shelley mentions are draped. If Prometheus can be made
effeminate, we must not be surprised that Keats is too.
But we may not like to think of the author of *Hyperion*, a
young man of flint and iron, as an angel soul, a gentle
child, a pale flower, a broken lily, lying in dewy sleep, with
a tear on the silken fringe of his faint eyes.

The fact is of course that the real subject of *Adonais* is
not Keats but Shelley, and the author sentimentalizes
Keats as he regularly sentimentalized himself. What fires
him is not so much the sense of personal or even poetic loss,
it is the belief that a young man of about his own age, a
poet and a liberal, has been hounded to death by Tory reviewers, has been another victim of established power and
prejudice. Shelley does lament the death of Keats, to be
sure, but the passion and force of *Adonais* are the outpour-
ing of his own accumulated bitterness. Hence the long
passage on himself as a herd-abandoned deer; in another's
fate he wept his own. How little Shelley is concerned with
the actual Keats is indicated in his choice of such mourners
as Byron, who had foamed at the mouth over "Jack
Ketch," and Moore, who had no relation to Keats what-

---

[77] *Phars.* viii. 621 (*Seque probat moriens*), and 626–27. See Paul Elmer More,
"Shelley," *Shelburne Essays*, Seventh Series (Boston and New York, 1910), p. 24.
   I have not observed in the commentators any mention of a probable echo, in
stanza xliv, of Wordsworth's sonnet *Brave Schill!* (published 1815).

ever; but Byron and Moore had been on the side of freedom against tyranny, they were allies, and might well be mourners, of Shelley. Of course *Lycidas* is about John Milton, but while Milton has a personal intensity his doubts and fears and hopes are those of any high-minded young poet; the poem makes a universal appeal. Similarly in the *Stanzas Written in Dejection*, Shelley is very conscious of his uniqueness as a lonely and frustrated idealist; in the invocation to Light, Milton's emotions are not individual and peculiar, and, though a rebel whose life had been in danger, he feels "from the cheerful ways of men Cut off."

Of the beautiful stanzas which stream like a comet's hair through the latter part of *Adonais* there is no occasion to speak. Starting from the pastoral motive of the contrast between the renewal of life in nature and the eternal sleep of the dead, a motive which Christian elegists had changed into a hymn of Christian immortality, Shelley soars upward into that Platonic heaven whose light for ever shines, for him. Here if anywhere he escapes from the trammels of life and death, the world and time, and almost compels us to believe that at last he has pierced the veil.

CHAPTER V

Minor Poets of the Early Nineteenth Century

WHILE we look back to Wordsworth, Keats, and Shelley as the creators of the mythological genre in the nineteenth century, many smaller poets reflected and in some degree fostered the growth of romantic Hellenism. Indeed some of the poorest of them were popular when the great poets were not. However, the reader will not be asked to crawl with me through the endless underbrush which envelops the foothills of Parnassus — some of it is faggoted in the Appendix — and most of this chapter, after the first few pages, is concerned with such more or less important minor poets as Hunt, Peacock, Hartley Coleridge, Hood, and Beddoes. We may observe, among other things, how constantly the mythological impulse is accompanied by, or springs from, Elizabethan enthusiasms. That note is dominant in such pioneers as Mrs. Tighe and Lord Thurlow. Mrs. Tighe, said Christopher North, was an angel on earth, "evanescent as her own immortal Psyche"; she was celebrated by Moore, and, in Mooreish strains, by the young Keats. In her long and languid allegorical poem of 1805, which has already been touched upon in connection with *Endymion*, Mrs. Tighe was more of an eighteenth-century Spenserian than a true romantic, though her sensuous coloring was softer and warmer than that of her predecessors. If Elizabethan ardor, and adaptations of Shakespeare and Spenser, could alone make a poet, Lord

Thurlow, the author of *Ariadne* (1814) and *Angelica* (1822), would have been one, and a man who thought the golden age of our language was that of Elizabeth was not entirely the fool Byron called him; but his *Ariadne* is as fantastic a romance as Henry Petowe's continuation of Marlowe's *Hero and Leander*.

A few better-known writers belong to the Hellenic rather than the Elizabethan revival. Mrs. Hemans, whose first volume appeared in 1808, began to celebrate Greek themes when still in pinafores. Her very literary Muse ranged far and wide, and might have groaned, with Aeneas, that the whole earth — and a large tract of heaven — was full of her labors. In her tepidly idealistic and romantic way Mrs. Hemans versified numerous bits of Plutarch, Mitford's *History of Greece*, Potter's *Archaeologica Graeca*, and similar books; her *Elysium* is headed by a quotation from Chateaubriand's *La génie du christianisme*. In *Modern Greece* (1817) she sang, a fluent, feminine, decorous Byron, of Greek freedom, art, and antiquities; the noble lord resented the infringement of his monopoly by a writer who had never been in Greece. Campbell eulogized the past, in his lectures on the poetry of Greece (1812), and to the modern struggle for independence he paid a tribute, not unworthy of his martial fire, in his *Song of the Greeks*. That charming friend of all the world, Tom Moore, translated Anacreon in 1800, with some aid from "Thomas Little," and then, as Thomas Little, drew from Anacreon a warmth of amorous sentiment which maintained his reputation for naughtiness well through the strict period of the Regency. No such adventitious interest helps to carry one through his *Evenings in Greece* (1825) and *Legendary Ballads* (1830). The thin treble of the songs is accompanied by a ponderous bass in the form of footnotes which testify to the multiplication of books of travel and antiquities, but Moore's reading did not prevent his Greece from bearing a close resemblance to the Orient of *Lalla Rookh*. His cheerfully inadequate notions of ancient Epicureanism were demolished by Peacock.

Three other writers must be included in these preliminary paragraphs, Thomas Wade, Mary Shelley, and Bryan Waller Procter. Of these the best poet was Wade, one of the earliest poetic admirers and imitators of Shelley; Keats also he admired, and Shakespeare's narrative poems.[1] As one would expect, his long *Nuptials of Juno* (1825) was what, since the time of Shelley and Keats, has been called a typical young man's poem, an exuberant mythological tapestry of rich color and sensuous warmth. This last phrase should be partly qualified with reference to the opening episode, based on a rather obscure myth; a cuckoo, after being fondled by Juno, turns into Jove, and there follow fourteen blameless lines of asterisks.

Mary Shelley's little dramas, *Proserpine* and *Midas*, were probably written in 1820; the former was first printed in 1832, the latter in 1922, in M. Koszul's excellent edition. They are not important, but they enable us to read Shelley's lovely lyrics in the setting for which they were designed. Apart from the question of comparative quality, the lyrics harmonize with the context, though the conclusion at least of the *Hymn of Pan* hardly warrants the adjectives of Tmolus and Midas, "blithe," "merry," "sprightly," and "gay." The fable of each drama sticks pretty closely to Ovid (whom Mary read with Shelley); there is the usual fanciful and descriptive elaboration. In *Midas* there is also a moral, that only a man who preferred earthly to divine music would be fool enough to crave unlimited gold. (If Mary had not been a devoted daughter, one might be tempted to see behind Midas the figure of her

---

[1] In addition to internal evidence in Wade's volumes of 1825 and 1835, see, in the latter, pp. 120–22, 234. This volume, *Mundi et Cordis*, was dedicated to Procter.

father, who for some time cared less for Shelley's poetry than for negotiable bits of his formal prose.) But Midas learns his lesson, and the conclusion anticipates the era when man, having lost the curse of gold, shall be "Rich, happy, free & great." In *Proserpine* Mrs. Shelley expresses her own spontaneous pleasure in the beauties of nature and myth, and, while she cannot take wing like her husband, she does at moments catch something of the pure Shelleyan limpidity.

The amiable gentleman of letters, Bryan Waller Procter, long outlived the numerous mythological poems of "Barry Cornwall." In his Elizabethan and Italian sympathies, and in his soft, smooth, luscious manner, he was closer to Hunt than to his great contemporaries. The effort to be Miltonic, in *The Flood of Thessaly* (1823), did something to brace his nerveless and invertebrate style, but the poem was a comparative failure. *Blackwood's*, which had praised Procter's early work, now reluctantly linked him with the "Greekish" Cockneys, "the lieges of Leigh the First." [2] In general Procter turned myths into pretty tapestries of descriptive luxuriance and delicate amorousness.[3] Mrs. Browning acknowledged his "genius," but said he had done a good deal "to emasculate the poetry of the passing age." [4] Both Shelley and Keats spoke well of Procter and

---

[2] *Blackwood's Magazine*, XIII (1823), 534; Richard W. Armour, *Barry Cornwall* (Boston, 1935), pp. 158–59.

[3] It was not always quite delicate, and Shelley was roused to unnecessary vehemence by Procter's imitation of *Beppo* and *Don Juan*, the pertly arch and vulgar *Gyges* (published in *A Sicilian Story*, 1820); see Shelley's *Letters*, ed. Ingpen (1914), II, 839, 847, 860. The birthmark with which Procter endows the queen, and which he compares with that of Imogen, seems to be a reminiscence of Spenser's tale of Pastorella (*Faerie Queene*, VI. xii. 7). It is to Procter's credit as an Elizabethan student, if not as a poet, that he quotes a "moral" from the story of Gyges in Painter's *Palace of Pleasure*.

[4] *Letters of Elizabeth Barrett Browning Addressed to Richard Hengist Horne*, ed. S. R. Townshend Mayer (1877), I, 233. See Procter's retrospective words, in *The Browning Box*, ed. H. W. Donner (Oxford University Press, 1935), p. 50.

ill of Barry Cornwall; Keats's words are kind and final.[5] But I may quote a more formal judgment from the *pontifex maximus* of criticism because it is a general characterization of the new mode in mythological poetry. In his belated review Jeffrey praised Keats highly, and linked him as a mythological poet with Barry Cornwall. These and other recent poets, he says,

sheltering the violence of the fiction under the ancient traditionary fable, have in reality created and imagined an entire new set of characters; and brought closely and minutely before us the loves and sorrows and perplexities of beings, with whose names and supernatural attributes we had long been familiar, without any sense or feeling of their personal character. We have more than doubts of the fitness of such personages to maintain a permanent interest with the modern public; — but the way in which they are here managed certainly gives them the best chance that now remains for them; and, at all events, it cannot be denied that the effect is striking and graceful.[6]

I. Leigh Hunt (1784–1859)

Our memory of Leigh Hunt's verse is often limited to *Abou Ben Adhem* and a bad couplet or two from *The Story of Rimini* — the damned "rural spot" will not out — but he wrote, to mention only what concerns us, one charming poem, *The Nymphs* (1818), and two partly good narratives, *Hero and Leander* and *Bacchus and Ariadne*, both of 1819. Though his instinct for mythological luxuries had appeared as early as his *Juvenilia* (1801), Hunt may, in this group of poems, have been emulating Keats.[7] We do not regret

---

[5] *Letters*, ed. M. B. Forman (1935), p. 471.

[6] *Jeffrey's Literary Criticism*, ed. D. Nichol Smith (Oxford University Press, 1910), pp. 183–84; *Edinburgh Review*, XXXIV (1820), 206–07.

[7] Louis Landré, *Leigh Hunt* (Paris, 1936), II, 287; for a discussion of Hunt's mythological essays and sketches in prose, see II, 370 ff. M. Landré's study appeared too late to allow more than a last-minute perusal—since there comes a time when one does have to stop reading—but I am glad to find that my few pages, so far as they go, are in sufficient accord with that massive and admirable work.

that, on hearing of Shelley's work, he abandoned a projected *Prometheus Throned*, since, as he wrote to Shelley, he was "rather the son of one of Atlas's daughters, than of Atlas himself." [8] But if Hunt the romantic and mythological poet flowered and died early, Hunt the critic, essayist, and book-maker continued to testify to his faith, for the endless misfortunes and endless labor of his later life seem hardly to have dimmed his youthful vision of the radiant antique world.

Before we consider Hunt's notions of myth a word should be said of *The Story of Rimini* (1816) because of its general influence on mythological poetry. Taking as his model the English poet whom at that time he found most delightful, John Dryden, Hunt set out, with a stronger sense of "the tender and the pathetic," and a more sensuous pleasure in nature and color, to tell a romantic story in verse of informal flexibility, which should combine rich decoration with something of realism in tone and sentiment.[9] As he candidly acknowledged later, *Rimini* was pitched in the wrong key — he was Ariosto's man, not Dante's — but, when all his lapses have been duly condemned and when the poem is compared with what had gone before rather than with what came after, it remains a notable piece of romantic narrative. For young writers of luscious tastes who inclined to the antique, *Laodamia* was too austere in

---

[8] Edmund Blunden, *Leigh Hunt and His Circle* (1930), pp. 140–41; *Correspondence of Leigh Hunt* (1862), I, 132.

Any reader of Hunt's original verse might predict the varying degrees of success he would attain in his numerous translations — that he would be happy in rendering most of the Italians (such as Tasso's *Aminta* and Redi's *Bacco in Toscana*), the Greek pastorals and Anacreontics, and similar congenial things, and that he would be less happy with Homer. (Hunt infuriated Byron, of course, by referring, in the preface to *Foliage*, to Pope's *Iliad* as an elegant mistake in two volumes octavo; see Byron's *Letters and Journals*, IV, 238.) Perhaps the only real anomaly is Hunt's unexpectedly virile rendering of Catullus' *Attis*, done in 1810.

[9] *Autobiography of Leigh Hunt* (World's Classics ed.), p. 310.

form and style, and *Rimini* did more than any other single
work to create the convention which Hunt himself, Keats,
and others more or less followed in their mythological
verse. If the fruits of that convention were sometimes
over-ripe, they were sometimes beautiful too.

While Hunt was grateful to Christ's Hospital (if not
especially to the renowned Boyer) for making him "acquainted with the languages of Homer and Ovid," gerund-
grinding developed no immediate love for any of the classics except Virgil (and one episode in him, that of Nisus
and Euryalus). His saturation in mythology began as a
boyish and extra-curricular enthusiasm, that kind of enthusiasm which seems so often to have been engendered by
primitive educational systems. Like Keats, Hunt reveled
in a trinity which look drab enough now, Lempriere's
Classical Dictionary, Spence's *Polymetis* (this for its plates
rather than its text), and above all Tooke's *Pantheon*, over
which he dreamed in the fields as well as in school.[10] Later
came such poetry as Spenser and the fifty-six volumes of
the *Parnaso Italiano* (which the cheerful martyr bought
while in prison) to fill his imagination with gods and
nymphs. In addition to the classical and modern literature that he might be expected to know, Hunt could
quote familiarly from such formidable mythographers as
Boccaccio, Natalis Comes, George Sandys, Bochart, and
others.[11] More important than knowledge was his rich
appreciation of mythology and the older poetic tradition,
and no critic of his time set forth with such full and in-
tuitive sympathy the esthetic and spiritual values which

[10] *Autobiography*, pp. 98–101, 108, 126, 138, 492.
[11] See especially the mythological papers included in the volume *A Day by
the Fire*, ed. J. E. Babson (Boston, 1870). These had appeared in *The New
Monthly Magazine* for 1835–36, and in other journals; see Luther A. Brewer, *My
Leigh Hunt Library* (Cedar Rapids, Iowa, 1932), pp. 96, 127, 165, etc. Hunt's
references to Sandys' *Ovid* in *A Day by the Fire* (pp. 195, 214) show that he used
the edition of 1640, the one Keats also referred to.

the romantic poets had re-discovered in myth. In the preface to *Foliage* (1818) Hunt expanded, with special reference to mythology, the anti-classicist doctrine of the preface to *Rimini*. Shakespeare

> felt the Grecian mythology not as a set of school-boy commonplaces which it was thought manly to give up, but as something which it requires more than mere scholarship to understand, — as the elevation of the external world and of accomplished humanity to the highest pitch of the graceful, and as embodied essences of all the grand and lovely qualities of nature.

Hunt rejoiced, then, that the living and life-giving tradition of Shakespeare, Spenser, and the rest had come up, on the other side of the eighteenth-century desert, in romantic poetry. In its serious essence Hunt's interpretation of myth is in harmony with that of *The Excursion*: [12] "There is a deeper sense of another world, precisely because there is a deeper sense of the present; of its varieties, its benignities, its mystery." [13] But, as we should expect, Hunt feels more esthetic and sensuous enjoyment than religious or mystical aspiration. Like Francis Thompson toward the end of the century, he was well aware of what modern poets, because of their very remoteness from pagan religion, added in the way of refinement and nobility to

[12] He refers admiringly to this passage in connection with his own poem of 1836, *Apollo and the Sunbeams* (*Poetical Works*, ed. H. S. Milford, Oxford University Press, 1923, p. 262). He had mentioned it in 1817 as the basis of Keats's myths in *I Stood Tip-toe*; see Edmund Blunden, *Leigh Hunt's "Examiner" Examined* (1928), p. 134; *Poems of John Keats*, ed. De Selincourt (1926), p. 390. Cf. Hazlitt, "On the Love of the Country" (*Works*, ed. Waller and Glover, 1902, I, 19), and Mr. C. D. Thorpe's edition of Keats (New York, 1935), pp. 56–57.

[13] "Spirit of the Ancient Mythology," *The Indicator*, January 19, 1820; *Essays. By Leigh Hunt* (Moxon, 1842); *Essays by Leigh Hunt*, ed. Arthur Symons (1888). This is one of a number of mythological pieces in prose which appeared in *The Indicator* during 1819–20.

ancient conceptions.[14] Moreover, his approach to the subject was not merely bookish:

He that would run the whole round of the spirit of heathenism to perfection [a phrase impossible for Coleridge, Wordsworth, or Keats or Shelley!], must become intimate with the poetry of Milton and Spenser; of Ovid, Homer, Theocritus, and the Greek tragedians; with the novels of Wieland, the sculptures of Phidias and others, and the pictures of Raphael, and the Caraccis, and Nicholas Poussin. But *a single page of Spenser or one morning at the Angerstein Gallery*, will make him better acquainted with it than a dozen such folios as Spence's Polymetis, or all the mythologists and book-poets who have attempted to draw Greek inspiration from a Latin fount.[15]

I have emphasized Hunt's views of myth because they are such a clear summary of what his betters were doing in poetry, and because he exerted so much personal influence; his influence as a noted liberal is another story. His poem *The Nymphs* is not altogether unworthy of his critical ideals. Indeed it may be counted Hunt's best poem, though he left it out of the canon. It delighted Shelley, and we can hardly read the song of the Nepheliads without feeling that it contributed something to the richer music and imagery of *The Cloud* and *Arethusa*.[16] The poem requires no investigation of sources; except for the names of the classes of nymphs and their general functions, it grows out of Hunt's lively senses.[17] "I write to enjoy myself,"

---

[14] *Ibid.*; and *A Day by the Fire*, pp. 58–59.

[15] "A Popular View of the Heathen Mythology," *A Day by the Fire*, p. 59.

[16] *Works*, pp. 328–30, ll. 135 ff.; and p. 322, ll. 131–33. See *Letters of Shelley* (1914), II, 589, 909; for a report of Shelley's less favorable opinion of Hunt's work in general, see Peck, *Shelley*, II, 409. Although, or because, *The Nymphs* so much resembles the early verse of Keats, the more philosophic Keats found it inadequate; see the *Letters* (1935), pp. 16, 25–26, 96.

[17] The less common as well as the common names and functions (apart from the Nepheliads) were described in a number of books Hunt was familiar with, from Tooke's *Pantheon* (ed. 1781, pp. 223–24) and Natalis Comes, *Mythologiae*,

he says in the preface to *Foliage*, and the statement indicates both his virtues and his limitations. "The main features of the book are a love of sociality, of the country, and of the fine imagination of the Greeks." Nowhere else does Hunt express so poetically, and with so few of his irritating faults, his sensitive joy in all the bright and happy phenomena of nature, his loving observation of wood and field and stream and sky, and, one may add, the female form. There is no explicit symbolism in the poem; it is mainly "a now" in luxuriant verse. To use a formula of the age which Hunt the critic handled with insight, *The Nymphs* has more of fancy than imagination; but there is visual imagination at least, and in peopling the natural world with lovely nymphs Hunt is true to his own conception of the Greeks and their direct, unsophisticated response to nature. He does achieve something of a primitive outlook,[18] though his more or less authentic tidings are of visible things. Hunt never wearied of quoting "Great God! I'd rather be . . . ," and he hazarded the guess that he had had far more sights of Proteus than Wordsworth; for Wordsworth, in occasional revulsions from ugly actuality, was only escaping into the world of imagination where he, Hunt, had habitually lived.[19] Granted the possible truth of the claim, it would help to account for Hunt's rank as a poet. He was a more active and courageous publicist than his great elders and juniors, and in his personal experience

V, xi–xii (ed. Padua, 1616, pp. 254–55), to the *Parnaso Italiano*; in this vast anthology, see, for instance, XVI, 197–98, 249, and XXIV, 194 (ed. Venice, 1784 *et seq.*). A prose analogue to the poem is Hunt's essay of 1836, "The Nymphs of Antiquity and of the Poets" (*A Day by the Fire*). A brief passage on nymphs in *Rimini* was based, Hunt says, partly on Poussin's picture of Polyphemus; see *Works*, p. 23, ll. 470 ff., and the preface to *The Story of Rimini*, 1817, p. xiii.

[18] Many years later Hunt remarked that the supernatural should not be weakly and mistakenly humanized by a poet: "His nymphs will have no taste of their woods and waters; his gods and goddesses be only so many fair or frowning ladies and gentlemen. . . ." (*Imagination and Fancy*, ed. 1870, p. 17.)

[19] *Autobiography*, pp. 492–93.

of life he bore perhaps as much trouble as any of them, yet his sunny temperament seems to have banished clouds, and his writing to a large extent remained outside the world of reality.

Such a lover of the Elizabethans as Hunt should have had qualms in undertaking to re-tell the story of Hero and Leander. He made no such additions to the legend as Marlowe had, though he treated it freely enough and apparently with little thought of reproducing the antique.[20] Indeed his sense of the modernity, or the timelessness, of the tale, which dictated his style and tone, is revealed in his thinking of the star-crossed lovers as he "would of two that died last night."[21] The manner is much like that of *Rimini*, though nothing is so good or perhaps quite so bad. Such lines as "And after months of mutual admiration" and "Strained to his heart the cordial shapeliness" represent the obverse side of Hunt's attempt at unaffected ease. There is compensation in some half-Tennysonian lines like that about the crane which "Began to clang against the coming rain," or "All but the washing of the eternal seas."

The first part of *Bacchus and Ariadne*, which narrates the heroine's discovery of Theseus' desertion, is mainly adapted from the tenth epistle of the *Heroides*. Hunt softens the high-pitched rhetoric of the original into his own key of pathetic sentiment, and pleasantly amplifies Ovid's touches of nature; a happy example is the picture of Ariadne in her leafy bower, wakening out of her dreams to the chirp of birds. But if the poem has any claim upon the modern reader, it is by virtue of a long and fine bravura

[20] In *Imagination and Fancy* (p. 122) Hunt mentions Marlowe's poem as "not comparable with his plays." In the same book (pp. 255, 263) he cites Coleridge's mythological paraphrases from Schiller, and he may have known Schiller's *Hero und Leander*. There is some resemblance, for example, between Hunt's *Hero and Leander*, ll. 179 ff., and Schiller, ll. 65 ff. (*Werke, Säkular-Ausgabe*, I, 79), but it may be only coincidence.
[21] *Works*, p. 683.

passage on the arrival of Bacchus and his throng. Though
marred of course by bits of flat or inept phrasing, and
though far inferior to Keats's Bacchic procession, it stands
comparison better than most of Hunt's work because Hunt
is at his best and Keats, while splendid, is merely descriptive. As for sources, Hunt would know Ovid and Catullus
and other renderings in verse and prose, not to mention
such paintings as Titian's and Poussin's.[22]

One cannot take leave of Hunt without quoting the
finest mythological image he ever struck out, one that his
greatest contemporaries might have been glad to own. In
the essay "A Walk from Dulwich to Brockham" he described a bed of poppies with dark ruby cups and crowned
heads, glowing with melancholy beauty in the setting sun:
"They look as if they held a mystery at their hearts, like
sleeping kings of Lethe."[23] Francis Thompson did not
equal that.

II. THOMAS LOVE PEACOCK (1785–1866)

Rhododaphne (1818) is an attractive if not important
poem, and it partly expresses an element in Peacock which
the reader of his lively prose might overlook. Though his
literary career covered the first two thirds of the nineteenth
century, Peacock was always an eighteenth-century aristo-
crat. His mellow (and sometimes belligerent) classical
scholarship, his Epicurean creed, which was both gustatory
and philosophic, his infinite common sense, his skeptical
mockery of all forms of irrationality and "enthusiasm,"
these things are of the eighteenth century, and, along with

---

[22] In *Sleep and Poetry*, Keats alluded to the prints on Hunt's walls, among
them "several, probably, of his [Poussin's] various 'Bacchanals,' with the god
and his leopard-drawn car, and groups of nymphs dancing with fauns or strewn
upon the foreground to right or left" (Colvin, *John Keats*, 1917, p. 54).

[23] *The Companion. By Leigh Hunt* (1828), p. 361; *Essays*, ed. Symons,
pp. 309–10; *Essays* (Everyman ed.), p. 85.

his mental agility and high spirits, they give to his books their unique sanity and sparkle and tang. As a largely self-trained classic, Peacock united to more than donnish crotchets the more than donnish passion for Greek with which he endowed such fine old pagan clerics as Dr. Folliott. In temperament he was closer to Lucian than to Plato, and, like most satirists, he attacked his own age because he had visions of a better one. But he was no martyr or crusader because, again like most satirists', his visions were of the past, not of the future. Greece, however, is not a mere refuge from reality, it is reality; it is the touchstone of truth and simplicity, of rational wisdom. In the Aristophanic comedy in *Gryll Grange*, Peacock, like Spenser, makes use of Plutarch's Gryllus, the victim of Circe who preferred to retain his hoggish nature; for the man of the Renaissance such porcine contentment is an affront to the dignity of the human soul, in Peacock it expresses a resolute Tory's contempt for modern boasts of progress.[24] If Gryllus belongs to the backyard of the Pantheon, Peacock employs mythology proper, along with medieval romance, in the prose fragment *Calidore* (1816). In this fantasy, which reminds us of Heine's *The Gods in Exile*, we learn that the Olympian deities were happy in their relations with humanity until men degenerated and began to call the gods Beelzebub and Astaroth, to sigh and groan and turn up the whites of their eyes. The Nonconformist conscience, as Mr. Beerbohm would say, had made cowards of them all, and the gods, disgusted with so unpleasant a race, retired to an undisturbed island.

The harmony which soon prevailed between the Olympians and their Arthurian visitors might be taken, allegorically, as a symbol of Peacock's combination of Hellenic rationalism with a genuine romantic strain. When in *The*

[24] *Faerie Queene*, II. xii. 86–87. See *Plutarch's Morals*, ed. W. W. Goodwin (Boston, 1878), V, 218 ff. ("That Brute Beasts Make Use of Reason").

Four Ages of Poetry (1820) he says, "We know too that there are no Dryads in Hyde-park nor Naiads in the Regent's-canal," he is not a rationalist rejoicing in the march of mind but a romantic mourning the decay of the spirit of wonder and mystery that progress has brought about. He feels, like Arnold thirty years later, how unpoetical the age is. And at the end of his life he was not merely the "whiteheaded jolly old worldling" whom Thackeray saw. The confession of faith that he put into the mouth of Mr. Falconer may stand as essentially his own; Peacock himself, strange as it seems, was a devotee of St. Catherine. Mr. Falconer feels the need of believing in some local spiritual influence, genius or nymph, to link him with the spirit of the universe, for the world of things "is too deeply tinged with sordid vulgarity."

There can be no intellectual power resident in a wood, where the only inscription is not "*Genio loci*," but "Trespassers will be prosecuted"; no Naiad in a stream that turns a cotton-mill; no Oread in a mountain dell, where a railway train deposits a cargo of vandals; no Nereids or Oceanitides along the sea-shore, where a coastguard is watching for smugglers. No; the intellectual life of the material world is dead. Imagination cannot replace it. But the intercession of saints still forms a link between the visible and invisible. . . .[25]

If this complaint has a touch of elderly sentimental peevishness — like "By the Ilissus there was no Wragg, poor thing" — Peacock's fundamental attitude, like the much more philosophic Arnold's, was sincere. His half-primitive and pagan belief, or desire to believe, was the closest approach to religious sentiment that his irresponsible intelligence permitted. But while in mythological poems Keats and Shelley, with their larger vision, did not lose sight of

[25] *Gryll Grange* (1861), ch. IX. See Carl Van Doren, *Life of Thomas Love Peacock* (1911), pp. 245–46; Jean-Jacques Mayoux, *Un épicurien anglais: Thomas Love Peacock* (Paris, 1933), p. 499.

the modern world, Peacock did in *Rhododaphne*. The critic of modernity who wrote the novels owed much to his commerce with the ancients; the Hellenism of the poem is wholly a romantic dream, a way of escape. The fable of the seven cantos can be briefly summarized. The maiden Calliroë suffers from a strange disease, and her lover Anthemion goes to a festival in honor of Love to make an offering on her behalf. He is enthralled by the beauty and magical power of Rhododaphne. He escapes to his own home, to find Calliroë well and radiant, but when he kisses her with the lips that have been kissed by the enchantress, she swoons, apparently in death. The stricken Anthemion rushes away. He is recaptured by Rhododaphne, who passionately insists that she holds sway over all things but his heart, and she must possess it. They live together in a magic palace, until Rhododaphne is slain by Uranian Love for profaning his altars. The palace vanishes, and Anthemion awakens to find himself at home in Arcadia, with the dead Rhododaphne beside him. But Calliroë appears, alive and lovely, to be reunited with him, and to weep for the fate of the loving Rhododaphne.

Peacock's main interest was in a tale of ancient magic and mystery and beauty. His imagination was too concrete, too simply romantic, for the symbolism that Keats and Shelley instinctively found in the antique, yet he went some way in that direction. The poem commences with a differentiation of threefold love, creative, heavenly, and earthly, and at the beginning of the last canto we are reminded that "Love's first flame," Anthemion's love for Calliroë, is "of heavenly birth," while the passion between him and the enchantress is earthly. The story of a young man torn between a supernatural and a human love will have recalled Keats's *Endymion*, which appeared a few months after *Rhododaphne*, and which Peacock did not like.[26] But Peacock did not work out his parable with anything like Keats's seriousness, so that his critics have generally failed to observe that he has one. The episode of the magic palace reminds us at once of *Lamia*, and, as we have seen, Keats apparently gathered some hints from Peacock. *Rhododaphne* contains, as Shelley said, "the transfused essence of Lucian, Petronius, and Apuleius," and the author's classical learning appears, unobtrusively, in and between the lines.[27] In comparison with *Endymion* and

[26] He complained because Keats's hero, instead of having an eternal sleep, went questing after shadows; see Peacock's *Works*, Halliford Edition, ed. H. F. B. Brett-Smith and C. E. Jones (1924–34), I, lxxxii. M. Mayoux (p. 317, note) says that to Peacock Keats would seem to have done violence to the classic ideal of repose, but Peacock's own narrative is hardly reposeful, and he was, moreover, contemptuous of *Hyperion* (*Works*, *loc. cit.*). In connection with Peacock's parable of love in *Rhododaphne*, M. Mayoux (p. 134) cites Shelley's *Prince Athanase*.

Peacock planned a nympholeptic tale, which "would obviously have been a second *Rhododaphne*" (Van Doren, pp. 110–11), but he gave it up on the announcement of Horace Smith's *Amarynthus, the Nympholept* (*Works*, I, lxxix).

[27] Shelley's *Letters*, II, 995; *Works*, ed. Ingpen and Peck (1926–30), VI, 273 ff. Peacock discusses these three and other ancient authorities in his preface and notes. He remarks that the song about Bacchus and the pirates in the fifth canto is based on the Homeric *Hymn to Dionysus*; see, to cite the most accessible edition, pp. 137 and 205 in *The Misfortunes of Elphin and Rhododaphne*, ed. G. Saintsbury (London, 1927). In the opening of the sixth canto Peacock paraphrases at length the reflections in Petronius (*Satyricon*, cxv) on a man lost at sea and the vicissitudes of human life (cf. the first section of Taylor's *Holy Dying*). A sentence from this passage of Petronius is the motto for the tenth chapter of *Gryll Grange*.

I cannot claim a close acquaintance with Peacock's beloved Nonnus — probably he did not wish that anyone should — but his animated description of Bacchic revels (p. 239), though the theme was stereotyped, may owe something to the *Dionysiaca*, xxii. 1 ff.; and see his reference to the twelfth book in a letter to Shelley (*Works*, VIII, 203). Magic palaces are also somewhat stereotyped, and Rhododaphne's apparently includes items from those of Alcinous (*Od.* vii. 100–02) and Psyche (*Rhododaphne*, canto vi, pp. 222, 225). For an account of similar palaces and gardens in Nonnus, see Lewis P. Chamberlayne, "A Study of Nonnus," *S.P.*, XIII (1916), 63–65. The transformation of a pirate crew into animals who prowl around the gardens (canto vii, p. 234) is an obvious reminiscence of Circe (*Od.* x. 212 ff.). The picture of Rhododaphne hurling the javelin (canto vii, p. 240) embodies some lines from Peacock's unpublished version of the dialogue *Phaedra and Nurse*, from Euripides (*Works*, VII, 413, 442).

Prometheus Unbound, if not in an absolute sense, the poem deserves Shelley's epithets, not yet overworn, of "Greek and Pagan," although, as Shelley went on to say, the love story is more modern than the spirit and scenery. The "strong *religio loci*" is partly in the substance of the tale, and so far may be called Hellenic, and partly it is in the way of modern and nostalgic comment. The most genuine emotion in the poem is felt in the expressions of wistful regret for the passing of the infant world and its divinities:

> The life, the intellectual soul
> Of vale, and grove, and stream, has fled
> For ever with the creed sublime
> That nursed the Muse of earlier time.[28]

Peacock's classical taste is everywhere apparent, not merely in the use of local color but in the crystalline clarity, definiteness, and objectivity of his narrative method, style, and imagery. We have no vagueness or fumbling, no Keatsian lapses in taste, no beating of Shelleyan wings. That is a merit, and it belongs partly to the ancients and partly to the eighteenth century; one may say of the poem what the East India Company's officials said of the author's examination papers, "Nothing superfluous and nothing wanting." But one is compelled to add that Peacock is not struggling to utter anything of much difficulty or importance. If we happen to begin *Rhododaphne*, we yield at once to its melodious charm and the freshness of its bright water-color pictures, but we retain no memory of it, and we may forget to pick it up again; the story of human love stirs no emotion, the diablerie causes no *frisson*. If we compare the description of Rhododaphne in the moonlit grove with parallel scenes in *Christabel*, we feel at

---

[28] Canto iii, ll. 1 ff., and iv. 13 ff. Part of the former passage was quoted by Poe, who found the poem "brim-full of music"; see his *Works*, ed. E. C. Stedman and G. E. Woodberry (New York, 1914), VII, 314.

once what the former lacks, or avoids.[29] When Peacock uses the simile "like the phantom of a dream," it has in its context something of Greek externality and distinctness which is quite different from the inwardness, the suggestion of reverie, in Shelley's "As suddenly Thou comest as the memory of a dream." [30] There seem to be echoes of the poem in Shelley's work, and it was doubtless association with Shelley that kindled a genuine poetic flame from the ashes of *Palmyra* and *The Genius of the Thames*. Yet Peacock remained himself, a modern Ovid.

III. HARTLEY COLERIDGE (1796–1849)

Hartley Coleridge discussed mythology in a prose essay much more lucid than his father's speculations.[31] Like Jeffrey, he linked together "Keats, Cornwall, and Shelley" — and he added Wordsworth — as poets who had breathed a new life into dry bones. Like Jeffrey also, he observed that the stern, simple gods of ancient paganism had acquired "new manners, and almost new faces"; they have become tender, radiant beings allied with "the gentler parts of nature." The most eloquent bits of the essay are largely an elaboration of the mythological passages in *The Excursion* and *The Piccolomini*, both of which are quoted. In Hartley's sympathetic view Greek myth lives on, at least for poets, because of its very humanity; it once was,

---

[29] *Rhododaphne*, canto iii; *Christabel*, ll. 58 ff., 279 ff.

[30] *Rhododaphne*, canto ii, l. 17; *Prometheus Unbound*, II. i. 7–8. Cf. also Peacock's lines on love, which rhyme "ocean" and "emotion" (canto vii, ed. Saintsbury, p. 245), and Shelley's use of the words and idea (*P.U.*, IV. 96–98). The second stanza of the *Hymn of Pan* seems to have echoes of Peacock's "Down Pindus' steep . . ." (canto iii, p. 176); see *Works of Shelley*, ed. Ingpen and Peck, IV, 402, and the opening of Shelley's review of *Rhododaphne*. For possible echoes in *Adonais*, see Peck, *Shelley*, II, 221, note 11 (and also I, 426, note 71).

[31] "On the Poetical Use of the Heathen Mythology," *London Magazine*, February, 1822, pp. 113 ff.; reprinted in *Essays and Marginalia*, ed. Derwent Coleridge (1851), I, 18 ff. The essay gave much pleasure to the Wordsworths (*Letters of the Wordsworth Family*, ed. Knight, II, 173).

and may still be, the beautiful or terrible expression of man's unchanging loves and fears, his yearnings and his passions. From a gifted poet thus inclined toward the symbolic use of myth, a poet with a keen love of nature and one who went up to Oxford, as Southey said, with Greek enough for a whole college, we might expect something distinctive. If Hartley's verse on classical themes (like much of his other verse) does not seem worthy of his powers, still we have such things as the sonnets on Homer,[32] *The Vale of Tempe*, *Diana and Endymion*, and the fragment of a dramatic poem, *Prometheus*.

In addition to the general causes which hindered the fulfilment of Hartley's poetic promise there was the fact that, in spite of his imaginative sympathy with mythology, his heart was divided. In the first place he inherited the paternal doctrine of the finite quality of Greek anthropomorphism.[33] That idea is touched, quite beautifully, in *The Vale of Tempe*, but at least between the lines of the sonnet appears a related and more fundamental anti-mythological instinct, also paternal, the religious pietism which found such sincere and usually unpoetic expression in Hartley's later poems. For a full statement of it we may turn back to the very essay in which he celebrated the poetic possibilities of myth:

Oh! what a faith were this, if human life indeed were but a summer's dream, and sin and sorrow but a beldame's tale, and death the fading of a rainbow, or the sinking of a breeze into quiet air;

---

[32] *Poems*, ed. Derwent Coleridge (1851), I, 144, II, 16. While Hartley's father, Wordsworth, and Southey "all leant to the Wolfian, or, as my brother called it, Wolfish and Heinous (Heyne) hypothesis respecting the origin of the Homeric poems, Hartley was always a stout and vehement upholder of the orthodox opinion" (*ibid.*, I, clvi). He said he had witnessed the Trojan war, being then "an insect which in these days is nameless," that took refuge in Helen's hair (Earl L. Griggs, *Hartley Coleridge*, University of London Press, 1929, p. 168).

[33] See *Essays*, I, 37; *Poems*, I, 37, 162, II, 212; Herbert Hartman, *Hartley Coleridge* (Oxford University Press, 1931), pp. 109–10.

if all mankind were lovers and poets, and there were no truer pain than the first sigh of love, or the yearning after ideal beauty; if there were no dark misgivings, no obstinate questionings, no age to freeze the springs of life, and no remorse to taint them.[34]

Such words, from Hartley Coleridge, are not mere rhetoric, and some of them have a parallel in the *Prometheus* which, in ignorance of Shelley's drama, he had begun at Oxford, apparently in 1820.[35] His scholarly equipment was admirable; he translated the *Medea* in 1820 and planned a prose version of Aeschylus. For many years he hoped to finish *Prometheus*, but of course he never did, partly on account of his constitutional infirmities and partly, perhaps, because he sank under the formidable exposition of the myth which his zealous father unloaded upon him.[36] The fragment, which has something over six hundred lines, consists mainly of a dialogue between the unconquerable Prometheus and a chorus of sylphs who wish to be allowed to plead with Jupiter on his behalf. As "a lovely child, a boy divine," Jupiter had sworn to make his reign a golden age, and the sylphs had sung of it. It is their music, says Prometheus, which deludes mortals into dreaming of a new world of peace

> Where beauty fades not, love is ever true,
> And life immortal like a summer day.

How the drama would have evolved we cannot tell, but the separate "Conclusion" gives a hint:

> Mortal! fear no more, —
> The reign is past of ancient violence;
> And Jove hath sworn that time shall not deface,
> Nor death destroy, nor mutability
> Perplex the truth of love.

---

[34] Cf. *Poems*, I, 117, and a piece in lighter vein, I, 152.

[35] See *Poems*, I, xciii, II, 280; Griggs, p. 93; Hartman, p. 81.

[36] That is, the lecture on the *Prometheus* of Aeschylus mentioned at the beginning of my second chapter. See *Unpublished Letters of Samuel Taylor Cole-*

The reign of love sounds Shelleyan, though not the idea of a reformed and beneficent Jupiter.[37] Hartley may have intended something like the Aeschylean solution, or, more probably, a development of the contrast between pagan and Christian ideals. In Bagehot's judgment the poem had no Greek severity of style, no defined outline, but one may think that in general concreteness and humanity of feeling it is closer to Greek drama than most English imitations except those whose severity is indistinguishable from *rigor mortis*.[38]

IV. THOMAS HOOD (1799–1845)

Hood's arduous maturity allowed little time for classical reading, but he must have absorbed some mythological lore during his brief schooldays.[39] The poems of his which concern us are notable examples of Elizabethan influence combined with that of some moderns, especially Keats. The least happy example is *Lamia*, which is Keats's poem made over into an Elizabethan play.[40] In the charming *Plea of the Midsummer Fairies* (1827) we are reminded not only of Shakespeare but of Spenser and Marlowe, and of

ridge, ed. E. L. Griggs (1932), II, 281, 336; and Derwent Coleridge's summary of the relevant part of the lecture (*Poems*, II, 282).

Apart from echoes of Aeschylus' Promethean drama in Hartley's poem, compare *Agam.*, ll. 717 ff., and *Poems*, II, 301; *Paradise Regained*, ii. 178 ff., and *Poems*, II, 295.

[37] Richard Garnett said that "although his brother attributes it to an earlier period, it is plainly composed under the influence of Shelley" (*D.N.B.*). Allowing for the identity of the fables, I do not think the internal evidence is so plain.

[38] See Bagehot's *Literary Studies* (Everyman ed.), I, 64. A reviewer in *Fraser's Magazine* (XLIII [1851], 611) complained, not quite justly, that the theme required an Aeschylus, not a Theocritus.

[39] See *The Irish Schoolmaster*, stanzas 22–23 (*Poetical Works of Thomas Hood*, ed. Walter Jerrold, Oxford University Press, 1920, pp. 64–65).

[40] The date of composition is uncertain; see my Appendix, under 1822. The allusion to the poor maiden that adored Apollo (i. 27; *Works*, p. 675) suggests *The Girl of Provence*, by Hood's friend Procter, which appeared in *The Flood of Thessaly* (1823), though the story was well known.

Keats by the rich coloring and the "hoary majesty" of Saturn.[41] The feeling that Hood here expressed for the old divinities of tree and stream [42] found further expression in the two classical narratives, *Lycus, the Centaur* (1822) and *Hero and Leander* (1827).

Both the theme and the sensuous detail of the former poem show the influence of Keats. The nymph who loves Lycus procures a charm from Circe to make him immortal, but, as she utters it and sees him becoming a horse, she breaks off in horror, and he remains a centaur. One thinks at once of the episode of Glaucus, Scylla, and Circe in the third book of *Endymion*; though Hood is concerned with the sensations of Lycus and not with humanitarian and ethical symbolism, he is closer to Keats than to Ovid.[43] Besides, as Mr. Elton remarks, *Lycus* seems to be influenced, in its slow-galloping meter, by Shelley's *Vision of the Sea*, and "perhaps also in its highly charged attempt at dreadfulness." [44] Hartley Coleridge wrote to Hood that the poem was "a work absolutely unique in its line, such as no man has written, or could have written, but yourself," and John Clare could not understand a word of it.[45] Something can be said for both opinions. The utterance of a man changed into a centaur may well be somewhat distraught and incoherent. But if Hood has the imagination, he has not the style to sustain horror and pity at the level he sometimes reaches.

[41] For Spenser and Marlowe, see stanzas cxii and lx. While Saturn is altered to suit a fanciful poem, such stanzas as lxiii-lxv, including the borrowed phrase, recall *Hyperion* (cf. i. 59 in particular). Keats's general influence on Hood was discussed, rather inadequately, by Federico Olivero, in *M.L.N.*, XXVIII (1913), 233-35.   [42] P. 116, st. xxiv.

[43] Cf. the myth of Cronus and Philyra in Apollonius Rhodius, *Argonautica*, ii. 1231 ff. Keats's *Lamia* is remembered in *Lycus*, ll. 56-57, and probably the first line of *Endymion* in ll. 154-55.

[44] *Survey of English Literature, 1780-1880* (1920), II, 288.

[45] Walter Jerrold, *Thomas Hood: His Life and Times* (New York, 1909), p. 197.

Hero and Leander contains some beauties, and its faults may be less irritating than those of Hunt's version. Hood avoided direct competition with Marlowe by inventing a large part of his story. He begins with the parting of the lovers in the morning. Leander, on his way back to Abydos, encounters a sea nymph who carries him down to her home, not knowing that gratification of her love means death to him; in the hope of restoring his life she brings him up to the shore, but the body is removed by fishermen and she returns to the water. This episode occupies ninety out of the hundred and thirty stanzas; only at the end does Hood resume the original tale in describing the grief and suicide of Hero. The theme of the episode is common property — it had been used lately by Hood's friend, J. H. Reynolds, in *The Naiad* (1816), and by Hood himself in *Lycus* — but the initial hint might have come from Marlowe's lines about Neptune's pulling Leander down to the depths where sweet singing mermaids sported with their loves. Hood's poem has some clear echoes of Marlowe.[46]

There are also clear echoes of *Venus and Adonis* — not to mention the sixain stanza — and of *The Rape of Lucrece*. The nymph's invitation to love, and her efforts to revive the drowned Leander, recall Shakespeare's Venus.[47] When she sees that Leander is dead, she denounces Night in a series of conceits parallel to those of Lucrece on the same theme, and her address to Death, in the latter part of the same speech, was doubtless suggested by the tirade of Venus.[48] But no list of actual reminiscences or imitations

[46] E.g., Hood, ll..403 ff., Marlowe, i. 347–48; Hood, ll. 493 ff., Marlowe, i. 375–76.

[47] See especially Hood, ll. 447–48, and Shakespeare, ll. 1127–28. In *Bianca's Dream* (*Works*, p. 76, l. 233) there is an acknowledged echo (see l. 234) of Shakespeare, l. 231.

[48] Hood, ll. 499 ff.; *Lucrece*, ll. 764 ff.; *Venus and Adonis*, ll. 931 ff. Hood doubtless knew the original of Lucrece's declamation on Night, *Faerie Queene*,

could begin to indicate the Elizabethan quality of the rhetorical speeches, conceits, gnomic lines, and the diction generally. The poem is probably the most remarkable example in modern verse of almost complete reproduction of the narrative manner of the Elizabethan Ovidians. One cannot quite dismiss as *pastiche* what is written with the youthful freshness and spontaneity of a contemporary of Shakespeare and Marlowe. Of course there is some obvious modernity of spirit and expression — and Keats is not forgotten [49] — but in general Hood seems to see and think and feel in the Elizabethan way, and he is as unconscious as Shakespeare and Marlowe were that it is often a bad way.

V. THOMAS LOVELL BEDDOES (1803–49)

That Beddoes was the last Elizabethan — more properly the last Jacobean — has long been a cliché of criticism, and the incidental mythology of the dramas recalls the main varieties of Elizabethan style. He can be soft and idyllic, in the Elizabethan-Romantic convention of his own day, though he seldom lapses into mere prettiness; he can let himself go in boyishly flamboyant rhetoric, like Marlowe and Shakespeare; or, like Donne, he can divest a decorative mythological image of its traditional glamor and give us an anti-romantic or ghoulish shock. Though Beddoes took classical prizes at school, and in later life continued to read Greek along with anatomy and German, most of his writing was decidedly "Gothic." And, for all his strange Elizabethan quality, his distinctive mythological allusions

---

III. iv. 55 ff. Hood's detailed description of the attitudes of the people watching the nymph (ll. 667 ff.) appears to be an imitation of Lucrece's account of the painting of Trojan scenes.

[49] For probable or possible echoes, see Hood, ll. 226–28, and *Isabella*, st. xxxiv; Hood, ll. 269–70, and Keats's sonnet on Leander (cf. Hood's sonnet and a comic piece on Hero and Leander, *Works*, pp. 194, 436); Hood, l. 376, and *Eve of St. Agnes*, st. xxxiii–xxxv; Hood, l. 620, and *Lamia*, i. 8.

could not be mistaken for early work; whether quiet or turbid, they are of the nineteenth century. Every critic quotes these lovely lines:

> Here's the blue violet, like Pandora's eye,
> When first it darkened with immortal life.[50]

The first line might have been uttered by Perdita, but not the second. For a less serene image, take the lines on Night with giant strides stalking over the world

> Like a swart Cyclops, on its hideous front
> One round, red, thunderswollen eye ablaze.[51]

While the Elizabethans and Jacobeans loved such large personifications, there is here a modern touch of conscious composition or aggregation. Beddoes is more characteristic in his sardonic or macabre vein. It is a far cry from, say, Portia's "Peace, ho! the moon sleeps with Endymion," to Isbrand's

> That wolf-howled, witch-prayed, owl-sung fool,
> Fat mother moon . . . ,

or from Shakespeare's or even Hunt's Cleopatra — "The laughing queen that caught the world's great hands" — to Beddoes' lines on the queen's cracked and battered skull.[52]

In addition to many allusions, Beddoes has some poems on classical subjects, from the genial, robust, and grotesque *Silenus in Proteus* to such a romantic whimsy as the *Song of the Stygian Naiades*.[53] His most ambitious effort in that vein was *Pygmalion* (1825), which most of his critics have

---

[50] *The Brides' Tragedy* (1822), I. i (*Works*, ed. H. W. Donner, Oxford University Press, 1935, p. 174; ed. Gosse, 1928, II, 406).

[51] *Ibid.*, III. iii (Donner, p. 204; Gosse, II, 442–43).

[52] *Death's Jest-Book*, III. iii and V. iv (Donner, pp. 423, 479–80; Gosse, I, 184, 246). In Isbrand's lyric on Harpagus and Astyages, which has nothing lyrical but the meter, a sufficiently grim incident from Herodotus (i. 119) is elaborated with gruesomely jocular details (Donner, pp. 90, 466; Gosse, I, 230).

[53] Donner, pp. 136–37; Gosse, II, 375, 398.

united in ignoring, perhaps in the belief that the author, who liked it at first, was right in looking back on it as "considerable trash." [54] In style the poem reminds one sometimes of Landor's *Hellenics*, sometimes of Keats; [55] it is at any rate not Elizabethan, unless the largely imagined and energetic conceits and the occasionally knotty texture have a parallel in Chapman. All that Beddoes retains of the Ovidian myth is the first part — how Pygmalion, scorning the women around him, made a statue and fell in love with it — and even that part is re-created; the conclusion, and the interpretation, are entirely modern. This poem is Beddoes' *Alastor* or *Endymion*. Pygmalion is a type of the lonely artist, the artist of an age of idealism, frustration, and *Weltschmerz*, whose life is apart from the world about him. The statue is so beautiful that its maker must be called divine, a giver of immortality greater than Jove, but he cannot pass the bars between his mortal self and the fragment of reality he has created. He prays that he may be spared from death and the grave, that the figure into which he has poured his soul may be endowed with life by the gods who have often wasted life "On the deformed, the hideous and the vile." [56] But the statue remains stone and the sculptor pines away; as his body dies the statue comes to life. Artist and work of art are united only in the immaterial world of eternity.[57]

[54] A letter of 1837 (Donner, pp. 662, 664; Gosse, I, 103, 105). For the poem, see Donner, pp. 78–83; Gosse, II, 346–52.

[55] Kelsall spoke of the "peculiar fascination" Keats had for Beddoes, and found "traces" of his influence in *Pygmalion*, "the sole instance of a direct impress from another mind, in the whole compass" of his friend's poetry; see his edition of the *Poems* (1851), pp. xxii–xxiii. Cf. Kelsall's letter of 1869, in *The Browning Box*, ed. H. W. Donner (Oxford University Press, 1935), pp. 85–86.

[56] In a letter of August 25, 1824, Beddoes wrote of Shelley: "What would he not have done, if ten years more, that will be wasted upon the lives of unprofitable knaves and fools, had been given to him" (Donner, p. 590; Gosse, I, 18).

[57] Though Beddoes went much beyond Rousseau's "Pygmalion," I think he owed somewhat more to it than Mr. Donner admits. See Rousseau's *Œuvres*

As poetry, *Pygmalion* is not one of the things by which Beddoes lives, yet as a document at least it is worth something. His skeptical, disillusioned brain and soul harbored a tormenting conviction of the emptiness of life, and he searched "with avidity for every shadow of a proof or probability of an after-existence, both in the material & immaterial nature of man." Nothing else could "satisfy the claims of the oppressed on nature, satiate endless & admirable love & humanity, & quench the greediness of the spirit for existence." [58] One other passage from a letter brings us close to the specific theme of *Pygmalion*:

Shakspeare, Dante, Milton, all who have come next to the human heart, had found no object in life to satiate the restless yearnings of their hearts & appease at the same time the fastidious cravings of their imaginations. Dissatisfaction is the lot of the poet, if it be that of any being; & therefore the gushings of the spirit, these pourings out of their innermost on imaginary topics, because there was no altar in their home worthy of the libation.[59]

And the conclusion of the last letter Beddoes wrote is the ultimate comment on *Pygmalion*: "I ought to have been among other things a good poet; Life was too great a bore on one peg & that a bad one. . . ."

These various minor writers show how ready the poetic soil was to foster the mythological seed sown by Keats and

---

complètes (Paris, 1870–74), V, 232–36; Donner, pp. 601, 754, and his *Thomas Lovell Beddoes: The Making of a Poet* (Oxford, 1935), p. 174. Leigh Hunt, in his version of Rousseau's work, remarked that the author "was a kind of Pygmalion himself, disgusted with the world, and perpetually yet hopelessly endeavouring to realize the dreams of his imagination" (*The Indicator*, May 10, 1820, pp. 241 ff.). Compare Beddoes' "Translation of the Philosophic Letters of Schiller," published in 1825 (Donner, pp. 549 ff.).

[58] A letter of April 20, 1827 (Donner, p. 630; Gosse, I, 64–65). For this question as a motive in his medical studies see Donner, *Thomas Lovell Beddoes*, p. 187.   [59] October 21, 1827 (Donner, p. 635; Gosse, I, 71).

Shelley (and Wordsworth), and no one dropped more gentle rain from heaven upon it than Leigh Hunt. Besides the abundant evidence in print of these young men's interests, it is pleasant to hear of Hunt, Peacock, and Hogg on Sunday afternoons "talking of mythology, and the Greeks, and our old friends." [60] Some of these poets are original and important figures, others, like Barry Cornwall and Mrs. Shelley, only testify to the ease with which, after a fashion, the new mythological conventions could be worked. Nearly all of them showed in their writing the influence of their Elizabethan enthusiasms. With such exceptions as Hartley Coleridge and Beddoes, they generally lacked the philosophic depth and symbolic power of Keats and Shelley, and were content, like most of the Elizabethans, with decorative story-telling and picture-making. And only one, Hartley Coleridge, revealed the cleavage, apparent in his father and in Wordsworth, between Christian and pagan ideals, a cleavage which was to persist and to widen during the rest of the century.

[60] Blunden, *Leigh Hunt and His Circle*, p. 139; *Correspondence of Leigh Hunt* (1862), I, 129 (March 9, 1819).

CHAPTER VI

Tennyson

OF LATE years, very happily, sniffs or sneers at Tennyson have ceased to be proof of a modern critical intelligence. The reaction of the earlier twentieth century against the Laureate was not in itself entirely modern. Some of our complaints had been made by Wilson and Lockhart, and, as the Victorian era advanced, most of the others were added; even the years of relative security after 1850 were not altogether a green lawn "where Alf, the sacred river, ran." As that great era receded into the past hostile voices increased in volume and shrillness, for |the white light of truth heated as well as illuminated the modern mind. Victorian literature could be damned outright as "pink pills for pale people," and its most complete and revered representative was the chief sufferer. The reaction was of course inevitable, and, in cutting Tennyson loose from a mass of dubious writing, from a partly adventitious and spurious reputation, it has left an indubitable poet standing on a smaller but firmer pedestal. Much of his work is dead beyond recall, but we still hear the wind sweep and the plover cry, and the sea breaking on the cold gray stones. For he lives mainly as a painter of landscape and water, as a poet of lyrical, especially elegiac, moments, and, within limits, as a superb artist in words, a maker of golden lines.

Tennyson's mind and career, some modern critics have thought, are paradoxical, and they have tried to find a formula which explains apparent changes in him. The common pattern of interpretation is something like this. Tennyson began as a genuine romantic poet and ended as a Laureate, a British minister for divine affairs, who aspired to see his Pilot face to face, "as gentleman to gentleman." The real poetic fire that he possessed was gradually extinguished, it seems, by a number of causes — native timidity and morbid sensitiveness to both praise and blame; the Apostles' contagious zeal for uplift; hostile reviewers; the thrusting, by misguided friends and pious public, of the rôle of *vates* or preacher upon a born singer; the paralyzing result of accepting and expounding the Victorian compromise; the taming influence of a wife who ruled his spirit from her sofa; prosperity and familiar acquaintance with Royalty.

Doubtless all these deleterious agencies and more were in operation, and some of them certainly left their mark, but the formula of the frustrated artist has been so widely used by modern biographical writers that one may grow suspicious of a well-worn pass-key. A complete survey of Tennyson's life from Somersby to Westminster Abbey does not suggest that he was notably warped, that he took or was pushed into the wrong road. Surely his temperament, his parentage, his early training and environment, made his future course almost certain. There are paradoxes in the mature Tennyson, but there were paradoxes in little Alfred, who was a combination of normal boy, scholar, poet, melancholist and mystic. In that astonishing play, *The Devil and the Lady*, which he wrote at the age of fourteen, in the midst of boyish high jinks and Elizabethan robustiousness (and Tennysonian landscape-painting), we have speculations about the mystery of evil and about "suns and spheres and stars and belts and systems." [1] If we must have a formula, a glance at the Tenny-

---

[1] *The Devil and the Lady*, ed. Charles Tennyson (London, 1930), pp. 65, 24.

sonian table of contents will furnish one that is far from novel. From the juvenilia to *Crossing the Bar* Tennyson was sometimes a poet, sometimes a preacher. Nor was the preacher wholly an encumbrance; if it was he who modulated "the last deliberate snuffle of 'the blameless king,'" he also gave strength to *Ulysses* and *In Memoriam*. We may wish that Tennyson had been, like Keats, a "natural man," so to speak, who had to make himself and his own spiritual world, instead of finding both ready made, but we must take him as he is. If one allows for the normal mellowing of maturity, Tennyson was at the end what he was at the beginning, an artist who had consummate powers of expression and not very much, except as an emotional poet, to say.

I

The earliest poem that we have shows Tennyson in the capacity of translator. Between his eleventh and fourteenth years he translated the first ninety-three lines of Claudian's *De Raptu Proserpinae* into a hundred and thirty-three lines of regular and often antithetical couplets. It was the work of a boy saturated in Pope's *Homer*, and it not unworthily inaugurated the long career of a poet who, whatever flickering lights sometimes misled him, never wavered in his loyalty to the ancients. Nearly threescore and ten years later we shall find him returning to the vale of Enna, and apparently to Claudian too.[2] Classical influence was much less potent in *Poems by Two Brothers* than the pseudo-orientalism of Byron and Moore. In the volume of 1830, along with much decorative and melodious romanticism — and the gloomy *Supposed Confessions* and the original *Mariana* and *The Kraken* — ap-

[2] See the discussion of *Demeter and Persephone*. The juvenile paraphrase is in *Unpublished Early Poems by Alfred Tennyson*, ed. Charles Tennyson (1931). For an early Ovidian poem see *Alfred Lord Tennyson: A Memoir* (1897), I, 40, note. This biography by the poet's son is henceforth cited as *Memoir*.

peared two classical pieces, *Hero to Leander* and *The Sea-Fairies*. The speech of Hero to her departing lover has the long tradition of the *aubade* behind it; the immediate suggestion may have come from Hood's *Hero and Leander*, which opens with a similar situation.[3] The passion is partly Shelleyan, but a little more authentic than in the earlier *Antony to Cleopatra*.

The Sea-Fairies is linked in theme and manner with the inferior *Merman* and *Mermaid* and with the remarkable *Hesperides* of 1833. The first three are light-hearted poems of escape; they show the only kind of audacity that remained with Tennyson to the end, metrical audacity. *The Sea-Fairies* is the first of his variations on Homeric motives, though the connection with Homer is slight;[4] these sirens are innocent creatures, almost angels in appearance, who invite, not to sin, but to a carefree holiday. If the later *Lotos-Eaters* has gained much in its long-drawn languors and inlaid gold of phrase, it has also lost something, the untroubled play of youthful fancy and the relative naturalness of lyrical style. The romanticism of *The Sea-Fairies* is quite external; *The Hesperides* is the purest piece of magic and mystery, and perhaps the only piece of myth-making, that Tennyson ever wrote. What opium was for the author of *Kubla Khan*, two lines of *Comus* were for our sober young bard; he did not reprint the result, though he later wished he had done so — and though he

---

[3] For the text, see W. J. Rolfe's edition of Tennyson's *Works* (Boston, 1898), p. 782, and *Early Poems of Alfred Lord Tennyson*, ed. J. Churton Collins (1900), p. 286. There does not seem to be any specific debt to the versions of Marlowe or Leigh Hunt; see, however, note 59 below.

[4] See *Odyssey*, xii. 39 ff., 181 ff. The early text is in Rolfe, p. 786, and Collins, p. 29. The revised text is in the standard editions, such as the one-volume *Works*, ed. Hallam, Lord Tennyson (1913). This edition, in the impression of 1931, is henceforth cited as *Works*.

I should mention *Ilion, Ilion*, apparently written in Tennyson's Cambridge days (*Unpublished Early Poems*, p. 47). Like most English poems in quantity, it has the air of a cat picking its way along the top of a fence, yet it does deserve the threadbare adjective "haunting."

reprinted *The Lord of Burleigh* and *The May Queen*. Nowhere else in his poetry is such strangeness added to beauty
as in this weird mythological incantation. But it is hardly
the work of "The Poet," and with such words Freedom
could not shake the world.[5]
So far in this slight sketch we have seen Tennyson as a
conscious and not altogether unworthy heir of the romantic poets. But his voluminous juvenilia reveal two instincts likely to impair the flow of lyrical emotion, one
moralistic and one stylistic; both might be taken as symp-
toms of lower poetic vitality than the romantics possessed.
The romantics, to be sure, had been both teachers and
artists, but they had lived more fully than Tennyson, had
earned a more valid right to expound what truth they had
attained; further, however ornate they might be, style remained a means, it did not become an end in itself. In *The
Palace of Art*, for instance, Tennyson poses much the same
question that had troubled Shelley and Keats: can the individual live in an intellectual and artistic world of his own,
or does he need the nourishment of ordinary human life
and sympathy with the common lot?[6] In spite of the artistic faults of *Alastor* and *Endymion*, no one can doubt
that Shelley and Keats are stirred to their depths by the
problem they try to solve. Tennyson is more palpably

---

[5] The poem is printed in *Works*, p. 873; *Memoir*, I, 61; Rolfe, p. 787; Collins,
p. 301. The specific allusions in the introductory stanza are based on the *Periplus*
of Hanno; see the translation by Wilfred H. Schoff (Philadelphia, 1912).

A reviewer, probably Bulwer, described *The Hesperides* and *Oenone* as "of the
best Cockney classic; and Keatesian [*sic*] to the marrow" (*New Monthly Magazine*, XXXVII [1833], 72). *The Hesperides* has lately been praised by Mr. Eliot
(*Essays Ancient and Modern*, 1936, pp. 176–78).

[6] Without disputing this traditional interpretation, which was that of Spedding and the poet's other friends, Mr. A. C. Howell argues that Tennyson,
compelled to leave Cambridge for "the world," was finding compensation in the
thought of his university as a beautiful home of sterile pedantry. This may well
be one of the "lesser meanings," though Mr. Howell seems inclined to make it
more than that. In any case, while the suggestion enriches the poem as a personal document, it does not, I think, give the poem as a poem any more moving
reality than it had before. See *S.P.*, XXXIII (1936), 507–22.

didactic — instead of Platonic idealism he has the religious inheritance of Somersby and the "Apostles' Creed" — but he is not struggling toward a glimpse of truth, he has apparently always known it. His poem, as a poem, does not move us at all, partly because it seems to have cost so little, partly because, as the endless revision testifies, the author is mainly concerned with the framing of exquisite panel pictures and the subtle arrangement of vowels and consonants.

These paragraphs, intended as a preface, have grown much too long, but one needs to emphasize the fact that all the elements, good and bad, of the mature and the aged Tennyson appear in his early work. If he was a poet *manqué*, the spoiling process had begun at a date too early for critical analysis; it was indeed partly pre-natal. At any rate there is probably no group of poems, outside of the great lyrics, so sure of a place in any Tennyson anthology as most of the long series of classical pieces.[7] In the verse of classical inspiration — and that includes hundreds of scattered lines and phrases — we have less of Tennyson's weakness and more of his strength than in any other part of his work, except, as I said, the small body of perfect lyrics. For the classical themes generally banished from his mind what was timid, parochial, sentimental, inadequately philosophical, and evoked his special gifts and his most authentic emotions, his rich and wistful sense of the past, his love of nature, and his power of style.[8]

[7] Since, as in my other volume, I am not discussing stage plays, I omit *The Cup*.

[8] Before going on to the volumes of 1842 I may mention a fragment of twenty-eight lines, written about 1835 and first printed by Tennyson's son (*Works*, p. xxv). It begins:

> "I wish'd to see Him. Who may feel
> His light and love? He comes. . . ."

Such words might be from the heroine of *St. Agnes' Eve*, but the speaker is Semele. The fragment is in the irregular lines and measures of a number of poems already noticed. The latter half is a prophetic picture of a Bacchic pro-

II

The first version of *Oenone* [9] contained many of the best passages that are familiar in the text of 1842, but it was much amplified and enriched in revision. The opening description of the vale of Ida (which of course is more Spanish than Asiatic) was at first cluttered with dubious compound words, of Greek, Miltonic, or Keatsian suggestion, and the scene was somewhat remote and indistinct; in 1842 the affectations of phrase disappeared, and the whole picture gained in composition, coherence, and rhythmical movement. Elsewhere in the poem the excision of slight irrelevances of descriptive detail substituted simplicity for mannered profusion, and the natural background was related more intimately to the theme and mood. The first version included some lines of epic breadth and dignity, but others were added in the second, such as those describing the majestic approach of Herè.

The story of the judgment of Paris had been told by countless writers, ancient, medieval, and modern, and how many of these Tennyson knew is a question; since his handling is freely original it is not a very important question.[10] Tennyson "purposely chose those classical sub-

cession, more rapid and more purely musical, and much less rich in color, than that of Keats.

9 Collins, pp. 79–83; Rolfe, pp. 800–01.

10 For a partial list of ancient versions see the *Library* of Apollodorus, ed. Sir James Frazer, II, 172–73. Colluthus' *Rape of Helen* seems to be neglected by the commentators on Tennyson, but its first two hundred lines are a full account of the judgment, and he was pretty well read in the lesser Greek poets. To mention one trifle, Tennyson's "married brows" is always related to his beloved Theocritus, but it appears in Colluthus also; see Theoc., *Id.* viii. 72; *Oppian, Colluthus, Tryphiodorus* (Loeb Classical Library), p. 548, l. 75.

The judgment is more fully described in Ovid's epistle of Paris to Helen than in the epistle of Oenone. The latter contains some hints for the heroine and her background, but Ovid's nymph is a somewhat priggish and maudlin creature who is conscious of having married beneath her.

Some parallels in description, phrasing, and moralizing can be found between *Oenone* and Beattie's dreary *Judgment of Paris*; one may think, and hope, that

jects from mythology and legend, which had been before but imperfectly treated, or of which the stories were slight, so that he might have free scope for his imagination." [11] Of course there are numerous adaptations of classical phrasing woven into the texture with the taste and skill of Tennysonian scholarship, and such things gave his earlier if not his modern readers the pleasure of recognizing old jewels in a new setting. For the general mode of treatment, the placing of a miniature epic in a luxuriant natural background, Tennyson was indebted to the Alexandrian idyll and epyllion, especially to his favorite Theocritus. [12] The device of a refrain and the repetition of words and phrases are also Theocritean.

The name of Tennyson's ancient master raises a question which concerns more poems than *Oenone*. Even in Theocritus' mythological idylls artifice is mingled with touches of realism; Tennyson is more obviously and consistently artificial. We wonder how many pipes he smoked over these delicately contrived embroideries of phrase and rhythm, which constantly call attention to their beauty. And the poem as a whole has something of operatic unreality when such elaborate, such perfectly poised narrative and description, are put in the mouth of the heartbroken nymph. If we turn to *Oenone* after *Endymion*, we are aware at once of Tennyson's cool and conscious artistic detachment; even where Keats is writing badly, the intensity may be mawkish and uncontrolled, but it is intensity, and he seldom fails to apprehend myth with warm

they are only accidental. Much closer than any of them is the parallel between the substance and language of Herè's offer to Paris and *Paradise Regained*, iii. 255 ff.

[11] *Memoir*, II, 13.

[12] Mr. W. H. B. Bird has recorded that as an undergraduate he once asked Hepworth Thompson about Tennyson's classical attainments. "The Master paused a moment and then said, 'He knew his Theocritus very well'" (*T.L.S.*, September 21, 1933, p. 631). For *Oenone*, see W. P. Mustard, *Classical Echoes in Tennyson*, pp. 35–36, and the article by F. J. Hemelt cited in my bibliography.

human sympathy. Tennyson's sympathy partly evaporates in a concern for style. What we remember is not Oenone and her wrongs, but the vale in Ida, Paris white-breasted like a star, leading "a jet-black goat white-horn'd, white-hooved," [13] the crocus breaking like fire under the feet of the goddesses, the rosy form of Aphrodite (though she is perhaps too much of a Victorian Royal Academy nude), "great Herè's angry eyes," the autumn rains that "flash in the pools of whirling Simois," and the

> tall dark pines, that plumed the craggy ledge
> High over the blue gorge. . . .[14]

Not that the poem lacks personal feeling. Oenone's weariness of life partakes of a central mood in the early Tennyson, who was generally more of a poet when seeking peace than when in possession of it. But Pallas is only too secure in her hold upon truth. The faith in moderation that Tennyson constantly expressed, though wholly sincere, is too ready-made and Polonian. "Self-reverence, self-knowledge, self-control," said Chesterton profanely, "These three alone will make a man a prig." The sound and prosaic wisdom of the goddess is so very Victorian that we become embarrassingly aware that she is undressed, apart from a spear, and it seems, to violate chronology and propriety, as if the Queen herself had started up in her bath

---

[13] Beautiful as the picture of Paris is, one may wish for something less refined. This is Sherburne's seventeenth-century translation of Colluthus (Chalmers, *English Poets*, VI, 618):

> "Low as his knee a mountain goat's rough hide
> Hung from his shoulders, flagging by his side:
> In's hand a neatherd's goad. . . ."

[14] Without disparaging Tennyson's fine clear water-colors one may recall Keats's magical picture in oils —

> "Far, far around shall those dark-cluster'd trees
> Fledge the wild-ridged mountains steep by steep."

and begun to address the Duke of Argyll.[15] Tennyson is so obviously sticking an edifying patch into the middle of his golden tapestry that we feel we have been beguiled by a sensuous poem that turns into a tract. Many years later, in connection with *Demeter and Persephone*, Tennyson said that when he wrote an antique he must put it into a frame, with something modern about it: "It is no use giving a mere *réchauffé* of old legends." [16] The principle was sound, as the whole of this book endeavors to show, and Tennyson was generally, if not in *Oenone*, too fine an artist to let the preacher get out of bounds. But how magnificently the poem ends!

> I will not die alone,
> Lest their shrill happy laughter come to me
> Walking the cold and starless road of Death
> Uncomforted, leaving my ancient love
> With the Greek woman. . . .

Tennyson rises above the level of the rest of the poem because he remembers, in his own great way, Aeschylus and Virgil. The concluding allusion to Cassandra points to its obvious source, but I do not think it has been observed that the lines quoted recall the despair of the abandoned Dido:

> agit ipse furentem
> in somnis ferus Aeneas, semperque relinqui
> sola sibi, semper longam incomitata videtur
> ire viam et Tyrios deserta quaerere terra. . . .[17]

---

[15] See the poem *To the Duke of Argyll* (*Works*, p. 562). There is a mitigating anecdote, about Pallas' speech, in the *Memoir*, I, 317–18.

According to the common classical tradition Pallas offered victory in war, but from Fulgentius onward her gift was wisdom. See my other volume, p. 17.

[16] *Works*, p. 993; *Memoir*, II, 364.

[17] *Agamemnon*, l. 1256; *Aen*. iv. 465–68. The allusion to Cassandra and the fire that dances before her may be sufficiently explained by Aeschylus, but the tone of the lines, and the "I will not die alone," suggest Quintus Smyrnaeus, though it is uncertain how much firsthand knowledge Tennyson had, now or later, of that author. See his *Fall of Troy* (Loeb Classical Library), xii. 540 ff.; cf. Ovid's epistle of Paris, ll. 121 ff.

Apart from the usual and beautiful echoes of classical phrases,[18] *The Lotos-Eaters* has only the faintest relation to Homer or anything ancient. The several lines in the proem about the coming of the lotos-eaters, and the thoughts of Ithaca in the sixth stanza of the choric song (a section added in 1842), are all that can be called Homeric. The concluding description of the gods who enjoy eternal ease, indifferent to the lot of man, is of course Lucretian. Tennyson, as his manner was, pointed out to Aubrey de Vere "the improvement effected" by the introduction of this passage on the Epicurean gods,[19] but it is too elaborate for the occasion. In itself it is an improvement on the original ending of 1833, which was in the fanciful, romantic manner of *The Sea-Fairies* and *The Hesperides*, but with more defects and less magic. It is no doubt legitimate, if a poet's aim is the creation of a mood, to abandon any attempt at dramatic verisimilitude, but artifice and refinement go deeper here than in *Oenone*. These singers who sit down on the shore and melodiously interweave the most delicate observations of nature with the most delicate analysis of modern ennui, these are not a band of tough, hairy, brine-stained Greek mariners eager for food and drink, but an operatic chorus, or at any rate a chorus of college-bred poets.

Even if such refining of the Homeric episode is in itself permissible, the poetic attitude which engenders it may extend to the treatment of the central idea. *The Lotos-Eaters* is not an isolated moral holiday, its plea for selfish

[18] They are taken chiefly from the Greek pastoral poets, with a few from Homer and Virgil. See Mustard, pp. 7–8, 32, 36–37, 63, 103, 143. There are some "turns" and parallelisms of phrase on the Theocritean pattern. For the Homeric echoes, see *Odyssey*, i. 245, 325, ix. 82 ff., xi. 114. One may assume the general or particular influence of *The Faerie Queene* (II. vi and xii), and *The Castle of Indolence.*

[19] *Memoir*, I, 504. See *De Rerum Natura*, ii. 646, iii. 18, v. 82, vi. 58; and note 33 below.

irresponsibility, for escape from the claims of duty and effort, is related to Tennyson's frequent personal expressions of weariness and disillusionment. But, while this poem and *Ulysses* are utterances of the poet's "two voices," the one is major poetry and the other is not, and the reason is not, of course, the difference between heroic and unheroic moods, it is the difference between serious and non-serious treatment of a serious theme. Despair becomes decorative, and *The Lotos-Eaters* in its total effect is an incomparably pretty account of spiritual disintegration. Additions in the earlier part of the poem deepened its moral significance, and the new Lucretian conclusion, in Spedding's solemn words, was "of still more awful import," for it showed "the effect of lotos-eating upon the religious feelings." [20] And the poet who felt called to be a leader, to turn his back on the sterile languors of a palace of art, whose mind revolved continually around death and immortality, assuredly put personal emotion into such lines as "Two handfuls of white dust, shut in an urn of brass" and "eyes grown dim with gazing on the pilot-stars." Yet we remember these only as beautiful lines, along with the pictures of three silent pinnacles of aged snow, of the full-juiced apple, waxing over-mellow, that drops in a silent autumn night, of the dark-blue sky vaulted o'er the dark-blue sea, and a multitude of other beauties of verbal ornament.

Whatever reservations are made in regard to the Lydian airs of *Oenone* and *The Lotos-Eaters*, there can be nothing but praise for the Doric strength and nobility and seriousness of *Ulysses*. The death of Hallam was of course the great crisis, indeed the only crisis, of Tennyson's life. Out of his grief and philosophic bewilderment the poem was born, and it expounds no ready-made moral lesson; the

[20] *Edinburgh Review*, LXXVII (1843), 379; *Reviews and Discussions* (1879), p. 284.

forces of order and courage win a hard victory over the dark mood of chaos and defeat. In speaking of *In Memoriam*, Tennyson said: "There is more about myself in 'Ulysses,' which was written under the sense of loss and all that had gone by, but that still life must be fought out to the end. It was more written with the feeling of his loss upon me than many poems in 'In Memoriam.'" [21] Both in spirit and in many details the poem is quite un-Greek. Homer's Ulysses, though he did linger some time with Calypso and Circe, was an old, tired man, eager to reach home and settle down on his own hearth, and his feeling was that of a normal Greek. In Plato's vision of the day of judgment, we may remember, when the shades are choosing their lives for the era to come, Ulysses hunts about for the life of a private citizen, for he is weary of toils and troubles. The Greek world had no room for a mind and soul questing after the unknown, and Tennyson's conception, derived from Dante,[22] becomes a noble expression of his belief in "the need of going forward, and braving the struggle of life." [23]

In the process of modernization Ulysses naturally loses his notable guile, and is endowed with a nineteenth-century elegiac sensibility and magnanimous reflectiveness, a ca-

[21] Sir James Knowles, "Aspects of Tennyson," *Nineteenth Century*, XXXIII (1893), 182.

[22] *Inferno*, c. xxvi. In Dante, Ulysses sets out on his western voyage after escaping from Circe. In echoing the exhortation to his comrades which Dante puts in the mouth of Ulysses, Tennyson forgets or prefers to forget that his hero, who sets forth from Ithaca, had lost all his fellow mariners — not that it matters. Tennyson would at least partly share Keats's view of the poetic "authenticity" of Dante's version of the story; see above, ch. III, note 59.

For early accounts of Ulysses' later travels, see Otto Gruppe, *Griechische Mythologie und Religionsgeschichte* (Munich, 1906), I, 714 ff.; Jane Harrison, *Myths of the Odyssey* (1882), pp. 110 ff.; G. M. Sargeaunt, "The Eternal Wanderer," *Classical Studies* (1929), pp. 1–16. On Dante and Tennyson, see T. S. Eliot, *Selected Essays* (1932), pp. 234–36. See also *Odyssey*, xi. 119–37, xii. 206 ff.; Virgil, *Aen.* i. 198 ff.; Horace, *Ep.* I. ii. 17 ff.; Byron, *Childe Harold*, III. lxxii; Shakespeare, *Troilus and Cressida*, III. iii. 151–53.

[23] *Memoir*, I, 196.

pacity for not only seeking experience but interpreting it. If in a few lines philosophizing threatens to become a little top-heavy for the vehicle, there are corrective elements throughout the poem. There is the stately but masculine and sinewy blank verse — even in grief Tennyson does not forget his vowels — and there is the incomparable phrasing, rich with the special beauty of classical associations and overtones. Epic echoes from the ringing plains of windy Troy give the modern-minded Ulysses a substantial and traditional setting, and in our ears is the sound of waves, for Tennyson, who can be so satiny, so weak and tame, is nevertheless the greatest English poet of the sea. The word "Doric" that I used above must be qualified, since Tennyson is much more "poetical" than either Homer or Dante; his simplicity is a finely wrought, a Tennysonian and Virgilian simplicity. The mood of heroic fortitude and resolution, however, does not melt into over-refinement or mere decoration.

Ulysses affords a capital example of a fact which many later poems enable us to verify. When Tennyson treats much the same subject in an ancient and in a modern setting he is almost invariably superior, greatly superior, in the former. The antique fable taps that authentic vein of his poetic inspiration, his classical memories; it limits the range of thought and allusion, forbids anything in the nature of modern realism, and compels concentration on the universal and more or less symbolic aspects of the theme. *The Two Voices* grew out of the same spiritual distress as *Ulysses*, it grapples directly with the modern problem, and, as a whole, it is a serious and moving poem; but the one hero's courage and hope are roused by thoughts of Troy and the Happy Isles and "the great Achilles, whom we knew," the other's by the sight of a father, mother, and little maiden pure, pacing churchward on Sunday morning! And in *Locksley Hall* the unpleasant and declamatory modern hero salves a wounded heart with hopes of scientific progress. Thus in modern treatments of the modern soul or the condition of England, Tennyson is likely to utter a journalistic bark or a clerical bleat. In *Ulysses* the assertion of positive faith and hope is neither bathetic nor strident; Penelope does not wear the rose of womanhood, and the hero is not touched by parochial piety or by thoughts of science (though science may be included in the symbolism of the voyage). In antique garb Tennyson becomes another man.

Tithonus was printed in 1860 but had been "written upwards of a quarter of a century" earlier. The main source was the brief episode in the Homeric *Hymn to Aphrodite*, where romance, tragedy, and comedy are blended; Tithonus grows senile and repulsive, and the vigorous young wife, with the realistic matter-of-factness of the early world, shuts him up as one might bottle an insect. Tennyson has a more exalted conception. *Tithonus* is perhaps the most Virgilian of all his poems, unless *Tears, Idle Tears* challenge first place — *To Virgil* of course is *sui generis* — not because of particular echoes, but because it is the purest emanation of that part of Tennyson, the most truly poetic part, which was akin to Virgil:

> Release me, and restore me to the ground;
> Thou seëst all things, thou wilt see my grave:
> Thou wilt renew thy beauty morn by morn;
> I earth in earth forget these empty courts,
> And thee returning on thy silver wheels.

The stately phrase and rhythm, the opulent but not profuse decoration, the conscious art that governs the curve of the whole poem and weighs every syllable, all this is Virgilian. Even the simplicity is a contrived simplicity: "Man comes and tills the field and lies beneath. . . ." [24]

²⁴ Such a line is less in the vein of Wordsworth than in that of Keats's "Of peaceful sway above man's harvesting" (*Hyperion*, i. 110). Keats's great influ-

Classical images, after passing through Tennyson's mind, emerge with a slower, more deliberate, more sophisticated beauty; one might compare his horses of the dawn, which "beat the twilight into flakes of fire," with their probable original in Catullus.[25]

But style and substance cannot in *Tithonus* be separated, as, to the detriment of each, they often can be in Tennyson. Here the verse, in diction and movement, is the perfect statement of the idea, and the result is a tone poem in gray and silver. The mythological situation is not of course a literally possible human experience (though the suitor of Emily Sellwood might in time have felt otherwise), and the poem is less obviously personal than *Ulysses*. But it was written in the period of *Ulysses*, *Morte d'Arthur*, and *Break, Break, Break*, and it expressed a very personal longing for release from the burden of life. Tennyson's own emotion is essential to the moving power of his realization of the timeless contrasts of youth and age and love and death. And the pathos inherent in the simple cycle of human life is felt and rendered not only with Virgilian dignity and beauty, but with Virgilian pity and tenderness.

---

ence on Tennyson was more stylistic than spiritual, and one must allow for some congenital similarity of taste. Reviewers after 1830 frequently linked them together; in addition to Hallam, Lockhart, and Wilson, we may remember Bulwer's line, "Out-babying Wordsworth and out-glittering Keats" (and see above, note 5). In conversation in later years Tennyson constantly put Keats on a pedestal, for example: "Keats, with his high spiritual vision, would have been, if he had lived, the greatest of us all (tho' his blank verse lacked originality in movement) . . . there is something magic and of the innermost soul of poetry in almost everything which he wrote" (*Memoir*, I, 152; see *ibid.*, I, 210, II, 70, 202, 286–87, 386, 421, 504). Tennyson's deafness to Keats's blank verse seems curious and perverse, for his own is far closer to Keats than to Milton.

[25] *Attis* (lxiii. 39–41):

> "sed ubi oris aurei Sol radiantibus oculis
> lustravit aethera album, sola dura, mare ferum,
> pepulitque noctis umbras vegetis sonipedibus. . . ."

Compare also some lines in the juvenile *Coach of Death* (*Unpublished Early Poems*, p. 22).

III

Lucretius (1868) may be considered from two points of view, that of classical scholars and that of critics of English poetry. It is, all scholars have agreed, a masterly condensation of, and commentary on, one of the world's greatest philosophical poems, and it is an intensely vivid portrait of the man its author may have been.[26] There is no need, and no space, to show here the astonishingly close Lucretian texture of Tennyson's lines, or the accuracy and imaginative spaciousness of his rendering of Lucretian ideas. He was evidently as steeped in Lucretius as Aristophanes was in Euripides, though the modern poet's fear of modernism did not include humor among its weapons. As a piece of English poetry, however, *Lucretius* has been both vehemently praised and vehemently damned. To mention only recent opinions, I prefer the critical eulogy of Mr. Lascelles Abercrombie, who is a poet, to the uncritical condemnation of Mr. Harold Nicolson, who is not;[27] and I should like to quote Mr. Abercrombie because his essay, read after this chapter was done, seemed to support one of its main (and of course not novel) theses. In showing that Tennyson lacks "structural inspiration," that in the main he gives us, not poems, but a "continual succession of splendid moments," the critic excepts *Maud* and *Lucretius*:

Both of these are splendid pieces of great imaginative structure, and in both the structure is given, not indeed by the intellectual life, but by the passion of a consistently objectified character. And in both we have those unique moments of sense, thought, and feeling all compounded together which are Tennyson's

---

[26] In addition to Mustard, see the bibliography to this chapter for discussions by Sir Richard Jebb, Churton Collins, Katharine Allen, Ortha Wilner, and others.

[27] Nicolson, *Tennyson* (1923), p. 14; *Revaluations*, by Lascelles Abercrombie, Lord David Cecil, *et al.* (Oxford University Press, 1931), pp. 68, 72.

peculiar property; and these enchant us not merely in themselves, but in the pregnant imaginative purpose with which they are charged.

Lucretius is of course very different from Tennyson's other poems of antique inspiration. The subject is "historical" and not mythological, it is Roman and not Greek. The poem lacks the classical poise of *Ulysses*, for the writer, like his hero — and not quite like the real Lucretius at the time he composed the *De Rerum Natura* — seems to be still engulfed in the swirling currents of immediate experience. As a mental thunderstorm with lurid flashes of lightning, *Lucretius* out-Brownings Browning. How much of the feverish intensity of Tennyson's manner is to be attributed to his conception of the subject, and how much to "spasmodic" and Swinburnian fashions in verse,[28] one cannot be sure. At any rate the poem is a very powerful picture of a noble Roman patriot who feels himself breaking along with the old republic; a Roman conscience which in its torments is more Hebraic and puritan than Greek; a Roman intellect which has sought with passionate honesty for the truth that delivers from evil and fear; a prophet and preacher of serenity whose creed has failed him; a poet and philosopher whose joy in nature has turned to ashes.[29]

Lucretius springs directly out of Victorian religious and ethical problems, and reminds us of numerous other poems, such as Arnold's *Empedocles*, and many of Tennyson's own. *In Memoriam* is full of similar questionings, though Hallam

[28] *Maud*, says Mr. Nicolson, had signalized Tennyson's consciousness of the spasmodics, and in *Lucretius* he thinks the poet had decided to mix a little Swinburnian wine with the limpid waters of Camelot (*Tennyson*, pp. 207, 230). But the Swinburnian element is confined to the two weakest passages in the poem, that is, the two which attempt to be boldest, the lines about the breasts of Helen and the naked Oread, and these might be justified in motive if not in manner by the last part of Lucretius' fourth book; see also i. 133 ff., iv. 33 ff.

[29] The Lucretius who only with the knife can woo the "Passionless bride, divine Tranquillity," carries us back to Tennyson's juvenile play *The Devil and the Lady*, where he had written of "Boyhood's passionless Tranquillity" (p. 65).

had "faced the spectres of the mind" and laid them, and had come at length "To find a stronger faith his own."[30] In 1866 Tennyson declared that he would commit suicide if he thought there was no future life,[31] and he treated that theme, in a modern setting, in *Despair* (1881), a poem which has not, I think, provoked any contradictory critical estimates. Further, if God and immortality are delusions, there is no armor against the lusts of the flesh. Tennyson's Lucretius had believed himself secure, but an abhorrent unseen monster laid "vast and filthy hands" upon his will. "Divine Philosophy" has pushed beyond her mark and become "Procuress to the Lords of Hell"; Lucretius (because of the love-philter, of course) has not fled "The reeling Faun, the sensual feast." [32] With these phrases from *In Memoriam* one might link the crude moralizing of *By an Evolutionist*, or that unfortunate drama *The Promise of May*, which gave the impression that Tennyson believed immorality the inevitable consequence of religious skepticism. I mention these various poems only to illustrate again the immense advantages, both positive and negative, which Tennyson derived from confining himself within a classical frame.

Such poems also help to make clear the modern implications of *Lucretius*, in which the nature of the treatment forbids any Christian answer to the despair of the materialist. To say that the modern moral does not come home to us, that the reading of *Lucretius* never settled a doubt, is not of course a damaging statement, though the poem would lack most of its force if Tennyson had not been dealing with what was to him and his age a living issue. He

[30] *In Memoriam*, xcvi.

[31] *Memoir*, II, 35. The dramatic use of storm and calm in *Lucretius* reminds one of Palgrave's account of the overwhelming effect of the reading of the *De Rerum Natura* late one night at Tennyson's house (*ibid.*, II, 500). Cf. Lucretius, i. 271 ff., vi. 281 ff.

[32] *In Memoriam*, liii, cxviii.

started from the Victorian predicament, but he surrendered himself with such imaginative passion to the presentation of Lucretius that the result was a great poem and not a harangue. Unlike *The Lotos-Eaters*, it is not a mosaic of beautiful lines but a whole, a serious and impressive picture of spiritual disintegration. And once more Tennyson reproduces that favorite vision of his, of the Homeric and Lucretian gods in their "sacred everlasting calm"; [33] here it is not so much a symbol of divine indifference to the world as of a divine lotos-land where all human doubts and fears are at rest.

Tiresias was published in 1885, though it had been written "many a year ago." [34] The main theme, the self-sacrifice of young Menoeceus, at the instigation of the aged prophet, for the saving of Thebes, is taken from the *Phoenissae* of Euripides. [35] The incident of Tiresias' surprising of Pallas was suggested by the fifth *Hymn* of Callimachus; and the last lines are based on Pindar. [36] *Tiresias* has perhaps received less than its due from critics of Tennyson, but it is obviously inferior to his best classical

[33] *Odyssey*, iv. 566, vi. 43; *De Rerum Natura*, iii. 18. When Rawnsley said of the passage, "Of course that is Homer," Tennyson replied, with that strange scientific naïveté of his, "Yes, but I improved on Homer, because I knew that snow crystallises in stars." See W. F. Rawnsley, "Personal Recollections of Tennyson," *Nineteenth Century*, XCVII (1925), 7.

[34] Tennyson's son says that it was "partly written at the same time as *Ulysses*" (*Works*, p. 974). A reviewer in *The Athenaeum* (December 26, 1885) said, on I know not what authority: "One-half of 'Tiresias' is new; the other half was written, we believe, just fifty years ago."

[35] Ll. 911 ff. From the same play are derived a number of details, such as the lines about Cadmus, the dragon, and the sphinx. The passage about the attack on the city seems to include items from Euripides, Aeschylus' *Seven Against Thebes*, and Virgil (*Georg.* i. 44, 65, *Aen.* vi. 591, viii. 596); for Virgil, see Mustard, pp. 96–97. Cf. Statius, *Thebaid*, x. 609 ff. At Somersby Tennyson "had written in Greek hexameters an Homeric book on the Seven against Thebes" (*Memoir*, I, 40, note).

[36] Callimachus, v. 70 ff. Line 72 had already been utilized in *Oenone*: "For now the noonday quiet holds the hill." For Pindar's threnody, see Sir John Sandys' volume (Loeb Classical Library), pp. 588–91; and Mustard, pp. 27–28.

poems in conception and, except in two or three passages, in details of execution. Possibly because of some loss in ourselves, the simple story of a golden deed may appear a less maturely human and universal theme than the unfaltering quest of truth or the longing for death. But, however sedentary we may be, we never cease to be stirred by the famous distich of Simonides or the funeral speech of Pericles.[37] The voluntary martyrdom of Menoeceus ought to have, in its degree, something of the moving power of *Samson Agonistes*, and it does not. One reason is that Tennyson seems to have looked about for a subject instead of being caught and possessed by an inspiration. For instance, the picture of Pallas emerging from her bath is fine enough in itself, and an allusion to the prophet's fatal glimpse of the naked goddess would not be irrelevant, but can we believe in the reality of a siege and heroic patriotism when Tiresias, with the enemy at the gates, indulges in such a studied description? Doubtless the author, feeling some bareness in a subject cut off from landscape painting, could not resist a bit of decoration, yet this and other unrealistic details imply that he has not made a complete surrender to his theme, and we do not surrender either.

The poem is not, however, without serious personal feeling. It is Tennyson who has yearned

> to scale the highest of the heights
> With some strange hope to see the nearer God.

("My most passionate desire," he said once, "is to have a clearer and fuller vision of God."[38]) It is Tennyson who would be a seer and a sage, who, in spite of his strain of jingoism, has been dismayed by the horrors of war, who has believed that the tyranny of one is prelude to the

[37] Tennyson may have been thinking of that speech when he wrote the noble lines beginning "No sound is breathed so potent to coerce. . . ."

[38] *Memoir*, I, 319–20.

tyranny of all, and that the tyranny of all leads backward to the tyranny of one. This last sentiment may sound obtrusively Victorian, but it is Hellenic enough; it is in fact thoroughly Platonic.[39] The trouble is that it does not grow naturally out of the theme and context. Finally, to quote the lines which their author justly regarded as a specimen of his best blank verse, it is Tennyson who prays:

> But for me,
> I would that I were gather'd to my rest,
> And mingled with the famous kings of old,
> On whom about their ocean-islets flash
> The faces of the Gods — the wise man's word,
> Here trampled by the populace underfoot,
> There crown'd with worship — and these eyes will find
> The men I knew, and watch the chariot whirl
> About the goal again, and hunters race
> The shadowy lion, and the warrior-kings,
> In height and prowess more than human, strive
> Again for glory, while the golden lyre
> Is ever sounding in heroic ears
> Heroic hymns, and every way the vales
> Wind, clouded with the grateful incense-fume
> Of those who mix all odour to the Gods
> On one far height in one far-shining fire.

Whatever the date of these beautiful lines, they are the utterance of a tired and disillusioned man, who had felt, for all his preaching of "the need of the Ideal," as if his life "had been a very useless life." [40]

To me often the far-off world seems nearer than the present, for in the present is always something unreal and indistinct, but the other seems a good solid planet, rolling round its green hills and paradises to the harmony of more steadfast laws. There steam up from about me mists of weakness, or sin, or despondency, and roll between me and the far planet, but it is there still.[41]

---

[39] See the *Republic*, 562–64.
[40] *Memoir*, II, 337.
[41] *Memoir*, I, 171–72 (and cf. I, 168). Tennyson considered the Norse my-

When Tennyson writes in Christian terms of some far-off
divine event, or in journalistic terms of a scientific future,
he is seldom a poet and not a very satisfactory preacher,
but when his longing for a quiet abode above the tumult
is translated into a picture of the life of the gods or of an
heroic elysium, how splendid a poet he can be! Such writing may be damned as poetry of escape, and perhaps it is.
At any rate the most influential poet and critic of our own
time, in making Tiresias an all-embracing modern consciousness, reveals a not altogether dissimilar nostalgia.
Mr. Eliot does not, like Tennyson, find alleviation or subli-
mation of his pain in weaving sumptuous Pindaric embroidery, but both modern and Victorian, oppressed by
an ignoble and sordid present, embody in the Theban
prophet a desire for an unattainable ideal, a remembered
or imagined vision.[42]

It was the aging Tennyson who felt with increasing
keenness the need of such support, and his last great utterance in that vein was *Demeter and Persephone*, which
appeared when the poet was eighty. It is as a whole, if not
in particular beauties, a finer poem than the *Oenone* of half
a century before. Tennyson had for the most part ceased
to labor under messianic responsibility. Whether he spoke
or kept silent, the world was going on its way, to ill, or, he
might still hope, to good. Not only his brother and his son,
but friend after friend, had followed one another from sunshine to the sunless land, and he whose mind had seldom
been free from thoughts of death and immortality was
himself approaching the end. Demeter's is not, as Mr.
F. L. Lucas says of Oenone's, a painted grief upon a

---

thology less beautiful than the Greek, but finer, and his reason was characteristic: "The Norsemen thought that there was something better in the way of
religion that would dawn upon the earth after the Ragnarok or twilight of the
gods" (*ibid.*, I, 256, note).

[42] Tiresias is a Protean character. In Mr. MacLeish's *1933* he appears as
Karl Marx; see his *Poems, 1924–1933* (Boston and New York, 1933), pp. 186 ff.

painted mountain; [43] a poet with a full life behind him is too much concerned with human experience to find solace in beautiful landscapes. Here myth is the vehicle for a truly and purely poetic questioning of the mysteries of love and life and earth and human destiny.

The Homeric *Hymn to Aphrodite* had supplied the bald story of Tithonus, in a manner antipathetic to Tennyson. The *Hymn to Demeter*, his main source for this poem, offered much more substance and also was written with a warm human sympathy that was entirely congenial. Tennyson utilized the general background of the underworld and its lord and the flowery vale of Enna, the mother's long search for her child and their happy meeting, the withering of harvests, and, after the reunion, the renewal of life throughout the earth. Many finely imaginative and emotional details were added, and classical reminiscences were interwoven with the accustomed grace; [44] Tennyson, as one would expect, was content to accept the myth in its traditional form, without emulating the bold inventiveness of Meredith's version of six years earlier. If one takes *Demeter and Persephone* simply as a mythological poem, one need not invoke *The May Queen* as a reminder of the difference between a modern and a classical treatment of the love of mother and daughter. There is no taint of sen-

[43] *Eight Victorian Poets* (Cambridge University Press, 1930), p. 16.

[44] Some items suggest that Tennyson had run through the poem he had partly translated in boyhood, Claudian's *De Raptu Proserpinae*. Neither the Homeric *Hymn* nor Ovid (except in *Metam.* v. 532, 534) makes use of the Fates, but they have a part in Claudian, though in a different connection (i. 48 ff., ii. 354; see *Unpublished Early Poems*, p. 3). Cf. Virgil, *Ecl.* iv. 46.

In the *Hymn* it is Helios who tells Demeter that Pluto carried off Persephone; in Ovid (*Metam.* v. 487 ff.) it is Arethusa (the Sun, in *Fasti*, iv. 583); in Apollodorus it is the people of Hermion (*Library*, ed. Frazer, I. v. 1); in Tennyson it is a dream or phantasm of Persephone herself, and the simile in the lines "Last, as the likeness of a dying man" is probably a reminiscence of the Lucretian theory of vision (*De Rerum Natura*, iv. 37). But the whole passage may have been suggested by Claudian's account (iii. 80 ff.) of the daughter's appearing in a dream to her mother. See also note 47 below.

timentality in the Demeter who feels "the deathless heart of motherhood" shudder within her. The very remoteness of the theme from the everyday world prevents any lapses into trivial middle-class domesticities, and, in a positive way, contributes a primitive greatness of maternal passion which is worthy of the earth-mother.

The poem is full of Tennyson's mellow Virgilian sense of the rhythm of the seasons and the life of man, but the "frame" which he thought essential to a treatment of myth contains something more distinctively, though not obtrusively, modern. If Browning had handled the myth, he would probably have argued from Demeter's love to God's greater love for man, from the imperfection of earth to the perfection of heaven. Over Tennyson's less buoyant optimism lies the shadow of the hard eternities, of the Fates who spin the lives of men and know not why they spin, and his hope of a better day is conceived throughout in mythological terms. Echoing Aeschylus,[45] and probably *Hyperion*, Demeter looks forward to an era of "younger kindlier Gods." Tennyson's faith in progress does not here rest on the advance of science, there is nothing of the modernism which is so quickly dated. The gods will grow beneficent, "and all the Shadow die into the Light";[46] the queen of death shall send her life along with her mother's "from buried grain thro' springing blade." No longer feared, they shall reap

> The worship which is Love, and see no more
> The Stone, the Wheel, the dimly-glimmering lawns
> Of that Elysium, all the hateful fires
> Of torment, and the shadowy warrior glide
> Along the silent field of Asphodel.[47]

---

[45] *Eumenides*, ll. 778, 808.
[46] Cf. Claudian (ii. 330–31):

> "Erebi se sponte relaxat
> squalor et aeternam patitur rarescere noctem."

[47] While the picture of sufferers in Hades is an ancient and modern common-

This picture of a happier world, it may be said, is only our old friend, the "one far-off divine event," in mythological dress, and it may be called a sentimental alleviation or evasion of life, but one must have an austere critical intelligence to be untouched by such beauty.

The Death of Oenone, the last of Tennyson's classical narratives, was published in 1892; he read the proofs just before he died. It is the one classical poem that has been unanimously abused, even by critics who ordinarily move on the level of adulation. One may or may not like the poem, though it is a remarkable achievement for a poet who really was a grand old man, but dislike is not an excuse for ignorant misrepresentation. Mr. Harold Nicolson, though aware of some two hundred and fifty books on the poet, including Andrew Lang's, does not seem to have consulted the relevant portions of Lang or Mustard, much less Tennyson's avowed source, Quintus Smyrnaeus. He is content to build a humorous edifice of his own around Stopford Brooke's uninformed remarks about "the husband and wife and widow business" in this poem and the poet's general obsession with domesticity.[48] Tennyson's notions of love do revolve too much around the ring and the cradle, but there is enough evidence against him without fabricating any. In regard to this poem he is an innocent victim of his own bad name. The upholders of a marital bond between Paris and Oenone were Ovid and Quintus Smyrnaeus; the latter has about twice as many

place, the whole passage in Claudian from which I quoted in the preceding note tells of the rejoicing in the underworld and the intermission of punishments; Ixion, Tantalus, Tityus, are at peace. Tennyson's conclusion may be a spiritualized condensation of Claudian. The last line and a half come from the *Odyssey*, xi. 538–39.

[48] Nicolson, *Tennyson*, pp. 201, 248; Stopford Brooke, *Tennyson* (1895), pp. 140–41. It is needless to mention other opinions of the same kind. Of course classical scholars such as Andrew Lang (*Alfred Tennyson*, 1901, p. 207), and Mustard (*Classical Echoes*, pp. 45–51), were not among the critics who repeated one another.

allusions as Tennyson to "wife" and "husband." [49] Marriage, it would appear, was not a purely Victorian or Tennysonian invention. Further, the whole situation in Quintus Smyrnaeus is more domestic than it is in Tennyson. It is the modern poet who places Oenone in her old cave on the hillside, and all the action occurs on the hill and in the valley. In the Greek poem Paris comes to the house where Oenone is living with her father and servants and is turned away from her door; she lies down on her former husband's bed; and at night she leaves her house secretly to go down to the pyre. [50]

Certainly *The Death of Oenone* has "more of the pure Greek simplicity" [51] than the warm, luxuriant pastoral of sixty years before, and its lack of a modern frame (apart from that supplied by the critics) suggests that the tireless experimenter was attempting something Landorian, or that the poet wished to write but had nothing to say. His unwonted objective severity is the result of coldness rather than restrained fire. The poem is inferior to its Greek original, it is inferior to all Tennyson's other antique pieces, partly because of the too conscious art — even the dying Paris weighs his syllables — but mainly because this

---

[49] *The Fall of Troy* (Loeb Classical Library), x. 265, 284, 286, 290, etc. Ovid uses *coniunx, marito, nubere, uxor* (*Heroides*, v. 1, 9, 12, 80, 108, 133). Apollodorus also says that Paris married Oenone (*Lib.* III. xii. 6).

[50] Tennyson's poem is about half as long as the episode in Quintus Smyrnaeus. He omits the details of battle, the talk of Hera with her attendants in heaven, the lamentations of Hecuba and Helen, and the classical tirade delivered by Oenone is reduced to two lines. Tennyson adds Oenone's dream of Paris that sends her down to their last meeting, her questions about the body on the pyre, and her cry of "Husband!" as she leaps into the flames. This last is a dubious alteration, not because of the domestic taint but because it is too obvious; in the Greek poem she acts in silence and we infer what she feels.

Tennyson's "Somewhat lazily handled" is less than just to Quintus Smyrnaeus. Against Jebb's "an exceedingly feeble and frigid writer" (quoted in *Works*, p. 1001) may be set the praise of Andrew Lang (see note 48 above) and of a greater critic, Sainte-Beuve (*Étude sur Virgile*, Paris, 1870, p. 426; quoted by Mustard, p. 45). [51] *Memoir*, II, 509. Cf. II, 386.

is the only one of the long series of classical poems which is not modernized and animated by personal emotion. It is related in theme and tone to such poems of 1889 as *Romney's Remorse, The Ring,* and others, and, while none of these has a line like "Thin as the batlike shrillings of the Dead," [52] for once it is impossible to say that the antique poem is on an immeasurably higher level than the modern ones. So the rule which has been observed throughout this sketch of Tennyson's classical poems is confirmed even by this one apparent exception. He had forgotten that "it is no use giving a mere *réchauffé* of old legends."

IV

Classical influence in Tennyson is not, of course, limited to the poems on classical subjects; it may appear anywhere in the great body of non-classical verse, more often in image and diction than in mythological allusion. (To mention one famous allusion, "Now lies the Earth all Danaë to the stars" seems to me, in spite of all the praise that has gathered round it, little better than a forced conceit.[53]) No poet since Milton has equaled Tennyson in the weaving of classical reminiscences into the texture of his own style, but that large province of his art needs no praise here. We must, however, take the briefest of glances at his relation to a few of his favorite poets. We have observed already the Theocritean richness and sweetness of such classical idylls as *Oenone* and *The Lotos-Eaters,* and shall not concern ourselves with the English idylls. The Theocritean analogues have frequently been pointed out,[54] and I am

---

[52] See the *Odyssey,* xxiv. 6 ff.

[53] *Works,* p. 208.

[54] E. C. Stedman, *Victorian Poets* (ed. 1894), pp. 217 ff.; Mustard, pp. 31 ff.; Robert T. Kerlin, *Theocritus in English Literature* (Lynchburg, Va., 1910), pp. 113 ff.; J. W. Mackail, *Lectures on Greek Poetry* (1911), pp. 220 ff.

disposed to let the matter rest, since, apart from occasional
lines, these English idylls are for us what sham-philosophi-
cal novels (and Ben Jonson) were for Tennyson, "like wad-
ing through glue." [55] The robust charm of ancient Sicily
may be over-refined in the classical idylls, but at least it is
not translated, to invoke the genial aid of Calverley, into
"the Hall" and Syllabub Farm and my aunt Vivian who
dines at half-past six.

Over-refinement, Tennyson's besetting sin, is less conspicuous in the classical poems than elsewhere; as E. K.
said of Spenser, "hauing the sound of those auncient
Poetes still ringing in his eares, he mought needes in singing hit out some of theyr tunes." But some degree of refinement is a prime essential of Tennyson's art, and the
process is illustrated in his handling of Homer. His devotion to Homer extended from the time when as a boy he lay
on the shore at Mablethorpe, fighting the Trojan war in
imagination, to the more troubled time when the evergreen
laurel was threatened by the "terrible Muses" of Astron-
omy and Geology.[56] The adaptations of Homer scattered
through Tennyson are often beautiful and seldom Homeric
in spirit or style; we have had notable examples already,
from *Ilion, Ilion* to *The Lotos-Eaters* and *Ulysses*. Here it
will be enough to mention the translations of Homer. To
call them Virgilian might be to overwork the word, yet
there is no briefer way of indicating the difference between
the forthright ease and spontaneity of Homer (not that
Homer was a primitive artist), and the slower movement,
the more involved and sophisticated language and syntax,
of Tennyson. Reacting, doubtless with Arnold in mind,
against lame hexameters as a medium for "the strong-
wing'd music of Homer," Tennyson made two fine experiments in blank verse. They are *tours de force*, for the author is trying not to be Tennyson, is trying to gain speed

---

[55] *Memoir*, II, 73, 372.   [56] *Works*, pp. xvi, 810.

and simplicity, yet the earlier one at least is pure Tennyson:

> As when in heaven the stars about the moon
> Look beautiful, when all the winds are laid,
> And every height comes out, and jutting peak
> And valley, and the immeasurable heavens
> Break open to their highest. . . .

We may agree that this is incomparable[57] without agreeing that it is Homeric. Homer can change, none more easily, from plainness to gorgeous radiance, but it is a different kind of gorgeousness.

In spite of his fondness for Greek poetry and Greek subjects, Tennyson had very little of the classical Greek about him. As a man and an Englishman he was much more of a Roman; as a craftsman also he was Roman, and, like most of the Roman poets, Hellenistic. His tributes to Catullus and Virgil are very different from *Lucretius*. *Frater Ave atque Vale* does not merely evoke the elegiac spirit of the tenderest of Roman poets; through the enchanting verbal melody is felt the throb of personal grief, for Tennyson had lately lost his own brother, his favorite. The poem is more moving than most of the lyrics of *In Memoriam*, since the author is content to remember, and to feel, and not to speculate about modern problems. The other poem, *To Virgil*, is, one need not say, the briefest and finest appreciation of Virgil ever written, and it is, indirectly, the best possible testimony to the nature of Tennyson's Virgilian inspiration. He also is a landscape-lover, a lord of language, he is, at moments, majestic in his sadness at the doubtful doom of human kind, and for him hope gleams like a golden branch amid the shadows.

Tennyson was not like Homer, we may guess, nor like Lucretius, nor was he quite like Theocritus, but apparently

---

[57] Arthur Sidgwick, in *Tennyson and His Friends*, ed. Hallam, Lord Tennyson (1912), pp. 327–28.

he was very much like Virgil. They both were and remained, even in the sunshine of court favor, shy provincial lads, and they never lost the truest kind of patriotic feeling, attachment to the *dulcia arva*. (The thought of Lincolnshire recalls the earthy anecdotes attributed to the decorous Laureate, and also the Priapean pieces which lovers of decorum refuse to accept as Virgil's.) They both revered an heroic national past and believed in the state, in order, in the old ways of piety, duty, and discipline. Both were uncommonly sensitive to the life and color of field and sky and sea, and recorded all the phenomena of nature in exquisitely finished pictures; and in nature and human life they saw the workings of Universal Mind. Both Virgil and Tennyson had absorbed a rich literary culture, and were the most scholarly and ornate stylists of their age. It must have been with a special feeling of august sanction for his own methods that Tennyson recalled

> Old Virgil who would write ten lines, they say,
> At dawn, and lavish all the golden day
> To make them wealthier in his readers' eyes.

Their best work is essentially elegiac, the product of a temperamental melancholy, a brooding, wistful sense of the past, an unappeasable *desiderium* which is deepened by troubled questionings about the present and the future. Tennyson has less than Virgil of universal pity, but he has a not altogether dissimilar note, a cry of profound sadness and bewilderment.[58] Such parallels might be prolonged, and of course they need to be qualified, but the point is that Tennyson, though not a world poet, is in so many ways akin to Virgil that one cannot, in some of his best writing, mark where Virgilian inspiration leaves off and Tennyson begins.

[58] See Mr. Eliot's comment on Tennyson and Virgil (*Essays Ancient and Modern*, 1936, p. 189).

We have no space for Tennyson's actual imitations of Virgil, which, like Virgil's echoes of his models, are fine re-creations, and it would need an ear as subtle as Tennyson's own to determine what he learned from the stateliest measure ever molded by the lips of man. But there is *Tithonus*, there is *Demeter and Persephone*, there is *Tears, Idle Tears*. One may call this lyric a series of inspired variations on Virgil's most familiar and untranslatable line,[59] but it comes from the center of Tennyson's own soul. Here he touches with untrammeled fingers one of the universal chords of poetry, and perhaps the most authentic note in his own poetic register, the passion of the past. Feelings that were strongest in his youth are remembered and expressed with the finality of a mature artist in one of those precious moments when he has forgotten science and God and edification. It is at such moments that he writes as Virgil would have written.[60]

---

[59] *Aen.* i. 462; also iv. 449, x. 465, and *Georg.* iv. 375. Mr. Mackail describes the lyric as "completely in the Theocritean manner," and related particularly to the twelfth idyll (*Lectures on Greek Poetry*, p. 222).

Tennyson's line, "The casement slowly grows a glimmering square," recalls Leigh Hunt's *Hero and Leander* (ll. 284–85):

"And when the casement, at the dawn of light,
Began to show a square of ghastly white. . . ."

I was quite confident that Tennyson was improving on Hunt until I found that the parallel had been observed by Churton Collins (*Illustrations of Tennyson*, 1891, pp. 83–84).

[60] For Tennyson's "passion of the past, the abiding in the transient," see the *Memoir*, I, 253, II, 73, 288, 319.

The only time FitzGerald ever witnessed tears in Tennyson's eyes was during the reading of Virgil (*Euphranor*, in *Letters and Literary Remains of Edward FitzGerald*, ed. W. A. Wright [1889], II, 53).

CHAPTER VII

Landor and Arnold

I. WALTER SAVAGE LANDOR

THE contrast between two such classicists as Landor and Arnold may, I hope, justify postponing discussion of the former beyond his proper time. There is indeed no great violence done to chronology, since the bulk of Arnold's poetry belongs to 1849–53, and Landor's first volume of *Hellenics* appeared in 1847. Besides, Landor's work is mostly of the kind that does not date. It may be more candid than tactful to say at the beginning that I am not one of that company, "few and select," who were to dine late in Landor's well-lighted dining-room. Probably no one should write about him except those who, like most of his critics, feel entitled to a couch in that august triclinium, and I must admit that I am only, like the Marchioness, squinting through the keyhole at the austere solitary within. But I have read Landor for a good many years, with abundant appreciation of the unsubduable old Roman's personality and of some aspects of his art, and I can do no more than set down the result.

"Poetry was always my amusement, prose my study and business," said Landor, at the beginning of that proud boast about dining late [1] — it is evidence of the man's stature that such boasts may provoke disagreement, but seldom a smile — and we must, however briefly, take some account of his great mass of prose. Its essential qualities

[1] *Complete Works of Walter Savage Landor*, ed. T. Earle Welby (1927 *et seq.*), VI, 37.

are the essential qualities of the verse also, and what is said of the one kind is largely true of the other. Most essays on Landor resolve themselves into inquiries about the general neglect of a monumental author, and the fault appears to be more ours than his; we cannot breathe at his altitude, our taste for the garish and the emphatic does not respond to classical and un-English virtues of architectonic form, definite line, and severe restraint. There is truth in that, for in England the way of the disciplined artist has never been easy. But, with full recognition of some great and rare excellences in Landor's prose, and without ringing the changes on "statuesque," "chiseled," and "marmoreal," one may venture to note some other characteristics which help to explain, and perhaps partly justify, the traditional neglect.

Certainly when we think of countless passages which deserve the stock adjectives, of the white light which bathes every corner of Landor's lofty porticoes and colonnades and well-kept gardens, we may exclaim that here as nowhere else in English is classical prose in the grand style. Then we may think of the best ancient prose, or of the plain force and fire of Swift, the urbane ease and flexibility of Dryden or Chesterfield, and we ask if Landor's prose is in the best tradition, if it is really classical, or if its classicism is akin to that of the statues in Westminster Abbey. At any rate, with its variations between the hard and the soft, the condensed and the diffuse, Landor's style seems to be not so much Attic as a mixture of the Laconic and the Asiatic. It is obviously highly mannered prose. When Landor ceases to be regal he frequently becomes deplorable. He irritates us by constantly wrapping a plain idea in an elaborate and studied metaphor. His English is not seldom puffed out with Johnsonese; in the midst of that moving dialogue "Tiberius and Vipsania," we are suddenly chilled when we read, in an allusion to the sun, of sailors drawing their shaggy hair across their eyes "to mitigate its effulgence." And though at times we feel the freshness of English or Italian air, probably no eminent writer of the century except Pater smells so continually of the lamp, is so lacking in naturalness and spontaneity. Nor is that greatly to be wondered at, for, while in one sense it is usually Landor who speaks through his interlocutors, in another sense the real, the whole Landor seldom speaks at all; he has subdued too much of himself in creating his auctorial personality. Thinking not merely of Landor's classical scholarship, his preoccupation with the niceties of Latinity, but of his temper and writing in general, Sir Leslie Stephen characterized him in a well-known phrase as "a glorified and sublime edition of the model sixth-form lad,"[2] the perfect product of Etonian tradition. And Landor's prose, as well as a good deal of his verse, has the pervading air of a translation, impersonal, well-bred, a little stiff, less concerned with matter than with manner.

Paradoxical as it may sound regarding a man of somewhat notable masculinity, there is a frequent strain of the effeminate and sentimental. We need not take him at his worst, when he is trying to be arch, but at his best, for example in this famous prose poem:

Laodameia died; Helen died; Leda, the beloved of Jupiter, went before. It is better to repose in the earth betimes than to sit up late; better, than to cling pertinaciously to what we feel crumbling under us, and to protract an inevitable fall. We may enjoy the present while we are insensible of infirmity and decay: but the present, like a note in music, is nothing but as it appertains to what is past and what is to come. There are no fields of amaranth on this side of the grave: there are no voices, O Rhodopè, that are not soon mute, however tuneful: there is no name, with whatever emphasis of passionate love repeated, of which the echo is not faint at last.[3]

---

[2] *Hours in a Library* (1907), III, 221.   [3] *Works,* I, 14–15.

This is beautiful, assuredly, but to feel what it lacks let us put beside it a familiar sentence from an age of greater vitality and more robust prose:

O eloquent, just, and mighty Death! whom none could advise, thou hast persuaded; what none hath dared, thou hast done; and whom all the world hath flattered, thou only hast cast out of the world and despised: thou hast drawn together all the far-stretched greatness, all the pride, cruelty, and ambition of man, and covered it all over with these two narrow words, *Hic iacet!*

Not only is Ralegh completely masculine, he stirs us profoundly because he is himself carried away by his vision of Death the Leveler. The superb orchestration, the way in which phrases widen out like ripples on water, seems the very height of unconscious art, the perfect rendering of the idea. By comparison the Landorian passage is artificial; in the first sentence we are made aware of a deliberate variation of movement, and throughout we are less conscious of the idea than of over-sweet chimes of words.

This mingled artificiality and sentimentality is not infrequent in Landor. His quite conscious idealizing of Greek life and manners springs, of course, from sincere devotion, yet he is one of the lineal progenitors of Pater and Wilde (who were sincere devotees too). His latest editor warns us, rightly enough, against looking for historical verisimilitude,[4] but nominal reproductions of antiquity which are not, except at moments, either antique or modern, seem to classify themselves as museum pieces. Pericles is the ideal aristocratic republican, Landor in Greek attire taking a series of graceful attitudes. Aspasia is the ideal of intelligent, cultivated, emancipated womanhood — decidedly not Mrs. Landor in Greek dress. If only, among these charming and dignified murals of a sort of Greek Versailles, we could have an Aristophanic whiff of a fried-

4 *Works*, I, viii.

fish shop! It must be said, though Landor's critics do not say it, that *Pericles and Aspasia* is very hard to get through. When we can turn to the realistic Greeks themselves, we may not feel inclined to perambulate a gallery in which some noble statues are greatly outnumbered by Leighton paintings.

The point of the whole matter is that, with some qualifications, Landor was a man of enormous and delicate literary sensibility, a unique craftsman in words, who had little or nothing to say. I am not unmindful of the hundreds of aphorisms strewn through his works, but these, however weighty in themselves, seem to be blank cartridges; they do not come home to our business and bosoms because we do not feel behind them any ordered philosophy, or even a seriously reflective attitude toward life. As Meredith said of the young Swinburne, "I don't see any internal centre from which springs anything that he does." [5] The nearest approximation to a philosophy in Landor is a serene Epicureanism, but it is not quite that of Epicurus; at the best it is an ideal of taste (which, to be sure, is not too common a possession to be underrated), at other times it is merely a becoming literary costume. If our neglect of Landor is not entirely due to our own lazy incapacity, here, one may think, is a fundamental reason for it. He was not of God, and so he could not stand.

This lack of a philosophic center, of philosophic depth, is very manifest in Landor's literary criticisms. No man ever had a more passionate devotion to Milton than he, but one capital obstacle had to be overcome: "Averse as I am to everything relating to theology, and especially to the view of it thrown open by this poem [*Paradise Lost*], I recur to it incessantly as the noblest specimen in the world of eloquence, harmony, and genius." [6] What Landor per-

---

[5] *Letters of George Meredith*, ed. W. M. Meredith (1912), I, 55.
[6] *Works*, V, 280.

ceives and intensely admires is Milton the craftsman; he has no ear for what Milton spent his life and his art in trying to say. There is no need to cite chapter and verse for his abhorrence of things metaphysical and his inability to understand things religious,[7] apart from ancient paganism, but that state of mind is allied with Landor's comparative indifference to literature's reason for being, and his preoccupation with details of technique. He often reminds us of those Renaissance humanists whose commerce with the ancients was much less a spiritual than a stylistic discipline. On general questions he has strong and sometimes violent opinions, but these, like his moral aphorisms, make little impact upon us because Landor has no body of doctrine, no critical point of view. He exists and thunders in a great void, so that in scanning English literature we can forget him entirely, as we could never forget classicists like Ben Jonson, Dr. Johnson, and Arnold.

Consistency is not one of Landor's foibles, but when a man consistently and vehemently disparages Plato and Dante, and consistently and extravagantly exalts Ovid and Boccaccio, he has pretty well defined himself and his view of literature. Since Ovid comes within our range, we may notice some remarks on him. The oratorical contest between Ajax and Ulysses in the *Metamorphoses* "is the most wonderful thing in the whole range of Latin poetry," and has more "continued and unabated excellence" [8] than anything in Dante. "Of all the ancient Romans, Ovid had the finest imagination." [9] "There is more invention and imagination in Ovid than in any poet between Homer and

---

[7] One brief item may be quoted. After an explosive attack, through the mouth of Porson, on the "conventicle" allusions in the first version of *Laodamia*, the speaker avows that he is "not insensible to the warmly chaste morality which is the soul of it, nor indifferent to the benefits that literature on many occasions has derived from Christianity" (*Works*, V, 163). The last phrase is unconsciously illuminating.

[8] *Works*, VII, 240, IX, 171.   [9] *Ibid.*, IX, 200.

Shakespeare." [10] Finally, for we cannot survey Landor's critical judgments, what are we to think of a man who singles out these lines from Milton as "the richest jewel that Poetry ever wore"?

> Yielded with coy submission, modest pride,
> And sweet, reluctant, amorous delay.

In these lines, especially the second, Milton lapsed into the style of his eighteenth-century imitators, and in fact that line was echoed again and again; [11] it indicates the weak side of Landor's eighteenth-century taste that he would rather have written these two lines "than all the poetry that has been written since Milton's time in all the regions of the earth." [12] It is true that he exalted Shakespeare, even above Milton — "a rib of Shakespeare would have made a Milton: the same portion of Milton, all the poets born ever since" [13] — but it is permissible to wonder how much of Shakespeare was visible to a man with such fatal blind spots.

Landor's first volume of poetry appeared in 1795, three years before the *Lyrical Ballads*, and his last in 1863, two years before *Atalanta in Calydon*. That first book showed a taste for classical narrative, in the semi-Ovidian *Pyramus and Thisbe* and in several episodes in *The Birth of Poesy*,

[10] *Letters and Other Unpublished Writings of Walter Savage Landor*, ed. Stephen Wheeler (1897), p. 59. Cf. H. C. Minchin, *Walter Savage Landor* (1934), pp. 76, 93.

[11] Mr. G. R. Potter records echoes in Collins, Blake, Erasmus Darwin, R. P. Knight, and Anna Seward (*M.L.N.*, XXXVII, 443). The names of Phineas Fletcher and Ovid may serve to suggest the kind of sweetness and rhetorical wit which momentarily misled Milton. In his unpublished *Epithalamium* (*Venus and Anchises*, etc., ed. Ethel Seaton, Oxford University Press, 1926, p. 28), Fletcher had written

> "Those feared ioyes and hoped paines
> But with fainting sweet delayes."

[12] *Works*, V, 249. Of course this is Landor's way of saying that he likes a thing very much; see his remark on Shelley (*ibid.*, V, 287).

[13] *Ibid.*, V, 280.

but the conventional eighteenth-century manner gave little promise of distinction. Landor's own early style, condensed, rugged, and often difficult, was fully displayed in the fragments of an epic, *The Phocaeans*, and the completed epic, *Gebir* (1798), announced, to a very few readers, the arrival of a highly original poet. A number of Latin idylls, later turned into English, appeared in 1815 and 1820. Many lyrics and dramatic scenes were included in *Pericles and Aspasia* (1836) and other prose works. Most of the classical idylls in English, the short narratives and dialogues by which, along with the lyrics, Landor's poetry is best known, were published in the *Works* of 1846 and the *Hellenics* of 1847 and later years. If poetry was his amusement, Landor toiled at it mightily, and the pursuit of perfection, which led to constant and often drastic rewriting, made his bibliography grow, like ballads, by incremental repetition. Poets such as Shakespeare and Milton, Wordsworth and Keats, need to be studied chronologically, but it matters relatively little whether we know the dates of Landor's poems or not. Though there were several somewhat different phases, we can say of him, as we cannot of the other poets, that he never grew, he was cast. Living in his own isolated and timeless world, surrounded by the stately figures of history and legend, he strove unceasingly to add weight and polish to his phrases. Not that he did not express himself, often with violence, upon public affairs as well as upon individuals, but it was usually a tempest in a library.

Landor began, however, with ambitious poems on historical and mythological themes which were fired by his revolutionary zeal. *The Phocaeans*, *Gebir*, and *Crysaor* [14] are all connected by tradition, or, in the case of *Gebir*, by Landor's manipulation, with ancient Iberia, and in these

[14] The fragments of *The Phocaeans* were probably written in or about 1795-96, *Gebir* in 1797, and *Crysaor* after 1797. See the Appendix, under 1802. The

works the man who was to rush to the aid of Spanish patriots proclaimed, a little darkly and indirectly, his republican faith, or at least his hatred of tyrants. In the first part of *The Phocaeans*, which in spite of some fine bits must surely be the worst-told story in the world, the arrival of Phocaean exiles at Tartessus inspires a description of the sufferings of the Tartessians; Phocaea's defiance of Persia is the subject of *Protis's Narrative*, which is based more fully on Herodotus and is quite lucid. Landor said that *From the Phocaeans* and *Gebir* were written "when our young English heads were turned towards the French Revolution, and were deluded by a phantom of Liberty, as if the French could ever be free or let others be." [15] Here and there we are conscious of that stimulus, especially in the Landor-like figure of Hymneus, the poet-liberator, but, at least in the first fragment, we may be too preoccupied with puzzling out our course to discern a red flag waving on the sea of glue. In *Gebir* the evils of kingship and aggression are contrasted, in the vein of eighteenth-century sentimentalism, with the idyllic love and unambitious rural peace of Tamar and his athletic nymph. If that serious theme at times emerges, we generally forget it in the atmosphere of pure romance, young love, royal magnificence, eastern magic, and above all in the endless series of clear hard pictures. And, though the thoughts may be "connected by flea-skips of association" (in William Taylor's very modern phrase [16]), Landor's inconsecutive method and excessive condensation are still real difficulties.

---

chronology of the Landor items is of course based on Messrs. T. J. Wise and Stephen Wheeler's *Bibliography of the Writings in Prose and Verse of Walter Savage Landor* (1919), and on the notes in the *Works* edited by Welby and Mr. Wheeler. My brief discussion of the early epics is indebted to the careful thesis of William Bradley, *The Early Poems of Walter Savage Landor. A Study of his Development and Debt to Milton* (1914).

[15] *Letters and Other Unpublished Writings*, ed. Wheeler, p. 135.

[16] John Forster, *Walter Savage Landor. A Biography* (1869), I, 182.

In the fragment *Crysaor* theme and fable are one and indivisible, and probably no modern English poem of comparable power is less known to the generality of readers. Crysaor, one of the Titans or giants who is ruler of Spain, defies Jupiter and asserts his own godlike authority over mankind. Jupiter, aroused against the race of mortals who are "criminal mostly for enduring crimes," calls upon Neptune to destroy the tyrant. Neptune with one blow severs Gades from the fruitful main; Crysaor, overwhelmed, curses the gods and dies. But emancipated mankind must still pay for its weak submission. One of the Titans had given birth to a daughter, and she, Superstition, is allowed to carry on another reign of tyranny. Thus the poem is one of romantic revolt, but Crysaor is not glorified as the Promethean rebel and superman, he is condemned as an oppressor of man. While the central incident might have been suggested by Ajax's defiance of Poseidon,[17] Landor's chief debt seems to be to *Paradise Lost*. Corresponding to Milton's God, Christ, Satan and his fallen angels, and Adam and Eve, we have Jupiter, Neptune, Crysaor and the fallen Titans, and mankind; Superstition has a Miltonic parallel in Sin.[18] The republican in Milton might have endorsed Landor's reading of the theme, that man incurs guilt by submitting to kings who usurp divine authority, and brings on as his own punishment further enslavement to superstition. This may not be the greatest of arguments — we remember Carlyle's remark that Landor's principle was mere rebellion — but it is not an ig-

---

[17] *Odyssey*, iv. 499 ff.; *Poems*, ed. Wheeler, I, 365–66. See also Colvin's note, *Selections from the Writings of Walter Savage Landor* (1920), p. 364. Crysaor sprang, with Pegasus, from the blood of Medusa. The offspring of his union with Callirrhoe was the monster Geryon, who inhabited the island of Erythia or Gadira (Cadiz). See Apollodorus, *Lib.*, ed. Frazer, I, 158–59, 210–13.

In general it has not seemed worth while to chronicle Landor's mythological sources, since they are often brief and obscure anecdotes. A few items are mentioned by Colvin in the volume just cited.

[18] Bradley, p. 98.

noble one, and Landor handles it nobly. Since we are approaching a very different body of Landor's verse, the point may be emphasized that the poem which Colvin and others have justly regarded as Landor's greatest achievement in classical narrative is a poem in which he is uttering the faith that is in him, and that in doing so, in using myth for propaganda, to put it crudely, he rises to the fullest strength and splendor of his poetical power.[19]

Crysaor is the third, then, of Landor's early attempts to set forth his love of liberty, and it cannot be said that any one of them is a complete success. Yet we may think that after this time he took the wrong turning. Many of the idylls, to be sure, are exquisitely done, but, apart from a very few, Landor no longer has much to say except that young love is sweet. The cold reception given to his early work may have led him to refrigerate his public sentiments; or he may have found a more congenial platform in the *Imaginary Conversations*, where, clad in mantle or toga, he is not averse to shaking a stick at contemporary statesmen. Whatever the cause, when Landor ceased to put his republican creed, elementary as it may have been, into his narrative and dramatic verse, most of the life went out of it. *Crysaor* with its rugged approaches to sublimity is major poetry; nearly all the *Hellenics* are definitely minor. The imperfect performer on the organ was content to become a consummate master of the flute.

However erratic Landor's critical judgments, in matters of form and expression he early evolved a theory which never ceased to govern his own practice. The Popeian manner did not survive his first volume (though he always

[19] The theme of the poem is clear enough, but in a note Landor says: "This poem describes a period when the insolence of tyranny and the sufferings of mankind were at the utmost. They could not be so without slavery. . . ." (*Poems*, I, 366). In regard to Superstition, one might quote "Epicurus and Metrodorus": "The goat of Ida will suckle new Jupiters when the elder is starved to death upon Olympus" (*Works*, I, 250).

remained in some essential respects an eighteenth-century man), and he forged for himself that closely packed, elliptical style which is illustrated in the early heroic poems.[20] We all know of Landor's youthful desire to emulate Pindar's "proud complacency and scornful strength . . . to be as compendious and exclusive,"[21] and we can only wish that the model had been Homer. Imitation of Pindar assuredly did knit Landor's poetic sinews, but it also knotted them, and he seemed to think he could achieve classic clarity and precision by striking out every other line. Thanks partly to Miltonic influence, one may suppose, this uneven and coagulated style became less lumpy in *Gebir* and *Crysaor*; and the study of Milton and Virgil may have helped to keep mythological allusions in *Gebir* lucid and relevant, unlike the obscure and far-fetched allusions in *The Phocaeans*.[22]

Landor was almost alone among the poets of his time in going directly to an ancient model, and during the romantic age and the Victorian he set himself in conscious opposition to the dominant fashions. "I found my company in a hothouse warmed with steam, and conducted them to my dining-room through a cold corridor with nothing but a few old statues in it from one end to the other."[23] His most famous phrase, a finely critical one, occurs in the preface to the *Hellenics* of 1859: "Poetry, in our day, is

[20] The rapid change is illustrated also, as Bradley says (pp. 4, 28, 61), in the Virgilian translation, *The Descent of Orpheus* (written in 1794, printed in 1841), and a piece on Medea later incorporated in *To Corinth*. See Forster, I, 36–40.

[21] Forster, I, 78. Commenting on the luxuriance of *Endymion*, Landor, though he admired Keats, wished that young poets might be apprenticed to Pindar (*ibid.*, II, 527).

[22] The demonstrable influence of Milton is slight, especially when one considers the degree and the duration of Landor's feeling for him; see Bradley, pp. 70–72, and Havens, *Influence of Milton*, pp. 293 ff. For Virgilian echoes in *Gebir*, see Elizabeth Nitchie, *Vergil and the English Poets*, pp. 207 ff.

[23] Forster, II, 345. In the preface to the *Hellenics* of 1847, Landor with mock modesty contrasted the popular style with his own "rude frescoes, delineated on an old wall high up, and sadly weak in coloring" (*Poems*, II, 315).

oftener prismatic than diaphanous: this is not so: they who look into it may see through." The style of Landor's later heroic poems and idylls is in the main that of *Gebir*, considerably relaxed and simplified, and lightened with more "air-bubbles." Compared with the normal post-romantic style, it may be called classical, but by any absolute standard, so far as there is such a thing, Landor's mature manner is more Hellenistic and Ovidian than Hellenic. Instead of an even texture, "fullness in the concise and depth in the clear," we often find, as in the prose, a mixture of the condensed and the diffuse, the hard and the soft. Compression may result in dramatic surprise, as in the lines on the transformation of Phineus into stone —

> when the sword
> Of Phineus, white with wonder, shook restrain'd,
> And the hilt rattled in his marble hand — [24]

but the hint here of a conceit becomes a certainty in that much-praised line in *The Hamadryad*, "And the axe shone behind him in their eyes."

There is indeed something like Ovidian wit in Landor, for instance in those ambiguous and epigrammatic conclusions which are a mannerism in the *Hellenics*. The incomplete, ironic ending may of course be very effective, but in Landor it is too obviously labored. Even in the moving *Death of Artemidora* the final "'twas not hers" seems studied, and I at least prefer the quiet completeness of the additional lines which Landor removed:

> With her that old boat incorruptible,
> Unwearied, undiverted in its course,
> Had plash'd the water up the farther strand.[25]

The best and briefest example of the art that does not conceal art is the epigram which Swinburne, in the Landorian

[24] *Gebir*, vii. 228-30.   [25] *Works*, X, 75; *Poems*, IV, 174.

manner that was also his own, pronounced "the very brightest (in my eyes at least) of all the jewels in Landor's crown of song":

> Stand close around, ye Stygian set,
> With Dirce in one boat convey'd,
> Or Charon, seeing, may forget
> That he is old, and she a shade.[26]

"The heart," Landor once said, "is the creator of the poetical world; only the atmosphere is from the brain." [27] *Dirce* was born in his heart, but dwelt too long in his brain. Not to mention the forced rhyme-word "set," whatever genuine pathos Landor felt in the extinction of youth and beauty has been ironed out in the achieving of epigrammatic neatness and indirectness. The result is clever, but one would not apply that adjective to, say, *Ternissa! you are fled.*[28]

Although both groups of classical idylls, the dramatic and the narrative, contain some lifeless members, the former maintains perhaps a higher level of vitality and poetical power. Some, like *Europa and her Mother*, are only charming trifles of light and sunny expansiveness. Others, like those concerned with the story of Agamemnon, are tragic, and more ambitious in their reading of character and passion. But even a short scene may be too much for Landor's dramatic faculty. In *The Shades of Agamemnon and of Iphigeneia* the girl whom her father had allowed to die greets him with eager questions about her loving mother who has murdered him. It is a great occasion for tragic irony — "I am tragedian in this scene alone," said Landor proudly, in words which show how deeply he could feel — but the situation, once presented, eddies around

---

[26] *Works*, X, 241; *Poems*, IV, 72; *Letters of Algernon Charles Swinburne*, ed. Gosse and Wise (1918), I, 134.
[27] *Works*, V, 308.   [28] *Poems*, II, 356–57.

without reaching a climax.[29] Landor is good in simple
strokes of characterization, though he is apt to play on one
string; in the scene of Iphigeneia's sacrifice pathetic simplicity becomes exaggerated naïveté. Incidentally, the
renderings in prose and verse of *Peleus and Thetis* and
Achilles and Helena on Ida afford illustrations of the general superiority of Landor's prose; the verse is not without
flatness and padding.[30]

In conception and execution the *Hellenics* are unique in
English, and they have no parallel in classical literature
unless in the late Greek mythological idylls and the individual tales of Ovid. Landor's narrative pieces are indeed
very Hellenistic and Ovidian not merely in their objective,
pictorial, and general "literary" qualities, but in their preoccupation with romantic love and the fate of young lovers. If these poems were serious studies of human passion,
one would hesitate to say that the author of *Crysaor* had
immensely narrowed his range, but since they are in the
main only decorative reproductions of the antique, one
does say so. One may "see through" them much too
easily. In spite of their usually admirable narrative pattern most of the idylls, in particular those translated from
Latin, leave no impression whatever; they are literary exercises. If we think of them as wholes, it is as clear bright
murals, and more often we remember only parts, a descriptive phrase, or a bit of the antique local color which Landor, unlike most English poets, could use with skill. He
expressed a strong dislike for what we call "pure poetry,"
saying that Shakespeare and Milton "stood among substantial men, and sang upon recorded actions," [31] but if, as
Arnold maintained, in classical art the subject is everything, in Landor it is next to nothing, for the recorded

[29] *Works*, X, 228; *Poems*, II, 211; *Agamemnon*, ll. 1555 ff.
[30] *Peleus and Thetis* is in *Works*, I, 240; *Poems*, II, 237; *Achilles and Helena*,
in *Works*, I, 1; *Poems*, II, 373.   [31] *Works*, V, 204.

actions of which he sings so artistically are seldom important.

It is a question whether a mythological subject can yield significant poetry when treated in Landor's way. He apparently wished to produce a poem which should read as if it had been written by an ancient poet, and his antique world is cut off from any intrusion of modernity, unless in regard to the sentiment of love. If that method is right, then the major poets from Chaucer to the present are wrong. For one main thesis of this book, a truism to be sure, is that mythological poetry is alive when myths are re-created, when they carry modern implications, and that mythological poetry in which myths are merely retold is, if not dead, at least of a very inferior order. The author of *Crysaor* had a message, the author of the *Hellenics* has none, and he has little of the Shakespearean substitute for a philosophy, a creative zest in life itself. Of course the idylls rest on the idea of the beauty and simplicity of ancient life and story, and Landor holds his Epicurean creed with pagan dignity, and it may be, as an admirable critic has said, that "it was Landor's achievement to bring into an age of romantic taste and sentiment, and of a growingly oppressive modernity, tortured with introspection and overburdened with its own problems, something of the peculiar nobility and fragrance of the antique world." [32] Yet one may think that a modern poet who withdraws from the modern world into an idealized antiquity can make no strong claim upon us. The bringing of antiquity, whether idealized or not, into the modern world is another matter.

No one who had read Landor's prose and discovered his abhorrence of the metaphysical and allegorical (though he

[32] Ernest de Selincourt, "Classicism and Romanticism in the Poetry of Walter Savage Landor," *England und die Antike*, ed. Fritz Saxl (Leipzig and Berlin, 1932), p. 243.

wrote some allegories) would expect him to reinterpret myth in the symbolic and ethical manner of his contemporaries. One has only to recall his beautiful lines on the shell, which he never wearied of belaboring Wordsworth for borrowing and spoiling.[33] For Landor the sound returned by the shell is an end in itself. For Wordsworth the immediate sensation is only a starting-point for reflection; the sound suggests authentic tidings of invisible things. If it were only a question of method, the objective or the interpretative, critical opinion nowadays would prefer the former, but, though here and there an idea is implicit in a poem, Landor's objectivity is not so much artistic restraint as it is the result of the limitations of his unphilosophical mind. He is, in fact, something of an Imagist,[34] and decidedly a romanticist, who lives less in whole works than in fine moments. His classicism is rather of the neoclassic than the ancient type. For classicism is not a matter of drapery and attitude but of inner discipline. The classical qualities of form, order, restraint, precision, are in themselves, after all, secondary qualities, not too difficult of attainment if an artist avoids grappling with the experience and the problems of his age. It was not in so doing that the great ancients became classical, and Landor himself did not so begin. He remains perennially interesting as a craftsman, but the root of the matter is not in him.

II. MATTHEW ARNOLD

Landor and Arnold are the great English classicists of the nineteenth century, and classicism almost ceases to

[33] *Gebir*, i. 170 ff.; *The Excursion*, iv. 1132 ff. One might compare *The Hamadryad* with the moralized conclusion of Shelley's *The Woodman and the Nightingale*.

[34] See Mr. Aldington's eulogy in his *Literary Studies and Reviews* (1924). When, in the course of some excellent remarks, the critic declares that in the *Hellenics* Landor is "never dull, never diffuse, never ignoble, never turgid and vague," one can only wonder how much he has read.

have a meaning when it harbors two men so completely unlike. There are resemblances, to be sure, some superficial, some less so. Both made prose their business but won high reputations as poets; if Landor lives mainly in his prose, Arnold's present fame rests largely on his poetry. Both were men of the world, good scholars, but gentlemen and amateurs. Both went to antiquity for their best inspiration and were true to what they conceived to be Greek ideals. Both in a sense repudiated the romantic age and both drew nourishment from romantic roots.

Yet even these statements need qualification. Landor beneath his pagan garb was always "a true-born and wrong-headed Englishman." It is one of Arnold's distinctions that he was an intellectual cosmopolite. Landor's classical culture, despite his liking for Greek themes, was chiefly Latin; Arnold's interest was mainly in Greek. Landor wished to walk with Epicurus on the right hand and Epictetus on the left (though Epictetus was generally a few yards in the rear); the son of Dr. Arnold walked, one might say, between Marcus Aurelius and Thomas à Kempis. But the fundamental differences all turn on this one fact, that Landor was a man of letters, a pure artist, while Arnold was a prophet and preacher. This fact of course determines their approach to the ancients, their whole conception of life and literature. In the classics one sought mainly literary, the other mainly intellectual and spiritual, discipline; and Arnold was indebted to his father not merely for his Hebraism but for something of his Hellenism too.[35] If Landor found classical sanction for the aristocratic Epicureanism of his temperament, in general he had more feeling for the *eloquentia* than for the philosophic import of the ancients. There are times when Arnold's classicism becomes literary and pedantic, but it is not the

[35] See, for example, *Essays in Criticism* (1895), I, 349; *Letters of Matthew Arnold*, ed. George W. E. Russell (1895), I, 253, 263, 362, 442, 455, II, 5.

poetry of Professor Arnold which is part of our experience.
What we remember best, to speak only of the poems which
concern us here, are Arnold's dreams of a primitive mythological world of simple joy and harmony. Again and again
such a world is opposed to the sick hurry of modern life,
not as a preferable or possible alternative or as a complete
ideal, for Arnold would not disown his intellectual heritage, however painful its responsibilities, but as a partial
corrective of ill-balanced modernity and as a cool refuge
for his perplexed and lonely soul. And his sense of the high
seriousness of life and poetry, his constant effort to see
himself and nature under the reign of law, prevent his
mythological visions from being mere poetry of escape.
Landor the author and Landor the man were almost two
different persons; only the former enjoyed serenity, and it
was the negative serenity of a pagan cloister, or, in part,
of an eighteenth-century man who feared "enthusiasm."
Arnold, grappling with the spiritual and intellectual problems of the modern world, and above all with the conflicting impulses in his own nature, tried to win serenity and
failed. His failure made him a poet; in his later years he
gained a partial victory and became a journalist and a
classicist.

Few poets in a first volume have declared themselves so
completely, in technique and substance, as Arnold did in
The Strayed Reveller of 1849. He had indeed formulated an
ambitious poetical program for the year, in which one item
was "a system of the Universe," a project partly realized
in the later *Empedocles*.[36] In most of the significant poems
of 1849 — and they are nearly all significant — we see, not
the future apostle of culture and reason opening the door
of Truth with smiling self-confidence, but a young man
who, for all his debonair dandyism in society, is groping

---

[36] Chauncey B. Tinker, "Arnold's Poetic Plans," *Yale Review*, XXII (1932–
33), 782–93.

his way uncertainly toward a rule of life, seeking always for unity and totality, for the peace of self-discipline. He is much concerned also, as he is in the letters of this time, with the responsible function, and hence with the method, of modern poetry. Although our knowledge of Arnold's formative years is less complete than it is in the case of any other major author of the century, we cannot miss the conflict in the young man who loved "Marguerite" — not to mention nature and the world — and who at the same time believed that, both as a human being and as a poet, he must govern his senses and emotions, must discover and follow a high and lonely road. It was Arnold's personal tragedy, and the source of his special quality and power, that he could not reconcile his poetry and his philosophy, for both were rooted in his instincts. The earliest poetic manifestations of that conflict differ of course in range and intensity. *The Strayed Reveller* exhibits his poetic susceptibility, the breadth and depth of his capacity for feeling. In *The New Sirens* he is aware, though perhaps not fully aware, of his sensuous and emotional impulses, and rebukes them. In *Mycerinus* the problem is in the moral sphere and only by implication in the poetical as well.

If Arnold sometimes lapsed into the baldly didactic, no English poet has proved more clearly that ethical ideas can be carried alive into the heart by passion, and he treated such ideas nobly in *Mycerinus*.[37] The remoteness and beauty of the setting, and the embodiment of the problem in one philosophic character, give the poem a dramatic

---

[37] In Herodotus (ii. 129–33), Mycerinus reproaches the oracle for injustice and receives an explanation. Egypt was fated to suffer a hundred and fifty years, and Mycerinus' predecessors had understood this, he had not. The king then proceeds to turn his allotted six years into twelve by burning the candle at both ends, converting nights into days. The tale is an anecdote of oriental ingenuity in cheating death rather than the statement of a moral problem. *Mycerinus* should be read, of course, along with *The Sick King in Bokhara*.

Arnold's poems are quoted from the Oxford edition, ed. Sir Arthur Quiller-Couch (1913).

quality which raises it above such pieces as *Self-Dependence* and *Morality*. The problem of Mycerinus is that of Job, though the king does not bow to God's will and gain a reward in the end. Contemplating the happy life of his iniquitous father and the divine sentence passed on his own blameless career, he reasons the question out. Are the gods mere ghosts who look with frozen apathy both on sensual pleasures and on the man who scorns them, or are they themselves "slaves of a tyrannous Necessity," or do they live in serene ease in heaven? His last six years, then, Mycerinus will deliberately give to "Revels more deep, joy keener than their own." But he is no sensualist, and, though Arnold refrains from saying the last word, we know that the king's royal soul was not satisfied.

Some lines in *Mycerinus*, such as "Splinter'd the silver arrows of the moon," remind us of Landor, and *The Strayed Reveller* is somewhat Landorian in its clear-cut images and phrasing and its antique verisimilitude. If the father of Landor's Rhaicos had allowed him to join the festive throng, he might have been this youth who at dawn snatched up his dappled fawn-skin, his vine-crown and fir-staff, all drenched with dew. Arnold never again created such a series of vivid pictures as those of the reveler himself, the cup of wine, Ulysses, the spare, dark-featured, quick-eyed stranger, and the mythological visions which sweep through the brain of the intoxicated youth, visions of the sad unheeded old prophet, Tiresias, the centaurs snuffing the mountain wind, the heroes sitting in the dark ship on the violet sea. Precision of outline is combined with romantic suggestion and fullness of detail. Arnold's manner is not that of any one ancient model, though he evidently always preferred Homeric and Sophoclean simplicity to Pindaric obscurity.[38] In his abstract theme

---

[38] In respect to the metrical form, Mr. Laurence Binyon observes that Arnold "no doubt imitated . . . Goethe's and Heine's free-verse poems, which I imagine

Arnold is concerned, if not very profoundly, with the nature of poetic experience. Thanks to Circe's draught, not here the agent of bestial transformation, the young reveler, like one of the gods, beholds visions of beauty with painless, irresponsible ecstasy, unmindful of the human grief and pain which lie behind. But he knows too that the bards who sing of these themes must become what they sing, must see the whole and not the part, must suffer with Tiresias and toil with the heroes. It is the condition, the glory, and the penalty of poetic power.[39]

If Arnold's somewhat maternal Circe is not in the tradition of antiquity and the Renaissance, his "new sirens," though modernized, are closer to the old symbols of fleshly delights. In the author's prose commentary on *The New Sirens*, the poet who interrogates. them says that he has dreamed of such beings as "the fierce sensual lovers of antiquity," but these new ones claim that their love is romantic and is "a satisfying of the spirit." [40] Wisdom, say the temptresses of the poem, is in feeling; the brain is dry and cold. But, replies the poet, the raptures of sense are momentary fires which leave only ashes behind them; mere emotion does not lead to truth, it brings satiety and languor and vain attempts to renew intoxication. The argument reminds us of one of Arnold's definitions of Hebraism as the most effective teacher of "the discipline

were in their turn modelled on a misunderstanding of Greek lyrics" (*Tradition and Reaction in Modern Poetry*, English Association Pamphlet No. 63, 1926, p. 12).

[39] The same general idea reappears in the *Epilogue to Lessing's Laocoön* (1867), ll. 129 ff. In *The Youth of Nature*, by the way, Wordsworth is likened to Tiresias. The strayed reveler's visions are not unified, they are aspects of varied experience; in *The Future* (1852) the brief parallel series of pictures — of Rebekah and Moses — develops out of the poet's nostalgic search for unity and peace.

[40] *Letters of Matthew Arnold to Arthur Hugh Clough*, ed. Howard F. Lowry (Oxford University Press, 1932), pp. 105–06. Mrs. Iris Sells thinks that Arnold found the theme of the poem in Senancour's *Obermann* (*Matthew Arnold and France*, Cambridge University Press, 1935, pp. 60 ff.).

by which alone man is enabled to rescue his life from thral-
dom to the passing moment and to his bodily senses, to en-
noble it, and to make it eternal."

Arnold's melancholy always of course had its religious
roots, but here, as often elsewhere, two other sources appear. First, there was the experience represented by the
shadowy "Marguerite," and the half-bitter, half-inspiring
return from the world of passion and romance to the work
and duties of life. Was that return a dedication of his
higher self, or was it a renunciation of his birthright? Was
love, emotion, a whirlpool which would engulf the undisciplined man, or was it a main stream of his buried life?
Arnold could not be sure; hence his mingled longing for,
and distrust of, the power of feeling.[41] A second element
of melancholy in *The New Sirens* is allied with this, but
belongs more to the author than the man. It arises from
his critical contemplation of the world, in particular the
poetical world — "how deeply *unpoetical* the age and all
one's surroundings are." [42] The best commentary on the
literary implications of the poem is contained in the letters
to Clough of 1848–52. Here we have repeated complaints
that Keats and Browning achieve, not "an Idea of the
world," but only "the world's multitudinousness"; that
Keats and Shelley have revived Elizabethan richness; that
Tennyson dawdles with the painted shell of the universe.[43]
"Those who cannot read Greek should read nothing but
Milton and parts of Wordsworth." Modern poetry,
which, like the ancient, must include religion and must be
"a complete magister vitae," cannot spend itself in "ex-

---

[41] In *To Marguerite* (*Poems*, p. 281), Arnold's allusion to Endymion is a world
away from Keats's poet-lover. Love has failed, and he rebukes himself for having forgotten that loneliness is his appointed destiny. The lines are poetically
felicitous, and very sincere, but perhaps not free from something like priggish-
ness.

[42] Lowry, p. 99. Cf. pp. 109–11.

[43] Lowry, pp. 63, 97, 100–01, 124, and *passim*.

quisite bits and images" but "can only subsist by its *contents*"; it must, then, be very plain, direct, and severe. But *The New Sirens* is not so confident, and it might stand as an epitome of Arnold's poetical life. For the poet is not deaf to the seductive voices; like Milton, he betrays his own sensuous instincts in castigating them, and the whip is entwined with vine leaves.[44]

The young Arnold, on account of his philosophic seriousness, was more strict than Landor, for Landor, with some reservations, warmly praised all four of the poets whom Arnold found wanting. Nearly twenty years after *The New Sirens*, he returned to its general theme in *Bacchanalia; or, the New Age*. In the early poem he had been at least half "pagan"; now, an unsympathetic elder, he sees the younger generation as a wine-flushed Bacchic rout invading the silence with noisy revelry, and, since the poem appeared in 1867, doubtless the leader of the revels was envisaged as a certain demonic youth with flaming hair. Like every generation, this youthful band is going to do greater things than were ever done before, but the poet is mindful of the past, of the eternal cycle of youth and age, and of the few achievements that survive the sound and fury of each confident epoch.[45] In this later poem the self-assured preacher is more audible than the troubled poet. Arnold begins in his best manner, with the quiet beauty of an evening landscape and the inrush of the Bacchic throng, but then he gives himself up to satire, which is saved by

[44] A remark by Edward Quillinan on the "*very* classical" *Memorial Verses* led to the prediction that Arnold "has a good deal of poetry in him; & it will come out in spite of all the heathen Gods & goddesses that hold him in enchantment." See *The Correspondence of Henry Crabb Robinson with the Wordsworth Circle*, ed. Edith J. Morley (Clarendon Press, 1927), II, 769; Lowry, p. 114.

[45] "I read his [Goethe's] letters, Bacon, Pindar, Sophocles, Milton, Th. à Kempis, and Ecclesiasticus, and retire more and more from the modern world and modern literature, which is all only what has been before and what will be again, and not bracing or edifying in the least" (*Letters*, ed. Russell, I, 18; January, 1851).

humor from middle-aged peevishness, though it does lapse into journalism.

These poems are essentially variations on one theme, the relative value of and the conflict between two ways of life and art, that of sensuous emotion and intuition and that of elevated and disciplined thought. Although the terms would need partial re-defining, especially in view of Arnold's ethical emphasis, the dilemma is parallel to that of Keats, and, like Keats, Arnold feels intensely the claims of both modes of experience. In 1852 came *Empedocles on Etna*, the most elaborate and impressive statement of the struggle between his poetic and his philosophic self. Callicles and Empedocles represent the two extremes at their best; Pausanias is only a foil, a representative of normal, uncritical humanity. The poem corresponds in the Arnoldian canon to Tennyson's *Lucretius* of 1868,[46] which showed Empedocles' materialistic disciple ending in suicidal despair. Superficially, Arnold's moral is not altogether dissimilar, but the real and partly unconscious implications are not so obvious. His reason for withdrawing the poem, that a situation involving mere endurance of distress which had no vent in action was essentially morbid, painful rather than tragic, was of course a sincere article in his classical creed, yet it may not have been the whole truth. Surely a more vital reason was a perception that he had said the opposite of what he believed he ought to have said. For years he had been trying to suppress his emotions in the interest of a higher intellectual and spiritual life, and *Empedocles* should have been a song of victory; instead it records the failure of the austere ideal his will had imposed upon himself. Whatever reminiscences of the his-

---

[46] In 1866 Arnold was disturbed by the news that Tennyson was at work on this subject, since he himself for some twenty years had been occupied with it (*Letters*, ed. Russell, I, 375). Mrs. Sells (pp. 149 ff.) sees much of *Obermann* in *Empedocles*.

torical Empedocles or other sources may be mixed up with it, the philosopher's stoic sermon is pure Arnold, but if it is preached as an adequate way of life, a fearless mind's guide through the darkness, then suicide seems quite illogical. It is of course no reflection on the poet's spiritual integrity that he himself did not jump into the Thames but lived to dine with the Rothschilds; if the subject was to yield its full value, Empedocles must be presented *in extremis*.

But Arnold is not merely Empedocles, he is also Callicles. In the poems of 1849 he had not been single-hearted in condemning the joys of sense and emotion, and Callicles is not so much an embodiment of the poet's lost youth as of a youth that he had never fully lived. That personal feeling runs everywhere through both letters and poems. "I am past thirty, and three parts iced over," he wrote to Clough in 1853.[47] And in Arnold's mind his own youth is constantly bound up with visions of a simpler and healthier age in the life of man, with remembrance of Wordsworth, priest to us all of the wonder and bloom of the world. He always saw and emphasized, of course, what might be called the Arnoldian elements in Wordsworth, and the poet in whose shadow he grew up was, like Marguerite, a symbol of a world now closed. In his last moments Empedocles recalls an older day, when thought had not killed sense but lived in happy harmony with it, when, to quote the most Wordsworthian lines in all Arnold,

> we receiv'd the shock of mighty thoughts
> On simple minds with a pure natural joy.

Thus, whatever Arnold the critic or moralist might say, Arnold the poet was, at least for the time, with the young singer. The inference would be dubious if based merely on

---

[47] Lowry, p. 128. "What a difference there is," he says in 1852, "between reading in poetry and morals of the loss of youth, and experiencing it!" (*ibid.*, p. 125). And see such poems as *Growing Old* and *The Progress of Poesy*.

the unwonted ease and beauty of the lyrics, as compared
with the rugged stanzas of Empedocles, for the contrast is
a dramatic necessity. But it is Callicles who touches the
springs of the philosopher's buried life; and, when Empedocles has plunged into the crater, when pure thought has,
however nobly, failed to win peace except in extinction,
the last word remains with the singer, a hymn of pure
natural joy. Between the lines, and often in them, the
whole poem is an anti-intellectual affirmation on the side
of simple feeling, sensuous intuition. But Arnold cannot,
as Keats sometimes can, surrender wholly to the one part
of himself; the dilemma remains a dilemma. And if life
were to be lived again, he would not know any better how
to retain possession of his whole being: "I feel immensely
— more and more clearly — what I *want* — what I have
(I believe) lost and choked by my treatment of myself and
the studies to which I have addicted myself. But what
ought I to have done in preference to what I have done?
there is the question." [48]

Callicles' function as the Pippa of this poem has been
partly indicated. He does not proclaim that God's in his
heaven, and he does not dissuade Empedocles from his
purpose, but the singer and his songs are much more than
decorative. By implication and contrast they supplement
and feed the nostalgic regrets of Empedocles. In the midst
of the philosopher's bleak picture of the universe and his
own mind come these interludes of untroubled beauty,
idyllic glimpses of the joys and pains of that primal world
from which he has long been exiled. These mythological

---

[48] Lowry, p. 136 (May 1, 1853). To his sister, in 1851, Arnold wrote: "The
aimless and unsettled, but also open and liberal state of our youth we *must* perhaps all leave and take refuge in our morality and character; but with most of us
it is a melancholy passage from which we emerge shorn of so many beams that
we are almost tempted to quarrel with the law of nature which imposes it on us"
(*Letters*, ed. Russell, I, 17). Cf. *Unpublished Letters of Matthew Arnold*, ed.
Arnold Whitridge (Yale University Press, 1923), p. 18.

lyrics recall the Proteus and Triton of Wordsworth's vision, for he too, though far less often than Arnold, could turn back to antiquity to find symbols of values that his own age had lost.[49]

Nor are the particular subjects wholly detached from the main theme. The first lyric tells how Chiron the centaur taught young Achilles of the gods, the stars, the tides, and the heroic life that leads to Elysium,[50] and this simple view of the whole duty of man is immediately followed by the modern-minded Empedocles' testament to Pausanias, with its very different conception of heroism and the heroic soul. The philosopher's concluding theme is the stoic version of *Carpe diem*; expect no bliss in heaven, but enjoy what earth affords, and fear not.[51] Then comes the lovely idyll of Cadmus and Harmonia, a green thought in a green shade. The ancient pair, once the happiest of mortals, had suffered calamity, and then had been granted the peace of Elysium, but not as human beings; they enjoyed happiness

---

[49] When Arnold tells us, in *Kensington Gardens*, that he was "breathed on by the rural Pan," we know what he means, though his Pan was not a goatish deity. Similarly in his allusions to the "Mighty Mother" in *The Youth of Nature* and *Thyrsis*, the idea is less of nature's fecundity than of the freshness and "rightness" of the early world "And all the marvel of the golden skies." In *Westminster Abbey* (1882), the same idea inspires a fine but over-elaborate allusion to the Mighty Mother and the child whom she wished to endow with more than human gifts; it suggests parallels with the Homeric *Hymn to Demeter*, Virgil's fourth *Eclogue*, and Milton's *Nativity*, which the infancy of Dean Stanley will hardly sustain.

[50] See Pindar, *Nem.* iii. 43 ff., *Pyth.* vi. 19 ff.; Statius, *Ach.* i. 106 ff., 184 ff., ii. 96 ff. We may remember that Arnold projected a poem on Achilles' voyage after death to the island of Leuce. See Pindar, *Nem.* iv. 49, *Ol.* ii. 68 ff.; Pausanias, III. xix. 11–13.

[51] The doctrine is of course very typical of Arnold but he must be recalling a passage from Pindar which he certainly remembered in *Cadmus and Harmonia*. After telling how Asclepius was struck down by Zeus for restoring a dead person to life (as in Arnold's poem Empedocles is popularly thought to have done), Pindar says: "We must seek from the gods for such boons as best befit a mortal mind, knowing what lieth before our feet, and knowing of what estate we are. Seek not, my soul, the life of the immortals; but enjoy to the full the resources that are within thy reach" (*Pyth.* iii. 59 ff., in Sandys' transla-

as snakes, "placid and dumb." [52] Since Arnold is so often, and not unjustly, accused of a defective ear, we might observe the beauty of the opening rhythm, a rich and subtle movement beyond Swinburne's compass.

When Empedocles, conscious that the world has broken him, approaches the crater and rouses himself to die before his soul is dead, Callicles sings of the rebel Typho who groans beneath the mountain while his conqueror feasts with the gods.[53] Empedocles catches up the truth that he discerns in the fable; the brave impetuous heart yields everywhere to the subtle, contriving head, the world of "littleness united" hates the simplicity of greatness. As he takes off his "fool's-armoury of magic" with the "Lie there" of a bitterly skeptical Prospero, Callicles sings of Apollo and the flaying of Marsyas.[54] The young Olympus had wept for the fate of his master — as Callicles himself stands apart, grieving for his admired Empedocles, another victim of Apollo. The poet-philosopher lays down his laurel bough, "Scornful Apollo's ensign." He has no choice between the two extremes, Apollo and the world,

---

tion). Arnold prized Pindar not so much for being "compendious and exclusive," but as one of the few great exemplars of "imaginative reason."

[52] Pindar (*Pyth.* iii. 88 ff.) tells of Cadmus and his wife, whose wedding the gods attended, as examples of the fate that overtakes prosperity. In his *Last Words on Translating Homer*, Arnold quotes the passage as a specimen of "the grand style in simplicity." See also the speech of Dionysus near the end of the *Bacchae*; Apollodorus, *Lib.* III. v. 4; Hyginus, *Fab.* vi; Ovid, *Metam.* iv. 563 ff.; *Paradise Lost*, ix. 505–06.

Mr. Aldington (*Literary Studies and Reviews*, 1924, pp. 144–45) compares this lyric with a passage from Landor's *To Corinth*, and condemns it as "prismatic," weakly emotional, and full of weak "literary" adjectives, "warm," "green," "happy," "fair," and so on. Landor's lines are admirably cool and diaphanous, but Arnold's purpose is different, and surely legitimate; and most of his adjectives might be defended as Homeric.

[53] See Hesiod, *Theog.*, ll. 820 ff.; Pindar, *Pyth.* i. 15 ff.; Aeschylus, *Prometheus Bound*, ll. 351 ff.; Ovid, *Metam.* v. 321 ff. For the allusion to "the Mount of Gore" (Mount Haemus), see Apollodorus, *Lib.* I. vi. 3.

[54] Hyginus, *Fab.* clxv; cf. Ovid, *Metam.* vi. 393–94. In some versions (*e.g.*, Apollodorus, I. iv. 2) Olympus is the father of Marsyas.

the intolerable loneliness of thought and intolerable life with his fellow men. He has outlived the happy time of his youth, when thought and feeling, the soul and the world, were wedded in simple harmony. Then, in the last proud consciousness that he has not been wholly enslaved, he returns to the elements, and, like the everlasting sea closing calmly over a noble wreck, there comes the singer's joyful, glowing vision of eternal things, the things Achilles had learned of from Chiron, Zeus and the gods and the action of men, toil and strife and rest and the stars. The Apollo of this swift, magnificent lyric is not the Apollo of Empedocles, the remote, austere deity of solitary thought, but the radiant leader of the Nine whose temple is the universal heart of nature and man.[55]

The lyrical and the ethical impulses in Arnold are represented, in their simplest form, in two of his best short classical poems, *Philomela* (1853) and *Palladium* (1867). Philomela, ever since Elizabethan days, had been sadly overworked in English verse; Cowper included her "mechanic woe" in a satirical list of poetic clichés.[56] But here, as always, an old theme has only to be felt freshly and intensely to become new. The ancient tale of lust and suffering, of the dumb sister's web, of hot cheeks and seared eyes, is set against a characteristic Arnoldian background, a moonlit lawn with cool trees beside the tranquil Thames.[57]

---

[55] John Bailey remarked (*The Continuity of Letters*, Clarendon Press, 1923, p. 108) that a line in the *Prometheus* of Aeschylus (ed. Sidgwick, l. 115) "finds perhaps its nearest English rendering in Arnold's 'What sweet-breathing presence . . . prime.'"

[56] *An Ode Secundum Artem.*

[57] Mrs. Sells (p. 201) observes that the nightingale's song had been to Obermann a "sublime expression d'une mélodie primitive, indicible élan d'amour et de douleur . . ." (*Obermann*, lxiii). Mr. H. W. Garrod regrets that Arnold revived the mythological associations of the bird, and finds in the poem "an individual elegance of melancholy" (*The Profession of Poetry*, Clarendon Press, 1929, p. 158). On ancient and modern confusions between Procne and Philomela, the nightingale and the swallow, see H. J. Rose, *Handbook of Greek Mythology* (1928), p. 263; Apollodorus, *Lib.* (ed. Frazer), II, 99–100.

Callicles' last song in *Empedocles* had been a moonlit mythological vision of a different kind, but the "eternal passion, eternal pain" of *Philomela* belongs no less to what will be for ever, what was from of old. If *Philomela* is a rare jet of pure feeling, *Palladium* is perhaps the most firm and finely rounded of Arnold's many poems in which morality is touched with emotion. It might, especially the last stanza, have been spoken by Empedocles in a melodious moment, and, as more than one critic has observed, it is very much in the vein of Clough. That a poem which, with almost the simplicity of a gospel hymn, first states the fable and then draws a lesson from it, should be so completely poetical is surely a triumph of sincerity. *Palladium* is as aloof and monumental, though not in the Landorian way, as the statue of Pallas herself, standing in the citadel above the roar of battle. There have been complaints that in his lectures *On Translating Homer* Arnold was more concerned with style than with substance — a charge which, even if true, would be disarmed by his title — but if we need any testimony to the depth of his feeling for Homer we have it in this poem:

> We shall renew the battle in the plain
> To-morrow; — red with blood will Xanthus be;
> Hector and Ajax will be there again,
> Helen will come upon the wall to see.[58]

Nothing could be more in the spirit of the great phrase of Goethe's that Arnold quoted near the beginning of his lectures: "From Homer and Polygnotus I every day learn more clearly that in our life here above ground we have, properly speaking, to enact Hell." [59] In *Palladium*, as in

---

[58] I quote the later version; in 1867 the first two words were "Men will."

[59] Arnold recalls the saying, in different words, in a letter to his sister of 1857 (Russell, I, 64). See also the stanza in his *Obermann* (1852) beginning "Yes, as the Son of Thetis said," where simple Homeric fatalism (cf. *Iliad*, xxi. 106 ff.) becomes a statement of the "centre of indifference" through which Arnold, like Carlyle, passed from the "me" to the "not-me."

Mycerinus, a classical symbol or example gives to the presentation of ethical ideas a distinctness, a substantial unity, an aura of noble associations, that we may miss in the poems of pure reflection.

Landor, as we have seen, lapsed from a major into a minor poet when he gave up the philosophic for the decorative; of only a very few *Hellenics* could it be said that the change was from the personal to the universal. Though Arnold wrote some fine things up to the last, there was in him a general decline from the authentic to the academic. The conflict between his soul and the world did not altogether cease — indeed it continued to inspire his best moments — but the gnawing pain subsided sufficiently to permit him to choose subjects instead of being chosen by them, to write poems according to a conscientious classicist theory. His moral and religious uncertainties found a partial relief in the apparent certitudes of classicism.

The classical doctrine expounded in the preface of 1853 and in many other parts of Arnold's prose is on the whole, despite some special pleading, permanently valid. The classicism of *Merope* (1858) is almost entirely factitious and synthetic. The post-romantics and spasmodics could not be curbed and guided by what was here the dead hand of antiquity. It may be readily granted for what it is worth that *Merope* is the most complete reproduction in English of the form and conventions of Sophoclean tragedy, even if the choruses mostly justify the famous similitude of a gamin drawing a stick along an area railing. But Arnold forgot his own "caution to poets":

> What Poets feel not, when they make,
>   A pleasure in creating,
> The world, in *its* turn, will not take
>   Pleasure in contemplating.[60]

---

[60] Lowry, p. 126. The quatrain appeared in the *New Poems* of 1867. As Mr. Lowry observes, Arnold "is reflecting upon his recent *Empedocles* and its failure to 'give joy.'"

The Arnold who stirs us is the Arnold who looked in his
heart, and mind, and wrote. He did so in his *Fragment of
an "Antigone"* — "Well hath he done who hath seiz'd
happiness" — and in the finer and more completely personal *Fragment of Chorus of a "Dejaneira."* [61] But the
author of *Merope* was a misguided Professor of Poetry who
had the *Poetics,* Sophocles' *Electra,* Hyginus and Pausanias
propped up before him. [62] Even *Gorboduc* of gloomy memory, and *Cato,* had the partial animation of patriotic and
political propaganda. In one chorus of *Merope* — "Much
is there which the sea . . ." — Arnold does speak with nobility and force on the dangers of autocracy in lines even
more pertinent nowadays than they were in 1858; if the
rest of the drama were on that level it would not go un-
read. But apart from this chorus, and from touches of
modern refinement and introspection in the chief characters, Arnold rivals Landor in confining himself within
the Greek world. Later he complained, in regard to *Atalanta in Calydon,* that "the moderns will only have the
antique on the condition of making it more *beautiful* (according to their own notions of beauty) than the antique:
i.e. something wholly different." [63] But the classicism of
Merope is untrue to Arnold's own best principles, not to
mention the ancients', and he is closer to Malherbe than

[61] These fragments appeared in 1849 and 1867 respectively. The *Dejaneira,*
which had moved Swinburne to rapture (*Essays and Studies,* 1875, pp. 160, 162)
moved Saintsbury to inept burlesque (*Matthew Arnold,* 1899, p. 113). Arnold
himself, writing in 1872 of the death of his son "Budge," says that his "main
feeling about him" is expressed in the poem (*Letters,* ed. Russell, II, 93); see the
last stanza especially.

[62] For details about structure and sources, see Churton Collins' edition of
Merope (2d ed., Clarendon Press, 1917).

[63] *Letters,* ed. Russell, I, 307. In his review of Arnold (pp. 160–62; see note 61
above) Swinburne gave some praise to *Merope,* but his real opinion appeared in
the epistolary comment: "As for Professor Arnold's *Merope,* the clothes are well
enough, but where has the body gone?" (*Letters,* ed. Gosse and Wise, 1918,
I, 32).

to his admired Sainte-Beuve.[64] His anxious defence of the play in his letters is, despite its apparent confidence, the fondness of a mother for a subnormal child.[65]

Sohrab and Rustum (1853) and *Balder Dead* (1855) lie outside our territory, but, in connection with *Merope*, they may be mentioned on account of their author's purpose. Modern stories in verse, like Keats's *Isabella*, to use Arnold's own illustration, were purple patches united by a thread of narrative; what they needed was the bracing and restraining influence of classical form, sobriety of style, and greatness of subject. The critics who have seen no good in *Merope*, and next to none in *Balder*, have rarely failed, even the lukewarm Arnoldians, to heap praises upon *Sohrab and Rustum*. I am not a lukewarm Arnoldian, but I cannot join the chorus. The narrative is admirably shaped, the writing is always good and sometimes beautiful, and our emotions are touched as they are not in the other two works. Yet *Sohrab and Rustum* also is academic, it has the defects of a poem written to illustrate a theory. In spite of the author's desire to make an effective whole, it is particular parts that we remember, for its unity is "not an organic thing, not the flow of flesh under the impulse of passionate thought."[66] In the first place, an artistic purpose is dubiously classical when it involves the adoption of an unnatural manner, and *Sohrab and Rustum* is more of a *tour de force* than *Hyperion*. The attempt to

---

[64] On Arnold's ranking ancient works above such things as *Hermann and Dorothea* and *Childe Harold*, Sainte-Beuve made some wise comments. While endorsing the principle on which the judgment was based, he insisted on the primary necessity "que le poëme ait vie, — une vie réelle à sa date et parmi les contemporains, et non pas une vie froide pour quelques amateurs dans le cabinet, — la nécessité d'un élément moderne, d'un intérêt moderne actuel et jeune, cet intérêt ne fût-il qu'adapté et comme infusé dans un sujet ancien" (*Étude sur Virgile*, Paris, 1870, p. 73). For Malherbe's doctrine of rigid reproduction of the antique, see my other volume, p. 123.

[65] *Letters*, ed. Russell, I, 66 ff.; *Unpublished Letters*, ed. Whitridge, pp. 35 ff.

[66] W. B. Yeats, "Art and Ideas," *Essays* (New York, 1924), p. 439.

write like Homer, even if one could, is a mistake in itself, and, though the poem is full of echoes, sometimes splendid, the general texture misses Homer's rapid simplicity, not to mention his fire and richness. The best sustained passage, the grand conclusion, is the one part in which we hear the authentic voice of Arnold, and it is that part which, in its style and in its half-symbolic use of the river Oxus, is most completely un-Homeric. Artificiality is most patent, of course, in the elaborate epic similes, which are usually more Miltonic and Virgilian than Homeric, and which, while often fine in themselves, are often also not integral parts of the poem but extraneous ornaments. (Arnold could forget his desire to be plain, direct, and severe, as in the two stanzas about the Tyrian trader at the end of *The Scholar Gipsy* [67] — not that one would wish them away.) In these similes we hear again the voice of the author, but he is counting his lines and saying that it is time for another one.

The question, however, goes beyond mere form and style. For a critic who rightly insisted on the supreme importance of the subject, Arnold was strangely misled in his efforts to provide inspiring examples for modern poets. The subject of *Merope*, at least as Arnold handles it, is simply insignificant. In *Balder* "the shadowy figures of a priestly mythology are impelled by unintelligible motives to inconclusive ends." [68] The subject of *Sohrab and Rustum*, the author would say, is thoroughly Homeric in spirit,[69] since it turns on the love of an heroic father and son, surely one of the great primary affections which subsist independently of time and place. But it is not so. The fatal combat is not, as dozens of Homeric episodes are, a universal and inevitable situation. Sophocles did not

[67] See E. K. Brown, "The Scholar Gipsy," *Revue Anglo-Américaine*, XII (1934–35), 219–25.
[68] Sir Edmund Chambers, "Matthew Arnold," *Proceedings of the British Academy*, XVIII (1932), 32.   [69] Cf. Lowry, pp. 136, 145–46; Russell, I, 34–35.

make a tragedy out of Oedipus' unwitting murder of his father; that was merely the factual beginning for much larger issues, the whole riddle of human life and the testing of human will. The subject of *Sohrab and Rustum* is a particular pathetic accident which is not brought about by qualities of character (though of course it displays them) nor, in any philosophic sense, by fate; hence it is not tragic, and it does not contain the large implications of Homer or Sophocles. Arnold would not wish to be tried by any lower standard.

Thus in his several attempts to furnish models of a serious subject treated with simplicity and severity Arnold missed the essential qualities that he most admired. He did, like Landor, achieve a high degree of classical sobriety and objectivity, but he did so, like Landor, by ignoring ideas and confining himself within a primitive antique world. It was not by that method that modern poetry could become a *magister vitae*, a criticism of life, the one hope and stay of a race that had lost religion. But in the many poems in which Arnold speaks — if he does not often sing — because he must, poems which reveal the many-sided struggle between his soul and the world, between Hebraism and Hellenism, between his wistful idealizing of the past and his effort to find guidance for the future, between his instinctive philosophic search for the One and his instinctive emotional response to the Many — it is in such poems, where he tries to achieve order, and not in his more or less academic exercises, where order is negative and ready-made, that Arnold comes closest to being a classical poet. And it is in such poems also that he shows what Swinburne described as "a sense of right resulting in a spontaneous temperance which bears no mark of curb or snaffle, but obeys the hand with imperceptible submission and gracious reserve." [70]

[70] *Essays and Studies*, p. 138.

CHAPTER VIII

Early Victorian Minor Poets

IN THE years just before and after Victoria's accession English poetry was in the doldrums. Wordsworth and Southey were alive, in a sense, but of the older generation of romantics Landor alone was flourishing. Tennyson was wrapped in gloomy silence and tobacco smoke; the bud of Browning's fame was nipped by *Sordello*. Elizabeth Barrett's position, though higher than that of her future husband, was not yet consolidated by the two volumes of 1844. The great poet of the day was Sir Henry Taylor, who, said Miss Barrett, was in her opinion "scarcely a poet at all"; and every drawing-room was fragrant with the volumes of Mrs. Hemans and L.E.L. But if greatness be measured by editions, the really dominant figure was Robert Montgomery, author of *Satan* and *The Omnipresence of the Deity*, who made a Roman holiday for Macaulay. And then came Martin Tupper.

For this was a serious age, an age of middle-class literature and the middle-class conscience. If the pagan serenity of the Olympian gods was not shaken by numerous hymn-writers' yearnings for a heavenly home, or by the bray of Exeter Hall, it was disturbed by more cultivated sounds. The young men of the new generation were feeling the influence of Wordsworth, Keats, and Shelley, for the stars of Byron and Moore had waned, but now there was another kind of leaven at work. The mystical monologues of the oracle of Highgate were dying away, though their effect was still potent, when there rose like a steam of rich distilled perfumes the voice of Newman. Keats and

Shelley, standing outside orthodox religion, had not been aware of a conflict between Christianity and paganism, but for a number of early Victorian writers, Mrs. Browning, Aubrey de Vere and others, the old conflict was revived, even before the advent of Rossetti and Swinburne made neo-paganism the only wear. These writers, or some of them, are united also by their sense of a conflict between the claims of the antique and the claims of modern realism. From representatives of that double strain we shall pass on to a more miscellaneous group, which includes the sturdy pagan evolutionist, Richard Henry Horne, Macaulay, whose soul is a mystery, Charles Kingsley, the muscular Christian, and "Owen Meredith," who was perhaps a better diplomat than poet.

I. Elizabeth Barrett Browning (1806–61)

Although Mrs. Browning's poetic treatment of myth has not much intrinsic importance, she is in several ways a symptomatic figure in the mythological and Hellenic tradition. All through her girlhood and later life, until marriage enlarged her activities, Greek literature, along with endless novels and modern poetry, fed the passions of a starved nature. But her Hellenic devotion was not entirely Attic. [1] She read every line of the three tragic poets, and all of Plato, and she enjoyed Greek literature for its own sake, but she enjoyed it far more when she could think of it as a vestibule to Christianity. [2] Hence

---

[1] On May 1, 1832, she made a record of the number of lines of Greek she could repeat. Of the 3280 lines of Greek prose, only 90 are from "Heathen writers," and 1860 are from Gregory Nazianzen alone. The total for Greek poetry is 4420, and Aeschylus comes first with 1800, Euripides is a poor third with 350; the second is Synesius, of whose hymns she knows 1310 lines. See *Elizabeth Barrett Browning: Hitherto Unpublished Poems and Stories, with an Inedited Autobiography*, ed. H. B. Forman (Boston, 1914), II, 134–35.

[2] *Letters of Elizabeth Barrett Browning*, ed. Sir Frederic Kenyon (1897), I, 101. Hugh Boyd, who had led her to the Greek Christian writers, would apparently

for the most part Mrs. Browning's Hellenism and her faith dwelt happily together, and in a series of prefaces (which also show her evolution from eighteenth-century classicism to romantic Hellenism) the young author found evidence that the pagan Greeks, from Homer onward, had sought the divine, though darkly.[3] *Prometheus Bound* is "one of the very noblest of human imaginations," but if Aeschylus had come later he would surely have turned from Caucasus to Calvary, from the theme of hate and revenge to love and forgiveness.[4] It was in some such spirit that, during 1841, Mrs. Browning — who of course was Miss Barrett until 1846 — in collaboration with Horne planned a lyrical drama on the birth and growth of the soul, *Psyche Apocalypté*, which was to end with a vision of the Cross; the extant drafts cause no regret that it was abandoned.[5] Still another attempt to blend Hellenism and Christianity was *A Drama of Exile* (1844), which shows what a Christian Aeschylus might have done with Adam and Eve; in spite of "Euripides the human," Mrs. Browning regarded Aeschylus as "the divinest of all the divine Greek souls,"[6] and, in her own wild way, she had something Aeschylean about her.

---

have confined her poetry "to the exclusive expression of Christian doctrine" (*ibid.*, I, 242, 247). Against this may be set his gift of Cyprus wine, which the pupil celebrated in verses of secular gusto.

[3] See the prefaces to *The Battle of Marathon* (1820) and the first version of *Prometheus Bound* (1833), in the *Poetical Works* (Oxford University Press, 1920).

[4] Preface to *The Seraphim* of 1838 (*Works*, pp. 78–80). Mrs. Browning's Shelleyan desire to make Prometheus into a perfect hero comes out in the discussion between her and her future husband of both the ancient drama and the one he suggested she should write. Browning, after explaining his notion of Greek realism, ends with "In your poem you shall make Prometheus our way." See *Letters of Robert Browning and Elizabeth Barrett Barrett* (1899), I, 35–40. This collection is cited henceforth as *Letters*.

[5] *Letters of Elizabeth Barrett Browning Addressed to Richard Hengist Horne*, ed. S. R. Townshend Mayer (1877), II, 61 ff.; *Hitherto Unpublished Poems*, etc., ed. Forman, II, 200 ff.; *Letters of Elizabeth Barrett Browning*, ed. Kenyon, I, 84–85.

[6] *Letters*, I, 35. She planned to write a monologue supposedly spoken by

So far Christianity is in harmony with Hellenism, a half-Christianized Hellenism. But Mrs. Browning's religion, a mixture of the evangelical, the "Platonic," and the poetic, was a central fact of her nature, and the love of Greek, for all its intensity, was in comparison an external accident; if challenged, the one romantic passion was strong enough to annihilate the other. In a poem which, whatever be thought of its general quality and its rhymes, is Mrs. Browning's most serious treatment of myth, the Greek gods are brought face to face with Christian truth and put to rout. The conflict between Christ and Pan had been revived for the early nineteenth century by Schiller's *Gods of Greece,* and Mrs. Browning, having read Mr. Kenyon's paraphrase, was roused to a passionate answer, *The Dead Pan* (1844). Milton, who was Hebraic enough even in youth, had celebrated the overthrow of the pagan deities at the birth of Christ, but he had been carried out of his Christian purpose by their sonorous names and glamorous associations. Mrs. Browning has no Renaissance paganism behind her, but, along with her own fervent instincts, all the strength of early Victorian pietism. "Pan is dead," she proclaims with ruthless exultation, the vain false gods of Hellas are silent evermore. In the concluding stanzas, to which, she said, all the rest were only a prelude, she exhorts poets to remember that "God Himself is the best Poet" and "the Real is His song"; "Truest Truth" is "the fairest Beauty." [7] In letters of equal

---

Aeschylus "just before the eagle cracked his great massy skull with a stone" (*ibid.*, I, 31). See below, ch. XI, note 12. Miss M. H. Shackford has suggested a relationship between the sufferings of Io and those of Marian Erle in *Aurora Leigh* (*E. B. Browning; R. H. Horne: Two Studies,* Wellesley, Mass., 1935, p. 15).

[7] *Works,* p. 306. Is the line "To think God's song unexcelling" (stanza xxxvii) an echo of Milton's "Sion's songs, to all true tastes excelling" in his tirade against Greek culture (*Paradise Regained,* iv. 347)?

The popular bard, Charles Mackay, wrote a *Dead Pan* (*Legends of the Isles,* 1845) on the same text, though Mrs. Browning did not feel that she had any

sincerity the author maintained her case against Mr. Kenyon's criticism; we do not live among dreams, and if the Christian religion is true, "the *poetry of Christianity* will one day be developed greatly and nobly." [8]

These bits of verse and prose suggest a third element in Mrs. Browning's poetic constitution which is antagonistic to myth, what may be called the modern and realistic. The poet's business is not "to rhyme the stars and walk apart" but to grapple with life. Books had always, for her, been "a substitute for living," and "nothing is more striking when at last she broke the prison bars than the fervour with which she flung herself into the life of the moment." [9] In the long meditated, intensely felt, and turbidly written *Aurora Leigh* (1857), which shocked the mammas of England, one comes upon mythological allusions which are strangely incongruous in such a setting. One may, like Oscar Wilde, see in them "the fine literary influence of a classical training," [10] or one may think merely that such things could not help running off a bluestocking's pen. At times even these partake of Mrs. Browning's excited realism. Compare Tennyson's "Now lies the Earth all Danaë to the stars" with these lines, in the vein of Mrs. Browning's husband, on a picture of

> A tiptoe Danae, overbold and hot,
> Both arms a-flame to meet her wishing Jove
> Half-way, and burn him faster down; the face
> And breasts upturned and straining, the loose locks
> All glowing with the anticipated gold.[11]

---

claims against him (*Letters*, I, 393, 398). And Robert Buchanan made a poetic comment on Mrs. Browning's poem; see his *Complete Poems* (1901), I, 185.

[8] *Letters*, ed. Kenyon, I, 128–29. On the question of her rhymes, which she says were a matter of principle and not of carelessness, see *ibid.*, I, 182–83, and *Letters to Horne*, II, 113 ff.

[9] Virginia Woolf, *The Common Reader*, Second Series (1932), p. 207. For Mrs. Browning's phrase about rhyming the stars, see *Letters*, ed. Kenyon, II, 382.

[10] *Works of Oscar Wilde*, Authorized Edition (Boston [1910]), XII, 257.

[11] *Works*, pp. 411–12.

A little overbold and hot for pre-Swinburnian verse, and a poetess too! But more instinctive and characteristic is a denunciation of mythology and an appeal to poets to express the meanings, human and divine, of the world about them:

> Never flinch,
> But still, unscrupulously epic, catch
> Upon the burning lava of a song
> The full-veined, heaving, double-breasted Age.[12]

These lines remind us that Mrs. Browning's modes of thought and feeling were no more disciplined by Greek than her Christian thought and feeling were disturbed by her early reading of eighteenth-century rationalists.[13] And the whole passage, along with other evidence, explains why she never wrote a mythological narrative or idyll as almost every poet and poetaster of her time did.[14] When, long before *Aurora Leigh*, her future husband tempted her for the moment with the subject of Prometheus, she put it away from her, partly because she did not dare to follow Aeschylus, but mainly because she was on principle opposed to the antique:

I am inclined to think that we want new *forms*, as well as thoughts. The old gods are dethroned. Why should we go back to the antique moulds, classical moulds, as they are so improperly called? If it is a necessity of Art to do so, why then those critics are right who hold that Art is exhausted, and the world too worn out for poetry. I do not, for my part, believe this: and

---

[12] *Ibid.*, pp. 449-51.

[13] Even in her paraphrases of the ancients she slipped easily into modernizing or sentimentalizing. For example, compare the passage "And if I read aright" (*Works*, p. 586) with Apuleius (*Metam.* v. 25); see Adolf Hoffmann, *Das Psyche-Märchen des Apuleius in der englischen Literatur* (Strassburg, 1908), p. 84.

[14] She perhaps approached such a thing in *The Enchantress*, which was apparently written in the early eighteen-thirties, but it was never completed or published. See *New Poems by Robert Browning and Elizabeth Barrett Browning*, ed. Kenyon (1914), pp. 78-82.

I believe the so-called necessity of Art to be the mere feebleness of the artist. Let us all aspire rather to *Life*, and let the dead bury their dead. . . . And then Christianity is a worthy *myth*, and poetically acceptable.[15]

The enthusiastic preoccupation with Greek which effervesces in Mrs. Browning's early works and letters almost disappears after marriage has given her a new life in the great world of men and women, Italian and French politics, and the still darker mysteries of séances. Her critical remarks on Greek authors, pagan or Christian, are mostly trite in comparison with her independent and sometimes keen estimates of her contemporaries. Pagan literature had been an imaginative and romantic escape from solitude, and the lady of Shalott — or, as a Grecian might have said, the dweller in Plato's cave — was sick of shadows. Apart from *The Dead Pan*, her poems on classical subjects are happy familiar verses on the joys of reading, and even such a pleasant reminiscence as *Hector in the Garden* ends with an injunction to shun dreams and be up and doing. Once, in a springtime near the end of her life, Mrs. Browning surrendered to myth, and sang with rarely melodious felicity of Pan by the river. Her reward from posterity has been that *A Musical Instrument* (1860) is one of her best-known poems.[16] But its serious theme is that of the earlier *Vision of Poets*, "the necessary relations of genius to suffering and self-sacrifice." While at first sight Pan might seem here to have conquered Christ, it is because, for Mrs. Browning, Christ includes Pan. "All truth and all beauty and all music belong to God — He is in all things; and in speaking of all, we speak of Him." [17]

[15] *Letters*, I, 45–46.
[16] One reward at the time was an anonymous letter from a person who had hitherto regarded her "as a great Age-teacher, all but divine," and now denounced this lyrical ebullition of her heart as immoral (*Letters*, ed. Kenyon, II, 406).
[17] *Letters*, ed. Kenyon, I, 247.

II. Aubrey de Vere, Clough, Cory, and Others

The essential problem of Christian and pagan, of modern and antique themes, is indicated in the sketch of Mrs. Browning, but it touched too many writers of the age to be dismissed without a few pages on some more or less notable names.[18] Aubrey de Vere (1814–1902) paid his chief poetical tributes to Greece in his middle twenties, and he lives not by them but by his poetry of Ireland and of religious faith; in 1851 he followed Newman to Rome. His lyrical masque, *The Search after Proserpine* (1843), appears in itself to be little more than a piece of decorative mythology, and one's opinion is not much altered by the prefatory account of the elaborate philosophic symbolism intended.[19] As a presentation of "a problem of our Humanity" the masque is only pretty tinsel compared with De Vere's poem on the Irish famine, *The Year of Sorrow* — he was himself active in relief work — and as a treatment of death and immortality it is frivolous beside the pages of his diary on the death of his father.[20] The

---

[18] One cannot take account of the small fry, since everyone learned to play variations on the contrasts between Christian and pagan ideals, but William Bell Scott and Augusta Webster may be mentioned. Contemplating the Elgin Marbles, Scott recognized the grand truths implicit in ancient fables, and, though the Cross has triumphed over all, the gods remain sublime revelations of the ideal toward which humanity must move (see my Appendix, under 1854). In *Athens* (*Blanche Lisle*, 1860, pp. 55–61), the scholarly Mrs. Webster celebrated the ancient city, but contrasted Zeus with "a greater God" and Athene with the Virgin Mary. The bulkiest contribution to the theme was Charles Kent's *Aletheia: or The Doom of Mythology* (1850), a poem of 139 pages with a mythological glossary of some 85. With picturesque and joyous exuberance the author conjures up all the figures of pagan myth, and then in the last few pages Aletheia appears to say that Pan is dead, that Truth and Love and the Christian God have banished "the Pagan devils."

[19] Landor's lack of discernment, or his native generosity, inspired a noble salute to the author in *Last Fruit off an Old Tree* (1853), p. 459; see *Poems*, ed. Wheeler, III (1935), 159, 180. For Landor's epistolary praise, see Wilfrid Ward, *Aubrey de Vere: A Memoir* (1904), p. 256, note. In connection with the symbolism, it is of some interest to find De Vere quoting Bacon's *Wisdom of the Ancients*.   [20] Ward, pp. 111 ff., 118 ff.

Proserpine volume included *Recollections of Greece*. As a poet De Vere was too much in love with the passionless bride, divine tranquillity, but he achieved energy and salience in some sonnets, such as *Aeschylus* and the monumental *Sun God* (called *Sunrise* in 1843). The main interest, however, of these poems on Greek themes is in the conflict they reveal. De Vere felt keenly the power of Greek beauty and wisdom, while as a serious Christian he recoiled from paganism and turned more and more to the Catholic Middle Ages, not as a refuge, but because "there was a positive religious insight in the Middle Ages, which the modern world was losing." [21] In the elaborate *Lines Written Under Delphi*, he finds the Greek gods far better than the gods of modern life, "Traditions, Systems, Passion, Interest, Power," yet nothing but the worship of the God of Truth with his whole being can redeem man from devotion to the idols of passion and sense. [22] In a number of critical essays of later years, when time and increasing security of faith had mellowed his anti-pagan convictions, De Vere returned to the subject of Hellenism, and no Victorian critic treated the mythological aspects of Spenser, Landor, Wordsworth, Keats, and Shelley with his combination of insight, breadth, and scholarship. This long but inadequate paragraph may be rounded off with a few remarks from the essay "Landor's Poetry" (1850). [23] "True poetry has ever a substratum of Religion in it," and Greek poetry owed its high character to the elements of truth in Greek religion, philosophy, and myth. But the modern world and its poetry are secular, not Christian. When Wordsworth would rather be an old pagan than a

---

[21] *Ibid.*, p. 317. Cf. De Vere's two dramas, *Alexander the Great* and *Saint Thomas of Canterbury*, and his *Recollections* (1897), pp. 358 ff.

[22] *Poetical Works* (1884), I, 82–94. Cf. *Wisdom* (*ibid.*, I, 59–60).

[23] *Edinburgh Review*, XCI (1850), 408–43; *Essays Chiefly on Poetry* (1887), II, 143–88, especially 180 ff.

modern Englishman, he is only affirming "that Triton is better than Plutus." Considering the want of spirituality in a large proportion of modern verse, De Vere asks — and the question sums up the great contribution of the romantics to mythological poetry — where in that body of writing is to be found so close a relation, "even through type or symbol, with religious ideas," as in the portion of it based on ancient myth?

Arthur Hugh Clough (1819–61) may be mentioned here as a symptom rather than as a mythological poet. His ironic temperament, the oppressive weight of religious difficulties, and a native instinct for the modern, realistic, and satirical in poetry, these all combined to turn him aside from the conventional post-romantic path. In print he rebuked not only Alexander Smith but his friend Arnold for being led away from the realities of human life by Keatsian luxuries or by classical models.[24] But Arnold himself was a perplexed modernist who at times found a refuge in the antique world or in dreams of the warm south, and Clough too, though rarely, felt a similar impulse. He shows his capacity for enchantment in the proem to the first canto of *Amours de Voyage*:

Come, let us go, — to a land wherein gods of the old time wandered,
Where every breath even now changes to ether divine.[25]

In Rome, thinking (like Gibbon before him, though with less untroubled detachment) of the Catholic ritual being performed under the "Dome of Agrippa," he repeoples the niches, not with the martyrs and saints and the rest,

[24] *Prose Remains of Arthur Hugh Clough* (1888), pp. 356, 368. The review appeared in *The North American Review*, LXXVII (1853), 1 ff.

[25] *Poems* (1890), p. 269. In the next lines he feels that, wherever we turn, the world "still is the same narrow crib."

Clough's one purely mythological poem was *Actaeon*, a dubious metrical experiment (*Poems*, pp. 423–24). It was apparently first published in the *Poems and Prose Remains* (1869), II, 467–68. See also ἐπὶ Λάτμῳ (1849) and *Selene*.

"But with the mightier forms of an older, austerer worship,"
and he goes on to render the Horatian lines about Apollo
of Delos and Patara.[26] The most poignantly ironical allusion, however, occurs in the fine opening of *The Shadow*:

> I dreamed a dream: I dreamt that I espied,
> Upon a stone that was not rolled aside,
> A Shadow sit upon a grave — a Shade,
> As thin, as unsubstantial, as of old
> Came, the Greek poet told,
> To lick the life-blood in the trench Ulysses made —
> As pale, as thin, and said:
> "I am the Resurrection of the Dead. . . ."

Although his few and brief mythological verses are not
of much account, William Johnson Cory (1823–92) is another symbol of mingled Hellenic and modern sympathies.
He lacked Clough's religious intensity, and Clough did
not have Cory's patriotic fervor, which was of the kind
nourished by the playing fields of Eton. But the melancholy of both was partly due to a sense of failure, to an
academic consciousness of being outside the large world
of actualities. Cory, the man of simpler nature, is the
schoolmaster on the sidelines of life, cheering the games
he cannot play, coveting the sword he cannot wield. His
reading, ancient and modern, is, like Elizabeth Barrett's,
a substitute for living. He is at one with Clough when he
declines to pray for dryads and prefers "the presence of
hungering, thirsting men."[27] In one of his two famous
pieces, *Mimnermus in Church*, he craves human life and
imperfect earth, not heaven and abstract perfection; Mimnermus is a mild, shy pagan, and a post-romantic one, an
enfant du siècle,[28] as Cory called himself. His classical

---

[26] *Poems*, pp. 274–75; Horace, *Od*. III. iv. 58 ff.

[27] *An Invocation (Ionica*, 1858). Cory exemplified his remark that one's feelings lose poetic flow soon after twenty-seven or so, and he virtually said his say
in this early volume.

[28] *Extracts from the Letters and Journals of William Cory*, ed. Francis Warre
Cornish (Oxford, 1897), p. 458.

studies did not much alter tastes determined by his own age and by personal idiosyncrasy. "Tennyson is the sum and product of the art that began with Homer." [29] And the elegiac grace and tenderness of Cory's *Heraclitus* are partly Tennysonian. The lyric is a particular expression of the central motive of *Mimnermus*, and it is a very Victorian bit of Hellenism. One may say, with Basil Gildersleeve, "A pretty poem, Mr. Cory, but you must not call it Callimachus"; [30] yet the poet probably knew what he was doing, if one may judge from his later comment on a rendering from Euripides by W. H. Mallock: "It gave me a new type of *romantic* translation, in which the modern versifier walks alongside of the classic poet, and has a colour of his own, and does not think it his duty to be concise." [31]

That a sensitive and exalted poetic nature could really be torn between Christian and Hellenic impulses one has pathetic proof in the case of Digby Mackworth Dolben (1848-67). Rugby was not the only school which nourished morbidly religious boys. Dolben's life, William Cory said, "was one gem," and Gerard Manley Hopkins knew enough of him to lament the extinction of his beautiful promise. Bridges described, though he did not print, the first section of a poem of 1864, *Vocation B.C.*, in which Dolben tried to harmonize his two loves and two worlds by showing "how a pagan might have a mystical love of God, anal-

[29] *Ibid.*, pp. 498-99. More remarkable, from a master of Eton, is the judgment that "Greek plays are to French plays what cold boiled veal is to snipe" and by French plays he means not Racine but Dumas and Sardou and their kind (*ibid.*, p. 458).

[30] *Selections from the Brief Mention of Basil Lanneau Gildersleeve* (Johns Hopkins University Press, 1930), p. 268 (and cf. pp. 243, 327). The poem was written in 1845.

[31] *Letters and Journals*, p. 565. See Mallock's *New Republic* (1877), II, 106-07, or his *Verses* (1893). On the lack of conciseness in Cory's lyric, see F. W. Bateson, *English Poetry and the English Language* (Clarendon Press, 1934), p. 124.

ogous to a Christian's emotion." [32] The reconciliation of Apollo and Christ was not final. In a third part of the poem, printed as *From the Cloister*, Brother Jerome hungers for the beauties of Greece and Greek myths — when we remember Dolben's idealization of his friend Manning we understand why the tale of Hyacinth is "dearest of them all" [33] — for "sunny Athens, home of life and love,"

> Free joyous life that I may never live,
> Warm glowing love that I may never know. . . .

Weary of this squalid holiness, these hot black draperies, the incense-thickened air and the inevitable bells, he wishes that Apollo, dear bright-haired god in whom he half believes, might catch him heavenward. But this mood is overcome by thoughts of the Passion, and Brother Francis is heard singing of Jesus and eternal love. During the short time that remained to him Dolben praised Homer and Aeschylus, translated from Sappho and Catullus and Ovid, and was able to rejoice that "The world is young today." But some of his latest poems reveal the strain of living between earth and heaven, of wavering (to quote *Ash Wednesday*) between the profit and the loss. From desolating weariness, "Tired sorrow, tired bliss," he turns for quiet to a Madonna-like Persephone, "with supreme compassion pale," and envies the gods in their palaces far above the shaken trees.[34]

Before his conversion Gerard Hopkins (1844–89) gave evidence of a power which might have braced the flaccid sinews of Victorian mythological verse. The prize poem of his schooldays, *A Vision of the Mermaids* (1862), critics have mostly been content to label Keatsian, a useful but vague epithet which fits better the mythological allusions

---

[32] *Poems of Digby Mackworth Dolben* (Oxford University Press, 1915), pp. lv ff. (and see pp. xcv ff.).

[33] Cf. the references to Hylas and Hyacinthus (*ibid.*, p. 85).

[34] Pp. 117–18, 122.

in a still earlier prize poem, *The Escorial* (1860).[35] The *Vision* is markedly and prophetically individual. Instead of the common romantic idealism and soft, idyllic prettiness of description, the young poet, with the eye of a painter, creates a sharp-edged pattern of hard, bright color and sinuous movement. Words may be strained but they are alive. If the lines

> Plum-purple was the west; but spikes of light
> Spear'd open lustrous gashes, crimson-white,

suggest an Imagist striving after novelty, they carry us on to "Kiss my hand to the dappled-with-damson west" and "Glory be to God for dappled things." It was doubtless better for English poetry that Hopkins' later visions should have been of God rather than mermaids, yet one may regret his stern asceticism.[36] Though he could praise the mythological poems of his friends Bridges and Dixon, he was opposed, on both religious and artistic grounds, to the introduction of pagan deities into modern poetry. He admitted, however, that allegorical treatment of myth might yield the most beautiful results; "the moral evil is got rid of and the pure art, morally neutral and artistically so rich, remains and can be even turned to moral uses."[37]

Thus some of these poets are linked together by their preference for the modern over the antique, and all are

[35] The *Vision* was first printed in full in the facsimile edition of 1929, and is included in Bridges' edition of the *Poems*, re-edited by Charles Williams (Oxford University Press, 1930), pp. 130 ff.

[36] There is the sonnet *Andromeda* (1879), which was intended to be Miltonic but reminds us of Chapman's *Andromeda Liberata*.

[37] *Correspondence of Gerard Manley Hopkins and Richard Watson Dixon*, ed. C. C. Abbott (Oxford University Press, 1935), pp. 145 ff.; *Letters of Gerard Manley Hopkins to Robert Bridges*, ed. C. C. Abbott (1935), pp. 109, 216 ff.

Hopkins' discussions of Keats, in letters to Patmore of 1887–88, are not only remarkably penetrating but, in view of the whole bent of the writer's mind and life, remarkably sympathetic. See G. F. Lahey, *Gerard Manley Hopkins* (Oxford University Press, 1930), pp. 71 ff.

on the side of Christ rather than Apollo or Pan. This sketch of the problem may end, for the present, with a reference to the youthful poems of another religious devotee. At fourteen Christina Rossetti wrote an *Ariadne to Theseus*,[38] and three years later, in 1847, an inevitably Tennysonian piece, *The Lotus-Eaters*.[39] But Christina was no Hellenist (though a much finer artist than most English Hellenists, from Mrs. Browning to Swinburne), and her girlish enthusiasm for mythology was soon extinguished by her passionate and austere religious faith.[40]

III. Horne, Macaulay, Kingsley, Robert Lytton

Richard Henry Horne (1803–84)

When a boy Richard Henry (later Hengist) Horne threw a snowball at John Keats as he sat in the surgeon's gig, and he survived, a quaint relic, to awaken the amused pity of Sir Edmund Gosse. His adventurous life was that of a Victorian Trelawny, though more poetical than piratical, and he carried into a pietistic age not only the humanitarian idealism of the second romantic generation but, from *Hecatompylos* (1828) to *The Last Words of Cleanthes* (1883), a half-pagan faith of his own. *Orion* (1843) was the most considerable mythological narrative since *Hyperion*, and, whatever publicity was due to its original price, it owed its many editions to more substantial causes.

One can hardly escape giving a brief outline of the poem, an outline in which allegorical continuity must compel the

---

[38] *Poetical Works of Christina Rossetti*, ed. W. M. Rossetti (1904), p. xli. Among other unpublished poems were two concerning Sappho, of 1846 and 1848 (*ibid.*, p. xlii).

[39] It was not published in her lifetime, but is included in the *Works*, p. 111. See *ibid.*, pp. xxxvii, 467; and *New Poems by Christina Rossetti*, ed. W. M. Rossetti (1896), p. 370.

[40] See *Works*, pp. xlvii, lxix. There is one late and slightly mythological sonnet, *Venus's Looking-Glass* (pp. 387, 487).

slighting of action and description.[41] Orion is one of a company of giants who are mostly crude, destructive, elemental beings; one, Encolyon, is a type of the obstinate reactionary, while Akinetos, the Great Unmoved, is almo'st sublime in his utter passivity and cynical indifference to the world outside himself. Orion has not been in spirit one of these. He is by nature a "builder-up of things, and of himself," and love of Artemis fires him with new energies, new dreams of human possibilities. But though Artemis becomes the guide of his humanitarian toil and of his spiritual progress "From tyrant senses to pure intellect," Orion is still too earth-bound and self-centered for complete happiness or attainment of his high, hard ideal. His chief lapse into the tyranny of sense is the passion he conceives for King Oenopion's daughter Merope, a beautiful creature of earth, and gratification brings vague discontent and sorrow; it brings too the loss of Merope and of his sight, for the king's soldiers remove her and put out his eyes.

Though physical passion has crippled Orion's purposeful life, it leads eventually, through blindness and distress, to wisdom and a renewal of beneficent activity. The counsels of Akinetos tempt him only for the moment to subside into apathy. Nature and Labor, represented by a shepherd and Brontes the Cyclops, direct him to Eos, goddess of the dawn. She restores his sight, and his soul, his belief in good, is reborn; "'Tis always morning somewhere in the world." Now, with re-awakened love, Orion begins to understand the mutual support and balance of body and soul. He is still grateful to Artemis, and to Merope, but this new love unifies and inspires his head, heart, and hand; it fills him with life and happiness, yet

---

[41] See Horne's "Brief Commentary" prefixed to the ninth edition (1872). I have used Mr. Eric Partridge's reprint of the first edition (1928). For the classical myths of Orion, see Apollodorus, *Lib.* I. iv. 3–5.

turns his sympathies to the ills of the world. In the midst of all his "fresh designs for human weal" he is struck down by the jealous Artemis, but she, repenting, goes with Eos to entreat Zeus to restore his life. Orion's task is finished, however, and he is set in heaven as a constellation, a symbol to men of "victory over life's distress." The work of the builder lives on, a fruitful inspiration to the world, while Akinetos is turned into stone.

In the author's own words, Orion "is meant to present a type of the struggle of man with himself, *i.e.* the contest between the intellect and the senses, when powerful energies are equally balanced. *Orion* is man standing naked before Heaven and Destiny, resolved to work as a really free agent to the utmost pitch of his powers for the good of his race." That is clear enough, but no reader of the poem, or even of a bald summary, can help exclaiming, "This is a combination of *Endymion* and *Hyperion!*"[42] Orion's progress from simple realities through dreams to higher realities, from selfish love to humanitarian sympathy and action, is a large part of what all modern critics see in *Endymion*. Further, Orion is spiritualized partly through his own activity, partly through the ardors and sorrows he experiences in his love for three female beings; the three symbols are differently handled, but in the end each hero cleaves to the one who, representing human reality, represents the ideal also. The influence of *Hyperion*

[42] Mrs. Browning defined Horne's subject as "the growth of a poet's mind" (*Athenaeum*, June 24, 1843, p. 583; see Horne's address to "the herald Poet," p. 82). That may also have been his subject in a narrower sense, for Horne had a lifelong thirst for fame. According to Mr. P. L. Carver's suggestion, Akinetos would be the immovable British public, Merope an earthly infatuation, Eos the poet's several humanitarian activities, and Artemis those studies in philosophy of which *Orion* was the intellectual product (*R.E.S.*, V [1929], 371). One may hesitate at such explicit personal symbols, though none is impossible, and such a secondary intention in Akinetos at least seems plausible. In the last sentence of her review Mrs. Browning playfully warned the public not to invite the fate of the Unmoved by neglecting the poem.

on the parable is less obvious, but there is a general similarity (a safer word!) in the conception of social progress and individual self-discipline; whether or not Horne understood the significance of Keats's Apollo, he had the same idea of a poet's rise to his full godlike power through the knowledge that is sorrow, the sorrow that is wisdom. The relation of art to life was not of course a problem of the romantic poets only; just before *Orion* had appeared *Sordello* and the revised *Palace of Art*. Keats's humanitarianism had been a poetic ideal, Horne's was a practical fact, though his social labors are best remembered because his report on conditions in mines and factories inspired Mrs. Browning's *Cry of the Children*.[43] Finally, *Orion* embodies something of Carlyle's gospel of work and leadership, and it anticipates Meredith's evolutionary and humanitarian ideals.[44] It anticipates also Meredith's mythological and philosophic "reading of life." Horne insisted that *Orion* was not merely a "spiritual epic," as Mrs. Browning called it, but a corporeal epic too; whereas Christian asceticism, in spite of modern physiology and psychology, had never allowed the legitimate claims of the body, he had given senses as well as intellect full scope, and set up as an ideal the harmony of the two. This is pure Meredith.

If we ask why a poem of such serious purpose does not, philosophically, come home to us, the answer applies to more and greater works than *Orion*. While Horne's faith

[43] The episode of the famine in Ithaca (*Orion*, pp. 15 ff.) is one admitted topical allusion, a palpable reminder of the Corn Law agitation ("Brief Commentary," p. x). In the early *Hecatompylos*, which seems to be entirely in the tradition of musings over antique ruins, Horne ends with an allusion to famine (*Athenaeum*, April 8, 1828, p. 361).

[44] Horne says that Meredith wrote to him about the poem ("Brief Commentary," p. vi, note). In 1872 Horne cites Darwinian doctrine, quite in the spirit of Meredith, as a basis for meliorist hope, not pessimism (*ibid.*, p. xvi). The Hegelian strain in Horne's work has been noticed by René Galland, *George Meredith* (Paris, 1923), p. 43, and Robert Sencourt, *Life of George Meredith* (1929), p. 23.

is sincere and humane, we do not feel compelled to share a hardly won illumination kindled by intense inward conflict. The poem is not an imaginative rendering of the quality of experience, it is a theoretical pattern imposed upon experience. We are not moved as we are by such various confessional poems as *Endymion* and *Hyperion*, or *The New Sirens* and *Empedocles on Etna*. A further reason for our indifference to the author's intention is the mere amplitude of narrative and ornament, which, as in most such poems, can be enjoyed without reference to the transparent symbolism. The style of *Orion* is largely in the tradition of *Endymion*, though particular echoes of *Hyperion* are more obvious. If Horne has no lines like "Or blind Orion hungry for the morn," he avoids Keats's youthful lapses in taste, and his story is rapid and coherent. Poe, the most erratic of critics, while disliking the moral, lost his head altogether over the poetical beauties of *Orion*.[45] There is an abundance of lucid and richly colored pictures, and they have a minute realism not often found in the vaguely standardized "Greek" scenes of Victorian verse. The Nymphs have "clear elastic limbs of nut-brown hue"; Sylvans and Fauns dip their heads into a stream "Deep as the top hair of their pointed ears"; at the giants' orgy the wine

> Bubbled and leapt, and streamed in crimsoning foam,
> Hot as the hissing sap of the green logs.

And there are touches of another kind of realism rarer still in a philosophic and mythological "epic," namely, comedy, in connection with "the bald sage" and especially Akinetos, who is an original gem, or rather monument, of satirical and humorous imagination.

As Gosse says, Horne "was a remarkable poet for seven

45 *Works*, ed. E. C. Stedman and G. E. Woodberry (New York, 1914), VI, 323–54, especially 344 ff.

or eight years, and a tiresome and uninspired scribbler for the rest of his life." [46] Yet one cannot help admiring the indomitable old man who, in the remote Australian bush, could sit down after his day's work to write *Prometheus the Fire-Bringer*, and, when the manuscript was lost, could write it over again.[47] Admiration, however, stops at that point, and alarm begins when we scan the *dramatis personae* and observe a "sub-chorus of troglodytes." *Prometheus* is in fact a feeble repetition of *Orion*; Horne's faith is still in him, but what fire he had has gone out. He left behind him a work he considered his masterpiece, *Ancient Idols; or, The Fall of the Gods*; it has never reached print. But *The Last Words of Cleanthes* was a not ignoble valedictory; looking back over an austere life of fearless thought, Cleanthes returns, a tranquil Empedocles, to the elements.

Thomas Babington Macaulay (1800–59)

Scott's influence on the translating and writing of heroic ballads showed itself most obviously in the proportion of Scotsmen who took a hand in it. But the only bard who needs to be mentioned here was the very Irish William Maginn (Thackeray's Captain Shandon), whose *Homeric Ballads* appeared in *Fraser's Magazine* in 1838.[48] Though Maginn himself was no disintegrator, his translations are a reminder that the theory of the ballad origin of the Homeric poems had become generally familiar. The year

[46] "'Orion' Horne," *Selected Essays*, First Series (1928), p. 196.
[47] Dedication of *Prometheus* (Edinburgh, 1864). The drama is discussed by Miss Shackford, pp. 63–66 (see note 6 above).
[48] They were not issued in book form until 1850. Moore's *Legendary Ballads* (1830), which included mythological pieces, were only drawing-room lyrics. J. E. Bode, in publishing his *Ballads from Herodotus* (1853), took pains to say that he had conceived the idea in 1841, and had printed one ballad in *Blackwood* in April, 1842, some six months before the appearance of Macaulay's *Lays*. His inspiration came from the English and Scottish popular ballads; one does not regret his failure to defeat Arnold for the Oxford Professorship of Poetry.

1842 brought books from such established favorites as Sir Henry Taylor and Robert Montgomery, not to mention Tennyson's two volumes and Browning's *Dramatic Lyrics*, but Macaulay led the field. No one can count the editions of the *Lays*, [49] or — still stronger proof of vitality and popularity — the parodies they have drawn from old and young. In every generation the *Lays* have caused for one kind of reader a heightened pulse, for another a heightened eyebrow. We need not take account of Arnold's sneer (which allowed relative merit to Maginn's often slipshod work), for Arnold has been demolished by a number of critics who, not being poets, are more disposed to maintain that the house of poetry has many mansions. It should be possible to acknowledge that Macaulay did what he set out to do better than anyone else, though doubtless anyone could do it "if he had the mind." And Macaulay has had some tributes from poets. The *Lays* roused Elizabeth Barrett from her sofa; Landor more than once praised their Roman spirit; and, though Macaulay has often been blamed for corrupting the childish ear for poetry, he did not irreparably damage Swinburne or Francis Thompson or Mr. Yeats.[50]

Macaulay had begun writing ballads as a disciple of Scott, and in his early *Battle of Bosworth Field* we see not only his style in process of development but particular parallels, notably in the battle itself, with *The Battle of the Lake Regillus*.[51] But he wisely abandoned a period that Scott had made his own for the remoter antiquity in

[49] Their popularity has not been confined to English-speaking countries. See the article by Tommaso Tittoni cited in the bibliography.

[50] See Mrs. Browning's *Letters to Horne*, ed. Mayer, I, 166; Landor's *Works* (1846), II, 673, and *Heroic Idyls* (1863), p. 147 (*Poems*, ed. Wheeler, III, 153, 205); G. Lafourcade, *La jeunesse de Swinburne* (Paris and London, 1928), I, 95; Everard Meynell, *Life of Francis Thompson* (1926), p. 9; W. B. Yeats, *Autobiographies* (New York, 1927), p. 57.

[51] *Macaulay's Lays of Ancient Rome and other Historical Poems*, ed. G. M. Trevelyan (1928), pp. vii–viii, 176 ff.

which he had spent a good part of his life. He showed instinctive tact in writing as an ancient Roman bard, reciting the great deeds of a simple heroic world, holding up to a later age the old ideals of *pietas* and patriotic valor. Macaulay's robust mind has perhaps been most tersely described, in the words of Aubrey de Vere, as having "no trace of originality, depth, breadth, elevation, subtlety, comprehensiveness, spirituality," [52] but, without stopping to qualify the judgment, one may say that he chose themes and settings which brought out all his strength and turned his limitations into virtues of dramatic verisimilitude. Livy was his main source, and a congenial one — for Macaulay, who dreamed of being the English Thucydides, was rather the English Livy — but a man with all classical literature in his prodigious memory could not fail to draw upon a multitude of authors. And sometimes he echoed moderns as well as ancients. Such lines as

> Unwatched along Clitumnus
> Grazes the milk-white steer,

take us to Virgil, and also to Byron:

> But thou, Clitumnus . . .
> Thy grassy banks whereon the milk-white steer
> Grazes. . . .[53]

But the question of sources would lead us far and wide, and must be left to the editors and commentators.

Many a passage of Macaulay's prose, however garish

---

[52] Wilfrid Ward, *Aubrey de Vere: A Memoir*, p. 75.

[53] *Georg.* ii. 146; *Childe Harold*, iv. 66 (*Works of Byron*, ed. E. H. Coleridge, II, 379). Byron's editor seems to overlook this item, but, in connection with *Childe Harold*, iv. 80 (*ibid.*, II, 391), he cites *The Prophecy of Capys*, stanza xxx. Aubrey de Vere remarks (*Essays Chiefly on Poetry*, I, 26) that the finest passages in Scott's *Lord of the Isles* and *The Prophecy of Capys* have their original in the scene between Britomart and the priest of Isis in *The Faerie Queene* (V. vii. 20 ff.). But prophecies are common in heroic poetry, and Macaulay's famous slip about the Blatant Beast suggests that Spenser was less firmly lodged in his mind than a few hundred other authors.

it now seems, testifies to his vein of romance, his boyish love of heroic scenes, of historical pomp and circumstance, and he revealed something more than that in *The Last Buccaneer* and the *Epitaph on a Jacobite*. Of pathos there is not much in the *Lays*, certainly not where we might expect to find it, in *Virginia*; we forget the heroine, but not Appius gnawing his lip as the crowd close in upon him. The *Lays* do, however, possess abundant romantic feeling, quite genuine within its range. Memory and historical imagination pour out realistic, concrete details on every page. It is all so rapid and effortless that we feel a shock when, once in a while, the illusion is broken by an undramatic touch of pedantry like "Traced from the right on linen white. . . ." Macaulay is most happily and surely romantic in his handling of proper names, whether of places or persons. *The Armada*, as Chesterton says, is a good geography book gone mad, and so are the *Lays*. Macaulay had not been born in Italy, but reading and travel had made the land as rich in historical associations for him as Scotland was for Scott. Again and again the "rhymed rhetoric" of the *Lays* rises into poetry in the sonorous suggestiveness of proper names —

> Sempronius Atratinus
> Sate in the Eastern Gate.

Although by their very nature the *Lays* stand outside the main body of romantic mythological poetry, they show in their way what is true of greater works, namely, that, other things being equal, mere imitations or reproductions of the antique are usually dead, while poems informed by a modern spirit, either personal or "propagandist," are usually alive. If Macaulay's *Lays* surpassed other men's [54] the reason was not merely superiority of talent. It is not in academic effusions that brains and

---

[54] His nearest rival was Aytoun, whose first Scottish lay appeared in *Blackwood* in 1843. Sir Theodore Martin said that so far as Aytoun had a model it was

blood and bowels are splashed about with such Homeric
joy as Macaulay displays. In an excellent essay Mr.
E. E. Kellett (after recalling what Leigh Hunt told Macaulay in his begging-letter, that the *Lays* "want the
aroma that breathes from the *Faerie Queene*") thus explains their unique force and fire:

Their moving impulse was perhaps political rather than ethereal. Proud Tarquin was to him a sort of James the Second;
Valerius an earlier Schomberg; Titus was the Duke of Berwick;
Julius was Sarsfield, and Regillus a luckier Steinkirk: nay, the
Sublician Bridge was the bridge over the Gette, which William,
retreating before Luxemburg, crossed so unwillingly. Had there
been no British significance in these old Roman stories, nay, had
they not possessed a specially Whig significance, Macaulay
would never have retold them with such spirit. But though his
inspiration thus came as much from Constitution Hill as from
Helicon, it is a high and genuine inspiration nevertheless.[55]

And we may remember the boyish cheer of Andrew Lang,
who, when he came to "But Titus stabbed Valerius A
span deep in the breast," scribbled in the margin, "Well
done, the Jacobites!" [56]

Charles Kingsley (*1819–75*)

Apart from a few brief experiments, such as Hawtrey's
famous rendering from Homer, English hexameters gener-

---

not Macaulay but Wilhelm Müller (*Memoir of William Edmondstoune Aytoun*,
1867, p. 76). About the same time Aytoun wrote an Ovidian ballad on Lycaon,
which was first printed in the *Memoir* (pp. 97–99). A couple of jocular mythological pieces were included in the Bon Gaultier *Ballads* (1845).

In his *Lays and Legends of Ancient Greece* (1857), John Stuart Blackie tried
feebly to mingle sweet the classic strain with Gothic minstrelsy. See also the
volume by Freeman and Cox (Appendix, under 1850).

[55] "Macaulay's Lay Figures," *Suggestions* (Cambridge University Press,
1923), p. 164. In connection with the bridge over the Gette, Mr. Kellett quotes
a passage from the twentieth chapter of the *History* which recalls the situation
in *Horatius* to the reader, and recalled it to the author, who refers to his old hero.
See the *History* (World's Classics ed.), IV, 460.

[56] R. S. Rait *et al.*, "Andrew Lang," *Quarterly Review*, CCXVIII (1913), 300.

ally remind us of Dr. Johnson's dictum on women's preaching, and among whole poems in that measure *Andromeda* (1858) stands high in relative rightness and ease. Kingsley spent great pains on the mechanics of the poem, and now and then he achieved sonorous perfection — "As when an osprey aloft, dark-eyebrowed, royally crested." Yet even he did not escape the inevitable pitfalls. Though he aimed at "Homer's average of a spondee a line," [57] *Andromeda* lacks spondaic variety, and the movement is less dactylic than anapestic.

The attractions of *Andromeda* are not merely metrical, even if it is only a poem for boys — and possibly the modern boy who reads poetry is an intellectual from the cradle. Arnold, hearing what Kingsley was about, complained, *a priori*, that he was too coarse a workman for poetry.[58] But Kingsley, if not subtle, was an outdoor man, with senses keenly alive. He loved the beauty of the myth and reveled in it more and more, making, as his habit was, dozens of pencil drawings before turning to words for "colour and chiaroscuro."[59] One need not forfeit one's adult status if one's eye and pulse respond to the description of the Nereids and Tritons (most of which was "rattled off in the last two hours, in the act of dressing and breakfasting") —

Onward they came in their joy, and before them the roll of the surges
Sank, as the breeze sank dead, into smooth green foam-flecked
marble —

or the roar of wind and water, the radiant swooping figure of Perseus, the approach of the sea-monster, bulky and

---

[57] *Charles Kingsley: His Letters and Memories of his Life. Edited by his Wife* (2d ed., 1877), I, 344.
[58] *Letters of Matthew Arnold to Arthur Hugh Clough*, ed. H. F. Lowry, p. 139. Arnold did not mention *Andromeda* in discussing hexameters in the lectures on Homer.
[59] *Charles Kingsley*, I, 339 (and 342).

black as a galley, "Lazily coasting along, as the fish fled leaping before it." [60] The poem is doubtless too long, but it seldom flags, and the Homeric echoes and similes are more spontaneous at least than those of *Sohrab* and *Balder*. While not at all a symbolist in the romantic tradition, Kingsley saw in the subject more than an excuse for heroic and sensuous objectivity. The myth was "a very deep one," and belonged to the primitive period of "human sacrifices to the dark powers of nature, which died out throughout Greece before the higher, sunnier faith in *human* gods." He wished to show Andromeda as "a barbarian" with "no notion (besides fetichism) beyond pleasure and pain, as of an animal. It is not till the thinking, sententious Greek, with his awful beauty, inspires her, that she develops into woman." Speaking of a difference in style between two parts of the poem, Kingsley said: "I felt myself on old mythic, idolatrous ground, and went slowly and artificially, feeling it unreal, and wishing to make readers feel it such. Then when I get into real *human* Greek life, I can burst out and rollick along in the joy of existence." [61] One may miss the underlying intention, but one cannot miss "the joy of existence," the genuine love for high adventure, for the brave heart and hand, that one expects from the author of *Westward Ho!* and *Hereward the Wake*. "I love these old Hellenes heartily," he said in the preface to *The Heroes*, and, in more philosophic strain, he confessed to Arnold, when thanking him for *Culture and Anarchy*, that he had been ashamed to catch himself, a clergyman, wishing he had been an old Greek rather than

[60] *Poems* (1880), p. 201. Kingsley was working at the poem in 1852 *et seq.* In Part IV of the story of Perseus in *The Heroes* (published 1855, dated 1856), the whole passage on the sea-monster is almost identical, except for its being in prose. For the personal observation that went into the simile of the osprey (*Poems*, p. 202), see *Charles Kingsley*, I, 339–40.

[61] *Charles Kingsley*, I, 338–40. For the original myth, see Ovid, *Metam*. iv. 663 ff., and Apollodorus, *Lib.* II. iv. 3.

an Englishman.[62] However, needless to say, Kingsley is no "pagan." Next to the romances of the Christian Middle Ages, "there are no fairy tales like these old Greek ones, for beauty, and wisdom, and truth, and for making children love noble deeds, and trust in God to help them through."[63] And the conclusion of *Andromeda* reflects not only the simple Homeric world that Kingsley loved, but something of the ideals of the author of *Yeast* and *Alton Locke*:

Chanting of order and right, and of foresight, warden of nations;
Chanting of labour and craft, and of wealth in the port and the garner;
Chanting of valour and fame, and the man who can fall with the foremost,
Fighting for children and wife, and the field which his father bequeathed him.
Sweetly and solemnly sang she, and planned new lessons for mortals:
Happy, who hearing obey her, the wise unsullied Athené.

Robert Lytton (*1831–91*)

If the faded copies of *Lucile* on the shelves of every secondhand bookshop in the English-speaking world were ever disturbed in their eternal repose, one might say that "Owen Meredith" still lived. While *Lucile* does not concern us, two of Lytton's other works, one popular and one stillborn, help to explain what happened, on the lower levels of mythological verse, to the post-romantic tradition, and to explain also the neglect of a number of poets whom we now read. The chief thing in his first volume (1855) was the drama *Clytemnestra*, part of which he had written before he left Harrow. In his fable and structure Lytton followed the *Agamemnon*, but substituted Victorian fullness of characterization for Aeschylus' religious and philosophic vision, and for a public unable to take Greek tragedy neat he provided plenty of romantic soda-water. Clytemnestra is not so much a grand, hard murderess as

[62] *Charles Kingsley*, II, 338.   [63] *The Heroes* (Cambridge, 1856), p. xvii.

one of the world's great lovers, the introspective heroine of a Victorian triangle in an exotic setting. She, who had "so much to give," found herself condemned to a loveless marriage; and she recalls the evening when she and Aegisthus lingered outside the city in the moonlight, unconscious of passing time. In this drama Lytton may be said to have won his spurs as perhaps the most notorious plagiarist of the century. Apart from Aeschylus, echoes range from *Macbeth* to Arnold's *Empedocles*, which Lytton greatly admired.[64] In the chorus describing the sacrifice of Iphigeneia, he contrives to use, and of course expand, every detail of Tennyson's picture in *A Dream of Fair Women*. This chorus makes a protracted and un-Aeschylean assault upon the feelings, a successful assault, apparently, since it drew tears from Leigh Hunt. Of the poet's taste for glossy diction, in which he was by no means alone, one specimen will be enough, a disastrous improvement on Marlowe — "Make me immortal with one costly kiss!"

Lytton's father, the novelist, was sincerely complimentary in expressing surprise at the merits of the drama.[65] That very busy man, and not injudicious critic, never ceased to urge Robert to aim at condensation and selection, and, as a means to that end, to study the Greeks, especially Homer.[66] Greek was, Robert wrote to Mrs. Browning, the

[64] *Poetical Works of Owen Meredith* (1867), I, 24; *Personal & Literary Letters of Robert First Earl of Lytton*, ed. Lady Betty Balfour (1906), I, 49–50.

[65] *Personal & Literary Letters*, I, 54.

[66] *Ibid.*, I, 206–07, 276; *Life of Edward Bulwer First Lord Lytton By his Grandson The Earl of Lytton* (London, 1913), II, 385–86.

Since Bulwer nowadays seldom gets even disapproving attention, one may observe, quite irrelevantly, that he condemned the "false sentiment" of *Enoch Arden* (*Life*, II, 431), which both Swinburne and Arnold considered the best thing Tennyson had yet done (*Letters of Algernon Charles Swinburne*, ed. Edmund Gosse and T. J. Wise, I, 35; *Letters of Matthew Arnold*, ed. G. W. E. Russell, I, 277); Arnold did not like *Tithonus* quite so well. Further, in view of recent changes of attitude, one may quote Bulwer's complaint: "I despair of fellow-feeling with an age which says Pope is no poet and Rossetti is a great one" (*Life*, II, 431).

only knowledge he did not regret the time spent in acquir-
ing,[67] but its "pure cool fountains" had almost as little effect upon his style as upon hers. Keats had been his first
love,[68] and his father, although since *The New Timon* he had
come to admire Keats greatly, believed, like Arnold, that
his influence had been unfortunate in fostering "the effeminate attention to wording and expression and efflorescent
description which characterise the poetry now in vogue."[69]
"The Elizabethan School has been overworked. Leave it
alone."[70] Bulwer constantly urged also that Robert should
try to be "popular," in the sense (the Arnoldian sense)
that Homer was; but his reference on one occasion to the
popular Charles Mackay, as compared with the neglected
Shelley and Keats, might well lead to misunderstanding.[71]
At any rate Robert produced *Lucile*. It cannot be said
that Bulwer's own volume of mythological poems, *The
Lost Tales of Miletus* (1866), furnished notable models
of the virtues he strove to inculcate, for Robert's facile
fluency and tinsel were a direct paternal inheritance.[72]

[67] *Personal & Literary Letters*, I, 84.

[68] *Ibid.*, I, 42.

[69] *Life*, II, 426–28.

[70] *Ibid.*, II, 385.

[71] *Personal & Literary Letters*, I, 55–56. Cf. *ibid.*, I, 146, and *Life*, II, 396 ff.

[72] For Bulwer's own comments on this work, see the *Life*, II, 362 ff. In 1844
he had published *The Poems and Ballads of Schiller*, which helped to popularize
Schiller's mythological pieces; their modern idealism was quite congenial to the
translator (see, for instance, Bulwer's notes on *Hero and Leander* and *The Complaint of Ceres*). Two years later he adapted *Oedipus Tyrannus* for the modern
stage, but arrangements for production fell through (*Life*, II, 84–85, 90–91).
The third volume (1853) of his *Poetical and Dramatic Works* included some short
classical poems, and it is rather surprising, at this date, to find one, *Ganymede*,
headed by a quotation from the *Mystagogus Poeticus* of Alexander Ross. Early
in his hard-working career Bulwer had essayed an historical work, *Athens, Its
Rise and Fall* (1836), but he wisely abandoned it after the success of Thirlwall
and Grote. He turned his considerable scholarship to not very valuable account
in the uncompleted historical romance, *Pausanias the Spartan* (published posthumously in 1876, but written twenty years earlier), and of course in the *Last Days
of Pompeii*.

Robert inherited also his father's versatile energies — his writing was the by-product of an active diplomatic career — and he was not content with the reputation of a popular drawing-room novelist in verse. In 1868 he published an ambitious two-volume work, *Chronicles and Characters*. The first book consisted of three tales from Herodotus, of which one at least, the inevitable *Gyges and Candaules*, might seem an odd part of what attempted to be a panorama of the development of the human mind.[73] From these tales of Greece, which the always hopeful and always disappointed father described as "pretty exercises, but not the spring of a great genius into the arena," we pass to the Crucifixion in the second book. The third confronts heroic paganism, in the person of Licinius, "Rome's last Roman," with Christianity, the new gospel of love. The treatment of this theme, which was not yet threadbare, pleased both the author and his father, and it was praised by George Meredith.[74] But Robert Lytton quite lacked the power to do justice to such an impressive scheme, and even in its own day the book was a failure.

Glancing back over this chapter, and omitting such healthy extroverts as Macaulay and Kingsley, we are aware that in minor poetry at least the "paganism" of Wordsworth, Keats, and Shelley has lost most of its original force, and that the Christian hostility to Hellenism which showed itself in the Coleridges (and Wordsworth) has be-

[73] The discreet but somewhat luscious rendering drew a parental admonition against being Swinburnian (*Personal & Literary Letters*, I, 206–08). "Keatsian" would have been more accurate, for the disrobing of Gyges' wife is a pallid imitation of *The Eve of St. Agnes*.

[74] See the Memorial Edition of Meredith's *Works*, XXIII (1910), 121. A similar theme had been touched in *Tannhäuser; or, The Battle of the Bards* (1861), by "Neville Temple" (*i.e.*, Julian Fane) and "Edward Trevor" (*i.e.*, Robert Lytton).

come a disturbing element in the Protestant Mrs. Browning and in a number of young men who took the path to Rome. Further, Keats and Shelley had instinctively treated modern and humanitarian themes through mythological symbols, but now the loss of their primitive imagination and the increasing pressure of modernism have made such attitudes and methods less possible or less instinctive. Minor poets, because they are minor, may reflect the *Zeitgeist* more clearly than great ones, and even this chapter indicates that we have left romanticism behind and are in the age of Victorian realism, pietism, and rationalism.

By 1850 Tennyson was seated firmly on his throne, Browning had an important critical following, and Arnold had published his first volume. The spasmodics (apart from that "she-spasmodic," Mrs. Browning) do not come into these pages, but we may observe that Aytoun did not forget mythology in his burlesque. We can hardly blame readers who saw no difference between the genuine article and *Firmilian*:

> Then came the voice of universal Pan,
> The dread earth-whisper, booming in mine ear. . . .[75]

The ruffled waters had hardly closed over the spasmodics before the literary public became aware that, to put it rather spasmodically, a fresh crew had manned the romantic craft, thrown out a good deal more ballast, and set out in a new direction. The creed of Rossetti, the master spirit, was that modern poetry had culminated in Coleridge and Keats, the poets of medieval color and enchantment, and his own early poems carried on that tradition,

---

[75] See the whole passage, *Poems of William Edmondstoune Aytoun*, ed. F. Page (Oxford University Press, 1921), p. 298. The advantage of this kind of writing, as the genial author remarked, is "that you can go on slapdash, without thinking!" (Martin, *Memoir*, p. 147).

with a minute unearthly realism. At Oxford, William Morris and his friends looked up to Tennyson, the early romantic Tennyson; one of Morris's favorite poems was *The Hesperides*. Since Rossetti's poems were not collected until 1870, the poetic landmark for the group, though few readers as yet perceived the fact, was *The Defence of Guenevere*. Although the Morris circle was imbibing the social gospel of Carlyle (and the esthetic gospel of Ruskin), neither Morris nor Rossetti approached "life" except at Browningesque moments. As for Anglo-Catholicism, it nourished in this group, not the scruples of Dolben and Hopkins, but devotion to Gothic and ritualistic symbolism, and as much of religion as was compatible with the belief that "there is no God and the Virgin Mary is His mother." As one would expect, classic myth was not the most immediate interest. Christina Rossetti, we have seen, was the first to begin and the first to leave off. Her brother's mythological pieces came late in his career. *Atalanta in Calydon* announced the arrival of Dionysus in 1865, and *The Life and Death of Jason* appeared two years after that. Meanwhile Morris had written, though he never published, his *Scenes from the Fall of Troy*. In these poems he was reviving a tradition older than Tennyson or Keats, the tradition of the classical romances of the Middle Ages. To Morris, accordingly, we now turn.

CHAPTER IX

William Morris

IF POETS were to be discussed in proportion to the bulk of their mythological verse, this chapter would be the longest in the book. If written solely from the critical standpoint of the present, it would probably be the shortest. For modern notions of poetry and the romantic tradition have left the diffuse and unintellectual Morris and most of his contemporaries (except the very different Hopkins and Patmore) in a backwater which seems to be more remote from us than the era of Donne or Marvell or Pope. Whether the Pre-Raphaelites contributed something distinctive and vital to English poetry, or only to the history of English poetry, the contribution was made over and over again in many volumes; and all the possible critical judgments on these writers have likewise been uttered over and over again in many volumes. But if there are no general readers extant with a sufficiently youthful intelligence to find or to have found some pleasure in Morris's story-telling, scholars at least are above hedonistic motives. And for more than one reason Morris is a significant figure in the mythological tradition.

Morris was never more than a fair classical scholar — compared, that is, with most Victorian poets, not with most modern ones — and the pace at which he composed his narratives was not impeded by a weight of literary or archaeological learning. The conventions he created had more or less antique flavor, and that, in his open-air tales, was enough. Although he said, in his downright way, that he loathed all classical art and literature, he meant classicism rather than things antique.[1] At any rate his tens of thousands of lines of mythological verse were the most voluminous tribute that any modern man has paid to the antique imagination. Morris's instincts did lead him to shun the whole neoclassic tradition, yet his own decorative manner, in verse and in the arts and crafts, was as much in the spirit of the late Renaissance as in that of the Middle Ages. And his hatred of classicism and rhetoric did not hinder his inventing another kind of rhetorical upholstery less durable than that of the seventeenth and eighteenth centuries.

While in the large sense Morris's mythological verse has a general uniformity of style and tone, there are in his technique several consecutive and fairly distinct phases, the dramatic, the simply narrative and pictorial, and the epic. The first, represented by the *Scenes from the Fall of Troy*, naturally coincides with the *Defence of Guenevere* volume (1858). The second phase includes most of the work of Morris's middle period, *The Life and Death of Jason* and the first three fourths of *The Earthly Paradise*. The epic tales, which probably few readers have arrived at and fewer still have reached the end of, appear in the last part of *The Earthly Paradise*, and indicate the turning of the author's mind toward northern saga and ancient epics.

I

The *Scenes from the Fall of Troy*, which Morris worked on in 1857 and at times during the next few years, were to have comprised twelve dramatic poems; he left six complete in manuscript, and drafts of two more.[2] These texts,

---

[1] J. W. Mackail, *Life of William Morris* (1899), I, 48, 180–81, 197–98, II, 171; *Collected Works of William Morris*, ed. May Morris (1910–15), XXII, xiii.

[2] Mackail, I, 166 ff. The *Scenes* were first printed in the *Works*, XXIV (1915), 3 ff. See *ibid.*, pp. xxvii–xxviii, and II (1910), xi, xiv. Plans for the Red House about this time included Trojan scenes to be done on the walls by Burne-Jones (Mackail, I, 158).

along with the full list of titles, show that Morris, like medieval redactors of the tale of Troy, was less concerned with epic than with romance. Although, unlike the romancers, he knew Homer and other Greek authors, he instinctively saw the Trojan story as it had come down from Dares and Dictys to Caxton and Lydgate.[3] With medieval freedom he mixed and greatly embellished his sources, so that the result was something quite new. In medieval fashion he emphasized romantic incidents, individual rather than national fortunes, and above all the feelings of the characters, especially in regard to love. Such a title as *The Wedding of Polyxena*, or such a scene as *Achilles' Love-Letter*, is scarcely less Homeric than Morris's treatment of actual Homeric material.[4] Indeed, except in the use of the dramatic form, which was probably inspired by Shakespeare's *Troilus and Cressida*,[5] the *Scenes* embody all the characteristics of Morris's lifelong attitude toward ancient story. Troy is a medieval town; the warriors are "knights"; Hector wears hauberk and "wambeson"; Troilus cries, "Ho you Sir Knight wearing a lady's glove" — a chivalric touch which carries us back to the Elizabethans nourished on Caxton.[6] Hecuba reminds Paris of

---

[3] For Morris's praise of the undiluted medievalism of Caxton's *Recuyell of the Historyes of Troye*, see H. Halliday Sparling, *The Kelmscott Press and William Morris Master-Craftsman* (1924), pp. 109–10.

In this chapter I owe much to Elisabet C. Küster, *Mittelalter und Antike bei William Morris* (Berlin and Leipzig, 1928).

[4] The first-named scene was not written. Landor wrote an *Hellenic*, *The Espousals of Polyxena*, Englished in 1847 and recast in 1859 (*Poems*, ed. Wheeler, II, 346, 406).

For the story of Achilles' enamorment and death, see Caxton's *Recuyell*, ed. H. O. Sommer (1894), II, 621 ff., 640 ff.; *Lydgate's Troy Book*, ed. H. Bergen (*E.E.T.S.*, 1906–10), iv. 723 ff., 3098 ff.; Dictys Cretensis, *Ephemeridos Belli Troiani Libri Sex*, ed. F. Meister (Leipzig, 1872), iii. 2–3, iv. 11.

[5] Küster, pp. 91–92. Cf. *Works*, I, 322; Mackail, I, 47.

[6] *Works*, XXIV, 4, 18–19. Cf. Shakespeare, *Troilus and Cressida*, V. iii. 96, iv. 27; Chaucer, *Troilus and Criseyde*, v. 1660–61. For similar allusions in Peele and Warner, see my other volume, pp. 51, 65. In Morris's un-Homeric account of the death of Hector (pp. 19–20), the hero, tired of battle and with his armor

the time when he rode with Helen through the streets of Troy.[7] If such medievalism seems an affectation, it was at any rate more sincere in Morris than it could have been for any other modern man.

In more essential ways Morris's attitude toward his material was quite un-medieval. The Middle Ages did not know that they were medieval and romantic; they did not need to make a cult of beauty to satisfy souls starved by the life around them. Medieval writers did not "escape" into the classical past; they used ancient stories because they were good stories, and they brought them very vividly up to date. For them the ancient characters were alive, but Morris by his very method of handling acknowledged that they were dead beyond recall; he wrote about ghosts of a glamorous past. While his psychologizing of Helen, Paris, and the rest is in the medieval tradition, the feelings delineated are almost entirely modern. Characters are endowed with the poet's own self-conscious devotion to beauty,[8] his own poignant sense of its impermanence. Pater's beautiful moments are already implicit, indeed explicit, in the verse of Morris. To-day melts quickly into yesterday, the future brings old age and death and nothingness, and the lover's crown of sorrow is remembering happier things. The scene called *Helen Arming Paris* is far from martial; it is a duet on the passing of life and love and Troy itself. In another scene Helen grows weary, growing old, and she sings a lyric of which the refrain is heard all through Morris's work:

> Kiss me sweet! for who knoweth
> What thing cometh after death?[9]

---

off, is surprised by Achilles. Cf. Shakespeare, *Troilus and Cressida*, V. viii; Caxton, II, 613; Lydgate, iii. 5373 ff.

[7] P. 28. Morris may have thought of Chaucer's Troilus riding up the street (cf. *Jason*, xvii. 21). See Caxton, II, 536; Lydgate, ii. 4108 ff.

[8] Cf. the reference to Helen in *Sir Peter Harpdon's End*, ll. 196 ff., and also *The Defence of Guenevere*, ll. 109 ff.

[9] *Helen's Chamber*, pp. 33, 40. The lyric, much altered but with almost the

Hecuba's song contrasts "the merry days of old" with her present lot as an abject slave, "An old woman by the sea." *The Defiance of the Greeks* opens with speeches less heroic than elegiac. Everywhere the spirit of futility and disillusion and decay broods over Morris's Troy.

The sense that all things, even the feelings of the characters, existed in some dead past does not make drama very dramatic or realism very realistic. The *Scenes* in general lack the "close-up" effects of *The Defence of Guenevere*. Shouts and the clash of arms are dimly heard, as in a dream. The episode of the wooden horse is taken quite out of the epic world of Homer and Virgil, which was romantic enough, when Helen sings

> O my merchants, whence come ye
> Landing laden from the sea? [10]

Morris's habitual romanticizing, idealizing, and softening go together, and are illustrated in his treatment of character. Paris and Helen, who live only for love, are a Lancelot and Guenevere, almost as remote from Homer's human pair as they are from the sophisticated Romans of Ovid's *Heroides*. Helen is a "fatal woman," but, like so many modern heroines, she is "good," no matter what she has done. She is afflicted by the consciousness that she has ruined Paris, her "poor kind knight," who has never thought of himself. He is the Browning who had taught

---

same refrain, was transferred to *Ogier the Dane* (*Works*, IV, 247–48). Compare, for example, "Love while ye may" (*The Doom of King Acrisius*, III, 229).

[10] For Homer's very different account of Helen and the Greek warriors, see *Od.* iv. 274 ff., xi. 523 ff. Morris's "some thirty men" in the horse (p. 43) suggests Quintus Smyrnaeus, who names thirty and says there were more (*Fall of Troy*, Loeb Classical Library, xii. 314 ff.), although Morris's brief list of persons differs somewhat. In later years at least Morris was acquainted with Quintus Smyrnaeus (Mackail, I, 167–68), and presumably he was at this time. See also Apollodorus, *Lib.* (*Epitome*, v. 14), ed. Frazer, II, 230–31. Caxton's horse contains a "thousand knyghtes" (*Recuyell*, II, 663); cf. Lydgate, iv. 6075.

this Elizabeth Barrett

> how to live, when long ago
> I had forgotten that the world was fair
> And I was fair.[11]

The best scene is the one between Menelaus and Helen. Homer was content to show Helen as a dutiful wife settled down at home again. Quintus Smyrnaeus, Euripides, and some other ancient authors told how Menelaus, intent on killing Helen, dropped his sword at the sight of her beauty.[12] Landor had dramatized the situation a dozen years before Morris, and the differences between the two versions are not merely what might be expected from a classicist and a romantic; despite his cool antique manner, Landor is the more sentimental. In his scene there is little atmosphere or physical background; his dialogue has the usual dignity, and the usual unrealistic stiffness. Menelaus, though he hardens himself, cannot finally resist Helen's thoughts of home and her child, her voice, her hair, his recollection of her as a bride, her anguished sobs. Morris attempts to realize Helen's feelings and the whole emotional and physical atmosphere. Only in the setting does she differ from the heroine of a modern triangle; it is not a "quadrangle," since Deiphobus does not count. In the silence of the warm night Helen rises, restlessly, from the side of Deiphobus, a hearty unspiritual husband, to think of the morrow and to wonder if she is growing old. She opens the window for air and stretches out her arm in the rain. Now that the Greeks are gone, she will live on quietly until age steals upon her. She had been young once, with Paris; when

---

[11] P. 4.

[12] Quintus Smyrnaeus, *Fall of Troy*, xiii. 354 ff., 385 ff., xiv. 39–70, 149–78; Euripides, *Andromache*, ll. 628 ff. (and *Trojan Women*, ll. 869 ff.); Aristophanes, *Lysistrata*, l. 155. Morris would get no help from Pausanias' *Description of Greece*, V. xviii. 3 (ed. Frazer, I, 264), or Apollodorus, *Epit.* v. 22. See Küster, pp. 225–26. Cf. Tennyson's *Lucretius* (1868), ll. 60 ff. For Landor's dramatic scene, see *Poems*, ed. Wheeler, II, 223.

spring comes round she will think of him "for a little while."
But Troy has fallen, and Menelaus appears; he forces her
to help him kill Deiphobus in bed.[13] Helen's bitter speeches,
like her self-pity, are modern. Menelaus, with no apparent thought of killing her, has "Come back to fetch
a thing" he left behind: "A-bed, Helen, before the night
goes by!" This — apart from the macabre elements of
the scene — is a revenge more cruel than the sword; it
might be Soames Forsyte with Irene. Then the personal
drama merges into the general uproar of the bloodthirsty
conquerors of the city. Thus Morris handles the myth
far more freely than Landor, and his re-creation is quite
unclassical, but it is alive. It is doubtless exaggeration
to say, as a modern poet does, that the *Scenes* "perhaps
contain his greatest poetry, and . . . are certainly at the
greatest heights of Victorian poetry,"[14] yet it would be
hard to think of any incident in *Jason* or *The Earthly
Paradise* which approaches the indelible effect of this scene.

II

The Life and Death of Jason (1867), which had been
designed for the beginning of *The Earthly Paradise*, grew
under the author's hand into the longest single mythologi-

[13] Morris somewhat heightens the gruesomeness, though mutilation is tradi-
tional, *e.g.*, Virgil, *Aen.* vi. 494 ff.; Dictys Cretensis, v. 12; see Lempriere's
Classical Dictionary, ed. Rev. T. Smith (1847). In Morris, Helen does not betray
Deiphobus to Menelaus, as she does in Lempriere and some ancient sources.

Miss May Morris has kindly informed me that she is unable to identify the
edition of Lempriere used by her father, but the items referred to in my notes,
though based on the 1847 edition just cited, seem to remain the same, or without
essential changes, in various editions, such as that of 1818 edited by Lempriere
himself.

[14] Mr. Gordon Bottomley, in his introduction to *Two Poems by William
Morris* (1930). One might almost mistake Mr. Bottomley's own poem, *The Last
of Helen* (1902), for part of Morris's sequence; here too Helen is a fragment of a
gray world of decay.

cal tale in modern English poetry.[15] In spite of its seventeen books it is "single," and moves at a steady if unhur-
ried pace to its destined goal. The unity of a biographical
chronicle of travel, adventure, and romantic love was not
of epic character, and Morris emphasized the romantic
elements. The loose frame was congenial, and, apart from
the central story, the episodes, allusions, and constant
decoration would furnish materials for a mythological
dictionary. Morris is on the whole a better story-teller
than Apollonius Rhodius, whose half-epic, half-romantic
Argonautica was his chief source, and he lightens and
quickens the narrative by omitting much antiquarian
and geographical lore. Apollonius' best moments, however, such as the incident of Prometheus' eagle, are beyond
Morris's imaginative reach.[16]

Apollonius begins with Jason's arrival at Iolchos, and
at once thrusts upon his readers an Alexandrian choke-
pear, a long list of the Argonauts. Morris postpones the
roll-call, which could not be left out of an heroic poem,
to his third book, where the momentum of the story carries
it along and where it adds more to the luster of the enterprise. The catalogue itself is sometimes more ample than
the original, and usually more readable; here and there the
recital of heroic distinctions is mixed with Chaucerian
details of personal appearance. In medieval style (sanc-
tioned by Apollodorus) Morris begins his story with Jason's
infancy and narrates everything in order. The first two
books, which describe Jason's early life with Chiron the
centaur, his journey to Iolchos and encounter with King

---

[15] The title may have been suggested by *The Life and Death of Hector* (1614),
which has been commonly but mistakenly attributed to Thomas Heywood;
see my other volume, p. 316. I am indebted in this section to H. Sybil
Kermode, "The Classical Sources of Morris's *Life and Death of Jason*" (see
bibliography).

[16] See J. W. Mackail, *Lectures on Greek Poetry* (1911), pp. 239–72, especially
258 ff.

Pelias, are based mainly on Pindar's fourth Pythian ode.[17] The outdoor life of a simple heroic age gives full play to Morris's invention and his pictorial instinct; while in Pindar the child is simply handed over to Chiron "at night," in Morris he plays with his father's black beard and laughs for joy "To see the war-horse in the red torch-light." [18]

From the catalogue of heroes to the winning of the golden fleece, Morris followed Apollonius, though with abundant changes. For the voyage homeward, which occupies books nine to fourteen, Morris abandoned Apollonius and Greek travel routes for a narrative in the spirit of *The Earthly Paradise*. The Argonauts find their way, by various rivers and by land, through the cold, rugged, and mysterious regions of Germanic barbarians, to the northern sea. The mystery is heightened by the absence of geographical names, which appears to have resulted from both the author's art and his uncertainty about the map.[19] In the last three books Morris returns, in part, to the classics; Medea's contriving of the death of Pelias follows Ovid in outline, but the tragic conclusion is quite remote from Euripides.[20]

Jason displayed a method of story-telling which was new in modern English mythological verse, and which was a new departure for Morris. The often Browningesque immediacy and intensity of *The Defence of Guenevere*, the

[17] One concrete item is Jason's two spears (*Jason*, ii. 8–9; Pindar, *Pyth.* iv. 79). My references to *Jason* are to the handy volume in the Oxford World's Classics.

[18] *Jason*, i. 111–13; Pindar, l. 115. See also the allusion to Diana's hunting in the moonlight (i. 267–84).

[19] When pressed by some earnest university students, Morris mentioned the Don or Dvina and the Vistula (*Works*, II, xxiv). In Apollonius the Argonauts return by way of the Ister (Danube), the Adriatic, the Eridanus (Po), the Rhone, and the Mediterranean. See *The Life and Death of Jason*, ed. E. Maxwell (Clarendon Press, 1919), pp. xix–xx, 609; and cf. Kingsley's *Heroes*, "The Argonauts," Part V (Cambridge, 1856), pp. 120–24, notes.

[20] *Jason*, xv; *Metam.* vii. 159 ff., 297 ff. Cf. Lempriere ("Medea," "Pelias"); Hyginus, *Fab.* xxiv; Apollodorus, *Lib.* I. ix. 27 (and Frazer's note, I, 121).

paler and half-retrospective drama of the Trojan *Scenes*, give place to a broad, clear stream of narrative whose smooth surface is hardly ever ruffled, except in the last book, by a dramatic moment. Most of the youthful magic and fantasy of the *Guenevere* volume has also vanished. Adventures and speeches are less salient in the memory than bits of the lyrics and some of the endless succession of pure, lucid pictures. Character, incident, description — there is more now of description than of vivid suggestion — all melt into the even uniformity of tapestry. This last word has of course more than its usual meaning here, for Morris, like Spenser and like no other English poet since Spenser, was familiar with the medievalized classical scenes in tapestry, and he carried their pictorial style and coloring into verse. (Everyone knows Morris's revealing dictum: "If a chap can't compose an epic poem while he's weaving tapestry, he had better shut up, he'll never do any good at all.")[21] The constant and generally pale greens and blues and grays and whites and golds of Morris's descriptions remind us, in their *simplesse*, not so much of epic style as of tapestries and murals. And these colors, to mix metaphors, are indicative of the key in which the whole poem is pitched. We can hardly refuse to surrender to the effortless ease and charm and frequent beauty of the performance, but it is not wise, as I have found several times, to read the poem at a sitting.

Morris has often been likened to Chaucer, partly because he avowed loving discipleship — though how could he speak of Chaucer's "dreamy eyes"?[22] — and partly be-

[21] Mackail, *Life*, I, 186. Mr. Sparling tells of Morris "bumble-beeing" the Greek of the *Odyssey* while sketching, and leaving the easel or sketchblock at intervals to write down what he had translated (*The Kelmscott Press*, p. 37). References to tapestry in Morris's tales are too numerous to mention. In *Jason*, see v. 44–45, vi. 477–85; and Küster, pp. 88–89, 93, 223–25.

[22] *Jason*, xvii. 11 ff.; *Earthly Paradise*, Prologue, 1 ff., and L'Envoi. Cf. Lydgate, *Troy Book*, ii. 4677 ff.

cause there have been very few forthright story-tellers in English verse. Most, though not all, of the phrases used in the preceding paragraph would be true of such a full-dress romance as the Knight's Tale, but they would be quite untrue of that great work, *Troilus and Criseyde*, which should more properly serve for comparison. The *Troilus* is a drama in five acts and innumerable scenes, which range from the subtlest comic to the most moving tragic irony; it is a drama of both psychology and destiny. Morris never approaches or tries to approach Chaucer's level of human reality and philosophic vision. As he said himself, his turn was "decidedly more to Romance than was Chaucer's." [23] In story-telling Morris's affinity is rather with Gower — and that is not a disparagement.

We have observed the idealizing of Paris and Helen in the *Scenes from the Fall of Troy*. The same process applied to the story of Jason makes Apollonius, the author of the first modern romance, appear a relentless realist. The Argonauts of the Greek tale are more fully individualized than they are in Morris, and they are a turbulent, unruly crew who would have preferred Hercules as their leader and who dispute Jason's authority. Morris's Jason is a completely ideal hero and commander who never weakens. (In both poems he suffers from being given supernatural aid at every turn; Aeneas is partly redeemed by the dignity of his Roman virtues and the greatness of his mission.) Morris once spoke of Tennyson's Sir Galahad as "rather a mild youth," and Jason is no less pallid in his perfection; the author's chief interest was in Medea. The idealizing is most obvious in the treatment of the love story; Morris's hero and heroine are the ingenuous youth and maiden of all romance who fall in love at first sight. Apollonius' Jason had already been the lover of Hypsipyle, and he approaches Medea at first as a self-seeking adven-

[23] Mackail, I, 197.

turer; and Medea herself, we may remember, was the proto-
type of Dido.[24] Morris's heroine has no scruples about be-
traying her father — unlike the Greek girl, but like Shakespeare's Jessica and most other damsels of romance held
in captivity by ogres. Further, the killing of Medea's
brother is so managed as not to lay a heavy burden of
guilt upon either her or Jason.

In leaving Apollonius for Euripides, Morris softens still
more the harshness of the myth. The last book has been
praised, by poets and others, as the finest of all; Mr. Drinkwater has even put it "among the supreme things in
poetry."[25] To me the last book seems a failure, but an interesting kind of failure. Glauce, who as a character is
Morris's creation, is a charming figure among his shadowy
women, a young and innocent Desdemona or Nausicaa,
who worships her hero; her fate would be moving if we
believed in it.[26] In his relations with her Jason is for the
first time standing on his own feet, and for the first time
has the semblance of a personality. For a while his new-
born love struggles with his conscience, and he feels
stricken by Medea's letter of farewell. He does not, like
Euripides' practical and cold-blooded Greek, try to prove
to a barbarian mistress the benefits which will accrue to
all concerned if he makes a prudent marriage. Morris's
Medea at the beginning had looked forward to the time

[24] Morris of course omits the affair with Hypsipyle (*Argonautica*, i. 609-909).
In the Greek poem Hera contrives to have Eros sent to inspire Medea with a
violent passion for Jason, and he, acting on the advice of a follower, goes to meet
the loving Medea in order to obtain her potent help in his enterprise; his heart
is not touched until she has given him a charm and has revealed her own feelings
with tears.

[25] *William Morris* (1912), p. 98. Cf. Swinburne, *Essays and Studies* (1875),
p. 120; Stopford Brooke, *A Study of Clough, Arnold, Rossetti, and Morris* (1908),
pp. 221-22; Alfred Noyes, *William Morris* (1908), p. 68.

[26] In addition to Euripides, see Apollodorus, I. ix. 28; Hyginus, *Fab.* xxv;
Pausanias, II. iii. 6. Lempriere gives the essential facts, including the name
Glauce.

when Jason would weary of her, and at the end, like
Chaucer's medieval saints of Cupid, she is more pathetic
and wistful than tragic and vindictive. She is one of those
countless women of fiction who give all for love and, when
love fails, can still love the man who casts them aside:

> Be happy! for thou shalt not hear again
> My voice, and with one word this scroll is done —
> Jason, I love thee, yea, love thee alone —
> God help me, therefore! [27]

These are the words of anguished sincerity, not hypocrisy,
and by all the laws of sentimental tragedy such a woman
is bound to "go out into the night." But excessive idealizing puts Morris in a dilemma, for the woman who says,
"Be happy... I love thee... alone," is preparing to
murder Jason's children (and hers) and his prospective
bride and father-in-law. The tigress of Euripides, whose
love has turned to hate, can kill the children and at the
same time mourn their death. Morris glosses over the
deed and makes it a sad necessity, which, for his still
loving heroine, it is not. He relies on the pathos of her
letter and her lament to blur the situation, to conceal
the unavoidable facts of the fable and preserve Medea to
the end as a wholly good woman, a great lover. [28]

Only in the case of the supplanted Medea does Morris
try to render intense emotion. The enamorment had been
pure romance, and few passages in the poem remain so
fresh in the memory as the picture of the happy lovers
stealing down in the star-light to the long white quays
lined with ships. [29] The episodes of Jason and Glauce and

[27] *Jason*, xvii. 842–45. For Medea's anticipation of Jason's deserting her,
see ix. 12 ff.

[28] The first lines of Medea's letter (xvii. 797–99) echo the opening lines of the
play. For the difference between realistic and literary pathos, compare *Medea*,
ll. 1021 ff., and *Jason*, xvii. 920 ff.

[29] *Jason*, ix. 214 ff. Cf. viii. 468 ff. In Apollonius (iv. 34 ff.) Medea flees to
the ship and begs Jason to take her on board.

Hylas and the nymph are sensuous, decorative idylls. Neither Apollonius nor Theocritus would have recognized a tale in which Hercules is of little account, in which Hylas dallies with a nymph robed in gold and fur like a courtly Red-Cross Knight or Cymochles with a Burne-Jones Duessa or Phaedria.[30] And Hylas' politely phrased suggestion that she cast off her "armour" as he has done reminds us of one strain of sensuousness which runs throughout the poem. Innumerable damsels appear, singly or in crowds, clad in raiment thin, and the desire is often expressed or felt to see them without the raiment. Morris's women do not have minds; one might almost say their bodies thought. He has, after his first volume at least, nothing of Rossetti's sensuous mysticism, nothing of Swinburne's sensual ardors; his interest in "slim bodies white" is a quite normal feeling, though it is expressed in a stylized and exotic way. Such a mode of treatment is perfectly suited to the tone and atmosphere Morris maintains, yet the continual estheticizing of elemental impulses may inspire an occasional yearning for Mrs. Bloom.

In *Jason* Morris carries on the medievalism of the Trojan *Scenes*, but usually with more restraint. The Argonauts are "heroes" and "seafarers," not "knights" — though Hercules offers in feudal fashion to become Jason's man [31] — and the armor is more or less classical. Aea, however, is a busy medieval seaport, much like Chaucer's London, and possesses not only a tournament hall and towers with bells but a temple to the deities of moon and sun.[32] Apart from some brief allusions, like that to the vanes on town

---

[30] *Jason*, iv. 381 ff.; *Argonautica*, i. 1207 ff. Hylas' "hair of gold" (l. 394) may come from Theocritus, xiii. 36. Cf. *Faerie Queene*, I. vii. 1 ff., II. vi. 12 ff.

[31] *Jason*, iii. 278–79, 301–04.

[32] *Ibid.*, vi. 273 ff. Cf. Lydgate's description of "Colchos" in the *Troy Book*, i. 1243–45, 1251–55 (Küster, pp. 120–21). For the tournament hall and towers, see *Jason*, viii. 46 ff., ix. 286–87; for the temple, vi. 420 ff. Miss Küster (p. 227) cites Pausanias, VI. xxiv. 6.

spires, Morris's only flagrant lapse into medievalism is
the description of the Argonauts embarking amid a shower
of roses rained from windows draped with purple, carrying wreaths on their spears and ladies' tokens in their
helmets, while their sweethearts are too sad to throw their
gathered flowers.[33] In general Morris preserves remarkably
well the set of conventions he devised; they are neither
ancient nor medieval but an artificial and sufficiently
harmonious blending of both.

The Greek deities also are of mixed composition. The
author makes them fairly credible by his adopted simplicity of outlook, and he provides them with realistic natural
settings and substantial, not too substantial, costumes.
The most unclassical divinity is Hylas' nymph, whom we
have met already. Juno appears at intervals, in various
disguises, to help Jason, but even when her function is parallel to that of Athene she is not Homer's almost matter-
of-fact elder sister; she has a touch of strangeness which
belongs to the *märchen*.[34] Virgil had gone some way in
that romantic direction, for instance, in the meeting between Aeneas and his goddess mother, but in Morris's
imitation of that incident Juno does not quite reveal the
true queen of heaven in her gait or manner. And in her
next appearance, as the old crone who carries Jason across
the river, she suggests the "loathly lady" of medieval
romance.[35] In spite of constant references to "the Gods,"
Morris's deities are feminine and decorative, and we have
no consciousness of a supreme ruler on Olympus. While

---

[33] *Jason*, iv. 10 ff. For the weather vanes, see i. 374.

[34] *Ibid.*, ii. 105 ff., iii. 81 ff., viii. 131 ff. In the long story of Phryxus and
Helle (ii. 345 ff.), Ino, while her behavior is authentic enough, reminds us of the
wicked stepmother of fairy tales. For the classical matter of this tale, see
Lempriere ("Argonautae"); Apollodorus, I. ix. 1; Hyginus, *Fab.* ii–iii. Pindar
and Apollonius make only brief references to the myth.

[35] *Jason*, ii. 30 ff. In Apollonius (iii. 72 ff.) Hera says Jason had carried her
(cf. Hyginus, *Fab.* xiii). In Lempriere ("Jason"), Juno, as an old woman, carries
Jason. For the imitation of Virgil, see *Jason*, i. 285 ff.

Homer's world was religious in its concrete way, and
Virgil's in its philosophic way, Morris's, being a modern
and romantic reconstruction, is altogether "pagan" and
esthetic.

The "pagan" melancholy of the *Scenes* is carried through
Jason. The poem ends on a note of hopeless disillusion and
frustration. Medea's fate we have seen. The once renowned Jason, "Of love, of honour, and of joy bereft,"
dies by a trivial and ironic accident, the fall of the *Argo's*
stempost.[36] And though the preceding sixteen books are
full of high adventure and romance, they are full of sadness too. The past cannot be recovered, in the present
the senses of youth offer only moments of joy, the blank
future contains no certainties but age and death, "death,
that maketh life so sweet." The hungering for "Saturn's
days of gold," when man knew no envy or strife or avarice
or pain or poverty, may take the form of thinly lyrical
nostalgia, and yet, knowing Morris, we cannot doubt his
sincerity and seriousness.[37] For Shelley the golden age
had commonly been an inspiring vision of the future. For
the Victorian, who sees men meshed within a smoky net
of unrejoicing labor, the golden age has returned to its
old place in the infancy of the world. In Morris's verse at
least it is a dream devoid of hope, and the Shelleyan millennium has dwindled to

> a little garden close
> Set thick with lily and red rose,
> Where I would wander if I might
> From dewy dawn to dewy night,
> And have one with me wandering.[38]

---

[36] See Lempriere ("Argo," "Jason"); and Euripides, *Medea*, ll. 1386–87.

[37] *Jason*, x. 467 ff., xii. 335 ff. Cf. v. 379 ff., xiv. 607–64, and *passim*.

[38] *Ibid.*, iv. 577 ff. See Mr. Eliot's comparison of this lyric with Marvell's
The Nymph and the Fawn (*Selected Essays*, 1932, p. 285). The thought of wandering hand in hand with a dream-mistress (which is also a Shelleyan *summum
bonum*) is recurrent in Morris. See *Jason*, i. 92–94, xiv. 209–12, and the lyric cut
out of *Bellerophon in Lycia* (*Works*, VI, xiv–xvi).

The most extended and familiar presentation of these moods is the antiphonal lyrics of Orpheus and the sirens.[39] From ancient times down the sirens, usually in connection with Ulysses, had been symbols of unmanly sloth and voluptuousness, to be resisted, as in Spenser and Daniel, by temperance and heroic resolution. In *Jason* the *Argo* keeps on its way as Orpheus answers the sirens, but his replies are almost indistinguishable in tone and substance from the invitations to give over pain and toil. The singer's armor against their seductive promises is of their own making, it is a catalogue of the sensuous delights of life in which heroic labor is a minor after-thought.[40] And even that recital is touched everywhere with languor and longing. Although this strain is so dominant in all the verse, it is a reminder that Morris the poet was only a fraction of the man.

III

The framework of *The Earthly Paradise* (1868–70) was perfectly adapted to Morris's narrative conventions. The central idea, of northern men wandering the western sea in search of the earthly paradise and arriving at last among people of Greek origin who had preserved their ancient lore, provided mouthpieces for both medieval and classical legends, and made natural the medieval coloring of the Greek tales. Further, the old age of both groups and the hard experiences of the wanderers dramatically justified the nostalgic melancholy no less inevitable in Morris than medievalism. The passing of the twelve months, marked

---

[39] *Jason*, xiv. 125 ff. Cf. *Argonautica*, iv. 891–921.

[40] Mr. Sparling tells of Morris snatching down his *Love Is Enough* and exclaiming: "There's a lie for you, though 'twas I that told it! Love isn't enough in itself; love *and work*, yes! *Work* and love, that's the life of a man! Why, a fellow can't even love decently unless he's got work to do, and pulls his weight in the boat!" (*The Kelmscott Press*, p. 100).

by the end-links as well as the lyrics, contributes a good deal to the total effect, and the quality of the verse in these interludes is generally finer than it is in the long stretches of narrative. But the framework is relatively static, and if Morris is not weighed down by the heavy moralizing of the *Confessio Amantis*, his reflections on youth and age and death do after a time come close to rivaling Gower's monotony.

Most of the myths are treated so freely that sources are of interest mainly by way of contrast. For a number of tales Morris would have needed little or nothing more than he could find in Lempriere.[41] The usual process of amplification and decoration involved countless invented incidents and changes; the most interesting and characteristic are those which idealize character, heighten romantic sentiment and atmosphere, and soften the sometimes harsh realism of the original myths.[42] In *Atalanta's Race* Morris carries further an Ovidian suggestion.[43] Ovid's Atalanta, touched by the hero's youth and by feelings which she does not recognize as love, urges him not to try; in Morris it is the king who attempts to dissuade him, while Atalanta

[41] I am indebted here and there to Julius Riegel, *Die Quellen von William Morris' Dichtung, The Earthly Paradise* (Erlangen and Leipzig, 1890), though the book does not go far toward showing what sources the poet actually used. Morris said that it taught him "a great deal about his stories he had not known before" (*Works*, III, xviii, note).

[42] Some facts about a few tales may be summarized briefly. It is perhaps not an accident that the only one in which Morris follows the original plot closely, *The Son of Croesus*, is the only one which contains no female figure; Atys' wife is merely alluded to. See *Works*, IV, 145 ff., and Herodotus, i. 34–45; Morris makes the conclusion more theatrical.

In *Acontius and Cydippe* hardly anything Ovidian is retained except the trick with the apple, which is the culmination of a series of original romantic situations. See *Works*, V, 124 ff., and *Heroides*, xx–xxi. Acontius' sailing to Delos, of which Morris makes a great deal, is in Lempriere and is suggested in Ovid.

For *The Golden Apples*, Morris would have found enough facts in Lempriere; the commandeering of a ship and the details are his own.

[43] *Metam.* x. 560 ff. The birth and infancy of Atalanta are recounted in Apollodorus (III. ix. 2) and Lempriere.

remains silent, austerely and remotely virginal, but she loses the race through being overcome by love rather than by a desire for the golden apples.

If a source can be named for *The Doom of King Acrisius*, it is probably Apollodorus.[44] Morris's inventions include both mythological "machines" and such intimately human episodes as the opening of the tale. The appearance of Jupiter in human form as he leaves Danaë, while natural enough in a modern version, may have been suggested by Caxton's long and courtly story.[45] In the business of Andromeda, Perseus does not, as he does in the sources, make a practical bargain for a bride before taking the trouble to rescue her.[46] *Pygmalion and the Image* is remote from the amorousness of Ovid, and of a conception such as Beddoes' of the aspiring creative artist there is only an occasional hint. Morris's tale of romantic passion for "The heavenly beauty that can ne'er pass by" is a model of decorum, well worthy of illustration by Burne-Jones.[47] Instead of warming the statue into life by his caresses, Pygmalion finds it alive on his return from the temple of Venus; and Venus herself, in his absence, has called and presented his love with the garments offered to herself by worshipers in the temple.

[44] *Lib.* II. iv. 1–5. Cf. Ovid, *Metam.* iv. 607 ff., 663 ff., v. 1 ff. In Apollodorus, Ovid, and Lempriere, Andromeda's mother boasts of her own beauty; in Hyginus (*Fab.* lxiv), Kingsley's *Andromeda*, and Morris, she boasts of her daughter's.

[45] *Recuyell*, I, 102 ff. Morris's description of Danaë's life with her maids is somewhat similar in its medieval coloring to Caxton's.

[46] His chivalry is equally spontaneous in Kingsley's poem and in his *Heroes*. Morris's account of the mental anguish of Medusa (*Works*, III, 203–04) might owe something to the tale of the Gorgon in George W. Cox's *Tales of Thebes and Argos* (1864), pp. 121–25. Cox's *Tales of the Gods and Heroes* (1862) was one of the books put in the Morris children's way by their parents (*Works*, IV, xviii).

[47] Among the many products of the artist's association with Morris are the four pictures based on the tale of Pygmalion; they are conveniently accessible in Malcolm Bell, *Sir Edward Burne-Jones* (1898), pp. 109 ff. The title of the last one is "The Soul Attains." For Morris's poem, see *Works*, IV, 189 ff.; Ovid, *Metam.* x. 243 ff. Only the opening stanzas, about Pygmalion's scorn for the women of Cyprus, are really Ovidian.

In *Rhodope*, Morris uses only the Cinderella part of the
classical stories, which is given in a sentence in Lempriere;
an eagle carried off one of her shoes while she was bathing
and the Egyptian king made her his wife when she appeared with the other.[48] All the rest is Morris's invention.
He ignores the most familiar fact about Rhodope, that
she was a famous courtesan, and makes her a rustic beauty,
a Eustacia Vye who longs for a larger life; nothing comes in
the dull round "To give us some bright dream before we
die."

Perhaps the most completely idealized tale is *The Love
of Alcestis*. The account of Apollo the herdsman and Admetus' winning of his bride is pure mythological romance,[49]
and it would be a dubious prelude to a realistic treatment
of death and self-sacrifice. At any rate Morris follows the
romantic path. Admetus is an ideal husband and king,
whose reign is "A fragment of the Golden Age." This
beloved father of his people in time falls ill and approaches
death; when he knows the decree of the Fates he simply
turns to the wall to die. Alcestis, unable to bear the thought
of life without him, lies down in his bed, praying for death.[50]
She dies, and Admetus awakes, restored to health and beneficent rule, though not to wedded happiness. In this very
simplified situation there is no Euripidean display of masculine egoism, no acceptance of a substitute; on the part
of Alcestis there is no human clinging to life, no practical
concern for the welfare of her children, nothing but un-

---

[48] The sentence is quoted by Miss May Morris (*Works*, V, xxii). In both the
1818 and 1847 editions of Lempriere the name is given as "Rhŏdŏpe, or Rhodō-
pis." The story comes from Aelian, *Varia Historia*, xiii. 33, and Strabo, *Geo-
graphica*, c. 808. In the version in Burton's *Anatomy* (Bohn's Popular Library,
III, 276), Rhodope is, as in Morris, a virgin. The tale of Acontius, which happens
to precede that of Rhodope in Morris, is told by Burton on p. 275.

[49] See Lempriere; Apollodorus, I. ix. 15; Hyginus, *Fab.* l–li.

[50] Gower has a somewhat similar half-rationalized dénouement (*Confessio
Amantis*, vii. 1937 ff.). For Browning's second version, see below, ch. XI,
note 18.

hesitating devotion. Euripides' play ends happily, with Heracles bringing Alcestis back, and in Morris's poem she remains dead, but the ancient work is, along with its satyric boisterousness, a piece of critical realism, while the modern version is sentimental and soft.

The Death of Paris is the only Trojan tale in The Earthly Paradise, and both the subject matter and the dramatic method carry us back to the Scenes. There is less medievalism, though the reference to Aeneas and Antenor perhaps recalls medieval versions of the Troy story, and Paris's blowing of his horn is in the vein of romance. But we have the same atmosphere of war-weary Troy, a little world in which nobility and heroism have died and everything is at an end. Paris, bereft of pride and all but life, is willing to be carried up to seek Oenone, his long-abandoned love, who alone can heal his wounds. Morris's attempt to render complexity of feeling in Paris and especially in Oenone is quite different from the simplicity of Quintus Smyrnaeus.[51] In the Greek epic the bitter Oenone mocks Paris's abject plea and sends him off; then, conscious that she still loves him, she goes down at night to join him on his funeral pyre. Tennyson, writing some twenty years after Morris, largely followed Quintus Smyrnaeus in fact and spirit. Landor, in his version of 1847, described no such revulsion of feeling as we have in the Greek.[52] Paris begs

[51] Works, V, 4 ff. Morris so completely re-created the incident that no literary source was needed, or perhaps available, since he was writing at a German watering-place (Works, V, xvi). The introductory lines in September ("The level ground . . .") describe the landscape of Ems (Mackail, I, 203). The locus classicus for the tale is Quintus Smyrnaeus, Fall of Troy, x. 231 ff., 411 ff. In Apollodorus (III. xii. 6) Oenone refuses to heal Paris, then repents, and, finding him dead, hangs herself. In Lempriere, Paris dies as he comes into her presence; she weeps and stabs herself.

[52] See Landor's Poems, ed. Wheeler, I, 113 ff. A version of this part of Corythos, with a separate title, appeared in 1859 (ibid., pp. 378 ff.). In Landor and Morris and Lempriere, though not in Quintus Smyrnaeus, Paris is carried up to Oenone on Mount Ida.

for pardon, not for help. Oenone utters "Nothing of anger or complaint"; what inward conflict she had felt is now over. She wishes to die first, and falls upon her dying lover with a "Give me one embrace. Paris is now my own." Such a version may be thought too simply pathetic, although, as usual, Landor's style gives the illusion of severity. In Morris, Oenone appears beside the litter of the wounded man, her heart full of "Pity and scorn, and love and hate." At first she thinks of her ten years of solitude and sorrow; then, softened by his plight, by thoughts of old love and hopes of its renewal, she begins to treat his wounds. But is she to heal him for Helen? Paris, though dying, cannot conceal his heart from her, and he must die. But Oenone kisses him before she leaves him to his fate. Paris rouses himself to give a blast on his horn, and with his last breath cries the name of Helen. Morris tells nothing further of Oenone, and Paris dies alone. This poem has more dramatic edge and vitality than most of the collection; Oenone is almost a woman, and her voice rises above the usual ghostly murmur.

What was spoken of at the beginning as the third phase in Morris's narrative technique received its great expression in *Sigurd the Volsung* (1876), and in some of the later tales of *The Earthly Paradise* he was feeling for a method and for subjects more massive and heroic than merely pictorial and romantic. The epic group includes *The Lovers of Gudrun* and the classical *Bellerophon at Argos* and *Bellerophon in Lycia*.[53] In the first of these two, King Proetus is

---

[53] One of the earliest poems designed for the collection was *The Story of Aristomenes*, which was written largely in 1866. See Mackail, I, 182–83; *Works*, XXIV, 171–238; Pausanias, IV. vi. 3 ff. (ed. Frazer, I, 187 ff., especially pp. 200–15). Pausanias' account of the Messenian liberator and his long guerilla warfare against the Spartans is full of romance and legend, which attracted Morris, but he felt hampered by the historical elements and by lack of first-hand knowledge of Greece, and he eventually gave up the poem. By virtue of its subject the long fragment has more of the epic about it than the tales of Bellerophon, though

the Potiphar, Potiphar's wife is Queen Sthenoboea, and Bellerophon is a spotless Joseph. When the queen falsely accuses him of violence, Proetus, unwilling to take the life of an honored guest, sends him to King Jobates of Lycia, Sthenoboea's father, with a request that he be put out of the way. In the second tale Jobates tries to carry out instructions by giving Bellerophon several hazardous enterprises, but the hero is victorious, and in the end he gains the esteem and confidence of the king. Throughout he is beloved by the king's daughter, Philonoë, who warns him of attempts on his life, and the ending is happy.[54] These poems are of great length, but otherwise their epic quality is not remarkable. However, the dominant tone is heroic and masculine, and characters and incidents are on a relatively human and realistic plane; we should be surprised if Bellerophon mounted Pegasus to attack the Chimera, and the supernatural monster itself is handled with finely indirect suggestion.[55] But there is much of the usual idealization, for in his classical tales Morris seems unable to yield to the stark barbarities and passions of northern saga — and even *The Lovers of Gudrun* and *Sigurd* are somewhat softened and romanticized.[56] The only bad

---

Morris develops such romantic incidents as Glauce's releasing Aristomenes from his captors. Like Rhodope, Glauce craves a fairer life than that of the daily round (*Works*, XXIV, 226).

[54] For the classical matter, see Lempriere; Homer, *Il.* vi. 155–97; Apollodorus, II. iii. 1–2; Hyginus, *Fab.* lvii. Hyginus says that Sthenoboea killed herself on hearing of Bellerophon's marriage with her sister; in Morris she displays less feminine and sisterly spleen, and commits suicide after Bellerophon sets off for Lycia.

[55] In general, though Morris is not averse to the supernatural, he changes some of its more naïve manifestations. In *Cupid and Psyche*, for instance, instead of the sisters' blunt theory that Psyche's husband is a serpent, they say they have been told of a serpent-bodied fiend which every hundred years assumes at night the form of a fair young man; and Psyche is given advice not by a speaking tower but by the voice of a queen imprisoned in the tower.

[56] Tremaine McDowell, "The Treatment of the Volsunga Saga by William Morris," *Scandinavian Studies*, VII (1923), 151–68.

character is the tired siren, Sthenoboea, and her badness, which adds a new element to Morris's simple patterns of romantic love, is more theatrical than convincing. Both the women of the poem recall Medea; Sthenoboea declares that she cannot help loving Bellerophon, even though he should weary of her and cast her off, and Philonoë loves the heroic stranger and helps him against her father.

The general characteristics of Morris's poetic and story-telling manner are all exemplified most freshly in *Jason*, and *The Earthly Paradise* is a long series of variations on the few familiar strings of his low-toned instrument. (Possibly one would turn that statement about if one happened to read *The Earthly Paradise* first.) There is the transparent copiousness of medieval narrative, and the pseudo-medieval air of dream-like enchantment envelops characters and action.[57] At times the author seems to share the weariness of his wanderers, and, like them, he must go on. There seems to be no end to his store of vague romantic phrases and sad, sweet rhymes. Morris's poetic conventions and poetic diction may on first acquaintance give real pleasure, especially if one is young and has some fear of intellectual and stylistic subtleties, but they are not for daily wear and in the long run become rather frayed. All eyes are gray, all hair is golden, all bosoms are hidden or half-bare, all legs are limbs, all feet are dainty. Morris avoids homely things and homely names almost as rig-

---

[57] I need mention only a few examples of medieval costume. The setting of *Atalanta's Race* is that of a tournament. Danaë's tower is of brass, but the four-square walls, small barred windows, and green hangings turn it into a medieval castle. The man who rescues Danaë when she is cast ashore had ridden forth with a hawk on his fist. Bells and gilded vanes reappear in *Cupid and Psyche*.

I have no space for Morris's translations of the *Aeneid* (1875) and the *Odyssey* (1887), and their general character is well known, even if they are not read. Troy is the "Holy Burg." Morris was literal enough, in a sense, but his attempt to make the poems something between romance and saga was quite fatal for one of them at least. What can be said on Morris's side has been said, with the charity of a scholar and translator of special authority, by Mr. Mackail (*Life*, I, 321–23, II, 180). See also W. Buchhorn, in my bibliography.

orously as Pope in his *Homer*. One could hardly imagine him, for all his social sympathies, writing a *Northern Farmer*, and if by any chance he had written *Jenny* the name, as Chesterton said, would probably have been "Jehanne."

Romantic trappings and royal magnificence are often essential to Morris's effects, of course, since the myths deal with kings and queens and their sons and daughters. But the instincts of a decorative craftsman may run away with him. There is in *Jason* and *The Earthly Paradise* an honest joy in all things made by men's hands, from ships and palaces to armor and cups, yet this really Homeric gusto is constantly mixed with something resembling over-ripe products of the Renaissance, such as the *Hypnerotomachia Poliphili* or the goldsmith's work of Cellini. In Apuleius there are many touches of drama and homely, robust realism, along with the romantic and the supernatural, and these varied qualities survived, with masculine vigor, in the Elizabethan prose of Adlington and the Caroline verse of Shakerley Marmion; in Morris's *Cupid and Psyche* there is little but sensuous materialism and feminine sweetness. Our senses are cloyed by the surfeit of luxuries, and the childlike seems to have become the childish when Psyche, planning entertainment for her sisters, assembles elephants, rhinoceroses, lions, leopards, tigers, eagles, peacocks, swans. . . . Even if this elaborate afternoon tea is an exceptional extravagance, the general texture of the writing is like the lion skin of Hercules in *The Golden Apples*; it was so wrought with gold that the fell showed but dim betwixt the threads. Thus one may not observe at first that the opening pages of *Rhodope* present exactly the same kind of family and background as the opening pages of Wordsworth's *Michael*. And in the midst of all the tinsel, which has its own charm of course, we are often refreshed by bits of pure earth and England. Admetus drives to Iolchos through "windings of the sweet-banked lanes." Pygmalion goes out to the woods through the fragrance of beanfields, past harvesters wielding the scythe, among swallows and partridges and bees murmuring in the clover. Atalanta's lover amid the beeches hears "the sweet familiar thrush," and his hounds' feet pattering over the dry leaves.

It is indeed a testimony to some genuine virtue in Morris that *The Earthly Paradise*, forty-two thousand lines with hardly a character or an idea, should be so readable as, in small doses, it is. To the reader of *Jason* very little is new except the fables themselves — and of course the Prologue and lyrics — and they, whatever their original differences in spirit, are nearly all transposed into one minor key. Morris was a subjective poet who regarded poetry as craftsmanship and whose slender vein, except at the beginning, was worked in a nominally objective way. *The Earthly Paradise* may be regarded as one interminable lyric on the memory of beauty and pain, the craving for rest, and the fear of death — *The Lotos-Eaters* on a vast scale. Although one theme which does not come into Tennyson's elegiac mood is central in Morris, namely, romantic love, it is bound up with the rest because it involves much less of joy than of anguish and longing.[58] The basic pattern of the love stories — that is, of the majority of the twelve classical poems — is the wish-fulfilment of all romance. An ideal young man and a beautiful maiden fall in love at first sight, and after toil and trouble and perhaps risk of life they are united. Particular fables may vary, but the characters seldom do; all the

---

[58] The most elaborate example did not get into the collection, *The Story of Orpheus and Eurydice* (*Works*, XXIV, 239–80). In permitting Orpheus to seek his bride, Hermes asks if his love can rise beyond earthly passion, and the tale ends, rather vaguely, with "earthly longing and defeat." The eight lyrics give the poem a somewhat operatic air. In some respects it is closer to the medieval *Sir Orfeo* than to a picture of the classical underworld.

young men are the same young man, nearly all the young
women are the same young woman. Except for the unfailing goodness of Morris's lovers and the usually happy
endings, much the same might be said of Ovid's twelve
dozen tales; but Ovid has such virtues as speed, brevity,
and variety, and in connection with *The Earthly Paradise*
it would be almost profane to think of Ovidian wit. Further,
in Ovid love is normally only healthy southern appetite,
not a consuming romantic passion for unattainable mysterious beauty. Morris endows the "hollow puppets" of his
rhymes with supposedly intense and exalted feelings, which
are described at great length but do not affect us as human
feelings. Hence the idealism seems thin and bloodless, and
not less so for being allied with sensuous desire.

Morris's religion of beauty is rooted in sense, but his
modern, self-conscious conception of beauty as a rare and
evanescent thing in an ugly world gives rise to his strain
of sophisticated melancholy. It is this which most obviously distinguishes his simply sensuous and unsymbol-
ical romanticism from that of *Hero and Leander* and *Venus
and Adonis*, for in those poems youthful senses are exuber-
antly alive and all-sufficient. Morris had closer affinities
with Keats than with any other modern poet,[59] at least
with the attenuated Pre-Raphaelite Keats, but there are
some fundamental differences; Keats's sensuous percep-
tions are so intense that they become intuitions of reality,
and, moreover, he is always striving to go behind the flux
to the idea. Morris's sensuousness tends to squander itself on white limbs and gold robes, wall papers and chintzes
and over-ornamental title-pages. When Chaucer wrote
mythological tales, in *The Legend of Good Women*, he, with
his zest for human realities, grew bored and gave up;
Morris was not bored, but he bores us. He made the
mistake, which even the poet of fairy-land avoided, of

[59] Mackail, I, 200, 219.

attempting to create a continuous illusion.[60] Love is a dream, grief a melody, death a dark cloud. This great body of verse from which the actual world is excluded lulls us into drowsy numbness as quickly as the earthly paradise itself would have done if men had ever found it.

Time was when the poetry resulting merely from this intense study and love of literature might have been, if not the best, yet at any rate very worthy and enduring: but in these days, when the issue is so momentous and the surroundings of life so stern that nothing can take serious hold of people, or should do so, but that which is rooted deepest in reality and is quite at first hand, there is no room for anything which is not forced out of a man because of its innate strength and vision.[61]

These words are not the verdict of a modern critic on Morris, they were said by Morris about Swinburne!

Spenser did not attempt a continuous illusion, a mere web of beautiful old tales, because, as a Renaissance poet, he had important things to say about all the elements of virtuous and gentle discipline, from holiness to courtesy, from ethics to politics and economics. His romanticism, for all its medieval wonders, chivalric manners, and devotion to beauty, does not grow out of thin soil, and it includes, like most great poetry, an element of prose. Spenser's commentary on the present is not limited to wistful visions of a beautiful past. In his best-known lyric Morris excuses himself, a dreamer of dreams, for not singing of heaven and hell, for not striving to set the crooked straight; he is only building

> a shadowy isle of bliss
> Midmost the beating of the steely sea,
> Where tossed about all hearts of men must be.[62]

---

[60] Mr. Elton puts Morris with Spenser in this respect (*Survey of English Literature 1780–1880*, 1920, IV, 37), but one may now and then differ with a critic who constantly compels agreement.

[61] Quoted by Mr. Mackail in a lecture on Swinburne (1909), in *Studies of English Poets* (1926), p. 221.

[62] When just beginning his life work, at the age of twenty-three, Morris said

The lyric is by no means a complete or just description of William Morris, but it does describe that part of him which expressed itself in *The Earthly Paradise* and in most of his poetry. His humanitarianism was not less earnest than Shelley's, it was certainly more steady, effective, and rational, but his poetic dream-world, cut off altogether from propaganda as well as from life, was far more unsubstantial than Shelley's.

Just because Morris was what he was, we may ask what degree of social consciousness is permitted to appear in his classical tales. The Prologue begins with those charming lines which take us back from the hideous town and six counties overhung with smoke to the fourteenth century, when men worked happily and beautifully with their hands. The wanderers do not find the earthly paradise, but they and their creator are always thinking of it. The one persistent allusion, here as in *Jason*, is to the golden age. Admetus ruled "in those old simple days" before the cravings of the rich sent men into peril; his reign was not darkened by conquest and war, it was a time of peace and plenty and healthy labor. Rhodope lived among simple folk in a similar world; all worked, few were poor, none were overrich, and none bore a great man's yoke.[63] Such pictures of a primitive Utopia are all that we get from the author of *News from Nowhere* and *The Dream of John Ball*, not to mention vigorous socialist speeches and chants. They do not go much beyond Macaulay's "Then none was for a party . . . ," and Macaulay never left the Albany for Hyde Park and Trafalgar Square.

Keats and Shelley tried to make the scope of poetry, mythological poetry too, commensurate with the whole

---

the same things in prose: "I can't enter into politico-social subjects with any interest, for on the whole I see that things are in a muddle, and I have no power or vocation to set them right in ever so little a degree. My work is the embodiment of dreams in one form or another." (Mackail, I, 107; and cf. II, 25.)

[63] *Works*, IV, 89–90, 114–16, V, 209, 222.

life of man, though there is a visible gulf between their large aims and their performance. In Morris the attenuation of romanticism is complete, and the divorce between poetry and life especially paradoxical, for he was not, like Rossetti, a secluded high-priest of estheticism. He not only transformed "the whole conception of the place of aesthetic values in the practical life of the modern world," but "gave a colour to socialism without which to-day it would be almost inconceivable." He was a great and inspiring "benefactor to humanity," "the sane man with his robust grip on the realities of human nature," the prophet whose "final message to us rests upon two words — Courage and Hope," whose spirit was "fundamentally revolutionary." [64] And this man of immense and versatile creative energy was the mild-eyed melancholy lotos-eater who spent part of that energy in composing an immense mass of verse most of which cannot appeal to modern readers after they have passed twenty. Was Morris's unceasing activity of hand and brain the result of some unsatisfied inner restlessness? "People always say," Miss Morris has remarked, "that my father was one of the happiest of men in his work: but who can know for sure?"[65] Was he, like his own Pygmalion, the craftsman who while looking on the sun may chide his useless labor never done, and yet

> For all his murmurs, with no other thing
> He soothes his heart and dulls thought's poisonous sting . . . ?

Was his heart too sick, as he suggests in the more personal lines of *November*, "To struggle any more with doubt and thought"? He has looked upon the real world, ruled at

[64] From tributes by Mr. Lascelles Abercrombie, Lord Snowden, Mr. Shaw, Mr. Mackail, and Mr. Herbert Read, in *Some Appreciations of William Morris*, ed. George E. Roebuck (Walthamstow, 1934), pp. 6, 22, 30, 32, 28.

[65] *Works*, XXIV, x. See Morris's letter quoted in Mackail, I, 327–28.

midnight by the silent moon, and has seen November
there:

> The changeless seal of change it seemed to be,
> Fair death of things that, living once, were fair;
> Bright sign of loneliness too great for me,
> Strange image of the dread eternity,
> In whose void patience how can these have part,
> These outstretched feverish hands, this restless heart?

CHAPTER X

Swinburne

NO MODERN English poet has been more saturated in Greek drama and poetry than Swinburne,
and none has been more essentially un-Greek in
spirit, form, and style. The paradox had already
had notable exemplars in English poetic history, from Chapman whom Swinburne praised to Mrs. Browning whom
he praised and parodied. Swinburne differed from these
two at least in the fact that he did, especially in his classical dramas, use enough Greek costume and idiom to create
a superficial illusion. But he was completely of his own
time, and his temperament transmuted everything into
the likeness of itself. He had a profound reverence for
the *Oresteia*, yet he employed the adjective "Aeschylean"
in sometimes curious ways. He could endow Sophocles
with "honey-heavy lips."[1] (He was less rococo and more
Hellenic, at any rate more Aristophanic, in his various
remarks about Euripides.) We hear little from Swinburne
of Greek authors "of the center"; for him the greatest
non-dramatic poet of Greece was Sappho, and her fair
fame has hardly recovered from the damage done by her
worshiper. The only Latin poets Swinburne included in
a list of the hundred best books were Lucretius, whom he
did not care for but admitted as an enemy of religion, and
Catullus, whose songs of love were different from those of
Tennyson, Browning, and Patmore.[2] Many modern artists,

---

[1] *Swinburne's Collected Poetical Works* (1924), II, 1045. This two-volume
edition is hereafter cited as *Works*.

[2] A letter to *The Pall Mall Gazette* (January, 1886), in *Letters from Algernon
Charles Swinburne to Sir Edward Lytton-Bulwer* (printed by T. J. Wise, 1913),

after they have passed through Swinburne's mind, may become unrecognizable. Michelangelo is interpreted in terms of Flaubert and Gautier;[3] Gautier himself is welcomed, presumably in Hades, by "all the crowned Hellenic heads." [4] Hugo and Baudelaire are given a classical setting; indeed the exiled Hugo is everything from Prometheus to Orpheus.[5] But we shall come upon many illustrations of Swinburne's generous Hellenism and the transforming power of his literary passions, and need not pursue the matter now.

I

Among the varied experiments of Swinburne's Eton days were several Ovidian poems, on Byblis, Clytie, and Apollo and Daphne (1849–50?).[6] The first subject would appeal to the precocious taste for lurid passions which at this time had been expressing itself in the Websterian and Tourneuresque drama, *The Unhappy Revenge*. In the very Shelleyan and slightly Aeschylean *Temple of Janus* (1857), Swinburne anticipated the *Tiresias* of *Songs before Sunrise*; the cause of Italy is the cause of freedom, and Janus turns into Mazzini.[7] Another experiment, of 1859,

---

p. 49. Like Byron and others, Swinburne disliked the compulsory Latin classics of the curriculum (Sir Edmund Gosse, *Life of Swinburne*, 1917, p. 25).

[3] Swinburne, *Essays and Studies* (1875), pp. 320–21; Mario Praz, *The Romantic Agony* (1933), p. 241.

[4] *Works*, I, 358. For a translation of Swinburne's Greek verses on Gautier, see William R. Rutland, *Swinburne: A Nineteenth Century Hellene* (Oxford, 1931), pp. 395–98. In commencing a brief survey of those aspects of Swinburne which are the subject of Mr. Rutland's large volume, I must pay my respects to his scholarship, taste, and enthusiasm, though I cannot share his estimate of Swinburne's Hellenic or poetic qualities.

[5] *Works*, I, 149, 870. On *Ave atque Vale* see Samuel C. Chew, *Swinburne* (Boston, 1929), pp. 145–49.

[6] Georges Lafourcade, *La jeunesse de Swinburne (1837–1867)* (Paris and London, 1928), I, 98, II, 13, 174; *Swinburne's Hyperion*, ed. G. Lafourcade (1927), p. 147. As footnotes will partly indicate, I share the obligations to M. Lafourcade which everyone who touches Swinburne must incur.

[7] Lafourcade, *Jeunesse*, II, 21 ff., 209–17; for the echoes of *Prometheus Bound*, see *ibid.*, p. 26; Rutland, pp. 265–66.

which M. Lafourcade in his elaborate edition has christened "Swinburne's Hyperion," is of special interest. This is an epic in two books, of slightly over five hundred lines, on the fall of the Titans. In style it shows Swinburne putting himself to school to Keats and to Keats's own master, Milton, and in such an imitative exercise original elements are not conspicuous. But the style of the conscious pupil, while forced and uneven, has more weight and edge than that of the mature Swinburne; indeed one may be reminded of *Gebir*. In later days Swinburne did not try to be Miltonic, and the most marked and permanent trace of his study of Keats was a love of compound adjectives.

For the fable Swinburne mainly follows *Hyperion*, with some additional matter from the first two books of *Paradise Lost*.[8] The bulk of the poem describes a council of the defeated Titans — a brief council among the victorious but agitated gods occurs toward the middle — and it ends, beyond the point where Keats stopped, with the Titans marching forth to renew battle. Hyperion is absent, and Apollo is only a lay-figure. Apparently Swinburne did not grasp the significance of Keats's parable of social, individual, and poetic progress,[9] but he introduced some philosophizing on his own account. Saturn explains, not in the manner of Keats's Oceanus, the workings of destiny, which here might be called "Necessity" or "the Life Force," according to one's taste.[10] He goes on to urge that

---

[8] The description of Tityus and other traditional sufferers in hell (pp. 139–40) is doubtless taken from Ovid, *Metam.* iv. 447 ff.

[9] In later life Swinburne had a good deal to do with propagating the pernicious notion of Keats as a pure artist. Being himself a serious preacher and prophet whose muse espoused various causes, including sadism and atheism, Swinburne increasingly condemned what he regarded as Keats's unmanly and unphilosophic estheticism — especially after the publication of the love letters had shown that Keats was not quite a gentleman and did not write as, say, an Eton and Oxford man would write to Emerson.

[10] The line "Which men call Time, or Fate, or Chance, or God" (p. 123) recalls Shelley's "Fate, Time, Occasion, Chance, and Change" (*Prometheus Unbound*, II. iv. 119; and cf. II. ii. 92).

the Titans, in their "inward power made strong," should conform to destiny, and so, "Sitting upon calm thrones of Knowledge," reign for ever in peace "And triumph in our being's perfectness." M. Lafourcade discerns here a more Hellenic attitude, and more philosophic depth and originality, than is visible to the naked eye, but his remarks on later developments may be quoted:

Swinburne's fatalism proceeds from his pantheism. It is because we are part of the "informing destiny" and "regent will" of the world that we cannot resist its decrees. Hence the folly of a revolt which Swinburne sometimes advocated (cf. *Atalanta*, etc.), but which he always condemned from the deeper and purely theological point of view (as in *Hertha* and the *Hymn of Man*).[11]

Certainly neither the doctrine nor the style of this poem prepares one for the work of Swinburne's next five or six years.

II

While *The Queen Mother and Rosamond* (1860) was, according to its author, the stillest of all still-born books, *Atalanta in Calydon* had, among the literary, a resounding success. Tennyson, with such reservations as one may imagine, admired the "strength and splendour," and even envied the "fine metrical invention." Everyone knows Ruskin's phrase, "the grandest thing ever yet done by a youth — though he is a Demoniac youth"; and he added the query, "Whether ever he will be clothed and in his right mind, heaven only knows. His foam at the mouth is fine, meantime."[12] Arnold, whose classical principles had not been relaxed by the fate of *Merope*, complained, quite justly, that *Atalanta* was wholly different from the antique. Our own reaction depends on whether we first

---

[11] P. 111.
[12] *Works of John Ruskin*, ed. E. T. Cook and Alexander Wedderburn (1903–12), XXXVI, 501; *Alfred Lord Tennyson: A Memoir* (1897), I, 496.

read the drama in youth, and whether we have reread it. At any rate this work of a young man of twenty-seven, though followed by a score of volumes, remains probably his finest major achievement. One might say either that Swinburne's artistic maturity was attained very early, or that his development was prematurely arrested. Indeed a survey of his great body of writing suggests that he passed from youth to old age without any intervening period.

Swinburne's remarks on *Atalanta* expressed a wholly literary ambition and intention:

I think it is pure Greek, and the first poem of the sort in modern times, combining lyric and dramatic work on the old principle. Shelley's *Prometheus* is magnificent and un-Hellenic, spoilt too in my mind by the infusion of philanthropic doctrinaire views and "progress of the species"; and by what I gather from Lewes's life of Goethe the *Iphigenia in Tauris* must be also impregnated with modern morals and feelings. As for Professor Arnold's *Merope*, the clothes are well enough, but where has the body gone? [13]

It was in the same spirit that Swinburne said in 1864 that he had rejoiced in Landor's poetry as a boy and was now "more than ever sure that the *Hamadryad* is a purer and better piece of work, from the highest point of view that art can take, than such magnificent hashes and stews of old and new with a sharp sauce of personality as *Oenone* and *Ulysses*."[14] But whatever he thought his intentions were, the author of *Atalanta* believed, most of the time, that poetry should be a criticism of life, and in his handling of the antique he was much closer to Shelley and Tennyson than to the pure artist, Landor. For though Landor

[13] *Letters of Algernon Charles Swinburne*, ed. Sir Edmund Gosse and Thomas J. Wise (1918), I, 31–32.
[14] *Ibid.*, I, 21.

represented pagan art, while Tennyson was "not a Greek
nor a heathen," a still stronger bond between the youngest
and the oldest singer was that Landor represented pagan
rebellion.[15]

In addition to these general literary impulses, we may
remember that *Atalanta* was begun and finished at the
seaside, and that the music of Handel as well as of the
waves passed into the choric rhythms. Further, the drama
was written under the shadow of personal grief, for the
death of Swinburne's sister Edith; and Landor died just
before it was finished. However, while he suspected that
"the funereal circumstances" had "a little deepened the
natural colours of Greek fatalism here and there," Swinburne "never enjoyed anything more" in his life "than
the composition of this poem, which though a work done
by intervals, was very rapid and pleasant." [16]

Swinburne admired Sophocles and detested Euripides
and borrowed from both; but he adored Aeschylus, and
some of his allusions suggest a not too pure or discriminating Hellenism. Thus Victor Hugo is a modern Aeschylus. The Titaness of *L'homme qui rit* who is revealed in
her "naked glory" is "a possible Astarte latent in an
actual Diana." In enlarging upon this, her maker's definition, Swinburne becomes dithyrambic: "We seem to hear
about her the beat and clash of the terrible timbrels, the
music that Aeschylus set to verse, the music that made
mad. . . ." She is "one of these Aeschylean women, a
monstrous goddess, whose tone of voice 'gave a sort of

---

[15] G. Lafourcade, *Swinburne's Atalanta in Calydon: A Facsimile of the First
Edition* (Oxford University Press, 1930), pp. viii–ix; *Swinburne: A Literary
Biography* (1932), p. 119. For a full and naturally somewhat one-sided discus-
sion see W. B. Drayton Henderson, *Swinburne and Landor* (1918).

[16] *Letters*, I, 32. The last 850 lines, apart from two or three insertions, were
written in four afternoons; see *ibid.*; Lafourcade, *Jeunesse*, II, 384; *Atalanta*,
ed. Lafourcade, p. x.

The passage on "old men honourable" (*Works*, II, 265–66) was, Swinburne
said, a reference to Landor (*Letters*, I, 31; *Atalanta*, ed. Lafourcade, pp. xi, 25–26).

Promethean grandeur to her furious and amorous words,'
who had in her the tragic and Titanic passion of the
women of the Eleusinian feasts 'seeking the satyrs under
the stars.'"[17] Another aspect of Swinburne's conception
of Greek tragedy is made clear in his study of Blake.
In Urizen, "'Father of jealousy'... are incarnate that
jealousy which the Hebrews acknowledged and that envy
which the Greeks recognized in the divine nature; in his
worship faith remains one with fear." As for the style of
Aeschylus, Swinburne speaks of passages in Blake "not
always unworthy of an Aeschylean chorus, full of fate and
fear; words that are strained wellnigh in sunder by strong
significance and earnest passion...."[18] Whatever we
think of Hugo and Blake in this connection, Aeschylus
was for Swinburne the poet who combined the lyrical with
the dramatic principle, and also combined Hellenic light
with Hebraic fire.[19] Such an Aeschylus was the inevitable
model for a lyrical dramatist steeped in the Bible and in
Greek; he was indeed the only one of the Greeks who could
in some sort be adopted by a devotee of Hugo, Blake,
Shakespeare, and the more sensational Jacobeans.

In the structure and details of *Atalanta*, Swinburne did
not strictly follow any one dramatist. In Aeschylus as
well as Euripides the choric odes are often related only in
a general way to the action, and most of Swinburne's are
of Aeschylean length and prophetic fervor; they are also
far more undramatic. (Unlike Arnold, Swinburne did not
attempt to give the effect of Greek choric meters but let
himself go on the billows of his rhyming anapests.) The
opening speech of the huntsman, whose soul is above his
occupation, resembles the usually less poetical Euripidean
prologue, and he reminds us also of the more realistic

[17] *Essays and Studies*, pp. 8–9; cf. p. 24.
[18] *William Blake* (1868), pp. 192–93, 195; (ed. 1906), pp. 213, 216.
[19] *Letters*, I, 31, 240.

watchman at the beginning of the *Agamemnon*. Another example of mixed influence or similarity is the lyrical lamentation at the end, which, in its length and antiphonal character and its voluptuous treatment of pain, is not altogether Hellenic. There is a partial parallel in Euripides' *Hippolytus*, where the dying hero is carried in like Meleager, is comforted by Artemis as Meleager is by Artemis' votary, and forgives his father as Meleager forgives Althaea; there is, too, the mourning at the tomb of Agamemnon in the *Choephoroe*, and Swinburne echoes both Euripides and Aeschylus.[20] Swinburne's rebellious and anti-religious spirit, which is expressed through both Althaea and the chorus, may be called Euripidean, but a more modern and accurate label will be encountered later.

For the main outline of the fable, and many details, Swinburne used Apollodorus. Ovid was the source next in importance, in general and notably in the description of the hunt, though Apollodorus was the chief source for this also. Swinburne's Meleager does not, as in the Greek versions, have a wife, but is a young man untouched by love until he sees Atalanta; this change, so much in harmony with the romantic and lyrical spirit of the drama, may have been suggested by Ovid. Among miscellaneous items, Swinburne wove in some of the fragments of Euripides' *Meleager*, the earliest source, apparently, in which Meleager's love for Atalanta was a prominent motive.[21] In the

[20] Compare Oeneus' "Thou shouldst die as he dies . . ." (*Works*, II, 326), and *Choeph.*, ll. 345 ff.; Meleager's "Let your hands meet . . ." (*Works*, II, 321), and *Hipp.*, ll. 198 ff., 1358 ff. Another general parallel is Sophocles' *Trachiniae*, ll. 972 ff. (Lafourcade, *Jeunesse*, II, 388).

[21] See Apollodorus, *Lib.* I. viii. 1–3 (and Frazer's references, I, 64–65); Ovid, *Metam.* viii. 260 ff.; Hyginus, *Fab.* clxxi–clxxiv; Diodorus Siculus, iv. 34. In Mr. Rutland's appendices (pp. 349 ff.) the sources are quoted, with translations. A number of discussions of Swinburne's structural and material borrowings are listed in my bibliography. In addition to Rutland (pp. 93 ff.) and Lafourcade (*Jeunesse*, II, 382–416), my sketch is chiefly indebted to the article of Mario Praz (*Atene e Roma*, III [1922], 157–89).

Classical sources do not include Althaea's dream of giving birth to a firebrand

tense dialogue between Althaea and the chorus after she has thrown the brand on the fire, Swinburne is obviously imitating the scene with Cassandra in the *Agamemnon*, and in following the supreme example of tragic horror in ancient drama he becomes, for once, almost Aeschylean; or rather, he would be if his climax possessed Aeschylean significance. Although materials and hints for his fable, not to mention countless echoes of poetic phrase, ancient and modern, are thus gathered from many sources, nowhere is there any sign of laborious documentation. Swinburne held the mass of mythological detail in solution, and had a crowd of figures vividly present to him, as Carlyle did, in the little theater under his hat. Not much energy, to be sure, was diverted from story to characterization; with one exception Swinburne's characters are paler silhouettes than any Greek play contains.

Whatever the Greeks may have made of the subject, in Swinburne's hands the external action is almost devoid of drama. One general reason is that all the persons speak in exactly the same style. What little drama there is takes place in the mind of Althaea, and that is not much. After the first choric ode, she complains of the ways of the gods, in particular of Artemis, who has not only afflicted the country but has inspired in her son a love for that human Artemis, Atalanta. In the next scene Althaea rebukes him for his infatuation, urging him to serve law and the gods and prosper as a great man.[22] Meleager protests that he is

---

or her subsequent dream of the brand bursting into flames. Critics have cited the *Choephoroe* (ll. 523 ff.), where Clytemnestra has a dream of her son which is parallel in its symbolism; and the dream of Atossa (*Persae*, ll. 176 ff.). They have not, I think, mentioned such a humble hint as the inaccurate remark of Falstaff's page: "Marry, my lord, Althea dreamed she was delivered of a firebrand . . ." (*2 Henry IV*, II. ii. 98). A firebrand being already in the story of Althaea and Meleager, Swinburne might naturally transfer the familiar story of Hecuba's dreaming of her son as a firebrand.

[22] With Althaea's picture of Elysium compare Pindar, *Ol.* ii. 68 ff., and Homer, *Od.* vi. 41 ff.

not a child but a man, one of the heroic Argonauts; besides, his feeling for Atalanta is not love but reverent
adoration. When Oeneus has tried to reconcile the two,
Althaea resumes her pleading; this time she begins with
the assertion that the gods smite good and bad alike.[23] Her
recollections of Meleager in his childhood are sometimes
touching, but both the son and the mother, apart from her
fierce possessiveness, are so noble and affectionate, and
their speeches are so diffuse and decorative, that what
might be a dramatic clash between them is muffled.

Atalanta now defends her status as a maiden huntress
against the gibes of Toxeus and Plexippus; she desires not
to rob them of honor or spoil, but only to serve her goddess and depart. Then, while the hunters attack the boar,
Swinburne attacks God. A herald returns to give a vivid
description of the hunt and of Meleager's prowess. Althaea rejoices, and the chorus sings in praise of Artemis;
it is that false dawn so beloved of the Greek dramatists.[24]
A second messenger reports the catastrophe; Toxeus and
Plexippus, attempting to deprive Atalanta of the spoils
Meleager presented to her, had been slain by him. At
once Althaea's mind turns to the thought of revenge and
of herself as an instrument of fate: "My dreams are fallen
upon me; burn thou too." In Ovid she has a mental conflict of a somewhat mechanical Euripidean kind. In Swinburne there is little real conflict. Althaea's tempestuous
grief for her loutish brothers — grief that we should but
cannot share — is heightened, like her former appeals to
her son, by tender recollections of their youth, and her
present enmity toward Meleager is mixed with flashes of

[23] Cf. *Seven against Thebes*, ll. 597 ff. Meleager's descriptive list of hunters
may have been partly suggested by the catalogue of chieftains in this play
(ll. 422 ff.). A more obvious model would be the scene in the third book of the
Iliad.
[24] Cf. *Oed. Col.*, ll. 668 ff.

reminiscence.[25] In a long series of speeches she lashes herself into a Titanic passion for vengeance; Swinburne wishes
to show her as a great victim of the great cruel powers she
has assailed. When she has cast the brand on the fire, and
is overcome by the realization of her act, she declares, like
Sophocles' Jocasta: "My lips shall not unfasten till I
die." There follows the lamentation of the chorus and
Meleager, who, it must be said, is an unconscionable time
a-dying. This *kommos* is a tissue, marvelous in its way, of
elegiac fancies, and is not at all dramatic or realistic. The
very movement of the stanzas, the ease and regularity with
which Meleager takes his turn, prevent our thinking of
him as a dying man. The lyrical symphony has its own
verbal and rhythmical magic, but one can only envy such
a critic as Mr. Harold Nicolson, who, though not in perfect sympathy with Swinburne, finds here "a cleansing of
the spirit, an almost overwhelming emotion of pity and
of fear."[26] Incidentally, the dying Meleager is a nineteenth-century pantheist who thinks of his life being
renewed in the life of the rain and dew on grass and
leaves.

The lyrical and undramatic character of *Atalanta* is too
commonplace a point to be labored, yet the poem was a
sun in the firmament of Victorian Hellenism, and the
reasons for its present eclipse must be considered. Splendors of style and rhythm have not been enough to keep it
alive; in the real sense of the word it never was alive. The
moment it is weighed in the scale of living dramas, *Atalanta*
labels itself "literature." As a mirror or interpretation of
life it does not touch us at all. When Gloucester says,
"As flies to wanton boys are we to the gods ... ," the

---

[25] Althaea's argument that a brother cannot be replaced is similar to Antigone's (*Antig.*, ll. 905 ff.), though the circumstances are not, and in Swinburne
the idea seems forced.
[26] *Swinburne* (1926), p. 88.

words have a terrible significance; when Althaea says

> what chance
> The gods cast lots for and shake out on us,
> That shall we take, and that much bear withal,

we hardly notice it, though it is a main text of the play. If we keep within *Atalanta's* particular and artificial genre, we may grant it second place in the list of English classical dramas — though that is debatable — but it is so far beneath *Samson Agonistes* that comparison would be absurd.

When there is no real dramatic pattern of life such as the Greeks had, and there are no characters or situations such as Shakespeare had, the "philosophy," since it does not reside in the fable, must be for the most part directly expounded by the author. If Swinburne's is to be measured by his flow of words, he has much to say. In the first serious choral ode, "Before the beginning of years," the theme is the greatness and the littleness of man; it is the theme of much great poetry, one might almost say of all great poetry, but one is not deeply stirred by Swinburne's melodious incantation.[27] As Mr. Eliot observes, "The chorus of Swinburne is almost a parody of the Athenian: it is sententious, but it has not even the significance of commonplace." The next chorus, "We have seen thee, O Love, thou art fair," contains almost a hundred and fifty lines, mainly on that favorite idea of Swinburne and his fellows, that Love is the mother of Death. After one has emerged from the verbal hallucination, it is an interest-

[27] More than one scholar has compared Swinburne's opening lines with the *Timaeus* (42a, 69c); see, for example, Paul Elmer More, *The Religion of Plato* (Princeton University Press, 1921), p. 184. The logic of Swinburne's transposition of Grief and Time, the tears and the glass, is censured by Mr. Eliot (*Selected Essays*, 1932, p. 312) and defended by Mr. I. A. Richards (*Practical Criticism*, 1929, pp. 195–96). See *Notes and Queries*, Twelfth Series, X (1922), 18, 54, 96, 136. Did Swinburne remember Landor's "Grief favours all who bear the gift of tears" (*Gebir*, vi. 78)?

ing study, since Love is personified, to follow the logical sequence of her biography in relation to the alleged conditions prevailing on earth. A relentless critic who did so concludes that "when the sheer contradictions have been cancelled out, it is hard to say whether anything intelligible remains at all, except the assertion that the coming of Love was calamitous."[28]

Atalanta's defence of herself gives no occasion whatever for the enunciation of the thesis of the play, the complaint about the wretched lot of helpless man and the arbitrary malice of the gods — a chorus of nearly a hundred and seventy lines ending with praise of silence — but the author has to get in what is more essential for him than Prometheus' curse of Jupiter was for Shelley. While Christina Rossetti deleted "The supreme evil, God," in her copy, that tremendous climax of blasphemy nowadays awakens hardly more than a smile; its evangelical zeal, though not its language, is that of a Hyde Park atheist, or a boy who has repudiated the Church of England. Whatever slight parallels can be found in Greek tragedy, especially in Euripides, the total effect is quite un-Greek. Swinburne wrests the idea of fate out of all likeness to a philosophical conception of the laws which never grow old, an eternal order which breaks the unruly or the unfortunate individual.[29] In the drama as a whole he does on a large scale what Hardy does briefly in the last paragraph of *Tess*; he makes Greek idiom and allusion the vehicle for a perversion of Greek sentiment.[30] Lord Houghton, in reviewing *Atalanta*, cited *Manfred* — he might have added *Cain* — and there is a similarity, though Swinburne denied any connection.[31] The real source, as he said, was one to which

[28] *T.L.S.*, December 11, 1930, p. 1060.
[29] Cf. *Athens* (*Works*, II, 624).
[30] For Hardy's phrase, "the President of the Immortals," see the Bohn translation of Aeschylus (1849), p. 7.
[31] *Edinburgh Review*, CXXII (1865), 214; Swinburne, *Letters*, I, 37–38.

Houghton himself had introduced him; he had been delighted to find in Sade confirmation of his own congenital
instincts. From Sade, Praz remarks, Swinburne took

the idea that God smites equally the just and the unjust, and
perhaps the former rather more than the latter; also the other
idea that pain and death are everywhere in Nature, that crime is
Nature's law; and the conception of God as a Being of supreme
wickedness ('the supreme evil, God'), and the revolt of man
against the divinity he disowns.[32]

While in *Atalanta* sadism largely takes the form of belaboring God, the sanguinary and erotic element is not absent.
It colors Althaea's thoughts about destroying her son's
life, and her picture of Atalanta,

> She the strange woman, she the flower, the sword,
> Red from spilt blood, a mortal flower to men,
> Adorable, detestable — even she
> Saw with strange eyes and with strange lips rejoiced,
> Seeing these mine own slain of mine own.

Atalanta, the "frigid virgin," is, as Praz says, one kind of
fatal woman; she is indirectly responsible for her lover's
death, and his dying under her eyes is a situation paralleled in that glossy piece of decadent sensationalism,
Salammbo.

Such ideas of God and human life as Swinburne sets
forth may, when differently felt and handled, be philosophically and emotionally moving — as some passages in the
Rubáiyát are, to go no higher — but even if the anti-religious fatalism of *Atalanta* is ineffectual, any modern idea
is better than no idea beyond reproduction of the antique.
We may read in a kind of hypnotic trance, but at least we

---

[32] *The Romantic Agony*, p. 225. Cf. Lafourcade, *Jeunesse*, II, 401–03. On the
similarity between this chorus and the "theological" passage in *Anactoria*
(*Works*, I, 62–63), see *Atalanta*, ed. Lafourcade, p. xiv; and Praz, pp. 89, 224,
279, note 54. Praz (p. 90) cites the speech of Ahasuerus in the seventh canto of
Queen Mab.

do not have to summon up the virtuous resolution with which we enter the chilly museum where so many pseudo-classic dramas repose. If there is hardly any real pity or terror, there is the animation of vigorous propaganda. And in addition to denouncing God, Swinburne glorifies "the holy spirit of man." This is the reverse side of his belief in the unholy spirit of God, and is perhaps no more solidly founded, though it partakes of his genuine love of liberty. Finally, whether such impulses give to *Atalanta* an authentic or an artificial fire, there is something else which is not merely Victorian and is not characteristic of Greek drama, the radiant freshness of morning and youthful beauty and strength and prowess. It is that impression, however blurred by rhetoric, which remains in our memories.

Along with his compliments Tennyson asked Swinburne if it was fair for a Greek chorus to abuse the Deity something in the style of the Hebrew prophets. But there seems to be no reason why saturation in the English Bible should make a modern poet's sentiments Hebraic any more than saturation in Greek makes them classical. When, for instance, Swinburne writes "a blast of the envy of God," we are at least vaguely conscious of what Traill called the "rum Old Testament ring," but the phrase in *Job*, "By the blast of God they perish," has been given a twist in accordance with Swinburne's view of the Deity and his notion of Greek and Hebrew views.[33] Swinburne's language itself, taken word by word, is almost a well of English undefiled — and so was Lyly's, to mention an earlier master of rhetorical tricks. It is Swinburne's combinations of words, and his inability to use one where a hundred will serve, which are the supreme evil. Generally his fault is not, any more than Shelley's, mere careless fluency, it is, as with Shelley, persistent vagueness. In

[33] *Works*, II, 322; *Job*, iv. 9. Cf. *Persae*, l. 362, and p. 334 above.

the classical dramas Swinburne can and does imitate the Greek tragic style, notably in the passages of stichomythy, and the force gained by unwonted condensation is immediately apparent. But ordinarily, and above all in the cascading choruses, an idea is lost in an iridescent foam of metaphors and adjectives, a nebula at once prismatic and diaphanous, if the last word may be used in a sense not quite Landor's. Take the famous opening lines:

> Maiden, and mistress of the months and stars
> Now folded in the flowerless fields of heaven. . . .

Starting probably from the Shelleyan phrases, "mother of the months" and "flock of the starry fold," Swinburne makes them even more soft and unsubstantial.[34] In the hands of a master like Gerard Hopkins alliteration can give strength and finality. Swinburne lulls us to sleep because his lines have little in them but sound, and their beauty does not wear so well as that of another famous opening:

> Before the starry threshold of Jove's court
> My mansion is, where those immortal shapes. . . .[35]

While Shelleyan language is wholly congenial to Swinburne (Arnold's "sort of pseudo-Shelley"), Greek and biblical phrases have outlines to lose. The first two words of "brown bright nightingale amorous" are an attempt to render Aeschylus' epithet, but the Aeschylean bird van-

---

[34] For the first phrase, see *The Revolt of Islam*, IV. i. 7; *Prometheus Unbound*, IV. 207; *The Witch of Atlas*, l. 73; for the second, Shelley's *Death of Napoleon*. This last passage Swinburne quotes in *Essays and Studies*, p. 258.

Swinburne's revisions of the second line show a concern for the sound rather than for a distinct idea or picture. "He began with 'happy,' rejected that in favour of 'rayless,' then tried 'sleepless,' and finally wrote the line as it stands" (*Atalanta in Calydon*, ed. J. H. Blackie, 1930, p. xii). The line is echoed, by the way, in Morris's *Jason*, vi. 105.

[35] One might quote another Miltonic line more clearly pictorial than Swinburne's — "And sow'd with stars the heaven thick as a field" (*Paradise Lost*, vii. 358). For Milton's probable original, see Spenser's fourth *Hymne*, l. 53.

ishes into musical syllables.[36] Homer's "clothed with impudence" and "clothed with might," and Ezekiel's "clothed with desolation," are concrete and instinctive metaphors; Swinburne's "He weaves, and is clothed with derision" is both more abstract and less logical.[37] Whatever Swinburne's own power over language, he must of course be held mainly responsible for infecting later Victorian poetry with that romantic jargon compounded of words like "sudden," "swift," "white," "bright," "fulfilled" (for "filled full of"), "perilous" (as in "perilous goddess"), and of properties like loathing and laughter, tears, years, flowers, flames, foam, fire, desire, and the rest. Swinburne was himself aware of his "tendency to the dulcet and luscious form of verbosity which has to be guarded against, lest the poem lose its foothold and be swept off its legs, sense and all, down a flood of effeminate and monotonous music, or be lost and spilt in a maze of what I call draggletailed melody."[38] One could not ask for a more eloquent description.

III

After praising the glories of *Atalanta*, critics have generally let *Erechtheus* (1876) go with the all-sufficient remark that it is more classical than its predecessor, by which they mean chiefly that it is less interesting. Some, including Swinburne, have found *Erechtheus* a more mature and satisfying whole.[39] One may lean toward both views but prefer to read *Atalanta*. In *Erechtheus* the impulse to skip is more frequent and irresistible, and indeed one may

---

[36] *Agam.*, l. 1142.

[37] *Works*, II, 260; *Ezekiel*, vii. 27; *Iliad*, i. 149, viii. 262. These examples, and some others, are taken from Praz's article in *Atene e Roma*, though he might disown my comments.

[38] *Letters*, I, 109; Gosse, *Life*, p. 208. Swinburne is speaking of the meter of his *Memorial Verses* on Gautier.

[39] *Works*, I, xiii; *Letters*, I, 240, 246.

turn over a couple of pages without noticing a break in continuity. For one thing, though the volume of words is immense, the fable, as Swinburne handles it, is thin and monotonous. Athens is threatened by Poseidon and the invading army of his son, Eumolpus, and the oracle demands the sacrifice of the king's daughter, Chthonia, if the city is to be saved. The sorrowing father tells the mother, the mother tells the daughter, and she goes forth to be slain by the priest. Chthonia's sisters refuse to survive her, the king is killed by the stroke of a divine hand — though these events are but dimly registered in our consciousness — and Praxithea is left alone. But the enemy are overpowered, the city is safe, under the blessing of Athena, and the name of Chthonia is for ever illustrious.[40]

Erechtheus has been much praised by Gosse and Welby, and treated almost as sacred literature by Mr. Rutland, but it makes a very faint impression upon me. The characters are little more than names, headings for different passages in one long lyric. What dramatic possibilities the story contains are all smoothed out. Father, mother, and daughter are completely perfect beings who outdo one another in family affection and in magnanimous devotion to Athens,

> The fruitful immortal anointed adored
> Dear city of men without master or lord.

(How remote, by the way, is this nostalgic feeling from the lines in the *Persae* that Swinburne echoes![41]) The result is the unrelieved nobility and unrelieved pathos of selfless patriotism. The trouble is not merely that we can

---

[40] See Apollodorus, *Lib.* III. xiv. 1, xv. 1–5; Hyginus, *Fab.* xlvi, etc. The chief fragment of Euripides' *Erechtheus* was in books that Swinburne had owned since his Eton days; it is quoted in Rutland, pp. 386–89. Rutland discusses Swinburne's borrowing, pp. 195–205, and quotes his violent protest against a reviewer's linking his drama with Euripides; see *Letters*, I, 247 ff., 260.

[41] *Pers.*, l. 242. For a different rendering see *Athens* (*Works*, II, 613).

have a surfeit of a single mood or motive, however exalted, but that that very motive, by such a method of treatment, is so attenuated that it fails of its effect. There are no obstacles, outward or inward, to be overcome, for the claims of public duty are met with sorrowful but unhesitating resolution. Even Chthonia has no mental struggle. As the two themes, regret for life blighted in the bud and glorification of the virgin martyr, are carried melodiously on through page after page, by Praxithea, the chorus, and Chthonia herself, we may think of such practical and realistic martyrs as Antigone and Alcestis, or, for a closer parallel, of the helpless Iphigeneia, who at first shows a natural human weakness.[42] And while these ancient characters are all involved more or less in a dramatic conflict, Chthonia and her parents from the beginning are, as it were, moving slowly forward together in a ritual procession. The lack of drama in the plot is heightened by lack of dramatic verisimilitude in details and in the poetic style. There is even less of Greek reticence and suggestion than in *Atalanta*; in *Erechtheus* everything possible is said, said again and again, about every aspect of the theme, and no amount of Greek idiom and allusion can take the place of hard salience of outline.

Swinburne declared that, "as far as it can be said to be modelled after anybody," *Erechtheus* was "modelled throughout after the earliest style of Aeschylus — the simple, three-parts-epic style of the *Suppliants*, *Persians*, and *Seven against Thebes*."[43] That is fairly clear, but the drama bears some resemblance to the manner of the despised Euripides, both in such external things as the *dea ex machina* and in the portrayal of a purely pathetic

---

[42] In making Chthonia courageous from the beginning Swinburne may have remembered Aristotle's criticism of Euripides' Iphigeneia (Chew, *Swinburne*, p. 128, note). One might mention another martyr, Macaria, in Euripides' *Children of Heracles*.

[43] *Letters*, I, 248.

situation. The critical spirit of Euripides is swallowed up in patriotic fervor. Instead of an attack on religion, for which the subject offers far better occasion than the subject of *Atalanta*, there is nothing but complete reverence for the gods, reverence more complete than even Sophocles would have thought necessary. One may indeed prefer the theatrical but sincere "atheism" of *Atalanta* to the pure but manufactured piety of *Erechtheus*, for the religious element, whatever may be thought of other elements, is assuredly *pastiche*. Since the days of *Atalanta* Swinburne had, to be sure, heard a call to messianic duty,[44] but, if one may mix metaphors, the leopard had not altogether changed his spots. Of course the celebration of Athens and freedom is intensely sincere, and "I praise the Gods for Athens" is one line, a very modern line, which rings true. Doubtless Swinburne, indifferent to fine distinctions, was willing to merge his own worship of Greece with Greek worship of the gods, who at least were not Christian.

Swinburne's Hellenic passion, strong as it was, would hardly save *Erechtheus* from being a death-mask if it were not combined with his passion for the Italy of Mazzini. (Even *Athens* includes an Italian impulse, though it is not enough to animate the grandiose tedium of the ode.) The drama may in fact be regarded as the longest of the *Songs before Sunrise*. But, if one may say it of the book which Swinburne set apart from all his others — "that one is myself"[45] — it takes a good deal of devotion to him and to Italy to get through the *Songs*; and the rigidly antique frame of *Erechtheus* keeps the Italian motive wholly between the lines, whereas the modern motive of *Atalanta* is overt and central. The story of *Erechtheus* is remote from our sympathies, and the author does not try to bridge the

---

[44] See the letter from Mazzini (1867) in Lafourcade, *Jeunesse*, I, 253–54; *Swinburne* (1932), p. 149.
[45] *Letters*, I, 233.

gap. His Italian ardor was given mythological embodiment in another poem which has been much praised, the
Tiresias of *Songs before Sunrise* (1871). Gosse links it,
Hertha, and *The Pilgrims* as three poems which show "the
most rapturous of troubadours transformed into one of
the great poetic intelligences of the modern world." [46]
I confess that I see no such matter. Swinburne's original
idea was of "Tiresias at the grave of Antigone — i.e.
(understand) Dante at the grave of Italia"; in the final
conception Tiresias is not only Dante but Michelangelo
and Mazzini, which may cause some initial confusion as
to who is who and when. In the picture of the Theban
prophet and other passages there is a calm, exalted dignity
not too common in Swinburne — a dignity which owes
much to echoes of Greek poetry — but the connection
between Greek and Italian themes appears artificial, and
this poem, like *Erechtheus*, leaves a shadowy impression
on what I must perforce call my mind.

Swinburne's love of Greece, Italy, and freedom, while
honest and intense, is not very satisfying, poetically or
philosophically. Although Mill's *Liberty* was "the textbook" of his creed "as to public morals and political faith,"
his expressed ideas are rather simple, as, for instance, in
one of his annual poems to Hugo:

> In the fair days when God
> By man as godlike trod,
> And each alike was Greek, alike was free. . . .[47]

If we think of the utterances of Swinburne, or Landor, in
comparison with the broad, deep, realistic spirit of civic
freedom which animates the prose and much of the verse
of Milton, or, to go to the fountain-head, which makes the

---

[46] *Life*, p. 177. Cf. Lafourcade, *Swinburne* (1932), pp. 170–71; Rutland,
pp. 300–06.
[47] *Works*, I, 144; see *Letters*, I, 153.

speech of Pericles what it is, the voices of Swinburne and
Landor are a wind in the reeds. Swinburne's passion for
liberty, when it was not a mere boyish impatience of restraint, seems to have been largely a somewhat rudimen-
tary individualism and nationalism finding release in verbal
orgies and impromptu ritual dances before the portraits of
his heroes. Indeed Swinburne's joy in trampling on popular deities was equaled only by his joy in abasing himself before his own idols; and such complete sacrifice as
he depicts in *Erechtheus* reminds us that his goddess of
liberty is a Lady of Pain not altogether unrelated to
Dolores.

IV

When *Poems and Ballads* (1866) dropped, as Hardy
said, like a garland of red roses about the hood of some
smug nun, the shock to public morals was great enough
to satisfy even the author, who was more impish than
satanic. After the lapse of time Swinburne's sexual per-
versities and pagan blasphemies seem worse than un-
speakably shocking, they are ridiculous.[48] It is impossible
to read the solemn and awful litany of Our Lady of Pain
with a straight face, unless one is young enough to share
the Hellenic raptures of Kipling's Muller in the Indian
jungle:

> Dough we shivt und bedeck und bedrape us,
>   Dou art noble und nude und andeek;
> Libidina dy moder, Briapus
>   Dy fader, a God und a Greek.

Little needs to be said here about the various poems
in which sadism appears in a pseudo-Hellenic disguise.

[48] I am speaking of the verse only, not of biographical facts. M. Lafourcade
has emphasized the connection, indicated by Swinburne himself, between such
things as *Dolores* and the personal experience which gave birth to *The Triumph
of Time* (*Jeunesse*, I, 204, 266, II, 465 ff.). See *Thalassius*, which is mentioned
below.

Though Swinburne seldom forgets that Venus was born of the sea, she is not the Uranian or even the Pandemic goddess; so far as she is classical at all she is nearer Cotytto. Really she is a modern creation, one of the "Mad mixtures of Frenchified offal," to use a fairly accurate phrase which the author intended as ironical.[49] Venus is the supreme type of the fatal woman, and in *Laus Veneris* Swinburne handles the Tannhäuser legend "with all the resources of a grim and satanic Pre-Raphaelite medievalism."[50] An outlawed deity in a Christian world, Venus has become the symbol of pagan beauty, passion, and cruelty:

> Lo, she was thus when her clear limbs enticed
> All lips that now grow sad with kissing Christ.

And, as Pater remembered, she has "The languor in her ears of many lyres."

In *Cleopatra* (published in 1866, though not in *Poems and Ballads*) we have another *belle dame sans merci*, as far from Keats as Keats is from Spenser. Phaedra, in the early dramatic fragment of that name, is one of the sanguinary sisterhood rather than Euripides' helpless victim of passion.[51] *The Masque of Queen Bersabe* (1862) has a whole procession of beautiful vampires, biblical and classical,

---

[49] *Poeta Loquitur*, in *The Italian Mother and Other Poems* (printed by T. J. Wise, 1918), p. 17.

[50] Praz, *Romantic Agony*, p. 228 (and pp. 243–44); see also Lafourcade, *Jeunesse*, II, 427 ff. Cf. the reference to Venus in *Ave atque Vale* (*Works*, I, 352). For the sources of *Laus Veneris*, see Clyde K. Hyder, *P.M.L.A.*, XLV (1930), 1202–13.

[51] Like Racine and Seneca, but unlike Euripides, Swinburne has Phaedra confront Hippolytus. For reminiscences of Beaumont and Fletcher's *Maid's Tragedy*, see Praz (*Atene e Roma*, III, 185, note); see also Lafourcade, *Jeunesse*, II, 445.

In an odd piece of exotic realism, *Pasiphae* (*Lady Maisie's Bairn and Other Poems*, printed by T. J. Wise, 1915), Phaedra's mother discusses with Daedalus the wooden cow he has made for her use somewhat in the manner of a housewife inspecting the plumber's repairs to the sink.

Cleopatra, Semiramis, Hesione, Myrrha, Pasiphae, Sappho, Messalina. . . . [52] In spite of the stately (and diffuse) *Sapphics*, it is really hard to forgive Swinburne for his treatment of Sappho, "the supreme head of song," as he calls her in *Ave atque Vale*.[53] The Sappho of *Anactoria* is not merely the descendant of Libitina and Priapus, she is the daughter of Sade. While Swinburne's sadistic women sprang from the head of the Olympian marquis, their costume was largely borrowed from the theatrical wardrobe of later French gods. In *Dolores, Faustine*, and elsewhere, as Praz remarks, "the vision of pagan antiquity, colossal and bloodstained, makes an accompanying *leit-motiv* to Swinburne's evocations of lustful pleasure, as it does to those of Gautier and Flaubert."[54] And one of these names is a reminder that *Hermaphroditus* is much more remote from Ovid than from Swinburne's beloved *Mademoiselle de Maupin*; in his very disingenuous defence of this poem Swinburne cited *The Witch of Atlas*. The lyric *Itylus* is almost equally remote from Ovid, in a different way; both the Ovidian myth and Arnold's "Eternal passion! Eternal pain!" are merely notes in a musical pattern.[55] In the midst of all the rococo paganism of *Poems and Ballads*, one comes with some surprise upon the early *At Eleusis*; here Swinburne has no thought of

[52] See Arthur O'Shaughnessy's imitation in *An Epic of Women* (1870). The heroine of Swinburne's *Rosamond* (1860) sees herself as the fatal woman of "all tales," as Helen, Cressida, and Guenevere. The lines are quoted in Mr. Nicolson's *Swinburne*, p. 65.

[53] Cf. *On the Cliffs* (*Works*, I, 614).

[54] Praz, *Romantic Agony*, p. 234; cf. p. 218. We may remember that at twelve or thirteen Swinburne had shown his own precocious sensuality and sadism in *The Unhappy Revenge*, a drama of intrigue and martyrdom in imperial Rome. See Lafourcade, *Jeunesse*, II, 114 ff.; *Swinburne* (1932), pp. 39–41; Swinburne, *Letters*, I, 285–86.

[55] For suggestions from Ovid (*Metam.* vi. 576–78, 646), Sappho, Aeschylus (*Agam.*, ll. 1140–49), and Homer (*Od.* xix. 518 ff.), see Lafourcade, *Jeunesse*, II, 448–50; Rutland, pp. 277–79.

"the women of the Eleusinian feasts 'seeking the satyrs under the stars,'" but is content with a simple Landorian, and somewhat Pre-Raphaelite, reworking of the Homeric *Hymn to Demeter.*

Swinburne's intoxicating neo-paganism gave a fresh and powerful stimulus, and a whole new vocabulary, to the old conflict between Christ and Pan which the names of Schiller and Mrs. Browning will recall. The antipathy to anything like Christian asceticism was bound up with that hostility to the Christian God which broke out in *Atalanta*, and the two passions were united in *Anactoria*. One result of the gospel of sensual rapture was the immense ennui of *The Garden of Proserpine*; Tennyson's mild lotos has given place to hashish. "Perversity," Swinburne said later, "is the fruit of weariness as weariness is the fruit of pleasure."[56] Meanwhile the evangel of deliverance from Victorian morality — into another kind of slavery — was proclaimed again and again by the new Dionysus. It is all contained in four famous lines of the *Hymn to Proserpine:*

Wilt thou yet take all, Galilean? but these thou shalt not take,
The laurel, the palms and the paean, the breasts of the nymphs in the brake. . . .
Thou hast conquered, O pale Galilean; the world has grown grey from thy breath;
We have drunken of things Lethean, and fed on the fullness of death.

Shelley's Christ is pale because Shelley's heroes are physically weak martyrs of humanity oppressed by brute power; Swinburne's is pale because, to this arm-chair sensualist, Christian morality is anemic. His various anti-Christian utterances contained more thunder than lightning, and

---

[56] *Essays and Studies*, p. 10. Not much more than the title of Swinburne's poem could have been suggested by Spenser's Garden of Proserpina (*Faerie Queene*, II. vii. 51–55). The apparent source for the theme, pattern, imagery, and versification was *Les Limbes* of Delavigne, though Swinburne made a piece of subjective paganism out of objective Catholicism. See Martha H. Shackford, "Swinburne and Delavigne," *P.M.L.A.*, XXXIII (1918), 85–95.

may be neglected, but he had no small share, though a devout Hellenist, in creating that deplorable conception of Greece as a Bohemian paradise of beauty, art, love, and no morals. That conception has not entirely vanished yet, for "Greek" and "pagan" are stock epithets among our reviewers; John Morley, speaking of Rossetti's being called "Greek," once observed that it was the blockhead's name for all that was not nineteenth-century British.[57]

Though neo-paganism continued, long after its author had outgrown it, to inveigle the feet of the young men into conscientious dissipation, Swinburne's own extravagances were less important than his religion of humanity. One respects such noble statements of it as the *Prelude* to *Songs before Sunrise* — "Because man's soul is man's God still" — even if they set the fashion for that sentimentally heroic despair which attracted later generations in Henley's *Invictus* and Lord Russell's essay "A Free Man's Worship." Although Swinburne's pagan fortitude and faith in man seems less of a philosophy than an attitude, it was the most positive inspiration of his later maturity. It appears, linked with "anti-Galilean fervour," in *The Last Oracle* (1876).[58] The opening lament for the overthrow of Apollo by the pale Galilean is followed by a declaration of faith in art and Apollonian man:

> God by God goes out, discrowned and disanointed,
> But the soul stands fast that gave them shape and speech.

Better known, probably, than the *Prelude* or *The Last Oracle* is the *Hymn of Man*, which M. Lafourcade calls "theological,"[59] and which doubtless is, though not much more maturely so than *Queen Mab*. In it the human David

[57] *Personal & Literary Letters of Robert First Earl of Lytton*, ed. Lady Betty Balfour (1906), I, 279.
[58] See Swinburne's account of the poem (*Letters*, I, 262); *Works*, I, 301; Lafourcade, *Jeunesse*, I, 55, note.
[59] See p. 331 above, and cf. *Swinburne* (1932), p. 174.

smites the divine Goliath and, exulting in his death, noisily proclaims: "Glory to man in the highest! for Man is the master of things." At the present time the sentiment seems tragically silly, and it was hardly less so in 1870.

There remains a group of nature poems classical at least in most of their titles. In the very Shelleyan *Thalassius* (1880) Swinburne uses myth for much the same purpose that his beloved Mrs. Gamp used Mrs. Harris. But any notion of personal conceit, about which he was apprehensive, really disappears as he recounts his debt to Landor — some critics see Hugo and Mazzini as well — for lessons in liberty and antique lore and indeed all the attributes of the ideal poet. Unhappy love led to dissipation, symbolized by the Bacchic rout;[60] but the child of Apollo and Cymothoe was restored to spiritual health by the sea, and he received the paternal blessing as a poet who had kept the faith. Landor is again remembered in the epigraph of *By the North Sea* — "We are what suns and winds and waters make us" [61] — and in *The Garden of Cymodoce* Swinburne puts his passion for the sea before his love of song and links it with his love of liberty. *Pan and Thalassius* (1889) carries us over from such poems to two others in which he reveals a more uneasy and incomplete passion for terrestrial nature. Here as elsewhere Swinburne has little or nothing of the mythological instinct of Keats and Shelley. Pan and Thalassius are decorative mouthpieces for arguing the claims of land and sea; Thalassius of course refuses to bow to Pan. In *A Nympholept* (1891) and *The Palace of Pan* (1893) Swinburne

[60] *Works*, I, 601–04. Cf. *Prelude* (*ibid.*, I, 666–67). The poem had been conceived some time before (*Letters*, II, 44).

[61] As Dottin remarks (*Revue Anglo-Américaine*, II [1924–25] 421), the third part of this poem (*Works*, II, 509–10) is one of the two or three places in which Swinburne reproduces the Greek conception of the underworld; see also *Atalanta* (*Works*, II, 309, 324, 333). Generally he thinks or feels in Catullian and neo-pagan terms of an eternal sleep. But the one attitude is no more or less literary than the other.

comes as near as he ever does to a mystical apprehension of nature, but even M. Lafourcade, who seldom admits a deficiency in his hero, concludes that he stops short of genuine pantheism. Swinburne's perception of a divinity in nature brings less of ecstasy than of a troubled feeling of mystery and fear, and instead of rising to belief in and rapturous communion with "some unseen Power," he shrinks back upon himself. Indeed all that we know of Swinburne's mind and temperament forbids the thought of any real kinship between his attitude toward nature and that of the romantics. "An earth-born dreamer, constrained by the bonds of birth . . . May hear not surely the fall of immortal feet."[62]

Of those permanent qualities of art which are called classical, obviously Swinburne has little. The "honey-heavy" excesses of his style he himself parodied, quite unnecessarily, and also described as

a maze of monotonous murmur,
Where reason roves ruined by rhyme.

Diffuse and undisciplined vagueness of emotion and expression make almost everything of Swinburne's pleasurable and forgettable; one remembers neither parts nor wholes. The high gods did not grant him architectonic power. Few of his long lyrical poems would suffer greatly from random rearrangement of the stanzas, fewer still from excision of every other one. In the classical dramas the Greek form did something to restrain him; as a rule he went on and on.

As for the spirit of Swinburne's Hellenism, it was always romantic, but it was not all of a piece. *Atalanta, Poems and Ballads*, and *Erechtheus* represent more or less different though not unrelated aspects. The very un-Hellenic elements in *Poems and Ballads* have no great intrinsic

---

[62] *A Nympholept (Works*, II, 976–77); see Lafourcade, *Jeunesse*, I, 62.

significance except that they naturalized in England the romantic agonies and pseudo-Hellenic poses of continental neo-pagans. This phase in Swinburne might have died earlier than it did if public outcry had not thrust upon him the congenial rôle of *enfant terrible*. That rôle had been voluntarily assumed when, in *Atalanta*, Swinburne put the metaphysic of Sade into superficially antique dress. The boyish and militant modernism of *Atalanta* gave place to the mature Hellenic pietism of *Erechtheus*, but that drama, though it could have been written only by a worshiper of Athens, owes much of what life it has to Swinburne's dreams of Italian freedom, his religion of humanity and the ideal state. A modern motive more exalted than that of *Atalanta*, and a stricter Greek form, should have resulted in a great play, yet *Erechtheus* is another romantic lyric, a beautiful idealism of moral excellence (to borrow Shelley's phrase), but fatally bookish, unrealistic, and verbose.

Swinburne's recent champions have not succeeded in showing that, with all his intense enthusiasms, he possessed a philosophic center or any real capacity for growth. His devotion to literature was somewhat like Keats's, but Keats was a bee, Swinburne was a chameleon. He never gives the impression, as William Morris does — to leave Keats out of account — that he was bigger and deeper than his literary work.[63] At an age when Morris was breaking through the social and esthetic shell in which he had grown up to become an active socialist, Swinburne was happily disentangling the minor Elizabethan dramatic collaborators; he was still an infant prodigy in a library. Various critics of late years have claimed Swinburne as a modern, on the ground that he was a poet of liberty, or that he had a modern sensibility and refused "to suppress

[63] I quoted above (ch. IX, p. 324) a judgment of Swinburne's poetry by Morris which might have been applied to his own, as he would doubtless have admitted. Swinburne seems to have had a similar feeling about the emptiness of *The Earthly Paradise*; see *Prelude* (*Works*, I, 665–66).

some of the deepest sexual tendencies of his nature."[64]
Such pleas, even if we accept the implied definitions of
modernism as adequate, are not convincing. Swinburne
remains a mid-Victorian romantic. And of his romantic
Hellenism he himself was well aware, if the following
words, as M. Lafourcade plausibly thinks, are his own:

Ne cherchez pas dans Phaedra, dans Hermaphroditus, et dans
l'Hymne à Proserpine, cette profonde intuition du passé que
révèlent les nobles poèmes de Leconte de Lisle. Swinburne est
païen, non pas comme un Grec du temps d'Aeschyle, mais comme
peut l'être un Anglais du 19ᵉ siècle.[65]

In being so completely of his own age Swinburne often
reminds us of some Italianate poets of the Renaissance.
They had, generally, little of his Greek, but they reached
out instinctively to all that was pagan and florid in decadent Greek and Latin and modern literature, and glorified what they took to be ancient ideals of freedom; often
they strove, in life and in writing, to outdo their models.
Marlowe, for instance, repudiated or tried to repudiate
medieval Christianity and bourgeois morality, and expounded the doctrines of a philosopher whom sixteenth-
century Protestants regarded as a Sade, one Machiavelli.
Atalanta, we might say, was Swinburne's *Tamburlaine*,
Poems and Ballads his *Hero and Leander* — but *Erechtheus*
was not a *Tragedy of Doctor Faustus*.

[64] Lafourcade, *Swinburne* (1932), pp. x–xi, 106.
[65] *Ibid.*, p. 242.

CHAPTER XI

Browning and Meredith

I. Browning

IT IS not customary to pass from Swinburne and Morris to Browning, who, by all the laws of textbooks and anthologies, should follow Tennyson as the night the day, but his place in our landscape is determined by the fact that almost all his poems on classical themes were written in the dozen years after 1870. This was indeed the energetic bard's most industrious period, both at the desk and the dinner table. The results of his restless productivity are oppressive in bulk and often in manner, and, though some of the short classical pieces are well known, one does not suppose that *Balaustion's Adventure* and *Aristophanes' Apology* are being much read nowadays; the latter apparently never was, except by hardened Browningites. The animating ideas of the classical poems were of a vintage much earlier than the eighteen-seventies, for Browning, in spite of his immense diversity of surface, did not really grow much more than Swinburne; he formulated his creed when still young and spent the rest of his life in applying it to everything. But if the student of Browning's once exalted philosophy and his methods finds little or nothing that is new in the poems from the antique, we at least may welcome them as original and vigorous variations in the romantic treatment of classical themes. The poems differ in merit as in length, but, unlike so many dozen Victorian tales and idylls and monologues, they could not, with perhaps one exception, have been written by anyone else. Browning started out as a belated romantic, and always remained one, of a nebulously Protestant sort. One thread of allusion in the first part of *Sordello* (1840) leads us into that maze of the Browning philosophy which has so many apparent turnings and needs only a simple clue. *Sordello* was his third effort to integrate his head and his heart, and, though a *Who's Who* of medieval Italy, it was his chief study of the function of a modern poet. As such, the poem corresponds to *Endymion* and the two *Hyperions*, to *Alastor*, to *The Palace of Art*, and, one might add, to *Sartor Resartus*. The name of Apollo recurs frequently in the early books, and it seems to be a symbol of Sordello in the harmonious but shallow completeness of the mere artist isolated from his fellow men. For Keats, Apollo is the ideal poet, the poet who has risen above artistic egoism and vain dreams to an intense social consciousness. Sordello (who at first resembles the Keats of Victorian criticism) is not content to inhabit an ivory tower, to be an Eglamor; as his soul grows, the Apollonian harmony gives place to a conflict between the self-centered artist and the humanitarian doer.

One of Browning's most insistent and familiar doctrines is the incompleteness of earth and the perfect fulfilment of heaven. His beloved Shelley, after striving to banish evil and make earth perfect, had taken refuge in radiant visions of the unattainable. Browning, in spite of *Sordello*, began almost at once to call in an ideal world to redress the balance of the actual, and his visions of ultimate perfection appeared more substantial than Shelley's because they had a realistic dress, because Browning exulted in this world of evil as "a moral gymnasium," because he was on terms of cheerful intimacy with God and was ready to bounce off joyously, like his own Europa, to share immortal life with the Great Lover. No conception of classic antiquity could have been more congenial to him than the romantic one we have encountered already in Coleridge,

Mrs. Browning and others, the contrast between the finite limitations of the Greek mind and Greek art and the groping and striving toward infinity of the modern soul. It was a thoroughly Browningesque philosophy of the imperfect that Ruskin set forth in his famous chapter on "The Nature of Gothic," and two or three sentences may be quoted here:

And therefore, while in all things that we see or do, we are to desire perfection, and strive for it, we are nevertheless not to set the meaner thing, in its narrow accomplishment, above the nobler thing, in its mighty progress; not to esteem smooth minuteness above shattered majesty; not to prefer mean victory to honourable defeat; not to lower the level of our aim, that we may the more surely enjoy the complacency of success.

·   ·   ·   ·   ·   ·   ·   ·   ·   ·   ·

The Greek sculptor could neither bear to confess his own feebleness, nor to tell the faults of the forms that he portrayed. But the Christian workman, believing that all is finally to work together for good, freely confesses both, and neither seeks to disguise his own roughness of work, nor his subject's roughness of make.[1]

Again and again, as in *Pippa Passes* (where the sculptor Jules breaks up his paltry classical models to begin art afresh), in *Cleon, Old Pictures in Florence, Imperante Augusto Natus Est*, and in poems to be discussed here, Browning rings the changes on the spiritual inadequacies of ancient paganism. That he could, in youth and in old age, delight in pagan myths and write of them at length involves no real paradox; he made them over in his own image.

For most readers the name of Browning does not at once call up classical poems and affiliations, but it is an odd fact, or at any rate a fair guess — since I have not

[1] *The Stones of Venice*, II. vi, 11 and 67.

actually weighed the material — that there have been more pages written on that subject than have grown up around almost any other modern English poet. These studies range from innumerable articles through several monographs to the seven hundred and fifty closely printed pages of Robert Spindler's *Robert Browning und die Antike* (1930). Since I had read all the lucubrations Spindler read, and have read Spindler besides, I might give the doctrine of the enclitic *De*, dead from the waist up. But one who lacks the moral fervor of scholarly members of the Browning Society can only describe the various mythological costumes the poet assumed for the exposition of a familiar creed.[2]

I

Artemis Prologizes (1842), all that we have of a drama on the subject of Hippolytus and Aricia, is, both chronologically and technically, a "freak." [3] It is the only mythological poem of Browning's earlier years, and the only one which might have been written by somebody else. Arnold, who seldom felt moved to praise the author, declared it "one of the very best antique fragments I know," and a modern poet, Mr. Sturge Moore, has gone so far as to call it "perhaps the most splendid 120 lines of blank verse in English." [4] Certainly it is a splendid *tour de force*, if not a vital poem. One does not expect the master of the realistic and grotesque to produce a speech of majestic stateliness which sounds like a translation, literal yet lofty, of

[2] Since Spindler gathers up the factual and critical matter of his predecessors, I have usually refrained from citing earlier studies, but I may mention Mr. Thurman L. Hood's monograph, *Browning's Ancient Classical Sources* (*Harvard Studies in Classical Philology*, XXXIII [1922], 79–180). Browning's poems are quoted from the edition of Charlotte Porter and Helen A. Clarke.

[3] See Euripides' *Hippolytus* and *Aen.* vii. 761 ff., and also Ovid, *Metam.* xv. 479 ff., *Fast.* vi. 733 ff.

[4] See Arnold's *Letters*, ed. Russell, I, 70; and Mr. Moore's "The Best Poetry," *Transactions of the Royal Society of Literature*, Second Series, XXXI (1912), 42.

some Euripidean prologue. It might be taken as allegorical that the poem was composed in bed, "much against my endeavour"; it needed illness to make Browning a classicist. Or perhaps he was able for once to subdue himself to objective classicality because he was here concerned with a straightforward recital of action, undisturbed by ideas. The cool, pure serenity of the opening in particular carries us back to Shelley's *Hymn of Apollo* and forward to "Maiden, and mistress of the months and stars"; most of all the poem may remind us of Landor. Only here and there does the poet betray his real self by such phrases as "sharp stub and spiny shell" and "the strips and jagged ends of flesh."

But the general style of *Artemis Prologizes* will not surprise those who have observed the quality of Browning's early mythological allusions. Amid the yeasty incoherences of *Pauline* (1833) there are moments of plastic lucidity which suggest Shelley and Keats. More than fifty years later, in *Development*, Browning recalled, or partly imagined,[5] the Trojan games and dreams of his childhood, before the skeptical scholarship of Wolf and the rest had spoiled his illusions. Here in *Pauline* the terribly aged, sinful, and serious young poet, who can no longer love anything, remembers how he had loved the old tales. They had been so real that he himself was a god "Wandering after beauty," and saw the morning break

> On the dim clustered isles in the blue sea,
> The deep groves and white temples and wet caves.[6]

He remembers Agamemnon "Treading the purple calmly to his death," and he lets himself go in a description of that engraving of Andromeda to which he was so devoted;

---

[5] W. Hall Griffin and H. C. Minchin, *Life of Robert Browning* (New York, 1910), p. 25, note 3.
[6] Ll. 321 ff.

one would almost think he had a premonition of himself
as the Perseus of the century.[7] The mythology in *Paracelsus* (1835) is much the same. The chief group of allusions occurs in the discourse of Aprile which teaches the
too intellectual Paracelsus the lesson of love. The artist
aspires to recreate "the forms of earth" and thus hold up
to men the loveliness of life, and, though he passes on to
nature and realism, he begins with romantic and idyllic
mythology:

> No ancient hunter lifted
> Up to the gods by his renown, no nymph
> Supposed the sweet soul of a woodland tree
> Or sapphirine spirit of a twilight star,
> Should be too hard for me. . . .[8]

In his later work Browning's mythological allusions did
not always lack his early decorative smoothness, but, as
he developed his own peculiar idiom of dramatic speech,
his mythology for the most part shared in the change.
The song of Ariel became the grunt of Caliban. Even in
Paracelsus we have such a bit of vivid anthropomorphism
as the allusion to strange groups of young volcanoes which

> come up, cyclops-like,
> Staring together with their eyes on flame.[9]

It is a far cry from Tennyson's picture of Europa to
"Bouncing Europa on the back o' the bull"; and if Count
Guido's fancy is not idyllic, still less is that of Tertium
Quid about curtaining Correggio carefully "Lest I be

[7] Ll. 568 ff., 656 ff. Of the mythological reminiscences in *Pauline*, the chief
source is Ovid.

[8] *Paracelsus*, ii. 422 ff. Browning's conception of Aprile is reminiscent not
only of Shelley himself but of Shelley's Prometheus and the progeny immortal
"Of Painting, Sculpture, and rapt Poesy." See *Prometheus Unbound*, III. iii.
53–54; Hall and Minchin, p. 67; *Letters of Robert Browning and Elizabeth Barrett
Barrett* (1899), I, 38 ff.

[9] *Paracelsus*, v. 660–62. See *The Witch of Atlas*, xi; Shelley's *Poems*, ed. C. D.
Locock (1911), I, 655; C. H. Herford, *Robert Browning* (1905), p. 263.

taught that Leda had two legs."[10] Finally, with the lines about Agamemnon in *Pauline* compare these, from Browning's notorious rendering of Aeschylus (1877):

> But if this seem so to thee — shoes, let some one
> Loose under, quick — foot's serviceable carriage!
> And me, on these sea-products walking, may no
> Grudge from a distance, from the god's eye, strike at!

Elizabeth Barrett had protested against the current view of Aeschylus as "a sort of poetic Orson, with his locks all wild,"[11] but Browning's Aeschylus seems to be a bear that walks, and tries to talk, like a man. Here and there one may prefer his "bronze-throat eagle-bark at blood" to the smooth "twitterings" of most translators; continuous reading is impossible. That impossibility, indeed, seems to have been part of Browning's intention. By showing Aeschylus in the Gothic nakedness of a literal translation he would confound the Arnolds who insisted that the Greeks were the unapproached masters of the grand style. The *Agamemnon* was a somewhat ponderous mode of argument.[12]

II

By the time Browning was nearly sixty it might have been assumed that, if not written out, he would at any rate not start off on a new path. But the poet who had set himself apart from his contemporaries by his avoidance of ancient themes now produced three bulky works, *Balaus-*

---

[10] *The Ring and the Book*, xi. 270–72, iv. 882–83.

[11] *Letters*, I, 35.

[12] See William C. De Vane, *A Browning Handbook* (New York, 1935), pp. 371–74.

The unfinished poem which has been called *Aeschylus' Soliloquy* is nearer to the style of *Artemis Prologizes* than to the forced ruggedness of the translation. It was first published in the *Cornhill Magazine*, XXXV (1913), 577 ff. For Elizabeth Barrett's intention of writing on the subject, see *Letters*, I, 31. The poem is noticed by Mr. De Vane, p. 514.

tion's Adventure (1871), *Aristophanes' Apology* (1875), and the translation of *Agamemnon*; a number of short pieces appeared in later volumes. Browning may have had a surfeit of his more or less modern and sordid realism, and the Countess Cowper's suggestion may have found him inclined to revive the old Hellenic enthusiasms he had shared with his wife — or at least with Elizabeth Barrett, for *Christmas-Eve and Easter-Day* does not suggest that the wife's influence was exerted on the side of the antique. Certainly he wished to vindicate their favorite Euripides against critical aspersions. Then, too, failing inspiration can always be postulated to account for a writer's choosing to interpret tales and characters which are to some degree ready made. Whatever the cause for Browning's change of direction, there was no failure of energy.

Indeed it was not so much a change of direction as a change of scene. Browning was not a poet of mythological imagination; the few moments in which he seems to deserve that name only emphasize his normal character as a novelist in verse. So in the two long poems which treat the stories of Alcestis and Heracles he is even less concerned with myths as myths than Euripides was. Browning's heart was always in the diverse spectacle of humanity, the concrete actualities of life and manners, the probing of human motives, the study of a soul's evolution from weakness to strength, and all this could be done as well with a Grecian as with an Italian or any other background. If Browning was intoxicated by "God's clear plan" for growth into eternity, he was intoxicated at the same time by the loves and hates, the talk and the clothes, the noise and bustle and smells of this earthly boarding-house. Realism has been defined as romanticism on all fours, and one might make the definition specific by saying that Browning was a kind of Shelley on all fours. The cosmic inebriacy of Browning the emotional sentimentalist is now at a discount, but his dramatic realism is as potent as ever. His treatment of Greek themes partakes of both elements. The power of his best non-classical poems, such as *The Bishop Orders his Tomb*, comes from the inspired massing of minute items of scholarly knowledge as well as from psychological intuition, and the classical poems possess the same archaeological actuality, whatever alien elements may be introduced. Landor had a good deal of that, but no English poet approaches Browning's exuberant delight in antique realism. His historical verisimilitude has of course a distinct boundary line; the Greece he presents is a mixture of the completely real and the completely unreal. Whatever solid properties can be seen or touched are Greek; the psychological motives he evolves are usually not Greek.

Our chief interest in *Balaustion's Adventure* is in Browning's interpretation of Euripides' *Alcestis*, but the romantic setting has its interest too. The initial idea came from Plutarch's anecdotes (at the end of his *Life of Nicias*) about the softening of the Syracusans' hearts when they found that Athenians or Athenian sympathizers could report some new bits of Euripides — a forcible reminder, by the way, that the ancient world was not ours. The flight of the ship from pirates and its reception at Syracuse are described with all Browning's verve and gusto; we have besides lines of such unquestionable authenticity as

> Agora, Dikasteria, Poikilé,
> Pnux, Keramikos; Salamis in sight. . . .

But when "the lyric girl," Balaustion, the enthusiastic devotee of Euripides, is brought forward to win over the Syracusans by reciting *Alcestis*, we may, without disparaging her radiant charm, scan Greek records in vain for such a mixture of bluestocking and Girl Guide. Even without Browning's several allusions to the not wholly felicitous eulogy of "Euripides, the human, With his droppings of warm tears, " we should know that we were back in Wimpole Street; Balaustion is "Ba," and the young man who sat each day by the temple steps to hear her had once sat beside a sofa.

The nature of Browning's sympathy with Euripides is suggested in the old phrase of his wife's. In comparison with the Titanic Aeschylus and the classic Sophocles, Euripides was an everyday realist, a debater and casuist, an explorer of sinful souls, a champion of women, a critic of stock opinions, a moral teacher, in short, an Athenian Browning. How far *Balaustion's Adventure* helps to justify such a label depends on our reading of Euripides' play, and that means our reading of the character of Admetus. Opinions have differed widely for generations, and probably the Athenians in 438 B.C. shared some of our uncertainties, for Euripides had a way of leaving his audiences troubled. There have been two main attitudes, held with varying degrees of moderation or with no moderation at all. According to one, Browning might be said to have done little more than fill in, with his own emphasis, what Euripides left to be inferred. A representative of this view is Mr. Gilbert Murray, whose discussion of Admetus, though it does not touch Browning, may be read with almost no change as an analysis of Browning's version.[13] The Admetus seen by such critics is a selfish coward and attitudinizer who is made to realize his baseness and emerges from his trial a changed man. On the other hand it has been often maintained that we must not read modern sentiment even into Euripides, that he presents Admetus, in a semi-satyric play with a happy ending, as a completely ideal king, *sans peur et sans reproche*, who is quite justified by ancient standards in expecting his subjects, including his relatives, to sacrifice their lives for his; and he is

[13] See the preface and notes to his translation (1915).

delivered from a terrible blow of fate simply because he is magnanimous enough to put the great virtue of hospitality above his private sorrow.[14]

It is impossible to take account here of all the valid arguments, much less the reckless statements, which have been used on both sides. It is true that Admetus has the love of Apollo and the friendship of Heracles, and that he receives nothing but sympathy and respect from the chorus, who, like Alcestis, complain of fate, not of the king. Alcestis deserves the highest honor for her voluntary sacrifice, but, as an ideal Greek wife and mother, submissive and practical, she cannot be said to show any lack of respect or trust. At the same time we have the scene with Pheres, which either is an unaccountable artistic blunder or constitutes an ironic exposure of Admetus. And a number of passages warrant the belief that Admetus, though a noble and pious and sincerely sorrowful king, is intended to appear at first as a too serene and complacent egoist; further, his tragic experience does, at least to some degree, open his eyes and leaves him a better man. Of course, as the continued existence of opposed views indicates, the Admetus of Euripides is nothing like so bad or so good as Browning's. In general modern criticism seems to take, not quite a middle road, but a road on Browning's side of the middle.

The translation of the *Alcestis* is clear, plain, and remarkably faithful, but Browning does sometimes omit, condense, or alter lines in accordance with his general bias.[15] In a more obvious and positive way he sets forth his reading of the drama in the eager descriptive and interpretative comments of Balaustion. Browning had the right

[14] A compendious statement of this view is given in Mr. E. A. Parker's edition of *Balaustion's Adventure* (1928). A number of other discussions are cited in my bibliography.

[15] Some examples are given by Mr. Frederick M. Tisdel, *P.M.L.A.*, XXXII (1917), 524–28.

every poet possesses to make over an ancient tale as he
pleased, but the way that pleased him is revealing. Fate
is slighted in order that the story may turn wholly on
human motives; little or no account is taken of the ordinary relations of a Greek husband and wife, of the fact
that Admetus is a king, or of the semi-satyric and fanciful
elements in the play. Browning's Admetus is a soft, weak,
selfish, cowardly man, and Alcestis, having in her last
hour the vision of the gods, sees through him; hence, says
Balaustion, her directions for the care of the children,
without a word of love to her husband, who is now be-
latedly weeping, muttering ineptitudes, and protesting
overmuch. Admetus is not insincere "but somehow childlike"; he had made the pact to save his own life long ago,
with his eyes open, and now that the time has come he
can grieve, but he cannot, and Alcestis knows he cannot,
rise to the height of repudiating the bargain and dying like
a man.

Then upon the house of mourning breaks in the high-
hearted lover and helper of men, Heracles, and no one can
tell him how selfish they all have been. Though Browning
admits the Euripidean motive of the king's unselfish regard for the duty of hospitality, he invents and emphasizes rather the contagion of magnanimity that Admetus
and all those present catch from the great exemplar of
service. But now, when Admetus has achieved a quietude
"Bent on pursuing its descent to truth," Pheres arrives
and he is plucked back again. Pheres, with his hard,
miserly clinging to life, brings out the worst in Admetus,
for he sees himself in his father and abhors what he sees.
Not only does he try to hide his weakness in bluster
against weakness, he is stricken by the consciousness
that Alcestis is still near him, on the bier, and yet is ir-
recoverably beyond his reach. But the wrangle with
Pheres leaves him "Only half-selfish now, since sensitive,"

and capable of rising higher. When Admetus returns from the burial to his empty house he is overcome by realization of the worthlessness of what he has gained and the infinite worth of what he has lost. But he attains in grief a solemn strength. Then Heracles comes back with the veiled woman and proceeds to test Admetus' new-born truth and loyalty of soul; when convinced that the king has won his fight with his old base self, he goes on to break the glad news. And Alcestis too, witnessing the trial, knows that her husband has risen to her level, that he has proved himself a comrade to live and die with.

Thus Admetus has become a typical Browning hero, rising from weakness to nobility, through evil to good. A mainly pathetic story is made over into a complex drama of the soul. As Swinburne said, "the pathos of the subject is too simple and downright for Browning's analytic method."[16] Greek manners and modes of feeling, conventions of the Greek stage, are disregarded in order to show the spiritual evolution through love and suffering of an unheroic man and to glorify the nobility of a perfect woman. The situation is in fact the stock theme of sentimental drama and fiction of an earlier age, the regeneration of a man through his experience of feminine goodness; no modern cynic, however, made Browning's Admetus the hero of another *Relapse*. No matter how firmly one may hold the Browningesque view of Euripides' play, the total effect of the modern version is quite different.

There is still Heracles. Both the drunken reveler and the happy ending belong not merely to myth but to the satyric convention. To Browning the *Alcestis* is "that strangest, saddest, sweetest song," and Euripides' comedy and contrasts disappear in a completely serious reading of the story. In the restoration scene Euripides doubtless in-

---

[16] Gosse, *Life*, p. 203. For Rossetti's similar comment, see *Dante Gabriel Rossetti: His Family Letters*, ed. W. M. Rossetti (1895), II, 241.

tended to recall Admetus' earlier and less heartfelt protestations, but there were also the elements of fairy-tale supernaturalism, pleasant mystification, and dramatic suspense before a happy reunion; Browning's emphasis, as we have seen, is on the final test of the king's changed soul. In Euripides, to be sure, Heracles is not the mere burlesque figure of a satyr play; he is a sturdy, lusty, heroic adventurer, a good-hearted *deus ex machina*. But whatever hints Euripides gives for Browning's conception are so multiplied and elaborated that Heracles becomes the supreme example of the poet's favorite mythological type, the divine helper of mankind. Again and again we are reminded that Heracles, unlike Admetus, toils unceasingly and at the risk of his life in the service of humanity; he is, as Dowden said, "a very saint of joyous effort," and his mere presence has an ennobling effect. The Heracles whom Tennyson admired as "a grand creation" is indeed Browning's King Arthur,[17] and he is a more attractive as well as a more muscular Christian. He is a combination of his mythological self and Perseus and Caponsacchi and Robert Browning, for of all great deeds the rescue of Alcestis from death would most deeply stir the poet's memory of how he had given back life to his own bride.

Altogether Browning creates an un-Greek set of values and emotions. Those who like the Browning gospel may like his version; others may prefer the less insistent and more ironic art of Euripides. But even one of the latter must grant that Browning's serious message gives his poem a vitality which is usually wanting in works praised as strictly classical. One might think that he had gone as far as a modern could in reinterpreting the myth, but the facts of Euripides, however altered, stopped short of complete idealism, and Balaustion adds her own unhampered

[17] *Memoir*, II, 109; E. A. Parker, p. xx. See *Aristophanes' Apology*, ll. 508 ff., and, for the satyric conventions, ll. 2383 ff.

version of what might have been. Here the poet of "lyric Love, half angel and half bird" is able to let himself go. In this postscript Admetus is an ideal king whose beneficent rule is about to be cut off; he prepares calmly to die, but he complains, like Mycerinus, of divine injustice. Alcestis reveals that she has made a secret agreement with Apollo to die in his stead, so that he may live and fulfill the gods' purposes in him. Admetus "in a passionate cry" refuses to think of such a sacrifice. But, with a last plea, on the ground of their perfect love and unity, that she is right, Alcestis dies. Her soul arrives at the throne of Persephone, but the queen of Hades sends her back to earth and life, since death has been cheated; the life and soul of Admetus have been doubled by the addition of his wife's. This is certainly a strange, sweet version of the story, yet one cannot blame Browning alone for soft sentimentalism; the idea of Alcestis' sacrifice being made without her husband's knowledge appears, for instance, in the versions of William Morris (1868) and John Todhunter (1879).[18] Nor can one lump these and other writers together as arrant Victorians. From Hans Sachs and Alexandre Hardy onward the authors of the numerous versions of the story have steadily refused to allow Admetus to accept his wife's sacrifice.[19] Of course Browning's con-

---

[18] Todhunter refers to *Balaustion's Adventure*; see also the *Admetus* (1871) of Emma Lazarus.

Since Browning's general influence on the mythological poem has been relatively slight, I may mention Edward Dowden's *The Heroines* (written in 1873, published 1876). Helena, Atalanta, Europa, Andromeda, and Eurydice represent five types of women and set forth their feelings about man and marriage. The monologues are not very dramatic, but the psychological analysis and the strenuous idealism are much in Browning's way. *Andromeda* is perhaps the best, and also the most Browningesque in its conception of the heroic moment; see Dowden's definition of such "eminent moments" in his *Robert Browning* (1905), p. 271. For Dowden's early views of Browning (and of marriage), see *Fragments from Old Letters: E. D. to E. D. W.* (1914), pp. 26–28, 51, 115.

[19] Karl Heinemann, *Die tragischen Gestalten der Griechen in der Weltliteratur* (Leipzig, 1920), I, 123 ff. In Hugo von Hofmannsthal's version (written in 1893,

ception of the mystical oneness of the wedded lovers is set forth with his own special fervor. The same theme of separation and reunion had, along with Leighton's picture, inspired that intense lyric of 1864, *Eurydice to Orpheus*.[20]

If this volume could take account of poems dealing with ancient life and thought, *Aristophanes' Apology*, the sequel to *Balaustion's Adventure*, would need a long chapter, but since we must stick to our muttons (Browningesque for "myths"), there is room for only a paragraph or two. The mere difficulty of reading the poem has been exaggerated, though in a good many places Browning's garrulous pedantry runs wild, and this lumpy and gritty erudition (which mostly came from a few well-remembered books)[21] is the mark of the prodigious and barbarian amateur rather than of the ripe scholar and artist who can refrain from telling all he knows. A few months after the time of composition only God knew what many of the allusions meant — and He might have been startled by one that is put into the mouth of the matronly defender of Victorian decency.

While in *Balaustion's Adventure* the framework remained a framework for the transcript and interpretation of the *Alcestis*, in *Aristophanes' Apology* the rendering of the *Heracles* may be called an interpolation of inartistic length. It is of interest as a translation and as further evidence of Browning's devotion to Heracles, and it has its immediate controversial value as a specimen of Eurip-

published in 1911), Admetus accepts the sacrifice on the ground that the life of the king is essential to the welfare of the state. This theory had been applied to Browning's Euripidean transcript by Richard G. Moulton in 1891; see bibliography.

[20] Leighton was the "great Kaunian painter" whose picture of Alcestis is alluded to at the end of *Balaustion's Adventure*.

[21] Frederick M. Tisdel, "Browning's *Aristophanes' Apology*," *University of Missouri Studies*, II (1927), 1–46. Cf. *Letters of Robert Browning*, ed. T. L. Hood (Yale University Press, 1933), p. 208.

ides, but it mars the continuity and lowers the dramatic temperature of the debate between Aristophanes and Balaustion. The poem as a whole is a eulogy of the noble art, the lofty idealism, of Euripides, who inspires a still deeper and fuller reverence in Balaustion the young wife than in Balaustion the wild-pomegranate-flower. Euripides and Athens have died together, as it were, to the sound of Aristophanes' flute-girls and dancing-girls, but the great soul lives and works in some heaven of truth and beauty above this world of falsehood and ugliness and greed and strife. For all its learning, relevant and irrelevant, the argument is alive. It is not a mere academic dispute on the merits of Aristophanes and Euripides, of comedy and tragedy, it embodies all that Browning passionately thought and felt about the ethical function of poetry and the conflict between flesh and spirit, sense and soul. In *The Ring and the Book* Euripides had appeared as nothing less than a Christian before Christ, and here, as Symonds said, he is a "burgher of no earthly city."[22] The exuberant genius of Aristophanes is acknowledged, if not quite to the satisfaction of his admirers, and he is allowed a copious defence of his own ideal of truth — after all, Browning's own withers were not unwrung by the attack on the poet of "solid vulgar life" — but a great deal of special pleading is required to depress the one dramatist and exalt the other. To quote Symonds again — his *Studies of the Greek Poets*, by the way, furnished a number of Browning's ideas[23] — "Aristophanes becomes the scape-goat of Athenian sins, while Euripides shines forth a saint as well as a sage."

The narrative and dialogue do not lack poetry and vivid

[22] *Academy*, VII (1875), 389–90. See *The Ring and the Book*, x. 1662 ff.

[23] The chief source of Browning's critical ideas was A. W. Schlegel, the "critic-friend of Syracuse" in *Balaustion's Adventure* (l. 2663), who had praised Aristophanes and damned Euripides. Browning was "no enemy of that Aristophanes" (*Letters*, ed. Hood, p. 193).

scenes — the desolation of Athens' magnificence, the
breaking in of Aristophanes and his revelers upon Balaustion as she mourns the death of Euripides, the "old pale-
swathed majesty" of Sophocles announcing that his next
chorus shall wear black, the singing, by Balaustion's
husband, of a chorus from *Electra* which stays for a little
while the vindictive hands of the Spartans.[24] And per-
severing readers will be rewarded by the fragmentary song
of Thamyris, which is about the only reminder in Browning's poem that Aristophanes was a Shelley as well as a
Rabelais; there is hardly any reminder at all that he was
also a combination of Gilbert and Lewis Carroll. Of incidental mythology there is not much that concerns us,
and nothing like the picture of Persephone in *Balaustion's
Adventure*, with

> the softened eyes
> Of the lost maidenhood that lingered still
> Straying among the flowers in Sicily.

But no less romantic in its way is the image Balaustion applies to Aristophanes, of the sea-god she had beheld in her
childhood, "large-looming from his wave . . . Divine with
yearning after fellowship." The comic bard, however, is no
forsaken merman; he is a god above, but below, all is
"tail-splash, frisk of fin."[25]

Browning's interest in Euripides spread beyond classical confines into such a modern monologue as *Fifine at the
Fair* (1872), but the appearances and implications of
Helen of Troy I leave to those who enjoy more than I do
that mass of wire-drawn casuistry about love, soul, and
sense.[26]

[24] Browning gives this act of a nameless Phocian to Balaustion's husband.
See Plutarch, *Lysander*, xv.

[25] Ll. 820 ff.

[26] See *Electra*, ll. 1278 ff., and *Helena*. For the same reason, and because the
poem is hardly mythological, I neglect *Numpholeptos* (*Pacchiarotto*, 1876) in the
following section on the shorter poems.

III

There remains a goodly bulk of miscellaneous poems and passages scattered through the volumes of Browning's last decade. His love of heroic action and the great moment, which attracted him alike to Heracles and to Hervé Riel — Casabianca had been preëmpted — inspired the vigorous *Pheidippides* (1879) and *Echetlos* (1880). Both poems present what we have seen to be Browning's favorite mythological situation, a god as the helper of man, and they embody a similar moral. In *Echetlos* the divine ally of the Greeks at Marathon is the rude god of the ploughshare, who performs his heroic task and vanishes.[27] "The great deed ne'er grows small." But the Greek leaders, Miltiades and Themistocles, whose patriotism was selfish and unstable, come to ignoble ends.

The story of Pheidippides' run to Sparta, the Spartan refusal of immediate aid, and the encounter with Pan, the patron of Athens, are the chief items derived from Herodotus; with these Browning combined a later legend, told by Lucian and Plutarch, of the herald who ran to Athens after Marathon and died in reporting the news of victory.[28] Apart from expansion of the speeches, Browning's changes are mostly in the way of dramatic compression, heightening, and realistic verisimilitude. His inventions include the branch of fennel, the promise of a reward and the talk with Miltiades, and the reference to the girl Pheidippides left behind him; this last item helps to make the herald a young and romantic as well as a heroic character. His humble, unselfish devotion to a great cause is contrasted directly with the mean jealousy which is attributed to the Spartans and, by implication, with the

[27] Pausanias, I. xv. 3, I. xxxii. 5. Some details come from Herodotus, vi. 111, 113–14, etc. See Hood, pp. 132–33, 158, 170; Spindler, II, 54–56.
[28] Herod. vi. 48, 105–06, 113. For details see Hood, pp. 131–32, 152, 157, 170; Spindler, II, 49–54; J. W. Cunliffe, *P.M.L.A.*, XXIV (1909), 154 ff.

great Miltiades. Pan, with his bearded cheek and "goat-thighs grand" and moss-cushioned hoof, is the Pan of the ancient legend, not a modernized or allegorized figure, except so far as he represents divine approbation of a godlike man.[29]

Pan and Luna (1880) has revealed to sundry Browning-ites the usual moral — love, aspiration, sympathy [30] — but the poem may be regarded without great loss as simply a bold and fanciful re-creation of the myth. In a brief allusion in the third *Georgic*, Virgil had told how Luna, beguiled by a snowy fleece of wool, yielded not unwillingly to the seductions of Pan. Browning's chivalrous idealism demands another interpretation. His Maid-Moon is abashed by the consciousness that heaven and earth behold with joy her naked beauty, and she glides into a fleecy cloud; but the cloud is Pan's contrivance, and she is caught and embraced by the rough red god. The contrast between the white, shrinking purity of the moon and her bristly half-brute lover is rendered with a primitive energy of imagination. It is all vivid and concrete, at once human and dream-like; the moon is female flesh, the cloud and even the blackness of the night are solid to the touch. But, for all its originality, the poem illustrates in brief compass the prevailing defects of Browning's later work and the un-Hellenic quality of his imagination. The display of breathless energy is itself oppressive. Nothing is seen quietly, everything is in confused commotion, and

[29] Herodotus apparently thinks of the encounter with Pan as occurring on the journey from Athens to Sparta; Browning's change to the return journey is an obvious improvement. Mrs. Browning had done the same thing in her juvenile *Battle of Marathon*, a poem Browning had not seen and even doubted the existence of; see Mrs. Browning's *Poetical Works* (Oxford University Press, 1920), p. 15, and Browning's *Letters*, ed. Hood, pp. 246, 298, 373. In Mr. Edward Thompson's *Pheidippides* (*John in Prison*, 1912; *Collected Poems*, 1930), the deity the runner meets is Christ.

[30] Spindler, II, 37. M. Paul de Reul cites several examples without accepting them (*L'art et la pensée de Robert Browning*, Brussels, 1929, p. 462).

no detail is too minute or irrelevant to be thrown in, from a scientific experiment with thickening poppy-juice to the method of caulking ships with sheep's hide "first steeped in pitch."

Unlike *Pan and Luna*, *Ixion* (1883) is a compendium of Browning's characteristic doctrines. It owes little to ancient sources, for the sermon does not grow out of the myth but is attached to it.[31] The poem might almost be called a condensed version of *Prometheus Unbound*, and in fact the myth of Prometheus would have been a better starting-point, but Prometheus was doubtless too familiar, and, for Browning, too innocent a character; he always preferred obscure and sinful heroes, so that they might, in Fuller's phrase, rebound the higher to heaven. Ixion on the wheel arraigns the revengeful injustice of Zeus, who keeps him in torment for ever. Now his soul is awakened to a sense of sin, yet punishment goes on. Browning's interest is rather in the soul's evolution than in the question of eternal punishment, although that attracted him; he would have eagerly endorsed the famous decision which dismissed hell with costs.[32] Ixion comes to see that he was deluded by his own poor conception of God; the tyrannical Zeus is not the true God but a figment of the limited human mind. Caliban had dimly felt a Quiet above Setebos, and Ixion has a more positive idea of a God above Zeus who permits evil as the condition of the soul's growth. Zeus is below the human level, he cannot grow. Like Shelley's Prometheus, though not sinless, Ixion, by the spiritual insight born of suffering, proves himself greater than the tyrant, and he rises out of the wreck "past Zeus to the

---

[31] Spindler (II, 30) cites the fragments of Euripides' drama on the subject, which embodied an arraignment of the gods, and the sixth of Lucian's *Dialogues of the Gods*. Browning would know of course the allusions in Virgil and Ovid. Both Spindler and Hood overlook Pindar's didactic version of the myth (*Pyth.* ii. 21 ff.).

[32] Cf. *A Camel-Driver* (*Ferishtah's Fancies*), and *The Inn Album*, iv. 358 ff.

Potency o'er him!" He has become, in short, a Christian,
of Browning's somewhat vaguely aspiring sect. What we
have is really the religion of humanity, for Browning's
God, while welcomed by generations of evangelical readers,
is not much more than a pot of gold at the end of the rainbow, a postulated *x* in the poet's emotional and optimistic
algebra. Philosophically the poem is not too coherent;
Browning seldom allowed the "soul's rush on the real"
to be obstructed by quiet meditation, he had to carry the
ramparts of truth by storm.

A much larger compendium of his lifelong convictions
was the *Parleyings* of 1887.[33] The prologue, *Apollo and the
Fates*, is, apart from the mythological frame, pure Browning. Apollo asks the Fates to prolong the life of Admetus.
They reply that death is a happy release for mortals,
whose only motive for living is the illusions and hopes that
Apollo bestows. He persuades them to drink of man's invention, wine, and they acknowledge that it transforms
life into radiance. But, Apollo argues, wine was really the
product of the anterior wisdom of Zeus, and man's reason
must labor to understand the divine mingling of good and
ill. The Fates, now intoxicated with the wine of imagination, proclaim that life is no defeat but a triumph. When
man drinks the same elixir, compounds fancy with fact,
the lost secret is found; man is not blinded by the actual,
he sees life in all its potential power. Though sobered by an
earthquake, the Fates recognize that they spoke the truth
when drunk. They cannot control destiny, but they know
that in spite of, or rather because of, obstacles and illusions
"Man learningly lives" until "death completes living,
shows life in its truth." They grant a reprieve to Admetus
on condition that someone for love's sake will die in his
stead, and they laugh mockingly as Apollo declares that
there will be no lack of volunteers.

[33] My discussion of parts of this work is much indebted to Mr. W. C.
De Vane's elaborate study (1927).

The "satyric" manner of the poem and the lolloping meter seem less suitable for an answer to the riddle of life than for a charade. As for the symbolism, one may think that Browning flung his everyday metaphysical garments on the nearest mythological chair — a property left over, perhaps, from *Balaustion's Adventure* — without much caring how they fell. But the central ideas are very clear and very familiar. That Browning should adopt, however allegorically, the principle *in vino veritas*, might suggest, allegorically, the position into which he had been driven. He had never really been an intellectual poet, and he became steadily more anti-intellectual. He could not, whatever he might say at times, have agreed with Donne that reason is our soul's left hand, even if faith is her right. The more his own intellect and others' refused to confirm his ingrained beliefs, the more he asserted the ultimate validity of his emotions and his imagination. One may say that is what the great mystics have done, but Browning was not a mystic, he was only misty; in the spiritual and ethical world he was somewhat like Heracles, a well-meaning, confused, energetic, irresponsible tramp. To maintain Browning's view of life does require perpetual intoxication, and Housman, for instance, has reminded us how difficult that is — "Could man be drunk for ever...." — and how painful the sober intervals of thought may be. Browning would not allow time for such intervals.

The doctrine set forth in the prologue receives further mythological illustration in several of the parleyings. "A myth may teach," Browning says in *With Bernard de Mandeville*, and he proceeds, after the manner of "Euripides not Aeschylus," to give an interpretation of Prometheus. His Titan is not the great rebel; the theme is man's inability to cram inside "his finite God's infinitude." All the earth felt and rejoiced in the beneficent power of the sun except man, whose nature craved real apprehension of

ultimate causes, an actual revelation of an actual bond
with the divine. Then Prometheus gave man a glass which
focused the rays of the sun and produced fire, and man,
seeing "The very Sun in little," could grasp the idea of
infinity. Every man is God in little, for, as Browning had
urged in *Saul* and many other poems, love in the human
heart is itself the best evidence of the providential love of
God.[34]

In *Mandeville*, Browning had been replying to Carlyle's
gloomy view of God's remoteness from the evil world. In
another poem he makes Francis Furini the stalking-horse
for a combined defence of the nude in art (his painter
son's work in particular) and an attack on the evolutionists. The two subjects seem far enough apart, but they
are related through the poet's faith in the close union of
body and soul, and, more specifically, through the symbolic figure of Andromeda. He is not now, as in *Pauline*,
mainly content with romantic picture-making (though he
does glance at a bathing nymph and Diana and Venus),
and Andromeda is not simply a beautiful girl rescued by a
heroic champion. Her body is the work of God which the
artist can see and make others see:

> God's best of beauteous and magnificent
> Revealed to earth — the naked female form.

When Browning turns upon the evolutionists, Andromeda
becomes more than that; she is indeed, as Mr. De Vane
says, the symbol of all his beliefs. He had been in youth,
and still was, an evolutionist of a kind, but he was very
militantly on the side of the angels. The scientists, preoccupied with biological origins, cannot see man's divine
soul striving upward through evil to good. Andromeda on
the rocks awaiting the serpent becomes the poet himself,

---

[34] Cf. the passage on Prometheus in *A Death in the Desert*, ll. 279 ff. See also
the discussion of a Promethean drama which Browning had meant to do himself
and then wanted Miss Barrett to write (*Letters*, I, 37 ff.).

standing on the firm ledge of his individual consciousness amid the wash and welter of ignorance, facing the monster of evil;[35] needless to say, the all-wise deliverer is God.

Poetically and philosophically, *With Gerard de Lairesse* is the most interesting poem in the collection. It is comparable in its way to *Paradise Regained*, for, like Milton in his old age, Browning feels that in his grand testament he must repudiate the Greece he has loved for the sake of a higher ideal; this is not to say that his ideal is the same as Milton's. Remembering his youthful debt to the book and the paintings of De Lairesse, Browning treats the artist with pious respect. Yet the poet of modern realism and the modern soul cannot really endorse or share the pseudo-classical fancy which, on too low a level, "composed the strife 'Twixt sense and soul." The moderns see the soul, not merely the body. Then, by way of beating the classicists on their own ground, the poet essays to imitate in words, in a series of purple patches, such mythological pictures as the painter's fancy had created; and in each he suggests what the mythological painter would not have felt, the limitations of Greek ideals. The series begins with Prometheus and the vulture in a night of lightning and thunder; here we have, in language reminiscent of Aeschylus and still more, apparently, of Shelley,[36] the traditional noble victim of a barbarous deity. Then, after the night of storm, radiant morning breaks on the figure of Artemis the huntress. She is not now the maternal patron of Hippolytus

---

[35] Cf. *Christmas-Eve*, ll. 306 ff.

[36] Echoes of the conclusion of Mrs. Browning's translation have been found here, and they would not be unnatural, but echoes of Shelley's drama seem more distinct. Like Shelley (*P.U.*, I. 432), Browning has "white fire" which splits a tree. Mrs. Browning's "Zeus's winged hound, The strong carnivorous eagle" seems less close to Browning (ll. 196–98) than Shelley's phrases are (I. 331–32); and Shelley uses "hound" more than once. Browning's "of scorn's unconquerable smile" recalls "I laugh your power . . . To lowest scorn" (*P.U.*, I. 473). "Thy pallid brow" and the symbolic golden dawn are also in Shelley's vein.

On the probable sources of these several mythological episodes, see De Vane, pp. 245 ff., and Spindler, II, 68 ff.

who had prologized nearly fifty years before; she is the
chaste and beautiful but cruel goddess whose envious
shafts have blighted many a marriage. But the description, if it lacks the lofty serenity of the early poem, is a
"close-up" of more concrete vigor and not less clarity of
line. The next picture brings hot noon, and a satyr not so
much lusting as yearning for the disdainful nymph, Lyda [37]
— Browning's version, one might say, of "the breasts of
the nymphs in the brake." Evening brings face to face
Darius and Alexander, contending for the mastery of the
world. And finally we have the pallid ghost of Greek
civilization and Greek religion. Though Browning intended these descriptive passages to be in a grandiose
bravura style, he did not contemplate what must be the
reaction of almost any reader; one is less impressed by
the supposed emptiness of such themes, not to mention the
anti-Hellenic morals, than one is by the poetical power
displayed in these mythological landscapes. Browning
vindicates what he set out to expose. The lurid vision of
Prometheus on the rocks, the poised grace of the huntress,
are perhaps the only memorable passages in the whole
volume.

Resuming his argument, Browning abjures the dead
past in the name of "the all-including Future" and the
endless progress of the soul. Who seeks for fire in Greek
lore finds only ashes. Poets must no longer

> Dream afresh old godlike shapes,
> Recapture ancient fable that escapes,
> Push back reality, repeople earth
> With vanished falseness, recognize no worth
> In fact new-born unless 'tis rendered back
> Pallid by fancy, as the western rack
> Of fading cloud bequeaths the lake some gleam
> Of its gone glory!

---

[37] Browning makes use, in his own way, of the brief tale of Moschus which
Shelley translated (*Works*, ed. Hutchinson, p. 715).

Browning is thinking of Swinburne and Morris[38] and the whole flock of Victorian Hellenists, above all, apparently, of Arnold, who had not only used antique themes but made a formal critical plea for them. Mrs. Browning, among others, had long before set aside myths in favor of modern themes, and Browning, a more romantic Christian and realist, had agreed with her.[39]

Such a repudiation of the antique, based on just such reasons, was the quite inevitable conclusion of Browning's poetic cycle. And yet he is certainly among the original figures in nineteenth-century Hellenism. His classical poems are distinctive mainly in two ways, both unclassical ways; they almost all embody his faith in man's heavenward progress and his zest for the motley texture of human life here and now. Browning's antique realism, his colloquial, vivacious learning, was a new phenomenon in English poetry, and his faith has the force and fervor which comes from the heart. One result is that his classical poems are not plaster façades, they are alive. Another result is that Browning is not a mythological poet in the way that Keats and Shelley were; his normal world is human and concrete, far from nature and Platonic idealism. He poured a stream of red blood into a kind of poetry always in danger of anemia; and, as someone has said, blood is reddest when it has not gone through the brain. For by any definition of Hellenism — and there have been many definitions — in his art, in his feeling, in what used to be called his philosophy, Browning was utterly un-Hellenic. He thought his vision of the infinite carried him, as a modern, beyond the finite rationalism of the Greeks — we need not ask here if the Greek mind was always finite and rational — but the fact is that he stopped short of that. He cannot

[38] For his opinions of the emptiness of both poets see *Letters*, ed. Hood, pp. 134, 136.

[39] *Letters*, I, 37, 443 (and above, ch. VIII). See also *Robert Browning and Alfred Domett*, ed. Kenyon (1906), p. 48.

forgive the Greeks their lack of a satisfying belief in Christian immortality, and he seems to conceive of immortality as incessant busyness. Whereas the Greeks were bound by their static sense of the laws which never grow old, Browning celebrates the dynamic power of love, or rather, of incessant loving. Insight into the nature of self and God and the universe is to be gained, not by religious and philosophic discipline, but by vigorous splashing in a sea, or even a tub, of spontaneous emotion. It was both his strength and his defect that he was, as Arnold said, absorbed in multitudinousness. In their various ways Keats and Shelley, Arnold and Tennyson, sought for philosophic unity, order, and meaning behind experience and appearances. Browning, lustily buffeting the waves of flux, solves all problems by shouting "God! Life! Love!"

In some matters which concern us Browning is quite close to his younger contemporary, George Meredith, whose reputation for philosophic modernity lasted longer than Browning's, though he too has gone under a cloud, and partly for similar reasons. Both believed in life as a high adventure, and made Greek myth the vehicle for evolutionary optimism, for a gospel of soul in harmony with flesh. Each missed the usual classical education of the period, and may be said to have brought to the Hellenic tradition the fresh, crude strength of a barbarian interloper. Both were rapid, excited, difficult writers, who often mistook mental agility for philosophic power; the noise and jar of a racing motor were a sufficient assurance of forward movement. But some differences will appear in the next section.

II. George Meredith

Exactly half a century separates the earliest and the latest mythological poems of George Meredith (1828–1909). The *Poems* of 1851, "my boy's book," as the author

later called it, had two tangible links with the past, a dedication to Peacock, his father-in-law, and an epigraph from
Orion. We have already noticed, in Chapter Eight, the
prophetically Meredithian character of Horne's ethical
and evolutionary parable, and Meredith's interest in it; but
though Horne's encouragement meant a great deal to the
young poet, his influence is not conspicuous in the classical pieces of this first volume. *The Rape of Aurora, Daphne,
Antigone*, and *The Shipwreck of Idomeneus* — a lyric, an
Ovidian idyll, a dramatic monologue, and a miniature epic
narrative — are mainly poetic experiments.[40] The vaguely
Keatsian *Daphne* is the most attractive, by virtue of its
fresh and exuberant open-air pictures; it is also, with its
conceits and pathetic fallacies, the most uneven. The
fleeing nymph suggests such a horrid image of bombard-
ment as this:

> On her rounded form ripe berries
> Dash and die in gory dew.[41]

As a riverside idyll *Daphne* falls far short of the lyrical
scene in *Richard Feverel*. A more mature product of the
same period was the strong and severe *Cassandra*.[42]

I may depart from my usual conscientious chronological
method and jump up to *A Reading of Life* (1901), which is
the most complete mythological exposition of Meredith's

[40] For brief comments on the first two, see *Letters of George Meredith, Collected and Edited by his Son* (1912), I, 8. The Widener Library has a copy of
the 1851 volume inscribed to Horne, "by whose generous appreciation and trusty
criticism these 'Poems' were chiefly fostered" (Robert E. Sencourt, *Life of
George Meredith*, 1929, p. 24).

[41] *Poetical Works*, ed. G. M. Trevelyan (1919), p. 39. This edition is cited
hereafter as *Works*. Charles B. Cayley, Christina Rossetti's suitor, has a number
of more astonishing lines in his *Daphne Transformed* (*Psyche's Interludes*, 1857),
such as this: "Her locks upturned, her bath adjourned. . . ."

[42] *Cassandra* was written in 1850–51 and published with *Modern Love* in 1862.
Meredith thought well of it (*Letters*, I, 7, 45). Whether or not he knew Schiller's
Kassandra, the two poems have no more than a general and inevitable resem-
blance. Praed's *Cassandra* (1830) is somewhat closer to Schiller.

fundamental creed. Youth, he says, must make "the vital choice" between Artemis, the virgin huntress, and Aphrodite, the persuader. "Each claims worship undivided," and each points to death as the penalty of disobedience or excessive devotion. Mr. Trevelyan takes Artemis as the "symbol here of our development of body, brain, and spirit in purity, in strife with the elements."[43] It is unsafe to question Mr. Trevelyan's admirable and "inspired" commentary, but can Artemis represent the ideal Meredithian triad and at the same time be partly condemned as one-sided and inadequate? While both deities are treated in a mainly favorable way, surely they symbolize those attitudes of which the Meredithian extremes are "the ascetic rocks and the sensual whirlpools."[44] *With the Huntress*, if less high-pitched and poetical, might almost be a presentation of the traditional English theory of "games." But Aphrodite, a radiant symbol of "Great Nature's stern necessity," can find the hidden weaknesses of "the race who mount the rose," that is, the red-cheeked athletes; in their avoidance of sex they are "irreverent of Life's design." Much of *With the Persuader* is a sort of idealistic manual for lovers, and Aphrodite, unlike Artemis, nearly disappears behind the author's interpretation. In the final section, *The Test of Manhood*, Meredith outlines his "pagan" view of the race's emergence from savagery through the mists of religious supernaturalism (a product of man's egoism) to a faith in the complete and disciplined man who follows Nature. Though he discarded Christian dogma, Meredith only held the more firmly to the moral ideal of Christianity; he did of course try to harmonize it with reason and biology. Obedience to either Artemis or Aphrodite alone means retrogression to the brute; a union

[43] *Works*, p. 614; *The Poetry and Philosophy of George Meredith* (1912), pp. 180–81.
[44] *Diana of the Crossways*, ch. XXXVII.

of flesh and spirit in which each has its due means endless struggle, but also endless and intelligent advance.[45] Thus the moral of this poem, and of many others, is virtually that of the romantic and decorative *Orion*; Meredith, however, enforces his doctrine with an earnest post-Darwinian realism.

When we look back over his other mythological poems we find that all the best ones are expositions of his central creed. Some classical pieces which are not, *Periander*, *Solon*, and *Bellerophon* (1887), must be neglected in this sketch. The interest of *Phaéthôn* (1867) is largely metrical, though it is a vivid narrative.[46] *The Cageing of Ares* (1899), which was "dedicated to the Council at the Hague," has not much interest of any kind, either as a mythological poem or as a serio-comic plea for peace. But there remains a group of mythological poems of unique originality and freshness. Meredith's religion of nature differs from Wordsworth's, among other ways, in being more simply pagan — one cannot escape damnable iteration of the word — and, even more spontaneously than Wordsworth, he can welcome myths as the products of a healthy, unsophisticated religious imagination seeking to explain the universe and man's relation to it. Those who dare to enter the woods of Westermain will find the old gods there. Such chosen spirits, like the "old bards, in nature wise," can see once more the "pageant of man's poetic brain," and believe that there is a life in orb and brook and tree and cloud. One who neighbors the invisible can think "the woods with

---

[45] Among the multitude of parallel utterances in Meredith, see the *Letters*, I, 33, 156–57, II, 409.

[46] Mr. Trevelyan remarks that Meredith's translations from Homer "have much of the spirit of the original," and that *Phaéthôn* similarly blends "rude primaeval vigour with beauty of imagination" (*Poetry and Philosophy of George Meredith*, p. 95, note). Meredith does avoid the common sins of tameness and flatness, but metrical difficulties cause a good deal of roughness and straining. See his review of Merivale's translation of the *Iliad* (*Works*, Memorial Edition, 1910, XXIII, 77–80).

nymphs alive"; he knows "the Dryad voices well." Thus Meredith's classic deities are not merely the graceful decorative beings of so much Victorian verse, but primitive and mysterious symbols of the life of earth.[47]

In *The Day of the Daughter of Hades* (1883) the myth of Demeter and Persephone is given a new turn. In the vale of Enna, now alive with the beauty of spring and the dawn, the mortal youth Callistes witnesses the reunion of the mother and the queen of the underworld; the tall figures by the chariot-wheel embraced like "Fellow poplars, windtaken. . . ." As the august pair move away, Callistes sees a maiden who has slipped out of Persephone's chariot. Though he does not know it yet, this is Skiágeneia, daughter of Persephone and Hades, of Spring and Darkness, who has escaped to the upper world. With Callistes she roams about, rejoicing in light and the teeming life and loveliness of earth. She has the key to its meaning, and reads clearly "the haunts of the beak and the claw," but she shuns the thoughts of cities and the waste of war which excite the heart of the still unenlightened Callistes. Toward evening she sings a rapturous "Song of Days," of furrow and seed and all growing things, of the unchanging cycle of the husbandman's life and labor. Her voice betrays her whereabouts to her father, and his chariot thunders up to carry her back to the realm of death. Callistes is left with a vision of beauty and wisdom which he can only long for till he dies. The daughter of Hades, in her brief happy day of life, has given to mortal man a reading of earth. In his old age Meredith put this at the head of all his poems.[48]

[47] See *The Woods of Westermain* (*Works*, p. 195); *The South-Wester* (p. 324); *Outer and Inner* (p. 340); *Ode to the Spirit of Earth in Autumn* (p. 173). Even the giant sons of Earth become Meredithian (*Hard Weather*, p. 321), and Meredith does not overlook Antaeus (*The Empty Purse*, p. 445).

[48] Desmond MacCarthy, *Portraits* (1931), pp. 176, 182. Mark Pattison, who damned so many things, damned the poem because it dealt with a classical myth,

Phoebus with Admetus (1880) and *Melampus* (1883) are briefer illustrations of the wise happiness and health which come with full-hearted acceptance and understanding of nature. The former is a "Song of Days" which tells how the god brought prosperity to Admetus' farm, how he led the whole round of work and rustic pleasures, and taught the shepherds new arts, from trapping wolves to music and dancing. (The matter-of-fact Apollodorus merely records that Apollo caused all the cows to drop twins.) [49] In its simpler way Apollo's year of service was for the household what Skiágeneia's day on earth was for Callistes, a renewal of "The union of our earth and skies" — to borrow a phrase from *The South-Wester*. The theme of *Melampus* is the same, though it starts from the union between man and the animal world. Meredith's portrait of the ancient sage is also a portrait of the artist. [50] For Melampus, who knows well "what the mystical woods disclose," the whole life of man and the creatures and things of earth is one. Nature and Apollo taught him sanity and wisdom, and he saw the harmony between nature and song. But he was no hermit. He dwelt as an Apollo among men, healing them, reclaiming them from aberrations with his "juice of the woods."

Meredith, who was afflicted by Hardy's twilight view of life, could not regard man, Earth's "great venture," as "the child of woe." His gospel of inspired sanity and robust optimism is a joyous gospel, not because he sees man and nature as wholly good, nor because man's imperfection is a guarantee of some heavenly fulfilment, but because the disorders, extravagances, and limitations of the individual and of society can be overcome with the aid

because Skiágeneia was "a thoroughly Burne Jones maiden," and because the poet was too diffuse (*Academy*, XXIV [1883], 37-38).

[49] *Library*, III. x. 4; cf. Callimachus, *Hymn to Apollo*, ll. 47-54. See Ford Madox Ford's sonnet in his *Collected Poems* (1914), p. 166.

[50] See Apollodorus, *Lib.* I. ix. 11, and Lempriere.

of man's mother, Earth, his "well of strength, his home of rest." "Contention is the vital force,"[51] the achievement of "the balanced mean" is a high and exciting adventure. Even death is not to be feared.

> Into the breast that gives the rose,
> Shall I with shuddering fall?

If these lines suggest that Meredith is a bedfellow of the cosmic sentimentalists, his sword of common sense lies between them. The comic spirit which is so essential an element in his creed is the foe of rose-pink optimism.

In nineteenth-century poetry, dominated by the romantic tradition, myth and the comic spirit are rarely found together. Meredith is "primitive" enough to be able to unite them, as in *The Appeasement of Demeter* (1887). While earth lies under the grieving mother's curse of sterility, her maid Iambe pities the dying things. Instinct prompts some animals to faint-hearted renewal of old frolics. The sight of a gaunt horse and mare trying to be gay awakens sudden mirth in Demeter, and the blighting spell is broken by laughter; the genial life of the sick earth is revived.[52] This is not the solution of *The Waste Land*. A more elaborate specimen of what is by implication more "thoughtful laughter" is the mythological extravaganza in the *Ode to the Comic Spirit* (1892). Momus, the over-bold satirist, is kicked out of Olympus; the gods, their conceit uncurbed, soon degenerate and fall to earth.[53] We

[51] *Hard Weather*, p. 320. Is the line a reinterpretation of Hesiod, *Works and Days*, l. 24?

[52] According to the myth, when Demeter sat down in the house of Celeus, the maid Iambe cracked jokes and made her smile. See Apollodorus, *Lib.* I. v. 1; Homeric *Hymn to Demeter*, ll. 192–205.

Another mythological mixture of comic and serious is *The Teaching of the Nude* (1892); see *Works*, p. 410.

[53] The mythology seems to be largely Meredith's. For Momus' criticism of the gods see Lucian's *Hermotimus*, 20; *Zeus Tragoedus*, 19 ff.; *The Gods in Coun-*

have a grotesque picture of them as a seaside orchestra, led by the limping mocker they had expelled from heaven. Zeus the thunderer is the trombone; Ares the bugler; the foam-born goddess of love is a carnal creature with "unholy oily leer." For the gods, like men, had a heart — "our throbber," as Meredith insists on calling it — and though the heart is a primary motive force, it will, when uncorrected, swell "To notions monstrous." In the contrast between "tyrant lust" and "barren fits of sentiment," between "red sensualist" and "pinched ascetic," we have the doctrine, already encountered in *A Reading of Life*, which runs through the poems and novels and provides the fundamental text of the *Essay on the Idea of Comedy*. Egoism, which is really man's refusal to obey the lessons of Earth, leads to sentimentalism or sensuality. The great corrective of the heart and the senses is the comic spirit, the sword which cuts away fatty or cancerous growths of egoism in man and the race. It assigns a rightful value to the claims of blood, brain, and spirit, making the individual an harmonious, disciplined whole, and, uniting men in true solidarity, it checks the retrograde instincts of the brute and points the way onward and upward. Meredith's emphasis on man's roots in earth, on his place in the biological scheme, whether or not it commends itself to scientific philosophers, separates him both from such optimists as Browning and from those who, like Swinburne, made an abstract deity of the spirit of man. And though Meredith, like Browning, believed in passionate love, he was, in his own full-blooded athletic way, too austere to confuse vagrant emotion with spiritual progress. On the other hand, in poetry at least he lacked Browning's incomparable genius for portrait-painting and

---

cil, 2 ff. (*Works*, trans. H. W. and F. G. Fowler, Clarendon Press, 1905, II, 52, III, 89 ff., IV, 165 ff.). For the critic's expulsion from heaven, see *Fabulae Aesopicae Collectae*, ed. C. Halm (Leipzig, 1852), Fab. 155.

boundless curiosity about all aspects of human behavior, so that he was more consistently and narrowly a preacher and moralist.

The early mythological poems, with the exception of *Cassandra*, showed few traces of that bright muscular idiom which Meredith developed for the expression of his philosophical ideas. Of his frequent obscurity and uncouthness we have had some slight examples already, and the mythological poems like the rest yield many more. Skiágeneia has "Not a sign of the torch in the blood"; that is, she is an unspoiled child of nature who does not blush. (Of late years this kind of writing, though damned in Meredith, has been praised in Mr. Ezra Pound.) The description of a predatory bird killed and hung up by shepherds —

> Hung the hooky beak up aloft the arrowhead
> Reddened through his feathers for our dear fold —

causes, in Johnsonian language, a sudden astonishment which may not be followed by rational admiration. At such times, however instinctive Meredith's manner was, we can only cry "Less brain, O Lord, less brain!" and wish that the style invented for the exposition of subtle ideas were not extended to simple ones as well. In Meredith generally poetry does not come as naturally as leaves to a tree; rather, there is the spirit of "Up, Guards, and at them!" The gracious serenity of *Melampus* is not common in verse of abounding energy. In the second stanza of *Phoebus with Admetus*, Meredith cannot be accused of imitating *Oenone* or the opening of *Hyperion* in his description of stillness; he charges along with the same splendid movement he had begun. The refrain of this poem, by the way, coming after such stanzaic rhythms, sounds like a clog dance done by a man with wooden legs. If Meredith's poetry seldom strikes us as a wording of our own highest thoughts, it is partly because he was an evangelist with a message, and partly because, as Chesterton said of Browning, his mind was like a piece of strong wood with a knot in it. But, with all his uncontrolled fecundity of glancing thought and image and didactic argumentation, Meredith had the virtues of his defects. He let in the sun and wind upon the often tame and literary mythological conventions of his time. No poet of the century makes us live so vividly in the outdoor world of trees and flowers, birds and bees, and "Bulls, that walk the pastures in kingly-flashing coats." Meredith is a worthy son of Pan; earth to him is young as the slip of the new moon.

Nowadays Meredith's poetry and novels, his philosophy and his style, once the shibboleths of the intellectual, have been condemned, or, worse still, ignored. As regards style, it may seem odd that a generation which has welcomed Hopkins should remain cold to the only Victorian poet whose manner (and whose love of earth) approached his.[54] For a time Meredith's brilliance and buoyancy were less attractive than the tragic pessimism and rugged plainness of Hardy. Then the defeatist mood of the war and postwar years pushed Meredith's faith in Earth and his strenuous evolutionary meliorism still further into the past. Since that dusty answer no longer satisfies, and since Hardy's philosophy has ceased, as a philosophy, to be impressive, we might expect Meredith to emerge from disrepute. But other obstacles have arisen. What mysticism has come out of the post-war period has been more or less Christian and especially Catholic, and to it Meredith's rational paganism and love of life are alien. Further, the younger generation has embraced Marxism, and the creator of Sir Austin Feverel and Sir Willoughby Patterne is not a proletarian author; in a deeper sense also, a partly

[54] Mr. Eliot compares the two, "altogether to Hopkins's advantage" (*After Strange Gods*, New York, 1934, pp. 52–53).

Greek and Stoic sense, Meredith is aristocratic. But even if the particular articles of his creed do not come home to us, though we seem able to accept creeds no more novel and much less arduous, at least the gospel of Earth carries a fine clean air with it, a wealth of natural beauty and a noble lyrical fervor.

CHAPTER XII

Minor Poets, Mid-Victorian
and Later

I

AUBREY DE VERE remarked, in 1882, that the
religion of nature, the religion of beauty, and
the religion of humanity, then so potent, had
all been launched sixty years before by Shelley.[1]
But Shelley was only one of the sources, and the three
religions had both lost the triple unity they once possessed and had undergone a change in their individual
character. Some minor poets accepted the Victorian compromise between religion and science, some followed the
Pre-Raphaelites in ignoring both. Evolution provided a
basis for the Christian meliorism of Roden Noel as well
as for the pagan meliorism of George Meredith; it also
contributed to the stark pessimism of James Thomson.
What especially concerns us, the mythological conception
of nature, had apparently died with Wordsworth, Keats,
and Shelley. In the latter half of the century there is
sufficient evidence that Pan is dead in the almost annual
assertions that he is not; and so far as Dionysus could be
said to have a renewal of life in the eighties and nineties,
the wine of the world was perhaps less potent in nature
than when put up in bottles.

The romantic religion of beauty was no longer the Platonic idealism of Keats and Shelley. Romantic ideas of the

[1] Wilfrid Ward, *Aubrey de Vere: A Memoir* (1904), p. 336.

poet as a creator of beauty, a person apart, were detached from their context, they were intensified and exaggerated in a positive way by French influence and in a negative way by hostility to the moral and utilitarian standards of the Victorian bourgeoisie. The doctrine of art for art's sake, enunciated by the earlier Swinburne and the Pre-Raphaelites, became a religion whose priests were Pater and Wilde. Sensuous ecstasy was not now an avenue to intuitions of universal beauty and truth, it was an end in itself, the precious possession, from moment to moment, of those choice spirits who could burn with a hard, gemlike flame — an occupation which has been likened to playing with fire but which sometimes suggests blowing into ashes. Keats's mature conception of beauty meant the unifying of experience, not the multiplication of experiences; it was also an apotheosis of the normal, an ideal growing out of the common life of man. The doctrine of the esthetes was relatively thin and esoteric, even when not tainted, as it often was, with decadent ideas of pain and evil. A distinction must be made, of course, between Pater himself, with his high (and vague) moral ideal, and the way in which his influence operated. The much less ambiguous Ruskin steadily proclaimed the oneness of beauty and morality, but a number of esthetes chose to take the cash and let the credit go. Arnold contributed more to the movement than he would have liked to think, though perhaps less than some hostile modern critics would have us think. As the foe of the British Philistine, the leader (if not the whole body) of the saving remnant, the exponent of Hellenic sweetness and light, of culture and the pursuit of perfection, of critical disinterestedness, Arnold supplied ideas and catchwords which, without his Hebraic checks and balances, lent themselves to exaggeration and perversion.

The religion of humanity had likewise become attenuated, at least in poetry. Major as well as minor Victorian poets generally lacked the large and positive humanitarian faith of the romantics, and at the same time they recoiled from the blatant commercial optimism of an age of prosperity and progress. For Keats and Shelley classic myths had been symbols with which to body forth a vision of man and a new world; now they became a means of withdrawal from the world. Swinburne's religion of humanity was mostly extravagant posturing. Rossetti rarely went outside his palace of art. William Morris, with his intense social passion, escaped from the shadow of the dark Satanic mills to the green and pleasant land of Greece. Thus in various ways and for various reasons the broad deep stream of romanticism had run thin, and what fresh showers of rain came down were not enough to revive the parched waste land; most of the poets were not aware that it was parched.

Meanwhile the small garden of classical mythology was being diligently cultivated by scholars and was yielding some remarkable growths. The learned rejoiced that the new etymological method had at last put comparative mythology on a scientific basis. Max Müller, like Francis Thompson's Shelley, got between the feet of the horses of the sun, and during the third quarter of the century almost everyone accompanied him on his celestial flights. "The siege of Troy," he said, "is but a repetition of the daily siege of the East by the solar powers that every evening are robbed of their brightest treasures in the West."[2] Most of the characters of mythology, from Achilles, Ulysses, Oedipus and Jason, to Helen, Europa, and Athene, all in fact "whose lives had not been wholly sedentary," as a hostile reviewer put it, "and who had not already been proved to be the night or the moon, were proved to be the dawn or the sun."[3] Müller himself was early disturbed by

[2] *Lectures on the Science of Language,* Second Series (1864), p. 471, and *passim*; see also p. 501.   [3] *Edinburgh Review,* CLIII (1881), 517.

the fact that all roads led to the sun, but there was the ir-refragable evidence of etymology, which was not yet very scientific, and the Vedic hymns. After reading Müller and his followers one is surprised by the scholarly modera-tion of Gladstone's proof that Homeric theology included relics of Scriptural traditions,[4] and of Ruskin's *Queen of the Air* (1869), which was very sound ethically if not etymo-logically. Only half a dozen years separate Ruskin's book from Pater's half-poetic, half-anthropological studies of Demeter and Persephone and Dionysus, but these belong to the scholarship and philosophy of another age. I mention this phase of mythological science merely as a reminder that, while Spenser and Chapman and others drew abundant and vital nourishment from the ethical mythographers of the Renaissance, the mid-Victorian poets who looked up to be fed would have been swollen with wind. However, the modern poet's contemplation of mythological truth has been, one might say, Buddhistic, and the inner consciousness has been assisted by the poetic tradition, more or less classical reading, and the multi-plying editions of Lempriere.

As we move on through the century these omnibus chap-ters, much to the distress of the writer as well as the reader, have to provide for increasing crowds of minor but not negligible writers, along with some who are not minor but have little to do with us. In the last third of the nine-teenth century, as in the last decade of the sixteenth, a mythological poem was the first impulse of the aspirant who had an itch to write something, and the number of the literate had been vastly enlarged. In addition to the end-less narratives or idylls in the Keats-Tennyson tradition, the production of mythological dramas was stimulated by *Atalanta in Calydon.* Along with De Tabley's *Philoctetes*

---

[4] *Studies on Homer and the Homeric Age* (Oxford University Press, 1858), vol. II.

(1866), there were such things as Thomas Ashe's pathetic *Sorrows of Hypsipyle* (1867) and the more austerely Hellenic *Prometheus Unbound* (1867) of George A. Simcox. Some men began with mythological poems and turned to other fields in which they did more original work. Robert Buchanan, whose early classical pieces were encouraged by the veteran Peacock, set up as a realist; John Todhunter became a poet when he deserted Hellenic for Celtic themes; Edward Carpenter, after *Narcissus* (1873), changed from a mythological to a social dreamer. Mrs. Tighe, Mrs. Hemans, and Mrs. Browning had successors in the increasing band of women, from the mild Jean Ingelow to such scholars as the strong-minded Augusta Webster and A. Mary F. Robinson; even George Eliot wrote a poem on Arion. And by this time romantic Hellenism had reached the British dominions. Ulysses and Polyxena arrived in Australia, to be rhymed with "kisses" and "Athena" by Adam Lindsay Gordon;[5] and Henry C. Kendall's *Leaves from Australian Forests* (1869) included a number of leaves from Boeotian woods. Canada was represented by an early volume of Sir Charles G. D. Roberts.

The writers who are taken in this chapter as representatives of all this mythological activity do not group themselves into a neat and coherent pattern. In manner they are all more or less decorative followers of Keats, Tennyson, and the Pre-Raphaelites. As regards substance and outlook, "textbook meaning," classification is difficult; it turns of course on their mythological poems, not on their work in general. First we may take some writers who in one way or another have a central relation to the conflict between Christianity and paganism. The second group begins with Rossetti and ends with Wilde, and, though the theme of conflict is not absent here, these poets represent art for art's sake. At the end we may put two men,

[5] See his *Podas Okus.*

one good and unpopular, the other bad and popular, who cannot be decisively linked with either group, that is, Lord De Tabley and Sir Lewis Morris.

II

In earlier generations, from the Coleridges senior and junior through Mrs. Browning and others, we encountered an hostility to myth based on such single or mixed motives as the supremacy of Christian truth and Christian infinities over Greek fables and finiteness, and the artistic and humanitarian claims of modern life and realism. All these contrasts continued to be felt and exploited by an increasing number of writers, sometimes as real personal problems, sometimes only as picturesque material.[6] After *Poems and Ballads* a new note became dominant, the conflict between Christian asceticism and Dionysian paganism. Whatever their degree of religiosity, most poets ranged themselves on the Christian side, usually with wistful backward glances at the vine-leaved and goat-footed gods. Both "father and son," one might say, contributed to Gosse's *Old and New* (1873), in which a vision of a Bacchic rout gives place to a vision of Christ and the cross and immortality;[7] in a number of later pieces, such as *May Morning*, the son alone celebrated "the antique world of wonder." Oscar Wilde's *Santa Decca* recorded his emergence from his brief phase of responsiveness to Catholicism; "Great Pan is dead, and Mary's son is King,"

6 For example, in *Philhellene* (1877) Ernest Myers turned back from a nostalgic eulogy of Greece to "our sad realities." His *Judgment of Prometheus* (1886), like the slightly earlier *Prometheus* of Bridges, ends with the hope of a new torchbearer for humanity who shall have a wisdom "wiser than Promethean." In "The Dumb Oracle," in Richard Garnett's volume of prose fantasies, *The Twilight of the Gods* (1888), Apollo himself points the young priest to "a more august service than Apollo's . . . the service of Humanity."

7 Cf. *Father and Son* (New York, 1908), pp. 276–77, 324. Gosse is noticed further in the third part of this chapter.

he wrote, but he hoped and felt that Pan was not dead. Even Alfred Austin's meditations on Apollo were disturbed by an ascetic black-robed priest and visions of torture.[8] Since we seem to have got away from poetry, it might save time to quote a suggestive bit of prose from a man who was deeply and frequently stirred by conflicting sympathies, John Addington Symonds. Once, walking about in the primitive Theocritean world near Mentone, half-expecting to encounter a Thyrsis or Daphne, he came upon a "Calvary set on a solitary hillock":

Thus I stepped suddenly away from the outward pomp and bravery of nature to the inward aspirations, agonies, and martyrdoms of man — from Greek legends of the past to the real Christian present — and I remembered that an illimitable prospect has been opened to the world, that in spite of ourselves we must turn our eyes heavenward, inward, to the infinite unseen beyond us and within our souls. Nothing can take us back to Phoebus or to Pan. Nothing can again identify us with the simple natural earth.[9]

Such feelings inspired many pages of Symonds' over-rich prose and verse; though his conception of the Renaissance is no longer satisfying, he would have been happier if he had lived among the Renaissance pagans he described. For the classical statement of the theme we turn to a greater writer than Symonds. Set La Gioconda, said Pater, "beside one of those white Greek goddesses or beautiful women of antiquity, and how would they be troubled by this beauty, into which the soul with all its maladies has passed!" Pater's reactions to the whole question of paganism and Christianity were equally serious, subtle, and elusive, and the compromise that he achieved

---

[8] *At Delphi* (1881), in *At the Gate of the Convent* (1885).
[9] *Sketches in Italy and Greece* (1874), p. 7. Cf. *Studies of the Greek Poets* (1873–76), I, 241–42, 318, 419–23, etc. See Van Wyck Brooks, *John Addington Symonds* (1914), especially pp. 18 ff., 96 ff., 215.

was hardly possible for less sensitively discriminating temperaments, as the writings of his disciples soon made clear. His faculty for reading himself into every period and person he touched led to his languidly beautiful perversions of Plato and Sparta, imperial Rome and the Renaissance. He was Hippolytus and Dionysus and Marius and Pico (and, as some have thought, the husband of La Gioconda), and all this had been to him but as the sound of lyres and flutes, and lives only in the delicacy with which it has molded the changing lineaments. . . . Pater's imagination had even freer scope in such avowedly romantic fantasies as "Denys l'Auxerrois" (1886) and "Apollo in Picardy" (1893). Starting from Heine's picture of the gods in exile, which had made a deep impression upon him, Pater mingled scholarship and poetic fancy in setting the Greek gods against a medieval and Christian background and translating their myths and attributes into medieval terms.[10] As for the whole body of his writings on classical themes, the reader hot for certainties might have been puzzled to know whether he was being initiated into the ritual of Christ or Apollo; on leaving the temple, however, he would have been in no doubt that he was in the garden of Epicurus, not Gethsemane.

But we must consider a few poets who represent various reactions to the problem. James Thomson (1834–82) contributed two quasi-mythological parables, *Life's Hebe* and *The Naked Goddess*.[11] Both are anti-ascetic pleas for a full, bold and natural enjoyment of life, but in the vein of Blake rather than of Victorian neo-pagans. Civilized men will not drink of Hebe's cup unless they adulterate it, and then they grow faint and sluggish; the poet alone unhesitatingly drains the pure nectar, and the cup fills again.

[10] See John S. Harrison, "Pater, Heine, and the Old Gods of Greece," *P.M.L.A.*, XXXIX (1924), 655–86.

[11] They were written in 1866–67 and published with *The City of Dreadful Night* (1880). See *Poetical Works*, ed. Bertram Dobell (1895), I, 218, 241.

The second poem is more picturesque and dramatic than merely allegorical, and has besides a dash of humor. The naked goddess, Nature, surrounded by beasts wild and tame, is confronted by a crowd of townspeople. A priest and a sage lecture and exhort her, but she refuses to wear the cramping robe of either a nun or a philosopher; she welcomes only the two children who, with instincts unspoiled, wish to stay with her and her animals. Thomson returned to the theme in a prose essay, "Great Christ Is Dead!" (1875), in which, starting with Plutarch's famous tale, he cited such friends of Pan as Swinburne, Leopardi, Schiller, and Heine.[12] The conclusion is that, as Christianity had killed the pagan mythology, so modern science has killed the Christian. The essay has about it something of the gritty rationalism of its age. Finally, in the *Proem* written just before his death, the man who had seen grim specters in the streets of London turns wistfully from a bleak scientific world stripped naked of mythological dreams to the bright beauty and joyous youthfulness of antique fables.[13]

Roden Noel (1834–94) had a very different kind of life from Thomson's, and a very different message. Perhaps the best approach is through his essay "On the Poetic Interpretation of Nature."[14] In the eighteenth century materialism had changed love into a sensation and man into a handful of dust, and had emptied the universe of ancient awe. Then came "Prophet-Poets, as very ministers of Heaven," to point men "to the World-Soul, commanding them once more to veil their faces before the swift subtle splendour of Universal Life." "I believe that Rousseau, Wordsworth, Byron, Shelley, Keats, Coleridge, were verily

---

[12] *Satires and Profanities* (1884), pp. 105–09. For Thomson's two versions of Heine's *Gods of Greece*, and his rendering of Goethe's Promethean monologue, see *Works*, I, 341–49, 357.   [13] *Works*, II, 61–63.

[14] *Essays on Poetry and Poets* (1886). The main ideas are repeated in the various essays on the romantic poets and Whitman.

prophets, to whom a new revelation was entrusted." This faith in a "Universal Life" that rolls through all things had been rolling through the nineteenth century — it had been a fairly heady stream in the eighteenth — and it rolls, somewhat turbidly, through Noel's poems. But with all his "enthusiasm" Noel differs from most of his spiritual ancestors in at least two major articles; his passionate gospel of nature is bound up with a passionate Christianity, and he has a post-Darwinian consciousness of the cruelty of nature.

Most of Noel's mythological verse expounds his vehement but cloudy mysticism. His second volume (1868) contained a long and involved poem on Mencheres (otherwise Mycerinus), which he had written in ignorance of Arnold's much shorter and finer piece.[15] Mencheres, though he has failed, has a vision of "a kinglier Man" than himself who will arise with a more dauntless faith, a diviner hope. It is by the wrong and suffering and failure of many individuals that "The dread World-Soul in darkness doth mature" its immeasurable ends. *Pan*, in the same volume, has nothing mythological but the title, with its traditional allegorical implications; the poem is a rhapsodic hymn to Being, "the whole harmonic scale of things" that the poet loves, from reptiles, birds, and beasts up to "the Son of Man." *Ganymede*, however, is a sensuous mythological idyll. One is prepared for the rich color of the nature-painting, but not perhaps for the luxuriant, indeed oppressively effeminate, description of Ganymede's bodily beauty. The details are a fault of taste, but the delight in "fair fleshly loveliness" is part of the poet's creed. Body and soul, he says in *Pan*, are indivisible; all comeliness of color and of form is the "Mere side reverse of spiritual grace." Noel shared this faith, as well as cosmic intoxi-

---

[15] The conclusion was evidently written with a knowledge of Arnold's *A Last Word*. See the *Collected Poems*, ed. Victoria Buxton (1902), p. 71.

cation, with the Whitman he admired. The same creed doubtless warrants the lusciousness of *The Water-Nymph and the Boy* (1872), which, though based on a German legend, is parallel to Ovid's tale of Salmacis and Hermaphroditus, and in manner is somewhat more Ovidian than Victorian.

Of the many high-souled Victorian attempts to interpret human life with Goethean comprehensiveness, Noel's *A Modern Faust* (1888) was one of the most earnest. Only a small part of this vision of a pilgrimage concerns us. Grief for the death of a child and the sufferings of ill-used children drive the hero to doubts of the goodness of God. (We may remember that personal sorrow inspired Noel's best volume, *A Little Child's Monument*.) He seeks distraction in the pleasures of sense, a phase set forth in the second canto of the third book, "The Flesh — Triumph of Bacchus." In a palace of sensual luxury the hero witnesses a "masque of Beauty" led by Dionysus (who is another Ganymede), and receives the ministrations of a ravishing damsel. Even in the concrete description of her the poet can hardly control his imagery and syntax. The preceding canto, founded on "cases dealt with by the excellent Society for the Prevention of Cruelty to Children," is one of many passages which show the author's capacity for genuine if over-wrought realism, but he knew less of human sensuality and this account of the flesh remains decorative mythology. The hero is warned against the bondage of sense, but he wishes to reconcile sense and spirit, and here Noel's exuberant and exalted pantheism finds utterance. A choir sings an ode on Pan, in reply to Schiller and Mrs. Browning. The poem is partly sensuous, in its mythological evocation of the myriad life of nature, partly mystical in its endeavor to harmonize a higher paganism with Christian faith.[16] As for the rest of the long work, Noel's

[16] See the author's note, *Poems*, pp. 504–05. Cf. *Essays*, pp. 8, 156–57, 167–68.

ultimate solution is found in a Christian religion of humanity. Through human service and human suffering the spirit of God and the World-Idea lead onward and upward. "From chaos ever nobler order grows."

Katherine Bradley (1846–1914) and Edith Cooper (1862–1913) are related to the theme of paganism and Christianity because, outwardly if not really, they began on one side and ended on the other. The first volume published under the name of "Michael Field," *Callïrrhoë: Fair Rosamund* (1884), seems to have had more success than later ones. Apparently interest in the new poet lapsed when he proved to be not only not a man but two women.[17] In spite of Michael Field's considerable if not compelling talents, a public indifferent toward drama in verse could not digest twenty-seven tragedies, a masque, and eight volumes of lyrics.

According to ancient story,[18] Coresus, a priest of Dionysus, loved Callirrhoë, and, when rejected by her, invoked a curse upon the city; the oracle declared that she must die unless a substitute could be found; when Coresus was about to slay the victim, he stabbed himself instead, and she, overcome by pity and shame, took her life. In dramatizing the story Michael Field followed, not the popular Greek mode, but the Elizabethan, even to the use of prose for realistic and humorous scenes; Elizabethan too is the crowd of minor figures, many of whom are killed

---

[17] The first joint production was *Bellerophôn* (1881), by "Arran and Isla Leigh." This volume was wholly mythological; it comprised a drama of a hundred and thirty pages and some eleven short pieces. Since I found the British Museum copy uncut (I did not leave it so), and since Michael Field, like the public, was content to forget the work, it is perhaps enough to say that the diffuse and incoherent drama is a tragedy of frustrated idealism. The authors acknowledge a large debt to Ruskin's *Queen of the Air*. Miss Bradley, by the way, was an ardent lover of Greek, but her niece "could not be coaxed on" in that subject, though she fully shared in the mythological collaboration. See Mary Sturgeon, *Michael Field* (1922), p. 18.

[18] Pausanias, VII. xxi. 1–5. For Landor's narrative versions see his *Poems*, ed. Wheeler, II, 330, 395. Landor's 1859 text was reprinted in 1876.

off by the plague. The two main motives of the play, the glorification of enthusiasm and of self-sacrificing love, express the authors' deepest instincts. Coresus pleads both for his own love and for the god who came to bring more abundant life: "We must be fools; all art is ecstasy." Callirrhoë has the desire to surrender to love and Dionysus, but she is a too timid and "apathetic slave of commonplace." Only after Coresus has given his life for hers does she realize that she has always loved him, and now she can "die his Maenad." Next to the hero and heroine the chief person is Machaon, the humorous skeptic, whose ultimate conversion to the worship of Dionysus is quite out of character but essential to the authors' thesis; the scene in which Machaon questions the young faun who is trying to outdance his shadow is a piece of irony somewhere between *We Are Seven* and *Peter Pan*.[19] Such a Dionysian drama, as Browning kindly put it, "recalls, to its disadvantage in certain respects, the wonderful *Bacchae* of Euripides." It recalls still more Pater's "Study of Dionysus" (1876).[20] But the authors' faith in enthusiasm was not derivative. They combined Victorian propriety of conduct with an ecstatic response to life and all the beauty and color of nature and art. Even their later devotional poems, as Mary Sturgeon has said, "have often the audacity and abandon of the worshipper of the vine-god. The poet is Maenad still."[21] Nor was their belief in "Love with its halo of self-sacrifice" merely a Victorian inheritance, but, as their lives were to show, a fundamental and passionate conviction. In spite of all their "pagan"

[19] This scene was the work of Edith Cooper; see *Works and Days: From the Journal of Michael Field*, ed. T. and D. C. Sturge Moore (1933), p. 3.

[20] For Browning's comments see *Works and Days*, pp. 2-3. Edith Cooper replied that her aunt "was the enthusiastic student of the *Bacchae*." She thought their respective shares in the "mosaic-work" were "almost even."

"Wouldn't one give much to surprise the Bacchant in Walter Pater!" Edith exclaimed after hearing a lecture (*Works and Days*, p. 120).

[21] P. 64.

qualities it would not have been difficult to prophesy that the authors of *Callirrhoë* would ultimately substitute Christ for Dionysus. There was evolution but no conflict. Both aunt and niece became Roman Catholics in 1907, and their latest writings were wholly and intensely religious. In the preceding thirty years they had been, as the elder said of herself in 1889, "Christian, pagan, pantheist, and other things the name of which I do not know."[22]

But I have already sinned against the canonical orthodoxy of the *Cambridge History of English Literature*, which assesses the bulky achievement of Michael Field in three sentences, and I can only mention the ambitious drama on the story of Lucrece, *Brutus Ultor* (1886), the pastoral masque *Noontide Branches* (1899), and the dozens of short mythological pieces; of these many were suggested by paintings. In *Long Ago* (1889) the authors yielded to the always dangerous temptation of embroidering Sapphic fragments; modern readers may not find in the volume the faultless flow, classic concision, and realist passion that Meredith found.[23] Our total impression of Michael Field's poetry is that it had more facility than economy and concentration.

III

Dante Gabriel Rossetti (1828–82), who combined the purest doctrine of art for art's sake with the mercenary hardness of a Philistine dealer, whose mystical conception of love rose, to borrow Donne's phrase, like a lily out of red earth, who was, rather than the English and noisily self-conscious Swinburne, the real high-priest of Victorian neo-paganism, undeniably had an untidy greatness about

[22] Sturgeon, p. 47. A good share of Miss Bradley's *The New Minnesinger* (1875) had been religious.

[23] *Works and Days*, p. 66. Mr. Sturge Moore has made generous claims for Michael Field's lyrics in his *Selection from the Poems of Michael Field* (1923).

him. That, however, does not prevent our finding it almost as difficult nowadays to read much of his poetry as art critics do to look at his paintings. His work in both kinds seems to belong too much to "literature," and, while we feel the power of great lines, in the end we are stifled and thirsty for reality. Rossetti's medieval and pseudo-medieval interests left little room for classical themes, but there are the ballad *Troy Town*, several sonnets in *The House of Life* (*Venus Victrix, Death's Songsters, Hero's Lamp*),[24] and some of the sonnets for pictures, such as *Pandora* and the two on Cassandra. The classical pieces were composed between 1865 and 1877, most of them in and about 1869. "The only classical poet," said Rossetti's brother, "whom he took to in any degree worth speaking of was Homer, the Odyssey considerably more than the Iliad,"[25] and in his few mythological poems two Homeric themes recur, the story of Troy and the story of the sirens.

The Helen of *Troy Town* is as yet untroubled, and the poet is equally untroubled in the creation of what one is expected to call pure plastic beauty. The pagan rapture of the senses rises here to no mystical heights, and there is no hint of transiency or decay. *Troy Town* has been much praised, and not merely by Swinburne; the author himself at one time pronounced it his "best thing."[26] But Rossetti shows in it a talent possessed by many smaller men of his time for making myths pretty, and not in the

[24] Sonnets xxxiii, lxxxvii, lxxxviii; see *Collected Works*, ed. W. M. Rossetti (1886), I, 193, 220–21. For comments see *The House of Life*, ed. Paull F. Baum (Harvard University Press, 1928). Mr. Baum observes (p. 201) that a penciled note in the MS. of *Hero's Lamp* refers to Burton's *Anatomy*; see Bohn's Popular Library ed., III, 248.

[25] *Works*, ed. W. M. Rossetti (1886), I, xxvi; *Works*, ed. W. M. Rossetti (1911), pp. xxiii ff. As a boy Rossetti did pen-and-ink illustrations of the *Iliad* for his sister Maria. Some of these, along with the classical paintings and drawings of his maturity, are reproduced in H. C. Marillier, *Dante Gabriel Rossetti* (1899).

[26] *Dante Gabriel Rossetti: His Family Letters*, ed. W. M. Rossetti (1895), II, 220.

fresh Elizabethan way. The simple theme of Helen's offering Venus a cup molded from her breast is overlaid with an embroidery of decadent literary and erotic conceits.[27] While the Helen of the ballad is happily sensual in her consciousness of physical beauty, the Helen of *Death's Songsters* is a symbol of fatality. Rossetti describes two occasions when Ulysses overcame temptation which would have ended in death; he kept his comrades silent when Helen sang outside the wooden horse, and he took his ship past the sirens. After these clear mythological pictures the sonnet ends with two lines of that labored rhetorical subtlety to which the author was increasingly addicted:

> Say, soul, — are songs of Death no heaven to thee,
> Nor shames her lip the cheek of Victory?

Whether he is thinking of life or poetry or both, it is not clear if he is rebuking himself for resisting or for being tempted by thoughts of death and seductive beauty.[28]

In his later poems and paintings Rossetti was more and more obsessed by the evil of beauty and the beauty of evil. One to whom the sonnets for pictures seem rather strained program notes may ease his conscience by mentioning Swinburne's rhapsody on *Pandora*.[29] The siren with her "imperial trouble of beauty" and "fatal face" has, in Rossetti alone, a variety of names and settings, in pieces about Lilith and her non-classical sisters, and in *The Wine of Circe, Aspecta Medusa, Venus Verticordia, A Sea-Spell,* and *Astarte Syriaca*.[30] Finally, in the elaborate prose text

---

[27] As the story appears in Pliny's *Natural History* (xxxiii. 81), the offering is made to Minerva. James Thursfield wrote to Rossetti in 1869 that he had been unable to trace the legend beyond Pliny or to find any mention of it in Greek authors (R. L. Mégroz, *Dante Gabriel Rossetti*, 1928, pp. 189-90). I have had no better fortune.

[28] See Baum, p. 200; Mégroz, p. 313; W. M. Rossetti, *Dante Gabriel Rossetti as Designer and Writer* (1889), pp. 247-48.

[29] *Essays and Studies* (1875), p. 90 (and pp. 375 ff.).

[30] *Works* (1886), I, 350, 357, 360-61. After "writing the sonnet [on Venus],

for a lyrical tragedy, *The Doom of the Sirens*, a Christian prince succumbs to the witcheries of Ligeia; later his son achieves a spiritual victory over the same beautiful enemy, but at the cost of physical death.[31] If Rossetti's preoccupation with the fatal woman seems only another chapter of decadent literary history, we may remember that in his own tragic experience life came close to imitating art.

We may turn from the swarthy Bohemian artist to the very English and respectable Richard Watson Dixon (1833–1900). While some of his contemporaries took the path to Rome, and his Oxford friends Morris and Burne-Jones abandoned holy for artistic orders, Dixon spent a long life as an unappreciated clergyman. His verse was largely unappreciated too, though it won praise from Rossetti and his fellows and from Bridges and Hopkins. Morris became a "pagan" mythological poet, and Hopkins condemned mythology and almost renounced poetry, but Dixon as an Anglican cleric had no trouble in reconciling Christ and Apollo. His present reputation, such as it is, owes little to his mythological poems, but two or three of them have some distinction; of course they reflect Pre-Raphaelite modes. *Proserpine*, which appeared in *Christ's Company* (1861), is mainly pictorial, though not in the conventional Keatsian way; Demeter, a figure of gold and silver, is set against a murky background of underworld rites streaked with fire and blood. *The Birth of Apollo* and *Orpheus*, in *Historical Odes* (1864), are poems of ideas. In the former a reminiscence of Oceanus' speech on progress in *Hyperion* illustrates Dixon's tendency toward uncouth or prosaic baldness; in *Orpheus* the metaphysical impulse, which gives vibrant overtones to his best odes and lyrics,

---

or rather christening the picture," Rossetti learned of the statement in Lempriere that "Verticordia" was one of Venus' titles "because she could turn the hearts of women to cultivate chastity." It was "awkward" that the picture did not suggest this particular attribute (*Family Letters*, II, 211).

[31] *Works*, I, 431 ff. Cf. *The Orchard Pit*, I, 377 ff., 427 ff.

is somewhat clogged, and the poem contains some of the most completely Chapmanesque lines to be found outside of Chapman. In these early pieces Dixon has something to say which may not be very lucid or important but gives a lumpy backbone to his work. *Cephalus and Procris*, *Apollo Pythius*, and the Theocritean *Polyphemus* (1884), are more idyllic and decorative than philosophical, yet some of the pictures have enough imaginative and stylistic energy to make an impression. Hopkins praised *Cephalus and Procris* and *Ulysses and Calypso* (1887).[32] In the latter Calypso offers Ulysses immortality and the untroubled joys of the gods, but he prefers a mortal lot with its human trials and human rewards. Such lines as these, if far from Homer, are not so far from Blake:

> That so, the world around,
>   Might death seem fair and gay:
> Jocund the tiger's bound,
>   Merry his bleeding prey.

A similar condensed clarity of suggestion animates the lyric *Mercury to Prometheus*.

Other writers of Pre-Raphaelite affiliations one would like to mention, such as Thomas Gordon Hake, whose *Birth of Venus* (1876) was praised by Rossetti, but there is room for only one. Mr. B. Ifor Evans, possibly the only living person besides myself who has read Eugene Lee-Hamilton's *Apollo and Marsyas* (1884), has pointed out its individual and un-Victorian quality.[33] The rôles given to the musical contestants may be described in Nietzschean terms as Apollonian and Dionysian. The god sings of noble deeds and everyday toil, of harvesters, women weaving, sailors singing at sea, a procession moving to a temple,

---

[32] *Correspondence of Gerard Manley Hopkins and Richard Watson Dixon*, ed. C. C. Abbott (Oxford University Press, 1935), pp. 49, 68, 143.

[33] *English Poetry in the Later Nineteenth Century* (1933), p. 368.

and the scenes he evokes are bathed in golden light. Marsyas loves all that is dark and mysterious and fearful, wild glens and woods and caves, the cries of lynxes and the screams of eagles, the echoes of his own flute, which "ape the voice of some wild wounded beast" or wail "Like souls in Hades wailing unreleased." He delights in thunder and howling winds, he feels the air full of grabbing hands and evil fancies. The poet reveals his Victorianism by unnecessarily underlining his intention in an introductory piece. The contest symbolizes the strife "That fills all Art, all Nature and all Life." Man's heart is alternately wooed "By Nature's carol or by Nature's sigh"; he responds to the "charm of bright serenity and mirth," and no less to the "charm of vague desire" and passion and shapes of fear. The author loves both lords but he half admits the stronger spell of Marsyas.[34]

Austin Dobson, Sir Edmund Gosse, and Andrew Lang are linked together not only by their cultivation of French verse forms but by their interest in classical themes. Dobson, the most finished artist of the group, was the least happy in his mythological excursions. The sometimes Horatian master of *vers de société* should have remembered Horace's *nec ... conamur, tenues grandia*, and not have strayed so far beyond the bounds of the Louvre and St. James's. A number of Gosse's shorter mythological pieces, however, are among his best, such as the sonnet in dialogue, *Alcyone*, which has a reticent dignity, if not quite deserving of Swinburne's breathless encomiums.[35] Most of his mythological verse may be described as English tea

[34] See Wilde's reference, near the end of *The Burden of Itys* (1881), to Marsyas' "troubled songs of pain," and, in *The Decay of Lying*, to Marsyas, not Apollo, as "the singer of life" (*Works*, Authorized Edition, Boston [1910], III, 45).

[35] *Letters of Algernon Charles Swinburne*, ed. Gosse and Wise, II, 40, 44. A number of long classical pieces were omitted, not unwisely, from Gosse's *Collected Poems* (1911).

just laced with Swinburnian brandy. In the quiet and respectable man of books ancient Greece seems to have inspired mainly a literary longing for Dionysus and his crew, for the old divine madness instead of petrifying knowledge and the niceties of art; a desire to escape from the "foolish world, too sadly wise," to the "ancient, innocent ecstasies" of Theocritean Sicily.[36] But, at least in his later years, Gosse would never have forsaken Mayfair for Maenalus. His *Hypolympia or the Gods in the Island* (1901), a long ironic fantasy mostly in prose, is rather too *fin-de-siècle* in manner to be a very serious vindication of life as it is. The Greek deities, driven from Olympus, took refuge in a northern island inhabited by Lutherans whose ways were not Hellenic; they even worshiped a God crowned with thorns. Many of the gods find a new happiness in exchanging the complete satisfactions of eternity and heaven for the vicissitudes, imperfections, and struggles of mortal life, although, on the report that the usurper of Olympus has fallen, they are all glad to go back; they leave behind them the Hope for which they have no further need. Thus the "moral" is a light variation on a stock romantic theme; the mythological fancy is in the tradition of Peacock, Heine, and Pater.[37]

Whatever may be thought of Andrew Lang's verse — and he himself came to think very little of it — he performed dashing service on behalf of myth and Homer. A young anthropological David, he laid low the Goliath of etymological and solar myths, Max Müller; and he fought stoutly for the unity of Homer, though he did not live to

---

[36] See *Impression, Theocritus: For A. Lang's Translation, The Maenad's Grave, Greece and England, The Praise of Dionysus, The Tomb of Sophocles*, etc. *Old and New* was mentioned at the beginning of the second section of this chapter.

[37] One might mention a similar though much more serious volume of the same year, Mr. H. W. Nevinson's *The Plea of Pan*, in which myths were the vehicle for characteristic expositions of the author's social creed. One piece, "The Fire of Prometheus," is in *The Bibelot*, XV (1909), 139–78.

see the final disintegration of the disintegrators. The Homeric translations in which he had a large share might be less disparaged nowadays if the privilege of sniffing were asserted only by people versed in the original. His verse, though voluminous, was mainly the by-product of a busy life, and his gay mind and melancholy soul found perhaps their most durable expression in familiar and elegiac pieces. The numerous classical poems, including his one ambitious work, *Helen of Troy*, have not worn well; indeed the first reception of *Helen* seems to have been a disappointment which threw Lang back on smaller and lighter themes.

There is room here for nothing but *Helen* and the sonnet on the *Odyssey*, though I might mention *Hesperothen* (1872), a lyrical and allegorical watering-down of *Ulysses*, *The Lotos-Eaters*, and *The Palace of Art*. The verse is of the vaguely mellifluous kind that everyone could write at the time, and the most interesting thing about the poem is that a number of its stanzas are quite indistinguishable from those of Lang's later piece, *The New Orpheus to his Eurydice*, a burlesque specimen of the way "We twanged the melancholy lyre ... When first we heard Rossetti sing." The sonnet *The Odyssey* (1879), after pleasing the uncritical for many years, has been damned of late by several persons. Housman took it as a sample of the "stale and faded prettiness" of nineteenth-century poetic diction. Mr. F. R. Leavis, after pointing out the presence of Swinburne, Morris, Tennyson, Arnold, and Keats, concludes that "it is the music of the languid hours that predominates in the sonnet."[38] Although Mr. Leavis is a critic who frequently

[38] *New Bearings in English Poetry* (1932), pp. 11–12; A. E. Housman, *The Name and Nature of Poetry* (Cambridge University Press, 1933), p. 22, note. Miss Sitwell's evidence for Lang's plagiarisms is, rather oddly, very close to Mr. Leavis's (*Aspects of Modern Poetry*, 1934, p. 74).

As an interesting parallel to the imagery of the sonnet I might quote a sentence from a letter of Edward Dowden's of 1872: "Altogether after Rossetti, one feels a longing for blown sea-breezes in verse, and sea-smells to restore vigour,

makes disagreement a pleasure, he seems to be right. Some allowance must be made for the author's legitimate intention, the conscious reproduction of the languors he is condemning, but that point could be urged with more confidence if this were Lang's only questionable poem; certainly one does wish for a more heroic evocation of Homer in contrast to the little bards with their low lutes of love. Perhaps one may find more of what Homer meant to him in such a sonnet as *Colonel Burnaby*.

Lang's chief model in *Helen of Troy* (1882) was William Morris. He is less sensuous and dreamy, but the fluent smoothness and lucidity, the strain of romantic melancholy, the whole scale of values and the tapestry effect, are much closer to Morris than to Homer and Quintus Smyrnaeus. The archaistic language is also akin to Morris's, and, especially in the Homeric passages, recalls Lang's prose translations. The story begins with the arrival of Paris at the court of Menelaus and ends with the return of Menelaus and Helen to Sparta. The fundamental defect is that the gallant champion of feminine and lost causes lets his chivalrous instincts run away with him. Whenever the tale seems about to provide an occasion for a display of character, for something more than costume romance, divine intervention endows Helen with a loss of memory. Lang preserves his heroine's innocence at the cost of her personality and, in consequence, at the cost of any substantial interest the poem might have had. Though he claimed some Homeric authority for the conception of Helen as an unwilling victim of the gods, his Helen is not the real woman of the *Iliad* — Homer's divine machinery does not destroy character — but a pale phantom, faultily faultless and not very splendidly null. Further, the adoption by a modern story-teller of a primitive simplicity

---

and the rough edges of rocks and salt on one's face seem the pleasanter" (*Fragments from Old Letters: E. D. to E. D. W.*, 1914, p. 28).

of outlook — not that Homer was either primitive or simple — almost automatically removes a work from the category of serious poetry. The fact that so devout, scholarly, and clear-eyed a lover of Homer as Lang was able in all good faith to commit such sins against the large candor and humane realism of Homeric art is a forcible illustration of what happens to Hellenism when it encounters romantic sentimentalism.[39] All this, however, is not to say that *Helen* does not make tolerable reading on a lazy afternoon, and Lang's interpretation of his heroine is perhaps no worse than the more modern habit of canonizing the prostitute with the heart of gold.

Oscar Wilde has been kept for the end of this section, and is given undeserved space, because his verse shows all the traditional elements of romantic Hellenism in all the refinement and purity of decadence, freed at last from any vulgar contact with life. He wrote of beauty, love and pain, religion, the religion of humanity, liberty, nature, pantheism and the cosmic soul, and of course mythology, all the themes consecrated by his predecessors from Keats and Shelley to Arnold and Swinburne. But, nursed in the hothouse of art, watered by two generations of English and French romanticism, what were only seeds (and not always unhealthy seeds) in Keats and Shelley have become frail languorous stalks drooping with exotic many-hued flowers. At moments they look like flowers of evil, until we see that they are only wax.

Wilde had traveled in Greece, he had attained higher academic distinction in classical learning than Arnold or

[39] Another variety of sentimentalism is illustrated in Gilbert's *Pygmalion and Galatea* (1871). The incomparable Victorian Aristophanes, who could mock so many sacrosanct things, has Pygmalion a wedded lover whose model for the statue is his wife. The statue comes to life, loves the sculptor, realizes that she is *de trop*, and turns voluntarily into marble again. This "sleek" contrivance moved Sir Ronald Ross to produce another version (Madras, 1883), but since, according to the author, no one ever bought a copy, I have not seen it. Cf. John Gawsworth, *Ten Contemporaries* (1932), p. 153.

Swinburne; he was a fortunate youth who, but for his blue china, might have seemed born to revive a somewhat anemic genre. But the *Poems* of 1881, far from being a manifesto and a challenge, were indeed a wax-work exhibition of mid-Victorian poetical modes. (The same year, by the way, yielded further evidence of the Irish instinct for decadence, George Moore's *Pagan Poems*, which included a sadistic dramatic sketch of Sappho.) In exploiting the conventions of his elder contemporaries Wilde showed his lack of originality and his genius for immediate success. "Nothing is so dangerous as being too modern," says Lady Markby in *An Ideal Husband*; "one is apt to grow old-fashioned quite suddenly." Wilde's themes, attitudes, and mannerisms were mainly Swinburnian, though the *élan* of Swinburne was subdued and softened by Arnoldian pastoralism. His innumerable borrowings were transferred rather than transformed, with an openness unrivaled except by Robert Lytton. Wilde rarely went beyond the poets of his own century, and, in spite of his classical lore, he echoed hardly any ancient but Theocritus. He was, moreover, not only Echo but Narcissus, for from the very beginning he continually repeated himself.[40]

The two rambling reveries, *The Garden of Eros* and *The Burden of Itys*, show that Wilde was far too thorough a Swinburnian to learn lessons of form and compression from the classics, though Swinburne cannot be blamed for his disciple's conceits. In the first the setting and the idea of a garden are derived from *The Scholar Gipsy* and *The Sensitive Plant*; the catalogue of flowers is a pretty *hortus siccus* gathered from Shelley, Arnold, Tennyson, Meredith, Wordsworth, and Shakespeare. The second part of the

[40] In a brief discussion of Wilde's verse one cannot do much more than draw upon the full researches of Bernhard Fehr, *Studien zu Oscar Wilde's Gedichten* (Berlin, 1918); I have preserved my self-respect by adding a few details. The poems are quoted from the edition of Robert Ross (*Works*, Authorized Edition, Boston [1910]).

poem is an address to the spirit of beauty and its votaries, Keats, Shelley, Swinburne, Morris, Rossetti, and Burne-Jones. In this age of clay the scientists have banished naiads and killed romance and wonder. These "new Actaeons" have spied on beauty (see *Adonais*), have analyzed the rainbow (see *Lamia*), and he, Oscar, "the last Endymion," alone gazes at the moon without a telescope. The eulogy of Swinburne is a reminder that the mood of religious sensibility expressed in *Rosa Mystica* was brief, though simultaneous publication of old and new made the volume of 1881 a queer medley. Swinburne has "sung the Galilaean's requiem" and restored the worship of Venus and "the Ancient Gods." Henceforth Christ and Christian symbols are only picturesque properties which set off the self-conscious paganism of a Greek born out of his time — until, in the late and sober pages of *De Profundis*, Christ is rehabilitated as the inaugurator of the romantic movement. It is rather confusing to turn from *The Garden of Eros* to *The Burden of Itys*, but one can always tell which poem one is reading by glancing at the title. Here also the old gods of Greece, old shapes of beauty, are contrasted with "the Gorgon eyes of Truth" and "The wan white face of that deserted Christ." Arnold's Oxford poems, along with *Philomela*, provide the setting and some details, the Maenad and the Bassarid carry a familiar trademark, and the pipe of Pan is Mrs. Browning's musical instrument. Wilde praises "the wondrous boy" who heard

> The horn of Atalanta faintly blown
> Across the Cumnor hills,

and we must grant that not everyone could, in ten words, recall Swinburne, Tennyson, and Arnold.

Charmides, being a narrative, has some sort of form. Lucian had told, in his *Erotes*, how a youth concealed himself in a temple for a night in order to gratify his passion

for a statue of Aphrodite, and how his profane violence
was punished. By expansion and alteration Wilde turned
the anecdote into a luxuriant mythological romance. His
admiration for *Laodamia* did not affect his own moral,
which is simply the glory of beauty and youthful physical
passion. The dryad who longs to be rid of "this pallid
chastity" is Gautier's Rosalinde in a Theocritean setting.[41]
Dr. Fehr pronounces the style thoroughly Keatsian, but I
think Wilde's chief model was William Morris.[42] There is
the usual quota of reminiscences from Arnold and others.

Such an embalmer of romantic themes could not escape
the fatal woman. In *The New Helen* the beautiful enchantress has the lineaments of Swinburne's Venus, Pater's
La Gioconda, and Lillie Langtry. But Wilde's chief contribution to the romantic agony was *The Sphinx* (published
in 1894). The poem could not well be less than a masterpiece of English decadent verse, since it was compounded
from *La tentation de saint Antoine*, *A rebours*, Baudelaire,
and Gautier. From a young man's love for the statue of a
goddess it was no great step to the erotic memories of the
half-animal sphinx. The decorative sensuousness is no
longer warm, soft, and English, but, thanks especially to
Flaubert, is lacquered and exotic. Such a panorama of
pagan splendors and horrors and colossal lusts can easily
topple over into the ridiculous, as we see sometimes in
Flaubert and very often in that sensual-sentimental Hel-

---

[41] The dryad's falling in love with a drowned youth recalls, among other
things, the *Hero and Leander* of Thomas Hood, a poet Wilde had some knowledge
of (Fehr, p. 145). One or two phrases in the account of Venus may have come
from the last stanza of *Venus and Adonis* (Fehr, pp. 145–46).

[42] Besides the general tone there are perhaps specific debts. A number of
details about the temple remind us of the temple scene in *Atalanta's Race*. The
business of Athena's appearance on Charmides' ship includes a detail or two from
Theocritus' *Hylas*, but seems to resemble the conclusion of Morris's episode of
Hylas (*Jason*, iv. 663 ff.). Charmides' leaping into the sea suggests Butes (*Jason*,
xiv. 442 ff.); both young men, in different ways, attract the beneficent sympathy
of Venus. Cf. also Charmides' "I come" and Marlowe's *Hero and Leander*,
ii. 154.

lenist, Pierre Louys; Wilde's strange beasts and gimcracks and sadistic visions hardly arouse the authentic shudder. Again, by the way, we have the wan Christ mourning for lost souls, since neo-paganism, in England at least, needs the ultimate refinement of a sense of sin.[43]

The bulk of Wilde's verse is oddly naïve in comparison with his brittle, sophisticated prose — though the critic's Paterian patches are very like the verse — and his mythological formula is a thin sentimental nostalgia, prettily dressed, and garlanded with purple flowers of passion. The wine of nineteenth-century Hellenism has lost all its body, and only a stale bouquet remains. Slavish imitation of Swinburne and others might incur the Platonic charge of being at least two removes from truth, but the poet would doubtless appeal to a higher authority and cite his own dictum that "all bad poetry springs from genuine feeling." His Lord Henry Wotton wished to write a novel "as lovely as a Persian carpet, and as unreal," [44] and Wilde, like any poet who sets out to be simply "the creator of beautiful things," ends as the collector of bric-à-brac. His continual yearning for the vanished gods and the age of gold springs

[43] In some prose works and in *The Sphinx* and *Itys* (*Poems*, pp. 76–77, 251), Wilde alludes to Antinous, the slave of Hadrian. As Dr. Fehr points out (pp. 113, 211), he knew the tale in *A Nile Novel*, by "George Fleming" (II, 195 ff.; see also the allusion to the sphinx, I, 82), and probably had read Symonds' essay on Antinous in *Sketches and Studies in Italy* (1879). But Wilde's references strongly suggest a knowledge of Symonds' poem *The Lotos-Garland of Antinous* (*Many Moods*, 1878), in which, among other parallels, the red lotos is a recurrent motif. Symonds' poems, and much of his prose, anticipated Wilde's taste for luxuries and heavy-scented flowers, and one might mention his treatise on a phase of Greek life in which Wilde had a more notorious interest.

To return for a moment to *The Sphinx*, the blameless Gosse's sonnet *On a Lute Found in a Sarcophagus* (1873) is a briefer and less erotic treatment of a similar theme, and includes such a Wildean touch as "the bare Black breasts of carven Pasht."

[44] Possibly the desideratum was met by Beardsley's *Under the Hill*, an imitation of that product of intoxicated Renaissance paganism, the *Hypnerotomachia Poliphili*. See Praz, *The Romantic Agony*, p. 342, and my other volume, p. 77.

partly from his admiration of ancient Greece and partly from his dislike of Victorian England. Such mixed motives, as usual, create a Greece which is an ideal and idyllic home of art, beauty, liberty, blithe serenity, and occasional ecstasy with free-hearted nymphs. Though Wilde the critic can be wise as well as clever, and though he can cite Aristotle for his purpose, his prose furnishes no great corrective to the paradisal reveries of the verse. The tired hedonist completes the Corinthian temple of estheticism which Landor, Arnold, Swinburne and Pater helped to build.[45] He carries to the last extravagant gesture the Hellenic gospel of Arnold and Pater, and perverts both, especially the former, since he discards the Hebraic three-fourths of Arnold (and Ruskin) and the less obvious but indubitable moral seriousness of Pater. It must be admitted that Arnold laid himself open to perversion — "By the Ilissus there was no Wragg, poor thing!" ("no Higginbotham," says Wilde, misquoting a phrase Arnold should have left for him). At any rate the austere and esthetic young monks of Pater's Lacedaemon and the artists and dreamers of Wilde's Hellenic rhapsodies breathe the perfume of pomegranates, and never find their noses in indignation at the odor of Athenian garlic and sausage.

IV

John Byrne Leicester Warren (1835–95), who became Lord De Tabley in 1887, is a remarkable example of poetic industry accompanied by poetic growth, though his workmanship was uneven and undisciplined to the last. No one detected or could have detected promise of distinction in his first four volumes (1859–62), which included some

---

[45] The large and complex background of the esthetic movement must of course be taken for granted. See the bibliography for recent works by Rose F. Egan, Albert J. Farmer, and Louise Rosenblatt, and, for Pater's influence on Wilde, the studies by Eduard J. Bock, Ernst Bendz, and J. Mainsard.

thirty mythological poems and a long chronicle-drama, *The Threshold of Atrides*. "George F. Preston" was succeeded by a better poet, "William Lancaster," whose writings (1863–67) contained a number of classical and other pieces which were preserved in the *Collected Poems* (1903). The success first gained by *Philoctetes* (1866) was quickly blighted by *Orestes* (1867), and De Tabley relapsed into obscurity, to be discovered and praised, for a while, in the early nineties. His main development was along the Keats-Tennyson line, though his work was colored by Swinburne, the Pre-Raphaelites, and Browning.[46]

Without *Atalanta in Calydon*, which De Tabley reviewed in the first number of the *Fortnightly*,[47] *Philoctetes* might not have been written, but the author stood on his own feet, and Sophocles'. In both dramatic and metrical form he was more strictly classical than Swinburne, and probably owed more to Swinburne's fine blank verse than to his dithyrambic choruses. Obviously *Philoctetes* lacks the color and rush and sound of *Atalanta*, but it has a sober strength and dignity. The first part of the drama is taken up with Philoctetes' bitter complaints of his wrongs; while Sophocles' hero inveighs chiefly against his human enemies, De Tabley's denounces the malignant gods, especially, in Promethean fashion, the "new god," Zeus. Whatever the degree of Swinburnian influence there may have been, such ideas seem too persistent and sincere to be merely borrowed; besides, before the appearance of *Atalanta* De Tabley had embodied the essential conception of his drama in the brief monologue *Niobe*, where the mother arraigns the gods and, as a free human soul, scorns their

---

[46] De Tabley said himself that "Tennyson, in his highest classical flights, such as *Tithonus* and *Ulysses*, or in his best lyrics, such as *Maud*," appealed to him more "both in youth and in middle age, than any other modern poet" (Hugh Walker, *John B. Leicester Warren, Lord de Tabley*, 1903, p. 49).

[47] The enthusiastic reviewer was upset by Lewes' editorial alterations (Gosse, "Lord De Tabley," *Critical Kit-Kats*, New York, 1897, p. 175).

cruelty.[48] With all the complaints of divine injustice and malice, Philoctetes does not rest in paralyzing fatalism. Though "this whole universe is mad with pain," he proclaims his faith in human dignity and courage:

> Spirit of man, to whom these petty stings
> Of pain, that seem so utterly mighty now,
> Are but the vestments robing the pure ray
> Of thy nobility. O life of man
> Greatly afflicted and so great indeed
> In spite of thine afflictions. . . .

After an interlude with the maiden Aegle, who has nursed her wounded hero, the drama takes a Sophoclean turn with the arrival of Ulysses and Pyrrhus. De Tabley follows Sophocles in contrasting Ulysses' unscrupulous duplicity with the young man's rectitude, though the latter's moral struggle is not here made a central theme. When about to sail home with Pyrrhus, Philoctetes has a vision of Heracles, who enjoins him to go to Troy and — this is less Sophoclean — to forgive his enemies. In a noble farewell to the Lemnians he reasserts his faith in man's unconquerable mind, which no god can break. De Tabley feels his theme deeply, and the note of pagan fortitude rings true. While the drama does not need biographical props, his own harassed life — "I have failed in everything in which it is possible for a man to fail" [49] — may at least guarantee full imaginative sympathy and sincerity in the treatment of Philoctetes.

Orestes (which has no connection with the *Oresteia*) is more of a play and less of a dramatic poem than its predecessor, and it has been praised by Gosse as De Tabley's best

---

[48] *Eclogues and Monodramas* (1864), p. 96; *Collected Poems* (1903), p. 106. *Niobe* is closer in spirit to the drama than is the monologue *Philoctetes* (*Praeterita*, 1863; *Collected Poems*, p. 30).

For Philoctetes' account of the agonized Heracles' last hours, see Sophocles, *Philoctetes*, ll. 670, 801, 1130–32, *Trachiniae*, ll. 749 ff., 1046 ff.; Diodorus Siculus, iv. 38; Ovid, *Metam.* ix. 159 ff.; Hyginus, *Fab.* xxxvi.

[49] Walker, p. 36.

work, but action and intrigue, not always well motivated, are a poor compensation for noble simplicity and philosophic breadth. The young and good characters are too pallid, and the dominating mother and her lover are not at all magnificent in sin. Several choruses, by the way, are more Swinburnian than anything in *Philoctetes*:

> From the fire of the fountains of God,
> Swift art thou as thunder or death. . . .

More than thirty mythological poems, written over the period 1859–95, appear in De Tabley's *Collected Poems*; most of his early efforts he allowed to die, or rather to remain dead, though some were recast. His devotion to classic antiquity was as lifelong as his favorite Tennyson's, and was based on real scholarship. At the end of the fragment *Phaethon* (1893) the usually impersonal poet wishes, "in a huckster age," for the inspiration of Greece and the gods which the wise critics of the city of smoke "Sneer at as wrack and lumber of the tombs." He began, to pass by the voluminous apprentice work, with a series of monologues more or less in the vein of *Ulysses* and *Tithonus*; the reflective element was much larger than the sensuous and mythological. Unlike most poets, De Tabley as he grew older grew more luxuriant; what Gosse calls "the brocaded magnificence of his style" appears to have been partly nourished by increasing devotion to Milton. The descriptions of nature only too inevitable in Victorian mythological verse are not commonplace in him. An expert botanist as well as a disciple of decorative poets, he painted appearances with loving accuracy and vivid color, and he also communicated a sense of the rich and mysterious processes of life on "this daedal and delightful earth." "He is Faunus; he is a woodland creature!" said Tennyson.[50] I can give only two scraps, from Bridges' "carefully chosen"

[50] Gosse, p. 166.

quotations. One is about Pan haunting the blue cork-
woods and

> the bulrush pits,
> Where the hot oxen chin-deep soaking lie;
> Or in the mulberry orchard grass he sits
> With milky kex and marrowy hemlocks nigh.

The other and less Keatsian picture is of a giant tulip in
Circe's flowery abode,

> A flaunting bloom, naked and undivine,
> Rigid and bare,
> Gaunt as a tawny bond-girl born to shame,
> With freckled cheeks and splotched side serpentine,
> A gipsy among flowers. . . .[51]

Though Circe is a fatal woman in a sensual paradise of far-
fetched luxuries, De Tabley's paganism went deeper than
neo-pagan affectations. One can imagine an ancient reading, if not writing, *An Eleusinian Chant*, and the tersely
gorgeous hymns to Astarte and Aphrodite remind us of
Lucretius' apostrophe to Venus as the source of life.[52] In
calling the roll of Victorian pessimists we may forget
De Tabley, but he is not a mere echo. "God withers in his
place," and

> Locked in blind heaven aloof,
> The gods are grey and dead.
> Worn is the old world's woof,
> Weary the sun's bright head.[53]

We have met a good deal of paganism in the course of
this chapter, but the devil did not have all the tunes, and

---

[51] *Poems*, pp. 148, 280; Bridges, *Collected Essays Papers, &c.*, VI–VII (Oxford University Press, 1931), 238–41. The *Ode to Pan*, as it appeared in *Rehearsals* (1870), was somewhat altered from its first form as a chorus in *Philoctetes* (*Poems*, p. 176). It would take a page to record the permutations and combinations of various parts of *Circe*; the lines quoted were in *Poems Lyrical and Dramatic* (1893), p. 36.

[52] These three poems appeared in 1901, 1893, and 1895 respectively.

[53] *Hymn to Astarte*. Compare the conclusion of *The Children of the Gods* (1865) and *A Song of Despair* (1894), in *Poems*, pp. 351, 458.

Victorian England was never in any more danger of becoming Dionysian than of becoming Apollonian. The average reader was a Hebraist, and he abhorred verse so obscure that he had to pause at times to grasp the meaning; he liked the bread of moral truth to be simply wrapped and delivered at the door. We could have no better evidence of the strength of the mythological fashion than the fact that such a popular purveyor of hearty platitudes as Charles Mackay felt moved to write *Studies from the Antique* (1864). But a still greater and more genteel popularity was that of Sir Lewis Morris, the "Tennyson *des enfants*." The most arresting line in my copy of *The Epic of Hades* (first published in 1876–77) is "Fortieth Thousand." That alone justifies the reserving of Morris for a climactic conclusion. The three books of the epic deal with the shades in Tartarus and Hades, and with the gods. A "high and delicate aroma of purity," to quote an early review, sustains us in the underworld and suffocates us on Olympus. The framework, especially in the first book, recalls, if not Dante, at least the *Mirror for Magistrates*. Tantalus, Phaedra, and Sisyphus, now repentant, confess their evil deeds; Clytemnestra, unexpectedly and happily, is still unregenerate. All the tales have a combination of moral earnestness, misty idealism, diffuse clarity, and glossy prettiness, which explains why Morris slew his tens of thousands, including John Bright and the Bishop of Gloucester and Bristol. We may take leave of him with the kind verdict of Edith Cooper, the younger half of "Michael Field." She found him a good-hearted man, "depressed with his fatal popularity, almost rebellious at the power Tennyson has had over his mind. . . . He loves Keats (ah, poor Keats, nauseous in his disciples!), Milton and Tennyson . . . he is dimly conscious he belongs to darkness." [54]

[54] *Works and Days*, p. 113.

CHAPTER XIII

From the Nineties to the Present. I

THIS chapter is devoted to a group of poets whose work in general and particularly in the mythological category has more or less family resemblance, and is commonly classified, with favorable or unfavorable intent, as traditional, literary, and academic. The antique poems and dramas of Robert Bridges, Mr. Sturge Moore, Mr. Gordon Bottomley, Mr. Laurence Binyon, Mr. Lascelles Abercrombie, and Mr. R. C. Trevelyan, constitute a formidable as well as a dignified and impressive body of writing, and, if one is to avoid a mere catalogue, one must slight some in order to discuss others, whose work in our genre is greater in bulk or importance, at something like decent length. As a general text for their aims and the best of their achievement we might take some words of Mr. Binyon's:

That we are over-busy with the surface of life is no reason for poetry and art to reflect that fever and bustle; rather should they embody, passionately embody, the interior, the imaginative life. The spirit of art is against the spirit of the age. Perhaps it has always been so. . . . We express our own age by resisting it, by creating something which will outlast its fevers and its disillusions.[1]

I

Mr. Bottomley we have met already, in connection with Morris's *Scenes from the Fall of Troy*, and he is linked with the Pre-Raphaelites by the macabre strain so notable in

[1] *Tradition and Reaction in Modern Poetry*, English Association Pamphlet No. 63 (1926), p. 15.

his dramas — *Laodice and Danaë* is an exotic pattern of cruelty and pain — by the primitive, magical dream-world he inhabits, and by his love of picturesque detail and color. *Daphne* is a series of designs by Burne-Jones, or Ricketts or Shannon. But one of Mr. Bottomley's central qualities is less Pre-Raphaelite, his love of the rich pageantry of the seasons and the homely realities of rural life. *The Dairy-maids to Pan* is as English as the poet's other rustic lyrics; the heroine of the poem *Phillis* is no sophisticated Ovidian lover, but the princess of an English folk-tale who milks cows and wears woolsy and prepares gay dresses for the wedding that never takes place. Mr. Bottomley can treat myths in the grand manner, as in *Kassandra Prophesies* (1899), but he is more attractive and original in the bucolic vein.

Apart from the slight play *Memnon* (1930), Mr. Binyon's mythological pieces came early in his career, and they do not in general represent his best work. The long narrative *Penthesilea* (1905) is a skillfully contrived tapestry. The theme of the one-act tragedy *Paris and Helen* (1906) had been handled by Landor, Morris, and Tennyson, and Mr. Binyon's unoriginal version seems to have no cogent reason for existing. Among the *Odes* (1901) we have, however, a well-worn theme re-imagined, in *The Dryad*, with a cool sweetness of pictorial beauty and a touch of unwonted magic; and *The Bacchanal of Alexander*, if less glowing and resounding than Keats's Bacchic ode, is a processional which combines opulent color with lucid design and movement. But more important than these poems is *The Sirens* (1925), which is not mythological though it derives its title and unity from the Homeric episode. In this spacious ode the unearthly music of the sirens becomes the symbol of the questing and conquering spirit of man which has led him to explore the seas and the stars, to build monuments of steel and of thought. The poem is not another nineteenth-century hymn to progress, for the poet is too much beset by doubts and fears, is too conscious of the blindness as well as the vision of man; it would have been approved by Sophocles, though Sophocles might have made it shorter.

Two poems in Mr. Abercrombie's *Twelve Idyls* (1928) have some essential affinity with *The Sirens*. In *Zagreus* the voice of the tortured god who lies in hell imagining mankind is the voice of a philosophic poet who, contemplating the machines man has created and the quality of modern life, believes that the darkness will pass, as it has done before, and that the spirit of beauty and joy will be born again. *The Olympians* is a variation on the Apollonian and Dionysian theme. When the gods withered in the Christian era, Bacchus, the man who refused to be a god, began to fill men with the strength and vision they needed; the eddying pattern of the world was broken by unchanging energy. But, says Apollo, though Bacchus will continue to lure men on with dreams of infinity, in time they will again perceive and desire the beauty of established order and new gods of shapeliness will arise to conquer eternal flux. This idealistic latter half of the poem might be called a modern *Hyperion*, but it is somewhat too abstract and mythological to make a deep impression; what we remember are the weird imaginings of the opening narrative.

Mr. Abercrombie's "tragicomedy," *Phoenix* (1923), is a very different sort of thing. The characters might almost have modern names, since their feelings and motives are more modern and theatrical than Homeric.[2] The queen resents her husband's infatuation with the amiable harlot Rhodope. The king's passion is not merely that of an old sensualist, it is a rebirth of romance; but Rhodope dislikes his sexual ardor and is bored by his romantic idealism.

---

[2] See *Il.* ix. 437 ff., and Apollodorus, *Lib.*, ed. Frazer, II, 74–75.

The prince, whose manliness and innocence bring him dangerously close to the public-school hero, is used by his mother to lure Rhodope from his father; he falls in love and worships the spotless virgin with a youthful idealism as extravagant as Amyntor's. When he discovers her relation to his father, and when both father and son discover that she has gravitated easily into the arms of the palace soldiers, whose love-making she understands, they feel that their lives are poisoned. Thus *Phoenix* is as far from the usual antique drama in substance as it is in form and manner. Shorn of some unrealities and especially of comedy, it might have been a cruel and moving thing; as it is, Rhodope is the most credible character, and the play, though skillfully composed, is neither fish nor flesh.

In a long series of mythological works Mr. R. C. Trevelyan has displayed virtues not quite compelling enough to make reading an experience as well as a scholarly pleasure. One personal poem I find harder to forget than any of the classical pieces, a wistful lament for having spent a poetic life in re-bottling old wines "While in rich clusters the living vintage was awaiting" a more adventurous hand.[3] Such a conviction of wasted effort, of estrangement from human realities, is not insignificant in a thoughtful literary poet who has outlived the apparent security of his youth and finds himself in a chaotic world, and most authors of the moment would applaud it; but possibly a stronger poet, for whom myths had been less an end than a means, would not have had occasion to feel regrets.

These paragraphs on some distinguished traditionalists hardly even approach the main body of their work but must serve to place them in our landscape. A fuller discussion is needed in the case of two poets who have made much more use of mythological subjects than most of the others, Robert Bridges and Mr. Sturge Moore.

[3] *Epistola ad A. W.* (*Rimeless Numbers*, 1932).

II. Robert Bridges (1844-1930)

Bridges' narrative *Eros and Psyche* and the four mythological dramas are perhaps generally regarded, like Tennyson's *Idylls*, as the sometimes beautiful mistakes of a born lyrist, and the multitude who bought but did not read *The Testament of Beauty* are not likely to discover the long poems written a generation and more ago. Yet these everywhere reveal the poet's special quality, and their defects as well as their virtues illustrate his attitude toward art and life. The scholarly traditionalist, the technical experimenter and contriver of subtle rhythms, the singer of love and joy and beauty, they are all here.

Eros and Psyche, first published in 1885, was revised in 1894; the original twelve "measures," containing three hundred and sixty-five stanzas, were named after the months of the year. Apart from countless verbal improvements, a number of the changes indicate somewhat less concern with mere narrative and more with philosophic interpolations. The first version lacked the faults, and the unforgettable felicities, of *Endymion*, because Bridges' artistry and taste were mature, and because his gospel of beauty was a quiet familiar possession rather than a new revelation. Keats thought, wisely enough, that further work on *Endymion* would be unprofitable; the minute revision of *Eros and Psyche* would not have been carried out by a less scrupulous artist than Bridges, or by a more inspired poet.

He described the work as "in all essentials a faithful translation of Apuleius' story," [4] but there are modifica-

---

[4] *Poetical Works* (1898-1905), I, 290. In a note in the 1885 volume Bridges said that he had never read any English version of Apuleius. He also acknowledged that he had borrowed plumes from Homer, Pindar, Plato, Moschus, Callimachus, the *Greek Anthology*, Lucian, Lucretius, Virgil, Dante, Petrarch, Botticelli, Titian, Raphael, Spenser, Wyatt, Shakespeare, and others.

I have used the one-volume edition (Oxford University Press, 1914), which is cited as *Works*.

tions on almost every page; since this section is not a thesis I can only indicate something of their general character. The Hellenizing of the story hardly goes beyond the substitution of Greek names for Latin ones. Bridges' choice of Crete instead of Apuleius' unlocalized setting permits allusions to Cretan places and myths, such as the unnecessary bronze giant Talos,[5] and a gorgeous sunset is composed of "the phenomena which followed the great eruption of Krakatoa."[6] As we should expect, the poet frequently and beautifully works in the natural background, sometimes for its own sake, sometimes, as in the account of the sacrificial procession, to heighten the pictorial vividness of the action. More obtrusive, though not often disagreeably so, are the incidental allusions to mythology. Spenser may have been the chief model, but Bridges' usual brevity is more Ovidian than Spenserian. The paintings on the walls of Psyche's room, which show "Love's victories over the gods renown'd," recall the more luscious pictures of "Cupids warres" in the house of Busyrane.[7] The descriptions of Eros, Pan, Hera, Aphrodite's chariot, and Hermes are elaborately pictorial passages for which Apuleius gives only hints.[8] The catalogue of the melodious

---

[5] *April*, 13–14. Not all of Bridges' details about Talos appear in the standard accounts: Apollodorus, I. ix. 26; Apollonius Rhodius, iv. 1638–88; Scholiast on *Odyssey*, xx. 302. Bridges places in Crete the contest between the Muses and the Sirens (*September*, 1–4; Pausanias, IX. xxxiv. 3).

[6] *March*, 24–26. See *Poetical Works*, I, 290; *Letters of Gerard Manley Hopkins to Robert Bridges*, ed. C. C. Abbott (Oxford University Press, 1935), p. 202.

[7] *May*, 18–20; *F.Q.*, III. xi. 29 ff. Such mythological decorations are merely suggested in Apuleius (v. 1). Bridges quotes (*February*, 27) a line from Spenser "in homage to his account of 'Cupid and Psyche' in the Fairy Queen" (*Eros and Psyche*, 1885, p. 157; *F.Q.*, III. vi. 50).

[8] *March*, 16–17 (see Moschus' first idyll); *August*, 12–14; *October*, 23–25; *November*, 5–6, 10–12. The second description of Eros (*July*, 20–22) is derived from Apuleius' own purple patch (v. 22), though Apuleius gives no warrant for Bridges' impression of the love-god's weaknesses. Hera receives three partly Homeric stanzas in place of Apuleius' *cum totius sui numinis augusta dignitate* (vi. 4; see *Iliad*, xiv. 178 ff.). Bridges remarks (ed. 1885, p. 157) that "the addi-

names of the sea-nymphs, which comes from Homer, attracted Bridges as much as Spenser.[9] Such ornamentations, if mostly pleasant in themselves, do not help to preserve the serious import of the story.

A number of elements contribute to the effect of sophisticated unsophistication. There is, as in William Morris, the general process of idealizing and refining, the softening of some harsh motives and circumstances of the original, the "gentler characterization of Psyche." Bridges does not rationalize the supernatural — the speaking tower remains a speaking tower — and he even introduces marvels on his own account.[10] A bit of science is less in harmony with the spirit of a fairy-tale; the younger sister's fall from the cliff inspires a definition of the law of gravity and accelerated motion.[11] In addition to mythological lists in the Elizabethan fashion we have a series of half-Elizabethan "sentences" on the power of love, and even an acrostic on Purcell.[12] Such things, along with the archaisms of diction, carry the suspicion of preciousness, of studied quaintness. *Eros and Psyche* has been called "if not the best, . . . the most beautiful narrative poem in the language,"[13] and Bridges' coolness, restraint, human feeling and delicate purity of style wear better than the dreamy sweetness and sensuousness of Morris. Yet, as the stanzas glide by in their ordered beauty, we may wish here also for the robust, racy spontaneity of Adlington's prose or Marmion's slipshod verse.

---

tion made to Homer's description of Hera's dress is an orientalism of the present writer."

[9] *March*, 27–28; *Il.* xviii. 39 ff.; *F.Q.*, IV. xi. 48 ff. Spenser's list comes from a Latin version of Hesiod, as Mrs. J. W. Bennett showed; see my other volume, p. 89, note 4. The roll-call of deities at Psyche's wedding (*February*, 17–20) is expanded from Apuleius. In Psyche's prayer to Hera (*October*, 20–22), Bridges omits the numerous ritualistic allusions of the original (vi. 4).

[10] See *December*, 14–16, 31; Apuleius, vi. 12–13, 15.

[11] *August*, 27.   [12] *March*, 18–19; *May*, 15.

[13] F. Brett Young, *Robert Bridges* (1914), pp. 196–97.

For a modern poet, however perfect his structure and style, cannot afford to be content with story-telling of deliberate simplicity. As Hopkins wrote to Bridges: "The story you have not elevated but confined yourself to making it please. Eros is little more than a winged Masher, but Psyche is a success, a sweet little 'body,' rather than 'soul.'" [14] We go back again and again to *Endymion* mainly because Keats was struggling to utter the faith that was in him. Bridges, to be sure, has his faith also, and it has been said that he devised his framework of months and days because he wished the symbolic implications of the story to be deeply pondered.[15] Although a formal scheme which invites, and rather often necessitates, padding may appear a dubious means to that end, still the symbolic implications are at times made explicit, in a manner highly characteristic of the poet. Beauty is the native food of man's desire "And doth to good our varying world control." Psyche's beauty purges passion of its earthly soil. She is more beautiful than Aphrodite because — here speaks the nineteenth-century romantic — she carries the immortal question in a mortal face, "The vague desire whereunto man is born." [16] And that Hedonè or Joy, the daughter of Eros and Psyche, means more in Bridges than the *Voluptas* of Apuleius we know, but we know it less from this poem than from his others. Thus while the few hints of a parable, including the grave benediction of the "envoy," add something to the story, they do not make a compelling reinterpretation of it. Hence the tenth reading of the poem yields no deeper pleasure than the first.

Professor Sidgwick of Cambridge is reported to have entertained "sincere but cold respect" for Bridges' dramas;

---

[14] *Letters*, p. 206.

[15] *T.L.S.*, May 1, 1930, p. 357.

[16] *March*, 6; *April*, 1, 4. Most of the lines in *April*, 1–7, the chief philosophic gloss in the poem, were added or rewritten in 1894.

"He would have been proud to be able to write them; but
he does not care so much about reading them." [17] Some
critics would endorse the whole of that statement, the majority perhaps only the latter half. Although Bridges
intended all his plays, except *Nero*, for the stage,[18] it is impossible to consider as acting dramas works so defective in
stagecraft and characterization. There remains "the
poetry," and, for those who do not like the frequently
Elizabethan idiom of the blank verse, there are the choral
lyrics, of which a number are worthy of the greatest modern lyrical poet. There is also the philosophy, which sometimes grows out of the fable and sometimes is grafted upon
it; in any case the dramas gave a fairly full presentation of
their author's view of the world long before *The Testament
of Beauty* was written.

All four of the mythological dramas have a prologue and
chorus, but only *Prometheus the Firegiver* (1883) approaches at all closely the Greek manner, and it, as "a
mask," has very little dramatic realism or conflict or suspense. Zeus is the tyrannical "new god" of *Prometheus
Bound*, who, having failed to destroy the human race, is
resolved to keep it on the level of brutes by withholding
fire. Prometheus brings the fire he has stolen from heaven
to the man best fitted to receive the momentous gift,
Inachus, the beneficent ruler of Argos. Prometheus' task
is to rouse Inachus from his too submissive piety toward
the god who is thwarting human development. The spirit
of man is not to be cowed by circumstance, it "wooeth
beauty," even though earth holds many things "Unblest
and fallen from beauty"; it is characteristic of the poet
that his definitions of good and evil involve such terms and
ideas. Man, Prometheus insists, has more power for good

---

[17] *Works and Days: From the Journal of Michael Field*, ed. T. and D. C.
Sturge Moore, p. 128.

[18] *Poetical Works*, III (1901), 262.

than Zeus for ill, and when man's mind is in firm accord
with eternal laws he should not deny his best reason and
instincts. Inachus is ready to accept fire and face the
wrath of Zeus. Prometheus expands his "vision fair of
Greece inhabited" with something of Shelleyan idealism
but with a more temperate conception of progress.[19] The
second part of the drama hardly maintains the large nobility of the first. Argeia, the wife of Inachus, fears the consequences of impiety, and rehearses with picturesque detail
the fates of some eight or nine mythological sinners, an
Alexandrian recital which reduces a high argument to the
dimensions of a prize poem. Argeia's objections are very
quickly overcome, and she joins her husband in his wish to
know the future. After a prelude on the greatness of man's
aspirations, which foreknowledge cannot subdue, Prometheus reveals the fate of Inachus' daughter, Io. Three
pages are given to the tale of her future wanderings, and
Prometheus does not seem to be describing torment but
mapping out a tour. In Aeschylus the geographical catalogue, which contains only a third of Bridges' place names,
is defensible or explicable on various grounds;[20] here one
can only wonder about the authenticity of the poetic impulse which can be diverted into such arid pseudo-classicism. To return to the plot, Inachus is still resolute, and
Prometheus kindles the pile of wood. Amid the excitement
he vanishes, after scoring out the name of Zeus on the altar
and substituting his own, and Inachus gladly acknowledges the primacy of the benefactor of man.

Of the choruses some are dramatic and decorative, some
less dramatic and more philosophical. The first two cere-
monial odes in honor of Zeus and Hera are admirably cool

[19] *Works* (1914), p. 25. Cf. *Prometheus Unbound*, III. iii. 40–62.
[20] *Prometheus Bound*, ll. 707 ff., 790 ff. Cf. *Suppl.*, ll. 540 ff. Bridges' list
seems to be compiled, with the aid of a map, from Pausanias or Strabo or
both.

and lucid mythological lyrics.[21] The ode on the spirit of wonder which concludes the first part of the drama is a beautiful and entirely modern utterance. Prometheus' prophetic picture of Io coming upon himself nailed to the rocks inspires an ode, also modern in feeling, on the miserable lot of man.[22] Even in treating the conception of self-sacrifice the poet finds no strength but the thought of duty, "Nor any solace but the love of beauty." The linking of such motives is of course fundamental in *The Testament of Beauty*. The drama ends, like the first book of the *Testament*, with a transition from Hellas to Judaea. The identity of the mythological being who was to arise and overthrow Zeus had already been foreshadowed by Prometheus, and the final odes return to that theme. The new deity is to rule in mercy and truth and love and peace.[23]

While Bridges avoided direct competition with his great predecessors, he reminds us at times of both Goethe and Shelley, and the theme of idealistic striving bears some resemblance to Calderon's *La Estatua de Prometeo*.[24] Bridges

---

[21] For details about Rhea and the birth of Zeus, see Hesiod, *Theog.*, ll. 468 ff.; Callimachus, *Hymns*, i. 42 ff.; Apollodorus, *Lib.* I. i. 5–7 (and Frazer's notes); Diodorus Siculus, v. 65; Ovid, *Fasti*, iv. 207 ff.; Scholia on Apollonius Rhodius, i. 1129 (*Apollonii Argonautica*, ed. R. Merkel and H. Keil, Leipzig, 1854). For the names of the Idaean Dactyls (Bridges, p. 10, ll. 254 ff.), see Hesiod (Loeb Classical Library), p. 76; Apollonius Rhodius, i. 1126, 1129, and the Scholia on these lines. Bridges has "Kermis" for the usual "Kelmis"; see Pauly-Wissowa, "Daktyloi." For the story of the golden apples given to Hera, see the Scholia on Apollonius, iv. 1396; Hyginus, *Poet. Astron.* ii. 3; Servius on *Aen.* iv. 484. Bridges' Hestia does not seem to be in the usual ancient lists of the Hesperides, but she appears in some old texts of Apollodorus, such as that of Heyne (Göttingen, 1803), p. 193; cf. Frazer, I, 220, textual note 3.

[22] The "far-off cry" that Io will hear (p. 37) was perhaps suggested by the great passage in Apollonius Rhodius (ii. 1247 ff.).

[23] Bridges' "For if there be love in heaven with evil to cope" (p. 46) suggests Spenser's "And is there care in heaven?" (*F.Q.*, II. viii. 1). See also Bridges, pp. 28–29, ll. 859 ff.

[24] While Bridges indicates his knowledge of other dramas of Calderon, he does not, I think, mention this one anywhere. Like Goethe, Calderon employs Epimetheus, Pandora, and Minerva, but the former deals with Prometheus' creation of human beings, the latter with the theft of fire, which is knowledge.

could not, presumably, have equaled them, but he could have made a finer drama than he did if he had been sufficiently possessed by his subject to follow them in completely reinterpreting it. As it is, he vacillates uncertainly between philosophic modernization and studious reproduction of the antique, and the symbolic parable appears intermittently among bits of flawless writing which are not alive. Except Prometheus — and he is not always an exception — the characters remain too merely mythological; even the fire stolen from heaven is a little too much in the nature of chemical combustion. Further, the action, though chiefly mental, is too simple for the implications of the theme. Still, with all its shortcomings, *Prometheus* is, as an extended and massive lyric, a beautiful performance. Bridges' idealism is not spurious or extravagant, and his exalted purity of tone does more than anything else to show that his faith in beauty and in good is a living faith.

The other three dramas must be noticed more briefly. *The Return of Ulysses* (1890) is the longest and, to me, the least attractive, though it has been praised by Mr. Yeats as "one of the most beautiful and, as I think, dramatic of modern plays." [25] In the main Bridges follows Homer closely, and loses the Homeric qualities without much gain in dramatic concentration; if the piece is impracticable for the stage, it makes small claim, since we have the *Odyssey*, upon the reader. While there is some refining of sentiment and atmosphere — Ulysses knows that imagination "hath a grasp of joy" finer than sense — the chief virtue of the other dramas, the infusion of the poet's meditative love of beauty, is almost entirely lacking here.

There is no such lack in the graceful heroic pastoral, *Achilles in Scyros* (1890). Bridges evidently consulted Statius, but altered the plot as well as the epic atmos-

---

[25] "The Theatre," *Ideas of Good and Evil* (*Essays*, New York, 1924, pp. 206, 244 ff.). For Hopkins' adverse opinion see *Letters*, pp. 216–18.

phere. [26] The dramatic possibilities of the chief incident, Achilles' unwitting revelation of his sex, are nullified by Ulysses' previous explanation of his plan, and the element of surprise is transferred to the love story. Deidamia cherishes an innocent friendship for Pyrrha-Achilles, whose sex is disclosed to her by Thetis only near the end; up till then they might be a pair of Shakespearean girl friends, with un-Shakespearean warmth of sentiment in place of realism and humor. An Elizabethan feature which is not altogether happy, even in a largely decorative scheme, is the appearance of Ulysses as an elderly Autolycus warbling of his wares. We have again a touch of pedantry in the catalogue of Greek ships at Aulis. [27] But neither Elizabethan nor antique elements detract much from the general effect of idyllic refinement and modern sensibility. Lycomedes is only at moments a king of the Homeric world. He recognizes the fighting instinct as natural, but

[26] See the *Achilleid*, i. 207 ff., and, for various details, Hyginus, *Fab.* xcvi; Ovid, *Metam.* xiii. 162 ff.; *Achilles in Scyro*, in the *Imagines* of Philostratus (*Philostratorum et Callistrati Opera*, ed. A. Westermann, Paris, 1849, p. 398; Philostratus, *Imagines*, etc., Loeb Classical Library, pp. 287 ff.); the fragmentary idyll of Bion; and Lempriere. The pastoral matter is Bridges' own, but may have been partly suggested by the festivals in Statius and by Calderon's *El Monstruo de los Jardines* (Bridges, *Poetical Works*, III, 263). The story of Achilles and Deidamia, by the way, has been treated in Mr. Edward Shanks' *The Island of Youth* (1921).

A word may be added about Bridges' *The Isle of Achilles* (*From the Greek*), which appeared among the new poems in the *Poetical Works*, II (1899); see *Works* (1914), pp. 359–62. It seems to be in the main an amplified version of the prose of Philostratus, *Heroicus*, xx. 32–40 (pp. 313–16 in the *Opera* cited just above). Some details are altered, perhaps from Pausanias, III. xix. 11–13. See Frazer's note in his edition of Apollodorus, II, 216–17. A more literal version of Philostratus, *Achilles' Island*, appeared in Sebastian Evans' *In the Studio* (1875).

My distress over the number and length of these footnotes was somewhat relieved when a learned journal rejected this discussion of Bridges as not scholarly enough.

[27] The fine passage which follows the catalogue was preferred by Henry Bradley to its original in Calderon's *Principe Constante*; see Bridges' *Poetical Works*, III, 204–05, 264, and *Three Friends* (Oxford University Press, 1932), pp. 178–79.

wonders if in time man may not throw off the baser passions. The perfecting of ourselves is our noblest task, and
it can be best achieved through meditation amid the quiet
beauties of nature — as at Yattendon or Boar's Hill. And
Hector has nothing to fear from the Achilles who has assured his love that it is not idleness to steep the soul in
nature's beauty; rather it is idle to let beauteous things go
by unperceived. The purest distillation of Bridges is the
lovely choral song of the gladness of earth in spring; man
works along with his Maker, who has set a beautiful end
before the world, and sorrow, disease, war, all the evils of
life, are only the shavings thrown off from His tools.[28]

In *Demeter* (1905) Bridges owed a general debt to *Comus*,
and a more specific debt to the Homeric *Hymn to Demeter*.[29]
In its main themes this "mask," like *Prometheus*, anticipates the doctrines more philosophically expounded in
The Testament of Beauty. Demeter, who in the beginning
was hostile to Zeus and man, learned to feel human sympathy; in nursing the infant Demophoön she nursed all
mortal nature. In the language of the *Testament*, she developed from Selfhood to Motherhood. Persephone also
undergoes a spiritual evolution. At first she is a happy,
unthinking child of nature, full of innocent joy in earth
and resentful of the larger and sadder wisdom of Athena.
But when she rejoins her mother after her sojourn below,
her spirit has been purged with salt and fire. She now
knows that the origin of all things is good, and the end
good, and that what appears as evil is as a film of dust
which may be brushed away. If *Demeter*, though it touches
major themes, is not major poetry, the reason is not merely
that decoration envelops and softens ideas, but that the

---

[28] Compare, for example, *The Growth of Love*, Sonnet 16.
[29] I cannot catalogue particular items from the *Hymn* or from other sources.
The names of the places Demeter visited in her search seem to be most closely
approximated in Ovid, *Fasti*, iv. 467 ff.; cf. *Metam.* v. 409 ff.

ideas are sentiments not proved on our pulses. The poet's intellect, temperament, and happy circumstances, if they did not disqualify him for grappling with the problems of good and evil, at any rate over-simplified those problems. If we pass by the youthful *Comus*, Milton's faith in reason, divine and human, was won in a long struggle, and victory was never entirely secure. Bridges' Reason is a name for the serene idealism and optimistic monism of a sequestered, untroubled student and lover of nature which satisfied him more completely than it may satisfy the less fortunate.

On the other hand we have a way of confusing the real defects of such a poet as Bridges with our own hasty or fashionable prejudices. He has suffered unduly from critics who, accustomed to "gross and violent stimulants," worship only demonic genius, regard a work of art as cold unless it boils over, and find the proof of inspiration in disorder. (Henry James, the Bridges of modern fiction, has suffered in the same way.) Bridges is academic and traditional in the good as well as the bad sense. When an artist does not deal with raw experience it may be that he has weakly recoiled from it; but it may be also that he has gone beyond it. Bridges' "classical gravity of speech," to quote Mr. Yeats again,

which does not, like Shakespeare's verse, desire the vivacity of common life, purifies and subdues all passion into lyrical and meditative ecstasies. . . . Had Mr. Bridges been a true Shakesperian, the pomp and glory of the world would have drowned that subtle voice that speaks amid our heterogeneous lives of a life lived in obedience to a lonely and distinguished ideal.

III. T. STURGE MOORE (1870–1944)

Of twentieth-century poets who have written in English Mr. Sturge Moore unquestionably stands first on our particular bead-roll, and his place in any general rank-list would be, or ought to be, high. While his preoccupation with antique subjects, classical and biblical, is an obvious mark of his traditional centrality, neither his imagination nor his manner is like that of anyone else. The peculiar quality, even more than the bulk, of his plays, long poems, and lyrics on mythological themes, forbids the full analysis which work of such fine integrity, meditative power, and technical accomplishment deserves. It cannot be said, so far as my reading goes, that many critics of Mr. Moore's volumes from 1899 to 1933 have penetrated very far within the august temple he has built, and a mere historian cannot hope to do more than indicate the existence of dimly illuminated vistas.[30]

Mr. Moore has expressly avowed his appreciation of the inexhaustible opportunities for poetry in the richly suggestive symbolism of ever-living myths; he has also deprecated attempts to confine a myth to one meaning or to "freeze" it with explanations — a warning the commentator has to disobey.[31] Mr. Moore's poems, especially the later ones, are tantalizing in their hints of things unsaid; indeed at times one could do with fewer threads of intangible and tangential suggestion than he provides. In the course of his long career there has been some general evolution, from pictorial richness and relative thinness of thought to stylistic and philosophic density, but even that statement must be qualified. At any rate, while his poetic creed has gained in breadth and depth, it has not altered, it has steadily ripened from within. Of the works which can be described here, some early ones may be said to be born of the senses and imagination, while in many later

[30] There are exceptions of course, but dozens of reviewers throughout the period of Mr. Moore's productivity have been content with rather casual comments on purely stylistic or peripheral matters. Two of the plays are well discussed in Miss Priscilla Thouless' *Modern Poetic Drama* (Oxford, 1934).

[31] *Poems*, Collected Edition (1931–33), IV, 72. Cf. *Armour for Aphrodite* (1929), pp. 160–61.

ones the tone is predominantly ethical and even metaphysical. But such categories are only a matter of emphasis, for Mr. Moore's poetic faith is a unity in which the
several elements are blended. Though his philosophy cannot be detached and neatly summarized, his idealism may
be said to rest on four pillars, beauty, good, love, and joy,
and the foundation is a courageous belief in the wholeness
and oneness of life. Mr. Moore is not, however, another
Bridges; his poetic thought is more subtle and oracular.
His creed is not a novel one, but it is not borrowed; it is the
integrated personal vision of a deeply meditative artist.
His "Platonic" gospel of beauty does not require a radiant
dream-world remote from ours, a nostalgic compensation
for ours; it grows out of close contact with this earth, and,
to mix metaphors, it is a steady beam of light in a modern
soul conscious of the vast darkness of the unknown. But
consideration of Mr. Moore's philosophy may wait until
we come to the plays, in which it is most fully embodied.

In such a sketch as this one must pass by a great deal,
in particular the multitude of short poems and lyrics,
which seem to be largely unknown to our multitude of
anthologists, and which range from the most richly sensuous to the most pregnantly thoughtful. One that has
achieved something like fame must be mentioned, the
Lines on Titian's 'Bacchanal' in the Prado at Madrid
(1904). Mr. Moore has been a loyal admirer of "Michael
Field," but none of Michael Field's poems on pictures
approaches this in controlled wealth of description and
largeness of imaginative suggestion. And I must pass by
that luminous golden mist called *Danaë*, a series of Pre-
Raphaelite paintings of ideal virginal beauty and awakening love, for the more masculine fancy, the more robust
outdoor invention, of the dramatic dialogues, *The Centaur's Booty* and *The Rout of the Amazons* (1903). In the
former the characters are two centaurs, the last of their

race. The younger, Medon, is a lover of women and beauty, while old Pholus has always despised and feared such weaknesses; but his iron heart is captured by the lusty baby boy Medon has carried off from a village, and the two centaurs gallop away with joy in the thought of their renewed life and strength. In the other piece we see, through the eyes of a faun, the ruthless slaughter of the Amazons when they invaded Attica. These poems are not conventional versions of conventional myths but virtually original tales involving the wilder and more primitive figures of the Greek imagination. They show a myth-making faculty very rare in modern poetry, and a good deal of the natural magic which Arnold over-praised in Maurice de Guérin.[32] Mr. Moore's borderland beings are re-created not so much by allusive scholarship but as living denizens of their world of nature, which the poet conceives with both the imaginative and the physical eye. He has always been a maker of pictures, and they always remind us that he is a practitioner of graphic art.

Further, the descriptions of the coming of the Amazon army, and of the wounded and the dead, are memorable not only for their beauty of design and detail but for their symbolic value. While the poet fills and satisfies the eye he is adumbrating a part of his fundamental creed. Even the half-barbaric faun cannot understand how men, whose lives are so brief and whose dulling senses do not renew themselves with the spring, can knowingly destroy such beauty, piercing and crushing those strangely lovely bodies. (A similar theme is touched, less richly but with a similar mixture of realism and unearthly suggestion, in *The Gazelles*; elegant aristocratic hunters destroy the shy, timid animals and "the meaningless beauty of their lives,"

[32] Mr. Moore published in 1899 a translation of *Le Centaure* and *La Bacchante*; if his own poem owes anything to the former piece, the debt is rather general than specific. See also Mr. Moore's prose poem *Blind Thamyris*.

a beauty "Unseizable, fugitive, half discerned.") Mr. Moore might have started from a page in "Hippolytus Veiled" where Pater comments on the destruction of innocent and lovely things which accompanies civilization and progress: "Centaur and Amazon, as we see them in the fine art of Greece, represent the regret of Athenians themselves for something that could never be brought to life again, and have their pathos." The poet may too have taken suggestions from Rubens' painting *The Battle of the Amazons*, and from Gautier's *Le Thermodon*, a poem not unlike his own, though shorter and less beautiful, of which the moral is: "Toujours l'esprit le cède à la force brutale." [33]

Perhaps the best key to the philosophy of the dramas is to be found in some passages of *The Powers of the Air* (1920). In this classic dialogue, when Plato is inclined to despair of ultimate truth in an unreal world of matter, Socrates accuses poets and artists of focusing their attention on sensible things. Their beauty is real, not a copy, yet it is not weeds moving in a stream or leaves in the wind which are themselves divine, "it is the flow which bends them . . . ; their movement is only an occasional index to a greater, purer, freer life." [34] A little later Socrates resorts to myth. Uranos once hesitated between the two goddesses, Ge and Nemesis. The former offered the beauty of actuality, clear and tangible but subject to change, and this as a living memory would become a part, though only a part, of the unalterable beauty of Nemesis which creates a permanent ecstasy. Uranos "gave vows to the bodiless Nemesis, and dallied none the less with the fair, substantial Ge." At last, distracted by the universe Ge created,

[33] Pater, *Greek Studies* (ed. 1910), p. 161; Edward Dillon, *Rubens* (1909) Plate CIV; *Choix de poésies de Théophile Gautier* (Paris, 1927), pp. 133–39. Mr. Moore would have got little help from classical sources, such as Plutarch (*Theseus*, xxvii) and Diodorus Siculus (iv. 28). Pausanias mentions a number of works of art which depicted the battle; see Frazer's index.

[34] *Poems*, IV, 319–20. Cf. Mr. Moore's *Correggio* (1906), p. 239.

he sought refuge with the immaterial goddess, and she brought forth the spiritual faculties which sift the material jumble, consistency, disinterested intelligence, intuition, divination and perception. So too the mature artist must turn his back on Ge, and, "treasuring a vivid memory of her beauty, set his heart on the unattainable Nemesis." [35]

Mr. Moore's ethics are esthetic and his esthetic is ethical, as indeed his use of Nemesis instead of Aphrodite Urania may suggest. Nemesis is not only a suprasensuous idea of immaterial, eternal beauty, she is also the idea of perfect responsibility, of experience enlarged "on the side of purpose and daring, not on that of logic and abstraction." The soul is tried by situations which evoke responsibility, and the strong soul goes forward; it is by the vigor of Nemesis that "the spirit both tests itself and all other things and dissipates inertia and ignorance as to its goal." After explaining that men need the ambiguity of a divine image, which suggests more than can be stated clearly, Socrates says that Nemesis is "'fire-white' because no gaze can focus the full implications of complete responsibility"; she is "'twin sister of Aphrodite' because this unseen perfection commands with even more authority than beauty seen"; she is "terrible" because she requires the uttermost loyalty; and she is "beneficent" because defeat is itself inspiration and proof that we have conceptions beyond our present grasp.[36]

All of Mr. Moore's mythological dramas depict souls caught in a crisis which brings out the strength or the weakness of their loyalty to Nemesis. For such a purpose mythological (and biblical) themes are peculiarly fitted, since they favor the isolation of essential things, and, having acquired traditional outlines, they make a familiar

[35] Poems, IV, 327–29. See, for example, Plato's Symposium, 210–11; Phaedo, 83; Phaedrus, 247.
[36] Poems, IV, 330–31. Cf. Mr. Moore's Correggio (1906), pp. 91–92.

and substantial basis for the author's inventions and implications. These implications are sometimes so riddling and oracular that one hazards guesses at their precise "meaning" with more trepidation than confidence, and with a memory of the author's remark about the freezing effect of explanations. An additional difficulty is that many generalized gnomic passages have no inevitable dramatic relevance but would be equally apposite in plays other than those they appear in. The mere bulk of Mr. Moore's work necessitates very summary treatment of most of it, and while the extracting of a series of bald morals has the effect of turning a highly imaginative and sensuous poet into a preacher, there seems to be no other way of indicating his ethical seriousness and consistency.

The title *Aphrodite against Artemis* announces a Euripidean conception of the rival goddesses, or impulses, fighting for possession of human souls, but in the course of the action the power of these divine agencies is hardly felt.[37] There are hints, however, of the author's special symbolism. Artemis is the goddess not merely of chastity but of responsibility, who seeks "To win mankind from bondage to what is." And Phaedra, a creature of the senses, of the here and now, exclaims in the bitterness of her repulse that Hippolytus may have a goddess then, "Nemesis fire-white purging even him." But the author's philosophic reinterpretation is thinner here than in his later plays, and his mythological invention is less active; he challenges Eurip-

---

[37] The text in the collected edition (vol. II) is an improvement, as a whole and in details, upon the first version of 1901. The play was staged in 1906.

Mr. Moore seems to have taken some hints from the *Phèdre*. As in Racine (and Swinburne's short dialogue), Phaedra pleads with Hippolytus for his love and at last commands him to kill her with his sword. Initial prominence is given to another Racinian motive, a false report of Theseus' death; in the 1901 version this came in late and awkwardly. The allusion to Aricia at the end of the early text (made vague in revision) may have been suggested by her place in the *Phèdre* and by the theme of Browning's fragment, which, as we have seen, Mr. Moore has praised.

ides and Racine too closely. In his partial modernization, in his mixture of symbolism and realism, he seems to fall, though gracefully, between two stools, for the play remains chiefly decorative.

The third and fourth volumes of the collected edition included one play, *Orpheus and Eurydice*, which had never appeared in book form, and another, *Omphale and Herakles*, which had never appeared at all.[38] In the latter Herakles divines in his last torments that, although he has opposed wrong, he has failed in uncompromising truth and singleness of heart. He has toiled at the gods' command and has been beguiled by hopes of freedom, pleasure, comfort; the conqueror of many a lawless beast has not conquered the one within himself. Our main impression, however, is not of tragic waste and spiritual victory, but of a decorative and discursive romantic episode in which myth is incompletely transmuted into symbol. *Orpheus and Eurydice* is a very elaborate and suggestive treatment of that well-worn myth. Orpheus returns a second time to fetch his wife, but she drinks a Lethean draught and will not go back to earth with him. If I understand the parable, Orpheus is the thrall of Ge, is the lover of earth, of immediate experience and actuality, who does not pierce the veil of eternal truth and beauty. So too is Eurydice at first, but she learns a higher wisdom and turns her back on Ge. Immortal beauty is not in experience itself, is not of the here and now, is not to be possessed in its wholeness by the ardent senses of man, but dwells in the ordered and timeless serenity of the spiritual world, the world of memory and art.

[38] The first was printed in the *Fortnightly Review* in 1909 but was much revised, the third act in particular being entirely recast. The second had been written still earlier, the author has kindly informed me, and was "greatly rehandled" for its first publication in 1933. In this there are some obvious debts to the *Trachiniae*, especially ll. 555 ff., 763 ff., 1157 ff. Cf. Mr. Moore's *Poems*, IV, 258 ff., 264.

Daimonassa (1930) is apparently an original adaptation of the myth of Danaus and his fifty daughters. The ousted tyrant of Orchomenos has prevailed on his daughters, Ferusa and Daimonassa, to marry the usurper's sons and murder them on the wedding night. When the moment comes the sisters are torn between loyalty to old hatreds and loyalty to young life and love. Ferusa breaks her oath to her father, Daimonassa fulfills hers, and triumphs as a true queen. The weaker one, who sacrificed all for dreams of the future, is left with nothing, while Daimonassa the realist faces life scarred, but with assured confidence and hope. This is not conventional poetic justice. The implication seems to be, as a critic of the play remarked, that "it is not by finding release for instinctive life that the spirit of man finds its growth; it is rather by cutting into life that the spirit grows in dignity and strength." [39] To feel such a parable as a moving reality, however, we need a story which is more than a series of violent and improbable incidents, characters who are more than silhouettes, and a heroine perhaps more sympathetic than Daimonassa.

Mr. Moore has illustrated both his own adventurousness and the flexibility of mythological subjects in several imitations of the Japanese Nō plays. Two of these, *Medea* (1920) and *Psyche in Hades* (1930), are of the author's best and most enigmatic work. Medea is not the tigress of common poetic tradition. After killing her children, as an atonement to Artemis for her marriage, she had returned to the forest to serve again the goddess of her youth. Now she leaves the chase seeking to communicate with the spirits of the children and obtain their forgiveness. [40] When she is alone the voice of her deepest thoughts, of her girlhood, speaks to her through the curtain bearer. She had been disloyal to Artemis in loving Jason, and now in yield-

---

[39] *New Statesman*, XXXV (1930), 414.
[40] Cf. Morris's *Life and Death of Jason*, xvii. 920 ff.

ing to maternal passion she is making a second and worse failure; her integrity has been betrayed by her senses and her heart. Medea tries to bring the children — who remain invisible, their voices being rendered by the curtain folders — to the object of her quest, but they are intent on their play, their "child's integrity of enjoyment," [41] and she cannot share fully in that. She is irrevocably sundered from these blithe spirits, these unspoiled children of Artemis, as she is from her own innocent youth. (It is perhaps a question if the tense, unearthly atmosphere gains or suffers from the very realistic treatment of the children, who laugh, play, hide, and chase rabbits; at any rate it is characteristic of the author, who is always reminding us, even by his angular rhythms and roughnesses of diction, of the solid earth and homely things.) Desperate, Medea feels at last that she must see them, must look into their eyes to win forgiveness, and she prays to "fire-white Nemesis," twin sister of Aphrodite, to restore them to life; [42] but at their cries of horror she revokes the prayer, and they fade away into their "snug graves." The play opens and closes on the note of pain and grief as elements of life. Rightly borne, such suffering refines and ennobles; but Nemesis condemns "weak longing," dependence upon others, and demands the undivided and unswerving loyalty of the entire soul. In seeking good first from Jason and then from her children Medea had been untrue to that solitary, austere, and even cruel ideal of individual responsibility and integrity.

Two dramatic poems about Psyche, published twenty-six years apart, are closely linked together. *Pan's Prophecy* (1904), along with the lyrical and pictorial color of

---

[41] The phrase is from *The Powers of the Air* (*Poems*, IV, 323).

[42] Medea's prayer should be read along with that in *The Powers of the Air*; see *Poems*, III, 50, and IV, 326. Some motives in the play are developed from the author's early monologue *Medea* (*Poems*, III, 27–32).

Mr. Moore's early verse, shows the beginnings of that condensed and elusive symbolism which we have encountered
already and which is carried further in *Psyche in Hades*
(1930). He will not take the fable of Psyche as an allegory
of the soul's attainment of immortality:

There is room for neither mystery nor faith where knowledge is
supposed to reign; yet to-day knowledge is admittedly inadequate and insecure. The soul and that which loves the soul are
idle talk or both must be presumed present in each individual;
their adventures are then inexhaustibly varied.[43]

Each work is a re-creation of one brief and concrete incident in Apuleius, though almost the whole story is brought
in by way of allusion. In the first, the despairing Psyche
encounters Pan after her attempt to drown herself. Pan is
a lover of earth and also a subtle philosopher of love,
beauty, and joy. Eros and Psyche were both at fault, he in
concealing his divinity from his human bride, she in not
trusting the intuitions of her happy heart. The experience
of joy means knowledge of the good, for the true lover loves
the thing revealed, and not the "form or face that did reveal." Both Eros and Psyche, then, had been lovers of
sense and not of soul; Pan himself has discovered the soul
in all things and become the universal friend. He tells
Psyche that she is not a mortal princess but the daughter
of Persephone; yet though she is immortal, she, and Eros
too, must learn by suffering. Psyche hastens away, somewhat too blithely, in search of her bridegroom.

In the play *Psyche in Hades*, a curtain bearer and two
folders are again employed, and the characters are masked.
Apuleius' tale of the descent to Hades is only the starting-
point for this "mystery." Psyche wishes to find Persephone, that other exile from joy, and tell her that she is
her child. Persephone, when we first see her, possesses the

[43] *Poems*, IV, 72.

large wisdom which Psyche has still to learn, that life's worth is not to be measured by its brief exultations and depressions, but by the whole sequence they have formed. To revert again to the author's Socratic myth, Psyche is still in the power of Ge, while her mother has at least a partial vision of Nemesis.[44] Though Psyche's grief had been alleviated by Pan, she is still full of horror for the past and dread for the future. After revealing the secret of her parentage, Psyche reveals also her overwhelming sense of her littleness and insecurity in relation to the vastness of unknown time and space; Eros too is not merely her lover but "the sensuously apprehended fragment of an occult immensity." They had known each other imperfectly, and love is of the whole. Psyche discerns no reality or continuity in life. What, she asks, is each moment, "each little *now*," but a drop of rain falling down into a fathomless past? Man is the dupe of ignorance and the inconstant flux of time, until he is caught by death.

Hermes now reports that Eros has won immortality for his bride and is seeking her. Anteros, the mocking enemy of love, enters and contrasts his own cool "unduped perspicacity," his sterile negations, with the ecstasies of lovers. From now to the end he and Persephone fight, as it were, for possession of Psyche; his approaches and retreats coincide with and symbolize the ebb and flow of love, insight, and courage in the souls of mother and daughter. Persephone cheers Psyche with a speech which contains the essence of this and other works of Mr. Moore's. As the body is beautiful in spite of its unbeautiful parts, so life, viewed as a proportioned whole, is greater than its moments of joy and pain; and the mature soul perceives the significance of the trials by which it has grown into mas-

---

[44] Socrates' whole discussion is relevant here; one particular remark is that man, seduced by his five senses, cannot concentrate on "purity of purpose and those limpid sequences of reason which flow past him" (*Poems*, IV, 328).

tery.[45] But Psyche still finds it hard to sink the painful
particulars in a sense of the grander reality and unity of
the whole, and her mother falters too; she can long for a
heaven where the perfect joyful moment may stand alone,
untrammeled by past or future.[46] But Anteros, who feeds
on their forebodings, vanishes when they rally their faith
in the quest of the whole and the good. Freed from fear by
the vision of eternity and unity, Psyche sets off to seek
Eros, but not in the spirit of her earlier search. *Psyche's
Passion* is completed in two short poems. Eros progresses
from the blind love of sense through "dismal, disillusioned,
inadequate mind," the numbing potency of Anteros,
through the mystery of the unknown, to a calm perception
of the ideal and to final reunion with Psyche. "To have
erred is at length to be," [47] and the individual, who contains both the soul and the lover of the soul, is born into
spiritual unity out of defeat and pain.

Such a summary of an enigmatic work, even if not inaccurate so far as it goes, involves the loss of all that gives
it its peculiar power, for Mr. Moore can seldom, and least
of all here, be paraphrased. Whatever the summary of
this and other dramas might suggest, there is a world of
difference between Browning's muscular confidence and
obvious romanticism and Mr. Moore's ever-present sense
of the dark and complex mysteries of life and the soul. (I
am comparing them, not as poets, but only in relation to
one main tenet of their ethical creed.) In this work Mr.
Moore embodies the essentials of his poetic thought more
completely and impressively than in any other that we
have considered, though we have had some partial paral-

[45] *Poems*, IV, 122.
[46] Compare the attitude of Orpheus, in the play already noticed, and *A
Sicilian Idyll* (*Poems*, IV, 181–85).
[47] In his *Correggio*, Mr. Moore quotes three times Mommsen's saying about
Julius Caesar: "The greatest men are not those who err the least" (pp. 150,
241, 247).

lels. Most poets have been content to retell the Apuleian fable with abundant decoration, to humanize the characters, and to suggest more or less of the traditional allegory. Mr. Moore's conception is his own, his characters are purely symbolic, and both his dramatic form and his style prevent lapses into conventional Victorian mythologizing. In fact what may be called the Chapman strain in him is here so dominant that, while it compels attention and continues to fascinate, it is constantly puzzling. But though one often feels conscious of having missed some of the manifold and subtle suggestions, one never loses a sense of at least partial communion with a mind of noble purity, nor does one lose faith in the reality of the poet's vision of beauty and good. This discussion has emphasized the philosopher at the expense of the artist, but I have read so much about the latter and so little about the former that distortion seemed pardonable if it would indicate the unswerving seriousness and integrity of the author's view of life and poetry.

CHAPTER XIV

From the Nineties to the Present. II

IF THE subject of this book were the classical tradition in poetry and so could embrace anything at all, these final chapters might take in some of the chief works of the twentieth century. *The Dynasts* would not be what it is without Greek tragedy. *Ulysses* might equally well be what it is without the *Odyssey*, since, whatever the writer owed to his underlying pattern, for the reader the parallels hammered out by the expositors are mere Alexandrianism; they add nothing to the significance of the book, for they are too remote to create by themselves a real effect of tragicomic parody. But we must stick to our last, and the problem of selection becomes more difficult than ever. There is in English no mythological poet of Carl Spitteler's epic stature, and of the overwhelming mass of contemporary mythological verse a great deal has been lyrical. It seems best to consider, as hitherto, the larger narrative and dramatic poems, and poets in whose work mythology has a more or less prominent place. When we think of Mr. Yeats's lifelong love of classical poetry and myth, and read such products of his later phase as *Leda and the Swan*, which vibrates with the resonance of Jove's own wings, or the opening lyric of *The Resurrection*, a fiercely ironic echo of the last chorus of *Hellas*, we may wish that the Celtic claims on his imagination had allowed fuller scope to the classical.

[1] See the Appendix, under 1928 and 1934, and note 10 below.

Two chapters extending from about 1890 to 1935 cover not merely forty-five years but several distinct generations. However, the bibliographical facts of life stand in the way of any simple division into Victorian, Edwardian, and Georgian, or even pre-war and post-war groups. Some loose or perhaps Procrustean categories there are. John Davidson may be called an exemplar of the thesis poem; and Mr. Aldington is put with him because his romantic Hellenism turned to realistic verse and prose with a "message." The tradition of the nineteenth-century romantic idyll or narrative is continued by Frederick Tennyson, Stephen Phillips, Maurice Hewlett, Mr. Aldous Huxley, and others. Of a vast amount of miscellaneous writing nothing can be said here. It ranges, to mention a few random examples, from Mrs. Meynell's eight lines of rejoicing in the Promethean light of the sun to Mr. W. W. Gibson's eight-line vision of Prometheus as a blind match-seller; [2] from the poems of Alfred Williams, the Wiltshire mechanic, to the glittering sophistications of Miss Sitwell's dream-world bric-à-brac and Mr. Sacheverell Sitwell's animated, immense, and unreadable *Canons of Giant Art*. But since the earnest reader may be lured into my Appendix by the game of discovering the few modern poets who are not there, I need not spoil the fun with a vain little catalogue now. We may turn then to some general aspects of romantic Hellenism which we have followed intermittently through the nineteenth century. One difficulty in these two chapters is that we have so often to journey backward and forward over the period 1890–1935; this method, though it seems unavoidable, is distressing to one whose devotion to chronology is almost pathological.

---

[2] *Poems of Alice Meynell* (1923), p. 131; W. W. Gibson, *Borderlands and Thoroughfares* (New York, 1914), p. 181.

I

The contrast or the conflict between Christianity and paganism has not ceased to attract the most diverse writers during the last half-century. We might start from Francis Thompson's early essay, "Paganism Old and New," the essay which led to the derelict author's appearing in Wilfrid Meynell's office; the defender of Christian civilization had neither shirt nor socks.[3] The moderns are wrong, said Thompson, who complain of modern materialism and yearn for antique beauty. "Heathenism is lovely *because* it is dead. To read Keats is to grow in love with Paganism; but it is the Paganism of Keats. Pagan Paganism was not poetical." "No pagan eye ever visioned the nymphs of Shelley." "We, who love the gods, do not worship them. The ancients, who worshipped the gods, did not love them." The beauty we see in ancient myth "came to it in dower when it gave its hand to Christianity." The Venus of the ancient poets was not the principle of earthly beauty. The English poetry of paganism "was born in the days of Elizabeth, and entered on its inheritance in the days of Keats." The fresh, primitive pagan religion cannot be restored, and a new paganism would be that of decadent Rome, a paganism "which already stoops on modern Paris, and wheels in shadowy menace over England." These scraps indicate Thompson's thesis, and his treatment of the Christian conceptions of love and nature indicates his debt to the prose and verse of Shelley. Apart from some special pleading, we may accept his argument, at least so far as it relates to the use of myth in modern poetry. Thompson's own mythology, as in the *Ode to the Setting Sun* (1889) and *Song of the Hours* (1890), is mostly in the vein of regret for the "old, essen-

---

[3] The essay appeared in *Merry England*, XI (1888), 99–109; see *Works*, ed. W. Meynell (1913), III, 38–51.

tial candours . . . who made The earth a living and a radiant thing," and the manner is quite Shelleyan or Swinburnian. The manner is even more so in *Daphne*, which might be called a brief parallel to *The Hound of Heaven*; the myth becomes an allegory of the struggle between a poet's ascetic dedication to his art and his craving for normal love and marriage.

The minor poets of the period continued to exploit the old contrasts in much the same fashion as their predecessors, and, in spite of Swinburne and Wilde and all the paganism of the nineties, most writers now as before took the Christian side, whatever their Hellenic nostalgias. The unhappy Lionel Johnson revealed his divided soul in *Julian at Eleusis*[4] and in more than one poem in which he distilled his love of the classics. The still more unhappy Ernest Dowson prayed to Aphrodite for deliverance from her service and to Persephone for the peace of Acheron, and also wrote of the peace of the Carthusians and of extreme unction. Pan was dead, lamented Lord Alfred Douglas (who later became a Catholic), and the world was "sad and brown."[5] John Payne, the candid translator of the *Arabian Nights*, Boccaccio, and Villon, started from Plutarch's tale of the death of Pan and reached "the New Covenant and the New Lord."[6] The religious and Celtic fervor of Eva Gore-Booth did not prevent her investing mythological subjects with mystical significance; in *The Three Resurrections* (1905) she dealt with Lazarus, Alcestis,

---

[4] *Ireland with Other Poems* (1897). The poem was written in 1886–87.

[5] *Hymn to Physical Beauty* (*Poems*, Paris, 1896).

[6] *The Death of Pan* (*Carol and Cadence*, 1908). Cf. *The Descent of the Dove*, III (*Songs of Consolation*, 1904).

In *A Lost God* (1891), Francis W. Bourdillon started from Plutarch and ended with Calvary, and he treated a similar theme in *The Debate of the Lady Venus and the Virgin Mary* (1908). Sir William Watson contributed *The Saint and the Satyr* (1894), a version of the well-known legend of St. Anthony. Arthur S. Cripps achieved an emotional reconciliation in having a faun, whose pipes Apollo scorned, receive the blessing of Christ in the wilderness (1900).

and Psyche. A mystic of another kind, Mr. De la Mare, in his own exquisite way denied the death of Pan, not, like most poets, in the name of facile pagan joys, but finding amid the violets "Tears of an antique bitterness."[7] In the same year as this brief lyric, 1906, appeared the six formidable volumes of *The Dawn in Britain*, which reaches, in the sixth book, the birth of Christ and the pagan gods; a description of the cave of Ashtareth [8] includes echoes of Spenser's piano and Milton's organ rendered on Doughty's own peculiar instrument, the giant Wurlitzer.

In recent years the theme has not died. Doughty's *Mansoul* (1920) takes us, in the fourth book, from the Athens of Socrates and the Eleusinian mysteries to Judaea. Such a title as *The Unknown God. I. Pheidias II. Paul* reminds us of many Victorians, but the poem is an early work of Mr. Humbert Wolfe. Mr. Robert Nichols, in his prose fantasy "Sir Perseus and the Fair Andromeda," made much of "the contrast between Romantic Mediaevalism and Romantic Hellenism" and "the contrast of Northern and Southern sentiment."[9] In a different category from these mainly literary contrasts between paganism and Christianity is Mr. Yeats's play *The Resurrection* (1934). A Greek and a Hebrew in Jerusalem debate the possibility of Christ's rising from the tomb, while in the street a Dionysiac throng proclaim the resurrection of their god. Christ appears, and the Greek, who had thought him a phantom, perceives that God and man die each other's

---

[7] *Tears* (*Poems*, 1906). Cf. *Sorcery*, also of 1906. See *Poems 1901 to 1918* (1920), I, 7, 8.

[8] II, 104.

[9] *Fantastica* (New York, 1923), p. 19. Mr. Nichols' friendly and talkative monster seems to be borrowed from Laforgue's "Persée et Andromède" in the *Moralités légendaires*.

The phrase *Vicisti, Galilaee* furnished a title for Mr. Alfred Noyes (*Collected Poems*, New York, 1913, I, 243–45), and, with a question mark, for Mr. J. D. C. Pellow (*Parentalia*, Oxford University Press, 1923).

life, live each other's death; the crucifixion has made vain all Platonic tolerance and Doric discipline.[10]

In the tired nineties paganism ran rather to nostalgia than to full-blooded revival of the antique joys of sense, but this creed had its poetical as well as its practical adherents.[11] Swinburnian and other forms of paganism, mythological, oriental, and occult, reached what ought to have been their last spasms in the early poems (1898–1905) of Aleister Crowley.[12] In later years paganism has not altogether lost the color of the Beardsley period, for British pagans can never quite shake off their excited consciousness of Mrs. Grundy, but the facts or the desires of the flesh have cast away most of their rococo draperies. The Powys brothers in their several ways have celebrated Pan and Priapus. Aphrodite Pandemos rose again to evangelize Bloomsbury and Chelsea from the Paphian shrine of the Fanfrolico Press. A more philosophical and less robustious pagan than Mr. Jack Lindsay is Mr. W. J. Turner, who set a young man to "reconcile Venus and Diana, Jesus and the Virgin Mary," and who in a later poem carries us, over a rather bumpy road, from the conflict of sensual and mythological paganism and Christian asceticism to a new paganism — it is not very new — in which

---

[10] Many comments on the lyrics (and on *Leda*) are cited in my book of 1968 mentioned above in the new preface.

[11] A few minor writers may be catalogued here. T. E. Brown, the Manxman, weighing Hellenism and Hebraism, praised the Greeks for "seizing one world where we balance two" (*Israel and Hellas, Old John*, 1893). Grant Allen's *The Return of Aphrodite* (1894) was the kind of anti-ascetic plea to be expected from the daring author of *The Woman Who Did*. We have already met Beardsley's pagan fantasy in prose, and along with it might be mentioned some of Charles Ricketts' *Unrecorded Histories* (1933), such as "The Transit of the Gods" and "The New God." A vivid picture of two worlds is suggested in Lady Dorothy Wellesley's *Jupiter and the Nun* (1932).

[12] One of the less exotic authorities Crowley quotes is Bacon's *Wisdom of the Ancients*, in connection with Orpheus; see *Works of Aleister Crowley* (1905–07), III, 158.

spirit and matter are one.[13] Even D. H. Lawrence, who abhorred poetical upholstery as well as civilization, could not forget the ancient gods and heroes when he glorified the delicious rottenness of medlars and sorb-apples, the rich instinctive life of crocuses, purple anemones, fig-trees, and baby tortoises.[14]

As in earlier periods, other forces than Christianity have threatened the poetic life of the Greek gods. To the romantically minded, ever since Coleridge and Keats and Poe, modern science (though it has its own world of fable) has appeared hostile to the spirit of wonder and mystery. Mr. Yeats, who as a boy dwelt with Homer and Helen and Amazons and centaurs, was loth to be disenchanted, to believe that the woods of Arcady were dead and their antique joy over; the world that fed on dreams has now "Grey Truth" for her painted toy, "Yet still she turns her restless head."[15] (As brief references have already partly indicated, the later Mr. Yeats, in his mythological symbolism as in other respects, has displayed a concentrated strength and irony which are not of the nineties.) "The gods are dead?" asked Henley; the world of prose was "Full-crammed with facts, in science swathed and sheeted," but the gods, he hoped, were alive in "some still land of lilacs and the rose." [16] This last phrase, more suggestive of Wilde than of its robust author, is especially significant

[13] *The Seven Days of the Sun* (1925); *Pursuit of Psyche* (1931).

[14] *Collected Poems* (1932), pp. 230, 354–56, 379, 391–93, 450. For other allusions, see pp. 92, 177, 206, 243–45, 483. I may quote an item from Dorothy Brett's *Lawrence and Brett* (Philadelphia, 1933), p. 285: "'Think,' you [*i.e.*, Lawrence] reply, 'of Pan, of the mythical Gods; think of all that old mythology; of Lorenzo the Magnificent. That is what Italy and Greece mean to me.'" See Lawrence's "Pan in America," *Southwest Review*, XI (1925–26), 102–15.

[15] *Song of the Last Arcadian* (*The Wanderings of Oisin*, 1889). See *Autobiographies* (New York, 1927), pp. 57, 69–72, 236, etc. Helen and Troy are alluded to in some lyrics in *The Green Helmet* (1910), *Responsibilities* (1914), etc.

[16] *Poems* (1898), p. 106; *Works* (1908), I, 111. Cf. *London Voluntaries*, v (*Works*, II, 95–96).

from one of the new realists who were bringing fresh air, in Henley's case hospital air, into an age of gas-lit romanticism.

The conflict between realistic modernism and romantic classicism is illustrated best perhaps in the drabness and dreams of a man of prose, George Gissing; that conflict was described a while ago by one of the modernists (Edwardian modernists) whose classical affinities have been limited to visions of Cloud-cuckoo-town, Mr. H. G. Wells.[17] And Gissing may remind us of an artist of more serene temperament and circumstances, George Moore, who went from verses of Swinburnian and Frenchified paganism to novels in the French naturalistic mode, and in his old age returned to Greece with *Aphrodite in Aulis*.[18] The enemies of mythology in modern verse have not added much to the arguments of Dr. Johnson and Whitman. Anna Wickham doubtless spoke for many when she declared that only a starveling singer seeks the stuff of songs among the Greeks, and that Persephone must give place to Reality.[19] Harold Monro, forgetting — or possibly remembering — his own first volume of mainly mythological poems, was aroused by the decorative exuberance of Mr. Robert Nichols' *A Faun's Holiday* to ask, "Who is to be bothered now with all these classical allusions? We have new Gods."[20]

Even if one doubts the inherent inferiority of myths as poetic symbols to such modes of reality as consist in numbering the hedges and daisies of English lanes or in cat-

[17] *Experiment in Autobiography* (New York, 1934), pp. 481 ff. For less lively and more scholarly studies see, in my bibliography, the books by Conrad F. Stadler and Samuel V. Gapp.

[18] For the Greek background of this book see P. J. Dixon, "Letters from George Moore," *London Mercury*, XXXI (1934), 14–21.

[19] *The Contemplative Quarry* (1915), p. 7.

[20] *Some Contemporary Poets* (1920), p. 171. See Mr. Nichols' rejoinder in *Fantastica* (New York, 1923), p. 15.

alogues of efforts to achieve chastity of soul by fleshly trial
and error, one might think that the reality of war would
have banished dreams of Hellas. Rather, it encouraged
such dreams.[21] Mr. Willoughby Weaving, invalided home
in 1915, poured out a whole stream of mythological poems.
While some men at the front had visions of Parisian
nymphs, Mr. Frederic Manning saw Aphrodite. Charles
Sorley conjured up, in France, radiant memories of the
Odyssey,[22] and Francis Ledwidge, with nothing of Sorley's
classical culture, pictured the Greek deities against the
background of his beloved Meath. Mr. Drinkwater's play
$X = O$ (1917), ostensibly about the Greeks and Trojans,
was a modern pacifist tract. It was perhaps easier for
romantic Hellenism to survive the war than the post-war
years, and a number of pagan hedonists, like Mr. Pound
and Mr. Aldington, turned to angry arraignments of things
in general. Before considering Mr. Aldington, whose work
seems less important in itself than as an epitome of some
typical phases and attitudes of the last twenty-five years,
we must go back to a man of the pre-war world who
abandoned the Victorian romantic-idyllic convention to
make classic myth subserve a more or less philosophic
criticism of modern civilization.

II

John Davidson (1857–1909) was an unknown and still
a tolerably happy man when he wrote his amusing and
original pantomime *Scaramouch in Naxos* (1888). Silenus,
drunk as usual, is saluted by his company as Bacchus and,
like another Christopher Sly, he enters into the rôle, de-
manding an Ariadne and a chariot. He praises drinking as

[21] See the Appendix.
[22] *Marlborough and Other Poems* (4th ed., Cambridge University Press, 1919),
No. xxxvi, pp. 81 ff. See Mr. Manning's *Reaction* (*Eidola*, 1917).

a madness less infernal than the madness caused by thinking. The showman Scaramouch, whose name "is not in
Lempriere, but . . . is a good name," arrives in Naxos with
the hope of engaging Bacchus for his troupe. The real
Bacchus appears, with Ariadne; they are still in the ardor
of romantic love. Scaramouch, with unabashed commercial effrontery, wants to hire Bacchus at his own price; his
occupation, he admits, is less honorable than godship, but
he flourishes in England, "land of shams and shows."
Bacchus transforms him into an ape, for exhibition, and
sets off for India with Ariadne. Thus the play is "a good-
natured night-mare," a blend of romantic beauty with
farce and satire of Elizabethan and Shavian vigor. Davidson's romance and humor were mostly to disappear in
satire and propaganda of stormy bitterness, of which, indeed, there are hints in the pantomime.

The Testament of John Davidson (1908) is the work of
a real if ineffectual Titan. The gospel which Davidson so
passionately proclaimed was an individual version of the
religion of humanity in which old religious, ethical, and
sexual values and standards were replaced by a new and
all-embracing materialism:

Thus I break the world out of the imaginary chrysalis or cocoon
of Other World in which it has slumbered so long; and man beholds himself, not now as that fabulous monster, half-god, half-
devil, of the Christian era, but as Man, the very form and substance of the universe, the material of eternity, eternity itself,
become conscious and self-conscious. This is the greatest thing
told since the world began. It means an end of the strangling
past . . . it means a new beginning . . . it means that there is
nothing greater than man anywhere; it means infinite terror,
infinite greatness. . . .

In intention, and sometimes in execution, Davidson was
not a minor poet. As for the poem, the representative of

invincible man encounters Diana and does not die; he tells of the only other men who have seen her, Actaeon, Orion, and Endymion. He tells too how he destroyed Aidoneus ("Hell") and Thor, "the mankind god"; against Apollo himself he had sung of "bisexual electrons," "passionate molecules," and "trellised protoplasm," of gods and God, the products of man's unenlightened mind, and as he sang of the evolving universe and evolving man Apollo had withered away. But the poet has partaken with Diana of her "Other World" food, that is, "the unreal essence of the spirit," and he is untrue to his material being in desiring to win the goddess instead of destroying her, in being seduced by the fantasy of the immaterial. He declares that the sin of heaven, which sapped Olympian power, was the cult of virginity. Diana is at first horrified, then inspired, by the thought of their uniting to create a greater race of men. After a night of passion the goddess dies, and the poet dies too; in loving Diana he had betrayed truth, himself, and the universe. The two awake in the hell where gods suffer, and he, who embodies all deities in himself, is crucified. But he has accomplished his great purpose of banishing the fear of hell, the worship of God and chastity, and all the other bogies which have hindered man from realizing his unfettered supremacy and his identity with the world of nature.

Critics have not failed to point out Davidson's partial kinship with Nietzsche, "the most powerful mind of recent times," as he is called in the dedication to the *Testament*. One might also say that the poem is a twentieth-century *Queen Mab*. But if Shelley sowed the wind, Davidson's reaping of the whirlwind was not the final reaping. His glorification of sex, of the liberated sexual energy of the triumphant superman, has only a specious resemblance to that of D. H. Lawrence, for Davidson's faith in scientific progress and the greatness of man leads very quickly and

directly to the anti-intellectual disillusionment, the sentimental primitivism, of Lawrence, to his despairing reliance
on the ultimate truth of the flesh; it leads also to the nihilistic nightmares of Robinson Jeffers. To come back to the
poem, the main ideas are unmistakable, though details of
the mythological symbolism are not always clear or coherent, and a reader may lose his way amid whirling words
and electrons. Davidson was far too intent on his single-
handed deliverance of a benighted world to be an artist,
and in the *Testament* nothing does more to control his
demonic energy and clarify his turbid imagination than
such relics of old religion and the strangling past as classic
myths. The mythological passages are written with a
force and careless splendor which set them apart from most
tame verse of the period.[23]

Chronologically, Mr. Richard Aldington started a little
beyond where Davidson left off, but he belonged to another
world. In intention and technique his early Hellenic-
Imagist poems were much the same as H. D.'s, but with a
more diffuse softness, a more openly Victorian weariness
and nostalgia. Greece was a symbol of the beauty of
nature and art, of freedom and amorous nymphs. *Choricos,*
which was too revolutionary for an English journal and

---

[23] A word may be said about Herbert Trench's *Apollo and the Seaman* (1907),
which, with its suggestions of *The Ancient Mariner*, is remote from Davidson's
Testament in conception and style, but is not so remote in its theme and thesis.
The simple and spacious allegory, of the loss of the old ship Immortality and the
superseding of Christian faith by the religion of humanity, has nothing of classic
myth about it except Apollo, who represents the *élan vital* or the Life Force.
Indeed one might find the positive text of the poem in the preface to *Man and
Superman* (New York, ed. 1912, p. xxxi: "This is the true joy in life. . . ."). But
Trench's faith in man as the agent of creative evolution was perhaps closer to
that of George Meredith, who had a marked influence upon him and who, incidentally, approved of this poem (*Letters of George Meredith*, 1912, II, 604).
Among other parallels which might be invoked I will mention only one, a work
which Trench translated and apparently absorbed, Merejkowski's *The Death of
the Gods*; see the preface to his translation (1901), and the text, for example,
pp. 81–82, 460.

consequently appeared in Miss Monroe's *Poetry* in 1912, was *The Garden of Proserpine* over again, without the Swinburnian music but with all the Swinburnian materials, melancholy regret, satiety, death and eternal sleep. *Images* (1915) was not wholly Greek; pictures of London streets and tubes and cinemas were realistic and angry. Then to the ugliness of peace was added a greater ugliness, and, as the poet had contrasted the statue of Eros and Psyche with the grime of Camden Town, so his images of war were mingled with visions of "beauty and the women of Hellas," the sea and olive gardens, fauns and "naked wanton hamadryads." But the mold of Mr. Aldington's Imagism was, along with other things, broken by the war. It was too delicate a vial for a wrath which one cannot condemn, though one may think an emotional indignation against all things established an inadequate creed for a serious writer. At any rate Mr. Aldington turned from Imagism to verse of the Pound-Eliot kind, and then to the novel, and has made a career of disillusioned bitterness.[24]

The phantasmagoric poem, *A Fool i' the Forest* (1925), contains one person split into three: the narrator, a modern man of artistic temperament who is struggling "to attain a harmony between himself and the exterior world"; the Conjurer, who represents "the intellectual faculties — age, science, righteous cant, solemnity, authority"; and Mezzetin, "the imaginative faculties — art, youth, satire, irresponsible gaiety, liberty." The trio visit Athens and discourse upon Greek culture. For a time the Greeks did possess that perfect harmony of mind and senses which yielded "Science and beauty reconciled with health." They accepted life; even their sensual excesses were disciplined by a sense of beauty. Our minds and senses, our science and art, are unbalanced, diseased, mechanized.

[24] Mythology appears even in the novels, for example, *Death of a Hero* (1929), pp. 147 ff., 172, and the opening of *All Men Are Enemies* (1933).

Finally, Mezzetin is killed in the war, through the Conjurer's blundering; back in London, the narrator throws the Conjurer into the Thames; and, left to himself, the lover of truth and beauty settles down as the complete suburbanite. Mr. Aldington's conception of Greece is here more realistic than it was, but it is still mainly emotional and sentimental. The evening star brings home the *Evening News* and the business man, "Sappho and Shelley you no longer bring"; such a line might have been written by Wilde.

Mr. Aldington has clung to a faith in life, which nowadays means love. His erotic philosophy is that of Lawrence enveloped in a mist of glamorous romantic idealism and classical allusion. In the neo-pagan idyll called *A Dream in the Luxembourg* (1930), the woman is a veritable wood-nymph "Because she is brave and frank and honest and herself" (as Shelley said, "frank, beautiful, and kind"), because (here the note is Swinburnian) such fair, uninhibited creatures fight against "The Jewish gloom and the gloomy Christ." Finally, there is *The Eaten Heart* (1933), a meditation on love, on an individual's escape from solitude to that complete union with another which yields complete satisfaction and enrichment. It is hard to discern any very felicitous aptness in the reinterpretation of Philoctetes as the symbol of "the dreadful inevitable loneliness of the human soul"; there is an unbridgeable gulf between the heroic masculine sufferer on the Lemnian isle and the modern lover's "weak squabble with despair." Altogether, Mr. Aldington is a sensitive romantic rebel who has found in Greek poetry, as any selective reader can find, support for his own temperament. He is superior to many such rebels in being aware of disharmony and confusion in himself. But he has always been, rather too self-consciously, a captive faun.[25]

[25] From the preface to *Poems* (New York, 1934), if not often from the poems

III

In this section we may gather together a number of narrative poems by writers who practised the Keats-Tennyson-Morris convention in the nineties, or carried it, with variations, up to our own day; Mr. Masefield's *Tale of Troy* hardly belongs here, but still less does it belong anywhere else. These poets are united by a predominant interest in romantic story-telling and picture-making. An idealistic message is often an ingredient; it had been more than an ingredient in Keats and Tennyson. It is much more than that in the first writer to be mentioned here, Tennyson's elder brother Frederick (1807–98), to whom FitzGerald transferred the faith he lost in Alfred. His verse, according to Browning, contained the proper stuff out of which poetry is made, but in a state of solution, not yet crystallized.[26] After a silence of thirty-six years he produced two thick volumes of classical poems, *The Isles of Greece* (1890) and *Daphne* (1891), in which the elements of poetry were still further from being crystallized; they were, rather, volatilized into a dense and sometimes Swedenborgian mist. The myths which formed the subjects were frequently lost in the enveloping sermons. The romantic faith in beauty and truth, in the "One Life, but one, that rolls through All," is set forth with a vague and earnest diffuseness which includes bits of genuine poetry, though they may not be an adequate reward for the search. Like a good deal of inspirational verse of the period, this might be indirectly summed up in two Delphic oracles which Sir

themselves, one understands that Mr. Aldington has had a genuine mythological "experience of certain places and times when one's whole nature seems to be in touch with a presence, a genius loci, a potency." Hence his allusions to Hellenic deities have not been mythological flourishes.

[26] *Personal & Literary Letters of Robert First Earl of Lytton*, ed. Lady Betty Balfour (1906), I, 50.

Owen Seaman once put into the mouth of that egregious sibyl, Marie Corelli:

> Surely there is Something, if we could but find out what it is.
> O unfathomable deeps!
> What is the Good? And what is the Beautiful? Who can say?
> All we know is that both terms are synonymous, the one quite as much as the other.[27]

Frederick Tennyson was, however, a scholar and a gentleman.

During the years just before and after 1900 Stephen Phillips (1864–1915) was said to be akin, among others, to Sophocles, Virgil, Dante, and Milton; he had brought back great themes and the grand style to poetry, and he was the savior of poetic drama. It was *Christ in Hades* (1896) which announced the new star in the firmament; *Marpessa* and subsequent works made it a constellation. But Phillips proved to be a meteor, or perhaps a rocket. His poetry was, to use a characteristic phrase of his own, one of the "over-beautiful, quick-fading things," and, although he was publishing to the last, his death in 1915 was almost unnoticed.

Christ in Hades has at least an initial largeness of conception, which results from carrying the medieval theme of the harrowing of hell into the Homeric and Virgilian underworld. The approach of Christ sends a quickening thrill through the ghosts in Hades, and the endless torments are suspended. Persephone, eager for the spring, thinks it is Hermes come to take her to the upper world.[28] She and her fellows, except the sadly philosophic Virgil, plead with the strange, silent figure; they long for the smell

---

[27] *Borrowed Plumes.*

[28] Persephone's eagerness to minister to the earth in springtime is the theme of a simple and attractive poem by Mr. Drinkwater (*Summer Harvest*, 1933). The contrast drawn between her thoughts of mortal life and Pluto's changeless immortality reminds one slightly of Phillips' favorite idea.

of earth and rain and the stir of life. One sufferer alone has not been freed from torture, Prometheus, the ante-type of Christ. He, the realist, warns Christ, the dreamer, of the strife and bloodshed which are destined to be enacted in His name, which will make the second martyr's anguish far greater than his own. Christ, contemplating the future of the faith He kindled, is stayed from His purpose of releasing the dead, and Hades resumes its interrupted life.

One theme which is touched in *Christ in Hades* — and had appeared in *Eremus* (1894) — is central in *Marpessa* (1897) and *Endymion* (1898), that is, the craving for the fullness of common human experience with all its sorrow. Marpessa, choosing between a divine and a mortal wooer, prefers Idas to Apollo.[29] The glorious life of untroubled serenity and power offered by the god she puts aside. (Part of her speech is not quite logical; forgetting the promised immortality, she dwells on the pain of fading into the neglected old wife of a husband eternally young.) What she desires is mortal life with the mortal Idas, the whole familiar cycle from the first passion to the peace and memories of age and finally death. In the drama *Ulysses* (1902) the central scene turns on the same motive. Tired of Calypso and slothful luxury, Ulysses rejects her offer of immortality; he longs for gaunt Ithaca, for earthly joys and sorrows, he will have life only on terms of death, "That sting in the wine of being, salt of its feast."[30]

Phillips felt this theme sincerely, but neither his vague idealism nor his craftsmanship was substantial or original enough to revivify an exhausted tradition. His mythological figures are little more than mouthpieces, and modern sentiment is more palpably imposed upon the fables than it usually is in his chief master, Tennyson. The set-

[29] See Apollodorus, *Lib.* I. vii. 8; Homer, *Il.* ix. 557 ff.
[30] Since Phillips was such an inveterate borrower, he might have read R. W. Dixon's *Ulysses and Calypso*, which was noticed in ch. XII.

ting of *Marpessa* is taken over from *Oenone* — *Endymion* of course has a Keatsian tinge—and Phillips' style, though capable at moments of sumptuous color and sweetness, is in general Tennyson diluted with sugar and water. His most notorious weakness is his dependence upon other poets, and in *Marpessa* he echoes not only Tennyson but Marlowe, Milton, Wordsworth, Keats, and Arnold. Plagiarism, according to a sound and venerable doctrine, is justified if the poet improves what he borrows, but the shade of Marlowe would not welcome

> Nor for that face that might indeed provoke
> Invasion of old cities,

and Arnold might complain of "And India in meditation plunged." A worse sin, however, is Phillips' instinct for that vague post-romantic diction which had been for some time the curse of small poets. What, for instance, is the meaning of the fifth line of *Marpessa*, "The mystic yearning of the garden wet"? Other things besides the garden which yearn in this poem are the sea, the soul, and the moon. Phillips is full of soft substitutes for emotion.

Before proceeding with long narrative poems we may notice several poets who did nothing of that kind, but whose lyrical work, so far as it concerns us, belongs in fact or in spirit to the nineties. Time has not dimmed the beauties of *A Shropshire Lad* (1896) and *Last Poems* (1922); it has, though, brought out more clearly the marks of their period, for the two volumes may be regarded as one. A rustic convention of artificial naïveté does not conceal a sentimental pessimism and stoic despair which may have been intensely personal but are also very *fin-de-siècle*. Classical scholarship contributed much, along with some modern influences, to the clean simplicity of Housman's form and diction, of his whole imaginative world, indeed, yet he is none the less another illustration of the familiar paradox that the poets most steeped in the classics may be the most unclassical in temperament. (One may perhaps suppose that his fiercely learned concentration on bad Latin poetry was itself an escape from emotional despair, that his sword ate into Manilius for lack of something else to hew and hack.) The evidence of the poems was more than confirmed by *The Name and Nature of Poetry*, which revealed an unregenerate anti-intellectual romantic and an admirer of Blake as the most poetical of all poets. Housman seldom touched myth, but he used ancient idiom and allusion with unique effect. A soldier of the queen echoes the Homeric speech of Sarpedon to Glaucus.[31] *To an Athlete Dying Young* begins in a region somewhat like Shropshire and ends among the strengthless dead of the underworld. In the *Epitaph on an Army of Mercenaries*, which makes some of the lovely lyrics seem just a little soft, the manner of the *Greek Anthology* and the atmosphere of the Greek world are a partial disguise for a bitter modern irony.[32] We may rejoice that so proud and angry a poet was able to write the incomparable *Fragment of a Greek Tragedy*.

One can neither pass by nor dwell long upon those two acquaintances who died young a few months apart, Rupert Brooke and James Elroy Flecker. Brooke's early *Ante Aram* is thoroughly in the feeling and style of the nineties. Of his two sonnets on Menelaus and Helen the first at least might have been written by Stephen Phillips —

> He swung his sword, and crashed into the dim
> Luxurious bower, flaming like a god.[33]

---

[31] *A Shropshire Lad*, lvi; *Iliad*, xii. 322. For some mythological allusions, see *A Shropshire Lad*, x, xv, xlii (and li); *Last Poems*, iii, xxiv, xxv. See also *More Poems* (1936), v, xv, xxxiii, xlv.

[32] See the sepulchral epigrams for dead soldiers in the *Greek Anthology* (Loeb Classical Library), II, 136–44 (nos. 242–59), and 236–42 (nos. 430–43), and also III, 162 (no. 304). This last is rendered in the Housman manner in Mr. Humbert Wolfe's *Others Abide* (1927), p. 86.

[33] Some lines in Brooke's *Kindliness*, on the dwindling of passionate love into habit, remind one very much of a portion of *Marpessa*.

The second sonnet exchanges the conscious splendors of high rhetoric for a conscious cynicism no less characteristic of the youthful Brooke. Helen, a prolific, scolding wife, and Menelaus, a garrulous, nagging husband, grew old in Sparta, while "Paris slept on by Scamander side."

Flecker sincerely loved Greece, or romantic mythological visions of Greece. Amidst the noise of London or in country lanes he heard Maenad melodies and tracked "the silver gleam of rushing feet." When he says, in *Oak and Olive*, that though born a Londoner and bred in Gloucestershire, he

> walked in Hellas years ago
> With friends in white attire,

we believe him more than we believe most minor poets. At the same time, as even this brief quotation suggests, the marks of the nineties are everywhere upon him. They appear in his ideal of art for art's sake, in his nostalgic escapist dreams of Greece and Bagdad and the golden road to Samarkand, in his love of exotic properties, in the decorative sadism (if not the excellent comedy) of *Hassan*, in the tone of his picture of Helen, the fatal woman, *Destroyer of Ships, Men, Cities*.[34] Flecker's fastidious Parnassian workmanship helped to keep him from being a mere Swinburnian echo, but his prose dialogue on education, "The Grecians," reveals a larger and deeper understanding of Greek and Roman antiquity than ever got into his verse.

Of the crowd of writers who carried the narrative modes of the nineteenth century into the twentieth, only a few can be noticed here. Mythological themes got their share of Mr. Alfred Noyes's melodious fluency, but his serious

---

[34] For this title see Aeschylus, *Agam.*, l. 689. Mr. Pound of course requires the Greek phrase; see *A Draft of XXX Cantos* (New York [1933]), c. ii, p. 6, c. vii, pp. 24–25.

things are less readable than *Bacchus and the Pirates* with its lively reminiscences of *Peter Pan* and *Treasure Island*. The numerous and voluminous idylls and tales of Maurice Hewlett run from about 1895 to 1916; in spirit they are nearly all of the nineties. In the dramatic trilogy *The Agonists* (1911), which Mr. Pound pronounced "if not the only, at least the most readable 'Greek Plays' in English,"[35] Hewlett tried to reach an ethical and metaphysical level beyond his philosophic and poetical powers. Most of his other pieces are graceful mixtures of sensuous scene-painting and sensuous love, in well-bred, flowing verse with a due measure of archaism. One would hardly guess from these pretty tapestries — though one might perhaps from the rustic realism of *Pan and the Young Shepherd* (1898) — that Hewlett would be capable of *The Song of the Plow*.

In 1913 a reviewer complained that one of Hewlett's mythological tales which purposed to express the "high mating of the mind" was in reality a celebration of concupiscence.[36] By 1920 this last word had dropped out of the critical vocabulary. In his *Leda* of that year Mr. Aldous Huxley was as Keatsian as a poet could be who had learned his letters from Krafft-Ebing. First we see the young Leda bathing in the cool Eurotas, a royal bride to whom love has brought only bitter disillusion; then we are carried heavenward to contemplate Jove sweating in his palace and devoured by an itching libido. His lustful eyes range over a varied panorama of scenes on earth, from the priapic revelry of a negroid holiday to savage Britain. The description of the actual encounter between Leda and the swan is relatively brief, though more candid

[35] *Poetry*, II (1913), 75.
[36] *Academy*, LXXXIV (1913), 679–80. In retrospect it seems a quaint anomaly that two volumes of new verse which the reviewer considered together were Hewlett's *Helen Redeemed* and the *Love Poems* of D. H. Lawrence. He did not know that he was standing on a watershed between two eras, though he did say that Hewlett had not realized what Lawrence had grasped "only too boldly."

than the similar incident of Thomas Wade a century earlier. This passage contains some parallels, perhaps accidental, with the prose *Lêda* of Pierre Louys, but the poem has nothing of Louys' symbolism. *Leda* is hardly an important work, yet it is an original combination of conventional mythological romanticism with animal and tropical heat and exotic color. Other poems in the volume, along with Mr. Huxley's many later writings, seem to confirm the suspicion that the romantic idealism and the modern sensuality of *Leda* are less harmonious than such elements are, say, in *Venus and Adonis*. Leda and the satyr Jove are mythological and remote; when in *Morning Scene* the author depicts a similar modern situation, with a red face "Fixed in the imbecile earnestness of lust," he recoils with loathing. The emancipated modern in Mr. Huxley has never subdued the angry puritan.

The war did not erase the memory of Helen and the little affair at Troy. Of the half-dozen long treatments of the story published since 1918, it will be enough to mention two, of very different character. Mr. W. J. Turner has grown into a philosophic poet of modernism, but in *Paris and Helen* (1921) he was an unabashed romantic. A reviewer facetiously observed that Mr. Turner might be accused of playing "Follow my *Leda*," although, as he went on to say, there is small resemblance between the poems. *Paris and Helen* is a tapestry of nature-painting, a series of backgrounds, with a shadowy thread of narrative and shadowy suggestions of unattainable Beauty and disillusioning Time. The indistinct outlines of persons and events give the whole a remoteness which sensuous beauties of detail do not bring into vivid life. It is a gravely lyrical tone poem that one enjoys and forgets.

The method of Mr. Masefield's *A Tale of Troy* (1932) is the exact opposite. Like some other pieces of the author's,[37] this poem was composed for recitation, and the device of putting various episodes into the mouth of various characters results in some discontinuity of narrative (and some prosaic rhythms), though it contributes to a realistic immediacy of impression. As a version of the greatest epic story in the world, the *Tale* is decidedly thin and unsatisfying, and it exhibits of course its author's distressing unawareness of slipshod commonplace and strained artifice. But it has the freshness of a saga told, as it were, for the first time. Like Dares and Dictys, Mr. Masefield was at Troy. His inventions are mostly harmonious, and he does not, like more learned poets, make one conscious of literary sources — an example which, for want of space, shall be followed here. The poem is mainly action, and a large part, the most stirring part, deals with the Greeks' perilous night in the wooden horse. As one would expect, Mr. Masefield is at his best in homely realism and in describing the things achieved by men's hands and by the courage of their souls. Both in such aspects of the tale, and in the modern sense of the causes and results of war, one sees not only the lover of ships and horses and the outdoor world but the author of *Gallipoli*.

A Tale of Troy ends with a speech of Christian piety and faith from Kassandra, but this incongruity is nothing compared with the story of Helen and Nireus, her unsuccessful lover, as narrated by choric figures called Rose-Flower and Moon-Blossom, at the end of the first four acts of a tragedy drawn from the Old Testament. Most of these Trojan choruses in *A King's Daughter* (1923) are facile and undistinguished, but one in short lines, at the end of the second act, is poetry; it describes how Nireus sailed to the island of the dead and saw Paris, whom he had killed, and the Trojan heroes. What is told of Nireus, Helen, and

---

[37] *Minnie Maylow's Story* (1931) includes *The Wild Swan*, a good deal of which is concerned with the fall of Troy, and *Penelope*, a paraphrase, with omissions, of the *Odyssey*, xix. 104–xx. 53.

Paris, in the first eight stanzas of the first chorus, is elaborated in a very unclassical prose romance of over a hundred pages, *The Taking of Helen* (1923). This, like *A Tale of Troy*, has the charm of freshness, an atmosphere of rural England, and it may be enjoyed by those who are young enough to share Mr. Masefield's love of a yarn. We have many little commentators on the universe, and much may be forgiven to a writer who has gallantly upheld a great tradition of story-telling.

As a critic Mr. F. L. Lucas has not shunned such romantic emotions as are permissible to a sophisticated man of the world, and he begins his *Ariadne* (1932) with a gibe at the Eliot school of poets. His own long poem is a romance which recalls *The Life and Death of Jason* in narrative method and often in style, and in its simple philosophy, more literary than primitive, of youth and love and death. Parallels are inevitable between tales of heroes befriended and loved by the daughters of their royal enemies, but Mr. Lucas' chief invention, the story of Aegle, heightens the resemblance. Theseus is torn between Aegle and Ariadne much as Jason is between Glauce and Medea, and in the end each hero is left alone. Though Theseus is untrue to Aegle, he does not, as in the myth, desert Ariadne; she, her dream over, leaves her fickle lover to follow Dionysus. The Minotaur becomes Minos in disguise, a change rather more dubious than the ancient rationalizing of the monster into a courtier, "Taurus."[38] In general, while Mr. Lucas brings the Morris manner up to date, and has his own virtues of artistic and scholarly ease, unfailing energy and speed, and a turn for bright, clear picture-making, *Ariadne* seems to prove more definitely than a poor poem would that this kind of writing is in our day only a pleasant recreation.

[38] See Plutarch's *Theseus*. This work of course contains a good deal of the material used in the poem, including the initial suggestion for the triangular love story (c. 20).

CHAPTER XV

American Poets

I

I DO not propose to give a systematic account of the mythological tradition in American poetry; whoever feels inclined to throw the first stone is invited to survey the chronological list of reasons in the Appendix. That list is not complete, and I begrudge no zealous young scholar the creative joy of discovering omissions, but it provides a sufficient panorama. Whitman and Emily Dickinson do not appear; almost everyone else does. To sum up the matter concisely, American mythological verse of the nineteenth and early twentieth centuries is a boundless, bottomless ocean of mediocrity; lighthouses are few and their rays are mostly dim. But what cannot for the most part be read can be roughly charted, and I shall try to indicate briefly the main currents or eddies of the period.

At the beginning stands a lone eagle, Philip Freneau, but *The Monument of Phaon*, written in 1770, looks back rather than forward. Romantic mythological verse began in the eighteen-twenties. Since, as Dr. Johnson said, there is no settling the point of precedency between a louse and a flea, the title of morning-star of song may be divided between the egregious James Gates Percival and the ineffable Mrs. Sigourney. In his *Prometheus* Percival wrote "freely on a variety of subjects," and in one of a number of poems on Greek themes, *The Mythology of Greece*, he subdued a regret for the fair humanities of old religion to a Christian note. American pietism has already given mythological verse a Victorian color, and that color was only to deepen in later years. In the eighteen-twenties also a writer of different quality, Edward Coote Pinkney, composed a fragmentary piece on the historical tale of Pausanias and Cleonice. N. P. Willis and Albert Pike, whose *Hymns to the Gods* (1839) won the praise of Christopher North, bring us to the first mythological moralizings of Longfellow and Lowell, and the dynamic and radiant *Bacchus* of Emerson. From now on there is a swelling tide of names, many of them respectable names, though respectable usually for other than mythological poems. All the ladies and gentlemen of New England possessed high ideals and a copy of Bulfinch. The more decorous Greek myths were part of the furniture of the Bostonian mind. "But my G-d," exclaimed Matthew Arnold in 1853, with less than his wonted urbanity and chivalry, "what rot did she [Margaret Fuller] and the other female dogs of Boston talk about the Greek mythology!" [1] Some years later Mr. Higginson invited a shy poetess to come down from Amherst and attend "a meeting of the Woman's Club at 3, Tremont Place," where he was to read "a paper on the Greek goddesses"; but she chose to stay at home and look in her heart.[2] Whitman besought American poets to turn away from Greece and Ionia and contemplate democratic vistas. The negative side of the plea at least was not much regarded. When Americans took up mythology they made it hum, and the latter half of the nineteenth century was filled with the murmuring of innumerable bees.

While in England, all through the century, a number of poets, great and less great, gave romantic Hellenism a series of fresh starts, in the United States a swarm of small

[1] *Letters of Matthew Arnold to Arthur Hugh Clough*, ed. H. F. Lowry (1932), p. 132.
[2] Genevieve Taggard, *The Life and Mind of Emily Dickinson* (New York, 1930), p. 213. See T. W. Higginson, "The Greek Goddesses," *Atlantic Monthly*, XXIV (1869), 97–108.

versifiers went on decade after decade playing the same tunes, that is, the tunes of the last or the next to the last generation of English writers. In all this activity there is something touching, something that might be called Elizabethan. For one discerns, along with inferior motives, a patriotic desire to prove and to forward the cultural maturity of a nation very conscious of its youth, to naturalize on American soil the great themes of so much great European poetry. What was needed was a Spenser, and nature provided only Gascoignes and Turbervilles. Then, too, when staid husbands and fathers persist in seeing nymphs, and wives and mothers and blameless spinsters harken to the pipes of Pan, one perceives a vague discontent with the drab stuffiness of American civilization; and writing mythological poems was as dignified a form of romantic revolt or escape as parading in red fezzes or listening to lectures.

But the mythological imagination could not grow out of shallow soil. Even in Europe the ancient myths have always been exotics, in spite of the long classical traditions of the Middle Ages and the Renaissance, and they were transplanted late to a new country. (One has often met the argument that American culture and art need nothing but native resources; one can only wonder what would have become of western Europe if it had taken that attitude toward its Graeco-Roman heritage.) The Pilgrim Fathers, some of whom might have bored Shakespeare or Virgil less than Arnold imagined, brought with them seeds of classical culture destined to fruitful growth. Perhaps the best evidence of that growth is in memoirs of many sober persons who read much and wrote little or nothing; or in old files of such magazines as *Harper's* and the *Atlantic Monthly*, which in the nineteenth and early twentieth centuries evidently ministered to a small and cultivated public — imagine the *Harper's* of to-day printing Pater's "Apollo in Picardy"! But, in spite of the classics' long hold upon New England, there seems to have been a steadily widening gap between professional scholarship and literature. The strength of the classical tradition in Europe has always been, and still is, the fact that it has not been the exclusive property of scholars, that it has been almost impossible for men of letters to forget the living presence of ancient literature. In the United States, which has had no Middle Ages, no Renaissance — only the Reformation — and, in the cultural sense, no eighteenth century, we have had much classical learning but not much of the humanities.

> When eras die, their legacies
> Are left to strange police.
> Professors in New England guard
> The glory that was Greece.[3]

Scholarship has suffered as much as literature from the divorce. To be sure, one can call up a number of names, past and present, which testify to a happy wedding of classical scholarship and creative talent, but the swallows are too few to make a summer; they do not alter the general fact that the American writer does not have the classics in his bones — and now that we are all proletarians he does not need to. When Poe, whose knowledge of Latin at least exceeded that of most modern American authors, reviewed Mrs. Browning, he ascribed the *Oedipus Coloneus* to Aeschylus; [4] in 1933 a well-known poet and critic commenced a somewhat lordly essay on Shelley, in a highbrow journal, with an allusion to "Sophocles' 'Prometheus.'" These may be slight straws (though others could be collected), but they imply a good deal; such things are not common in Europe.

---

[3] Clarence Day, *Thoughts Without Words* (New York, 1928), p. 113.
[4] *Works of Edgar Allan Poe*, ed. E. C. Stedman and G. E. Woodberry (New York, 1914), VI, 358. Mrs. Browning's comment was that Poe "sits somewhat loosely, probably, on his classics" (*Letters of Elizabeth Barrett Browning Addressed to Richard Hengist Horne*. ed. Mayer, 1877, II, 176).

A few paragraphs must be given to some individual poets whose general stature raises them above the multitude. One early link with the English romantics is Poe's sonnet *To Science* (1830), a complaint that analytical science is the blight of poetry, that it has dragged Diana from her car and driven the nymphs from tree and flood; Poe is echoing the first lines and the "rainbow" passage of *Lamia*.[5] One cannot mention Poe without recalling *To Helen* and "those Nicéan barks of yore," a romantically vague allusion which has exercised scholars, and above all the worst lines in the lyric, about the glory that was Greece and the grandeur that was Rome. These household words are not the meaningless jingle of a journalistic vulgarian, they are the tinsel or plaster rhetoric of a man of genius. Indeed in the poem as a whole the magic of the romantic nostalgia is in the rhythms, not in the meretricious, rococo images and diction.[6]

But impulses toward mythological romanticism were few and thin, and they were quickly merged, or submerged, in the earnest but pallid Victorian moralizing of such poets as Lowell and Longfellow. Some of Lowell's short pieces are not unpleasant trifles, though they all have their moral, but the longer ones, like the early *Prometheus* and the late *Endymion*, are diffuse and undistinguished. Even *Rhoecus*, in addition to its imaginative and stylistic remoteness from Landor's *Hamadryad*, is overweighted with its obvious lesson. One wonders how these, and many other poems of Lowell's, could ever have been written by the author of *A Fable for Critics* and *The Biglow Papers*, but one remembers the lines in the former on himself and his inability to learn "the distinction 'twixt singing and preach-

---

[5] *Poems*, ed. Killis Campbell (Boston and New York, 1917), pp. 169–70.

[6] See Mr. Aldous Huxley's rendering of Milton's "Not that fair field of Enna . . ." in the manner of Poe ("Vulgarity in Literature," *Saturday Review of Literature*, VII [1930], 158).

ing." He was much less vigorous in handling myths in verse than in attacking in prose the "modern antiques" of Swinburne, Arnold, and Landor.[7]

For Longfellow, as for Lowell, a myth was rather a text than an inspiration. In *Prometheus* (1858) we have the "Poet, Prophet, Seer," made wise by suffering, carrying on the torch of progress; the companion poem, *Epimetheus*, records poetic disillusion conquered by Hope. The elaborate sequence of scenes and lyrics, *The Masque of Pandora* (1875), was actually adapted for the stage, and it is perhaps more of a libretto than a poem. In two ways it has some mild interest. The contrast between Prometheus the humanitarian toiler and Epimetheus the esthetic dreamer, one inheriting the father's strength and the other the mother's weakness, suggests the two dominant inherited impulses of Longfellow himself.[8] Further, the same contrast has a partial parallel in Goethe, though otherwise this play is remote enough from Goethe's dramatic treatments of Pandora and Prometheus.[9] Longfellow may have merely embroidered Hesiod, and he may have taken a hint or two from Hawthorne's juvenile version in his *Wonder Book*.

Of the American poets of his time Emerson is the only one who seems to have an authentic spark of the mythological imagination, the only one who really heard the

---

[7] See the essay "Swinburne's Tragedies"; and *Letters of James Russell Lowell*, ed. C. E. Norton (Boston and New York, 1894), I, 357.

[8] My friend Odell Shepard speaks, with no reference to this work, of precisely these two diverse strains of inheritance in Longfellow as never outgrown and never reconciled (*Henry Wadsworth Longfellow: Representative Selections*, New York, 1934, p. xiv).

[9] Mr. James Taft Hatfield gives this summary: "The *Masque of Pandora*, derived chiefly from the Greek tragedy, has suggestions of the Second Part of *Faust*, especially in the chorus of Oreades, Waters, Winds, and Forests. Goethe's *Prometheus* was not drawn upon. The Chorus of the Eumenides suggests Goethe's *Iphigenie*" (*New Light on Longfellow*, Boston and New York, 1933, p. 136). Mr. Hatfield observes (p. 174) that *Pegasus in Pound* "is much like Schiller's *Pegasus im Joche*."

gods talk in the breath of the woods and the shaken pine.[10]
The clerical sage was primitive as well as prim. He was
no Hellenist, either by instinct or by learning, and he had
nothing of romantic delight in mythological tales and
luxuries; his allusions are relatively few and bare, and
they are nearly all in one vein of symbolism. One can
roughly indicate Emerson's mythological position by saying that he belongs to the line of Collins, Akenside, and
Wordsworth. His favorite deity is Pan, and Wordsworth
is "Pan's recording voice."[11] In short, Emerson's occasional allusions arise in connection with his perennial theme,
"the universal beauty to which every part and particle
is related; the eternal One." [12] His sense of unity in nature
and the soul of man is not more powerful than austere,
and his Pan is no embodiment of lawless vitality but
"ought to be represented in the mythology as the most
continent of the gods." [13] It is Pan "Who layeth the
world's incessant plan," and for ever doth escape into new
forms "Of gem, and air, of plants, and worms." [14] And
the oneness and beauty of Being is revealed both in the
myriad forms of nature and in "heroes, prophets, men,"
who are

> But pipes through which the breath of Pan doth blow
> A momentary music.[15]

For no poet more instinctively than for Emerson is Pan the
"universal All" of the allegorists, and these related ideas
and emotions receive concentrated and ecstatic expression

---

[10] *The Poet* (*Poems*, p. 311) in *Works*, Centenary Edition, ed. Edward W.
Emerson (Boston, 1903–04). Cf. *Waldeinsamkeit* (p. 250).

[11] *The Harp* (p. 240).

[12] "The Over-Soul."

[13] "Nature" (*Essays*). It may be added that few Renaissance poets ever
passed from "the hue and cry after Cupid" to such exalted abstractions as
Emerson embodies in *Initial, Daemonic and Celestial Love*.

[14] *Woodnotes* (*Poems*, p. 58).

[15] *Pan* (p. 360).

in *Bacchus*. "I become a transparent eyeball; I am nothing; I see all; the currents of the Universal Being circulate through me; I am part or parcel of God."[16] Most ancient followers of Dionysus may be supposed to have fallen short of the Emersonian conception of this wine of wine, blood of the world, this power of experiencing the essence of life, and in fact the inspiration of the poem, so far as it was not original, was Persian rather than classical or Neo-Platonic.[17] Pantheism is not in favor nowadays, but Emerson's wears better in his poetry than in his prose, and this poem of 1846, like many of his poems, remains remarkably modern.

In England, as we have seen, there was through most of the nineteenth century, and there has been up to the present, a conflict between the claims of the antique and of modern realism. In the United States the same conflict has gone on from the beginning, and here the relative weakness of the classical tradition, along with the modern and American sympathies of the major writers, Emerson, Lowell, Whitman and others, might have seemed sufficient to extinguish mythological verse. Even such a representative of the genteel tradition as Thomas Bailey Aldrich repudiated the mythological dreams of his youth for the realities of prostitution.[18] There was also a conflict between religion and "paganism" which could become significant in such a poet as William Vaughn Moody, but for the most part did not go beyond an innocent faith in the loveliness of love and nature.[19] Instead of the naughty

[16] *Nature: Addresses and Lectures* (*Works*, I, 10).

[17] Frederic I. Carpenter, *Emerson and Asia* (Harvard University Press, 1930), pp. 163, 168–69, 188–89; Arthur Christy, *The Orient in American Transcendentalism* (Columbia University Press, 1932), pp. 147–49, 152. See Edward Emerson's notes, *Poems*, pp. 443–45. Mr. Alfred Noyes eulogizes *Bacchus* in *Some Aspects of Modern Poetry* (New York, 1924), pp. 69 ff.

[18] *Andromeda* (*Unguarded Gates*, 1895).

[19] One might mention Mr. Thornton Wilder's novel, *The Woman of Andros*

nineties — for whatever American life and politics might be, American verse remained pure — we have the melodious and edifying musings of Madison Cawein and Edith M. Thomas. But neither realism nor puritanism dried up the springs of Helicon. With a few exceptions, one may say that all the well-known American poets of the last two or three generations, good and bad, romantic and realistic, sophisticated and unsophisticated, have paid their tribute to ancient myth. They range from the academic George Woodberry and William Alexander Percy to the author of *The Man with the Hoe* and Max Eastman, from such unabashed romantics as the brothers Benét to the ultra-intellectual Yvor Winters and Allen Tate. The list of mythological poets includes even novelists of such varied achievement as Rupert Hughes, John Erskine, Amélie Rives, Alice Brown, Willa Cather, and Mrs. Wharton; in their verse they are not very far apart. Some writers, as in England, worked off mythological measles in youth and then turned realist, while Mr. Edgar Lee Masters, after inaugurating the new realism (with an imitation of the *Greek Anthology*), has persisted indefatigably in publishing mythological poems.

Of recent as well as the older American verse the large bulk, if not the most important part, has continued the romantic, idyllic, or moralistic conventions of Victorian poetry in England. If that fact generally exempts one from reading it, wholesale condemnation may be checked by the thought of Miss Millay, whose handling of myth in allusions and in such a sonnet as the one on Endymion[20]

(New York, 1930), which, in the style of a somewhat earlier day, begins and ends with references to Judaea.

[20] *Fatal Interview* (1931), Sonnet LII. See Mr. Allen Tate's review, *New Republic*, LXVI (1931), 335–36; or his *Reactionary Essays on Poetry and Ideas* (New York, 1936), pp. 224–25. For more appreciative comments see Elizabeth Atkins, *Edna St. Vincent Millay and Her Times* (University of Chicago Press, 1936), pp. 231–33.

shows what rich beauty a supposedly exhausted vein can yield to a genuine poet. It is not a fatal charge against Miss Millay that, apart from the accent of the modern emancipated woman, her mythological poetry might have been written in the nineteenth century, since future readers will not care about such questions, but it is true that she rather arrays traditional myths in her own golden eloquence than re-creates their symbolic value. In the less traditional contemporary poetry, which is mainly lyrical, the treatment of myth has of course shared in the general changes in modern writing. Moral striving has turned to disillusion or frustration, optimistic idealism to ironic negations, emotionalism to intellectuality (or at least a more intellectual kind of emotionalism), transparent statement and symbol to the frequent obscurity of a private symbolism, idyllic picture-making and verbal music to taut economy and sharp edges. Here in various ways such influences as the Imagists, Mr. Pound, Mr. Eliot, and their masters, have counted.[21]

H. D., Mr. Pound, Mr. Eliot, and Mr. Jeffers, who appear to be the most distinctive mythological poets of recent years, will be discussed later. (I approach the present time with the diffidence proper to an academic person who cannot possibly understand anything written since about 1910 — to cite a fundamental axiom of the American literary journalists who have read nothing written before that date.) If the limits of this book were less rigorous, one might take in *Mourning Becomes Electra*, which shows that a semi-Greek pattern and intense seriousness are not enough to win a tragic catharsis from a Freudian casebook. And what, if one were not tethered at the foot of

---

[21] During the last forty years or so even our limited genre has revealed some French as well as the normal English affiliations, from Richard Hovey's *The Faun* (1894), an adaptation of Mallarmé, to Mr. Malcolm Cowley's *Leander* (1929), an imitation of Rimbaud's *Bateau Ivre*. See the critical study by M. René Taupin cited in the bibliography.

Olympus, would one do with such a truly classical poet as Mr. Frost, whose clear-eyed sanity and craftsmanship are not merely instinctive but owe much to his early passion for Latin and Greek? [22] As for the miscellaneous mass of recent verse, it is far too large to be discussed, and before we come to the quartet mentioned above we must take account of a group of ambitious poets of a generation ago.

II

Trumbull Stickney, William Vaughn Moody, and George Cabot Lodge all died prematurely, and they were united in life by ties of friendship, by aristocratic culture and classical learning, and by their efforts to treat major themes on a large scale. The Promethean dramas of Stickney and Moody are related to each other, so that we may begin with an unjustly brief glance at Lodge (1873-1909), who seems to be the least remembered of the three. Lodge's *Herakles* (1908) is certainly the longest of American mythological dramas. In spite of the author's use of Diodorus and Euripides and other sources, it is not in the ordinary sense a mythological poem, for there is nothing antique about it except the names of the characters and parts of the slight frame of action. It is a modern pilgrim's progress in which the hero not merely leaves his wife and children but, in accordance with the myth, slays them. Herakles is a god and savior, an incarnation of the soul or will. He turns away from the spurious values and successes of the world because he has a vision of truth, but he has still to learn the price of truth, to win the right to his divine mission. Through self-sacrifice he rises to ulti-

---

[22] While Mr. Frost's avowed debt to the classics has been recorded by various critics, I may mention an especially interesting interview in the *Harvard Crimson* (March 9, 1936). As a young man the poet had more wisdom than the molders of American college curricula; he took no English courses which required daily themes, but did take voluntary courses in Greek and Latin composition.

mate victory; by that sacrifice he links himself, and humanity, with the infinite will which rules the world. *Herakles* has profound sincerity, but its dramatic and poetical moments are not enough, perhaps, to sustain most of us at the required pitch of moral elevation through twelve scenes and two hundred and seventy pages.[23] The fact may be more of a reflection upon the reader than upon the writer.

Trumbull Stickney (1874–1904), the first American to receive a Paris doctorate (in Greek), wrote some monumental sonnets on Greek scenes, which we must pass by, and the one-act drama *Prometheus Pyrphoros* (1900).[24] The fable is based on Hesiod and Apollodorus. In a dark world bereft of fire the hopeless Deukalion and the faintly hopeful Pyrrha are enduring their fate.[25] In pity for them Prometheus steals fire from heaven and gives an epic account of his exploit. While he rejoices that he has lit the world, that he has vindicated the purposeful human will and "the majesty of life," darkness falls again and the ministers of Zeus claim him for punishment. He remains defiant, trusting in the light of hope and effort that he has kindled in the world, and his faith in life is echoed in the last words of Pyrrha. But in its total effect the drama is far from bracing, in the obvious sense. There clings to it, as Moody said,

something of the gray disheartenment of the "Works and Days." The heroic deed of the Titan brings with it no joy, rather at best only the courage to live and to Deukalion not so much, merely the hard necessity. The triumph lies in the deed itself and in the magnanimity which achieved it. It is very characteristic of

---

[23] *Poems and Dramas of George Cabot Lodge* (Boston and New York, 1911), II. *Herakles* is fully discussed, and highly praised, in Henry Adams' *Life of George Cabot Lodge* (1911), pp. 162 ff.

[24] *Poems of Trumbull Stickney*, ed. George Cabot Lodge, William Vaughn Moody, and John E. Lodge (Boston and New York, 1905).

[25] The pair had been treated in Bayard Taylor's ambitious, facile, and unreadable *Prince Deukalion* (Boston, 1878).

Stickney's line of thought that he should have given this turn to the great story.[26]

But what we remember is the somber atmosphere of the whole, the sense of human helplessness and pain and pity, the vaguely poignant lyrics of Pandora, Epimetheus weighed down by memories of the past, and Prometheus facing the torments of the future.

William Vaughn Moody (1869–1910) wrote *The Fire-Bringer* (1904) between *The Masque of Judgment* and the fragmentary *Death of Eve*, but logically it is the first member of the massive trilogy in which he attempted to assert eternal human passion and justify the ways of men to God.[27] He knew and loved the whole body of Greek tragedy, he had beheld Greece with his own eyes, he was steeped in the great tradition of English poetry, he had a native grandiloquence fitted for the treatment of heroic themes, and, since those four possessions are no guarantee against academic frigidity, he had a large personal vision and a positive modern faith to utter. *The Fire-Bringer*, consequently, is not classical, calm, and dead, though now and then in the texture of the writing and the symbolism there may be some vague remoteness.

In his manipulation of the fable Moody did not challenge comparison with Aeschylus, Goethe, or Shelley. His chief classical debt was to the *Bacchae* of Euripides; the symbol of Dionysiac ecstasy is recurrent in *The Fire-Bringer* and is used even in the biblical *Masque of Judgment*. For much of the general pattern of his story, the choice of his principal characters, and the giving of incidental lyrics to Pandora, as well as various details,

[26] "The Poems of Trumbull Stickney," *North American Review*, CLXXXIII (1906), 1018.

[27] Among studies of the whole trilogy, see Mr. J. M. Manly's introduction to the *Poems and Plays* (Boston and New York, 1912); *Selected Poems*, ed. Robert Morss Lovett (Boston and New York, 1931); David D. Henry, *William Vaughn Moody: A Study* (Boston, 1934).

Moody was indebted to the drama of his friend Stickney, but he re-created what he borrowed, and his large symbolism, especially in its application to the problem of good and evil, and the fundamental optimism of the whole, are his own.[28] Prometheus is absent, in the body, a good part of the time, Zeus is a harsh power in the background, and the action revolves mainly around the more or less passive Deukalion and Pyrrha and the nameless survivors of the flood. The stone men and earth women whom Deukalion and Pyrrha created symbolize the spiritual deadness of mankind, while Pandora, whose lyrics include some of Moody's best, alone keeps alive some embers of passion, courage, and hope in a crumbling and rotting world. The wayward energies and impulses of humanity, pride, lust, and wrangling, had troubled the harmony the gods enjoyed, and the water and darkness sent by Zeus upon the physical world have extinguished all spiritual light. The fire that has been lost is not knowledge, the arts of civilization, but the divine fire of the heart and soul, "the triple madness or passion of Plato's Phaedrus."[29] After a bold attempt to steal fire from heaven Prometheus returns, wounded, to earth. He rejects Deukalion's counsels of humble submission to the gods and, roused by Pandora's song of victory in defeat and by her love, he sets forth again in quest of fire.

The frightened flock of people seek to propitiate Zeus by sacrificing the daughter of Lykophon and the son of Deukalion and Pyrrha, but Pyrrha — the woman being a more effectual rebel than the man — delays the sacrifice

[28] For a detailed comparison see Henry, pp. 155 ff., and the briefer remarks of Charlton M. Lewis, *Yale Review*, II (1913), 688–703. In a note in Stickney's *Poems* (p. 105), Moody acknowledges his own "deep obligation" to *Prometheus Pyrphoros*; see also his *Letters to Harriet*, ed. Percy Mackaye (Boston and New York, 1935), p. 179. As a prose argument for his drama Moody quotes Apollodorus (*Lib.* I. vii. 1–2).

[29] Paul Shorey, "The Poetry of William Vaughn Moody," *University of Chicago Record*, XIII (1927), 184.

until Prometheus shall come back. Meanwhile the regeneration of humanity begins. Fanned by thoughts of Prometheus and by the voice of Pandora, there quickens in the bolder spirits a renewed spark of love and life, of will, purpose, desire. Heaven and earth become alive with joy and dazzling light, and Pandora sings of the inspiring trinity, Dionysus, Eros, and Apollo.[30] Prometheus returns, bearing fire, and through the boy and girl who were to have been sacrificed the race is endowed with "the passion of this element." In the third act Prometheus, before he undergoes his punishment, proclaims that the cycle of the seasons and of human life, of time and space and change, of passion, thought, and will, is re-established. In short, every man must be his own Prometheus, must kindle in his own heart the divine fire of abundant life.

Thus although Moody conceived of the Promethean drama, and of the whole trilogy, in terms of the inseparableness of God and man, we hear much less about God as a spiritual entity and reality than we do about man and a brave love of life, life in which the human and divine are fused. In the large sense Moody is with Goethe and Shelley and not with Aeschylus in affirming his faith in life and man and in treating God as a negative force or idea, a denier of life, to be opposed by man. Hence, as the author said, though not in these words,[31] the theological and metaphysical mythology of the biblical plays, while it gives spaciousness to the stage of the human drama, has nothing of the substance and significance that it had for Milton;

[30] In addition to the *Bacchae*, Shorey cites Nietzsche's essay on the origin of Greek tragedy. Of Pandora's song, "Because one creature of his breath" (*Poems and Plays*, I, 233-34), Shorey remarks that it is "the one poem in all modern literature which can be fairly matched with the Lucretian prelude as an expression of the love-life and genial spirit of universal nature and the creative evolution which culminates in man." Compare *The Moon-Moth*.

[31] *Some Letters of William Vaughn Moody*, ed. Daniel G. Mason (Boston and New York, 1913), pp. 131-34; Henry, p. 114. On Milton's influence, see Lovett, *Selected Poems*, pp. xxxviii, xliii.

Milton's influence, by the way, was potent, both on the imaginative and artistic side and, so far as Milton was counsel for the other party, on the philosophical. But what chiefly matters in the *Masque* is the sympathy felt by Raphael and Uriel for the passionate dreams and desires, the strivings and the pains, of puny man. The whole work, then, though it was to culminate in the reconciliation of God and Man, is not really a cosmology; in emphasis at least it is in the idealistic, optimistic, and — according to one's definition of the terms — humanitarian or humanistic tradition of the nineteenth century. It is also a document in the conflict between "pagan" naturalism and Christianity. Moody had a genuine vein of religious mysticism and a consciousness of the warfare between flesh and spirit, along with an exceptionally rich sensibility and a love of nature and the arts. He was pleading here — though early reviewers complained of the antique, un-American subjects — for that unified and passionate enrichment of life which had been divided by American puritanism or extinguished by American progress and prosperity. In the last chorus of *The Fire-Bringer*, as if pricked by a puritan conscience and a fear of being misunderstood in his glorifying of passion and sensuous life and joy, Moody allowed himself only a glance at the ecstasies of Eros and Dionysus and paid his worship to Apollo, who alone sets the prisoned spirit free.[32]

Whatever their individual differences, Lodge, Stickney, and Moody were passionate idealists. If their poetry does not exercise a compelling power upon us, perhaps the best general explanation is to be found in some informal words of Mr. Santayana's. In speaking of *The Last Puritan*, Mr. Santayana has named these three, along with some lesser Harvard poets of their time, as contributing to the tragedy

---

[32] See *Letters to Harriet*, pp. 161–62, and the comments on this chorus of Manly (p. xxxviii) and C. M. Lewis (p. 692).

of Oliver, who had a profoundly spiritual vocation and "nothing to pin his allegiance to." "Now, all those friends of mine, Stickney especially, of whom I was very fond, were visibly killed by the lack of air to breathe." [33] On the literary side, most recent writing has turned us against poets who work with a big brush, and most other American poets have not had the sinews to grapple with such great and greatly traditional arguments. Moody died in 1910, and his masculine voice was soon obscured by the multitudinous twitterings of the Imagists, his ardent affirmation of life was submerged by the flood of critical and uncritical pessimism.

III

Imagism as a movement died young. Indeed, as Mr. Leavis has observed, it amounted to little more than a recognition that something was wrong with poetry. The only member of the group who has survived, as an Imagist, is H. D. Her poetry may be approached through her translations, which provide a concrete if limited criterion for estimating her methods of re-creating the Greek world. Mr. Eliot's condemnation of the popular Mr. Murray and his praise of the highbrow H. D. have of course been echoed by critics less qualified to judge of the merits of the case.[34] Without disputing the general truth of Mr. Eliot's strictures, one may think that he is somewhat unkind to Mr. Murray and more than kind to H. D. The former had to frame a style which would serve for the rendering of whole plays, not merely "romantic crumbs"; the style he chose may be easily damned as vague, lush Swinburnese, but a

---

[33] Letters to Mr. W. L. Phelps (*Scribner's Magazine*, XCIX [1936], 379–80).

[34] *Selected Essays* (1932), p. 63. In the preface to her *Choruses from Iphigeneia in Aulis*, H. D. remarked that a literal version would be useless, that "a rhymed, languidly Swinburnian verse form is an insult and a barbarism," and that her own "rhymeless hard rhythms" seemed "most likely to keep the sharp edges and irregular cadence of the original."

whole play done in H. D.'s manner would be less readable and probably even less Greek. (It is likewise conventional nowadays to damn the Lang translations of Homer, but one shudders at the thought of the *Odyssey* done in the staccato strut of H. D.'s "chorus" specimen.[35]) Further, Mr. Murray was under obligation to translate all of his author's text, at least as much of it as any translator in verse can compass. One might expect that a translator who uses free verse would be invariably more faithful than one bound by, or rather stretched on, a fluent pattern of rhyme, but it is not always so; I wish there were space to illustrate the fact, but our concern must be with H. D. herself.[36]

Her alterations of detail are everywhere, and the total effect is not Euripidean; Euripides was an ancient Greek, not a modern Imagist. One of the Greek qualities commonly praised in H. D. is the clear white light in which everything is seen. In the translations that effect is partly authentic and partly a peculiarity of poetic diction. To lapse into statistics, in the translations from Euripides and the *Odyssey* in the *Collected Poems* the word "bright" occurs nine times. In three cases there is no corresponding word in the Greek, but the adjective may be more or

[35] As a specimen of reviewing at least one may quote another opinion: "Certainly the surge and thunder of the *Odyssey* has never been more finely caught a.id wrought into English verse than in the beautiful translation of the opening lines" (Irwin Edman, *Nation*, CXIX [1924], 527).

[36] For instance, the first of H. D.'s fragments from *Hippolytus* is less close to the Greek than Mr. Murray's version. The first chorus of *Iphigeneia in Aulis* shows some odd treatments of Euripides. H. D. expands the epithet "reed-nourishing" into two lines of a dozen words, in which the river Eurotas becomes "the strait," presumably "Euripos' strait" of her opening lines. Euripides alludes (as in the second chorus of his *Andromache*) to the three goddesses bathing in one of the many fountains of Mount Ida before they faced Paris for judgment. H. D. seems rather cruel in having them judged while standing in the water, and apparently the notorious current of the Euripus at that, for the third appearance of the "strait," in comparison with Euripides' three different localities, suggests an excessive fondness for unity of place. See H. D.'s *Collected Poems* (New York, 1925), pp. 105–06.

less fairly derived from the context. In the other six instances "bright" is the rendering of "with goodly locks," "golden," "dappled," "noble," "keen-sighted," and "beautiful." The poet has subtle ways of achieving brightness, but this is not one of them.

In the preface already quoted, H. D. refers to Euripides' "sharp edges" and to the presence, in the choruses of *Iphigeneia*, of "something of that rocky quality, of that imaged clarity, which are so admirable in the earlier lyric poets." Here again H. D.'s hardness and sharpness are partly authentic and partly not. Rocks and ledges are favorite stage properties in her original poems, and she introduces them freely into her translations. Even Homer is hardened in the same way. Although H. D. has her own fixed epithets — "bright" is not the only one — she avoids Homer's repeated phrase, "in the hollow caves," by means of two variations, neither of them accurate or attractive. One does not like to think of Calypso "yearning in the furrowed rock-shelf," or of Thoosa lying with Poseidon "among the shallow rocks"; but these nouns and adjectives are stock items in H. D.'s highly mannered poetic diction.

Another notable characteristic of the poet which the translations show in clear relief is her instinct for visual impressions of movement. Euripides' "the waters of far-famed Arethusa near the sea" — to quote the literal prose of E. P. Coleridge,[37] lest one's own be suspected of bias — becomes

> Arethusa twists among the boulders,
> Increases — cuts into the surf.

Prosaic "sailors" are turned into "men slashed with waves." Everywhere persons and things incessantly

[37] *The Plays of Euripides Translated into English Prose from the Text of Paley* (1904–06), II, 395–96.

"cut" and "dart" and "flash" and "strike." Indeed there are so many added words expressing motion that our eyes grow tired as they did in the days when moving-pictures flickered. Thus the translator seems to have found Euripides too unpoetical, in the Imagist sense, and the result is not so much the critics' "economy" as continual over-writing.

Such over-writing is not limited to description, it extends to the modernizing and heightening of emotion. The Greek chorus speak of visiting the armament at Aulis: "Next I sought the countless fleet, a wonder to behold, that I might fill my girlish eyes with gazing, a sweet delight." They are only normal, curious women, but in H. D.'s rendering they become modern poets, very like H. D.:

> This beauty is too much
> For any woman.
> It is burnt across my eyes.[38]

There are similar effects in the choruses translated from the *Bacchae* and *Hecuba* in *Red Roses for Bronze*. These are less bright and rocky and stiff than the earlier experiments, and more verbose — the one chorus from *Hecuba* has a hundred and thirty words in Greek and four hundred and fifty in English — but they are more attractive, thanks partly to H. D. and partly to Euripides. H. D. is generally superior to Mr. Murray in salience, energy, and speed, yet the two come together when they find an occasion to turn simple, concrete, human sentiments into an eighteen-ninetyish cult of Beauty. Mr. Murray writes of being set free from fear and hate, and loving loveliness for ever; H. D. celebrates escape from the hunting pack and the knowledge that wisdom is best and beauty sheer holiness.[39]

---

[38] The phrase about the fleet which comes next, "The line is an ivory-horn," is another of those clear hard images in which Euripides is deficient.

[39] Cf. *Bacchae*, ll. 877 ff.; Coleridge, II, 114.

It is something of a shock to discover how much less spiritual Euripides is than his translators: "What is true wisdom, or what fairer boon has heaven placed in mortals' reach, than to gain the mastery o'er a fallen foe? What is fair is dear for aye." At the end of the same chorus Euripides says: "But him, whose life from day to day is blest, I deem a happy man." While Mr. Murray keeps fairly close to the text, H. D. envelops the plain Greek idea in romantic overtones and romantic diction, with repetitions of "mysterious" and "mystical." These paragraphs do not pretend to do justice to the poetical merits of H. D.'s translations, they only attempt to suggest the degree of remoteness from the letter and spirit of Euripides. The translations produce almost exactly the same effect as many of H. D.'s original poems, and if there is one thing certain in the realm of poetry it is that Euripides was not like H. D.

Most of what has been said about the translations may be applied to the original poems. The pictures and emotional symbols, the "Greek" world of the feminine eye and the feminine heart, are mainly composed of waves, rocks, trees, and flowers. A fresh outdoor world of sun and wind, one might say, if the total effect were not curiously indoor and static, as of a seascape and landscape modeled in wax. H. D.'s phrasing and picture-making have a quality best described in her own words (slightly altered), rare, of pure texture, beautiful space and line, marble to grace her inaccessible shrine. But what is one to say of a kind of beauty which vanishes the moment one's eye leaves the page? As an early critic observed, H. D. "combines in a remarkable degree precision of detail and clear presentment of the symbol with a kind of mystification as to the nature of the thing symbolized." [40] Such a quality is scarcely Greek. H. D.'s clear bright light plays over sur-

[40] *T.L.S.*, January 5, 1922, p. 8.

faces, it seldom strikes into the depths; one is not always certain that there are depths.

H. D.'s original works include the lyrical pieces in the *Collected Poems* (1925) and *Red Roses for Bronze* (1931), the lyrical tragedy *Hippolytus Temporizes* (1927), and the prose "novels," *Palimpsest* (1926) and *Hedylus* (1928). Thus almost everything she has written has a Greek setting and most of the poems are more or less concerned with Greek myth. H. D. has had, nevertheless, enthusiastic tributes from numerous poets and critics, chiefly American, of wholly modern and realistic sympathies. (There may have been a patriotic factor at work, since H. D. has shown Europeans that an American poet may be able to read Greek.) We have been told again and again that she is the most authentically Greek of modern poets, that she sees and feels and writes like a Greek, that she is a startled dryad in this alien modern world. If all this were true, H. D. would not be a poet but a chameleon; she is something of a chameleon, but she is also, in her own narrow way, a poet.

One dominant and personal motive is love, the love that is woman's whole existence. Almost every theme and every myth lead to Eros and Aphrodite. Circe, Penelope, Cassandra, all alike are longing for love; even a centaur is a saint of love. Names change, but the characters all speak with the same voice. That voice grows more directly emotional in the course of H. D.'s work, and at no time is she much concerned with dramatic fidelity to a mythological character or situation; in early as in late poems there is both clarity and vagueness, and on the whole vagueness prevails. It is an essential if often an irritating element in the poet's romantic and suggestive art. In *Red Roses for Bronze*, Greece is rather the poet's conventional backdrop than her home, and the dramatic mask becomes inadequate for the protracted pains of unrequited passion. We have the same properties, the same eurhythmic attitudes, the same mythology, but now, instead of remote isolation and "cold splendour of song," there is a jarring discord between antique elements and modernity of feeling expressed in sometimes colloquial language. However dubious the authenticity of H. D.'s Hellenism, this volume shows the extent of her debt to it, for the partial abandonment of her Hellenic draperies exposes a somewhat monotonous and turbid romantic emotionalism. H. D. has disciplined her technique more than her poetic character.

In *Hippolytus Temporizes*, H. D. objectifies on a large scale some of the conflicts adumbrated in her short poems, especially the conflict between the energies and cravings of the flesh and the discipline and aspirations of the spirit. She retains the Euripidean idea of Phaedra and Hippolytus as representatives and symbols of the antagonistic powers of Aphrodite and Artemis, but her fable and interpretation are remote from the Greek play. Hippolytus is not merely a chaste devotee of Artemis and, like his mother, a haunter of her woods, but a modern poet (and apologist for free verse) who rejects the lures and the claims of the world in order to follow his elusive ideal. Artemis becomes really the chief character; she appears to symbolize a spiritual fire and beauty which the worshiper can have glimpses of but never possess. Phaedra, a sensual creature of the warm south, seduces Hippolytus by a trick. In Euripides, of course, he is not seduced, and Phaedra, after falsely accusing him to Theseus, hangs herself; the suicide of H. D.'s now contented embodiment of the flesh seems less logical.[41] Hippolytus, filled with rapture by the

[41] A reviewer of the play in *The New Republic* (LII [1927], 25) remarked, with the large omniscience characteristic of that journal: "In treating the material, she follows previous models, except that Phaedra seduces Hippolytus by means of a ruse instead of the usual love-potion." These interesting models were not identified. H. D. might have got some general hints from Mr. Sturge Moore's *Aphrodite against Artemis*.

thought that he has embraced Artemis, refuses to believe that it was Phaedra. He drives forth in his chariot to seek an outlet for his intoxication by flouting the waves and not, as in Euripides, because he is sent into exile. The last act is a debate between the two Olympians, Artemis and Helios. The former wishes Hippolytus to die, that she may "shelter him turned to a spirit"; Helios wishes to save his body and restores him temporarily to life. Hippolytus sees his goddess again as the true cold Artemis and dies with her kiss on his lips. She retires into her old inaccessibility, repeating the speech with which the play had begun; she must for ever dwell apart from man and mortal prayers.

It cannot be said that the symbolic intention is always clear or that, when clear, it is effectually carried out. The abstract theme is great enough, and the myth is a means of isolating and refining its essential elements, yet the poet does not do much to intensify our thoughts and feelings about it. Modernization is natural and desirable, but the result here is attenuation; Euripides' concrete, human, and ethical drama becomes vague, unhuman, and esthetic. We are not moved as we are by such treatments of a parallel theme as *Endymion* and *Alastor*, which, for all their romantic extravagance, are less literary and less remote. H. D.'s drama is really a series of antiphonal lyrics, in which there are moments of cool loveliness and august mystery, though the lyrics are mostly more tenuous than the Hippolytus-Phaedra pieces included in the *Collected Poems*. An increasingly tyrannous mannerism of the poet's, the repetition of identical one-word lines, often approaches and sometimes topples over the brink of the ridiculous; in the space of two pages, for instance, there are eighteen lines consisting of "aye," "yes," and "no." As dramatic or lyrical dialogue such writing lacks passion and variety; not even a ritualistic play can achieve high tension by such means.

H. D.'s devotion to Greece is obviously instinctive and
sincere, yet the instinctive effort of a twentieth-century
poet to write like a Greek indicates, no matter what the
degree of success, a fundamentally romantic and precious
conception both of Greece and of poetry. It represents
a new and very sophisticated species of primitivism. If
H. D. has any ancient affiliations at all, they are with
Sappho — so far as one can judge of Sappho — and with
the lyrists of the *Greek Anthology*. But the Greece she
dwells in has no real connection with the Greece of historic
actuality. Most of her poetry has the air of an exquisitely
chiseled reproduction of something, though it is a reproduction of something that never existed. While H. D. is
in the main a "pure" poet, in such "impure" poems as
Cities and *The Tribute* she reveals, more directly than elsewhere, a sensitive mind oppressed by the ugliness and
barbarism of modern life, by the belief that modern civilization has no room for beauty, and she invites choice spirits
to worship at her own secluded shrine. Such a creed, if
broadly and deeply based on human life, can give birth to
major poetry, but the poet must convince us that he has
known and surmounted the world, not simply turned away
from it. H. D. is a poet of escape. Her refuge is a dream-
world of ideal beauty which she calls Greece; her self-
conscious, even agonized, pursuit of elusive beauty is quite
un-Greek. Critics have found in her limitations evidence
of artistic integrity, but

> this beauty,
> beauty without strength,
> chokes out life.

The fact is that the hard bright shell of H. D.'s poetry
partly conceals a soft romantic nostalgia which, however
altered and feminized, is that of the Victorian Hellenists.
H. D., moreover, has been mainly content to inhabit the
ivory tower which those Hellenists were always break-

ing out of. Whatever their pseudo-Hellenic sins, Landor, Morris, and Swinburne testify their consciousness of the modern world, of a world outside themselves; H. D. never quite doffs her antique and individual mask. Her Greece, the paradise of beauty and beautiful lovers, is essentially the Greece of Pater and Wilde (who were scholars), and of Isadora Duncan (who was not).

IV

Mr. Pound (1885–) and T. S. Eliot (1888–1965), if very different in some fundamental respects, have been at one in their adaptation of modern French technique and in their hostility to romantic and "poetical" conceptions of poetry. While their younger disciples in the main have dropped classical baggage and, like Petulant, rely on their parts, the schoolmasters of modernism are devoutly, sometimes ostentatiously, rooted in the European tradition, and they dwell in imposing edifices of polyglot learning. Mr. Eliot's is the more sober and shapely building, and of late years it has acquired a likeness to St. Paul's. Mr. Pound's spiritual home is a more flamboyant affair, a Provençal castle with a Roman portico and some features of a pagoda; since his erudition impresses highbrow critics, it would be idle for a mere scholar to look behind the façade. Mr. Pound's verse, like that of his beloved Propertius, bristles with mythology; Mr. Eliot's allusions are few, but always suggestive and significant. If these two poets, who have aimed at a synthesis of the modern consciousness, were defending their use of myth, they would appeal, not to the nineteenth-century Hellenic tradition, but to Propertius and Ovid and Dante and Donne. Mr. Pound has been, however, a disciple of Browning, and he once celebrated Swinburne as "High Priest of Iacchus." [42] Since Mr.

[42] *Salve Pontifex* (*Ripostes*, 1912). Cf. Mr. Pound's "Swinburne versus Biographers," *Poetry*, XI (1917–18), 322–29.

Pound, the literary technician and amateur, deviates into poetry as seldom as Mr. Eliot departs from it, I shall give most of this section to the latter.

Mr. Pound's handling of myth might be illustrated from the *Cantos*, which are apparently designed to revolve around two main themes, the descent into Hades from Homer and a metamorphosis from Ovid,[43] but that work, though regarded by Mr. Eliot and others as the author's great monument, may seem to the less intelligent an extremely unattractive farrago of pedantry, the pedantry of realism as well as of bookishness. In the simpler and shorter *Hugh Selwyn Mauberley* (1920), which shows Mr. Eliot's influence, we have a disillusioned stock-taking by a studious poet who, out of key with his time, has striven to revive a rigorous ideal of art. "He has devoted his life to aesthetic discrimination and technical perfection while life slipped by," [44] and he has won no poetic diadem. Since full quotation is impossible and snippets are useless, one can only recall the brief, jerky, sardonic allusions to Capaneus,[45] the adventures of Odysseus, the metamorphosis of Cephalus' hound and its quarry into stone, which suggest the poet's rash ambition, his eclectic literary enthusiasms, and his sense of frustration.[46] Mr. Pound can be a poet — "Faun's flesh is not to us, Nor the saint's vision . . ." — but most of his mythological allusions are too tight and dry, too laboriously contrived and condensed.

At any rate this compressed, colloquial, witty expression

[43] W. B. Yeats, *A Packet for Ezra Pound* (Dublin, 1929), p. 2.

[44] F. R. Leavis, *New Bearings in English Poetry* (1932), pp. 141 ff. For a prose parallel — "I may have been an ensanguined fool to spend so much time on mediaeval literature . . ." — see Mr. Pound's *Pavannes and Divisions* (New York, 1918), p. 206; *Make It New* (1934), p. 113. For the poem see *Personae* (New York, 1926), pp. 187 ff.

[45] To cite references only in three of Mr. Pound's favorite poets, see Ovid, *Metam.* ix. 404; Propertius, II. xxxiv. 40; Dante, *Inferno*, xiv. 63 ff.

[46] See *Odyssey*, xii. 189, etc.; Ovid, *Metam.* vii. 787 ff. For Cephalus, see *Personae*, p. 200 (and also the allusion to Daphne, p. 196).

of romantic irony is far removed from the nineteenth-century method of handling mythological reference. The poetic experience described is less remote from that misguided period. This confessional poem by a leader of the left wing recalls Keats's condemnation of himself as a romantic dreamer who has shrunk from the realities of life; but, while Keats is whole-hearted in his conviction of sin, Mr. Pound, who has never been accused of humility, is condemning the age, which prefers pianolas to Sappho and drives a good poet to a sense of defeat. And if Mr. Pound's scorn for a commercialized civilization recalls "The world is too much with us," one may think his esthetic reaction closer to Wilde than to Wordsworth.[47] According to the common modernist creed, the nineteenth-century poets, especially the Victorians, are damned because they inhabited dream-worlds, whereas Mr. Pound and others have given poetry a new and comprehensive realism and a new direction. One may, with reservations, accept that view, and yet one may ask if Mr. Pound's exotic culture, which in so much of his verse seems to flourish for its own sake, has not served him as something of a dream-world, a romantic refuge from the ugly present. Mr. Eliot has insisted that Mr. Pound is not one of those writers who mistake literature for life, but his defence furnishes a good many arguments for those who think otherwise.[48]

Mr. Eliot was born five months after the death of Matthew Arnold. Though one would hesitate to suggest a transmigration of souls (certainly one would not suggest it to Mr. Eliot), and though fundamental differences are at least as marked as resemblances, no one else has come so close to being what Arnold was or what a twentieth-century Arnold might have been. While Mr. Eliot's classicism is less classical, more eclectic and modern, than

---

[47] See John Sparrow, *Sense and Poetry* (1934), pp. 123 ff.
[48] *Ezra Pound: Selected Poems*, ed. T. S. Eliot (1928), p. xi, and *passim*.

Arnold's, as critics they are linked together by their fine taste, their cosmopolitan, anti-provincial, anti-romantic conception of literature, their faith in the living value of tradition, authority, standards, discipline. In both has been seen, rightly or wrongly, a cleavage between the groping, disillusioned, romantic poet — to speak only of Mr. Eliot's earlier secular poems — and the confident, dogmatic, classicist critic. The poetry of both has revealed a conflict between a sensuous love of life, a consciousness of natural impulses denied, and a puritan and academic fear of life coupled with a desire for a stable anchorage. The general sources of their poetic pessimism are not unlike, though the emphasis differs, and Mr. Eliot's disillusion, like that of his age, has led him into fields which most Victorians did not feel called to explore. Both Arnold and Eliot have seen a mechanized and commercialized world of spurious or sordid values, a world of parched or greasy souls. But Arnold's solution of the Victorian religious problem, and his setting up of poetry as the new religion, have brought him severe (and one may think unjust) castigation from Mr. Eliot, who has himself taken, according to some opinions, the path of Bishop Andrewes, or, according to others, the path of disillusioned romantics of the early or the late nineteenth century.

Both poets have been called escapists — Mr. Eliot seems to regard Arnold as one [49] — and the charge is both true and untrue. Arnold was inevitably immersed, up to the neck at least, in the stream of the romantic tradition. If Mr. Eliot has done more than any individual to dry up that stream (and some might say he had only diverted it), the names of T. E. Hulme and Mr. Pound remind us that in the nature of things romanticism had run its course and

[49] *The Use of Poetry and the Use of Criticism* (Harvard University Press, 1933), pp. 98–99.

that a number of minds were giving poetry a fresh start.[50] At any rate Arnold and Mr. Eliot have had partly similar inward correctives to their nostalgic longings in their high seriousness, their effort at totality of vision, their belief that poetry must grapple with the realities of modern life, and that such poetry must be stripped of "poetical" ornament.[51] These are not marks of the ordinary escapist. Such parallels, which could be expanded and qualified indefinitely, may serve to show that both poets resort to classic myth from a partly identical impulse, the hunger for a glimpse of the ideal felt in the midst of arid and ugly actuality.

Their methods of course are utterly unlike. Compared with most Victorian Hellenists, such as Swinburne, Arnold is restrained and severe; compared with Mr. Eliot, he seems to wear his nostalgic heart on his sleeve, to let himself go in lush, idyllic pictures of the antique world with its fresh, natural unity and harmony. Mr. Eliot's heart, however, is not entirely concealed by his hard, terse, impersonal brevity. His pattern is sudden contrast, and since it is usually the Flaubertian contrast between the physical and spiritual squalor and artificiality of modern urban, bourgeois civilization and some ideal vision of the past, mythological allusions contribute their heroic, glamorous, idealistic associations to that vision. But Mr. Eliot's idealistic nostalgia is romantic with a difference. Arnold turned to myth as to a world outside of and unspoiled by his modern disillusion; Mr. Eliot likewise turns to that world, yet his mythological figures are made contemporaneous with his own and are embraced in the same view. Whatever his technical debt to Mr. Pound, Mr. Eliot is a poet of much

---

[50] See, for example, J. R. Daniells, "T. S. Eliot and his Relation to T. E. Hulme," *University of Toronto Quarterly*, II (1933), 380–96; F. O. Matthiessen, *The Achievement of T. S. Eliot* (Boston and New York, 1935), pp. 70–71, 144–45.

[51] See Matthiessen, p. 90, and above, ch. VII, pp. 251–52.

larger and more comprehensive soul, of much greater emotional, verbal, and rhythmic power, of more serious and philosophic integrity, and he combines romantic and modernist qualities to produce a unique effect. His mythological allusions are magical (though far from meaningless) incantations in a frame of irony. They comprise only two or three dozen lines, but they have weight and significance, and they remain indelibly etched in the memory. They are almost the only passages in Mr. Eliot's earlier poetry which can, in something like the ordinary sense of the word, be called beautiful.

In that everyday tragedy of triviality and futility, *The Love Song of J. Alfred Prufrock* (1917), the unheroic hero, the unconquering lover, might easily have been sentimentalized, but his pity for himself, and ours for him, are checked by his own self-mocking irony. The heroic dream of appearing as a young fashionable at a seaside resort leads at once to the mermaids' song, and we think at the same time of all the tales of alluring sea-maidens and of this fastidious, timid, aging suburbanite, who has measured out his life with coffee spoons, and in whose little soul the little flame of romance is extinguished. In periods and in poets of greater vitality the sirens were symbols of slothful or fleshly pleasures which distracted man from his virtuous or heroic purposes; witness the sirens or the Circe of Homer and Horace, Spenser and Milton.[52] Here they, or their cousins, have become, in contrast with modern anemic timidity, symbols of adventure, freedom, and fulfilment. The remaining lines of the poem, in spite of the modern twist with which they end, are more of a romantic mythological picture than the author has commonly al-

---

[52] For Horace, see *Ep.* I. ii. 17 ff. One might add Samuel Daniel's *Ulysses and the Siren*, or Mr. C. Day Lewis' poem on the sirens (*Collected Poems*, New York, 1935, p. 114). Of this last Miss Sitwell says: "He regards the intrusion of physically sensual life as dangerous. The physical world is his enemy, imperilling his spiritual vision" (*Aspects of Modern Poetry*, 1934, p. 245).

lowed himself; the chief suggestions seem to come from Laforgue.[53] If Mr. Prufrock is defeated by himself and his surroundings, Mr. Apollinax is not. Amid the tinkling decorums of a Boston afternoon tea, the foreign visitor with his pointed ears is a passionate disturbing force from a primitive world; he calls up thoughts of Priapus, the centaurs, the laughter, irresponsible, submarine, and profound, of the old man of the sea hidden under coral islands.

In later poems Mr. Eliot uses myth in a more typical manner and with more typical symbolic values. Princess Volupine, Burbank the naïve American, Bleistein, "Chicago Semite Viennese," and the wealthy winner of the Princess' favors, Sir Ferdinand Klein, are a tawdry crew who represent the modern heritage of Venice. But the poet does not muse upon departed grandeur in the style of *A Toccata of Galuppi's*. His characters are described, in a mixture of realistic and ironically "poetical" language (the irony does not exclude beauty), in terms of the horses of the sun, Mark Antony, and the burning glory of Cleopatra's barge.[54] Allusion is handled in the same way in *Sweeney Erect*. In Mr. Eliot's private mythology Sweeney is of course the symbol of gross, vulgar, sensual man, the unthinking human animal who lives by his appetites. Sweeney and the epileptic are a modern "Nausicaa and Polypheme," and his callous indifference to her recalls Theseus' desertion of Ariadne. The scene in the dubious lodging-house, where dingy drabness envelops a moment of ghastliness, is preceded by two stanzas on the myth which catch astonishingly in English the plangent resonance of Roman rhetoric.[55]

[53] Edmund Wilson, "T. S. Eliot," *New Republic*, LX (1929), 342; *Axel's Castle* (New York, 1931), p. 97. Cf. *Revue de littérature comparée*, VII (1936), 391–92.

[54] See *Antony and Cleopatra*, II. ii. 198 ff., IV. iii. 16–17; *The Phoenix and the Turtle*, l. 14.

[55] See the epistle of Ariadne in the *Heroides*.

These short poems cannot be called more than clever, uniquely, superlatively clever. The poet's sense of a vanished perfection, his vision of some greatness or beauty which the modern world has lost or degraded, is an uncertain implication in a tissue of satire, and the mythological allusions, however effective in themselves, are contrived and stuck on rather than organic and inevitable. *Sweeney Among the Nightingales* is more than clever, and that "more" is due to the sudden lift at the end, the allusion to the murder of Agamemnon prepared for by the epigraph.[56] The scene is a low dive where some of the disreputable habitués are intriguing against Sweeney; a number of words keep their animality before us. Then we come to the nightingales singing near the Convent of the Sacred Heart. Such is Mr. Eliot's power of concentrated suggestion that he can call up, in one apparently casual descriptive phrase, the two great traditions of civilization, the Christian and the classical. He makes us realize for ourselves that after two thousand years of Christianity this sordid intrigue is going on in a brothel near a convent.[57] And the song of the nightingale, for Mr. Eliot as for Keats and Arnold, carries across the gulf of time to link classical and modern worlds. The allusion to the bird associated with Greece in many Greek poets, and particularly in the *Agamemnon*, where it bewails Itys and the sensual crime of Tereus, leads up to the sensual crime of Clytemnestra.

[56] Mr. Matthiessen quotes (p. 129) Mr. Eliot's interesting remark that all he consciously set out to create was a sense of foreboding. Some of the items which contribute to that effect may have been suggested by the *Agamemnon*, although, apart from the nightingales (*Agam.*, ll. 1142–49), only one is a close parallel; cf. "the Dog . . . veiled" and *Agam.*, l. 967. "The circles of the stormy moon" might have started from the watchman's opening allusion to the stars, and with "Death and the Raven drift above" compare ll. 48 ff., 136–38, 1473, though the general idea is a commonplace.

[57] Browning needed a good many words to get a similar effect in *Fra Lippo Lippi*, in the lines about the murderer who has taken sanctuary in church, and Browning underlined his idea.

We feel a shock not merely of contrast but of elevation when we turn from the scheming of these idle wastrels to the death of the conqueror of Troy at the hands of a super-human murderess.

On the other hand, critical orthodoxy sees here a notable instance of Mr. Eliot's poetic counterpoint in a secondary (but really primary) realization forced upon us of the essential likeness; stripped of their antique greatness and glamour, is Clytemnestra so far from the demi-mondaines, is not Agamemnon another Sweeney? [58] It may well be so, for Mr. Eliot is often as subtle as his critics, but my own reaction, which is doubtless obtuse, remains what it was before I had read any comments. I cannot feel here that the poet's simultaneous double vision is limited to the "objective correlative," that Agamemnon is equated with Sweeney. The plotted death of such a creature arouses in me no sympathy or sense of human tragedy; (it would probably be illegitimate to remember that Sweeney lives to visit Mrs. Porter in the spring). The exaltation and the simple magic of phrase and rhythm carry us far beyond Sweeney to the universal lot of man, to such great Renaissance commonplaces as "The glories of our blood and state. . . ." And in such transcending of space and time Mr. Eliot, like Keats and Arnold, affirms in his own way eternal beauty and mortality, eternal passion and pain.

The mythological matter of *The Waste Land* (1922) has often been explained, up to a point, and, since it is not detachable, its character and function can only be briefly recalled to the initiated reader; to the uninitiated this particular dry stone can give no sound of water. Here we have classic myth, in addition to medieval and occult lore, used

[58] See, for example, R. P. Blackmur, "T. S. Eliot," *Hound and Horn*, I (1928), 208; Hugh R. Williamson, *The Poetry of T. S. Eliot* (1932), p. 166; Matthiessen, pp. 129–30. My remarks on the various poems are especially indebted to the last two critics.

not only for reference but for frame and background. There is Adonis, the slain vegetation god, who is merged with Christ; but Adonis has more to do with Frazer than with Venus and must be passed over here. Tiresias, however, "the most important personage in the poem," retains something of his mythological character. Since the prophet had been both man and woman — "throbbing between two lives" — he can be used as an all-embracing modern consciousness through which the poem is projected and unified. He sees and has "foresuffered all" the manifold experience, especially of sex, which constitutes the panorama of degradation and sterility in modern life and the modern soul. Since the poem is in one of its major aspects an inferno of the lustful, whose gnawing obsessions are contrasted with the harmony and fecundity of primitive life, Mr. Eliot may have been reminded of Tiresias by Dante as well as by Ovid and general mythological lore.[59]

One dark thread in the poem is the story of Tereus' rape of Philomela, which seems to be an example of crude fleshly lust and also, if the idea is not too nineteenth-century for Mr. Eliot, an example of the world's callous crushing of beauty. In "A Game of Chess" the upper-class woman of the first part and Lil, the lower-class woman of the second, are sisters under the skin, both aimless, restless neurasthenics, both denying life. The vapid cravings, the sterile ennui, of the first are contrasted with her luxurious surroundings in a passage of studied magnificence which includes allusions to Cleopatra and Dido.[60] Then we have

[59] *Inferno*, c. xx; *Purg.*, c. xxii.

[60] The resemblance which has been noticed (Matthiessen, pp. 85, 94) between these lines and Keats's picture of the banquet-hall in *Lamia* may be partly explained by the fact that Keats evidently recollected, along with other things, the Virgilian passage to which Mr. Eliot explicitly refers (see above, ch. III, note 49). But while Keats does not let his conception of Lamia affect his enjoyment of sensuous opulence, Mr. Eliot's description of concrete objects suggests spiritual aridity.

a rural vignette, of a sort, a glimpse of an antique past which suddenly becomes contemporary. Even if the poet, who cites Ovid, is not recalling again the nightingale in *Agamemnon*, his vaguely poignant change of tense in "pursues" corresponds with Cassandra's shift from the bird's fate to her own:

> Above the antique mantel was displayed
> As though a window gave upon the sylvan scene
> The change of Philomel, by the barbarous king
> So rudely forced; yet there the nightingale
> Filled all the desert with inviolable voice
> And still she cried, and still the world pursues,
> "Jug Jug" to dirty ears.

The Miltonic "sylvan scene" suggests Eden, as yet uncorrupted, and the inviolable voice rises above the world of pain and evil to declare the existence of some inviolable perfection man did not make and cannot mar; the lines have all the beauty of romantic poetry, and something besides.[61] The Elizabethan "Jug jug" is repeated in "The Fire Sermon," after a brief allusion, in sharply ironic vein, to the story of Actaeon and Diana. The idyllic mythological fancy of John Day becomes

> The sound of horns and motors, which shall bring
> Sweeney to Mrs. Porter in the spring.

The hunting horns are changed into symbols of mass production and progress. For the creatures of a mechanized world and mechanized appetites the spring is not the season when the slain god revives and the waste land receives

---

[61] The phrase "withered stumps of time," which comes just after the lines quoted, suggests the repeated allusions to the "stumps" of the ravished and mutilated Lavinia and her use of Ovid's story of Tereus (*Titus Andronicus*, II. iv. 4, III. ii. 42, V. ii. 183). But the phrase describes other old pictures on the walls, and, since the poet has just cited the first book of Virgil, one may think of the pictures at which Aeneas gazed, pictures of heroic action. Such queries may be quite fanciful, but Mr. Eliot awakens many echoes, whether always consciously or not.

rain; the cycle of human life is only "Birth, copulation, and death."

The theme of *The Waste Land* requires that much more should be suggested than could be stated, and if its suggestions were readily intelligible they would lose their infinite range and potent ambiguity. At the same time it is possible to think that Mr. Eliot's technique here somewhat overreached itself, that his vision of life, or our apprehension of his vision, is needlessly obscured by an intricate tangle of far-fetched learning. Of course an author can always insist that a poem "came that way," and leave the reader to brood upon his own defective mentality, but Mr. Eliot's notes, however inadequate, are themselves an admission that the poem cannot stand alone. It might have been written, like the *Prometheus Unbound* of a poet Mr. Eliot especially dislikes, for five or six persons, and others may read it for bits of "poetry" rather than for the austere import and art of the whole. Those five or six persons might maintain that this major work of our chief classicist, probably the major poetical work of our time, is truly classical. Others, not insensitive to its haunting magic and poignancy, might say that, for all its hold upon reality and evil, it is a twentieth-century version of romantic primitivism, a nostalgic vision of perfect purity, harmony, and fullness of life, an anguished cry that there might be shed

> On spirits that had long been dead,
> Spirits dried up and closely-furl'd,
> The freshness of the early world.

Yet such a view, if partly warranted by the poem itself and by its predecessors, must be modified in the light of the later poems, which have shown that the author has been steadily moving out of the flux, not backward into sentimental dreams but upward into dogmatic faith. There are those who would see no antithesis between such dreams and such faith, but a more sympathetic judgment would be that Mr. Eliot's nostalgia has been too deep and too intellectual to feed on self-deceiving illusions. A concluding passage of *The Waste Land* is thus summarized by Mr. Matthiessen: "The individual locked in his solitary identity can escape from this obsession only by self-surrender and by sympathy with others." [62] That sentence is also a summary of Keats's *Endymion*, yet definition of the terms would indicate how far Mr. Eliot has moved from the nineteenth-century religions of beauty and humanity.

V

The contemporary American poets who chiefly concern us have all recoiled with pain and disgust from modern civilization. H. D. and Mr. Pound (in spite of the all-embracing *Cantos*) may be called esthetic escapists; Mr. Eliot found a rock of spiritual order on the farther side of the waste land. Neither an esthetic nor a religious solution, not even the despairing sensual faith of D. H. Lawrence, could relieve the savage Titanism of Robinson Jeffers (1887–1962). It may be observed that H. D., Mr. Pound and Mr. Eliot have chosen to live abroad; Mr. Jeffers has shut himself in a tower of stone, or ivory,[63] in California. From his blasted heath, his universe of horrors, horrors which would have chilled Webster or Tourneur, there would seem to be no logical escape except suicide. Mr. Jeffers has, however, endured, and his waste land has yielded an annual or biennial volume; his curses on the human race and prayers for annihilation are collectors' items; and an expensive bibliography and a doctoral thesis seem to have established his classical status,

[62] P. 138.
[63] Morton D. Zabel, *New Republic*, LXXVII (1934), 230.

though he first flamed across the sky as late as 1924.[64] But that, however ironical, is the way of the world, and there is no question of Mr. Jeffers' tremendous sincerity, though there may be of his philosophic depth and poetic art.

I did not realize that this long survey of myth in poetry was destined to end with a bang, but Mr. Jeffers is a portent for us as well as for readers in general. In him, the latest poet of our latest decade, we have the most undisciplined soul and mind that we have yet encountered, the most striking of the many proofs we have had that Latin and Greek cannot make a classical artist out of a romantic, in this case a decadent romantic. While Mr. Jeffers began to read the ancient languages at an early age, he has said that most of whatever acquaintance he has with the classic spirit came from reading English poetry [65] — and that, as my two books have partly labored to show, is a generally dubious medium. Moreover, his first passions in English poetry were Rossetti and Swinburne — how many of our most advanced contemporaries started from the Pre-Raphaelites! — and these were followed by Shelley, Milton, and many others. Later, and less happily, came science and Spengler and Freud and Jung; Nietzsche was an early antidote to inherited Calvinism.

Although the classics have not wrought order out of Mr. Jeffers' stormy broodings on the plight of humanity, they have led him to ancient myth. As he has said, in words that many a traditional poet would subscribe to: "We turn to the classic stories, I suppose, as to Greek sculpture, for a more ideal and also more normal beauty, because the myths of our own race were never developed, and have been alienated from us." [66] And one cannot fail

---

[64] Volumes of 1912 and 1916 attracted little or no attention.

[65] S. S. Alberts, *A Bibliography of the Works of Robinson Jeffers* (New York, 1933), pp. 24–27; Lawrence C. Powell, *An Introduction to Robinson Jeffers* (Dijon, 1932), ch. I.

[66] Alberts, p. 27.

to observe the relative sobriety, firmness, and philosophic clarity of the mythological poems — the word "relative" must be emphasized — in comparison with most of the narratives of the California coast. In that madhouse world the uninstructed reader, despite occasional hints, may not penetrate to the symbolism which lies behind characters who, though partly unhuman, are also creatures of everyday realism, and behind the lurid welter of cruelty, sensuality, incest, and murder. It is not without reason that critics have turned to *The Tower Beyond Tragedy* for an exposition of the writer's creed.

This dramatic poem is a very free rehandling of the first two plays of the *Oresteia*.[67] It begins with Clytemnestra's welcome of her lord, and the murder follows at once. The rest of the first part depicts her on the palace steps, holding at bay the king's soldiers until Aegisthus shall come to support her. She is fighting against Agamemnon too, for the spirit of the dead man possesses the body of Cassandra and through her mouth urges on the men to slay the she-wolf. Clytemnestra's defence of herself is partly Aeschylean, but, as the soldiers grow more threatening and she grows more desperate, she resorts to what is known in a lower form of drama as a "strip tease" — a scene of grandiose, barbaric sensuality which would have shocked Aeschylus but might have appealed to Flaubert. Then, after "hours, hours," Aegisthus comes. In some long speeches, which carry us forward eight years into the second part, Cassandra mocks at the queen's and all human delusions of security in a world of ceaseless change and decay; individuals and empires are bubbles that burst and wander "On the stream of the world falling," and Cassandra prays

---

[67] *Roan Stallion, Tamar, and Other Poems* (New York, 1925). Mr. Jeffers has said that the origin of the poem "was probably in the rich voice and Amazon stature of a German-Jewish actress" who "recited one of the more barbaric Scotch ballads magnificently in private" (Alberts, p. 27).

to Death to make her grass, stone, air, to cut humanity out of her being. When Orestes and Electra meet after the murder of Clytemnestra and Cassandra, she, like her mother before her, is jubilant over the winning of peace, kingship, godship, but he is unhappy, he has grown apart from her. To make him happy, and to hold him, Electra offers herself as a lover, but Orestes will not waste inward upon humanity, he has found a fairer object. All the activities of the race have turned inward, their desires are incestuous. He, Orestes, is freed from human trammels, he has become one with the primeval life of nature; he has "fallen in love outward," has

> climbed the tower beyond time, consciously, and cast humanity,
> entered the earlier fountain.

Though less sensational and more coherent than most of the author's wholly original fables, *The Tower Beyond Tragedy* is plainly not an organic unit. Until near the end, except for the speeches of Cassandra which conclude the first part, the story seems to exist for its own sake, and then Orestes surprises us with the announcement that he has become a pantheistic extrovert. But if Mr. Jeffers is more explicitly didactic than implicitly symbolic, his intention is all the clearer. While Electra, like Clytemnestra, remains tangled in human relationships, and Cassandra finds peace in death, Orestes alone learns the lesson which the author has expounded in poem after poem. I may quote his prose statement of his view of life and his effort "to uncenter the human mind from itself":

There is no health for the individual whose attention is taken up with his own mind and processes; equally there is no health for the society that is always introverted on its own members, as ours becomes more and more, the interest engaged inward in love and hatred, companionship and competition. . . . All past cultures have died of introversion at last, and so will this one, but the individual can be free of the net, in his mind. . . .

I have often used incest as a symbol to express these introversions, and used it too often. . . .[68]

So for Mr. Jeffers the peace that passeth understanding is to be found in a return from "Civilization, the enemy of man," to the earlier fountain, the unconscious life of earth and water and air (and hawks), the timeless physical universe which reduces humanity to insignificance. It is needless to point out the gulf between this sub-rational evasion and the religious philosophy of Aeschylus. In fact it is only too easy to pigeonhole Mr. Jeffers' type of sentimental primitivism; apart from the violence of his presentation, and his somewhat clouded consciousness of modern science, it is all very old and familiar. If Irving Babbitt had ever read Mr. Jeffers, which may be doubted, he would not have needed to go further for an example *par excellence* of the nihilistic death-spasms of the romantic tradition. But Mr. Jeffers' "Everlasting No" is the inevitable sequel to Whitman's "Everlasting Yea," the sequel also, since we encountered another demonic Titan in the last chapter, to the scientific *hybris* of John Davidson.

The author's central theme receives mythological illustration in other poems and passages which must be noticed more briefly. Shelley, "Actaeon-like," had "gazed on Nature's naked loveliness"; for the modern, after a century of scientific progress, Actaeon is introverted man, who in his conquest of nature has begotten unmanageable giants and foresees his own destruction.[69] In *The Humanist's Tragedy*, Pentheus, who believes in progress, in increasing "the power, collectedness and dignity of man," confronts

[68] Powell, pp. 196–97; Alberts, p. 38.

[69] *Science* (*Roan Stallion*). While there is no space for random echoes, I may mention the adaptation in *Fauna* (*ibid.*, pp. 216 ff.) of Theocritus' tale of pastoral wooing (*Id.* xxvii).

Dionysus, who first glorifies the peace of death, and then exhorts the living to break prison of themselves "and enter the nature of things and use the beauty. . . . Only to break human collectedness." [70]

I must pass by *At the Fall of an Age*, a piece of romantic sadism with a vague philosophic gloss,[71] for a more complex work, *At the Birth of an Age*.[72] Here another tale of revenge, from the Nibelungen saga, is the vehicle for a view of civilization and a more positive expression of the author's faith than he has been wont to utter. He sees the Christian era, which is now on the eve of decline, as one of tension between the two poles of western blood and superimposed oriental religion, though in modern times the second pole has shifted from faith to ethics. Gudrun, who married Attila to gain power to wreak revenge on her brothers, the slayers of Sigurd, represents that restless tension and disintegration in her alternate impulses toward revenge and forgiveness; she has grown "passive, corrupt, merciful." After she has killed herself, her ghost turns from Christ to recognize in Prometheus the primitive power of her uncorrupted barbarous past and the spirit of a new future. Mr. Jeffers' Hanged God is not, like Mr. Eliot's, linked with a message of self-surrender ("Give, sympathise, control"), but with the opposite. Even Christ, though he reasserts the power of Christian ethics, is repentant for having deluded the world and admires the

---

[70] *Dear Judas* (New York, 1929). In *The Loving Shepherdess (ibid.*, p. 101), Clare has a vision of the peace of preëxistence, "Near the heart of life," which recalls Homer's descriptions of Elysium and Olympus (*Od.* iv. 563 ff., vi. 41 ff.).

[71] *Give Your Heart to the Hawks* (New York, 1933). For the story of Polyxo's revenge on Helen Mr. Jeffers cites Pausanias (III. xix. 9–10). He remarks that "The story of Achilles rising from the dead for love of Helen is well enough known," but it is not well known to me. There are familiar tales of the hero's living in marriage with Helen in the islands of the blessed (Pausanias, III. xix. 11; and above, ch. XIII, note 26), and of his ghost rising from the grave to demand the sacrifice of Polyxena (see Apollodorus, *Lib.*, ed. Frazer, II, 240).

[72] *Solstice and Other Poems* (New York, 1935).

terrible beauty of Prometheus, who has no righteousness, no mercy, no love. Prometheus is the spirit of reality, of all life, of strength and endurance, who instead of the perfect freedom of annihilation has chosen the heroic beauty of being,

Being; therefore wounds, bonds, limits and pain; the crowded mind and the anguished nerves, experience and ecstasy.[73]

For all Mr. Jeffers' massive earnestness, one cannot say that this "pagan" stoicism, this apotheosis of Life, goes much beyond such celebrations of the Man-God as *The Testament of John Davidson*, and his Prometheus has a large and sinister infusion of Woden and Nietzsche — an impression confirmed by the poet's more personal utterances.

The poem *Solstice* localizes in a California ranch the story of Medea's murder of her children; the witch-princess' chariot becomes Mrs. Bothwell's battered automobile, and other things are changed accordingly. Compared with Medea, Mrs. Bothwell is a primitive savage, though a not unnatural product of the author's worship of strength; he seems to delight as much in pain inflicted as in pain endured. I cannot discover any sufficient reason for the writing of this modernized and scarcely motivated version of a great theme. Whatever the intention, it shows in high relief what is plain enough in most of the California tales, that characters who exist and act in a moral vacuum have no tragic significance. When we think of Medea and then of Mrs. Bothwell, we may be glad that the ancients had got beyond behaviorism.

On the whole, though Mr. Jeffers has always been a vivid story-teller, the possessor of a keen visual sense and

[73] In a review of Miss Babette Deutsch's *Epistle to Prometheus*, Mr. Jeffers wrote of Prometheus as "the most inclusive symbol of the progressive striving of mankind as this time of the world sees it, free and yet hopelessly bound, patient and baffled, triumphant and despairing" (*New Freeman*, III [1931], 42).

a loose power over words, and though his vision of life has been serious and ambitious, his many volumes have not shown much evidence of growth. He may be said to have advanced, at least in emphasis, from eighteenth-century primitivism to the nineteenth-century religion of humanity. It is not surprising that many American reviewers should have hastened to deify the apostle of such a new evangel. Most Greeks would have considered him an unbalanced barbarian.

Conclusion

THE pattern of the Renaissance tradition in mythological poetry is obvious, almost too neatly rounded to be true. The pattern of the romantic tradition, at least from our present perspective, seems a less complete cycle, though the modern return of realistic wit and irony, after the long reign of nineteenth-century idealism, is a partial parallel to the impact of Donne upon the idyllic and idealistic mythology of the Elizabethans.[1] (Whether the modern metaphysical movement will give place to another Milton is a speculative question.) To begin with the eighteenth century, our one great classical age is, in the matter of classic myth, a desert of dry bones with a number of grassy oases fertilized by wit and with two or three flowers of imagination. During that period many critics said that mythology was dead and could never be revived. But Adonis, in spite of his annual wounds, administered in a hundred volumes of *Poems on Several Occasions*, was reborn. The fundamental reason for the mythological barrenness of the eighteenth century was the dominance of rationalism and realism, and the fundamental impulse of the mythological renascence was contained in the romantic protest against a mechanical world and mechanical verse stripped, as it seemed, of imagination and emotion, of beauty and mystery. The romantic revival, which included an Elizabethan and a Hellenic revival, brought ancient myth and the myth-making faculty to life once more. Poetic style, if less

[1] A parallel to the mythological burlesques of the Restoration may lie ahead of us, or perhaps lies behind us, in the works of Planché, the Broughs, and Francis Talfourd.

robust than the Elizabethan, rivaled it in decorative prodigality and went beyond it in sensuous refinement, and was as remote as ever from the Hellenic. The old allegorical tradition, which had never quite died, took fresh root in romantic idealism and flowered again in rich mythological symbols. Wordsworth found in the primitive myth-making instinct a vindication of natural religion. Into myth Keats put his deepest questionings of himself, of art, and of the world, and Shelley his most vivid pictures of hideous actuality, his most passionate dreams of perfectibility. The religion of nature, the religion of beauty, and the religion of humanity received their finest expression through myth.

At present the romantic tradition in mythological poetry, though not extinct, is obviously outside the main movement. During the last twenty-five years we have lived through the end of one era and into the beginning of another, and only a devout modernist would say that the fruits of the new one outweigh those of the single year 1819. A good many contemporary critics and poets, who can always sink minor differences and befuddlements in uniting to condemn the romantic movement, do not sometimes appear sufficiently conscious that sound modern views and comprehensive realistic intentions are not the same thing as poetic genius. Much of this volume has been concerned with a body of writing which may still without apology be considered among the permanent glories of English poetry. The existence of that golden book of mythological poems must not be forgotten, even though the decay of the romantic tradition demands a brief survey of some of its weaknesses, weaknesses which of course became much more evident in the period of exhaustion than during the fresh prime.

Recent attacks on the romantic movement remind us in more than one way of the young Keats's attack on the school of Boileau. The romantics were right in liberating poetry from bondage to the actual, and the moderns are right in reaffirming the claims of the actual. But the romantics' real purpose was not to give the imagination free reign over an empire of chimeras, it was to include the actual, to include all life and science, in a wider and deeper view of the scope and function of poetry. If romanticism had followed that course, if it had not succumbed to what Dr. Johnson called "the dangerous prevalence of imagination" — or what we might call wish-fulfilment — if, in short, it had been less romantic, its achievement would have been more substantial, its decline less inevitable. As it was, poets of the romantic movement, with all their philosophic, humanitarian, and realistic aspirations, laid themselves open to the charge that they did not know enough, and to the still commoner modern charge of being divorced from life. They did not have the critical humanism, religious or non-religious, of the ancients; they did not have the Christian faith which gave a steady light to Dante and Chaucer, Spenser and Milton; and the romantic substitutes, the religions of nature, beauty, and humanity, though they accomplished a great awakening, may seem, *sub specie aeternitatis*, to have been a false dawn. The religion of nature meant a rich quickening of man's senses, but on its highest plane it was a form of auto-intoxication.[2] The religion of beauty, without Plato's comprehensive ethical realism, was "too thin breathing." As for the religion of humanity, the ardent optimistic idealism of the revolutionary period soon faded, and belief in progress and in Man as God has become increasingly difficult. Altogether, the romantic creed was an insecure foundation for

[2] See the comprehensive study, *The Concept of Nature in Nineteenth-Century English Poetry* (New York, 1936), by Mr. Joseph Warren Beach. This illuminating book did not appear in time for my earlier pages to profit by it, except for a few footnotes.

a century to build on. No modern narrative poem or drama, whether mythological or not, has the human breadth and depth, the creative reality, of *Troilus and Criseyde* at the beginning of the Renaissance or *Samson Agonistes* at the end of it.

During the Victorian age the romantic decoration and reinterpretation of myth were carried on by almost all the greater poets and by scores of lesser ones. Mythology ought no doubt to have been killed by Darwin and industrialism as the Renaissance tradition had been killed by Descartes and puritanism — to over-simplify matters for the moment — and certainly little of the myth-making imagination survived Keats and Shelley. But myths were used more abundantly than ever for the treatment of serious themes. Much of that moral seriousness was on a low didactic level, and even in the great Victorian poets there was less of poetic vision, of imaginative experience, than of comment, sad or hopeful, on man, life, and God. With the Pre-Raphaelites and their followers came the progressive dissociation of poetry and ideas, and the result can be measured by the distance between Keats and Morris and Wilde. The mythological poem, like the historical novel, cannot live by its costume. It has been evident throughout this survey, to enunciate a truism for the last time, that, other things being equal, the mythological poems which are alive are those in which a myth is invested with a modern significance, whether personal or social, and that the dead ones are plaster reproductions of the antique.[3]

---

[3] In a series of essays, "Three Types of Poetry," which seem to combine acute precision with vague incoherence (not to mention a quite wanton use of Plato's name), Mr. Allen Tate has diagnosed the allegorical or propagandist instinct in the nineteenth century as an ineffectual substitute for the scientific will or control over nature. While one may assent to parts of the argument about the romantic poet as a frustrated allegorist or scientist, the critic's plea for a higher type of poetry comes suspiciously close at times to a modern and sophisticated version of art for art's sake — a suspicion which is not weakened by his concluding reference to Landor. See *The New Republic*, LXXVIII (1934), 126–28, 180–

Since romantic idealism and wish-fulfilment found natural expression in mythological symbols, even the best and most serious mythological poems have incurred, along with the whole body of nineteenth-century poetry, the charge of being an unrealistic escape from life into an idyllic dream-world. The charge may be partly accepted, even though, to echo Burke, one does not know the method of drawing up an indictment against a whole century, and though some considerable qualifications are strewn through preceding pages; further, as the last two chapters remind us, some of the most advanced and radical poets of our time must take their place at the bar also. Artists who are conscious of standing on solid ground, of having a place and function in society, do not usually seek to escape, and many writers in the romantic tradition who felt lost in this world preferred to lose themselves in a world of their own making. The flat-footed but not unintelligent Bulwer-Lytton declared that Wordsworth, Keats, and Shelley were genuine poets who "failed to be great because they were nothing but poets," whereas Shakespeare, Milton, and Byron were practical men of affairs who took "prose life with all its bearings into their poetic alchemy." [4] We may endorse the principle at least, and beside Lytton's verdict we may put a representative modern statement:

The task of the poet of the future is to win back the ground that has been lost by the romantic movement: that is to say he has to apply himself minutely to observe the life of people round him, and he has also to understand and to feel in himself the development of recent history.[5]

82, 237–40, or Mr. Tate's *Reactionary Essays on Poetry and Ideas* (New York, 1936).

[4] *Personal & Literary Letters of Robert First Earl of Lytton*, ed. Lady Betty Balfour (1906), I, 280–81. See the similar though more discriminating remarks, made in connection with Keats, in the letters of Gerard Hopkins (G. F. Lahey, *Gerard Manley Hopkins*, pp. 71 ff.).

[5] Stephen Spender, "The Artistic Future of Poetry," *New Republic*, LXXVIII (1934), 269.

One may find Lytton's words of 1871 more challenging than those of Mr. Spender and other recent critics of romanticism, for Lytton reminds us of the poet-citizens of antiquity, the Middle Ages, and the Renaissance, men who took an active part in the world's work and whose poetry was much the stronger because they were not merely observers.[6] A good many poets and critics nowadays sit among their books and condemn the romantics for ignoring life, and invite special sympathy for themselves because they feel lonely in an industrial, commercial, scientific, and barbarous world; one young American writer for a number of years made a career out of being "the lost generation." Instead of the proud sense of carrying on a great tradition of leadership, which inspired Spenser and Milton, we have a multitude of poets seeking for something to cling to, something to give them a consciousness of roots and a rightful place in the world. The most solid support at the moment seems to be Marxism, which may or may not prove as illusory as the romantic religions; at any rate in some manifestations the Marxist nostalgia is not unlike the Hellenic.

Hellenism came in with the tide of romantic primitivism and naturally ebbed along with it; more recent forms of primitivism have worn scientific disguises. If German Hellenism lost its early fervor, the name of Nietzsche reminds us that even a period of decline could give birth to demonic force. The French, in comparison with the Germans and the English, have never had "la tête mythologique," yet, as M. Henri Peyre says, "L'histoire de la poésie française de 1843 à 1870 se confond presque avec

[6] One might mention a romantic and heroic figure who seems to belong to the history of the ancient world, the young Italian poet-patriot, Lauro de Bosis, whose Sophoclean tragedy *Icaro* gained the Olympic prize for poetry in 1928, and who in 1931 sacrificed his life, as another Icarus, in a flight over Rome to scatter anti-Fascist leaflets. See Ruth Draper's translation of the play, with a preface by Gilbert Murray (Oxford University Press, 1933).

l'histoire du rêve hellénique"; [7] and since 1870 Hellenism
in France has attracted numerous devotees and decadents.
In general, while Hellenism, English Hellenism in particular, owed something to the mere momentum of the
classical tradition and to reaction against a desiccated neoclassicism, its appeal in the nineteenth century was largely
in the allurements it offered to those who abhorred a
materialistic civilization insensitive to beauty, or who recoiled from a religion which seemed both moribund and
oppressive, or who had no religion at all and wanted one.
It is not always easy to discern when Greece ceases to be a
positive humane ideal and when it becomes an idyllic or
naturalistic refuge, and not all Hellenic idealists have been
sentimental escapists or pagans. But, needful and fruitful
as it was in its day, the Hellenic movement contained from
the beginning the germs of Swinburne and Pater and
Wilde, and, one may add, of half of Bridges, of H. D. and
Robinson Jeffers. However substantial and critical the
creed of some individual Hellenists, the Greece of the revival was not the Greece of Aeschylus or Socrates but a
romantic mirage. There was from the first a frequently
significant antagonism between different pagan ideals, the
Apollonian and the Dionysian or Faustian, but much more
fatal, if one thinks of the remoter past, was the failure to
achieve a Christian humanism like that of the Middle
Ages and the Renaissance. The earlier movement of course
had its own weaknesses, from paganism to pedantry, and
some of them led on to the delusions of romantic optimism,
yet its aim was order, not rebellion, and it was at best a
universal and realistic combination of classical sanity and
Christian piety. To speak in such terms in relation to
modern problems is doubtless a grotesque anachronism, or
another kind of romantic nostalgia, for it is much easier

[7] *Bibliographie critique de l'hellénisme en France de 1843 à 1870* (Yale University Press, 1932), p. 71.

to see what in the past the classical and Christian traditions owed to each other, and what each lost when they fell apart and decayed, than it is to imagine how the Christian humanism of Erasmus or Milton could have been carried on into our agnostic and unclassical world.[8] Contemplating our rag-bag of indiscriminate knowledge and confused values, the fruitful products of science and democracy, we may look back with envy to even the eighteenth century with its aristocratic classical culture and positive ethical standards. If during the nineteenth century the classics on the whole came to mean less and less a way of life and thought and more and more the outer costume of a gentleman, they had not yet been deposited in a museum for the use of scholars. The conceptions of Hellenism which inspired the Germans, or Arnold and Pater, or Lowes Dickinson and Mr. Gilbert Murray, may have embodied fallacious ideas and ideals, yet they meant something in the world.

But I must return from disposing of the problems of civilization to the problems of poetry. Throughout the nineteenth century the dominant influence was that of Keats, though his unique magic and intensity were subdued by the cooler and more imitable art of Tennyson; it is hardly fair to blame either poet for the vast amount of mediocrity they called forth. But Keats's richness of sensibility and color did make him a dangerous model, and certainly to modern taste the most serious poetry of the period seems to lose in seriousness through excess of decoration and illustration, as Arnold, for one, clearly saw. Further, though Keats's creed was in him neither soft nor cheap, it has led countless minor poets up to our own day to swoon at the word "Beauty." Mr. Eliot has damned

---

[8] See Mr. Eliot's recent plea for a revival of Christian humanism, for the classics as educational instruments in association with religion (*Essays Ancient and Modern*, 1936, pp. 161–74).

most nineteenth-century poets for failing to fuse emotion with intelligence — a theory which may be right, though it can scarcely be proved by quotations from the metaphysical poets at their best and from Browning and Tennyson at their worst.[9] That is not a question I could undertake to settle, but it may be said that Wordsworth and Keats, Tennyson and Arnold, were keenly aware of the necessity of philosophic intelligence, that they were not wholly without it, and that they often made thought sensuous, even if they often failed to make sensuousness intellectual. The radical changes in modern taste and technique have not dulled the genuine gold in nineteenth-century poetry; they have exposed the gilt, and the taste of the future may reveal some spurious elements in the poetry of our time which is now taken as an absolute.

In spite of the modern poet's conscientious devotion to glands and girders, my Appendix indicates no falling off in the number of mythological poems, either English or American, and that list can give no notion of the amount of mythological reference in the thousand or so of contemporary poets who matter. In 1635, in 1735, in 1835, and doubtless in 1935, a large number of critics and poets were firmly convinced that classic myth was dead; it seems, however, to have nine lives. While the decline of classical education may be deplored on various grounds,[10] it does not necessarily involve the decline of myth; such symbols may be all the more precious when they are not a commonplace possession. Partly because of a distaste for old symbols, including myths, and partly because of the complexities and subtleties of the modern mind (the modern euphemism for intellectual confusion), a number of recent

---

[9] *Selected Essays* (1932), pp. 272 ff.

[10] In an earlier age an eminent critic might not have printed and reprinted an essay (on Keats's Chapman sonnet) beginning with the remark that great poems often spring like Jove from the head of Minerva.

poets have taken to private codes. This is an obvious sign of unhealthy inbreeding; poets cannot hope to lead mankind by taking in one another's washing. None the less the continued vitality of myth in our time is proved by a great mass of more or less distinctive writing, from the epics of Spitteler to the mythological pieces of such sophisticated moderns as Valéry, Gide, and Cocteau. If space allowed, one could cite many notable poets and poems in English, and, since nearly all American mythological verse of the nineteenth century was painfully derivative and insipid, it may be observed that in the last twenty or thirty years American writers have in general shown more independence and freshness in the handling of myth than the English; it is hardly an accident that the best-known of these Americans became Europeans by early adoption. Literary history indicates the unwisdom of prophecy, but it is no hazardous guess that during the next century poetic reports on the condition of the nervous and the social systems will not banish classic myth. Of late years we have had several new modes of treatment which suggest endless possibilities, in capable hands. There is the method of transposing ancient story into modern terms which is illustrated in *Ulysses* and *Mourning Becomes Electra*. Then the dramas and poems of Mr. Sturge Moore contain too much that is new to be dismissed as merely traditional; while poets for many generations have been rewriting *Endymion* and *Alastor*, in Mr. Moore's work we have a strongly individualized and muscular version of Platonic idealism. More typical of recent mythological poetry is the concentrated mingling of idealism with disillusioned irony and even wit, a method best exemplified in such leaders of the modern movement as Mr. Eliot and the later Mr. Yeats (and, if you like, there is the telegraphic garrulity of Mr. Pound). Besides, there is always room for writers who can simply re-create the fundamental ancient stories with a compelling vision and intensity. No observer of the New York theater could have predicted Mr. Robert Turney's drama, *Daughters of Atreus*, which — I speak perforce at second hand — has lately stirred serious critics. Altogether, after surveying the modern authors who have evoked fresh beauty and significance from classic myth, the most conservative reader may take heart in the belief that now no less than a hundred or three hundred years ago the old instinct brings back the old names.

APPENDIX

APPENDIX

The list of mythological poems in my former book aimed at completeness, the present one does not; a full catalogue would require another volume, and another compiler. But I have tried to record all the significant authors and poems, and a good many insignificant ones for the satisfaction of the scholarly appetite; "'tis enough, 'twill serve." The list does not ordinarily include formal translations and paraphrases, works in prose, non-classical burlesques with mythological "machines," popular and juvenile abridgments, stage plays, operas, masques, cantatas, pastorals, fables, or lyrical and short pieces; this general rule, especially in regard to the last category, has been somewhat relaxed for the late nineteenth and the twentieth centuries. Some poems on classical but not mythological subjects are included. The list begins at 1680, where the former one left off. Lack of space forbids description of pieces not discussed in the text, and of course the character of most modern poems forbids it also; almost all the travesties and burlesques up to 1750 are described by A. H. West and R. P. Bond (see Bibliography). In the case of authors who received titles from the Crown, consistency has generally been favored at the expense of chronology. The first section of the list includes citizens of Great Britain and the dominions, the second those of the United States. Unless it is otherwise indicated, places of publication are London and New York (or Boston and New York) respectively.

PART I. GREAT BRITAIN AND DOMINIONS

1681. Anon., Homer alamode, the second part, in English burlesque: or, a mock-poem upon the ninth book of Iliads.

1681. Anon., Deuteripideuteron: the second part of the second part of

Homer alamode. Or, a mock-poem on the ninth book of the Odysses.

1682. [Nicholas Brady], The giants wars. 1682. Some passages preceeding the giants war, translated out of a Greek fragment. . . . By Dr. B—— (*State-Poems; Continued From the time of O. Cromwel, to this present Year 1697* [1697], pp. 23–30). [A political satire.]

1682. John Oldham, The passion of Byblis in Ovid's Metamorphosis imitated in English.

1683. Thomas Hoy, Agathocles the Sicilian usurper. A poem.

Nominally an historical poem, but really a religious and political satire. Hoy also wrote some classical paraphrases, *Two Essays. The former Ovid. De Arte Amandi.* . . . *The First Book. The later Hero and Leander of Musaeus. From the Greek* (1682).

1684. Anon., Part of Lucian's dialogues, (not) from the original Greek, done into rhyme.

Lucian's dialogues, (not) from the Greek; done into English burlesque. The second part.

1684. [John Harington], The Grecian story: being an historical poem, in five books. . . . By J. H. Esq;.

A pseudo-classical romance of 321 pages.

1689. James Farewell, The Irish Hudibras, or Fingallian prince, taken from the sixth book of Virgil's Aenaeids, and adapted to the present times.

A travesty much closer to "the present times" than to Virgil.

1690. P. K., ΛΟΓΟΜΑΧΙΑ: or, the conquest of eloquence: containing two witty orations, the first spoke by Ajax: the second by Ulisses. . . . As they may be read, Ovid Metamorph. Lib. 13.

A relatively serious travesty.

1692. Anon., Acteon, or the original of Horn-Fair; The story of Orpheus burlesqu'd (*The Gentleman's Journal: or the Monthly Miscellany*, February, 1691–92, pp. 22–25, and June, 1692, pp. 8–10; reprinted in *Oxford and Cambridge Miscellany Poems*, ed. E. Fenton, 1708).

1692. John Crowne, The history of the famous and passionate love, between a fair noble Parisian lady and a beautiful young singing-man. . . . An heroic poem. In two canto's. Being in imitation of Virgil's Dido and Aeneas.

A tale more romantic than mock-heroic, with Virgil somewhat in the background. It "was design'd for an Epsode" in Crowne's *Daeneids*, which was based on Boileau's *Lutrin*.

1692. John Dennis, The passion of Byblis, made English. From Ovid. Metam. Lib. 9.

While Oldham had "not meddled with the Catastrophe," Dennis retains it, condensed into five lines and altered, "for to make it moving it was necessary to make it credible."

1692. John Dennis, The story of Orpheus burlesqu'd (*Poems in Burlesque*).

1692. James Smyth (?), Scarronnides, or, Virgil travestie. A mock-poem, on the second book of Virgil's *Aenaeis*. In English burlesque.

1694. M.L.M., Andromeda's deliverance by Perseus out of Manilius (*The Gentleman's Journal*, April, 1694, pp. 85–88).

A version of Manilius, *Astronomicon*, v. 541 ff.

1695. Charles Hopkins, The history of love. A poem: in a letter to a lady.

The title poem contains numerous mythological tales, chiefly from the *Metamorphoses*, in which Ovid is sometimes translated, "but for the most part . . . only kept . . . in View." This volume, like Hopkins' *Epistolary Poems* (1694), also includes isolated tales translated from the *Metamorphoses*.

1696. The works of Capt. Alex. Radcliffe in one volume. . . . The third edition augmented.

The *Ovid Travestie* of 1680 and 1681 contained travesties of five Ovidian epistles, and, according to the *D.N.B.*, had first appeared in 1673. The 1696 volume included fifteen epistles, which reappeared in 1705 as *Ovid Travestie. . . . The Fourth Edition*.

1700. John Dryden, Fables ancient and modern; translated into verse, from Homer, Ovid, Boccace & Chaucer: with original poems.

1700. John Hopkins, Amasia, or, the works of the muses.

The book contains *Hero*, *Priestess of Venus*, "paraphrastically imitated from the Greek of Musaeus," and numerous paraphrases from Ovid's *Metamorphoses*.

Before 1701? Sir Charles Sedley (?), Venus and Adonis: or the amour of Venus.

A poem of 235 lines, first published in Sedley's *Works* of 1722. See *Poetical and Dramatic Works*, ed. V. de Sola Pinto (1928), I, xx–xxiv, II, 198–203.

1701. Edward Ward, The revels of the gods: or, a ramble thro' the heavens.

A piece of celestial Billingsgate in *The Second Volume of the Writings of the Author of the London-Spy* (1703), pp. 78–91. The burlesque was first published, according to the *D.N.B.*, in 1701.

1703. David Crauford, Ovidius Britannicus: or, love epistles. In imitation of Ovid. . . . To which are added. Phaon's answer to Sapho and Theseus answer to Ariadne, which are wanting in Ovid's epistle.

1704. Tarquin and Tullia. By Mr. D——n (*Poems on Affairs of State, From 1640. to this present Year 1704*, III [1704], 319-23).
There is not much classical matter in this Jacobite attack on William III and his queen.

1704. Thomas D'Urfey, Abradatus and Panthea, or love and honour in perfection (*Tales Tragical and Comical*).

1704. William King, Orpheus and Euridice. [A travesty.]

1704. B. M. [Bernard Mandeville?], Typhon: or the wars between the gods and giants: a burlesque poem in imitation of the comical Mons. Scarron.
From the first part of Scarron's *Typhon*.

1707. Anon., The story of Europa (*The Adventures of Catullus. . . . Intermixed with Translations of his Choicest Poems. . . . Done from the French*, pp. 337-42).
See *Histoire d'Europe* in *Les Amours de Catulle, Œuvres du Sieur de la Chapelle* (Paris, 1700), I, 149-55.

1709. William King, The art of love. [A travesty.]

1709. Jonathan Swift, Baucis and Philemon: imitated from Ovid. [A travesty.]

1712. Anon., The history of the three goddesses, and the golden apple of prince Paris and prince Avaro.
A broadsheet satire, in verse, on the Duke of Marlborough.

1712. William Diaper, Nereides: or, sea-eclogues.
Fourteen pieces, including such figures as Glaucus and Proteus.

1713. Henry Carey, The marriage of Bacchus. From Ovid (*Poems on Several Occasions*).
The volume includes six cantatas on Ovidian themes.

1713. William Diaper, Dryades; or, the nymphs prophecy.
Nocturnal nymphs are mouthpieces for discourses on their own functions and on nature, morality, and public affairs. Reprinted as *The Dryads; or Wood-Nymphs* in *The Poetical Calendar*, ed. Francis Fawkes and William Woty, IX (1763-64), 17-46.

1714. John Gay, The fan. [Mock-heroic.]

17—? John Gay, The story of Cephisa.
See *Poetical Works*, ed. G. C. Faber (1926), pp. xxiv-xxix, 127 ff.

1715. Anon., Homer in a nut-shell: or, the Iliad of Homer in immortal doggrel. By Nickydemus Ninnyhammer. [A travesty of *Il.* i–iii.]

1716. Anon., Hero's complaint to Leander (*The Second Part of Miscellany Poems* [Dryden's *Miscellany*] . . . *The Fourth Edition*).

1716. [Sir Thomas Burnet and George Duckett], Homerides: or, Homer's first book moderniz'd. By Sir Iliad Doggrell. [A travesty of *Il.* i.]

1717. Elijah Fenton, Phaon to Sappho (*Poems on Several Occasions*). An original epistle following a translation of Ovid's *Sappho to Phaon.*

1719. [John Durant Breval], Ovid in masquerade. Being, a burlesque upon the xiiith book of his Metamorphoses, containing the celebrated speeches of Ajax and Ulysses. . . . By Mr. Joseph Gay.

1720. Anon., The story of Cinyras and Myrrha, in burlesque (*A New Miscellany of Original Poems, Translations and Imitations. By the most Eminent Hands, Viz. Mr. Prior, Mr. Pope, Mr. Hughes* . . . *&c.*). [An Ovidian travesty.]

1720. William Meston, Phaethon: or the first fable of the second book of Ovid's Metamorphoses burlesqu'd (Edinburgh).

1721 *et seq.* Thomas Parnell (d. 1718), Hesiod: or, the rise of woman; Bacchus; etc. (*Poems on Several Occasions*, 1722 [1721], and subsequent editions of Parnell).

1726. Anon., The Lifty: a table. In imitation of the Metamorphosis of Ovid. The author is also imitating Spenser's "incomparable Fable" on the Mulla (*Colin Clouts Come Home Againe*, ll. 104 ff.).

1729. Thomas Cooke, Philander and Cydippe (*Tales, Epistles, Odes, Fables, &c.*). A romantic pseudo-classical tale.

1731. Anon., Timoclia, or the power of virtue: an heroic tale for the ladies (*A Collection of Poems; Consisting of Odes, Tales, &c. as well Originals as Translations*).

1731. Samuel Boyse, Cynthia and Endymion. A tale (*Translations and Poems Written on several Subjects*, Edinburgh).

1732. Hildebrand Jacob, Chiron to Achilles. A poem.

1732. Bezaleel Morrice, The amour of Venus: or, the disasters of un-licens'd love. A poem. In four parts.

1737. Richard Glover, Leonidas. A poem.

1737. William Meston, A Grecian tale [Saturn and Jupiter]; Tarquin and Tullia. A Roman tale (*Old Mother Grim's Tales*). Burlesque satirical pieces. The work first appeared, according to the *D.N.B.*, in 1737.

1738. Anon., Achilles to Chiron. By the right honourable the lady＊＊＊＊ Occasion'd by the reading a poem, call'd Chiron to Achilles.

This, like Jacob's work (1732), is much less classical than moralistic.

1741. William Shenstone, The judgment of Hercules. A poem.

1742. Thomas De la Mayne, Love and honour. A dramatick poem: taken from Virgil. In seven cantoes.

1742. Robert Forbes, Ajax his speech to the Grecian knabbs. From Ovid's Metam. Lib. xiii. . . . Attempted in broad Buchans. By R. F. Gent. . . . M.DCC.XLVIII.

A travesty said, in the 1869 edition (Aberdeen and Edinburgh), to have been first published at Aberdeen in 1742.

1742. Thomas Gray, Sophonisba Massinissae. Epistola.

A Latin fragment included in a letter to West (*Correspondence of Gray, Walpole, West and Ashton,* ed. Toynbee, II, 44–47; *Correspondence of Thomas Gray,* ed. Toynbee and Whibley, I, 211–13.

1742. William Melmoth the younger, The transformation of Lycon and Euphormius (*Letters on Several Subjects.* By the late Sir Thomas Fitzosborne, II, 1749, Letter lxxii, pp. 215–22; pp. 151–55 in the eleventh edition, 1805).

A pseudo-classical tale in nineteen Spenserian stanzas. The first edition appeared in 1742 (*D.N.B.*).

1744. William Whitehead, Atys and Adrastus, a tale in the manner of Dryden's Fables.

1746 (pub. 1758). Mark Akenside, Hymn to the naiads.

1746. Lord Hervey, Flora to Pompey; Arisbe to Marius junior (Dodsley's *Museum,* 1746, I, 92–95, II, 14–19; reprinted in Dodsley's *Collection,* 1755 et seq.).

Epistles taken from Fontenelle's *Lettres à l'imitation des Héroïdes d'Ovide.*

1747. Anon., Paris to Oenone (Dodsley's *Museum,* III [1747], 209–13).

The "Epistle by Sabinus . . . is here rather imitated than translated."

1747. Robert Bedingfield, The education of Achilles (Dodsley's *Museum,* III, 127–31).

1747. Robert Lowth, The choice of Hercules (Spence's *Polymetis,* 1747, pp. 155 ff.).

1747. Gloster Ridley, Psyche: or, the great metamorphosis. A poem, written in imitation of Spencer (Dodsley's *Museum,* III, 80–97).

1749. "Henry Fitzcotton," A new and accurate translation of the first book of Homer's Iliad. . . . Dublin printed: London reprinted. [A travesty.]

1750–51. Anon., The quarrel between Venus and Hymen: an heroisatyrical mythological poem, in imitation of the antients: in vi. cantos.

"'Tis a severe Satyr against Lewdness in general."

1751. Richard Owen Cambridge, The Scribleriad. An heroic poem.

The adventures of Scriblerus in this mock-heroic poem are based on those of Aeneas.

1752. Anon., The tryal of Hercules, an ode on glory, virtue, and pleasure.

1755. Samuel Boyce, Paris; or, the force of beauty: a poem, in two cantos.

This poem on the judgment of Paris was reprinted in *Poems on Several Occasions* (1757).

1757. William Thompson, Coresus and Callirhoe (*Poems on Several Occasions*, Oxford).

1757. William Wilkie, The Epigoniad, a poem.

1758. [John Ellis], The canto added by Maphaeus to Virgil's twelve books of Aeneas, from the original bombastic, done into English Hudibrastic.

A travesty intended to be closer to the original than Cotton's travesty of Virgil (preface, pp. ix–x).

1759. Henry Fielding, The lover's assistant, or, new year's gift; being, a new art of love, adapted to the present times.

A prose travesty of the first book of the *Ars Amatoria*, "begun many Years ago, though altered in some Places by the Author, before his Death." Ovid's mythological tales are retained.

1762. "Cotton, junior" [Thomas Bridges], Homer travestie: being a new translation of the four first books of the Iliad.

Revised and enlarged in later editions.

1763. Rowland Rugeley, Venus and Mars taken in adultery; with the story of Phoebus and Leucothoe; burlesqued, from the fourth book of Ovid's Metamorphosis (*Miscellaneous Poems and Translations from La Fontaine and Others*, Cambridge, 1763).

1765. William Wither Beach, Abradates and Panthea. A tale, extracted from Xenophon.

A youthful rendering, in 304 lines, of the story in the *Cyropaedia*, V. i. 2 ff., VI. i. 31 ff., etc.

1765. James Beattie, The judgment of Paris. A poem.

1769. Anon., The heathen heroes; or, Vulcan cuckolded by Mars (*A*

Collection of Scots Poems, by "the late Mr Alexander Penne-cuik, Gent. and Others," Edinburgh, 1769).

Earlier editions in the British Museum are incomplete; this piece may have appeared before 1769.

1769. William Dunkin, The judgment of Hercules (*Poetical Works*, Dublin).

1770. James Graeme, Hero and Leander. In two books. From the Greek of Musaeus (*Poems on Several Occasions*, Edinburgh, 1773, pp. 7–26).

A free adaptation of the original, dated 1770. Reprinted in Anderson, *Poets of Great Britain*, XI (1794), 461–64.

1770. [Richard Shepherd], Hector, a dramatic poem.

Pp. 1–75. "A piece not built on the fable of the wooden horse, but on the authority of the only two prose historians, that have treated the subject, Dictys Cretensis and Dares Phrygius" (Dedication, p. iv).

1772. Michael Wodhull, To the dryads (1762) (*Poems*).

1774. [Rowland Rugeley], The story of Aeneas and Dido burlesqued: from the fourth book of the Aeneid of Virgil (Charleston [South Carolina]).

The author cites Scarron and, though not too prim himself, regrets Cotton's indelicacy.

1775. Robert Hill, Poems on several occasions.

A "juvenile Production" which contains numerous mytho-logical poems, the chief model being avowedly Dryden. The author's learning seems to be drawn mainly from Boyse's *Pantheon*.

1781. Gloster Ridley, Melampus: or the religious groves.

1789. Thomas Russell (d. 1788), Sonnet suppos'd to be written at Lemnos (*Sonnets and Miscellaneous Poems*, Oxford).

1789. William Woty, Orpheus and Euridice [burlesque] (*Poetical Amusements*, Nottingham).

1792. Frank Sayers, Pandora. A monodrama (*Poems*, appended to the second edition of *Dramatic Sketches of Northern Mythology*).

1793. Robert Southey, Sappho. A monodrama (*Poems*, Bristol, 1797).

1794. Lady Burrell, The Thymbriad (from Xenophon's Cyropoedia).

A somewhat Miltonic epic on the story of Panthea. The same volume contains a poetical version of the first seven books of Fénelon's very popular *Télémaque*. This earnest moralizer had her moments of facetious mythology (*Poems* [1793], II, 7, 230 ff.).

1795. Walter Savage Landor, Pyramus and Thisbe (*Poems*, 1795).

A free adaptation of Ovid. The chief poem in the volume, *The Birth of Poesy*, has more or less elaborate mythological episodes, such as that of Orpheus (pp. 19 ff.).

1796. Anon., Hymn to the dryads inscribed to Dr. Turton. (Pp. 4–32.)

1796–97. Robert Southey, Othryades, a mono-drama; Aristodemus A monodrama (*The Monthly Magazine, and British Register,* II [1796], 566; III [1797], 294).

1799? (pub. 1817). Samuel Taylor Coleridge, The visit of the gods. Imitated from Schiller.

1799. Hudson Gurney, Cupid and Psyche. A mythological tale from the Golden Ass of Apuleius.
Reprinted several times, e.g., in the Bohn volume of Apuleius.

1799. Robert Southey, Lucretia. A monodrama (*The Annual Anthology,* Bristol [1799–1800], II, 20–22).

1801. John Ogilvie, Britannia: A national epic poem, in twenty books (Aberdeen). [Brutus, etc.]

1802. Sir William Drummond, Byblis, a tragedy.

1802. Walter Savage Landor, Story of Crysaor; From the Phocaeans; Part of Protis's narrative (*Poetry By The Author of Gebir,* 1802).
The last two pieces are fragments of a projected epic, *The Phocaeans.* See additional fragments in *Poems,* ed. Wheeler (1933), I, 79, 89.

1802. William Sotheby, Orestes, a tragedy, in five acts.

1805. Mary Tighe, Psyche; or the legend of love.

1806. Robert Bland, Paris and Oenone (*Translations Chiefly from the Greek Anthology, With Tales and Miscellaneous Poems,* pp. 171–83).

1806. Walter Savage Landor, Pudoris ara (*Simonidea*).
This Latin idyll was Englished as *The Altar of Modesty* (see under 1847).

1806. Thomas Moore, The fall of Hebe. A dithyrambic ode (*Epistles, Odes, and Other Poems*).

1810. Anon., Hero and Leander; a poem (Bath).
A long and curious version, full of moralizing, and quite remote from Musaeus.

1812. John Galt, The tragedies of Maddalen, Agamemnon, Lady Macbeth, Antonia and Clytemnestra.

1814. Edward Lord Thurlow, Ariadne: a poem, in three parts.

1814. William Wordsworth, Laodamia (*Poems,* 1815).

1815. Walter Savage Landor, Corythus; Dryope; Pan et Pitys; Coresus et Callirhöe.
These four Latin idylls, along with *Helena ad Pudoris Aram*

(see under 1806), appeared in *Idyllia Nova Quinque Heroum atque Heroidum* (Oxford, 1815).

1816. Lord Byron, Prometheus (*The Prisoner of Chillon*).

1816. George Colman, Fire! or the sun-poker (*Eccentricities for Edinburgh*, Edinburgh).

A burlesque tale of Pandora, Prometheus, and the gods.

1816. J.P.H., Psyché, a mythological poem; from the Latin prose of Lucius Apuleius. (Pp. 3–77.)

1816 (pub. 1817). John Keats, I stood tip-toe upon a little hill.

On an engraved gem of Leander was printed in 1829.

1816 (pub. 1820). William Wordsworth, Dion (*Poems*).

1817 (pub. 1818). John Keats, Endymion. A poetic romance.

1818. Leigh Hunt, The nymphs (*Foliage*).

1818. Thomas Love Peacock, Rhododaphne: or the Thessalian spell.

1818–19 (pub. 1820). John Keats, Hyperion: a fragment.

The fragmentary *Ode to Maia* (1818) was printed in 1848.

1818–19 (pub. 1820). Percy Bysshe Shelley, Prometheus unbound. A lyrical drama in four acts.

1819? (pub. 1820). Elizabeth Barrett, The battle of Marathon.

1819. Leigh Hunt, Hero and Leander; Bacchus and Ariadne.

Apollo and the Sunbeams appeared in 1836. A number of mythological tales in prose appeared in Hunt's various journals, *The Indicator, The Companion*, etc. Most of them are collected in *Tales by Leigh Hunt*, ed. William Knight (1891), and listed in Luther Brewer, *My Leigh Hunt Library*.

1819 (pub. 1820). John Keats, Ode to Psyche; Ode on a Grecian urn; Lamia.

The Fall of Hyperion: A Vision (1819) was printed in 1856.

1819. Thomas Moore, Account of the milling-match between Entellus and Dares, translated from the fifth book of the Aeneid, by one of the fancy (*Tom Crib's Memorial to Congress*).

A travesty of *Aen.* v. 426 ff.

1819. Bryan Waller Procter ("Barry Cornwall"), Lysander and Ione; The dream (*Dramatic Scenes*).

1819 (pub. 1820). Percy Bysshe Shelley, Oedipus tyrannus or Swellfoot the tyrant. . . . Translated from the original Doric.

On the Medusa of Leonardo da Vinci (1819) was printed in 1824.

1820. Walter Savage Landor, Cupido et Pan; Catillus et Salia; Veneris pueri; Ulysses in Argirippa.

These four Latin idylls appeared in *Idyllia Heroica* (Pisa, 1820), along with revised versions of five which had been printed in *Idyllia Nova* (1815). *Sponsalia Polyxenae* was printed at Pistoia in 1819.

1820. Bryan Waller Procter ("Barry Cornwall"), The rape of Proserpine (*Marcian Colonna*, 1820); The worship of Dian; Gyges; The death of Acis; etc. (*A Sicilian Story*, 1820).

1820. Mary Shelley, Proserpine (pub. 1832); Midas (pub. 1922).

1820. Percy Bysshe Shelley, Hymn of Apollo; Hymn of Pan; Arethusa (all pub. 1824); Song of Proserpine (pub. 1839); Orpheus (pub. 1862); The witch of Atlas (pub. 1824).

1820 *et seq.* (pub. 1851). Hartley Coleridge, Prometheus.

1821. Edwin Atherstone, The last days of Herculaneum; and Abradates and Panthea.

1821. Robert Stephen Hawker ("Reuben") Lucretia; Diana (*Tendrils*, Cheltenham, 1821).

1821. Percy Bysshe Shelley, Adonais; Hellas (pub. 1822).

1821. Horace Smith, Amarynthus, the nympholept: a pastoral drama, in three acts. With other poems [Including *Sicilian Arethusa*, pp. 231–32].

1822. Gems, principally from the antique, drawn and etched by Richard Dagley . . . with illustrations in verse by the Rev. George Croly.
Brief pieces, mainly mythological.

1822. Thomas Hood, Lycus, the centaur (*London Magazine*, VI [1822], 141–47).
See also under 1827. *Lamia*, presumably an early work, was printed in *The Autobiography of William Jerdan* (1852), I, 249–94.

1822. Edward Lord Thurlow, Angelica; or, the rape of Proteus: a poem.
Another tale "carried on from the Tempest of Shakespeare" (see above, under 1814).

1823. George Darley, Olympian revels (*London Magazine*, 1823, pp. 297–306).
A "dramaticle" in the vein of high jinks.

1823. Felicia Hemans, Elysium; Greek songs (The storm of Delphi; etc.). (*The Siege of Valencia.*)
Other poems from the antique appeared in volumes of 1808, 1812, 1819, etc.

1823. Bryan Waller Procter ("Barry Cornwall"), The flood of Thessaly; The fall of Saturn; Tartarus (*The Flood of Thessaly*).

1824. Rev. Peter Potier [pseudonym?], Vulcan, a tale (*Fugitive Pieces*). [A burlesque, pp. 1–5.]

1825 (pub. 1851). Thomas Lovell Beddoes, Pygmalion the Cyprian statuary.

1825. Thomas Moore, Evenings in Greece.

1825. Horace Smith, The shriek of Prometheus. Suggested by a passage in the second book of Apollonius Rhodius.

In *Gaieties and Gravities* (1825), III, 180–85; reprinted in *Poetical Works* (1846), I, 24–34.

1825. Thomas Wade, The nuptials of Juno (*Tasso and the Sisters*, pp. 21–46).

Mundi et Cordis (1835) included the brief *Nymphs*.

1827. Thomas Hood, Hero and Leander; Lycus the centaur (1822) (*The Plea of the Midsummer Fairies*).

1827. William and Mary Howitt, The maid of Sestos (*The Desolation of Eyam*, pp. 203–05).

1830. Thomas Moore, Legendary ballads.

The volume includes songs on Cupid and Psyche, Hero and Leander, and Cephalus and Procris.

1830. Winthrop Mackworth Praed, Cassandra.

In *Poems*, ed. Derwent Coleridge (1864), I, 346–49.

1830. Alfred Tennyson, Hero to Leander; The sea-fairies (*Poems, Chiefly Lyrical*).

1830. Charles Tennyson (Turner), On a picture of the Fates; etc. (*Sonnets and Fugitive Pieces*, Cambridge).

A couple of other pieces had appeared in *Poems by Two Brothers* (1827).

1831. Thomas Kibble Hervey, Psyche; Hebe; Cupid and Psyche (*Gems of Modern Sculpture*).

The poems accompany plates of Canova and Westmacott. Some classical pieces had appeared in Hervey's *Poetical Sketch Book* (1829).

1831. Francis Hodgson, Mythology for versification: or, a brief sketch of the fables of the ancients, prepared to be rendered into Latin verse, and designed for the use of classical schools.

Byron's prolific friend rendered the ascent to Parnassus still easier by turning the book into Latin (1832).

1832. Thomas Kibble Hervey, Mercury and Pandora; Hebe; Arethusa; Venus; Narcissus; Prometheus; The sleeping nymph (*Illustrations of Modern Sculpture. A Series of Engravings, with Descriptive Prose, and Illustrative Poetry, by T. K. Hervey*).

The artists represented include Canova, Flaxman, and Thorwaldsen. Hervey's poems of 1829, 1831, and 1832, are reprinted,

along with some classical "Illustrations to Pictures," in his
Poems, ed. Mrs. Hervey (Boston, 1866).

1832–34. Benjamin Disraeli, Ixion in heaven; The infernal marriage
[Pluto and Proserpine]. (Prose burlesques in Bulwer-Lytton's
New Monthly Magazine, XXXV [1832], 514–20; XXXVII [1833],
175–84; etc.)

1833 [1832]. Alfred Tennyson, The Hesperides; Oenone; The lotos-
eaters (*Poems*).

ca. 1833–35. Alfred Tennyson, Semele (pub. 1913); Ulysses (pub. 1842);
Tithonus (pub. 1860).

1834. Arthur Hallam, Lines spoken in the character of Pygmalion.
Written on the occasion of a represented charade (1832) (*Remains,* 1834).

1834. Richard Monckton Milnes, later Lord Houghton, Memorials of
a tour in some parts of Greece: chiefly poetical.
The volume includes a score of classical and mythological
poems, of varying length, mostly reprinted in *Memorials of
Many Scenes* (1844) and *Poetical Works* (1876).

1835. Letitia E. Landon, Classical sketches (Sappho; Bacchus and
Ariadne; Leander and Hero; etc.) (*The Vow of the Peacock*).
Among other things were *Arion* (*The Improvisatrice,* 1824),
and *Subjects for Pictures,* including *Calypso Watching the Ocean,*
etc.

1836. Walter Savage Landor, The shades of Agamemnon and of
Iphigeneia (*Pericles and Aspasia,* 1836); The death of Clytemnestra (*Friendly Contributions,* 1836; reprinted in *Pentameron
and Pentalogia,* 1837, and incorporated in *Pericles and Aspasia,*
1846).

1837. George Darley, Syren songs (*The Tribute,* 1837).
The Dryads, a poem of 32 lines, appeared in Darley's *The
Labours of Idleness. . . . By Guy Penseval* (1826), pp. 64–65.
The dazzling *Nepenthe* (1835) has a good deal of incidental
mythology, but hardly comes within our range.

1837. Walter Savage Landor, The madness of Orestes (*The Tribute,*
1837; reprinted in *Pentameron and Pentalogia,* 1837, and incorporated in *Pericles and Aspasia,* 1846).

1838. Alexander William Crawford Lindsay, Lord Lindsay, later Earl
of Crawford and Balcarres, The nereids' cave. A fragment; in
imitation of Alfred Tennyson (*Poems and Poetical Fragments*
[Wigan, 1838], pp. 82–85).
This poem, dated "8 Dec., 1832," is the earliest imitation of
Tennyson I recall. It is more pictorial than mythological.

1838–42. John Ruskin, The Scythian grave; etc.
Seven poems based on Herodotus appeared in annuals, 1838–42, and were reprinted in Ruskin's *Poems* (1850). See *Poems of John Ruskin*, ed. W. G. Collingwood (1891), II.

1839. John Edmund Reade, Arethusa; The dance of the nereids; Achilles' description of Hector; Prometheus bound (*The Deluge*). Some more or less classical pieces had appeared in volumes of 1825, 1827, and 1829.

1839. John Sterling, Aphrodite; Daedalus (*Poems*).

1840. Sir Francis Hastings Doyle, The syrens; Dido's answer to Aeneas in Hades; etc. (*Miscellaneous Verses*). Some classical pieces in this volume had first appeared in one of the same title in 1834.

1840. [Helen Lowe], Cephalus and Procris (*Poems, Chiefly Dramatic*). [Not seen.]

1842. William Edmondstoune Aytoun, Endymion, or, a family party on Olympus. [Prose skit.]

1842. Robert Browning, Artemis prologuizes (*Dramatic Lyrics, Bells and Pomegranates, No. III*).

1842. Walter Savage Landor, The hamadryad (*The Foreign Quarterly Review*, XXX [1842], 183–90; printed in *Works* [1846], II, 478).

1842. Thomas Babington Macaulay, Lays of ancient Rome.

1842. John Edmund Reade, A record of the pyramids: a drama, in ten scenes [Prometheus]. Shorter mythological pieces by this prolific writer appeared in volumes of 1840, 1849, 1852, and 1863; see also under 1839.

1842. Alfred Tennyson, Oenone (revised); The lotos-eaters (revised); Ulysses (*Poems*).

1842. Richard Chevenix Trench, Orpheus and the sirens (*Poems from Eastern Sources*, pp. 173–83; reprinted, with several other classical pieces, in *Poems* (New York, 1856), and volumes of 1865 and 1885).

1843. Aubrey de Vere, The search after Proserpine, recollections of Greece, and other poems.

1843. Richard Henry Horne, Orion: an epic poem.

1843 (pub. 1860). William Caldwell Roscoe, Ariadne (*Poems and Essays*, ed. R. H. Hutton, 1860, I, 14–17).

1844. Elizabeth Barrett, Wine of Cyprus; The dead Pan (*Poems*). *A Musical Instrument* appeared in *Last Poems* (1862).

1844. Richard Monckton Milnes, later Lord Houghton, Delphi; The tomb of Laius; etc. (*Palm Leaves*).

Some other more or less classical pieces were included in
Poems, Legendary and Historical (1844).

1846. The works of Walter Savage Landor. In two volumes.[1]
New pieces (in Volume Two) are: *The Death of Artemidora*
(pp. 389, 483); *The Prayer of Orestes*; *Thrasymedes and Eunöe*;
Drimacos; *Theron and Zoe*; *Damaetas and Ida*; *Lysander, Al-
canor, Phanöe*; *Hyperbion*; *Icarios and Erigonè*; *The Hamadryad*
(see under 1842); *Enallos and Cymodameia*; *Iphigeneia*; *Menelaus
and Helen at Troy*; *To Corinth* (first printed in 1824).

1847. Walter Savage Landor, Hellenics ("Enlarged and completed").
In addition to nearly all the pieces named under 1846, this
volume included: *Acon and Rhodope*; English versions of the ten
Latin idylls (*Cupid and Pan*; *The Altar of Modesty*; *The Espousals
of Polyxena*; *Dryope*; *Corythos*; *Pan and Pitys*; *Coresus and
Callirhöe*; *Catillus and Salia*; *The Children of Venus*; *The Last of
Ulysses*; see under 1806, 1815, 1819, 1820); *Silenus*.

1847 (pub. 1896). Christina Rossetti, The lotus-eaters.

1849. Matthew Arnold, Mycerinus; The strayed reveller; Fragment of
an "Antigone"; The new sirens (*The Strayed Reveller*).

1849. William Edmondstoune Aytoun, Hermotimus (1839); Oenone
(*Lays of the Scottish Cavaliers*).
The ballad *Lycaon* was printed in Martin's *Memoir* of Aytoun
(1867).

1850. Edward A. Freeman and George W. Cox, Poems, legendary and
historical.
Each author wrote four on classical and mythological subjects.

1850. Thomas Hawkins, Prometheus. [Not seen.]

1850. William Charles Kent, Aletheia: or the doom of mythology.
Among "other poems" is *The Golden Apple* [Acontius and
Cydippe].

1850. Mrs. H[enry] R[oscoe] Sandbach, Aurora; Antigone; Penthesilea; etc. (*Aurora*).

1851. George Meredith, The rape of Aurora; Daphne; Antigone; The
shipwreck of Idomeneus (*Poems*).

1852. Anon., The siege of Oxford. Fragments from the second book of
the "Nova Aeneis" (Oxford).
A travesty (pp. 1–7) of the second book of Virgil, on the in-
vasion of Oxford by German culture.

---

[1] In the various Landor entries it is impossible to take account of the constant and often drastic revisions; and ordinarily only mythological or quasi-
mythological narratives and dialogues are listed.

1852. Matthew Arnold, Empedocles on Etna, and other poems.
Poems (1853) included *Philomela*.

1853. Sir Edwin Arnold, Iphigenia; The sirens (*Poems Narrative and Lyrical*, Oxford).

1853. J. E. Bode, Ballads from Herodotus.
Seventeen ballads, *Cleobis and Biton, Atys and Adrastus*, etc. Four more were added in 1854.

1854. William Bell Scott, Lines, written in the Elgin Marble Room, British Museum (*Poems*).
Several brief pieces appeared in volumes of 1875 and 1882.

1855. Robert Lytton, later Earl of Lytton ("Owen Meredith"), Clytemnestra (*Clytemnestra*, etc., pp. 1–122).

1857. William Cox Bennett, Pygmalion; Ariadne; The judgment of Midas; Cassandra speaks (*Queen Eleanor's Vengeance*).
Poems (1850) contained *The Triumph for Salamis*.

1857. John Stuart Blackie, Pandora; Prometheus; etc. (*Lays and Legends of Ancient Greece*).

1857. Charles B. Cayley, Daphne transformed; Psyche lamplit; etc. (*Psyche's Interludes*).

ca. 1857 et seq. (pub. 1915). William Morris, Scenes from the fall of Troy.

1858. Matthew Arnold, Merope. A tragedy.

1858. William Johnson (Cory), Iole; The daughter of Cleomenes; Asterope; etc. (*Ionica*).
Ionica II (1877) included a Euripidean paraphrase, *Phaedra's Nurse* (1866).

1858. Charles Kingsley, Andromeda and other poems.

1858. Walter Savage Landor, The ancient idyl (Europa and her mother); The descent of Orpheus; Achilles and Helena on Ida (*Dry Sticks*).
The Descent of Orpheus (written in 1794, first printed in 1841) is a translation of Virgil, *Georg.* iv. 464–515.

1859. Thomas Ashe, Acis; Delos; Numa (*Poems*).

1859. Richard Garnett, Io in Egypt; Aegisthus; etc. (*Io in Egypt*).

1859. Walter Savage Landor, Hellenics (new edition, enlarged).
New pieces: *Homer and Laertes*; *The Famine in Etruria*; *Penelope and Pheido*; *Peleus and Thetis* (a recast of the prose scene printed in *Imaginary Conversations*, Second Series, 1829); *The Death of Paris and Oenone* (corresponding in substance to the last part of *Corythos*, 1847); *Hercules, Pluto, Alcestis, Admetos*.

1859–62. John Byrne Leicester Warren, later Lord De Tabley.
Four volumes were issued under the pseudonym "G[eorge] F.

Preston": *Poems* (1859); *Ballads and Metrical Sketches* (1860); *The Threshold of Atrides* (1861); *Glimpses of Antiquity* (1862). The first two and the fourth contained about thirty mythological poems; the third was a sequence of dramatic scenes on Trojan episodes. Hardly anything from these volumes was reprinted in *Collected Poems* (1903).

ca. 1860? (pub. 1869). Arthur Hugh Clough, Actaeon.

> See also ἐπὶ Λάτμῳ (1849) and *Selene*.

1860? H. Hamilton, Midas, a poetic, mythological play in three acts (Privately printed, Frome, Somerset).

1861. Anon., Prometheus' daughter. A poem.

1861. Thomas Ashe, Dryope; Typhoeus; The myth of Prometheus (*Dryope*).

1861. Sir Joseph Noel Paton, Syrinx; Pan and Syrinx; Circe; Ariadne; The song of Silenus; Narcissus; Hymn to Aphrodite (*Poems by a Painter*).

> *Spindrift* (1867) contained *Ulysses in Ogygia* and *Actaeon in Hades*.

1862 (pub. in full, 1929). Gerard Manley Hopkins, A vision of the mermaids.

> The sonnet *Andromeda* was written in 1879.

1862. George Meredith, Cassandra (*Modern Love*).

1863. Robert Buchanan, Ades, king of hell; Pan; etc.

> A dozen mythological poems in *Undertones*. The second edition (1865) added two more, with some revision of old ones. Several other pieces appeared in later volumes.

1863. Jean Ingelow, Persephone (*Poems*, 1863).

1863. Walter Savage Landor, Heroic idyls, with additional poems.

> Among new pieces were: *Homer, Laertes, Agatha* (three scenes expanded from one of 1859); *Hippomenes and Atalanta*; *Theseus and Hippolyta*; *Eucrates to the God Sleep*; *Pan*; *Niobe*; *A Greek to the Eumenides*.
>
> *Endymion and Selene* and *The Marriage of Helena and Menelaos*, written before 1864, were printed in Forster, *Life* (1869), II, 579 ff. Additional fragments of *The Phocaeans, Sappho to Phaon*, and a *Hymn to Proserpine* were printed in *Letters and Unpublished Writings of Walter Savage Landor*, ed. S. Wheeler (1897); reprinted in *Poems*, ed. Wheeler (1933–35).

1863–65. John Byrne Leicester Warren, later Lord De Tabley.

> Three books, issued under the pseudonym "William [P.] Lancaster," may be lumped together: *Praeterita* (1863); *Eclogues and Monodramas* (1864); *Studies in Verse* (1865). They con-

tained some sixteen mythological pieces, nearly all reprinted in *Collected Poems* (1903).

1863. Philip Stanhope Worsley, Phaethon; Narcissus (*Poems and Translations*).

1864. Richard Watson Dixon, The birth of Apollo; Orpheus (*Historical Odes*).

   Christ's Company (1861) included *Proserpine*.

1864–68 (pub. 1911). Digby Mackworth Dolben, From the cloister; etc.

1864. Richard Henry (Hengist) Horne, Prometheus the fire-bringer (Edinburgh).

1864. Charles Mackay, Studies from the antique and sketches from nature.

   Twenty-two mythological pieces. Several others had appeared in earlier volumes.

1864. Alfred Tennyson, Tithonus (*Cornhill Magazine*, 1860; *Enoch Arden*, 1864). See under *ca.* 1835.

1864. Charles Tennyson (Turner), Christ and Orpheus (Three sonnets in *Sonnets*, 1864).

   Five or six other classical sonnets appeared in volumes of 1868, 1873, and 1880.

1865. Thomas Ashe, Pictures [Cupid and Psyche]; Merope (*Pictures*).

1865. William J. Linton, Eurydice (*Claribel*, pp. 95–103).

   Other volumes include a number of short pieces, mainly lyrical.

1865. H. C. G. M[oule], Apollo at Pherae, a dramatic poem after the Greek model (Cambridge).

   A miniature drama, in Miltonic style, "finished long before" the author knew of Swinburne's *Atalanta*.

1865. Algernon Charles Swinburne, Atalanta in Calydon. A tragedy.

   The early lyric *Echo* was printed in *Posthumous Poems*, ed. Gosse and Wise (1917); *Pasiphae* was printed by Wise in *Lady Maisie's Bairn* (1915).

1866. Sir Francis Hastings Doyle, The vision of Er the Pamphylian; Titus Manlius Torquatus (*The Return of the Guards*).

1866. Sir Edward Bulwer-Lytton, The secret way; Death and Sisyphus; Corinna; The fate of Calchas; The oread's son; The wife of Miletus; Bridals in the spirit land; Cydippe (*The Lost Tales of Miletus*).

   Four short classical pieces are included in the *Poetical and Dramatic Works*, III (1853).

1866 (pub. 1915). William Morris, The story of Aristomenes; The story of Orpheus and Eurydice.

These tales, intended for *The Earthly Paradise*, were first printed in the *Works*, XXIV (1915), 171–238, 239–80. A fragment of *Aristomenes* had appeared in *The Athenaeum* (May 13, 1876), and was privately printed as a pamphlet in the same year.

1866. Algernon Charles Swinburne, Laus Veneris; Phaedra; Itylus; Anactoria; Hymn to Proserpine; Hermaphroditus; The garden of Proserpine; Sapphics; At Eleusis (*Poems and Ballads*, First Series).

1866. John Byrne Leicester Warren, later Lord De Tabley, Philoctetes: a metrical drama, after the antique. By M. A.

1866–67 (pub. 1880). James Thomson, The naked goddess; Life's Hebe (*The City of Dreadful Night*, 1880).

Proem (1882) appeared in the *Poetical Works* (1895), II, 61–63.

1866–69 (pub. 1880). William Hurrell Mallock, Aeneas to Dido; From an unfinished drama, called Aeneas and Dido; Ariadne; Pygmalion to his statue, become his wife (*Poems*, 1880).

1867. Matthew Arnold, Thyrsis; Fragment of a chorus of a "Dejaneira"; Palladium; Bacchanalia (*New Poems*).

1867. Thomas Ashe, The sorrows of Hypsipyle.

1867. Arthur H. W. Ingram, The doom of the gods of Hellas, and other poems.

1867. William Morris, The life and death of Jason.

1867. Edmund Ollier, Bacchus in the east; Proserpina in the shades; Proteus; Eleusinia; Pan (*Poems from the Greek Mythology*).

Ollier quotes Bacon's *Wisdom of the Ancients* (pp. 22, 33).

1867. George Augustus Simcox, Prometheus unbound. A tragedy.

Poems and Romances (1869) included some short pieces and sonnets.

1867. John Byrne Leicester Warren, later Lord De Tabley, Orestes: a metrical drama, by William P. Lancaster.

1867. Edward Yardley, Prometheus; Electra (*Melusina*).

Supplementary Stories and Poems (1870) included *Bacchus and Ariadne* and *Circe*.

1868. Robert Lytton, later Earl of Lytton, Tales from Herodotus (Opis and Arge; Croesus and Adrastus; Gyges and Candaules) (*Characters and Chronicles*).

1868. William Morris, Atalanta's race; The doom of king Acrisius; The story of Cupid and Psyche; The love of Alcestis; The son of Croesus; Pygmalion and the image (*The Earthly Paradise*, Parts I and II).

1868. Roden Noel, Mencheres; Ganymede; Pan (*Beatrice*).

1869. Henry Clarence Kendall, Daphne; The voyage of Telegonus; Ogyges; Syrinx; Merope (*Leaves from Australian Forests*, Melbourne).

1870. William Morris, The death of Paris; The story of Acontius and Cydippe; The story of Rhodope; The golden apples; Bellerophon at Argos; Bellerophon in Lycia (*The Earthly Paradise*, Parts III and IV).

1870. Arthur W. E. O'Shaughnessy, The wife of Hephaestus; Cleopatra; Helen (*An Epic of Women*).

1870. Dante Gabriel Rossetti, Troy town; Aspecta Medusa; Death's songsters; The wine of Circe; Venus [Verticordia]; Cassandra; Pandora (*Poems*).

1870. Francis Reginald Statham ("Francis Reynolds"), Cephalus and Procris; Hero (*Glaphyra*).

1870 [1869]. Alfred Tennyson, Lucretius (*Macmillan's Magazine*, 1868; *The Holy Grail*, 1870 [1869]).

1870. John Byrne Leicester Warren, later Lord De Tabley, Pandora; Daphne; "Maga Circe"; etc. (Some thirteen poems, new and old, in *Rehearsals*; mostly reprinted in *Collected Poems*.)

1870. Augusta Webster, Medea; Circe (*Portraits*).
       Mrs. Webster's *In a Day* (1882) was a non-mythological drama with a Greek setting, *The Sentence* (1887) a Roman drama.

1871. Robert Browning, Balaustion's adventure: including a transcript from Euripides.

1871. Wathen Mark Wilks Call, The legend of Ariadne: a Greek romance (*Golden Histories*, pp. 1–72).
       Reverberations (revised ed., 1875) included *Alcestis* and *Admetus*.

1871. Richard Crawley, Venus and Psyche.
       Three cantos (pp. 3–166) of partly facetious Byronic narrative, loosely Apuleian in outline.

1871. Francis Turner Palgrave, Alcestis (*Lyrical Poems*, pp. 23–39).
       Amenophis (1892) contained an historical "ballad," *Pausanias and Cleonicé* (1886).

1871. Algernon Charles Swinburne, Tiresias; Eurydice (*Songs before Sunrise*).
       Celaeno appeared in *Songs of Two Nations* (1875).

1872. Andrew Lang, Hesperothen; Two sonnets of the sirens; The shade of Helen (*Ballads and Lyrics of Old France*).

1873. Edward Brennan, The witch of Nemi [Apollo] (*The Witch of Nemi*).

1873. John Brent, Atalanta, Winnie, and other poems.

1873. Edward Carpenter, Narcissus; Persephone; Venus Aphrodite; Sleeping Venus; The veiled Isis (*Narcissus*).

1873. John Byrne Leicester Warren, later Lord De Tabley, Medea; Ode to the sun (*Searching the Net*).

1874. "George Eliot," Arion (*The Legend of Jubal*).

1875. Wilfrid Scawen Blunt, Adonis (*Sonnets and Songs. By Proteus*).

1875. Robert Browning, Aristophanes' apology including a transcript from Euripides being the last adventure of Balaustion.

1875. Sebastian Evans, Achilles' island (*In the Studio*).

1876. Anon., Pan; or, the myth of Eubulus (*The King's Sacrifice*).

1876. Thomas Ashe, The gift of Herè [Aeolus and Deiopea]; Psamathe; Cleobis and Bito (*Songs Now and Then*).

1876. Edward Dowden, The heroines (Helena; Atalanta; Europa; Andromeda; Eurydice); etc. (*Poems*).

   Poems (1914) included *Imitated from Goethe's "Ganymede."*

1876. Joseph Ellis, A chase of Echo. An idyl (*Caesar in Egypt*).

1876. Dora Greenwell, Demeter and Cora (*Camera Obscura*).

1876 [1875]. Thomas Gordon Hake, The birth of Venus (*New Symbols*).

   Legends of the Morrow (1879) included *Venus Anadyomene*.

1876. Alexander [Lindsay], Earl of Crawford and Balcarres, Argo: or, the quest of the golden fleece.

   A free reworking of Apollonius Rhodius, in 298 pages.

1876. Algernon Charles Swinburne, Erechtheus: a tragedy.

1876. J. C. Westervale, Hero and Leander [burlesque] (*Wild Rhymes*).

1877. [William Cox Bennett], Prometheus the fire-giver: an attempted restoration of the lost first part of the Promethean trilogy of Aeschylus.

1877. Austin Dobson, A case of cameos [Seven short pieces]; The prayer of the swine to Circe; A tale of Polypheme (*Proverbs in Porcelain*).

   Vignettes in Rhyme (1873) included *The Death of Procris* (1869).

1877. Sir Lewis Morris, The epic of Hades.

   A volume with this title (1876) became the second of three books in the completed work. Some isolated poems appeared in other volumes.

1878. T. Waddon Martyn, Theseus, and other poems and translations.

1878. Algernon Charles Swinburne, The last oracle (1876) (*Poems and Ballads*, Second Series).

1878. John Addington Symonds, Callicrates; The lotos-garland of

Antinous; Love and death [Cratinus and Aristodemus]; Inclusam Danaen (*Many Moods*).

1879. Robert Browning, Pheidippides (*Dramatic Idyls*).

1879. Sir Edmund Gosse, The gifts of the muses; The praise of Dionysus; The praise of Artemis; Alcyone; The waking of Eurydice; etc. (*New Poems*).
On *Viol and Flute* (1873) contained *Old and New*.

1879. John Todhunter, Alcestis: a dramatic poem.
Laurella (1876) included *Scenes from the Masque of Psyche*, etc.

1880. Robert Browning, Echetlos; Pan and Luna (*Dramatic Idyls*, Second Series).

1880. Andrew Lang, Ballade of the voyage to Cythera; In Ithaca; The mystery of queen Persephone (*XXII Ballades in Blue China*).
The sonnet *The Odyssey*, printed with the translation (1879), appeared in the *Ballades* of 1881.

1880. Sir Charles G. D. Roberts, Orion; Ariadne; Memnon; Sappho (*Orion*, Philadelphia).

1880. Algernon Charles Swinburne, Thalassius (*Songs of the Springtides*).

1880. John Addington Symonds, Leuké; Hesperus and Hymenaeus; Prometheus dead; etc. (*New and Old*).

1881. Katherine Bradley and Edith Cooper, Bellerophôn. By Arran and Isla Leigh.
In addition to the drama the volume included eleven shorter pieces. Some twenty early mythological poems by Edith Cooper were printed in *Dedicated* (1914).

1881. George Moore, Sappho (*Pagan Poems*).

1881. Agnes Mary Frances Robinson (Duclaux), The gardener of Sinope; Before a bust of Venus; Philumene to Aristides (*The Crowned Hippolytus Translated from Euripides, with New Poems*).

1881. Dante Gabriel Rossetti, Venus victrix; Hero's lamp; A sea-spell; Astarte Syriaca; Proserpina (*Ballads and Sonnets*).

1881. [Francis Terrell], Sappho: a dream.

1881. Oscar Wilde, The garden of Eros; The new Helen; The burden of Itys; Endymion; Charmides; etc. (*Poems*).
The Sphinx appeared in 1894.

1881. Thomas Woolner, Pygmalion.

[1882]. Anon., Orpheus and Eurydice. A poem. Dedicated to J. E. C. (Pp. 3–28.)

1882. George Francis Armstrong, The satyr; Orithyia; Selemnos; The closing of the oracle; etc. (*A Garland from Greece*).

1882. Andrew Lang, Helen of Troy.

1882. Virginia Vaughan, Orpheus and the sirens: a drama in lyrics.
1883. Robert Bridges, Prometheus the firegiver (Oxford).
1883. Robert Browning, Ixion (*Jocoseria*).
1883. Isabella Harwood ("Ross Neil"), Orestes; Pandora (Verse plays, in *Andrea the Painter*).
1883. J. W. Mackail, In Scheria (*Love in Idleness*).
 Part I of the poem first appeared in *Mensae Secundae* (1879); both parts were reprinted, as *Nausicaa* and *The Return of Ulysses*, in *Love's Looking Glass* (1891).
1883. George Meredith, The day of the daughter of Hades; Phoebus with Admetus (1880); Melampus (*Poems and Lyrics of the Joy of Earth*).
1883. [Charles J. Pickering], Kallirrhoe; Lykophron (*The Last David*).
1883. Sir Ronald Ross, Edgar or the new Pygmalion and the judgment of Tithonus (Madras). [Not seen.]
 Poems (1928) included *Calypso to Ulysses* (1890) and *To Aphrodite in Cyprus* (1913).
1884. Katherine Bradley and Edith Cooper ("Michael Field"), Callirrhoë.
1884. Richard Watson Dixon, Cephalus and Procris; Apollo Pythius; Polyphemus (*Odes and Eclogues*, Oxford).
1884. Eugene Lee-Hamilton, Apollo and Marsyas, and other poems.
 Two pieces about statues of Venus appeared in *Poems and Transcripts* (1878), and a version of the Tannhäuser legend in *Gods, Saints, and Men* (1880).
1884. Amy Levy, Medea. A fragment in drama form, after Euripides (*A Minor Poet*).
 Xantippe was the title poem of a volume of 1881.
1884. Stephen Phillips, Orestes (Privately printed, 1884; revised version in *Primavera: Poems. By Four Authors*, Oxford, 1884, and in *New Poems*, 1908).
1884. Earl of Southesk, Theseus: a ballad; Andromeda: a ballad (*The Burial of Isis*, Edinburgh).
1884. Thomas Woolner, Silenus.
1885. Sir Edwin Arnold, The hymn of the priestess of Diana (*The Secret of Death*).
 Lotus and Jewel (1887) included *Atalanta*.
1885. Robert Bridges, Eros and Psyche (revised ed., 1894).
1885. Sir Edmund Gosse, The island of the blest; Timasitheos; The sons of Cydippe (*Firdausi in Exile*).
 In Russet and Silver (1894) included *The New Memnon*, *Philomel in London*, and *The Death of Procris*.

1885 [1884]. Andrew Lang, The fortunate islands; Pisidicê; Cameos. Sonnets from the antique (*Rhymes à la Mode*).

1885. Edward C. Lefroy, Echoes from Theocritus and other sonnets.
The book included mythological sonnets, mostly reprinted from booklets of 1883–84.

1885. Alfred Lord Tennyson, Tiresias and other poems.
The Cup was printed in 1881, and published in 1884.

1886. Katherine Bradley and Edith Cooper ("Michael Field"), Brutus ultor.

1886. W. G. Hole, Procris (*Procris*, pp. 1–39).

1886. Ernest Myers, The judgment of Prometheus; Rhodes; The Olympic Hermes (*The Judgment of Prometheus*).
Poems (1877) included *The Liberation of Dorieus*, etc.

1886. Sir Charles G. D. Roberts, Actaeon; The pipes of Pan; Off Pelorus [Ulysses and the sirens]; etc. (*In Divers Tones*, Boston).

1886. John Todhunter (d. 1916), Helena in Troas.
A *Sicilian Idyll* (1890) was an antique pastoral play. *The Wooing of Artemis* was published with *Trivium Amoris* in 1927.

1886. Thomas Woolner, Tiresias.

1886–87 (pub. 1897). Lionel Johnson, Julian at Eleusis (*Ireland*, 1897).
Poems (1895) included *A Dream of Youth, Lucretius, The Classics*, etc.

1887. Robert Browning, Apollo and the fates; etc. (*Parleyings with Certain People of Importance in their Day*).

1887. William Canton, The god and the schoolboy [Asclepius]; Comfort on Pelion [Chiron] (*A Lost Epic*).

1887. Richard Watson Dixon, Ulysses and Calypso; Mercury to Prometheus (*Lyrical Poems*, Oxford).

1887. Robert Earl of Lytton, Prometheia. (Freedom of speech and press, et caetera.) (*After Paradise or Legends of Exile*.)
A mythological satire, pp. 159–91.

1887. George Meredith, Periander; Solon; Bellerophon; Phaéthôn (1867). (*Ballads and Poems of Tragic Life*.)
The Appeasement of Demeter (1887) appeared in *A Reading of Earth* (1888); the *Ode to the Comic Spirit* in *Poems* (1892).

1887. Octavius Ogle, Idylls of Ilium, and other verses (Oxford).

1887. [Charles J. Pickering], Orpheus; Glaukos; Kodros (*Metassai: Scripts and Transcripts*, Glasgow, privately printed).

1888. Stopford Brooke, Hylas; The faun and the dryad; Endymion; Proteus; Phoebus the herdsman; Glaucon (*Poems*).

1888. Archibald Lampman, An Athenian reverie (*Among the Millet*, Ottawa).

Poems (ed. D. C. Scott, Toronto, 1900) included *Sostratus, Phokaia,* etc.

1888. Roden Noel, The flesh — triumph of Bacchus (*A Modern Faust,* second canto).

1889. Katherine Bradley and Edith Cooper ("Michael Field"), Long ago.

1889. John Davidson, Scaramouch in Naxos: a pantomime (*Plays,* Greenock).

1889. Caroline FitzGerald, Ophelion; Hymn to Persephone; Hymn to Apollo (*Venetia Victrix*).

1889. Sir Frank T. Marzials, Pygmalion; Orpheus and Eurydice; etc. (Six sonnets in *Death's Disguises*).

1889. Alfred Lord Tennyson, Demeter and Persephone (*Demeter*).

1889–90. Francis Thompson, Ode to the setting sun (1889; *New Poems,* 1897); Daphne (1890; *Works,* 1913); Song of the hours (1890; *Works,* 1913).

The sonnet *Hermes* appeared in *New Poems*.

1890. Laurence Binyon, Persephone: the Newdigate poem, 1890.

Lyric Poems (1894) included *Niobe* (1887).

1890. Robert Bridges, The return of Ulysses: a drama in five acts in a mixed manner; Achilles in Scyros: a drama in a mixed manner. [Published separately.]

1890. Richard Garnett, Iphigenia in Delphi: a dramatic poem.

Among the prose fantasies in *The Twilight of the Gods* (1888) were the title piece, "The Dumb Oracle," and "The Poet of Panopolis." "Pan's Wand" and "Truth and Her Companions" were added in 1903.

1890. Frederick Tennyson, The isles of Greece.

Fifteen sections, headed *Sappho, Alcaeus, Sappho and Alcaeus. Days and Hours* (1854) included *Death and the Shepherd.* The *Lament of the Wood-Nymphs* (1853) was reprinted in *The Shorter Poems of Frederick Tennyson* (1913).

1891. Francis William Bourdillon, A lost god [Pan and Christ].

Sursum Corda (1893) included *Helen* and *Eurydice.*

1891. James Dryden Hosken, Phaon and Sappho, a play, etc. (Penzance).

The Betrothal of Venus (1903) employs the motive of the ring given to Venus.

1891. Mary P. Negreponte, Io and other verse.

1891. James Rennell Rodd, later Lord Rennell, The violet crown.

Many short pieces on Greek scenes and themes. *Songs in the South* (1881) included *Endymion.*

1891. Frederick Tennyson, Daphne; Pygmalion; Ariadne; etc. (*Daphne*).

1892. Katherine Bradley and Edith Cooper ("Michael Field"), Sight and song.
Several more mythological pieces appeared in *Underneath the Bough* (1893).

1892. Alfred Lord Tennyson, The death of Oenone, Akbar's dream, and other poems.

1893. Charles D. Bell, Berenice's hair; The birth of Venus (*Poems Old and New*).

1893–95. Lord De Tabley, A hymn to Astarte; Phaethon; Circe (*Poems Dramatic and Lyrical*, 1893); Orpheus in Hades; A hymn to Aphrodite; Circe; The death of Phaethon (Ditto, Second Series, 1895).

1893. Richard Garnett, Nausicaa; Echo and Narcissus; Apollo in Tempe; etc. (*Poems*).

1893. Bryan C. Waller, Perseus with the Hesperides. [Not seen.]
Echo and Other Poems appeared posthumously (Oxford, 1936).

1894. Grant Allen, The return of Aphrodite (*The Lower Slopes*).

1894. T. W. H. Crosland, To Cynthia; Iris and the water-lilies; Aphrilis (*The Pink Book*, Brighton).

1894. Algernon Charles Swinburne, A nympholept; The palace of Pan (*Astrophel*).
Pan and Thalassius appeared in *Poems and Ballads*, Third Series (1889).

1895 and earlier (pub. 1901). Lord De Tabley, Orpheus in Thrace; The lament of Echo; An Eleusinian chant; A daughter of Circe; etc. (*Orpheus in Thrace*, 1901).
Fragments of *A Daughter of Circe* had appeared before, and were reprinted as separate pieces in the *Collected Poems*.

1895–98 (pub. 1909). Maurice Hewlett, Leto's child; The Niobids; Latmos; Hymnia's wreath (nine sonnets) (*Artemision: Idylls and Songs*, 1909).

1895–97. Edward Henry Pember, The voyage of the Phocaeans; Adrastus of Phrygia (Privately printed, 1895 and 1897).

1896. Maurice Hewlett, A hymn to Artemis; The Cretan ode; Ariadne forsaken; Prometheus; Ballad of Clytié; etc. (*Songs and Meditations*).
Pan and the Young Shepherd (1898) is almost wholly in prose.

1896. Stephen Phillips, Christ in Hades.

1897. James Renwick, Ariadne at Naxos; Aristomenes; etc. (*Poems and Sonnets*).

1898. Ernest Hartley Coleridge, Pygmalion's bride (*Poems*).

1898–1905. Aleister [i.e., Edward Alexander] Crowley, The tale of Archais (1898); The Argonauts (1904); Orpheus: a lyrical legend (1905); etc. (Collected in *The Works of Aleister Crowley*, 1905–07).

1898 [1897]. Stephen Phillips, Marpessa (*Poems*).
In *Who's Who* this poem was regularly dated 1890, but I have not seen any earlier edition than that of 1898.

1898. William Ernest Henley, The gods are dead (*Poems*).

1898. Robert Calverley Trevelyan, Epimetheus; Archilochus; Orpheus; etc. (*Mallow and Asphodel*).

1898. Theodore Watts-Dunton, Apollo in Paris [Hérédia]; Ancestral memory: The deaf and dumb son of Croesus (*The Coming of Love*).

1899. Katherine Bradley and Edith Cooper ("Michael Field"), Noontide branches (Oxford).

1899. W. Wilfred Campbell, The dryad; Pan the fallen (1893); Phaethon (*Beyond the Hills of Dream*, Boston and New York).

1899. Ernest Dowson, Villanelle of Acheron; Libera me [Aphrodite]. (*Decorations*.)

1899. T. Sturge Moore, Semele; Io; Daphne; The sibyl; Niobe; The home of Helen; A chorus of Dorides; Sappho's death; etc. (*The Vinedresser*).

1899. John Cowper Powys, Calypso; Ares and Aphrodite; etc. (*Poems*).
Several pieces appeared in *Odes* (1896); several more in *Mandragora* (New York, 1917).

1899. Elinor Sweetman, Pastoral of the faun; Pastoral of Kyprios; etc. (*Pastorals*).
Several other pieces appeared in *Footsteps of the Gods* (1893).

1900. Arthur Gray Butler, The choice of Achilles; The choice of Heracles (*The Choice of Achilles*).

1900. Arthur Shearly Cripps, Christ in the wilderness; Eurydice (*Titania*).

1900. Gilbert Murray, Andromache: a play in three acts [prose].

1901. Laurence Binyon, The dryad; The Bacchanal of Alexander; Amasis; Orpheus in Thrace (*Odes*; reprinted in *Odes*, 1913).

1901. Sir Edmund Gosse, Hypolympia or the gods in the island: an ironic fantasy. [Mostly prose.]

1901. George Meredith, A reading of life (The vital choice; With the huntress; With the persuader; The test of manhood); The cageing of Ares (1899) (*A Reading of Life*).

1901. Cosmo Monkhouse, Pasiteles the elder and other poems.

1901. T. Sturge Moore, Aphrodite against Artemis: a tragedy.
1901. Edward Henry Pember, The finding of Pheidippides; Pausanias and Cleonice (*The Finding of Pheidippides*, privately printed).
1901. Lady Margaret Sackville, Pan and the maiden; The helots; Themistocles (*Poems*).
1901. Lily Thicknesse, Eurydice to Orpheus (*Poems*).
1901. Robert Calverley Trevelyan, Polyphemus: a dramatic poem; etc. (*Polyphemus*).
1902. Alfred Austin, Polyphemus (1898) (*A Tale of True Love*).
        At Delphi (1881) appeared in *At the Gate of the Convent* (1885); *Sisyphus* in *Sacred and Profane Love* (1908).
1902. W. G. Hole, The naiad to the hamadryad; Gyges replies to the queen (*Poems Lyrical and Dramatic*).
1902. Rudyard Kipling, Pan in Vermont.
        See also *Poseidon's Law* (1904) and *The Bees and the Flies* (1909).
1902. John Payne, The last of Hercules; Anchises (*Poetical Works*, 1902, I, 363–73, 394–99).
1902. John Swinnerton Phillimore, Mantis [Cassandra]; etc. (*Poems*, Glasgow).
        Things Old and New (London, 1918) included *Pan* (*After the Russian of Maikov*).
1902. Stephen Phillips, Ulysses: a drama in a prologue and three acts.
1902. Arthur K. Sabin, Typhon; Orion; Clymene; Ida (*Typhon*).
1903. Maurice Baring, Circe (1899) (*The Black Prince*).
1903. Bliss Carman, The pipes of Pan; Legends of the reed (Marsyas; Syrinx; The magic flute; A shepherd in Lesbos); Daphne; The lost dryad; The dead faun; Hylas; At Phaedra's tomb (*The Pipes of Pan*).
        Later volumes included a few lyrics. *Sappho: One Hundred Lyrics* appeared in 1904 (Boston).
1903. R. C. K. Ensor, Pan in the Pennine (*Modern Poems*).
1903. Arnold Graves, Clytaemnestra: a tragedy.
1903. T. Sturge Moore, The centaur's booty; The rout of the Amazons; Danaë (first printed 1893, revised 1903).
        All published as separate volumes.
1903. Arthur Stringer, Hephaestus, Persephone at Enna, and Sappho in Leucadia.
1904. Gordon Bottomley, Prophesy (1899); The last of Helen (1902); The dairy-maids to Pan; Daphne (1899); The stealing of Dionysos (1903); Phillis (1902) (*The Gate of Smaragdus*).
        Some lyrics appeared in *Poems at White-Nights* (1899).

1904. T. Sturge Moore, Theseus, Medea and lyrics; Pan's prophecy; To Leda.
    Published as separate volumes. *The Gazelles* (1904) included *Lines on Titian's "Bacchanal."*
1904. George W. Russell ("A. E."), Aphrodite (*The Divine Vision*).
    The Mask of Apollo (prose) belongs to the same year.
1904. Ruth Young, Orpheus (*Verses*).
1905. Laurence Binyon, Penthesilea. ,
    The short *Queen Venus* appeared in *The Death of Adam* (1904).
1905. Robert Bridges, Demeter: a mask (Clarendon Press).
    The Isle of Achilles appeared in 1899; *Narcissus* (1913), in *October* (1920).
1905. Ethel Clifford, Demeter of Anthela; A song of Artemis; A song of Apollo; etc. (*Love's Journey*).
1905. Eva Gore-Booth, The three resurrections (Lazarus; The return of Alcestis; Psyche in Hades); Narcissus; etc. (*The Three Resurrections and The Triumph of Maeve*).
    The One and the Many (1904) included two short pieces on Proserpine. *The Death of Orpheus* and other poems appeared in *The Agate Lamp* (1912).
1905. Lady Margaret Sackville, A hymn to Dionysus; Philomena and Procne; Peirithous (*A Hymn to Dionysus*).
1906. Laurence Binyon, Paris and Oenone: a tragedy in one act (*Fortnightly Review*, 1905).
1906. Walter de la Mare, Tears [Pan]; Sorcery [Pan] (*Poems*).
    The Sunken Garden (1917) included *Alexander*.
1906. John Drinkwater, The death of Leander and other poems (Birmingham).
1906. Harold Monro, Clytie; Pausanias; Ariadne in Naxos (*Poems*).
1906. Arthur K. Sabin, The death of Icarus and other poems (Glasgow).
1907. Arthur Dillon, Orpheus.
1907. Bernard Drew, Prometheus delivered (pp. 13–101).
    Cassandra (1906), in addition to the title poem, contained *Orpheus and Eurydice*.
1907. James Elroy Flecker, On Turner's Polyphemus; The ballad of Hampstead Heath; The bridge of fire; Narcissus; Destroyer of ships, men, cities (*The Bridge of Fire*).
    Collected Poems (1916) included *Lucretia* (1904).
1907. Alfred Noyes, The net of Vulcan; The ride of Phaëthon; Niobe; Orpheus and Eurydice; The last of the Titans (*Forty Singing Seamen*).

Echo and Narcissus appeared in *The Loom of Years* (1902). *The Last of the Titans*, revised, appeared as *Atlas and Medusa* in *Collected Poems*, IV (1927).

1907. Herbert Trench, Apollo and the seaman (*New Poems*). *Poems* (1918) included *Milo*.

1908. J. Redwood Anderson, The legend of Eros and Psyche. *The Mask* (1912) included *Götterdämmerung*.

1908. Maurice Baring, Proserpine: a masque (Oxford). *Diminutive Dramas* (1919) included *Pious Aeneas*, *The Aulis Difficulty*, etc.

1908. Dudley Beresford, Io and Jupiter; etc. (*Lyrics and Legends*).

1908. Francis William Bourdillon, The debate of the lady Venus and the virgin Mary; Chryseis (1894); The statue (*Preludes and Romances*).

1908. Katherine Bradley and Edith Cooper ("Michael Field"), Wild honey. Some two dozen lyrical pieces.

1908. John Davidson, The testament of John Davidson.

1908. Eleanor Farjeon, Pan-worship; Apollo in Pherae (*Pan-Worship*).

[1908]. John Garth, Psyche, odes, etc.

1908. John Payne, The death of Pan; The wrath of Venus; Hector (*Carol and Cadence*).

1908 [1907]. Stephen Phillips, Endymion (1898); Iole (*New Poems*).

1908. Robert Calverley Trevelyan, Sisyphus: an operatic fable.

1909. T. Sturge Moore, Orpheus and Eurydice (*Fortnightly Review*, Literary Supplement, December, 1909, pp. 1–26). This play, and *Omphale and Herakles* (written earlier), were revised for publication in the *Collected Edition*, III and IV (1932, 1933).

1909. R. H. Mottram ("J. Marjoram"), Pygmalion and the image (*New Poems*).

1909. Alfred Noyes, Bacchus and the pirates; Actaeon (*The Enchanted Island*).

1909. Rachel Annand Taylor, Hades; Dirge for Narcissus; The dryad; etc. (*Rose and Vine*).

1909. Sir Robert Vansittart, The gods of yesterday (*Songs and Satires*).

1909. Alfred Williams, Paris and Oenone; Penelope to Phemius; Helen; etc. (*Songs in Wiltshire*). *Nature* (1912) included *The Story of Acestes* and *The Cyclops* from an early work, *Aeneas in Sicily*.

1910. Kitty Balbernie, Arion of Lesbos and other poems.

1910. Ralph Cheever Dunning, Hyllus: a drama.

1910. Joseph Heaton, The yoke of youth (Venus and Urania) (*Poems*, Hampstead).

1910. W. G. Hole, The chained Titan: a poem of yesterday and to-day.

1910. Richard Le Gallienne, Orestes: a tragedy (New York).
    The Lonely Dancer (1914) included *Alma Venus*.

1910. Frederic Manning, Theseus and Hippolyta; Kore (*Poems*).

1911. Clifford Bax, Echo and Narcissus (*Poems Dramatic and Lyrical*).

1911. Henry Bryan Binns, The adventure: a romantic variation on a Homeric theme [Ulysses and Circe].

1911. Rupert Brooke, Ante aram; Menelaus and Helen; The goddess in the wood (*Poems*).

1911. Roger M. Heath, Achilles (Oxford).

1911. Maurice Hewlett, Minos king of Crete; Ariadne in Naxos; The death of Hippolytus (*The Agonists: A Trilogy of God and Man*).

1911. Eden Phillpotts, A litany to Pan; Hymn to Pomona (1905); Hamadryad; etc. (*Wild Fruit*).
    Other short pieces are collected in *A Hundred Lyrics* (1930). One may mention the series of prose works with antique themes or settings, such as *The Girl and the Faun* (1916), *Evander* (1917), etc.

1911. Arthur K. Sabin, Medea and Circe and other poems.

1911–12. Lady Margaret Sackville, The wooing of Dionysus; The pythoness; Tereus; The return of Ganymede (*Bertrud*, Edinburgh, 1911); A poet at the court of Pan; etc. (*Lyrics*, 1912).

1911. Elinor Sweetman, The faun; The dancers; Rhoecus (*The Wild Orchard*).

1911. Wilfrid Thorley, The dead dryad; The crippled faun; etc. (*Confessional*).

1912. Sir Reed Gooch Baggorre, The fates; Genesis of the gods; The war with the giants; Cadmus; etc. (*Mythological Rhymes*).

1912. Patrick R. Chalmers, Pan-pipes; Pomona; Daphne; A song of Syrinx (*Green Days and Blue Days*).
    Other pieces of *Punch* character appeared in *Away to the Maypole* (1927).

1912. Francis Coutts, Psyche.
    Poems (1896), by "F. B. Money-Coutts," included *Hercules and Hylas*, *Tithonus*, and *Butes*.

1912. Bernard Drew, Helen; Hymn to Demeter; Endymion and Selene; Penelope forsaken (*Helen*).

1912. Norman Gale, Dream and ideal [Diana]; The cherry of Lucullus (*Song in September*).

    Orchard Songs (1893) included *Hannibal, Sagunto Capto, Loquitur.*

1912. James Roxburgh McClymont, Theseus in Crete; The golden age; etc. (*Metrical Romances and Ballads*).
    The Land of False Delight (1913) included *Hera in the Hesperides.*

1912. Richard Middleton, Hylas; Pan; Narcissus; To Diana (*Poems and Songs*, Second Series, ed. Henry Savage).

1912. Sir Henry Newbolt, The faun (*Poems: New and Old*).

1912. J. E. Patterson, Daughters of Nereus (*The Lure of the Sea*).

1912. Edward Thompson, Child of Achilles; Pheidippides (*John in Prison*).
    A few brief pieces appeared in *The Knight Mystic* (1907).

1912. Robert Calverley Trevelyan, The bride of Dionysus: a music-drama.

1913. James Elroy Flecker, In Phaeacia; etc. (*The Golden Journey to Samarkand*).
    Collected Poems (1916) included translations from the *Aeneid* (1914) and a fragmentary *Ode to the Glory of Greece* (1913).

1913. Phyllis Gleadow, Phyllis to Demophoön (*Philomela*).

1913. John Helston, Aphrodite at Leatherhead (*Aphrodite*).

1913. Maurice Hewlett, Helen redeemed; Hypsipyle; Oreithyia (1897); The Argive women; Gnatho (*Helen Redeemed*).
    The Ruinous Face, a prose tale of Helen, appeared in 1909.

1913. Marjorie L. C. Pickthall, The little fauns to Proserpine; To Alcithoë (*The Drift of Pinions*).

1913. Lady Margaret Sackville, Syrinx; The coming of Hippolytus; Orpheus among the shades; etc. (*Songs of Aphrodite*).
    The title poem in *Ariadne by the Sea* (1932) is dated 1913.

1914. Bliss Carman and Mary Perry King, Earth deities and other rhythmic masques (New York).
    The same authors' *Daughters of Dawn* (1913) included *Sappho.*

1914. John Mavrogordato, Cassandra in Troy [prose drama].

1914. T. Sturge Moore, The sea is kind; The thigh of Zeus; The young man's fondest foe; A prayer; The song of Cheiron; etc. (*The Sea Is Kind*).

1914. Clara Burdett Patterson, The dryad.

1915. Richard Aldington, To a Greek marble; Argyria; Choricos; At Mitylene; Hermes, leader of the dead; etc. (*Images, 1910–1915*).

1915. Herbert Asquith, Ares, god of war (*The Volunteer*).

1915. Charles Cunningham Brend, Marsyas; Icarius; Erigone; The Cretan fisherman; etc. (*Freshets of the Hills*).

1915. Alfred Noyes, Enceladus; The inimitable lovers [Antony and Cleopatra] (*A Salute from the Fleet*).

1915. Stephen Phillips, Penelope to Ulysses; Semele; Helen to Paris (*Panama*).

1916. Frank Betts, The deathless; Dionysos in Inde (*The Iron Age*, Oxford).

1916. Maurice Hewlett, Iocheaira; The veiled lover; In the forest; Daphne and Leukippos; etc. (*Gai Saber: Tales and Songs*).

1916. Rowland Thirlmere, Polyclitus and his wife Cleora (*Polyclitus*).

1916 *et seq*. Willoughby Weaving, Numerous short pieces in *The Star Fields* (1916); *The Bubble* (1917); *Heard Melodies* (1918); *Daedal Wings* (1920); and *Spoils of Time* (1934); all published at Oxford.

1917. M. St. Clare Byrne, Autonoë. A prologue (*Aldebaran*, Oxford).

1917. Ivar Campbell, Odysseus and Calypso (*Poems*).

1917. John Drinkwater, X = O: A night of the Trojan war (*Pawns: Three Poetic Plays*).

1917. Robert Graves, Faun; Escape (*Fairies and Fusiliers*).
   Over the Brazier (1916) included *The Dying Knight and the Fauns*.

1917. Francis Ledwidge, A dream of Artemis; The departure of Proserpine (*Songs of Peace*).
   Last Songs (1918) included *Pan*.

1917. Frederic Manning, Reaction; The faun; Danae; Demeter mourning (*Eidola*).

1917. Robert Nichols, A faun's holiday (1914–17); Fragments from a drama on the subject of Orestes (1914–16); Danaë: mystery in eight poems (1912–13) (*Ardours and Endurances*).
   Aurelia (1920) included *Closing Lines from "Polyphemus his Passion: A Pastoral"* (1917). The prose "romance of idea," "Sir Perseus and the Fair Andromeda," appeared in *Fantastica* (1923).

1917. Charles Williams, Proserpina; Troy [sonnets on Andromache, Helen, Hecuba, and Cassandra] (*Poems of Conformity*).
   Several other sonnets appeared in volumes of 1920 and 1925.

1918. Martin Armstrong, Phaethon [written before September, 1914] (*Thirty New Poems*).
   The Bird-Catcher (1929) included *The Naiad*.

1918. George Rostrevor Hamilton, Orpheus (*Escape and Fantasy*).
   Some short pieces appeared in volumes of 1910, 1917, etc.

1918. Eleanor Deane Hill, Demeter (Oxford).

1919. Richard Aldington, Bromios; Eros and Psyche; The faun captive; etc. (*Images, 1919*); An earth goddess (*Images of War, 1919*).

1919. William Gerard, Sappho; Achilles and Helen in Elysium (*Dramatic Vistas*).
Hellas Once More appeared in 1925.

1919. Laurence Housman, The wheel [Apollo in Hades; The death of Alcestis; The doom of Admetus].
The third of these plays appeared in 1916 as *The Return of Alcestis*.

1919. Donald F. Goold Johnson, Persephone; Hylas (*Poems*, Cambridge University Press).

1919. Alice Law, Cupid and Psyche and other poems.

1919. Edmund Willan, Hector and Andromache (*Mary Queen of Scots*, Oxford University Press).

1920. Gordon Bottomley, Laodice and Danaë (1909) (*King Lear's Wife*).
Rehearsal of Medusa appeared in *Frescoes from Buried Temples. By James Guthrie. With Poems by Gordon Bottomley* (Pear Tree Press, 1928).

1920. Aldous Huxley, Leda.

1920. T. Sturge Moore, Danaë: Aforetime: Blind Thamyris [*Danaë* is revised from the 1903 version; *Blind Thamyris* is mainly in prose]; Medea; Niobe (*Tragic Mothers*); The powers of the air [Prose, with some mythological poems].

1920. Evan Morgan, Psyche: an unfinished fragment (Oxford).

1920. Cecil Roberts, Phyllistraton (1913); Strayed Hylas (1914); Andromache (1915); Helen of Troy (1917) (*Poems*).
These had appeared in earlier volumes.

1920. Humbert Wolfe, The unknown god; The Sicilian expedition; etc. (*Shylock Reasons with Mr. Chesterton*, Oxford).

1921. Teresa Hooley, The pipes of Pan; The plea of Syrinx (*Songs of the Open*).

1921. Laurence Housman, The death of Orpheus.
The Love Concealed (1928) included the brief *Orpheus and the Phoenix*.

1921. William Jeffrey, Prometheus returns and other poems.

1921. Edward Shanks, The island of youth [Achilles and Deidamia] (*The Island of Youth*).
An "Epilogue" to this poem appeared in *The Shadowgraph* (1925). The brief *Pursuit of Daphne* was included in *Poems* (1916).

1921. Walter J. Turner, Paris and Helen.
   See also Cantos II–III of *Pursuit of Psyche* (1931).

1922. Arthur St. John Adcock, Gods in exile (Part I of *The Divine Tragedy*).

1922. E. H. W. Meyerstein, Philinnion (*In Merlin's Wood*, Oxford).

1922. Hon. Eleanour Norton, Narcissus and Echo; To Diana (*Magic*).

1922. Peter Quennell, Procne; The lion of Nemea; In Aulis (*Masques and Poems*, Waltham Saint Lawrence, Berks.).

1923. Lascelles Abercrombie, Phoenix: tragicomedy in three acts.

1923. Geoffrey Dearmer, The death of Pan (*The Day's Delight*).

1923. Kenneth Hare, Salmacis; Glaucus (*New Poems*).

1923. Eleanor Deane Hill, Polyphemus; Song of Bacchanals (*The Questing Prince*).
   The Jest on Marsyas appeared in 1929.

1923. John Masefield, Choruses in *A King's Daughter*; The taking of Helen [prose].
   The lyric *Fragments* was in *Ballads and Poems* (1910).

1923. Osbert Sitwell, Neptune in chains; The jealous goddess; Bacchanalia (*Out of the Flame*).
   Song of the Fauns appeared in *Argonaut and Juggernaut* (1919).

1924. James Cleugh, The kiss of Proserpine and other poems.

1924. Bernard Drew, Helen of Troy: a play.

1924. Sacheverell Sitwell, Eurydice; The Venus of Bolsover Castle; Daphne; Variation on a theme by John Lyly [Pan and Syrinx]; The sea god; The river god; etc. (*The Thirteenth Caesar*).

1924. William Vokes, The labours of Heracles.

1925. Richard Aldington, The voyage of Telemachus; The manifestation of Pallas; Greek scene — pagan sensuality (*A Fool i' the Forest*).

1925. Lord Gorell, The spirit of happiness [Deucalion].

1925. Edwin Muir, Ballad of Hector in Hades (*First Poems*).

1925. Sir Charles Sherrington, Cyrus and Panthea (*The Assaying of Brabantius*).

1925. Edith Sitwell, The child who saw Midas; Pandora's box (*Troy Park*).
   A number of other pieces appeared in *The Wooden Pegasus* (Oxford, 1920), *Bucolic Comedies* (1923), *Gold Coast Customs* (1929), etc.

1926. Archibald Y. Campbell, Lyrical extract from *The Fall of Troy* (*Poems*).

1926. John Drinkwater, Persephone (New York); reprinted in *Summer Harvest* (1933).

1926. Frank Fleetwood, Sappho; Antigone; Electra; Pan (*The Threshold*).

1926. A. G. McL. Pearce Higgins, Hecuba (Part I in *Marcellus*, Oxford, 1926; Part II in *Hecuba*, 1928).

1926. William Jeffrey, The doom of Atlas and other poems.
  The Wise Men Come to Town (1923) included *Andromeda*, etc.
  The Nymph appeared in 1924 (Porpoise Press).

1926. Naomi Mitchison, The laburnum branch.
  Some classical pieces, mainly Roman.

1926. Frank Morgan, Daphne; Hero and Leander; Theseus and Ariadne; Jason and Medea (*The Quest of Beauty*).

1926. Marian Osborne, Sappho and Phaon: a lyrical drama (Toronto).
  Brief pieces about Sappho appeared in volumes of 1914 and 1923 (London).

1926. Herbert Read, The white isle of Leuce (*Collected Poems*, 1926).

1926. Robert Calverley Trevelyan, Epimetheus; Lucretius (*The Deluge*).
  The brief *Helen* appeared in *Poems and Fables* (1925).

1927. Robert Graves, Pygmalion to Galatea (*Poems 1914–1926*).
  Whipperginny (1923) included *An Idyll of Old Age* [Baucis and Philemon]; *Poems 1926–1930* (1931) included *The Age of Certainty*. *Ulysses* and *As It Were Poems* appeared in *Poems 1930–1933* (1933).

1927. L[oyd] H[aberly], The sacrifice of spring: a masque of queens [Alcestis] (Long Crendon, Bucks.).
  Poems (Oxford University Press, 1931) included *Orpheus at Hell's Gate Speaks.*

1927. Wilfranc Hubbard, Dionysus in Megara (*Tanagra Figures*).

1927. Jack Lindsay, Helen comes of age: a lyric drama.

1927 [1926]. E. H. W. Meyerstein, Diomede and Cressid [pp. 3–8].

1927. Wallace B. Nichols, Prometheus in Piccadilly. [Not seen.]

1927. Sacheverell Sitwell, The Farnese Hercules; The Laocoon; The Hermes (*The Cyder Feast*).

1927. Robert Calverley Trevelyan, Meleager; Cheiron [Poetic dramas published separately].
  The drama *Sulla* (*Three Plays*, 1932) is based on Plutarch's tale of Sulla's encounter with a satyr.

1928. Lascelles Abercrombie, The Olympians; Zagreus (*Twelve Idyls*).

1928. James Urquhart, Hero and Leander; etc. (*Athens o' the North*, Edinburgh).

1928. Mary Webb (d. 1927), The ancient gods (*Poems and The Spring of Joy*).

1928. David R. Williamson, The sacrifice of Iphigenia; etc. (*Collected Poems*).

1928. Humbert Wolfe, Ilion; The sirens; What the sirens sang; Psyche (*This Blind Rose*).
  Troy (28 ll.) was issued separately (1928). Some brief pieces appeared in *The Unknown Goddess* (1925) and *Snow* (1931).

1928. William Butler Yeats, Two songs from a play; Leda and the swan (1923); Colonus' praise; From "Oedipus at Colonus" (*The Tower*).

1929. Gerald Gould, Helen (*Collected Poems*).

1929. George Henderland, Marsyas; Sarpedon (*Dawn*).

1929. Charles R. Jury, Love and the virgins.

1929. Frank L. Lucas, The elms of Protesilaus; Coresus and Callirrhoe (*Time and Memory*).
  Marionettes (1930) included *The Destinies* and *Pygmalion to Galatea*.

1929. Evan Morgan, The lament [Ganymede]; An incident in the life of Ganymedes, son of Tros (1920) (*The City of Canals*).

1929-30. Ranald Newson, Sappho: a lyrical drama (1929); Apollo and Marsyas: an idyl (1930).

1929. Mary Devenport Oneill, Prometheus and other poems.

1929. William Plomer, Three abductions [Europa; Persephone; Ganymede] (*The Family Tree*).

1929. Edward Thompson, The Thracian stranger.
  This poem about Dionysus had been begun "a quarter of a century ago."

1929. Alice Wills, Orpheus; Ulysses; Oenone (*Orpheus*).

1930. Alfred Gordon Bennett, Ulysses (*Collected Poems*).

1930. Laurence Binyon, Memnon (*Three Short Plays*).

1930. Eric Linklater, Silenus (*A Dragon Laughed*).

1930. T. Sturge Moore, Psyche in Hades; Daimonassa (*Mystery and Tragedy*).

1931. Audrey A. Brown, Laodamia; etc. (*A Dryad in Nanaimo*, Toronto).

1931. Anthony Crossley, Tragedy under Lucifer [Marsyas].
  Several pieces appeared in *Prophets, Gods and Witches* (1930).

1931. Robert Gathorne-Hardy, Glaucus (*Village Symphony*).

1931. Alice Law, Iphigenia: a tragedy (Altham, Accrington).

1931. John Masefield, The wild swan [Brutos and Lykaon]; Penelope [Homeric paraphrase] (*Minnie Maylow's Story*).

1931. Richard Rowley, Apollo in Mourne [acted 1926] (*Selected Poems*).

1931. Geoffrey Scott, The Skaian gate (*Poems*, Oxford University Press).

1931. Alberta Vickridge, Goatfoot; Tamer of horses; etc. (*Goatfoot*, Bradford).

1931. Elizabeth Wordsworth, The apple of discord [burlesque] (*Poems and Plays*, Oxford University Press).

1932. J. Redwood Anderson, Icarus (*Transvaluations*).

1932. Laurence Dakin, Theseus; Psyche (*Poems*, Paris).

1932. Frank L. Lucas, Ariadne (Cambridge University Press).

1932. John Masefield, A tale of Troy.

1932. Ranald Newson, Helen of Argos. A play in two parts (*Opus Eight*); Apollo in Galilee (*Interrupted Serenade*); Procris and the faun (*For Saxophone and Harpsichord*).

1932. Dorothy (Lady Gerald) Wellesley, Jupiter and the nun.

1932. Laurence Whistler, The new Olympus; The old faun's tale; etc. (*Armed October*).

1933. Richard Aldington, The eaten heart. [Mythology *passim*.]

1933. William Macneile Dixon, In Arcadia.
       A number of short classical and mythological pieces.

1933. Oliver St. John Gogarty, Europa and the bull; Leda and the swan; etc. (*Selected Poems*).

1933. G. Laurence Groom, Grecian nocturne.
       Numerous short pieces on Greek scenes and themes.

1933. T. Sturge Moore, Omphale and Herakles: in seven scenes (*Poems*, Collected Edition, IV).
       See under 1909.

1933. Sacheverell Sitwell, The Farnese Hercules (1927); Landscape with the giant Orion; The Hermes of Praxiteles (1927); Fugal siege; The Laocoon of El Greco (1927); Aeneas hunting stags upon the coast of Libya; The royal hunt and storm in the forest; Agamemnon's tomb; Bacchus in India; Battles of the centaurs; Cephalus and Procris (*Canons of Giant Art: Twenty Torsos in Heroic Landscapes*).

1933. William Butler Yeats, Lullaby; The Delphic oracle upon Plotinus; From the "Antigone" (*The Winding Stair*).

1934. A. Hugh Fisher, Callisto (Chicago).

1934. Yvonne Ffrench, The Amazons; Andromache bereaved; etc. (*The Amazons*).

1934. R. R. Sreshta, Narkissos; A scene in Olympus (*The Stratagem of Isis*, Cambridge).

1934. William Butler Yeats, The resurrection (*Wheels and Butterflies*).
Cf. *Two Songs from a Play*, under 1928.

1934. Joan R. Young, The return: a tale in verse [Cephalus and Procris] (Oxford).

1935. Gilbert Coleridge, Pygmalion and other poems.

1935. Peri Cotgrave, The little centaur and other verses (Centaur Press).

1935. Frank Eyre, The naiad and other poems (Oxford).

1935. James Kennedy, Psyche and Eros: Romeo and Juliet.

1935. B. Cyril Windeler, King Minos of Knossos (Oxford University Press).

PART II. UNITED STATES

1786. Philip Freneau, The monument of Phaon (1770); The prayer of Orpheus (*Poems*, Philadelphia).
The *Poems* of 1795 included *Minerva's Advice*.

1821. Henry C. Knight, Psyche bathing. A vision (*Poems*, Boston).

1823. James Gates Percival, Prometheus (*Poems*).
The first part of *Prometheus* appeared in *Poems* (New Haven, 1821); *Prometheus: Part II* in 1822.

1825–28 (pub. 1926). Edward Coote Pinkney, Cleonice (*Life and Works*, ed. Thomas O. Mabbott and Frank L. Pleadwell, 1926).

1827. James Gates Percival, Greece from mount Helicon; The mythology of Greece; etc. (*Clio . . . No. III*).
A few pieces appeared in *Clio . . . No. I* (Charleston, 1822).

1827. Lydia Huntley Sigourney, Invocation to Greece; Ancient tradition from the island of Lesbos; etc. (*Poems; by the Author of "Moral Pieces in Prose and Verse,"* Boston).

1829 (pub. 1830). Edgar Allan Poe, To science.

1830 (pub. 1836). Oliver Wendell Holmes, The meeting of the dryads (*Poems*, Boston).

1831. Nathaniel Parker Willis, Parrhasius (*Poem Delivered Before the Society of United Brothers . . . with Other Poems*).
Fugitive Poetry (Boston, 1829) included *Psyche, before the Tribunal of Venus*.

1839. Albert Pike, Hymns to the gods.
Eight hymns appeared in *Blackwood's Magazine*, XLV (1839), 819–30. Twelve, and the poem *Latona*, were included in *Hymns to the Gods* (privately printed, 1872), and in *General Albert Pike's Poems*, ed. Mrs. L. P. Roome (Little Rock, Ark., 1900).

1842 [1841]. Henry Wadsworth Longfellow, Endymion (*Ballads*, Cambridge).

Poems (Philadelphia, 1845) included *The Occultation of Orion*. *Pegasus in Pound* appeared in *The Seaside and the Fireside* (1850 [1849]).

1844 [1843]. James Russell Lowell, Prometheus; The shepherd of king Admetus; Rhoecus (*Poems*, Cambridge).

A Year's Life (Boston, 1841) included *The Syrens*.

1847 [1846]. Ralph Waldo Emerson, Bacchus; Merops (*Poems*, Boston).

1847. William Wetmore Story, Prometheus; Clytie (*Poems*, Boston).

1848. Henry B. Hirst, Endymion. A tale of Greece (Boston).

Some short pieces appeared in volumes of 1845 and 1849.

1848 [1847]. James Russell Lowell, Hebe (*Poems*, Second Series, Boston).

Poems (Boston, 1849) included *Eurydice*.

1848. Harriette Fanning Read, Medea (*Dramatic Poems*, Boston).

1851. Benjamin West Ball, Ionia; The song of Eneas' men; Pan and Laïs; etc. (*Elfin Land*, Boston).

1851. Mrs. Sara J. C. Lippincott ("Grace Greenwood"), Ariadne; Pygmalion (*Poems*, Boston).

1852. George Henry Boker, The vision of the goblet [Dionysus] (*The Podesta's Daughter*, Philadelphia).

1852. Richard Henry Stoddard, Arcadian hymn to Flora; Arcadian idyl (*Poems*, Boston).

1853. Thomas Holley Chivers, Astarte's song to Endymion (1836) (*Virginalia*, Philadelphia).

1855. Howard H. Caldwell, Evadne; Artemisia (*Oliatta*).

1855. Erastus W. Ellsworth, Ariadne; Cupid and the wasp (*Poems*, Hartford).

1855. Franklin W. Fish, Prometheus (*Poems*, New Haven).

1855. N. L. Frothingham, Odysseus and Calypso (*Metrical Pieces*, Boston).

1856. [John Witt Randall], Lament of Orpheus (*Consolations of Solitude*, Boston).

Poems of Nature and Life (Boston, 1899) included *The Dream of Orestes*.

1857. Paul Hamilton Hayne, Ancient fables; Song of the naiads (*Sonnets*, Charleston).

Poems (Boston, 1855) included *The Temptation of Venus*, a version of the Tannhäuser legend.

1857. Estelle Anna Lewis, The last hour of Sappho (*Poems*).

1857. Thomas Buchanan Read, Hero and Leander. In marble by
Steinhauser (*Sylvia*, Philadelphia).
Poems (London, 1852) included the brief *Endymion*.

1857. Richard Henry Stoddard, The fisher and Charon; The search for
Persephone (*Songs of Summer*, Boston).
The Book of the East (1871) included *The Wine-Cup* and *The
Children of Isis*.

1858. Henry Wadsworth Longfellow, Prometheus; Epimetheus (*The
Courtship of Miles Standish*, Boston).
Tales of a Wayside Inn (Boston, 1863) included *Enceladus*.

1859. Sidney Russell, Hebe and Ganymede; Alcestis (*Poems*, Philadelphia).

1860. William H. Holcombe, Circe for Calypso (*Poems*).

1860. Edmund Clarence Stedman, Penelope; Apollo (*Poems*, *Lyrical
and Idyllic*).
Alice of Monmouth (1864) contained *Alectryôn*.

1861. John Godfrey Saxe, Phaëthon; Pyramus and Thisbe; Polyphe-
mus and Ulysses; Orpheus and Eurydice; The choice of king
Midas (Travesties, in *Poems*, Boston).
Some other facetious pieces appeared in volumes of 1865 *et seq.*
The Masquerade (Boston, 1866) included the serious *Pan
Immortal*.

1862. [William George Caldcleugh], Thessalia; Pan, the wood-god;
Alcyon; Echo; Sappho; etc. (*The Branch*, Philadelphia).

1863. Bayard Taylor, Passing the sirens; Icarus (*The Poet's Journal*,
Boston).
Hylas and *Sicilian Wine* appeared in *A Book of Romances,
Lyrics, and Songs* (Boston, 1852). *Poems of the Orient* (1855) in-
cluded *An Epistle from Mount Tmolus*.

1864. Arthur Malachi Lee, Atalanta (*Fashion*).

1868. Edward Rowland Sill, Semele (*The Hermitage*).

1868. William Wetmore Story, Cassandra; Pan in love; Orestes;
Praxiteles and Phryne; Europa (*Graffiti d'Italia*, Edinburgh and
London).
A few other pieces were included in *Poems* (Boston, 1886).

1870. George Hill, Circe and Telemachus; etc. (*Titiania's Banquet*,
Pictures of Woman, third edition).
Some poems on Greek scenes had appeared in volumes of 1831
and 1839.

1870. Helen Hunt (Jackson), Oenone; Ariadne's farewell (*Verses*,
Boston).
The 1874 edition included *Demeter*.

1870. Margaret J. Preston, Alcyoné; Erinna's spinning; The flight of Arethusa; Rhodopé's sandal; The quenched brand (*Old Song and New*, Philadelphia).

1870. [Theodore F. Vaill], A free and independent translation of the first and fourth books of the Aeneid of Virgil (Winsted, Connecticut).

A travesty "in modern American."

1871. Emma Lazarus, Admetus; Orpheus (*Admetus*).

Poems and Translations (1867) included *Daphne, Penelope's Choice, Clytie*, and *Aphrodite*.

1872. Paul Hamilton Hayne, Daphles. An Argive story; Aëthra; Cambyses and the Macrobian bow; The story of Glaucus the Thessalian (*Legends and Lyrics*, Philadelphia).

The Mountain of the Lovers (1875) included *The Vengeance of the Goddess Diana*, a reworking of the author's early *Avolio* (1860).

1875. Arthur W. Austin, Jupiter and Hebe (*The Woman and the Queen*, Cambridge).

1875. Christopher P. Cranch, Atalanta; Iapis (*The Bird and the Bell*, Boston).

1875. George Parsons Lathrop, Helen at the loom (*Rose and Roof-Tree*, Boston).

1875. Estelle Anna Lewis ("Stella"), Sappho: a tragedy in five acts (London).

1875. Henry Wadsworth Longfellow, The masque of Pandora (Boston).

1876. Robert Kelley Weeks, Andromeda's escape. A dramatic poem (*Twenty Poems*).

1877. Samuel P. Putnam, Prometheus: a poem.

1877. Edmund Clarence Stedman, News from Olympia (*Hawthorne*, Boston).

The Blameless Prince (Boston, 1869) included *Pan in Wall Street*.

1878. Henry A. Beers, The rise of Aphrodite; Narcissus (*Odds and Ends*, Boston).

1878. Alice Wellington Rollins, Andromeda (*The Ring of Amethyst*).

1878. Bayard Taylor, Prince Deukalion (Boston).

The Masque of the Gods (Boston, 1872) included Apollo. Some short pieces were collected in *Poetical Works* (Boston, 1880).

1879. Sarah Helen Whitman, Proserpine to Pluto in Hades; The Venus of Milo (*Poems*, Boston).

1880. Oliver Wendell Holmes, The first fan (*Poetical Works*, Boston).
1880. W. N. Lockington, Venus and Vulcan [burlesque]; Lucrece (*Day-Dreams*, San Francisco).
1880. Denton J. Snider, Delphic days (St. Louis).
1881. Annie Fields, The lantern of Sestos; Helena; Herakles; Artemis; Antinous; Achilles; etc. (*Under the Olive*, Boston).
   Several short pieces appeared in *The Singing Shepherd* (Boston, 1895).
1881. William Gibson, Persephone; Sibylla Cumana (*Poems of Many Years and Many Places*, Boston).
1881. John Boyle O'Reilly, Prometheus — Christ (*The Statues in the Block*).
1883. Charles Leonard Moore, Herakles; Prometheus (*Poems Antique and Modern*, Philadelphia).
1883. Henry Peterson, Helen, after Troy; The legend of Curtius (*Poems*, Second Series, Philadelphia).
1884. Ralph Waldo Emerson, Nature; Pan (*Poems*, Boston).
1884. Henry Niles Pierce, The death-chant of Orpheus; Eurydice (*The Agnostic*).
1885. Luman Allen, The sage of Mentor (Chicago).
1885. Masson Pell Helmbold, Thisbe's lament and other poems (Philadelphia).
1885. Elizabeth Stuart Phelps, Galatea; Eurydice (*Songs of the Silent World*).
1885. Denton J. Snider, Agamemnon's daughter: a poem (Boston).
1885–87. Edith M. Thomas, Syrinx; Demeter's search; Persephone; etc. (*A New Year's Masque*, 1885); Fighting the wind; Moly; Apollo the shepherd; The homesickness of Ganymede; Marsyas; Glaucus (*Lyrics and Sonnets*, 1887).
1886. Clinton Scollard, The dryad; The death of Orion; Pomona (*With Reed and Lyre*, Boston).
   Pictures in Song (1884) included a number of short pieces.
1886. George Harrison Van Zandt, The sleep of Endymion; The lotos-eaters; etc. (*Poems*, Philadelphia).
1887–89. Madison Cawein, The dead oread; Aphrodite; Persephone; etc. (*Blooms of the Berry, The Triumph of Music, Accolon of Gaul*, Louisville, 1887, 1888, 1889).
1887. Louise Imogen Guiney, The white sail; Tarpeia; The last faun; Aglaus (*The White Sail*, Boston).
   Some short pieces appeared in *A Roadside Harp* (1893) and *Happy Ending* (1909).

1887. Frank Dempster Sherman, Bacchus; Come, Pan, and pipe (*Madrigals and Catches*).
    Lyrics for a Lute (1890) included *The Naiad's Cup*.

1888. [Allen R. Darrow], Iphigenia; a legend of the Iliad, and other poems (Buffalo). [Not seen.]

1888. Payne Erskine, Iona: a lay of ancient Greece (Boston).

1888. Harry Lyman Koopman, Orestes, a dramatic sketch: and other poems (Buffalo).

1888. James Russell Lowell, Phoebe (1881); Endymion (*Heartsease and Rue*, Boston).
    The Finding of the Lyre appeared in *Under the Willows* (Boston, 1869 [1868]).

1888. Edward Rowland Sill, The Venus of Milo (privately printed, 1883) (*Poems*, 1888).
    Hermione (1899) included *The Lost Magic*.

1888. David Atwood Wasson, Orpheus (*Poems*, Boston).

1889. Channing Moore Huntington, A day in the Homeric age (*A Bachelor's Wife*, Utica).

1890. Edna Duncan Proctor, Cleobis and Biton (*Poems*).

1890. George Edward Woodberry, Agathon (*The North Shore Watch*).

1891. Isabella T. Aitken, Orpheus and Eurydice; Pandora; Adonis; The sea-nymph (*Bohemia*, Philadelphia).

1891. Frank W. Gunsaulus, Phidias and other poems (Chicago).

1891. Denton J. Snider, Homer in Chios: An epopee (St. Louis).

[1892]. Marguerite E. Easter, Clytie; Antigone's farewell to Haemon; Selene; etc. (*Clytie*, Boston).

1892. Edward W. Evans, The shadow in stone (*Walter Savage Landor*, pp. 191–209).

1892. William Rufus Perkins, Bellerophon; Hadrian's lament over Antinoüs (*Eleusis*, Chicago).

1893 *et seq.* Madison Cawein, Numerous pieces in *Red Leaves and Roses* (1893), *Intimations of the Beautiful* (1894), *Myth and Romance* (1899), *New Poems* (1909), etc.

1893. Henry Hanby Hay, Rhaecus; Flight of Daphne; etc. (*Created Gold*, Philadelphia).

1893. Walter Malone, Narcissus; Orpheus and the sirens (*Narcissus*, Philadelphia).
    The Outcast (Cambridge, 1886) included *Song of the Dying Orpheus*.

1894. William Entriken Baily, The sacrifice of Iphigenia; Priam, king of Troy; Andromache in captivity; The daughters of Oedipus (*Dramatic Poems*, Philadelphia).

Classical Poems (Cincinnati, 1892) included *The Choice of Alcides*, etc.

1894. Hugh McCulloch, The quest of Heracles; Hermaphroditus; Antinoüs; Phaeton (*The Quest of Heracles*, Cambridge and Chicago).

Written in Florence (London, 1902) included *The Triumph of Bacchus* and *The Death of Pan*.

1894. Robert Cameron Rogers, The dancing faun; Hylas; Blind Polyphemus; Odysseus at the mast; The death of Argus (*The Wind in the Clearing*).

For the King (1899) included *Charon*.

1894. George Santayana, Lucifer (*Sonnets*, Cambridge and Chicago).

A Hermit of Carmel (1902) included *Before a Statue of Achilles*.

1895. Thomas Bailey Aldrich, Andromeda (*Unguarded Gates*).

1895. John McDowell Leavitt, Ariston (*Visions of Solyma*).

1896. Eugene Field, Pan liveth (*Songs and Other Verse*).

[1896]. James B. Kenyon, Hylas and Hercules; etc. (*An Oaten Pipe*).

1896. Edith M. Thomas, Ulysses at the court of Alcinous; Antaeus (*A Winter Swallow*).

Fair Shadow Land (1893) included *Atys*.

1897 *et seq*. Lloyd Mifflin, Innumerable pieces, mainly sonnets, in *At the Gates of Song* (Boston, 1897), *The Slopes of Helicon* (Boston, 1898), *Echoes of Greek Idyls* (1899), *Castalian Days* (1903), and other volumes.

1898. Florence Earle Coates, Psyche; Dryad song; Hylas; etc. (*Poems*).

Other short pieces appeared in volumes of 1904 and 1912.

1898. Julia P. Dabney, Tmolus; Tithonus; Orpheus sings; etc. (*Songs of Destiny*).

1898. Richard Hovey, The faun (1894) (*Along the Trail*, Boston).

1898. Charles Camp Tarelli, Persephone and other poems.

1898. Edward W. Watson, The cry of Prometheus; etc. (*Songs of Flying Hours*, Philadelphia).

1900. Annie Fields, Orpheus: a masque.

1900. William Norman Guthrie, The vision of Demeter; The coming of Dionysus; etc. (*Songs of American Destiny: A Vision of New Hellas*, Cincinnati).

1900. Sara King Wiley, The faun; Apollo and Daphne; Endymion; Clytie; etc. (*Poems Lyrical and Dramatic*).

1901. Henry Abbey, Phaëthon (Kingston, N. Y.).

Volumes of 1884–85 included *The King and the Naiad* and *Bellerophon*.

1901. Rupert Hughes, Gyges' ring: a dramatic monologue.
1901. Edwin Markham, The story of Bacchus (*Lincoln*).
       Two slight pieces appeared in *The Man with the Hoe* (1899).
1901 *et seq.* Cale Young Rice, The dead gods; The youth and the god (*Song-Surf*, Boston).
       Other short pieces appeared in volumes of 1909, 1912, 1917, 1922, 1925.
1902. Elizabeth Akers, The pipe of Pan; Phaon, the ferryman; etc. (*The Sun-set Song*, Boston).
1902. Gerda Dalliba (d. 1913), A sea myth; A prayer to Orithyia (*Fate and I*).
       Poems, Second Series (London, 1933), included *Endymion*.
1902. Maud Menefee, Ceres and Persephone: a child play (Chicago).
1902. Edwin Arlington Robinson, As a world would have it [Alcestis] (*Captain Craig*).
       The Children of the Night (1905) included *The Chorus of Old Men in "Aegeus."*
1902. Trumbull Stickney, Kalypso; Prometheus Pyrphoros (1900) (*Dramatic Verses*, Boston).
1902. Stephen Henry Thayer, Aurora's gift to Tithonus (*Songs from Edgewood*).
1903. Willa Cather, Antinous; Winter at Delphi; Lament for Marsyas (*April Twilights*, Boston).
       Reprinted in a volume of the same title, 1923.
1903. Joseph Cook, Orpheus and the sirens; The completion of Apollo (*Overtones*).
1903. Edgar Fawcett, Actaeon; Helen, old; Oedipus and the sphinx (*Voices and Visions*, London).
       Fantasy and Passion (Boston, 1878) included *La Belle Hélène* and *Medusa*.
1904. Guy Wetmore Carryl, The passing of Pan (1896); Phoebus Apollo (1900); Narcissus (1896) (*The Garden of Years*).
1904. Ethel Louise Cox, The hamadryad; Narcissus; Prometheus; Circe; Hymn to Diana; etc. (*Poems Lyrical and Dramatic*, Boston).
1904. William Vaughn Moody, The fire-bringer.
1905. Amélie Rives, Princess Troubetzkoy, Seléné.
1905. Sara King Wiley, Alcestis; Iphigeneia (*Alcestis*).
1906. Lee Wilson Dodd, To the gods of Greece; Adonis to Aphrodite; Fragment of an "Electra"; Cypselus; Circe (*A Modern Alchemist*, Boston).

1906. Charles Gibson, Orpheus and Eurydice; Hero and Leander; etc. (*The Spirit of Love*, Boston).

1906. William Ellery Leonard, Archilochus; Euris; Heraclitus, the obscure (*Sonnets and Poems*, Boston).

One may mention the poem to Virgil, *The Dawn* (1919), reprinted in *A Son of Earth* (1928).

1906. Louise Morgan Sill, Pan and Echo; etc. (*In Sun or Shade*).

1906. Alice Wilson, Actaeon's defence and other poems (Boston).

The Lutanist (Boston, 1914) included *Hero to Leander*.

1907. John Erskine, Actaeon; Iphidamus; etc. (*Actaeon*).

1907. Arthur Davison Ficke, Demeter; Dionysus; Cytherea; The elder gods; Foam around Delos; etc. (*From the Isles*, Norwich, England).

1907. Percy MacKaye, Sappho and Phaon: a tragedy.

1907. Louis Alexander Robertson, Orpheus and Eurydice; Phryne; Helen; etc. (*Through Painted Panes*, San Francisco).

The title poem of *The Dead Calypso* (1901) is only faintly classical.

1908. Grace Denio Litchfield, Narcissus; Semele to Jupiter (*Narcissus*).

1908. George Cabot Lodge, Herakles.

The Great Adventure (1905) included the sonnets *Odysseus* and *Kalypso*. *Poems (1899–1902)* included *The Greek Galley* and *Tannhauser to Venus*.

1908. Frank Justus Miller, Two dramatizations from Vergil: I. Dido — the Phoenician queen II. The fall of Troy. Arranged and translated into English verse (University of Chicago Press).

Dido first appeared in 1900.

1908. Martin Schütze, Hero and Leander: a tragedy.

1908. Charles Wharton Stork, Ganymede; The wanderings of Psyche; Philemon and Baucis; etc. (*Day Dreams of Greece*, Philadelphia).

The Queen of Orplede (Philadelphia, 1910) included *Actaeon*.

1908. Howard V. Sutherland, Prokris and Kephalos; Melas and Anaxe; Acis and Galataea; Oeme and Oeonus (*Idylls of Greece*, Boston).

Idylls of Greece, Second Series (1910), contained four more tales, *Phyllis and Demophoon, Pan and Pitys*, etc.

1908. Edward Lucas White, Rhampsinitos; The titan; etc. (*Narrative Lyrics*).

1909. Richard Edwin Day, Ino; The voyage of Bacchus; The conquest of Thebes; The fall of Dionysus (*New Poems*).

1909. Carlota Montenegro, Alcestis: a drama (Boston).

1909. Ezra Pound, An idyl for Glaucus (*Personae*, London).

Canzoni (1911) included *Canzon: The yearly slain. Pan is Dead* appeared in *Ripostes* (1912).

1909. Edith M. Thomas, The cloak [Horatius]; etc. (*The Guest at the Gate*, Boston).

1909. Arthur Upson (d. 1908), The silver flute (A chronicle of ancient Greece); Capaneus (*Collected Poems*, Minneapolis, 1909, II, 153-65, 220).

1909. Edith Wharton, Artemis to Actaeon; The Eumenides; Orpheus (*Artemis to Actaeon*).

1910. Anna Hempstead Branch, Selene (*Rose of the Wind*).
    A Song from Ganymede appeared in *Sonnets from a Lock Box* (1929).

1910. Theodosia Garrison, The faun; Pan (*The Earth Cry*).
    The Joy o' Life (1909) included *A Dream of Thessaly*.

1911. Benjamin R. C. Low, Penelope; Galatea; etc. (*The Sailor Who Sailed*).
    Broken Music (1920) included *Pygmalion to Galatea*.

1911. Sara Teasdale, Helen of Troy; Sappho; Erinna; Anadyomene; To Erinna; To Cleïs (*Helen of Troy*).

1911. Blanche Shoemaker Wagstaff, Alcestis, a poetic drama.
    Atys and *Narcissus* were the title poems of volumes of 1909 and 1918 respectively.

1912. Zoë Akins, Sappho to a swallow on the ground; Calypso; Circe (*Interpretations*).

1912. Percy Stickney Grant, The return of Odysseus: a poetic drama in four acts.
    The brief *Hero at Sestos* appeared in *A Fifth Avenue Parade* (1922).

1912. George Campbell Ogden, The trap for Venus; Pirithous transfixed (*Poems*, ed. C. H. Fisk, privately printed, Cincinnati).

1912. Robert Haven Schauffler, Marsyas (*Scum o' the Earth*).

1912-14? (pub. 1916). Alan Seeger, Tithonus; Antinous (*Poems*).

1913. William Rose Benét, The lost gods abiding; Song of the satyrs to Ariadne; The winning of Pomona; The halcyon birds; The centaur's farewell; etc. (*Merchants from Cathay*).

1913. Max Eastman, Child of the Amazons and other poems.

1913. John Gould Fletcher, Dionysus and Apollo (*Fire and Wine*, London); The Bacchanal; The flocks of Pan (*The Book of Nature 1910-1912*, London).

1913. John Myers O'Hara, The hushed gods; etc. (*Pagan Poems*, Portland, Maine).
    Other short pieces appeared in *Threnodies* (Portland, 1918).

1914. Walter C. Arensberg, Chryseis; Atalanta (*Poems*).
   Idols (1916) included *The Night of Ariadne*.
1914. Francis Wendell Butler-Thwing, The death of Penelope (*First-Fruits*, privately printed).
1914. John Jay Chapman, Homeric scenes: Hector's farewell and the wrath of Achilles.
   Cupid and Psyche appeared in 1916.
1914. Louis V. Ledoux, Persephone: a masque (*The Shadow of Aetna*).
1914. George Edward Woodberry, Proserpine; Demeter; etc. (*The Flight*).
1915. Grace Hazard Conkling, Proserpine and the sea-nymphs; To Hermes (*Afternoons of April*).
1915. Adelaide Crapsey (d. 1914), Birth-moment; Cry of the nymph to Eros (*Verse*, Rochester, New York).
1915. Robert Frost, Pan with us (*A Boy's Will*).
1915. William Alexander Percy, Sappho in Leukas and other poems (Yale University Press).
1915. Sara Teasdale, Sappho (*Rivers to the Sea*).
1916. H. D. (Hilda Doolittle), Sea gods; Acon; Sea iris; Hermes of the ways (*Sea Garden*).
1916. Hermann Hagedorn, The great maze [Clytemnestra] (*The Great Maze and The Heart of Youth*).
1916. Louis V. Ledoux, The story of Eleusis: a lyrical drama [Demeter].
1916. Percy MacKaye, Dionysus; The chase [Diana] (Three dance motives imagined for dances of Isadora Duncan, *Poems and Plays*).
1916. Edgar Lee Masters, The vision; Helen of Troy (*Songs and Satires*); Marsyas; Apollo at Pherae; The apology of Demetrius (*The Great Valley*).
1916. Antoinette De Coursey Patterson, The son of Merope and other poems (Philadelphia).
1917. Alice Brown, Pan; Love denied [Endymion]; The shepherds [Admetus] (*The Road to Castaly*; first edition, 1896).
1917. John Erskine, The sons of Metaneira (*The Shadowed Hour*).
   Collected Poems (1922) included *Penthesileia*; *Achilles and the Maiden*; *Paris, Helen's Lover*.
1917. Robert Silliman Hillyer, Antinous (*Sonnets and Other Lyrics*, Harvard University Press).
   Some brief pieces appeared in *The Five Books of Youth* (1920) and *The Seventh Hill* (1928).

1917. Grace Denio Litchfield, The song of the sirens.
  Collected Poems (1922) included *Icarus* and *Semele* (1910).
1919. William Frederick Allen, Hyacinthus; The faun (*Monographs*, Boston).
1919. Amelia Josephine Burr, Calypso; On Latmos (*Hearts Awake*).
  Several short pieces appeared in *The Roadside Fire* (1912) and *Life and Living* (1916).
1919. Harry Kemp, Cresseid; Helen in Hades; To Atthis; The mirrored Venus (*The Passing God*).
  The Sea and the Dunes (1926) included a number of short pieces on Helen.
1919. Ezra Pound, Three cantos; Homage to Sextus Propertius (1917) (*Quia Pauper Amavi*, London).
  Some brief pieces appeared in *Lustra* (1916).
1919. Clement Wood, Aphrodite Enoikia (*The Earth Turns South*).
1920. Stephen Vincent Benét, The first vision of Helen; The last vision of Helen (*Heavens and Earth*).
  Young Adventure (Yale University Press, 1918) included *Winged Man*.
1920. Witter Bynner, A canticle of Pan; A canticle of Bacchus; The singing faun; etc. (*A Canticle of Pan*).
  Grenstone Poems (1917) included several brief pieces.
1920. J. L. McLane, Hyacinthus; Demeter's lament; etc. (*Spindrift*, Boston).
1921. Hervey Allen, Hylas; Bacchus is gone (*Wampum and Old Gold*, Yale University Press).
1921. H. D. (Hilda Doolittle), Hymen; Demeter; Thetis; Circe; Leda; The islands; Sea heroes; Phaedra; etc. (*Hymen*).
1921. Elizabeth Huntington, Endymion; Psyche in Cupid's palace; Proserpine; etc. (*The Playground of the Gods*, Boston).
1921. Edgar Lee Masters, Ulysses; Invocation to the gods; Pentheus in these States (*The Open Sea*).
  Starved Rock (1919) included *Pallas Athene*.
1921. Edna St. Vincent Millay, Prayer to Persephone (*Second April*)
  The brief *Daphne* appeared in *A Few Figs from Thistles* (1922)
1921. Brookes More, Orpheus and Eurydice (*The Beggar's Vision*, Boston).
1921. George Sterling, The death of Circe (*Sails and Mirage*, San Francisco).
  Several other brief pieces appeared in volumes of 1904, 1911, and 1914.

1922. John Peale Bishop and Edmund Wilson, The death of the last centaur (*The Undertaker's Garland*).

1922. Thomas Stearns Eliot, The waste land.

1922. Raymond Holden, Calypso (*Granite and Alabaster*).

1923. Louise Bogan, Medusa (*Body of this Death*).
    Dark Summer (1929) included *Cassandra*.

1923. James Oppenheim, Nausicaa (*Golden Bird*).

1924. Richard Edwin Day, Songs of Silenus; The Furies to Alcmaeon; The gift of Hercules (*Dante*, Yale University Press).

1924. H. D. (Hilda Doolittle), Holy satyr; Lais; Heliodora; Helen; Nossis; Oread; Thetis; At Ithaca; After Troy; Cassandra; Toward the Piraeus; At Eleusis; Telesila; Orion dead; Charioteer; The look-out; Odyssey; Hyacinth; etc. (*Heliodora*).
    Some of these pieces, with new ones, were included in the series called *The God* (*Collected Poems*, 1925).

1924. Dorothy Dow, Echo; To Atalanta; Eternal Diana (*Black Babylon*).

1924. Harry Kemp, Calypso (*Boccaccio's Untold Tale, and Other One-Act Plays*).

1924. Charlton Miner Lewis, Pygmalion (*Poems*, Yale University Press).

1924. John U. Nicolson, The sainted courtezan [Phryne] (Chicago); A lady lived in Lesbos; Sapphics (*King of the Black Isles*, Chicago).

1924. John Crowe Ransom, Prometheus in straits; Philomela (*Chills and Fever*).

1924. Margaret Sherwood, Psyche (*The Upper Slopes*).

1924. Arthur Weightman Spencer, Prometheus unbound and other experiments in verse (Brookline, Mass.).

1925. Hervey Allen, The fire thief (*Earth Moods*).

1925. John Gould Fletcher, The death of Prometheus [prose]; On a moral triumph [Helen and Menelaus; prose]; Towards Olympus (*Parables*, London).

1925. Lincoln Hulley, Fables and myths from the sibyl's book (De Land, Fla.).

1925. Robinson Jeffers, The tower beyond tragedy (*Roan Stallion, Tamar, and Other Poems*).
    The Women on Cythaeron appeared in *Poems* (San Francisco, 1928), and, as *The Humanist's Tragedy*, in *Dear Judas* (1929).

1925. Archibald MacLeish, The pot of earth.
    Tower of Ivory (Yale University Press, 1917) included *Our Lady of Troy* [Faust story] and *Jason*.

1925. Roselle M. Montgomery, Ulysses returns, and other poems. [Not seen.]

1925. Edwin Arlington Robinson, Dionysus in doubt; Demos and Dionysus (*Dionysus in Doubt*).

1926. Joseph Auslander, Ulysses in autumn; Mother of Helen; Ixion (*Cyclops' Eye*).
      Letters to Women (1929) includes a *Letter to Sappho*.

1926. Samuel Loveman, The hermaphrodite (Athol, Mass.).
      Poems (Cleveland, 1911) included odes to Dionysus and Ceres, and *Oedipus at Colonus*.

1926. Clarence W. Mendell, Prometheus unbound (*Prometheus*, Yale University Press).

1926–27. Brookes More, Hero and Leander (Boston, 1926); Myrtella: a romance of ancient Greece (Boston, 1927).

1926. Genevieve Taggard, Galatea again (*Words for the Chisel*).

1926. Hugh Western, The return of Dionysios; Actaeon (*Serenade*, Chicago).

1926. Merle St. Croix Wright, The apparition of Pan; Venus Anadyomene; etc. (*Ignis Ardens*).

1926. Agnes Yarnall, Pandora, and other poems (Philadelphia). [Not seen.]

1927. Charlotte F. Babcock, Nausicaa; etc. (*Echoes*, Boston).

1927. Robert P. Tristram Coffin, Lamps once were being lit in Troy; The house of Jason (*Dew and Bronze*).

1927. H. D. (Hilda Doolittle), Hippolytus temporizes: a play in three acts.

1927. George O'Neil, Young Icarus (*The White Rooster*).

1927. H. Phelps Putnam, Ballad of a strange thing [Pan and Syrinx] (*Trinc*).

1928. Wallace Gould, Aphrodite; Endymion; Drunken Heracles (*Aphrodite*).

1928. Rolfe Humphries, Europa; For good Greeks; Aeolus (*Europa*).

1928. Mark Van Doren, Tiresias; The dinner (*Now the Sky*).

1929. Malcolm Cowley, Leander (*Blue Juniata*).

1929. William Griffith, Greek gestures.

1929. Gertrude Huntington McGiffert, A Greek cycle (*Cast in Bronze*, Portland, Maine).

1929. Roselle M. Montgomery, Marpessa; Atalanta; Daedalus; etc. (*Many Devices*).

1929. Merrill Moore, Pandora and the moon (*The Noise That Time Makes*).

1929. Helene Mullins, I will love Apollo; Psyche again (*Earthbound*). A couple of other short pieces appeared in *Balm in Gilead* (1930).

1929. L. B. Pemberton, Prometheus unbound; etc. (*The Dance at the Spring*, Boston).

1930. Conrad Aiken, Venus Anadyomene (*John Deth*).

1930. Henry Bertram Lister, Ancient fables interpreted; etc. (*A Hindoo's Tale: The Vestal's Choice: Hamadryad of the Redwood Tree*, San Francisco).

1930. Charles Norman, Telemachus (*The Bright World*).

1930. William Alexander Percy, Medusa; A legend of Lacedaemon [Castor and Pollux]; etc. (*Selected Poems*, Yale University Press).
    Enzio's Kingdom (1924) included *Calypso to Ulysses* and *Siren Song*.

1930. Ezra Pound, A draft of XXX cantos (Paris, 1930; New York, 1933).
    Eleven New Cantos XXXI–XLI appeared in 1934.

1930. Chard Powers Smith, The quest of Pan: beginning a trilogy of evolution.

1931. Babette Deutsch, Epistle to Prometheus. [Not seen.]
    Some brief pieces appeared in *Banners* (1919).

1931. George Dillon, Weep, Aphrodite, for Adonis dead (*The Flowering Stone*).

1931. H. D. (Hilda Doolittle), Myrtle bough; Choros sequence from *Morpheus*; etc. (*Red Roses for Bronze*).

1931. Frederick Faust, Dionysus in Hades (Oxford).

1931. Leonora Speyer, The maid Medusa; Again, Medusa (*Naked Heel*).

1931. Eda Lou Walton, Leda, the lost (*Jane Matthew*).

1931. Yvor Winters, Satyric complaint; Apollo and Daphne (*The Proof*).
    See also *Theseus: A Trilogy*, in *Hound and Horn*, VI (1932–33), 635–39.

1932. Edwin Markham, A prayer at the altar of Hermes; Hellas again; Divine Aphrodite; Pan encountered (*New Poems*).

1933. William Rose Benét, Ghost Actaeon; Fastidious Artemis; Young Apollo; Sung to Persephone (*Starry Harness*).
    Golden Fleece (1935) included *Riddle for Polyphemus*.

1933. Horace Gregory, New York, Cassandra (*No Retreat*).

1933. Robinson Jeffers, At the fall of an age [Helen and Polyxo] (*Give Your Heart to the Hawks*).

1933. Archibald MacLeish, Selene afterwards; 1933 [Odysseus and Elpenor] (*Poems, 1924–1933*).

    Selene Afterwards had appeared in *Streets in the Moon* (1926).

1933. Edgar Lee Masters, Prometheus; Song for the dead gods (*The Serpent in the Wilderness*).

    Invisible Landscapes (1935) included *Persephone*.

1933. Martin Wright Sampson, Pan; Odysseus; Voices of the forest (*Voices of the Forest*, Ithaca).

1934. Edna St. Vincent Millay, Sappho crosses the dark river into Hades (*Wine from these Grapes*).

    Fatal Interview (1931) included the sonnet *Oh, sleep forever in the Latmian cave.*

1934. Allen E. Woodall, The curse of Dido (Utica, New York).

    A sequel to *Aeneas* (privately printed, 1930).

1935. Leonard Bacon, The voyage of Autoleon: a fantastic epic.

    See also the pieces numbered xv, xx, xxi, in *Animula Vagula* (1926).

1935. Robinson Jeffers, At the birth of an age; Solstice (*Solstice*).

1936. Allen Tate, Aeneas at Washington (*The Mediterranean*).

    First printed in *Hound and Horn*, VI (1932–33), 445–46.

BIBLIOGRAPHY

BIBLIOGRAPHY

While I have owed at least as much to general studies as to special articles and monographs, it is obviously impossible to give a bibliography of the criticism of English poetry from 1680 to the present. Works of general criticism, especially the more or less standard ones, have generally been omitted, though this rule has been relaxed in the case of some poets whose mythological poems constitute a large part of their output. It has likewise been impossible to include many general and particular discussions of classical influence, since a number of these have little to do with the subject of this book. Reviews of recent volumes of poetry have not ordinarily been cited, since they are listed in the annual bibliographies of the Modern Humanities Research Association (1921 *et seq.*). The resulting list is inevitably arbitrary, and the learned reader is asked, before he pounces on omissions, to remember the difficulties of selection.

Authorities cited in more than one chapter, and some miscellaneous items, are mostly assembled in the first general section. This section includes also a very few books from the voluminous literature of German and French Hellenism.

In the bibliography, as in the footnotes, the place of publication of books is London, unless another place is named. Abbreviations used here and in footnotes are these:

A.J.P., American Journal of Philology; ELH, English Literary History; J.E.G.P., Journal of English and Germanic Philology; M.L.N., Modern Language Notes; M.L.R., Modern Language Review; M.P., Modern Philology;

P.M.L.A., *Publications of the Modern Language Association of America; P.Q., Philological Quarterly; R.E.S., Review of English Studies; S.P., Studies in Philology; T.L.S., London Times Literary Supplement.*

GENERAL

Aeschylus, The Prometheus Bound, Edited with Introduction, Commentary and Translation by George Thomson. Cambridge University Press, 1932.

Anon., "The Last Voyage of Ulysses" [Bridges, Phillips, Tennyson, Dante]. *Edinburgh Review*, CXCVI (1902), 84–96.

Herbert Antcliffe, "Prometheus in Literature." *Nineteenth Century*, XCVI (1924), 815–24.

Apollodorus: The Library, with an English Translation by Sir James George Frazer (Loeb Classical Library). 1921.

John Bailey, "Prometheus in Poetry." *The Continuity of Letters* (Clarendon Press, 1923), pp. 103–38.

Edward Baldwin (i.e., William Godwin), *The Pantheon: or, Ancient History of the Gods of Greece and Rome.* 1806.

Joseph Warren Beach, *The Concept of Nature in Nineteenth-Century English Poetry.* New York, 1936.

Karl Borinski, *Die Antike in Poetik und Kunsttheorie von Ausgang des klassischen Altertums bis auf Goethe und Wilhelm von Humboldt.* Leipzig, 1914–24.

A. C. Bradley, "Old Mythology in Modern Poetry." *Macmillan's Magazine*, XLIV (1881), 28–47.

Wilmon Brewer, *Ovid's Metamorphoses in European Culture* (Books i–v). Boston, 1933.

Friedrich Brie, *Ästhetische Weltanschauung in der Literatur des XIX. Jahrhunderts.* Freiburg, 1921.

Anna R. Brown, "The Lotus Symbolism in Homer, Theocritus, Moschus, Tennyson, and Browning." *Poet Lore*, II (1890), 625–34.

Huntington Brown, *The Classical Tradition in English Literature: A Bibliography. Harvard Studies and Notes in Philology and Literature*, XVIII (1935), 7–46.

E. E. Burriss, "The Classical Culture of Charles Lamb." *Classical Weekly*, XVIII (1924–25), 1–3; "The Classical Culture of Robert Louis Stevenson." *Classical Journal*, XX (1924–25), 271–79.

Douglas Bush, "English Translations of Homer." *P.M.L.A.*, XLI (1926), 335–41.

E. M. Butler, *The Tyranny of Greece over Germany*. Cambridge University Press, 1935.

René Canat, *La renaissance de la Grèce antique (1820–1850)*. Paris, 1911.

William Chislett, "Stevenson and the Classics." *J.E.G.P.*, XV (1916), 267–81.

William Chislett, *The Classical Influence in English Literature in the Nineteenth Century*. Boston, 1918.

Helen A. Clarke, "A Sketch of the Promethean Myth in Poetry." *Poet Lore*, IV (1892), 135–44.

Helen A. Clarke, *Ancient Myths in Modern Poets*. New York, 1910.

J. Churton Collins, *Greek Influence on English Poetry*. 1910.

Sir Sidney Colvin, "Penthesilea." *Cornhill Magazine*, XLIV (1881), 537–54.

W. L. Courtney, "Mr. Thomas Hardy and Aeschylus." *Fortnightly Review*, CVII (1917), 464–77, 629–40; *Old Saws and Modern Instances*. 1918.

Fernand Desonay, *Le rêve hellénique chez les poètes parnassiens*. Paris, 1928.

Jean Ducros, *Le retour de la poésie française à l'antiquité grecque au milieu du XIXᵉ siècle*. Paris, 1918.

Dwight L. Durling, *Georgic Tradition in English Poetry*. Columbia University Press, 1935.

B. Ifor Evans, *English Poetry in the Later Nineteenth Century*. 1933.

Oliver Elton, *A Survey of English Literature 1730–1780* (1928); *A Survey of English Literature 1780–1880* (New York, 1920).

Robert Faesi, *Spittelers Weg und Werk*. Frauenfeld and Leipzig, 1933.

Georg Finsler, *Homer in der Neuzeit von Dante bis Goethe*. Leipzig and Berlin, 1912.

Finley M. K. Foster, *English Translations from the Greek*. Columbia University Press, 1918.

Charles M. Gayley, *The Classic Myths in English Literature and in Art*. Boston and New York, 1911.

Stuart Gilbert, *James Joyce's Ulysses: A Study*. New York, 1931.

Basil L. Gildersleeve, "The Legend of Venus." *Essays and Studies* (Baltimore, 1890), pp. 161–205.

H. W. Gilmer, "The Classical Element in the Poems of Rudyard Kipling." *Classical Weekly*, XIV (1920–21), 178–81. Cf. *ibid.*, XV, 32.

Hedwig L. Glücksmann, *Die Gegenüberstellung von Antike-Christentum in der englischen Literatur des 19. Jahrhunderts*. Hannover, 1932.

George Gordon, "Virgil in English Poetry." *Proceedings of the British Academy*, XVII (1931), 39–53.

Arturo Graf, *Prometeo nella Poesia*. Torino, 1920.

Harley Granville-Barker, "Exit Planché—Enter Gilbert." *London Mercury*, XXV (1931–32), 457–66, 558–73; *The Eighteen-Sixties*, ed. John Drinkwater, Cambridge University Press, 1932.

H. J. C. Grierson, *The Background of English Literature*. 1925.

Otto Gruppe, *Geschichte der klassischen Mythologie und Religionsgeschichte während des Mittelalters im Abendland und während der Neuzeit*. Leipzig, 1921.

Edward C. Guild, *A List of Poems Illustrating Greek Mythology in the English Poetry of the Nineteenth Century*. Bowdoin College Library Bulletin, No. 1 (1891), pp. 15–31.

Johanna F. C. Gutteling, *Hellenic Influence on the English Poetry of the Nineteenth Century*. Amsterdam [1922].

Elizabeth H. Haight, "On Certain Uses of Apuleius' Story of Cupid and Psyche in English Literature." *Poet Lore*, XXVI (1915), 744–62; *Apuleius and His Influence*. New York, 1927.

Raymond D. Havens, *The Influence of Milton on English Poetry*. Harvard University Press, 1922.

Karl Heinemann, *Die tragischen Gestalten der Griechen in der Weltliteratur*. Leipzig, 1920.

Adolf Hoffmann, *Das Psyche-Märchen des Apuleius in der englischen Literatur*. Strassburg, 1908.

George Howe and G. A. Harrer, *A Handbook of Classical Mythology*. New York, 1929.

Walter W. Hyde, "The Place of Winckelmann in the History of Classical Scholarship." *Classical Weekly*, XII (1918–19), 75–79.

Franz Jakob, *Die Fabel von Atreus und Thyestes in den wichtigsten Tragödien der englischen, französischen und italienischen Literatur. Münchener Beiträge*, XXXVII (1907).

Franklin P. Johnson, "Neo-Platonic Hymns by Thomas Taylor." *P.Q.*, VIII (1929), 145–56.

John Kelman, "The Gods of Greece." *Among Famous Books* (1912), pp. 1–37.

Robert T. Kerlin, *Theocritus in English Literature*. Lynchburg, Virginia, 1910.

A. H. J. Knight, "Some Reflections on Spitteler's 'Prometheus und Epimetheus.'" *M.L.R.*, XXVII (1932), 430–47.

A. H. J. Knight, *Some Aspects of the Life and Work of Nietzsche, particularly of his connection with Greek Literature and Thought*. Cambridge University Press, 1933.

Casper J. Kraemer, "The Influence of the Classics on English Literature." *Classical Journal*, XXII (1926–27), 485–97.

Helen H. Law, "The Name Galatea in the Pygmalion Myth." *Classical Journal*, XXVII (1931–32), 337–42.

Helen H. Law, *Bibliography of Greek Myth in English Poetry*. Service Bureau for Classical Teachers, Bulletin XXVII (New York, 1932).

J. Lempriere, *A Classical Dictionary*. *The Sixth Edition, Corrected*. 1806; *A New Edition, Revised and Considerably Enlarged, by Rev. T. Smith*. 1847.

Harry Levin, *The Broken Column: A Study in Romantic Hellenism*. Harvard University Press, 1931.

Marie L. Lilly, *The Georgic: A Contribution to the Study of the Vergilian Type of Didactic Poetry*. Baltimore, 1917.

H. C. Lipscomb, "Stevenson and the Classics." *Classical Journal*, XX (1924–25), 564–66.

J. W. Mackail, *Studies of English Poets*. 1926.

Dougald MacMillan, "Planché's Early Classical Burlesques." *S.P.*, XXV (1928), 340–45. Cf. *P.Q.*, VIII (1929), 255–63.

B. Magnino, "Oreste nella poesia tragica." *Atene e Roma*, N. S., IX (1928), 146–54.

Lily E. Marshall, "Greek Myths in Modern English Poetry: Introduction." *Studi di Filologia Moderna*, IV (1911), 255–80; "Greek Myths in Modern English Poetry: Orpheus and Eurydice." *Ibid.*, V (1912), 203–32; VI (1913), 1–32.

Marshall Montgomery, *Friedrich Hölderlin and the German Neo-Hellenic Movement*. Oxford University Press, 1923.

Horace M. Moule, "Achilles and Lancelot." *Macmillan's Magazine*, XXIV (1871), 344–56.

James F. Muirhead, "Carl Spitteler and the New Epic." *Essays by Divers Hands: Being the Transactions of the Royal Society of Literature*, N. S., X (1931), 35–57.

Gilbert Murray, "What English Poetry May Still Learn from Greek." *Essays and Studies by Members of the English Association*, III (1912), 7–31.

Gilbert Murray, *The Classical Tradition in Poetry*. Harvard University Press, 1927.

W. P. Mustard, "Virgil's Georgics and the British Poets." *A.J.P.*, XXIX (1908), 1–32; "Later Echoes of the Greek Bucolic Poets." *Ibid.*, XXX (1909), 245–83.

Elizabeth Nitchie, *Vergil and the English Poets*. Columbia University Press, 1919; "Vergil and Romanticism." *Methodist Review*, CXIII

(1930), 859–67; "Horace and Thackeray." *Classical Journal*, XIII (1917–18), 393–410.

Fred Otto Nolte, *German Literature and the Classics: A Bibliographical Guide*. Harvard Studies and Notes in Philology and Literature, XVIII (1935), 125–63.

Eileen O'Rourke, *The Use of Mythological Subjects in Modern Poetry*. University of London Press, 1912.

Eugene Oswald, *The Legend of Fair Helen as told by Homer, Goethe, and Others*. 1905.

A. Peretti, "Nausicaa nella poesia." *Atene e Roma*, N. S., IX (1928), 193–217.

Henri Peyre, *Bibliographie critique de l'hellénisme en France de 1843 à 1870*. Yale University Press, 1932.

Frederick E. Pierce, "The Hellenic Current in English Nineteenth Century Poetry." *J.E.G.P.*, XVI (1917), 103–35.

Courtenay Pollock, "Lord Elgin and the Marbles." *Essays by Divers Hands: Being the Transactions of the Royal Society of Literature*, N. S., XI (1932), 41–67.

Mario Praz, *The Romantic Agony. Translated from the Italian by Angus Davidson*. Oxford University Press, 1933.

Frederick C. Prescott, *Poetry and Myth*. New York, 1927.

John G. Robertson, *The Gods of Greece in German Poetry*. Clarendon Press, 1924; *Essays and Addresses on Literature* (1935), pp. 118–44.

Sir Rennell Rodd (ed.), *The Englishman in Greece: Being a Collection of the Verse of many English Poets*. Clarendon Press, 1910.

H. J. Rose, *A Handbook of Greek Mythology*. 1928; *Modern Methods in Classical Mythology*. University Press, St. Andrews, 1930.

John Ruskin, *The Queen of the Air*. 1869.

Ovids Metamorphosis Englished, Mythologiz'd, And Represented in Figures. . . . By G[eorge] S[andys]. 1640.

Sir John E. Sandys, *A History of Classical Scholarship*. Cambridge University Press, 1903–08.

G. M. Sargeaunt, "The Eternal Wanderer" [Ulysses]; "Faust and Helen of Troy"; "Classical Myths in the National Gallery"; "Winckelmann in Rome." *Classical Studies*. 1929.

Fritz Saxl (ed.), *England und die Antike. Vorträge der Bibliothek Warburg (1930–31)*. Leipzig and Berlin, 1932.

J. T. Sheppard, *Aeschylus and Sophocles: Their Work and Influence*. New York, 1927.

Thomas K. Sidey, "Echoes of the Classics in Kipling." *M.L.N.*, XXIV (1909), 217–18.

F. Seymour Smith, *The Classics in Translation*. 1930.

Kirby F. Smith, "The Literary Tradition of Gyges and Candaules." *A.J.P.*, XLI (1920), 1–37. Cf. *ibid.*, XXIII (1902), 261–82, 361–87.

Herbert Weir Smyth, *Aeschylean Tragedy*. University of California Press, 1924.

Joseph Spence, *Polymetis: or, An Enquiry concerning the Agreement Between the Works of the Roman Poets, And the Remains of the Antient Artists. The Second Edition.* . . . 1755.

Eduard Stemplinger, "Die Befruchtung der Weltliteratur durch die Antike." *Germanisch-Romanische Monatsschrift*, II (1910), 529–42.

Fritz Strich, *Die Mythologie in der deutschen Literatur von Klopstock bis Wagner.* Halle, 1910.

Mary R. Thayer, *The Influence of Horace on the Chief English Poets of the Nineteenth Century.* Yale University Press, 1916.

Francis Thompson, "Paganism Old and New." *Works of Francis Thompson*, ed. W. Meynell (1913), III, 38–51.

J. A. K. Thomson, *The Religious Background of the Prometheus Vinctus. Harvard Studies in Classical Philology*, XXXI (1920), 1–37.

O. J. Todd, "The Character of Zeus in Aeschylus' *Prometheus Bound.*" *Classical Quarterly*, XIX (1925), 61–67.

Andrew Tooke, *The Pantheon, Representing the Fabulous Histories of the Heathen Gods, and Most Illustrious Heroes.* . . . 1781.

Humphry Trevelyan, *The Popular Background to Goethe's Hellenism.* 1934.

Willem Van Doorn, *Of the Tribe of Homer: Being an Enquiry into the Theory and Practice of English Narrative Verse Since 1833.* Amsterdam, 1932.

L. Vincenti, "Prometeo." *Leonardo*, III (1932), 97–101.

Sherard Vines, *The Course of English Classicism from the Tudor to the Victorian Age.* 1930.

Oskar Walzel, *Das Prometheussymbol von Shaftesbury zu Goethe.* Munich, 1932.

Bibliothek Warburg, *Kulturwissenschaftliche Bibliographie zum Nachleben der Antike*, ed. Hans Meier, Richard Newald, Edgar Wind, Vol. I (1931). Leipzig and Berlin, 1934.

Sir Herbert Warren, *Essays of Poets and Poetry Ancient and Modern.* 1909.

Carl J. Weber, "Thomas Hardy's 'Aeschylean phrase.'" *Classical Journal*, XXIX (1933–34), 533–35.

Friedrich Wild, *Die Batrachomyomachia in England. Wiener Beiträge*, XLVIII (1918).

Edmund Wilson, "James Joyce." *New Republic*, LXI (1929), 84–93; *Axel's Castle.* New York, 1931.

Julius Wirl, *Orpheus in der englischen Literatur. Wiener Beiträge*, XL (1913).

George E. Woodberry, "The Titan Myth." *The Torch* (New York, 1905), pp. 57–109.

CHAPTER I

THE EIGHTEENTH CENTURY

Flora R. Amos, *Early Theories of Translation*. Columbia University Press, 1920.

John Bell, *Bell's New Pantheon; or, Historical Dictionary of the Gods, Demi-Gods, Heroes, &c.* 1790.

Thomas Blackwell, *An Enquiry into the Life and Writings of Homer. The Second Edition.* 1736; *Letters Concerning Mythology.* 1748.

Richmond P. Bond, *English Burlesque Poetry 1700–1750.* Harvard University Press, 1932.

Samuel Boyse, *A New Pantheon: or, Fabulous History of the Heathen Gods, Heroes, Goddesses, &c. Explain'd in a Manner intirely New.* 1753.

Marion K. Bragg, *The Formal Eclogue in Eighteenth-Century England. University of Maine Studies,* Second Series, No. 6, 1926.

Friedrich Brie, *Englische Rokoko-Epik (1710–1730).* Munich, 1927.

Jacob Bryant, *A New System, or, An Analysis of Ancient Mythology: Wherein an Attempt is made to divest Tradition of Fable; and to reduce the Truth to its Original Purity.* Second edition, 1775.

Douglas Bush, "Musaeus in English Verse." *M.L.N.*, XLIII (1928), 101–04.

A. F. B. Clark, *Boileau and the French Classical Critics in England.* Paris, 1925.

Hardin Craig, "Dryden's Lucian." *Classical Philology*, XVI (1921), 141–63.

C. V. Deane, "Virgil and his Translators: Dryden and Warton"; "'Pictorial' Description and Landscape Art." *Aspects of Eighteenth Century Nature Poetry.* Oxford, 1935.

John W. Draper, "The Theory of Translation in the Eighteenth Century." *Neophilologus*, VI (1921), 241–54.

D. L. Drew, "Gray's Elegy and the Classics." *Classical Weekly*, XIX (1925–26), 109–11. Cf. *Anglia Beiblatt*, XLII (1931), 31–32; *Notes and Queries*, CLXV (1933), 370.

Harold W. Gammans, "Shenstone's Appreciation of Vergil." *Classical Weekly*, XXII (1928–29), 90–91.

Sir Samuel Garth *et al.*, *Ovid's Metamorphoses in Fifteen Books. Translated by the most Eminent Hands.* 1717.

Caroline Goad, *Horace in the English Literature of the Eighteenth Century.* Yale University Press, 1918.

Richard F. Jones, "Eclogue Types in English Poetry of the Eighteenth Century." *J.E.G.P.*, XXIV (1925), 33–60.

William King, *An Historical Account of the Heathen Gods and Heroes; Necessary for the Understanding of the Ancient Poets. . . . The Fourth Edition. . . .* 1727.

George Kitchin, *A Survey of Burlesque and Parody in English.* Edinburgh and London, 1931.

Levi R. Lind, "Lucian and Fielding." *Classical Weekly*, XXIX (1935–36), 84–86.

Arthur O. Lovejoy, "On the Discrimination of Romanticisms." *P.M.L.A.*, XXXIX (1924), 229–53; "Optimism and Romanticism." *Ibid.*, XLII (1927), 921–45; "The First Gothic Revival and the Return to Nature." *M.L.N.*, XLVII (1932), 419–46; "The Parallel of Deism and Classicism." *M.P.*, XXIX (1931–32), 281–99.

Charles Macpherson, *Über die Vergil-Übersetzung des John Dryden.* Berlin, 1910.

Grace H. Macurdy, "The Classical Element in Gray's Poetry." *Classical Weekly*, IV (1910–11), 58–62.

M. J. Minckwitz, "Pope als Übersetzer der Ilias." *Anglia*, XXXVI (1912), 221–82; XXXVIII (1914), 227–49; XXXIX (1915–16), 121–74.

C. A. Moore, "The Return to Nature in English Poetry of the Eighteenth Century." *S.P.*, XIV (1917), 243–91.

Federico Olivero, "Virgil in XVII and XVIII Century English Literature." *Poetry Review*, XXI (1930), 171–92.

The Travels of Cyrus. In Two Volumes. To which is annex'd, A Discourse upon the Theology and Mythology Of the Ancients. By the Chevalier Ramsay. . . . The Third Edition. . . . 1728.

Walter Richter, *Der Hiatus im englischen Klassizismus.* Schramberg (Württ.), 1934.

Oskar Seeger, *Die Auseinandersetzung zwischen Antike und Moderne in England bis zum Tode Dr. Samuel Johnsons.* Leipzig, 1927.

La Rue Van Hook, "New Light on the Classical Scholarship of Thomas Gray." *A.J.P.*, LVII (1936), 1–9.

Austin Warren, *Alexander Pope as Critic and Humanist.* Princeton University Press, 1929.

Austin Warren, "A Note on Pope's Preface to Homer." *P.Q.*, IX

(1930), 210–12; "Pope on the Translators of Homer." *M.P.*, XXIX (1931–32), 229–32.

Albert H. West, *L'influence française dans la poésie burlesque en Angleterre entre 1660 et 1700.* Paris, 1931.

R. C. Whitford, "Juvenal in England 1750–1802." *P.Q.*, VII (1928), 9–16.

Lois Whitney, "English Primitivistic Theories of Epic Origins." *M.P.*, XXI (1923–24), 337–78; "Thomas Blackwell, A Disciple of Shaftesbury." *P.Q.*, V (1926), 196–211.

Basil Willey, *The Seventeenth Century Background.* 1934.

A. S. P. Woodhouse, "Collins and the Creative Imagination." *Studies in English by Members of the University of Toronto* (University of Toronto Press, 1931), pp. 59–130.

CHAPTER II

(a) COLERIDGE AND WORDSWORTH

Leslie N. Broughton, *The Theocritean Element in the Works of William Wordsworth.* Halle, 1920.

Douglas Bush, "Wordsworth and the Classics." *University of Toronto Quarterly*, II (1933), 359–79.

C. C. Bushnell, "A Parallelism between Lucan and Lines in *Tintern Abbey*." *J.E.G.P.*, IV (1902), 58.

Lane Cooper, "Wordsworth's Knowledge of Plato." *M.L.N.*, XXXIII (1918), 497–99.

A. C. Dunstan, "The German Influence on Coleridge." *M.L.R.*, XVII (1922), 272–81; XVIII (1923), 183–201.

John L. Haney, *The German Influence on Samuel Taylor Coleridge.* Philadelphia, 1902.

Herbert Hartman, "The 'Intimations' of Wordsworth's *Ode*." *R.E.S.*, VI (1930), 1–20.

Anna A. Helmholtz (Mrs. A. A. von Helmholtz Phelan), *The Indebtedness of Samuel Taylor Coleridge to August Wilhelm Schlegel. Bulletin of the University of Wisconsin, Philology and Literature Series*, III (1907), 273–370.

William Knight, "A Lost Wordsworthian Fragment" [On Harmodius and Aristogeiton]. *Classical Review*, XV (1901), 82.

K. Lienemann, *Die Belesenheit von William Wordsworth.* Berlin, 1908.

Frederick E. Pierce, "Wordsworth and Thomas Taylor." *P.Q.*, VII (1928), 60–64.

J. P. Postgate, "Two Classical Parallels [Lucan, v. 219 ff., and *Intimations of Immortality*]." *Classical Review*, XXIII (1909), 42.
John D. Rea, "Coleridge's Intimations of Immortality from Proclus." *M.P.*, XXVI (1928-29), 201-13.
F. W. Stokoe, *German Influence in the English Romantic Period*. Cambridge University Press, 1926.
Una V. Tuckerman, "Wordsworth's Plan for his Imitation of Juvenal." *M.L.N.*, XLV (1930), 209-15.
James W. Tupper, "The Growth of the Classical in Wordsworth's Poetry." *Sewanee Review*, XXIII (1915), 95-107.

(*b*) BYRON

Karl Brunner, "Griechenland in Byrons Dichtung." *Anglia*, LX (1936), 203-10.
L. M. Buell, "Byron and Shelley [Prometheus]." *M.L.N.*, XXXII (1917), 312-13.
Samuel C. Chew, "Byroniana." [Cf. Buell above.] *M.L.N.*, XXXIII (1918), 306-09.
E. S. De Beer and Walter Seton, "Byroniana: The Archives of the London Greek Committee." *Nineteenth Century*, C (1926), 396 ff.
O. E., "Byron and Canova's Helen." *T.L.S.*, September 23, 1926, p. 632.
H. J. C. Grierson, "Byron and English Society." *The Background of English Literature* (1925), p . 167-99; *Byron, the Poet*, ed. Walter A. Briscoe (1924), pp. 55-85.
R. G. Howarth, "Byron's Reading." *T.L.S.*, March 15, 1934, p. 194.
Sir Richard Jebb, "Byron in Greece." *Modern Greece* (1880), pp. 143-83.
F. Maychrzak, "Lord Byron als Übersetzer." *Englische Studien*, XXI (1895), 384-430.
F. H. Pughe, "Byron, Wordsworth und die Antike." *Studien über Byron und Wordsworth*, ch. III. *Anglistische Forschungen*, VIII (1902), 40-54.
Helene Richter, "Byron. Klassizismus und Romantik." *Anglia*, XLVIII (1924), 209-57; *Lord Byron* (Halle, 1929), pp. 126 ff.
Walter F. Schirmer, "Zu Byrons 'klassizistischer Theorie.'" *Archiv*, CLI (1926), 84-85.
Harold Spender, *Byron and Greece*. 1924

CHAPTER III

KEATS

Lascelles Abercrombie, "The Second Version of Hyperion." *John Keats Memorial Volume*, 1921.

Hermann Anders, *Die Bedeutung Wordsworthscher Gedankengänge für das Denken und Dichten von John Keats*. Breslau, 1932.

Joseph W. Beach, "Keats's Realms of Gold." *P.M.L.A.*, XLIX (1934), 246–57.

Edmund Blunden, "Keats and his Predecessors: A Note on the *Ode to a Nightingale*." *London Mercury*, XX (1929), 289–92.

Margaret P. Boddy, "Stepping like Homer." *T.L.S.*, February 2, 1933, p. 76; cf. *ibid.*, p. 92.

Robert Bridges, "A Critical Introduction to Keats." *Collected Essays Papers &c.*, IV (Oxford University Press, 1929).

Leonard Brown, "The Genesis, Growth, and Meaning of *Endymion*." *S.P.*, XXX (1933), 618–53.

Douglas Bush, "Notes on Keats." *P.Q.*, VIII (1929), 313–15; "The Date of Keats's *Fall of Hyperion*." *M.L.N.*, XLIX (1934), 281–86; "Notes on Keats's Reading." *P.M.L.A.*, L (1935), 785–806.

James R. Caldwell, "The Meaning of *Hyperion*." *P.M.L.A.*, LI (1936), 1080–97.

H. L. Creek, "Keats and Cortez." *T.L.S.*, March 21, 1936, p. 244.

Sir Sidney Colvin, *John Keats*. 1917.

Alexander W. Crawford, *The Genius of Keats*. 1932.

Helen Darbishire, "Keats and Egypt." *R.E.S.*, III (1927), 1–11.

Poems of John Keats, ed. Ernest de Selincourt. Fifth edition, 1926.

G. R. Elliott, "The Real Tragedy of Keats." *P.M.L.A.*, XXXVI (1921), 315–31; *The Cycle of Modern Poetry* (Princeton University Press, 1929).

B. Ifor Evans, "Keats and the Golden Ass." *Nineteenth Century*, C (1926), 263–71; "Keats's Approach to the Chapman Sonnet." *Essays and Studies by Members of the English Association*, XVI (1931), 26–52.

Claude L. Finney, "Drayton's *Endimion and Phoebe* and Keats's *Endymion*." *P.M.L.A.*, XXXIX (1924), 805–13; "Keats's Philosophy of Beauty: An Interpretation of the Allegory of *Endymion* in the Light of the Neo-Platonism of Spenser." *P.Q.*, V (1926), 1–19; "The Fall of Hyperion." *J.E.G.P.*, XXVI (1927), 304–24; "Shakespeare and Keats's *Hyperion*." *P.Q.*, III (1924), 139–58.

Claude L. Finney, *The Evolution of Keats's Poetry*. Harvard University Press, 1936.

H. W. Garrod, *Keats*. Clarendon Press, 1926.

Raymond D. Havens, "Concerning the 'Ode on a Grecian Urn.'" *M.P.*, XXIV (1926), 209–14; "Unreconciled Opposites in Keats." *P.Q.*, XIV (1935), 289–300.

James Hinton, "'Ditamy,' *Endymion*, I, 555." *M.L.N.*, XXXII (1917), 440–41.

Grace W. Landrum, "More Concerning Chapman's Homer and Keats." *P.M.L.A.*, XLII (1927), 986–1009.

Charles A. Langworthy, "Dryden's Influence on the Versification of *Lamia*." *Research Studies of the State College of Washington*, II (1930), 117–24.

Amy Lowell, *John Keats*. Boston and New York, 1925.

John L. Lowes, "Keats and the Argonautica." *T.L.S.*, September 28, 1933, p. 651; "The 'pure serene.'" *Ibid.*, October 12, 1933, p. 691 (cf. *ibid.*, p. 774); "'Hyperion' and the 'Purgatorio.'" *Ibid.*, January 11, 1936, p. 35.

John L. Lowes, "Moneta's Temple." *P.M.L.A.*, LI (1936), 1098–1113.

J. Middleton Murry, *Keats and Shakespeare*. Oxford University Press, 1925.

J. Middleton Murry, *Studies in Keats*. Oxford University Press, 1930.

Edward T. Norris, "Hermes and the Nymph in *Lamia*." *ELH*, II (1935), 322–26.

J. L. N. O'Loughlin, "Coleridge and 'The Fall of Hyperion.'" *T.L.S.*, December 6, 1934, p. 875.

Charlotte Porter, "The Import of Keats's 'Lamia' in Contrast with Coleridge's 'Christabel.'" *Poet Lore*, VI (1894), 32–40.

Maurice R. Ridley, *Keats' Craftsmanship: A Study in Poetic Development*. Clarendon Press, 1933.

John H. Roberts, "Did Keats Finish *Hyperion*?" *M.L.N.*, XLIV (1929), 285–87; "Poetry of Sensation or of Thought?" *P.M.L.A.*, XLV (1930), 1129–39; "The Significance of *Lamia*." *P.M.L.A.*, L (1935), 550–61.

Takeshi Saito, *Keats' View of Poetry*. 1929.

Takeshi Saito, "Keats and Collins." *T.L.S.*, November 20, 1930, p. 991.

John A. Scott, "Keats and the Epic Cycle." *Classical Journal*, XVIII (1922–23), 569–70.

Martha H. Shackford, "*Hyperion*." *Sewanee Review*, XXII (1925), 48–60.

Margaret Sherwood, "Keats' Imaginative Approach to Myth." *Undercurrents of Influence in English Romantic Poetry* (Harvard University Press, 1934), pp. 203–64.

Mary E. Shipman, "Orthodoxy concerning Keats." *P.M.L.A.*, XLIV (1929), 929–34.

Paul Shorey, "Keats and Lucan." *Classical Philology*, XXII (1927), 317.

Royall H. Snow, "Heresy concerning Keats." *P.M.L.A.*, XLIII (1928), 1142–49.

Paul Starick, *Die Belesenheit von John Keats*. Berlin, 1910.

Joseph Texte, "Keats et le néo-hellénisme dans la poésie anglaise." *Études de littérature européenne* (Paris, 1898), pp. 95–145.

Clarence D. Thorpe, *The Mind of John Keats*. Oxford University Press, 1926.

C. D. Thorpe, "Wordsworth and Keats — A Study in Personal and Critical Impression." *P.M.L.A.*, XLII (1927), 1010–26.

C. D. Thorpe (ed.), *John Keats: Complete Poems and Selected Letters*. New York, 1935.

John H. Wagenblass, "Keats's Chapman Sonnet." *T.L.S.*, January 25, 1936, p. 75.

Sir Herbert Warren, "Keats as a Classical Scholar." *Nineteenth Century*, XCIII (1923), 62–68.

Earle V. Weller, "Keats and Mary Tighe." *P.M.L.A.*, XLII (1927), 963–85; *Keats and Mary Tighe*, New York, 1928.

The John Keats Memorial Volume, ed. G. C. Williamson. 1921.

Paul Wolters, "Keats' Grecian Urn." *Archiv für das Studium der neueren Sprachen und Literaturen*, CXX (1908), 53–61.

CHAPTER IV

SHELLEY

Richard Ackermann, *Quellen, Vorbilder, Stoffe zu Shelley's Poetischen Werken*. *Münchener Beiträge*, II (1890).

Richard Ackermann, "Studien über Shelley's Prometheus Unbound." *Englische Studien*, XVI (1892), 19–39.

Florian Asanger, *Percy Bysshe Shelley's Sprach-Studien. Seine Uebersetzungen aus dem Lateinischen und Griechischen*. Bonn, 1911.

Marjory A. Bald, "Shelley's Mental Progress." *Essays and Studies by Members of the English Association*, XIII (1928), 112–37.

Ellsworth Barnard, *Shelley's Religion*. University of Minnesota Press, 1937.

Allen R. Benham, "Shelley's Prometheus Unbound: An Interpretation." *Personalist*, IV (1923), 110–20.

C. A. Brown, "Notes for *Prometheus Unbound*." *P.Q.*, VII (1928), 195–98.

Eli E. Burriss, "The Classical Culture of Percy Bysshe Shelley." *Classical Journal*, XXI (1925–26), 344–54.

Douglas Bush, "Notes on Shelley." *P.Q.*, XIII (1934), 299–302.

Olwen Ward Campbell, *Shelley and the Unromantics*. 1924.

A. S. Cook, "Notes on Shelley." *M.L.N.*, XX (1905), 161–62.

Lane Cooper, "Notes on Byron and Shelley: *Adonais*, Stanza 55." *M.L.N.*, XXIII (1908), 118–19.

W. C. Douglas, *The Pastoral Elegy in English*. Oxford University Press, 1934. [Pp. 1–18.]

Adolf Droop, *Die Belesenheit Percy Bysshe Shelley's nach den direkten Zeugnissen und den bisherigen Forschungen*. Weimar, 1906.

Arthur E. DuBois, "Alastor: The Spirit of Solitude." *J.E.G.P.*, XXXV (1936), 530–45.

Elizabeth Ebeling, "A Probable Paracelsian Element in Shelley." *S.P.*, XXXII (1935), 508–25.

B. Farrington, "The Text of Shelley's Translation of the 'Symposium' of Plato." *M.L.R.*, XIV (1919), 325–26.

Allen H. Gilbert, "A Note on Shelley, Blake, and Milton." *M.L.N.*, XXXVI (1921), 505–06.

Carl Grabo, "Electricity, the Spirit of the Earth, in Shelley's *Prometheus Unbound*." *P.Q.*, VI (1927), 133–50; "Astronomical Allusions in Shelley's *Prometheus Unbound*." *Ibid.*, pp. 362–78.

Carl Grabo, *A Newton Among Poets*. University of North Carolina Press, 1930; *The Meaning of The Witch of Atlas*. *Ibid.*, 1935; *Prometheus Unbound: An Interpretation*. *Ibid.*, 1935.

J. F. C. Gutteling, "Demogorgon in Shelley's *Prometheus Unbound*." *Neophilologus*, IX (1924), 283–85.

T. P. Harrison, "Spenser and Shelley's 'Adonais.'" *University of Texas Studies in English*, XIII (1933), 54–63.

H. W. L. Hime, *The Greek Materials of Shelley's 'Adonais.'* 1888.

A. M. D. Hughes, "Shelley's 'Witch of Atlas.'" *M.L.R.*, VII (1912), 508–16.

O. Intze, *Antike Einflüsse bei Percy Bysshe Shelley*. Erlangen [1912].

Claude E. Jones, "Christ a Fury?" *M.L.N.*, L (1935), 41.

E. E. Kellett, "Imaginative: 'The Witch of Atlas'"; "The Plastic Stress." *Suggestions*. Cambridge University Press, 1923.

A. Koszul, "Les Océanides et le thème de l'amour dans le Prométhée de Shelley." *Revue Anglo-Américaine*, II (1924–25), 385–93.

Benjamin P. Kurtz, *The Pursuit of Death: A Study of Shelley's Poetry.* Oxford University Press (New York), 1933.

Charles W. Lemmi, "The Serpent and the Eagle in Spenser and Shelley." *M.L.N.*, L (1935), 165–68.

George G. Loane, "Shelley and Livy." *T.L.S.*, September 10, 1931, p. 683.

Henry G. Lotspeich, "Shelley's 'Eternity' and Demogorgon." *P.Q.*, XIII (1934), 309–11.

Paul Elmer More, "Shelley." *Shelburne Essays*, Seventh Series (Boston and New York, 1910), pp. 1–26.

George Norlin, "Greek Sources of Shelley's Adonais." *University of Colorado Studies*, I (1902–03), 305–21.

James A. Notopoulos, "Shelley and Thomas Taylor." *P.M.L.A.*, LI (1936), 502–17.

Walter E. Peck, *Shelley: His Life and Work.* Boston and New York, 1927.

Walter E. Peck, "The Source-Book of Shelley's 'Adonais.'" *T.L.S.*, April 8, 1921, pp. 228–29.

D. Pesce, "Il classicismo di P. B. Shelley." *La Nuova Italia* (Florence), January, 1934, pp. 11 ff., February, pp. 56 ff. [Not seen.]

Melvin M. Rader, "Shelley's Theory of Evil Misunderstood." *Western Reserve Studies: A Miscellany*, New Series, XXXIII (1930).

Herbert Read, *In Defence of Shelley and Other Essays.* 1936.

William M. Rossetti, "Shelley's Prometheus Unbound." *Shelley Society's Papers* (1888 *et seq.*), I, 138–79.

P. B. Shelley, *Adonais*, ed. W. M. Rossetti and A. O. Prickard. (Oxford University Press, 1924); *Prometheus Unbound*, ed. Vida D. Scudder (Boston, 1892); ed. Richard Ackermann (Heidelberg, 1908); *Poems*, ed. C. D. Locock (1911); *Complete Poetical Works*, ed. Thomas Hutchinson (Oxford University Press, 1927); *Works*, Julian Edition, ed. Roger Ingpen and W. E. Peck (1926–30).

Floyd Stovall, *Desire and Restraint in Shelley.* Duke University Press, 1931.

Archibald T. Strong, *Three Studies in Shelley.* Oxford University Press, 1921.

Henry Sweet, "Shelley's Nature-Poetry" (1888). *Collected Papers of Henry Sweet*, ed. H. C. Wyld (Clarendon Press, 1913), pp. 229–84.

E. M. W. Tillyard, "Shelley's *Prometheus Unbound* and Plato's *Statesman.*" *T.L.S.*, September 29, 1932, p. 691; George Sampson, *ibid.*, p. 762.

Theodor Vetter, "Shelley als Übersetzer des homerischen Hymnus ΕΙΣ

EPMHN." *Sonder-Abdruck aus der Festgabe für Hugo Blümner* (Zürich, 1914), pp. 523–39.

Newman I. White (ed.), *The Best of Shelley.* New York, 1932.

Newman I. White, "The Historical and Personal Background of Shelley's Hellas." *South Atlantic Quarterly*, XX (1921), 52–60; "Shelley's *Prometheus Unbound*, or Every Man His Own Allegorist." *P.M.L.A.*, XL (1925), 172–84.

Lilian Winstanley, "Platonism in Shelley." *Essays and Studies by Members of the English Association*, IV (1913), 72–100.

W. B. Yeats, "Prometheus Unbound." *The Spectator*, CL (1933), 366–67.

Hans Zettner, *Shelleys Mythendichtung.* Leipzig, 1904.

CHAPTER V

Minor Poets of the Early Nineteenth Century

Edmund Blunden, "Leigh Hunt." *T.L.S.*, November 16, 1922, pp. 733–34; reprinted, as "Leigh Hunt's Poetry," in *Votive Tablets* (1931), pp. 205–18.

Leigh Hunt, *A Day by the Fire; And Other Papers, Hitherto Uncollected*, ed. J. E. B[abson]. Boston, 1870.

Louis Landré, *Leigh Hunt (1784–1859): Contribution à l'histoire du romantisme anglais.* Paris, 1936.

Jean-Jacques Mayoux, *Un épicurien anglais: Thomas Love Peacock.* Paris, 1933.

Grete Moldauer, *Thomas Lovell Beddoes. Wiener Beiträge*, LII (1924).

Federico Olivero, "Hood and Keats." *M.L.N.*, XXVIII (1913), 233–35.

Proserpine and Midas: Two unpublished Mythological Dramas by Mary Shelley, ed. A. Koszul. Oxford University Press, 1922.

CHAPTER VI

Tennyson

Katharine Allen, "Lucretius the Poet, and Tennyson's Poem 'Lucretius.'" *Poet Lore*, XI (1899), 529–48.

G. Bertoni, "Ulisse nella 'Divina Commedia' e nei poeti moderni" [Tennyson; Graf; D'Annunzio; Pascoli]. *Atti dell' Accademia degli Arcadi*, V–VI, N. S. (1930), 19–31.

Friedrich Brie, "Tennysons *Ulysses.*" *Anglia,* LIX (1935), 441–47.

Douglas Bush, "The Personal Note in Tennyson's Classical Poems." *University of Toronto Quarterly,* IV (1935), 201–18.

Curtis C. Bushnell, "Some New Material dealing with the Classical Influence on Tennyson." *Proceedings of the American Philological Association,* XL (1909), xxii–xxv.

D. Laurance Chambers, "Tennysoniana" [*Lucretius*]. *M.L.N.,* XVIII (1903), 231–32.

J. Churton Collins, *Illustrations of Tennyson.* London, 1891.

Albert S. Cook, "The Literary Genealogy of Tennyson's Ulysses." *Poet Lore,* III (1891), 499–504.

Edmund D. Cressman, "The Classical Poems of Tennyson." *Classical Journal,* XXIV (1928–29), 98–111.

Sir Richard Jebb, "On Mr. Tennyson's 'Lucretius.'" *Macmillan's Magazine,* XVIII (1868), 97–103.

Harro De Wet Jensen, "Tennysons *Ulysses.*" *Englische Kultur in sprachwissenschaftlicher Deutung. Festschrift für Max Deutschbein* (Leipzig, 1936), pp. 130–43.

Elizabeth H. Haight, "Tennyson's Use of Homeric Material." *Poet Lore,* XII (1900), 541–51.

Francis J. Hemelt, "Points of Resemblance in the Verse of Tennyson and Theocritus." *M.L.N.,* XVIII (1903), 115–17.

Wilfred P. Mustard, *Classical Echoes in Tennyson.* New York and London, 1904.

Herbert Paul, "Aspects of Tennyson: The Classical Poems." *Nineteenth Century,* XXXIII (1893), 436–53; *Men and Letters.* 1901.

[R. D. B. Rawnsley], "Tennyson and Virgil." *Macmillan's Magazine,* XXXIII (1875–76), 43–49.

G. M. Sargeaunt, "The Eternal Wanderer" [Ulysses]. *Classical Studies* (1929), pp. 1–16.

A. Shewan, "Repetition in Homer and Tennyson." *Classical Weekly,* XVI (1922–23), 153–58, 162–66.

T. K. Sidey, "Some Unnoted Latinisms in Tennyson." *M.L.N.,* XXXV (1920), 245–46.

— Straede, *Tennyson's „Lucretius." Erklärung des Gedichtes, Verhältnis zu dem lateinischen Lehrgedicht „de rerum natura" des Lucretius.* Schlawe, 1905.

The Works of Tennyson, with Notes by the Author, edited with Memoir by Hallam, Lord Tennyson. New York, 1931.

Alfred Lord Tennyson: A Memoir. By His Son. 1897.

R. Y. Tyrrell, "Lucretius." *Atlantic Monthly,* LXXIV (1894), 56–66

Sir Herbert Warren, "Virgil and Tennyson: A Literary Parallel." *Essays of Poets and Poetry Ancient and Modern* (1909), pp. 172–216.
Ortha L. Wilner, "Tennyson and Lucretius." *Classical Journal*, XXV (1930), 347–66.

CHAPTER VII

(a) LANDOR

Richard Aldington, "Landor's 'Hellenics.'" *Literary Studies and Reviews*. 1924.
Anon., "Walter Savage Landor." *T.L.S.*, July 19, 1928, pp. 525–26; "Landor's Poems." *Ibid.*, August 24, 1933, pp. 553–54.
John Bailey, "Some Notes on the Unpopularity of Landor." *Essays by Divers Hands: Being the Transactions of the Royal Society of Literature*, V (1925), 63–85.
William Bradley, *The Early Poems of Walter Savage Landor. A Study of his Development and Debt to Milton.* [1914.]
Selections from the Writings of Walter Savage Landor, ed. Sir Sidney Colvin. 1920. (First published 1882.)
Ernest de Selincourt, "Classicism and Romanticism in the Poetry of Walter Savage Landor." *England und die Antike*, ed. Fritz Saxl (Leipzig and Berlin, 1932), pp. 230–50.
Aubrey de Vere, "Landor's Poetry." *Edinburgh Review*, XCI (1850), 408–43; *Essays Chiefly on Poetry* (1887), II, 143–88.
Edward Dowden, "Walter Savage Landor." *Studies in Literature 1789–1877* (1878), pp. 159–90.
Edward W. Evans, *Walter Savage Landor.* 1892.
Hermann M. Flasdieck, "Walter Savage Landor und seine *Imaginary Conversations.*" *Englische Studien*, LVIII (1924), 390–431.
Ruth I. Goldmark, *Studies in the Influence of the Classics on English Literature.* Columbia University Press, 1918. [Jonson, Landor, Arnold.]
Elizabeth Nitchie, "The Classicism of Walter Savage Landor." *Classical Journal*, XIV (1918–19), 147–66.
I. A. Richards, "Fifteen Lines from Landor." *The Criterion*, XII (1932–33), 355–70. Cf. *ibid.*, pp. 661–65.
Helene Richter, "Walter Savage Landor." *Anglia*, L (1926), 123–52, 317–44; LI (1927), 1–30.
Sir Leslie Stephen, "Landor's Imaginary Conversations." *Hours in a Library* (1907), III, 179–226.
Arthur Symons, "The Poetry of Landor." *Atlantic Monthly*, XCVII

(1906), 808–17; *The Romantic Movement in English Poetry* (1909), pp. 172–89.

Stanley T. Williams, "The Sources of Landor's *Gebir*." *M.L.N.*, XXXVI (1921), 315; "The Story of Gebir." *P.M.L.A.*, XXXVI (1921), 615–31; "Echoes of Walter Savage Landor." *Texas Review*, VII (1921–22), 43–53; *Studies in Victorian Literature* (New York, 1923); "Walter Savage Landor as a Critic of Literature." *P.M.L.A.*, XXXVIII (1923), 906–28; "Landor's Criticism in Poetry." *M.L.N.*, XL (1925), 413–18.

George E. Woodberry, "Landor." *Makers of Literature* (New York, 1909), pp. 63–90; *Literary Essays* (New York, 1920), pp. 17–34.

(*b*) ARNOLD

Anon., "The Poetry of Matthew Arnold." *Edinburgh Review*, CLXVIII (1888), 337–73.

Anon., "Matthew Arnold." *T.L.S.*, December 21, 1922, pp. 849–50.

Matthew Arnold. Early reviews: *Blackwood's Magazine*, LXVI (1849), 340–46; *Fraser's Magazine*, XXXIX (1849), 575–80; XLIX (1854), 140–49; *Westminster Review*, LXI (1854), 146–59.

Matthew Arnold, *Merope*. Review: *Fraser's Magazine*, LVII (1858), 691–701.

Matthew Arnold's Merope: to which is appended the Electra of Sophocles translated by Robert Whitelaw, ed. J. Churton Collins (2d ed.). Clarendon Press, 1917.

John Bailey, "Ancient Tragedy and Modern Imitations" [*Merope*]. *Poets and Poetry* (Clarendon Press, 1911), pp. 170–80.

Sir Edmund Chambers, "Matthew Arnold." *Proceedings of the British Academy*, XVIII (1932), 23–45.

Frank L. Clark, "On Certain Imitations or Reminiscences of Homer in Matthew Arnold's Sohrab and Rustum." *Classical Weekly*, XVII (1923–24), 3–7.

Milo G. Derham, "Borrowings and Adaptations from the 'Iliad' and 'Odyssey' in Matthew Arnold's 'Sohrab and Rustum.'" *University of Colorado Studies*, VII (1909–10), 73–89.

G. R. Elliott, "The Arnoldian Lyric Melancholy." *P.M.L.A.*, XXXVIII (1923), 929–32; *The Cycle of Modern Poetry*. Princeton University Press, 1929.

H. W. Garrod, "The Poetry of Matthew Arnold." *Poetry and the Criticism of Life* (Harvard University Press, 1931), pp. 23–66.

Ruth I. Goldmark: see under Landor.

Ralph E. C. Houghton, *The Influence of the Classics on the Poetry of Matthew Arnold*. Oxford, 1923. [Pp. 3–39.]

W. P. Mustard, "Homeric Echoes in Matthew Arnold's 'Balder Dead.'" *Studies in Honor of Basil Lanneau Gildersleeve* (Johns Hopkins University Press, 1902), pp. 19–28.

T. S. Omond, "Arnold and Homer." *Essays and Studies by Members of the English Association*, III (1912), 71–91.

John A. Scott, "Matthew Arnold's Interpretation of *Odyssey* iv. 563." *Classical Journal*, XVI (1920–21), 115–16.

Iris E. Sells, *Matthew Arnold and France: The Poet*. Cambridge University Press, 1935.

A. C. Swinburne, "Matthew Arnold's New Poems." *Essays and Studies*. 1875.

Chauncey B. Tinker, "Arnold's Poetic Plans." *Yale Review*, XXII (1932–33), 782–93.

C. B. Tinker and H. F. Lowry, "Arnold's *Dover Beach*." *T.L.S.*, October 10, 1935, p. 631.

Stanley Williams, "The Poetical Reputation of Matthew Arnold"; "Matthew Arnold and his Contemporaries"; "Three Aspects of Matthew Arnold's Poetry"; "Theory and Practice in the Poetry of Matthew Arnold." *Studies in Victorian Literature* (New York, 1923).

CHAPTER VIII

EARLY VICTORIAN MINOR POETS

D. Caclamanos, "Mrs. Browning's Translations of the Odyssey." *Notes and Queries*, CLV (1928), 355 (and 391).

P. L. Carver, review of *Orion*, ed. Partridge. *R.E.S.*, V (1929), 367–71.

Poems of Digby Mackworth Dolben Edited with a Memoir by Robert Bridges. Oxford University Press, 1915.

John Drinkwater, "William Cory." *Essays by Divers Hands: Being the Transactions of the Royal Society of Literature*, New Series, IV (1924), 1–31.

Sir Edmund Gosse, "'Orion' Horne." *Portraits and Sketches* (1913); *Selected Essays*, First Series (1928).

Orion: by R. H. Horne: With an Introduction on Horne's Life and Work, ed. Eric Partridge (1928).

Bernhard Jacobi, *Elizabeth Barrett Browning als Übersetzerin antiker Dichtungen*. Münster in Westfalen, 1908.

E. E. Kellett, "Macaulay's Lay Figures." *Suggestions* (Cambridge University Press, 1923), pp. 155–65.

William G. Kingsland, "An Unknown Poem of Mrs. Browning's" [*The Battle of Marathon*]. *Poet Lore*, III (1891), 281–84.

Federico Olivero, "On R. H. Horne's *Orion*." *M.L.N.*, XXX (1915), 33–39.

Edgar Allan Poe, "Horne's 'Orion.'" *Works*, ed. E. C. Stedman and G. E. Woodberry (New York, 1914), VI, 323–54.

John C. Rolfe, "Macaulay's *Lays of Ancient Rome*." *Classical Journal*, XXIX (1934), 567–81.

Tommaso Tittoni, "La Profezia di Capi di T. B. Macaulay." *Nuova Antologia*, CCXLVI (1926), 351–64.

George E. Woodberry, "The Poetry of Aubrey de Vere." *Makers of Literature* (New York, 1909), pp. 124–38; "Aubrey de Vere on Poetry." *Ibid.*, pp. 139–57.

CHAPTER IX

WILLIAM MORRIS

Wilhelm Buchhorn, *William Morris' Odyssee-Übersetzung*. Königsberg, 1910.

H. Sybil Kermode, "The Classical Sources of Morris's *Life and Death of Jason*." *Primitiae: Essays in English Literature by Students of the University of Liverpool* (Liverpool and London, 1912), pp. 158–82.

Elisabet C. Küster, *Mittelalter und Antike bei William Morris: Ein Beitrag zur Geschichte des Mediaevalismus in England*. Berlin and Leipzig, 1928.

Andrew Lang, "The Poetry of William Morris." *Contemporary Review*, XLII (1882), 200–17; "Mr. Morris's Poems." *Longman's Magazine*, XXVIII (1896), 560–73.

Karl Litzenberg, "William Morris and the Reviews." *R.E.S.*, XII (1936), 413–28.

Percy Lubbock, "The Poetry of William Morris." *Quarterly Review*, CCXV (1911), 482–504.

J. W. Mackail, *Life of William Morris*. 1899.

J. W. Mackail, "William Morris" (1910). *Studies of English Poets* (1926), pp. 173–97.

J. W. Mackail, "Apollonius of Rhodes and the Romantic Epic." *Lectures on Greek Poetry* (1911), pp. 239–72.

Paul Elmer More, "William Morris." *Shelburne Essays*, Seventh Series (Boston and New York, 1910), pp. 95–118.

William Morris, *The Life and Death of Jason*, ed. E. Maxwell. Clarendon Press, 1919.

Charles Eliot Norton, "The Life and Death of Jason." *The Nation*, V (1867), 146.

Alfred Noyes, *William Morris*. 1908.

Augustus Ralli, "The Earthly Paradise." *North American Review*, CCXXII (1925), 299–310; *Critiques* (1927), 19–33.

Julius Riegel, *Die Quellen von William Morris' Dichtung, The Earthly Paradise*. *Erlanger Beiträge*, IX (1890).

[John Skelton], "William Morris and Matthew Arnold." *Fraser's Magazine*, LXXIX (1869), 230–44.

A. C. Swinburne, "Morris's Life and Death of Jason." *Essays and Studies* (1875), pp. 110–22.

W. B. Yeats, "The Happiest of the Poets" (1902). *Ideas of Good and Evil (Essays*, New York, 1924, pp. 64–78).

CHAPTER X

SWINBURNE

Gerhard Buck, "Über Swinburnes „Atalanta in Calydon."" *Germanisch-Romanische Monatsschrift*, XXIII (1935), 426–44.

Samuel C. Chew, *Swinburne*. Boston, 1929.

J. B. Leicester Warren [Lord De Tabley], "Atalanta in Calydon." *Fortnightly Review*, I (1865), 75–80.

Paul Dottin, "Swinburne, poète grec et latin." *Revue Anglo-Américaine*, II (1924–25), 328–30; "Swinburne et les dieux." *Ibid.*, pp. 419–27.

Paul Dottin, "Les poèmes de Swinburne et les légendes héroïques de la Grèce." *Revue de l'enseignement des langues vivantes*, XLII (1925), 9–15; "La littérature et l'histoire anciennes dans les poèmes de Swinburne." *Ibid.*, pp. 145–54.

Sir Edmund Gosse, *Life of Algernon Charles Swinburne*. 1917.

W. B. Drayton Henderson, *Swinburne and Landor*. 1918.

Clyde K. Hyder, "Swinburne's *Laus Veneris* and the Tannhäuser Legend." *P.M.L.A.*, XLV (1930), 1202–13.

Clyde K. Hyder, *Swinburne's Literary Career and Fame*. Duke University Press, 1933.

Georges Lafourcade, "Atalanta in Calydon: le manuscrit; les sources." *Revue Anglo-Américaine*, III (1925–26), 34–47, 128–33.

Georges Lafourcade, *La jeunesse de Swinburne (1837–1867)*. Paris and Oxford University Press, 1928.

Georges Lafourcade, *Swinburne: A Literary Biography*. 1932.

J. W. Mackail, "Swinburne" (1909). *Studies of English Poets* (1926), pp. 201–25.

Harold Nicolson, *Swinburne*. 1926.

Federico Olivero, "On Swinburne's *Atalanta in Calydon*." *Studies in Modern Poetry*. Oxford University Press, 1921.

Olivia Pound, *On the Application of the Principles of Greek Lyric Tragedy in the Classical Dramas of Swinburne*. *University of Nebraska Studies*, XIII (1913), 341–60.

Mario Praz, "Le tragedie 'greche' di A. C. Swinburne e le fonti dell' 'Atalanta in Calydon.'" *Atene e Roma*, N. S., III (1922), 157–89.

Mario Praz, "Swinburne." *La Cultura*, I (1921–22), 536–53; "Il manoscritto dell' „Atalanta in Calydon.'" *Ibid.*, VIII (1929), 405–15; "Swinburniana." *Ibid.*, IX (1930), 11–23.

Paul de Reul, *L'œuvre de Swinburne*. Brussels, Paris, and Oxford University Press, 1922.

William R. Rutland, *Swinburne: A Nineteenth Century Hellene*. Oxford, 1931.

William R. Rutland, "Swinburne Revisited" [*Thalassius*]. *T.L.S.*, August 20, 1931, p. 633.

H. K. St. J. S., *et al.*, "Time with a gift of tears." *Notes and Queries*, Twelfth Series, X (1922), 18, 54, 96, 136.

Martha Hale Shackford, "Swinburne and Delavigne." *P.M.L.A.*, XXXIII (1918), 85–95.

Swinburne's Atalanta in Calydon: A Facsimile of the First Edition, ed. G. Lafourcade. Oxford University Press, 1930.

Swinburne, Atalanta in Calydon, ed. J. H. Blackie. 1930.

Swinburne's Atalanta in Calydon and Erechtheus, ed. Marion C. Wier. Ann Arbor, Michigan, 1922.

Swinburne's Hyperion and Other Poems, with an Essay on Swinburne and Keats By Georges Lafourcade. 1927.

T. Earle Welby, *A Study of Swinburne*. 1926.

Marion Clyde Wier, *The Influence of Aeschylus and Euripides on the Structure and Content of Swinburne's Atalanta in Calydon and Erechtheus*. Ann Arbor, Michigan, 1920.

CHAPTER XI

(a) BROWNING

Helen A. Clarke, "An Interpretation of Browning's 'Ixion.'" *Poet Lore*, V (1893), 626–30.

Edmund D. Cressman, "The Classical Poems of Robert Browning." *Classical Journal*, XXIII (1927–28), 198–207.

John W. Cunliffe, "Browning and the Marathon Race." *P.M.L.A.*, XXIV (1909), 154–63.

William C. De Vane, *Browning's Parleyings: The Autobiography of a Mind*. Yale University Press, 1927.

William C. De Vane, *A Browning Handbook*. New York, 1935.

Thurman L. Hood, *Browning's Ancient Classical Sources*. *Harvard Studies in Classical Philology*, XXXIII (1922), 78–180.

Carl N. Jackson, *Classical Elements in Browning's Aristophanes' Apology*. *Harvard Studies in Classical Philology*, XX (1909), 15–73.

John Kelman, "Robert Browning the Greek." *Prophets of Yesterday and Their Message for To-day*. Harvard University Press, 1924.

George D. Latimer, "A Study of Browning's 'Ixion.'" *Poet Lore*, IV (1892), 243–54.

W. C. Lawton, "The Classical Element in Browning's Poetry." *A.J.P.*, XVII (1896), 197–216; *Boston Browning Society Papers* (1897), pp. 363–87.

Andrew Marshall, "Balaustion and Mrs. Browning." *Cornhill Magazine*, LI (1921), 586–93.

Horace M. Moule, "The Story of Alcestis." *Fraser's Magazine*, N. S., IV (1871), 575–85.

Richard G. Moulton, "Browning's 'Balaustion' as a Beautiful Misrepresentation of the Original." *Browning Society's Papers*, XIII (1890–91), 148–67.

Philip S. Moxom, "Balaustion's Opinion of Euripides." *Boston Browning Society Papers* (1897), pp. 411–37; partly printed, under different title, in *Poet Lore*, VIII (1896), 425–32.

J. A. Nairn, "Robert Browning's Debt to Classical Literature." *Transactions of the Royal Society of Literature*, Second Series, XXIX (1909), 71–94.

Elizabeth Nitchie, "Browning's Use of the Classics." *Classical Weekly*, XIV (1920–21), 105–10.

Edward A. Parker (ed.), *Balaustion's Adventure*. London, 1928.

Vida D. Scudder, "The Greek Spirit in Shelley and Browning." *Boston Browning Society Papers* (1897), pp. 438–70.

George A. Simcox, "Balaustion's Adventure." *The Academy*, II (1870–71), 409–10.

T. C. Snow, "Robert Browning as a Scholar." *Classical Review*, IV (1890), 58–61.

Robert Spindler, *Robert Browning und die Antike*. Leipzig, 1930.

John Addington Symonds, "Aristophanes' Apology." *The Academy*, VII (1875), 389–90.

Frederick M. Tisdel, "*Balaustion's Adventure* as an Interpretation of the *Alcestis* of Euripides." *P.M.L.A.*, XXXII (1917), 519–46.
Frederick M. Tisdel, "Browning's *Aristophanes' Apology.*" *University of Missouri Studies*, II (1927), 1–46.
C. A. Wurtzburg, "The 'Alkestis' of Euripides and of Browning." *Poet Lore*, II (1890), 345–60.

(*b*) MEREDITH

René Galland, *George Meredith: Les cinquante premières années (1828–1878)*. Paris, 1923.
The Poetical Works of George Meredith, ed. G. M. Trevelyan. 1912.
G. M. Trevelyan, *The Poetry and Philosophy of George Meredith*. 1912.

CHAPTER XII

MINOR POETS, MID-VICTORIAN AND LATER

Anon., "De Tabley's Poems." *T.L.S.*, April 24, 1924, p. 251; "Lord De Tabley." *Ibid.*, April 25, 1935, p. 268.
Ernst Bendz, *The Influence of Pater and Matthew Arnold in the Prose-Writings of Oscar Wilde.* Gothenburg and London, 1914.
Eduard J. Bock, *Walter Pater's Einfluss auf Oscar Wilde. Bonner Studien zur englischen Philologie*, VIII (1913).
Robert Bridges, "Lord De Tabley's Poems." *The Speaker*, December 12, 1903, pp. 272–73; *Collected Essays Papers &c.*, VI–VII (Oxford University Press, 1931).
Poems by the late Rev. Dr. Richard Watson Dixon, ed. Robert Bridges. 1909. (Introduction reprinted in Bridges' *Three Friends*, Oxford University Press, 1932.)
Lord De Tabley, *Orestes*. Reviews: *Athenaeum*, July 27, 1867, p. 122; *Spectator*, XL (1867), 781–82.
Lord De Tabley, *Philoctetes*. Reviews: *Athenaeum*, May 26, 1866, p. 702; *Saturday Review*, XXII (1866), 213–15; *Spectator*, XXXIX (1866), 720–21.
Select Poems of Lord De Tabley, ed. John Drinkwater. Oxford University Press, 1924.
Rose F. Egan, *The Genesis of the Theory of "Art for Art's Sake" in Germany and England. Smith College Studies in Modern Languages*, II, No. 4 (1921), 1–61; V, No. 3 (1924), 1–33.
Albert J. Farmer, *Le mouvement esthétique et "décadent" en Angleterre (1873–1900)*. Paris, 1931

Bernhard Fehr, *Studien zu Oscar Wilde's Gedichten. Palaestra*, vol. 100 (Berlin, 1918).

George Gordon, *Andrew Lang*. Oxford University Press, 1928.

Sir Edmund Gosse, "Lord De Tabley." *Critical Kit-Kats* (New York, 1897), pp. 165–95.

John S. Harrison, "Pater, Heine, and the Old Gods of Greece." *P.M.L.A.*, XXXIX (1924), 655–86.

Merritt Y. Hughes, "The Immortal Wilde." *University of California Chronicle*, XXX (1928), 305–24.

Andrew Lang, *Helen of Troy*. Reviews: *Academy*, XXII (1882), 251; *Athenaeum*, October 7, 1882, pp. 455–56 (reply by Lang, p. 530); *Saturday Review*, LIV (1882), 541–42; *Spectator*, LVI (1883), 87–88.

Richard Le Gallienne, "The Poetry of Lord de Tabley." *Nineteenth Century*, XXXIII (1893), 899–904.

Herbert C. Lipscomb, "Horace and the Poetry of Austin Dobson." *A.J.P.*, L (1929), 1–20.

J. Mainsard, "L'esthéticisme de Walter Pater et d'Oscar Wilde." *Études*, CXCIV (1928), 525–52.

T. Sturge Moore (ed.), *A Selection from the Poems of Michael Field*. 1923.

Paul Elmer More, "Walter Pater." *The Drift of Romanticism* (Shelburne Essays, Eighth Series). Boston and New York, 1913.

Walter Pater, "Apollo in Picardy." *Harper's Magazine*, LXXXVII (1893), 949–57; *Miscellaneous Studies* (1895).

Walter Pater, "The Bacchanals of Euripides." *Macmillan's Magazine*, LX (1889), 63–72; *Greek Studies* (1895).

Walter Pater, "Denys l'Auxerrois." *Macmillan's Magazine*, LIV (1886), 413–23; *Imaginary Portraits* (1887).

Walter Pater, "Hippolytus Veiled." *Macmillan's Magazine*, LX (1889), 294–306; *Greek Studies* (1895).

Walter Pater, "Lacedaemon." *Contemporary Review*, LXI (1892), 791–808; *Plato and Platonism* (1893).

Walter Pater, "The Myth of Demeter and Persephone." *Fortnightly Review*, XXV (1876), 82–95, 260–76; *Greek Studies* (1895).

Walter Pater, "A Study of Dionysus." *Fortnightly Review*, XXVI (1876), 752–72; *Greek Studies* (1895).

Walter Pater, "Winckelmann." *Westminster Review*, LXXXVII (1867), 36–50; *Studies in the History of the Renaissance* (1873).

R. S. Rait, S. Reinach, Gilbert Murray, J. H. Millar, "Andrew Lang." *Quarterly Review*, CCXVIII (1913), 299–329.

Louise Rosenblatt, *L'idée de l'art pour l'art dans la littérature anglaise pendant la période victorienne*. Paris, 1931.

George Saintsbury, "The Poems of Andrew Lang." *Quarterly Review*, CCXL (1923), 262–75.

Alexander Shewan, *Andrew Lang's Work for Homer*. Oxford University Press, 1929.

Mary Sturgeon, *Michael Field*. 1922.

Hugh Walker, *John B. Leicester Warren, Lord de Tabley: A Biographical Sketch*. 1903.

Homer E. Woodbridge, "Oscar Wilde as a Poet." *Poet Lore*, XIX (1908), 439–57.

CHAPTER XIII

FROM THE NINETIES TO THE PRESENT. I

Lascelles Abercrombie, *Phoenix*. Reviews: *Nation and Athenaeum*, XXXIV (1923), 157–58; *New Statesman*, XXII (1923–24), 214; *Spectator*, CXXXI (1923), 520–21; *T.L.S.*, September 27, 1923, p. 633.

Laurence Binyon, Reviews: *Odes* (1901): *Academy*, LX (1901), 29; *Odes* (1913): *Academy*, LXXXV (1913), 684. *Penthesilea*: *Academy*, LXVIII (1905), 412.

Robert Bridges, Reviews: *Prometheus the Firegiver*: *Academy*, XXVI (1884), 334–35; *Athenaeum*, January 24, 1885, p. 115. *Eros and Psyche*: *Saturday Review*, LXXIX (1895), 41–42.

Edward Dowden, "The Poetry of Robert Bridges." *Fortnightly Review*, LXII (1894), 44–60; *New Studies in Literature* (1895).

Alfred Gilde, *Die dramatische Behandlung der Rückkehr des Odysseus bei Nicholas Rowe, Robert Bridges und Stephen Phillips*. Königsberg, 1903.

Llewellyn Jones, "The Poetry and Criticism of T. Sturge Moore." *First Impressions*. New York, 1925.

Harold A. Larrabee, "Robert Bridges and George Santayana." *The American Scholar*, I (1932), 167–82.

Herbert C. Lipscomb, "Lucretius and *The Testament of Beauty*." *Classical Journal*, XXXI (1935–36), 77–88.

Arthur McDowall, "The Poetry of Mr. Sturge Moore." *London Mercury*, V (1921–22), 607–16.

T. Sturge Moore. Reviews of early works: *Academy*, LVII (1899), 253; LXI, 147; LXVI, 350; LXVII, 337, 589; *Athenaeum*, January 7, 1905, p. 12; May 20, 1905, p. 620; *Saturday Review*, XCVII (1904), 335–36; XCVIII, 732–33; *Spectator*, XCVI (1906), 756.

T. Sturge Moore, *Danaë*, etc. Reviews: *Athenaeum*, October 15, 1920,

p. 515; *Nation* (London), XXVIII (1920–21), 244; *T.L.S.*, October 29, 1920, p. 695.

T. Sturge Moore, *Tragic Mothers* [*Medea; Niobe*]. Reviews: *New Statesman*, XVII (1921), 192–93; *T.L.S.*, March 18, 1921, p. 175.

T. Sturge Moore, *Mystery and Tragedy* [*Psyche; Daimonassa*]. Review: *New Statesman*, XXXV (1930), 414.

T. Sturge Moore, *Poems, Collected Edition* (1931–33). Reviews: see M.H.R.A. bibliographies.

Ezra Pound, "Hark to Sturge Moore." *Poetry*, VI (1915), 139–45.

Priscilla Thouless, *Modern Poetic Drama*. Oxford, 1934.

Yvor Winters, "T. Sturge Moore." *Hound and Horn*, VI (1932–33), 534–45.

W. B. Yeats, "The Return of Ulysses." *Ideas of Good and Evil* (*Essays*, New York, 1924, pp. 244–49).

CHAPTER XIV

From the Nineties to the Present. II

Anon., "The Poetry of Mr. Stephen Phillips." *Edinburgh Review*, CXCI (1900), 51–75.

Anon., "Some Recent Verse" [Phillips, Hewlett, Trench, Noyes, *et al.*]. *Edinburgh Review*, CCX (1909), 378–99.

Paull F. Baum, "Mr. Richard Aldington." *South Atlantic Quarterly*, XXVIII (1929), 201–08.

Cloudesley Brereton, "A Poet Philosopher: Herbert Trench." *The Quest*, XVI (1924–25), 169–87.

H. P. Collins, *Modern Poetry*. 1925. [On Housman, pp. 67–77.]

P. J. Dixon, "Letters from George Moore: The Greek Background of 'Aphrodite in Aulis.'" *London Mercury*, XXXI (1934), 14–21.

Samuel Vogt Gapp, *George Gissing: Classicist*. University of Pennsylvania Press, 1936.

H. W. Garrod, "Mr. A. E. Housman." *The Profession of Poetry* (Clarendon Press, 1929), pp. 211–24.

Stephen Gwynn, "The Masque of 'Ulysses'" [Stephen Phillips]. *Nineteenth Century*, LI (1902), 434–43.

S. B. Liljegren, "Die Dichtung Stephen Phillips'." *Englische Studien*, LVII (1923), 213–49.

Levi R. Lind, "Additions to a List of Classical Echoes in the Poetry of A. E. Housman." *Classical Weekly*, XXIX (1935–36), 56.

F. L. Lucas, "Few, but Roses" [Housman]. *New Statesman*, XXII (1923–24), 45–47; *Authors Dead and Living* (1926).

John Masefield, *A Tale of Troy*. Reviews: *Bookman* (New York), LXXV (1932), 748–49; *New Statesman and Nation*, IV (1932), 378; *T.L.S.*, September 22, 1932, p. 661.

Arthur McDowall, "The Poetry of Mr. W. J. Turner." *London Mercury*, XI (1924–25), 158–68.

May Sinclair, "The Poems of Richard Aldington." *English Review*, XXXII (1921), 397–410.

Charles Forster Smith, "Stephen Phillips." *Sewanee Review*, IX (1901), 385–97; "Mr. Stephen Phillips's 'Ulysses.'" *Ibid.*, X (1902), 320–24.

John Sparrow, "Echoes in the Poetry of A. E. Housman." *Nineteenth Century*, CXV (1934), 243–56.

Conrad F. Stadler, *Die Rolle der Antike bei George Gissing*. Quakenbrück, 1933.

Arthur Symons, "Mr. Stephen Phillips." *Quarterly Review*, CXCV (1902), 486–500; *Studies in Prose and Verse* (1904).

C. B. Tinker, "Housman's Poetry." *Yale Review*, XXV (1935–36), 84–95.

Cornelius Weygandt, "Lionel Johnson, English Irishman." *Tuesdays at Ten* (University of Pennsylvania Press, 1928), pp. 62–73; "The Poetry of Mr. Stephen Phillips." *Sewanee Review*, XVII (1909), 66–83; "The Rise and Fall of Stephen Phillips." *Tuesdays at Ten*, pp. 210–29.

CHAPTER XV

AMERICAN POETS

George O. Ackroyd, "The Classical in Robert Frost." *Poet Lore*, XL (1929), 610–14.

Nelson F. Adkins, "The Poetic Philosophy of William Vaughn Moody." *Texas Review*, IX (1923–24), 97–112.

S. S. Alberts, *A Bibliography of the Works of Robinson Jeffers*. New York, 1933.

Anon., "Poets' Translations" [H. D. *et al.*]. *T.L.S.*, November 21, 1919, p. 666; "Uniqueness, with a Note on Vers Libre" [H. D.]. *Ibid.*, January 5, 1922, p. 8.

John W. Beach, "A Perfumed Sea" [Poe]. *Classical Journal*, XXIX (1933–34), 454–56.

Richard P. Blackmur, "Masks of Ezra Pound." *Hound and Horn*, VII (1933–34), 177–212.

Ronald Bottrall, "XXX Cantos of Ezra Pound." *Determinations*, ed. F. R. Leavis (1934), pp. 179–98.

Friedrich Brie, "Eugene O'Neill als Nachfolger der Griechen (Mourning

Becomes Electra)." *Germanisch-Romanische Monatsschrift*, XXI (1933), 46–59.

Anna S. C. Brinton, "Vergilian Allusions in the New England Poets." *Classical Journal*, XXI (1925–26), 29–39, 85–99.

G. S. Bryan, "American Renderings of the 'Aeneid.'" *Sewanee Review*, XV (1907), 208–14.

Henry S. Canby, "Scarlet Becomes Crimson" [*Mourning Becomes Electra*]. *Saturday Review of Literature*, VIII (1931–32), 257–58.

Barrett H. Clark, "Aeschylus and O'Neill." *English Journal*, XXI (1932), 699–710.

H. P. Collins, *Modern Poetry*. 1925. [On H. D., pp. 154–202].

John Corbin, "O'Neill and Aeschylus." *Saturday Review of Literature*, VIII (1931–32), 693–95.

H. D., *Hymen*. Reviews: *Bookman* (New York), LVI (1922–23), 225–26; *Dial*, LXXII (1922), 203–07; *Literary Review, New York Evening Post*, January 21, 1922, p. 364; *New Republic*, XXIX (1921), 134; *Poetry*, XIX (1921–22), 333–37.

H. D., *Heliodora*. Reviews: *Literary Review, New York Evening Post*, August 23, 1924, p. 980; *Nation*, CXIX (1924), 526–27; *Nation and Athenaeum*, XXXV (1924), 250; *New Statesman*, XXIII (1924), 572–73; *Poetry*, XXV (1924–25), 160–64; *Saturday Review of Literature*, I (1924), 260; *T.L.S.*, July 3, 1924, p. 416.

H. D., *Collected Poems*. Reviews: *Bookman* (New York), LXII (1925), 80–81; *Dial*, LXXIX (1925), 170–72; *Literary Review, New York Evening Post*, May 23, 1925, p. 4; *Nation*, CXXI (1925), 211–12; *Poetry*, XXVI (1925), 268–75; *Yale Review*, XIV (1924–25), 590–91.

H. D., *Hippolytus Temporizes*. Reviews: *Dial*, LXXXIV (1928), 63–65; *Hound and Horn*, I (1927–28), 48–52; *New Republic*, LII (1927), 24–25.

H. D., *Red Roses for Bronze*. Reviews: *Nation*, CXXXIV (1932), 264; *Poetry*, XLI (1932–33), 94–100; *T.L.S.*, December 31, 1931, p. 1052.

J. R. Daniells, "T. S. Eliot and his Relation to T. E. Hulme." *University of Toronto Quarterly*, II (1933), 380–96.

Frank A. Doggett, "H. D. A Study in Sensitivity." *Sewanee Review*, XXXVII (1929), 1–9.

T. S. Eliot, "Euripides and Professor Murray." *The Sacred Wood*, 1920; *Selected Essays*, 1932.

Henry R. Fairclough, *The Classics and Our Twentieth-Century Poets*. Stanford University Press, 1927.

Basil L. Gildersleeve, *Hellas and Hesperia: or The Vitality of Greek Studies in America*. New York, 1909.

Earl L. Griggs, "Five Sources of Edgar Allan Poe's 'Pinakidia.'" *American Literature*, I (1929–30), 196–99.

Richard M. Gummere, "Apollo on Locust Street." *Pennsylvania Magazine of History and Biography*, LVI (1932), 68–92.

David D. Henry, *William Vaughn Moody: A Study*. Boston, 1934.

Thomas Wentworth Higginson, "The Greek Goddesses." *Atlantic Monthly*, XXIV (1869), 97–108.

Glenn Hughes, *Imagism and the Imagists*. Stanford University Press, 1931.

David K. Jackson, "Poe Notes: 'Pinakidia' and 'Some Ancient Greek Authors.'" *American Literature*, V (1933–34), 257–67; "'Some Ancient Greek Authors,' a Work of E. A. Poe." *Notes and Queries*, CLXVI (1934), 368.

J. J. Jones, "Poe's 'Nicéan Barks.'" *American Literature*, II (1930–31), 433–38.

F. R. Leavis, *New Bearings in English Poetry*. 1932.

Charlton M. Lewis, "William Vaughn Moody." *Yale Review*, II (1913), 688–703.

Selected Poems of William Vaughn Moody, ed. Robert Morss Lovett. Boston and New York, 1931.

F. O. Matthiessen, *The Achievement of T. S. Eliot*. Boston and New York, 1935.

H. E. Mierow, "A Classical Allusion in Poe." *M.L.N.*, XXXI (1916), 184.

William Vaughn Moody, "The Poems of Trumbull Stickney." *North American Review*, CLXXXIII (1906), 1005–18.

Emma K. Norman, "Poe's Knowledge of Latin." *American Literature*, VI (1934–35), 72–77.

Lawrence C. Powell, *An Introduction to Robinson Jeffers*. Dijon, 1932.

John P. Pritchard, "The Autocrat and Horace." *Classical Weekly*, XXV (1931–32), 217–23; "Horace and Edgar Allan Poe." *Ibid.*, XXVI (1932–33), 129–33; "The Horatian Influence upon Longfellow." *American Literature*, IV (1932–33), 22–38.

Ernest Riedel, "A Possible Classical Source of Poe's Poem, The Raven." *Classical Weekly*, XX (1926–27), 118.

Paul Shorey, "The Poetry of William Vaughn Moody." *University of Chicago Record*, XIII (1927), 172–200.

May Sinclair, "The Poems of 'H. D.'" *Fortnightly Review*, CXXVII (1927), 329–45.

James Stinchcomb, "Classical Mythology in Contemporary American Poetry." *Classical Weekly*, XXVI (1932–33), 81–84.

Allen Tate, "Ezra Pound's Golden Ass." *The Nation*, CXXXII (1931), 632–34.

René Taupin, *L'influence du symbolisme français sur la poésie américaine (de 1910 à 1920)*. Paris, 1929.

René Taupin, "The Classicism of T. S. Eliot." *Symposium*, III (1932), 64–82.

Arthur H. Weston, "The 'Nicean Barks' of Edgar Allan Poe." *Classical Journal*, XXIX (1933–34), 213–15. Cf. *ibid.*, p. 454.

Hugh R. Williamson, *The Poetry of T. S. Eliot.* 1932.

Edmund Wilson, "T. S. Eliot." *New Republic*, LX (1929), 341–49; *Axel's Castle.* New York, 1931.

Stark Young, "Mourning Becomes Electra." *New Republic*, LXVIII (1931), 352–55.

Morton D. Zabel, "A Prophet in His Wilderness" [Robinson Jeffers]. *New Republic*, LXXVII (1933–34), 229–30.

INDEX

INDEX [1]

[1] It has not appeared practicable to index the Appendix.